HOME FOR A REFUGEE

Home for a Refugee
An Autobiography by DEVI MOHAN (www.devimohan.com)

For privacy reasons, some names may have been changed.

Credits:
Cover Photography: Marko Brainovic
Cover Design: Ana Berner
Editing: Aariyah Kaur and Geeta Iyer

1st Edition published February 2023 by:
Gurulight
Email: info@gurulight.com
Web: www.gurulight.com

Gurulight

HOME FOR A REFUGEE

An Autobiography by

DEVI MOHAN

Gurulight

To Mohanji

Contents

Foreword

This book will touch your heart. It will raise the awareness and the power of people around the world, especially women. It will help them understand what they have to do and what their role in the world truly is as strong and brave women.

Devi Mohan is an angel and a true spark of the Divine. She has come down to help people through unconditional love. I always appreciate her and even Appa and Amma [Sage Agastya and Lopamudra] appreciate her and her husband Mohanji. She is my child forever and ever.

Blessings,
Devi Amma

Preface

Pain is a Powerful Teacher

"I am NOT a victim! I am NOT this poor little refugee!"

With that volcanic declaration, a new expanded me was born amidst the raging fires of fratricidal war in former Yugoslavia. It was November 4th, 1991, my 14th birthday, when the agonies of my refugee days reached their crescendo, and this powerful realization erupted from the previously unfathomable depths of my being. To this day, that intense inner experience and the pain that triggered it stand out as the best birthday gifts I have ever received!

Deep pain introduces us to ourselves in a way that is primordial and immeasurably profound. The dreamer jolted awake by pain is left heartbroken, lonely, and disappointed by the dream world once known and trusted. Coping skills vanish and the inner compass spins beyond control. But there is a hidden gift in pain – when Ego loses its footing in unknown territory, true breakthrough is possible. Our "a-ha moments" and astounding insights often come at the very brink of despair, during moments of raw pain.

When embraced, the pain makes us authentic in our vulnerability. It liberates us from our intense defense mechanisms and ushers in the blessing of clarity. The heavy curtains of the ego draw back, and brilliant rays of eternal wisdom and purest love permanently enter our reality.

The Guru Principle

When the student is ready, the teacher appears. The essence of brightness, the brightness of consciousness, enters the illusion as Gu (darkness) – Ru (He who dispels). The principle of the Guru, called Guru Tattva since the ancient times of Vedic India, is alive in all of us. The right guidance through synchronicities, intuition, telepathic guidance, or through a living being, a man or a woman pure and empty enough to embody the essence of Guru Tattva, will lift you from darkness into the light. This has been my direct experience! It is my absolute joy to now share with you how Guru Tattva appeared in my life and held me like a drop of dew on a flower petal, nurturing and strengthening me through every experience that expanded my horizons.

Dear reader, dear friend, my intention in writing this book is to open an inner passage to your own expanded states of consciousness by sharing authentic experiences from the deepest recesses of my heart. Let us explore together what will be revealed within us on the journey through these pages.

As you enter the sacred space of my heart's temple, know that I open myself to you sincerely and with the utmost feminine vulnerability. The frequency of this unpretentious vulnerability is the true source of strength, courage, and power within both men and women. You are likewise invited to draw upon that power and be completely vulnerable in the space that my heart holds for our shared connection and deep communion.

May this interaction inspire us as a human family to face and process any wounds of irreparable loss and humiliation, any illusion of hopeless separation, or any fear rooted in the misconception of death as the end of our existence. May we become even greater expressions of love in action and of our unique divinity that chose to incarnate at this special time on Earth to attain completion.

I also invite you to become aware of that cunning tendency of the mind and ego to place others into preconceived frames, coupled with the "I've seen it all" attitude that destroys wonder and childlike openness. If you choose to lay down your ego and enter this temple, please know that I will feel you within the shared field of consciousness and that I will welcome you with all my heart.

Before reading this book, I have a small request. I invite you to drop everything and stand before a mirror. Take a couple of abdominal breaths, and look deeply and lovingly into your own eyes, which are the mirrors of your soul. Aim to recognize the unique spark in your eyes. Smile through your eyes and see that spark shine brighter. Observe it with the awareness that this unique spark has always been the same, throughout all your life stages and journeys.

I started this brief introduction by sharing the darkest moment from my refugee days because that was the moment when I encountered a divine presence at the depth of my being, in the darkest of the caves within me. The warmth of that overwhelming love from within kept coursing through my veins, through my entire body, in stark contrast to the cold, windowless room that housed me then. In the coldest winter of my life, my soul was set on fire and I found the courage to continue – not as a victim, but as a sovereign of my inner world, claiming the throne with dignity, love, and power!

What followed was the realization of being something much greater than what my mind perceived myself to be till then. This eruption of energy also felt like it was not individual; it was not only about me. Contemplating this mystical experience over the years, I began understanding why it felt collective, ancestral, and archetypal. This supremely precious and pivotal experience was meant to be shared with the world, and finally, the time for sharing has come.

That moment of realization instantly lifted me to a different track in life, as if a whole new timeline had been created in my inner and outer reality. I entered the mode of assuming responsibility and creating a new life rooted in love and dignity. There was no thinking involved at that moment, only a change in my operating frequency. This change came with overwhelmingly huge willpower armed with a grace that transcends individual existence, a grace that chose to express itself through me. It called for firm commitment, discipline, and determination to take the next simple, solid step – to do what I could within the given circumstances to restore my dignity.

Moreover, the grace of that moment called for the courage to open my heart, and I made that commitment to myself right there and then. It is very daring to do that, but it is only from the sacred space of the open heart that one can create a different reality. In truth, it was more than a commitment, it was a sacred vow. Deep within me, I found the strength to open my heart amidst utmost pain and humiliation, for only those who dare to open their heart can serve the cause of peace and unity.

Little did I know that less than two decades later, I would ride the momentum of that inner breakthrough and sacred vow to a life beyond my wildest imagination. Little did I know that my journey was one of adding value to societies across the globe by transforming pain into purpose, a journey of divinity within humanity.

Union for a Higher Purpose

Sixteen years later, in the surreal city of Dubai, I met a man who had lost even more than I had, a man plunged into an even deeper abyss of pain. This man had lost everything he held dear, everything that defined him till then. The loss of his most beloved daughter, killed in an accident at only four years of age, was the first devastation. And the slaps continued. He lost his marriage, career, wealth, and health.

However, amid this unbearable pain and loss, not only did he find meaning, but he attained a powerful breakthrough in consciousness. Freed from all attachments in life, he mastered his mind. He became pure brightness, lighting up all other beings that come close to such a presence, especially those that are sufficiently dry and empty of concepts, theories, prejudice, and doubt. Such brightness cannot remain hidden. Its purpose is to shine for others, to lead many people into lasting transformation in consciousness. I was called to support the process of his introduction to the illusory world of noise and confusion, by offering a precious and perfectly timed nudge at the precise moment when he was ready to step out from the bliss of introversion.

His name is Mohanji.

When Mohanji made that step, he joined the world of noise as Silence. He made, is making, and will forever continue to make the most precious and desperately needed contribution one can make. Silence walks in the world of noise with determination, offering clarity and freedom to all, fully supported by the grand Tradition of Masters.

During one of our initial conversations, Mohanji captured my heart when he said, "I wish that all your hardships, pains, traumatic experiences, fears, betrayals, disappointments, and failures become stepping-stones towards the brightness of ultimate glory." Everything about him pressed all the right buttons in me and my joyful presence complemented his deep silence, leading us to our journey of higher purpose and unconditional togetherness.

Mohanji became my inspiration, the bright star in my inner sky that continues to guide me across the ocean of worldly illusion, through many ups and downs and against all odds. He is my beloved husband and the father of our precious daughter Mila, a true flower of Love. Mohanji, Mila, and I are a trio, our own little trinity, that is an essential part of a much larger spiritual family.

The teachings and methods of beloved Mohanji connect our global family across more than 80 countries. Built on the principles of unconditional love, purity, selflessness, and liberation from the gravitational pull of worldly existence, this family is dedicated to adding value to our respective communities, countries, and the world at large through the simple and eternal power of unconditional giving.

Even though our spiritual work transcends all barriers, including that of gender, my main role is in the awakening, healing, and empowerment of women. Our world needs strong, authentic, brave, educated, skilled, fulfilled, and loving women who are the spine of the sacred family unit and anchors of peace across the globe. To that end, I lead by example as Global Ambassador of the Mohanji Foundation and Global President of our charity, the ACT Foundation, active in 25 countries (and counting), that has touched more than 20 million lives to date. In the name of Mohanji, I give everything that I am, fully and wholeheartedly, while remaining rooted in my own, authentic, powerful feminine expression.

I dedicate this book to the consciousness that operates through Mohanji, for it was he who inspired me to write this book and share my heart with the world. This consciousness cannot be limited to a person or a personality. It represents the very heart of Guru Tattva, a tangible, brilliant, transformative, and uplifting flow from the Source. This is what Mohanji is to me – beyond the frames of marriage, relationships, the mind's games, and expectations. That consciousness lives as a flame of pure love, beyond all transactions and boundaries of human relationships.

All in all, this autobiography is an invitation into a higher vision and experience of life, a heart-to-heart invitation to all those who have suffered or continue to suffer from abuse of any sort, misfortune, humiliation, injustice, disillusionment, or meaninglessness. This book is an invitation to transformation for all people who feel they are victims of circumstances beyond their control, as well as those of you who may have attained the comforts of life, but deep inside feel something is grossly missing.

I want you to know that you are worthy of a life with endless wonders and possibilities. Just as higher education offers a multitude of new employment options, higher awareness reveals new horizons. It offers so many new possibilities to experience the true joy and multidimensional beauty of life. I want you to know that you are worthy of a fulfilling life that you create from your beautiful heart, backed by crystal clarity rooted in an awareness that is yours forever.

Dear friends of past, present, and future, thank you for connecting with me on this beautiful human journey of ours. Let us walk together into a new perspective and higher purpose so that we can, as Mohanji says, "live liberated and leave liberated."

There was an autobiography that mystically entered my life in 2004, changing it forever. This was not just a book – it was a living instrument of Guru Tattva – it spoke to my heart like no other book ever did. I dare to dream that this autobiography will touch you, dear reader, with the same grace.

Writing this book has required, by far, the deepest surrender of my life. During the Covid lockdown in 2020, I recorded a YouTube video series called "My Journey With Mohanji." For the first time, I openly shared some of the most intense trials and triumphs of my journey with Mohanji. In this book, I dive deeper, sharing things I have never dared to share before. I also revisit the experiences shared in those videos, but from a much deeper level of intimacy and insight.

I have written from my heart with absolute surrender to the Divine. May you enjoy the gifts of clarity, empowerment, and love these written words are here to provide. May all that I share with you be a catalyst for transformation in your life. May you also be inspired to pay the blessing forward by sharing the story of your own transformation.

With that, my heart welcomes you to the journey Home.

—Devi Mohan

Devi the pioneer, 1985

Dana, Grandma and Devi, 1981

Devi and father dancing, 1984

The House - Slatina, 1990

Happy, colorful childhood - Devi with best friend Sanja and her sister Tina

Devi's 20th birthday - in hug with sister Dana, Tovarnik 1997

Devi with her Lithuanian and Jordanian UN colleagues, Ilok, 1997

Lonely work days at the Hyatt Regency Hotel, Belgrade, 1998

Devi at her UN office in Kosovo, 1999

Translating for HH Patriarch Pavle, Kosovo, Easter 2000

Devi with Bishop Teodosije, KFOR representative and Father Peter, Kosovo, 2000

HH Patriarch Pavle reading, The Patriarchate of Peć, April 2000

Devi with Father Sava and dignitaries, Monastery Dečani, Kosovo, 2000

Graduation Day - Devi with President James Creagan and Dean Pavoncello, Rome, 2003

Devi with Martha and friends, Notre Dame, Indiana 2004

Salsa dancing at the Mexican Club, Indiana, USA, 2004

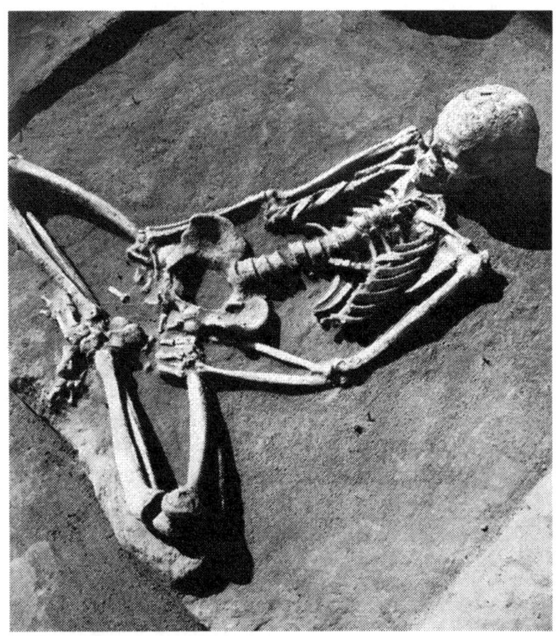

Lepenski Vir, Serbia - proof of a millennia old yogi in the Balkan region (Sourced from the net)

Devi's first media appearance - Dubai 2007

Image of Jesus, Materialised by Sai Baba,
(Sourced from the net,
enhanced by Marko Milović)

Devi, Mohanji, Devi's parents and family,
wedding day, 18 April 2010

Devi with Little Branko, Novi Sad, 2011

Mohanji and Devi under the historic mulberry
tree, Patriarchate of Peć, 2021

Introduction

"I," Devi

The woman described in this book bore many labels before arriving at Devi, her true name and highest destiny. To understand the dimensions of her sacred and powerful calling, she was made to witness extreme highs and lows on her life journey. This is the story of a woman finally settled in the shoes of "Devi," who is ready to expose her most intimate truth, inviting the revelation of true feminine vulnerability rooted in primordial wisdom that calls to be revealed and sanctified again.

> For I am the first and the last.
> I am the honored one and the scorned one.
> I am the whore and the holy one.
> I am the wife and the virgin.
> [...]
> I am the midwife and she who does not bear.
> I am the solace of my labor pains.
> [...]
> I am the utterance of my name.[1]

The power of this story is in its naked truthfulness, in its depth, and in the mirror that such depth offers to all who are ready to undergo their own personal transformation. The exquisite pains and immense blessings described on the following pages are the story of my awakening and self-actualization, the traps I encountered along the way, and my experience of the ultimate alchemy – the transmutation of selfish impulsiveness into the purity of emptiness and unconditional service. Descriptions of such experiences carry the authentic energy of experience-based truth that can metamorphosize everyone it touches.

This story is filled with pain that awakens light, pain that is the threshold to the passage of many "little deaths," to transformation through alchemical trial by fire. The many ups and downs, successes and failures, praises and defamations, joys and pains of life have all been refining fires, revealing ever more precious personal essence. Each experience was a necessary rite of passage to the highest version of myself, teaching the art of giving, opening my heart to the flow of divine love, and delivering me to the pure maiden who cannot be defiled, to Devi.

---

1 The Thunder, Perfect Mind, Nag Hammadi Scriptures. http://gnosis.org/naghamm/thunder.html

Chapter 1

A Childhood Lost

"In case of any shooting, let us all hide in the vineyards." That was the master plan.

In northeastern Croatia's Slavonia region, in a small city called Podravska Slatina, all the neighbors on Milice Križan street held a meeting. It was the early summer of 1991 and the threat of a serious conflict between Serbs and Croats in Croatia loomed above us like a dark, heavy cloud. We took some comfort in jointly deciding on the vineyards. It sounded like a good idea.

Biba-Riba

While growing up in Slatina, I enjoyed a perfect childhood. In 1991, I was one of the happiest 13-year-olds one could find, hopping around with endless joy, spending all my free time after school playing outdoors with my friends. Either my best friend Sanja or someone else was always available to play.

I loved learning the folk dances of Croatia, Serbia, Slovenia, and other parts of Former Yugoslavia. Due to my height, talent, and consistent practice, I was able to train with the more advanced dancers one or two years ahead of my age group. Our fast footwork and circular movements were exhilarating and energetically uplifting, while also grounding, connecting us with the ancestral spirit of the entire region.

Occasionally we traveled to other Yugoslav cities to perform our choreographed routines. Once we went to a lovely town in south Serbia called Guča, where our dances added color and sounds of joy to their famous annual trumpet festival. I remember dancing so intensely that my necklace broke, sending beads all over the stage. Luckily nobody slipped on them, but we still laughed about it for days.

I also participated in regional math competitions. It seemed that my brain was simply wired for math. I had the special ability to silence my mind, dig deep, and intuitively find solutions to complicated mathematical word problems. I remember spending my winter break from school solving word problems. I loved the challenge! Each time the solution to a complex mathematical problem would simply come to me was such a thrill.

While my parents were working, my elder sister Dana and I were in the care of Grandma Ana and Grandpa Pero. We loved them dearly, but we always looked forward to the weekends when Mom would bake a cake or one of her special recipes for lunch. Sometimes she would try to make something secretly and hide it in the freezer, but we would sniff out her creation and scream from excitement upon discovering it.

Mom was soft and caring but also tidy and organized, with an incredible work ethic. She had had a tough childhood with not much support from her parents, yet she always did her best for us. Her job was in the textile sales department of a big department store in the center of our small town. Though she had to stand all day long at work, she never complained of sore legs and continued working the moment she returned home, constantly caring for all of us.

We loved visiting her at work. It was a special treat to see all the latest clothing samples arrive at the store. But the real fun was extracting a couple of coins from Mom and joyfully running across the street with Dana to buy our favorite ice cream!

I remember laying my head in my mom's lap countless times, listening to her stories while she gently caressed my cheek. I especially enjoyed the story of my birth. She said I was always bubbly and full of life. Even my entry into this world was dramatic! She was rushed by ambulance to the maternity ward in the nearby city of Virovitica. I was eager to make my debut and my mom was sure I would be born in the elevator. She managed to make it to the delivery bed, but there was not enough time to remove her stockings, only to lower them. I arrived the very moment they laid her on the bed! (Nowadays, whenever my mom sees me packing, unpacking, and rushing to various events or the airport, she likes to remind me that I had arrived in this world in the same fashion – in a mad rush, but full of joy.)

Everyone called me Biba, short for Biljana, except my dad. To him, I was "Biba-Riba." *Riba* translates to fish and was added to my nickname concoction only because it sounded silly, rhyming with Biba. My dad was always teasing me, but he was never cruel. A big man with an even bigger heart, a tear would well in my dad's eyes whenever he spoke about anything or anyone he loved. My dancing, laughing, and sense of humor are definitely traits inherited from him.

Years later, while living in Serbia, I discovered that *riba* is slang for "a chick." After that, I hushed my dad whenever he tried to use my nickname in public. Being introduced as "Biba the chick" was beyond embarrassing for a young adult and gave my dad irrevocable teasing power for years to come.

The House

Fond memories of my childhood days revolve around a beautiful, three-story house at the top of a small hill, glowing in the warm light of a street lamp. Surrounding it was my mother and father's lovingly cultivated garden, bursting with colors and sweet fragrances. Mom gave Dana and me the arduous task of watering the countless pots on our balconies each day. We whined that there were too many pots, but we loved how the house looked and learned early in life that good looks require serious maintenance effort.

The house had a small orchard of organic apples and fifteen other fruit trees of which our dad was especially proud. He also loved tending to the hedge border surrounding our big yard of soft grass.

The yard was perfect for our improvised gymnastics and all sorts of outdoor play. A decade later, when I started practicing yoga, I understood where I got the base for my flexibility and proficiency in yoga *asanas* – right there on that grass! While my propensity for yoga surely originated long before this lifetime, the yogic knowledge lying deep within used to come out spontaneously during play.

Dana and I loved playing in the yard and generally loved everything about our house and neighborhood. I remembered the day when Dad was laying concrete on the big stairs between the house entrance and the summer kitchen near the basement. With a matchstick, he ceremoniously wrote "Dana & Biba" on the wet cement. That engraving remains on that staircase to this day, a testament to the beautiful childhood that once existed there.

The house had a special meaning to everyone in the Radonić family; it was our anchoring point. My parents and grandparents built this house from their sweat and blood. They toiled every day but never complained. The suffering and poverty of the Post-World War II years motivated them to work hard and prove their worth by creating such a large home. I remember that we once participated in a contest for the most beautiful house in Slatina. To our great joy, our house was among the top ten. That made my parents even more proud and eager to make it even more special.

The house was as old as I was. Only one room was usable when I was born in 1977. The whole family was housed in that single room, my cradle right in the middle, except for Dana who initially stayed with our grandma's sister in a nearby village. When the rest of the house was completed, that room became the basement.

Later in life, I would see that room several times in vivid, soul-stirring visions. It took a lot of spiritual seeking and contemplation to discover why my consciousness kept returning to that one room. Most notably, it reappeared in 2008 during a profoundly insightful non-hypnotic regression session with Dr. Yogesh Choudhary in Delhi, India.

I woke up suddenly, lying in a cradle on my back in a completely dark room. I was in the body of a small baby, all alone in the darkness. I cried in fear, as loud as I could. Suddenly, I was aware of a pleasant, tangible, loving presence. Two beings with a smooth, pearl-like complexion and golden glow floated into the room, hovering above me. They were similar to human beings, except that they had no hair and their slim waistline and neck were a bit elongated. Their heads had an unusual shape, like that of a human head with a cake on top (remains of similarly shaped skulls have been found, dating back to ancient Egypt). The most prominent feature on their faces was their large eyes, exuding so much love that I became instantly mesmerized and breathless. They could communicate through their eyes, without any facial expressions or words. Such communication is so effective and is felt very deeply.

For a time they just held me in their gaze and I felt incredibly comforted and loved. That was my first memory of telepathic communication. I recognized the truth that so much more can be conveyed in this way, much more than any spoken language. I stopped crying immediately to stare into those big eyes transmitting pure love into the very core of my being. Both beings were so incredibly dear and familiar to me. Deep in my heart, beyond anything my mind could fathom, I knew without a doubt that they are my parents and I their beloved child, in a different body and different time-space continuum.

This topic is very delicate and its interpretation requires special attention. For the time being, we shall remain with horizontal time on Earth and my childhood memories.

The Milice Križan Street Family

The street we lived on was truly something special – full of friendly neighbors and bubbly kids, with so many outdoor games to enjoy each day. All the neighbors were so connected that we felt like one large family. Indeed, the Milice Križan street family was rocking! Never before and never after have I seen such cohesion and family-like connection on one street. We used to gather once a month on a green meadow near our house, grown-ups and children alike. We would light up a campfire and have fun baking potatoes and corn kebabs in its flames. We spent our time together singing, dancing, laughing, and overall having a great time.

A journalist on our street used to come to those gatherings with his guitar and entertain us with his freshly composed, superbly satiric songs. He had an amazing talent for bringing out the rhyme in combination with some hilarious detail highlighting every family on our street. He had a knack for finding the perfect trait in each family about which to tease them. And we loved it so much!

With great anticipation, each family awaited their turn to be highlighted. We would all sing the refrain together, clapping to the beat, and then he would introduce a stanza for the next family that would make us all break into laughter. The last one I remember was *"Radonićke, kućne maze, samo svoju baku paze."* (The literal translation being: "Radonić girls [referring to my sister and me], remain home, always busy taking care of their grandma.")

Our love for our grandma was obvious to everyone. Even though she was short and often rather slow due to her weight and weak heart, grandma was the star of our childhood sky. She was the one who would take us to the dentist, doctor, or wherever needed, the one to cook for us on the weekdays and watch over us in all our mischief. Dana and I loved her to bits! She was also street-smart and very observant.

One winter, while ice skating across the frozen brook near our house, my right leg went through a layer of thin ice and sank into the freezing water up to my knee. My sister and I immediately devised a plan to hide this all from Grandma. Dana brought some cotton napkins and a rope and wrapped my leg up to the knee. While hopping into the yard on one foot, I enacted a scene from a movie to make Grandma believe that we were only playing a game in which I had to act wounded. Giving us a stern look, she said, "You better get that wet leg warmed in the kitchen right away before you catch a cold!"

Gunfire and My Brave Grandma

As the tension of looming war grew, the tone of those street family gatherings around the campfire changed from jovial to serious. All the neighbors agreed to stick together in case of any serious gunfire. We planned to run up the hill to hide in the vineyards which soon proved to be completely naïve. War always comes with unexpected twists, along with tremendous fear and chaos. Boom! It just takes over and nothing in life remains the same. Plans and certainty do not exist in war. And there are no winners. When it hits, you lose the very ground you stand on. That's exactly what happened to us.

The first shots we heard came from the very vineyards that were supposed to be our refuge! There was nowhere to run to so we opted to lay low and hide in our homes. Our family happened to have guests that night. My aunt and uncle from Osijek and their two children were with us when loud shots woke us in the middle of the night. I remember hiding behind the washing machine, under the stairs of the first floor with my sister. We laughed wildly, imagining we were caught up in an exciting action movie. But maintaining that positivity for long was not possible. At some point, the rush of adrenaline wore off and we crawled fearfully in our pajamas through the yard to the basement. We hid among the sacks of potatoes, waiting for the shooting to stop.

As we hid, our little cousin complained, "I'm so thirsty…" Grandma instantly sprang into action.

"Stay put," she said, "I will go to the kitchen and fetch you some water." The kitchen was across the yard, which meant she would be exposed to the bullets randomly shot from the hills. I still remember the expression on her face and the determination in her loving blue eyes. Prior exposure to war had made her gritty and it was clear she was unafraid to die.

At that moment all of us shouted, "No, grandma, no! They can shoot you from the hills!" But she just smiled. She simply had to get water for her grandson. Luckily, nothing happened to her that night and the shooting subsided at some point. But that experience of her poised, fearless demeanor, courage, and love stayed with me.

While our sweet Grandma Ana was short and chubby in physique, she was a giant in terms of her courage. She would sometimes share her WWII stories with us. Once we watched some partisan film from WWII about the battles of ordinary villagers against the heavily armed Nazis, narratives of true courage and sacrifice. Grandma added her own stories and observations. "Please know that these movies are not exaggerating anything," she said. "All that you saw in that movie did actually happen. The courage and defiance among the common people, oh well, it was simply outstanding. The Germans were well-armed and we hardly had anything – just some sticks and shovels. But we were defending our homes and we were not afraid to die!"

Another time, Grandma shared her own experience from the war, when she was imprisoned by the Nazis. She was taken with a group of approximately 20 people to a smaller concentration camp from which they eventually transported all the prisoners to one of the main concentration camps. This is how Grandma described her experience:

> "We were crammed into a room with several piles of horse dung. It smelled so terrible in there that we could hardly breathe. Yet, we were forced to sleep on that dung. That was

part of the overall humiliation agenda by the Nazis that went with the imprisonment. Every evening we would wonder whether we'd live to see another day.

"In the morning, we were shouted at and given tasks. It was usually some hard labor, regardless of gender and size. I was barely 17 and as short as I was, I was given the exhausting task of walking to a nearby spring and carrying two big metal buckets of water. They would put a wooden stick across my shoulders, with those two heavy buckets on each side for balance. I would somehow manage to start walking and then just continue, step by step, carrying all that weight. Each step was a torment. My entire body hurt from the exertion and my stomach from hunger and malnourishment.

"The same guard would stand in front of our quarters each day. One day, an idea just came to my mind. I challenged myself to fill my heart with as much love as I could, then looked at the guard softly, and beamed all that love on him. I knew I had nothing to lose by trying to reach out to him through love. Eventually, he responded. He liked my gaze. I could feel that he found me beautiful. This exchange of soft glances happened several times.

"One night I managed to speak to him, whispering from behind the bars: 'I'm going to tell you a secret. I have a couple of golden coins hidden in my bra. Please let us go and I will give you those coins.' I looked deep into his eyes with utmost love, invoking compassion in his heart through a continuous gaze.

"He paused for a moment, then smiled and said, 'Ok, I will let you go.'

"I was happy but could not bear the thought of leaving all the other people behind to die. Mustering all the strength I had in me, I decided to risk it further by pleading, 'Not just me, please let ALL of us go.'

"He kept looking into my eyes and finally said, 'Ok, but go right now before I change my mind.'

"As quickly as humanly possible, I woke everyone up. I was shivering inside, worried that the guard might change his mind. Like ghosts, we quietly slipped through the door that he unlocked. I gave him the golden coins and exchanged the final soft glances that conveyed my gratitude, along with a whisper, 'You are a good man. Thank you.'

"It was a huge risk, but I was glad that I had trusted my intuition. All of us ran in different directions that night, dispersing as fast as we could, desperate to reach the warmth of our homes. It felt amazing to be free again. I was especially joyous because I knew the lives of those twenty or so people had been saved because of me. That felt amazing and so deeply fulfilling."

Wow! Grandma Ana, the war heroine! This story stayed with me and took on a life of its own in my heart and memory. I used to contemplate whether I would have had the strength to do the same had I been in her situation. Would I have been able to find the love in my heart, a love powerful enough to thaw the ice in the heart of the security guard? And would I have saved myself alone? Or would I have had the guts to take the ultimate risk of losing that chance by asking the guard to release all the other people as well?

I was especially inspired by the way she had transformed the guard with love. I always had this innate knowledge that the heart is incredibly powerful, much more than our mind can fathom, and this story only confirmed it. Not many people could ever bring themselves to feel love for a guard that made their lives miserable. And yet, my grandma understood he was just a young man doing his job. She knew that behind his stern appearance, there was a soft heart that could be reached. I am filled with admiration for my grandma, my hero, who exhibited so much selflessness and such exceptional bravery.

I hoped to be like her when I grew up and told her this once, while cuddled in her lap. She said to me, "*Golubice bakina* (my dearest dove), but you are so brave already. Do you remember what you did when you were only six, how you wanted to save my life?" Since I only recalled the event vaguely, Grandma then shared the story of our walk across the meadow just beyond a little brook that separated our land from that of our neighbors and Grandma's cousin, Jela.

The two of us had been walking alone across the meadow when Grandma suddenly started wheezing and breathing heavily. My grandma suffered from a challenging heart condition called *Angina Pectoris*. She shared with me how deeply touched she was when I looked into her eyes and bravely proclaimed with total seriousness, "Grandma, do not worry. If you fall, I will carry you." I was so small, but totally confident that I could do it. She knew I meant it which is why she found my gesture so touching and sweet.

Her heart warmed and her spirit uplifted by this expression of purest love and courage, Grandma Ana felt better instantly. We slowly continued walking and reached Grandma Jela's house. She recounted this experience many times to different people. I too remember the moment – the heat, the grass, and that feeling when casting aside all fear I told her with utmost conviction that I would carry her. I wonder what propelled me: was it the spirit of my ancestors, my intense love for my grandma, or just my own heart overruling the mind?

Tito and the Yugoslav Woman

One year after this expression of courage, it was time for me to enroll in school. I couldn't wait! I could already read, add and subtract, and would read my sister's books, gathering knowledge from other subjects as well. I especially loved memorizing poems written for children. One day I walked around the house twice and memorized a poem about a frog in a pond. I was able to memorize it quite easily. As I recited it for grandma, she said that reminded her of some poem-related drama from my dad's childhood. Smiling, with that special glow in her eyes, she shared the story as follows:

> "When your father was approximately your age, one day I found him walking around the big mulberry tree in our yard, memorizing a song called 'Mother and the Child'. He was to recite it on stage at the upcoming school event. God only knows how many times he walked around that tree, reciting the poem endlessly. This went on for days. Surely even the birds on the trees would have learned it.
>
> "Finally, the day of the school event arrived. When 'Milan Radonić' was called to the stage, your father climbed up the steps proudly and ceremoniously like a child-sized Napoleon,

head up and spine straight. He then proceeded to loudly recite the title of the poem, his voice resounding through the hall: 'Mother and the Child!'

"There was an awkward pause. Some moments elapsed before he repeated the title, this time a bit softer, but still confident 'Mother and the Child!'

"Another round of awkward silence followed, this time even longer. Finally, he ended with a final proclamation - 'Mother and the Chiiiiiiild!' In the middle of this declaration he burst into tears provoking the audience's immediate laughter. There was something indescribably funny about this scene! It may have been because his entry was so dramatic. A wave of laughter circled the hall. I must admit that I would have laughed as well had I not been his mother.

"Of course, I felt bad for him and went to hug and console him. But he really did make people laugh, more than anyone who would have tried to achieve that effect intentionally. This is why I'm happy to see that you got your intelligence and diligence for studies from your mom. Thank God. But if you make people smile, you should know that could be a trait from your dad."

This adorable story remained with me and during any recitals I witnessed in the future, I would giggle and imagine my dad as a kid, proudly reciting the poem's title and progressing no further. That was so my dad – hilarious.

When the first day of my school arrived, I remember all of us standing up and introducing ourselves to the class. When my turn came, I got up and humbly said, "Biljana Radonić."

Soon after me, a blond girl stood up and said a name that created a similar effect to that of my dad's recital. "Dunja Breskvić," said the sweet girl. The literal translation is Quince Peach-ich. (The ending syllable 'ić' is typical for most Serbian family names.) We were shocked into laughter that her parents would name her Dunja, as if it was not bad enough that another fruit was her last name! The poor girl had to cope with endless teasing at school. At that moment, I vowed that, should I ever become a parent, I would give my child a simple, elegant name, easily pronounced by all.

This outburst also revealed how sweet my primary school teacher Helena was, how skillfully she calmed us down and continued with introductions. I loved sitting as close as I could to my teacher, mainly in the first or second row, following everything attentively. I was not nerdy, but my strategy was simple and meaningful: to learn as much as I could at school, finish homework as soon as I came home, and then go out and play for the rest of the day. The "work hard, play hard" policy worked for me.

One event stood out as a powerful experience at the onset of my education - when I joined the Union of Pioneers of Yugoslavia and became Tito's Pioneer. The pioneer movement was for all children of age seven and older. The goal of the program was for Pioneers to be responsible and respectful and to study hard as the future generations of the nation. I took the famous Pioneer oath very seriously. It brought to mind all the children who died in WWII and never got a chance to grow up, not to mention going to school and enjoying life.

There was a song about a girl called Marija who never got to grow up ("*Marija nikada odrasla nije*"), with her yellow coat sleeves remaining too long for her. That song always got to me, as well as any mention of the mass killing of children by the Nazis in the Serbian city of Kragujevac during WWII. The very thought of people, children especially, dying in war, made me sad and solemn. That is why I took my Pioneer title and responsibility very seriously.

While taking the oath, I felt the spirit of the ancestors in me, the spirit of all selfless people who had given their lives for the country. The words of this oath remain engraved in my memory:

> Today, when I am initiated as a pioneer
> I give the pioneer's word of honor
> That I shall learn and work hard and be a good friend;
> That I shall love our self-governed homeland, the Socialist Federal Republic of Yugoslavia;
> That I shall contribute to brotherhood and unity and the ideas Tito fought for;
> That I shall respect all people of the world who want freedom and peace!

I honestly loved the spirit of former Yugoslavia and the principles of brotherhood and unity. I loved the enthusiasm with which people were uniting in their joint effort to rebuild the country ruined by war, creating anew in the joy of togetherness. There was so much humor, talent, celebration, and unity in diversity between different ethnic groups and republics of Former Yugoslavia. To this day, most people from the Balkan region carry that Yugo-nostalgic feeling in their hearts.

Unity and dedication to a higher cause have always been my vibe. And nobody could invoke the feeling of Yugoslav unity better than the Yugoslav music icon of the 1980s – Lepa Brena. With her beautiful long legs, stunning smile, and amazing voice, Lepa Brena had a charm that appealed to everyone. One could say that she was Yugoslavia's Tina Turner since she is still active as a singer and still looks stunning in a mini skirt.

Born in Bosnia as Fahreta Jahić, Lepa Brena was a true bridge between the ethnic divide among Yugoslav people, as well as the traditional-modern and rural-urban divides (her disco pop songs were played on the accordion, a traditional folk instrument from the Balkan peninsula). Using her feminine charm and suggestive, elegant eroticism, she challenged the traditional patriarchal moral codes ingrained deep in the Balkan mentality. Her dress code was seductive and quirky, but completely appropriate even for children to watch. Brena was simply adorable and acceptable to all.

The first time I ever went to the cinema was in the late 1980s, to watch one of the three feature films from the musical comedy film series "Hajde da se volimo" (Let's Love One Another) by Lepa Brena and her band Slatki Greh (Sweet Sin). I remember how the laughter, music, and sweetness warmed the hearts of all present in the movie theater. Again, the movie was appropriate for all age groups, all ethnicities, all social strata – for everyone. That is when I first noticed and was impressed by how effectively feminine energy expressed through music, humor, and overall celebration of life can serve the cause of peace and unity. This insight has stayed with me.

Her song "Jugoslovenka" (A Yugoslav Woman) will always remain one of the most famous Yugoslav pop songs. It evokes nostalgia instantly. Moreover, it remains a powerful beacon of women's emancipation through music and film, not only in former Yugoslavia, but far and wide. I remember the thrill and goosebumps all over my body when I first heard the song, in which Lepa Brena celebrates unity in diversity in the most innovative way, reinforced by three prominent male co-singers from different ethnic and religious backgrounds: Montenegrin music star Danijel Popović, Croatian Vlado Kalember (who represented Yugoslavia at Eurovision 1984), and Bosnian Alen Islamović, the iconic lead singer of Bijelo Dugme, the most famous music band from Bosnia & Herzegovina.

To each one of them, Lepa Brena responds in the chorus, as a female personification of Yugoslavia, through her melodious voice in a beautiful physical body:

> My eyes are the Adriatic Sea,
> My hair is the Pannonian ears of grain,
> The Slavic soul is my sister -
> I am a Yugoslav woman.

When Yugoslavia crumbled under the heavy boot of brutal fratricidal war, Lepa Brena disappeared from the music scene for some time, until her return a couple of years later. One can freely say that she never succumbed to nationalistic pressures and remained the graceful personification of Yugoslav unity. While her music was not to my personal taste, I honor Lepa Brena as a phenomenon.

The music I really got into was *Sarajevska škola,* the Sarajevo school of pop rock. Sarajevska škola collectively refers to the amazing popular music created between 1960 and 1991 by artists and bands native to Sarajevo, the capital of Bosnia and Herzegovina, which was then one of the six republics of Yugoslavia. The music created in this period had a huge influence on the entire region and helped create a distinct identity for modern Sarajevo. Yugoslav rock really rocked! Bands like Bijelo Dugme, Zlatna Jabuka, Plavi Orkestar, Merlin, Zabranjeno Pušenje were among my favorites. Their music immediately brings feelings of nostalgia. Sarajevo was a city that embodied the spirit of unity, art, music, comedy, and the beauty of humanity.

The South Slavic Soul

I cannot close this topic without mentioning the famous Serbian pop-folk singer, songwriter, and recording artist Tomislav "Toma" Zdravković. In 2022, I watched the movie "Toma" about the life of this outstanding man, a true bohemian and poet, whose songs were a unique mix of French *chansons* and Serbian folk music. His warm baritone voice is truly inimitable and touches the depth of the heart. I watched this movie in one breath, without moving an inch. As the movie ended, tears flowed and took their time to stop. Built-up emotions created a long squeeze until my heart expanded so much that the inner call had to be answered – that of looking deep into these illogically strong emotions and their true message.

Toma Zdravković sang and composed from the depth of his soul. He spoke of the soul, at a time when this word was not very popular within Communist ideology. His songs touch the heart so indescribably deeply only because he lived at that depth, at that frequency. He indeed walked that sacred ground and that is why he could convey that which is indescribable.

Toma embodies the South Slavic soul, the unbearable depth of pain and unimaginable heights of love, the courage of vulnerability, the beauty of untamed creativity, and the magnificence of expressing one's uniqueness from the deepest space of the heart. He was a man deeply in touch with the feminine principle within and expressed it so beautifully.

As the war in former Yugoslavia was starting, regardless of his health condition, he traveled throughout the country, lighting up hearts through a series of live concerts. His doctor and surgeon recognized the importance of this calling, this higher mission of Toma's, and helped him fulfill it by personally driving him to all his performances. Powerful ripples of Love were created and his songs and message live on.

The reason his life's work touched me so deeply was my innermost feeling that former Yugoslavia (meaning, the land of the Southern Slavs) was not just a country. It was a platform that provided space for the expression of the soul of the Southern Slavs, the beauty of unity in diversity, the ideal of being more than the ordinary, and the calling to rise above one's selfish need-based existence. In former Yugoslavia, everyone gave something for the greater good. Comedians, singers, actors, various artists, as well as the common citizens of all other professions, all expressed their best within the available platform of unity in diversity.

The joy of heart-centered living was incredibly high, which is why many people remained "Yugo-nostalgic" long after the fratricidal war that tore this platform apart. Wherever we go, we may find better roads, economy, and administrative or governance systems, but we cannot seem to find that joy, warmth, and depth of connection between people. Everyone from former Yugoslavia who lives and works abroad comes to that same conclusion. This ideal is embedded in our South Slavic genome and is thousands of years old, predating Christianity by more than five millennia. Recent genetic studies based on Haplotypes and Haplogroups are now raising some poignant questions in this regard, questions that may lead to a complete revision of the historical narrative of South Slavs in the Balkan region. Paleolithic excavations in Lepenski Vir in Serbia (the first discovered urban settlement in Europe which is 8.5 millennia old) and Neolithic excavations done in Vinča (5.7 millennia old, located mainly in Serbia, but also several other surrounding countries in the region), are the proof of the beautiful civilization that once blossomed on the Balkan peninsula, especially around the Danube river.

Architect Pavlović, a recognized Serbian expert on the culture of Lepenski Vir, explains that "the Lepenians must have possessed a great knowledge of symmetry, geometry, right angles, even the Golden ratio, which is visible in the exterior and, even more, in the interior of the buildings. [...]

"Researchers at the site, including Pavlović, believe that the 'House 49' [discovered at Lepenski Vir] was a perfectly constructed 'energetic machine'. They explained it has a way in which air circulates through a shell-shaped house providing a comfortable environment for its inhabitants – also known as 'thermal comfort' in architecture. Architect Pavlović also maintains that Lepenski

Vir is the first planned settlement in Europe due to the exceptional creativity and knowledge of the indigenous people of the site."[2]

I was intrigued by the story of Vinča's discovery near Belgrade in the 1960s.

> "When the mighty Danube returned to its river bed a century ago, it revealed a great treasure. An old man named Panta from Vinča found a strange clay figurine on the river bank. This curious old man had never seen anything like it, so he took his figurine to the National Museum in Belgrade to find the explanation. He couldn't have even imagined that in his hands he was holding a figurine that had been made by an early man in the late Stone Age.
>
> "Since then the archaeological excavations have been revealing numerous cultural layers of a civilization preserved in a seemingly just an ordinary hill in Vinča. Archaeologists concluded that it was the largest Neolithic settlement in Europe, dating back more than 7,000 years B.C.
>
> "The archaeological treasure of Vinča was found at 10.5 meters of depth and it contains numerous layers of civilizations dating from the Neolithic Period over the Bronze Age to the tombs from the Middle Ages."[3]

My heart sends out a sincere calling to the souls of true historians destined to prove that which I already know deep inside. The truth of the South Slavic people, my ancestors, has much greater depth than the sixth-century migrations and that which is currently put forth as our history. Our pre-Christian ancestors valued the Sacred Feminine and embraced the essence of Vedic teachings, as evidenced by their ideals, values, beliefs, and lifestyle of deep connection with Mother Nature that lives on to this day. I would like to reiterate that I am not a historian and cannot provide detailed scientific or historic proof to this claim, but merely rely on my intuition (which has never failed me) and the hints received through recent studies.

Connection with Vedic teachings and ancient India is best seen through language. Numerous words are the same or similar in the Serbo-Croatian language and Sanskrit, in addition to some major grammatical rules. There is no possibility of a coincidence when it comes to language. Such similarities in language prove a connection between my ancestors from the Balkan region and ancient India. In Lepenski Vir in 2020 they also discovered the remnants of a man seated in a lotus pose. Was this a yogi who left his body in Samadhi on the territory of modern Serbia seven millennia ago? I was deeply touched by this discovery.

It is only a matter of time before the values that our pre-Christian ancestors embodied will be given their proper historic connotation and recognition. I see those values as the cause of the special talents, depth, beauty, and strength of the South Slavic people. These values are very much alive

---

2 Source: https://brewminate.com/the-culture-of-lepenski-vir-in-prehistoric-siberia/

3 Source:http://www.serbia.com/visit-serbia/cultural-attractions/archaeological-sites/vinca-the-cradle-of-european-civilization/

and I strongly believe they will become ever more activated through the consciousness and DNA of the Southern Slavs from the Balkan region.

The bridge between South Slavic joy and Vedic teachings, between the Balkans and India, is indeed alive in my heart. Everything that the Mohanji Foundation stands for is in service of such values – selflessness, non-violence, unconditional love, life in harmony with nature, and sacred duty towards one's family and society – values that are far beyond the boundaries of the mind.

I have always felt powerfully attracted to the very notion of unity and the unity of East and West. The connection between Vedic teachings and Southern Slavs is what stirs the greatest joy in my heart. Only after my near-death experience in 1999 did I gain sufficient clarity to understand why I felt such a pull toward unity. For the time being, we shall remain with the pre-war events in Slatina.

Discovering My Ethnicity

A huge wave of nationalism swept across Croatia and Serbia in the spring of 1991, heating up with each passing summer day and the media-fueled it to the maximum. As a 13-year-old girl in primary school, I didn't quite understand what was happening. One day at school, I heard some of the kids asking, "What's your favorite football team?" Some boys would immediately answer "Red Star" while others shouted, "Dinamo!" Aside from these being the two most popular football teams in Croatia at the time, there was a hidden polarization behind these answers, something I was yet to discover.

I remember when one boy insisted that I reply to his question about my favorite football team. I did not understand what the big deal was. I did not follow football at all, but since red was never my favorite (probably because it reminded me of blood), I replied without thinking, "Dinamo." Their color was blue, which was much better.

When I came home that day, I shared this seemingly insignificant experience with my parents at the dinner table. I remember how my father's face froze that very second. He paused, dropped his fork and knife, and then said in a serious tone, "There is something that you and your sister need to know at this point in time." He hesitated for a second and then continued with a sigh, "We are Serbian."

"What?! How's that possible? We live in Croatia, and the Serbs – well, they live in Serbia."

Dad replied that we were ethnically Serbian, even though we lived in Croatia. "Your mother's ancestors are Serbs from the Lika region and my ancestors are Serbs from the Slavonia region of Croatia. You should know this because there's a lot of nationalistic talk going on at this time. You should know your roots."

I was in a state of shock, to say the least. At that moment, I didn't want to be Serbian. I had heard some people say bad things about Serbs and that all Serbian people should be kicked out of Croatia. It was then that I understood that most Dinamo football fans were staunch Croats, while most Serbs were cheering for Red Star. With my new understanding, I would be careful to never say that I was a Dinamo fan or any club's fan for that matter. I quickly learned to swiftly and diplomatically extricate myself from such conversations.

The discovery of my ethnicity opened many topics for deeper discussions at home. Many of the stories that came up were horrific. One had to have the stomach for such stories. I remember the day when my Grandpa Pero shared with us how his father had been tortured and killed by the Ustaše[4] before his very eyes! At age seventeen, all he could do was helplessly listen to his father's screams. Hiding behind a nearby pillar, he witnessed his father's eyes being plucked out, among other horrors. I will return to this story later when speaking about ancestral karma, as it may be too early to delve into such darkness at this point.

It was very painful to see my grandpa so deeply shaken by the recollection of this traumatic event. As I leaned forward to hug him, I could see immense horror reflected in his teary eyes.

He looked at me and said, "I debated telling you this since you are still so young. But yes, you need to know who the Ustaše were and what they were capable of. You have to be aware. I could never understand where such sadism came from - what have we, Serbian people in Croatia, done to them to deserve this? But it was there, it happened, and it should never be forgotten. And now they are waving the same flag in front of my eyes. The other day I even heard the same slogans that the Ustaše used. The same evil has resurfaced. It is unbearable."

During my studies, I learned that the amygdala, the brain's alarm system, cannot tell time. That is why by merely seeing the symbols of the Ustaše, my grandpa was being plunged into the emotional depth of reliving his trauma. Triggers can stir up unprocessed trauma memories, which then activate the amygdala. This is why symbols should never be taken lightly.

I must say I was in a state of shock, if not disbelief, that one of my immediate ancestors had experienced such horrific abuse and injustice. "My goodness," I thought. "Have I entered a twilight zone or is this really happening?" This was the first time I had ever learned of ethnic-based hatred and violence.

This story had a deep impact on me because this atrocity had been committed not by the Nazi Germans or some malevolent foreigners, but by the people we lived with, our neighbors and countrymen, who spoke the same language and shared the same land. I simply could not understand how an ordinary human being could turn into a monstrously violent one in the blink of

---

4 In short, the Ustaše were the ultranationalist Croatian revolutionary movement responsible for the systematic persecution and mass extermination of mainly Serbs, but also Jews, Roma, and political dissidents, in WWII in a bid to make Croatia "ethnically clean." Large-scale massacres were committed and concentration camps were built, the largest one being the Jasenovac, which was notorious for its high mortality rate and the barbaric practices which occurred in it. These ultranationalists used the Nazi occupation of Croatia at the onset of WWII to declare the Independent State of Croatia, a puppet state of German Nazis and Italian Fascists, while other Croats joined Tito and the Yugoslav Army that formed in 1942.

an eye. My immediate next thought was about human nature and my wonderful Croatian neighbors – could any of them suddenly turn into Ustaše?

This was the moment that introduced me to the cycles of violence within my ancestral lineage and the collective consciousness of the Balkan people. This is the moment I return to when speaking about these perpetual cycles of violence that have tainted the wonderful, joyous, colorfully diverse people of the Balkan region, people of immense potential, talent, and heart. These cycles are rooted in the frequency of victimhood that brews within, taking its own time to boil over before inciting more acts of violence. Then when the right triggers activate the amygdala of enough people, they bring to the surface collective or individual violence justified by previous sufferings.

However, violence is never truly justified. And violence is never the answer. It completely destroys the firewall of our conscience. After engaging in violence, it is difficult to return to a balanced, higher-frequency energy. That frequency is the precondition or launching pad to our highest divine potential. Even in the case of self-defense, the act of inflicting pain on another should be the very last option, not the first one.

This victimhood phenomenon within the collective consciousness of the Balkan people created a deep longing within me to understand it, to study it, and most importantly, to transcend it within myself before even attempting to speak about it to others in any way. Throughout my studies and years of spiritual inner work, I wanted to make sure that I never observed any Croat I encountered through the prism of my grandpa's traumatic experience with the Ustaše who murdered his innocent father.

Indeed, I return to this moment with my grandpa as the entry point of the shadow of victimhood into my energetic structure, coming from both collective and ancestral energy. Just like a weed that quickly spreads, ruining what once was a beautiful garden, the energetic shadow grows when unattended and suppressed. The more we try to push it down and ignore it, the stronger it becomes. Its ugly head peeks out during our emotional reactions and moments when the limbic brain takes over.

Carl Gustav Jung, the famous Swiss psychologist whom I respect immensely, opened my eyes to the profundity of the truth of the shadow aspect that all of us carry within. It consists of all unpleasant, negative impressions and memories of life experiences that were too painful to process. They get left behind, dismissed, and therefore remain unconscious. But even when a shadow is ignored, it does not disappear. We will return to this topic when describing the experiences of my own encounter with the inner shadow.

In all confidence, I have reached a point in my spiritual journey where I can say that I can stand before a person of any ethnicity (and being of Serbian ethnic background, the most challenging in that sense would be Croatian and Kosovo Albanian nationalists, who create the strongest triggers within the Serbian historic dynamic), and state: "I do not hate you. I see a spark of the Divine in your eyes. May the violence end with me."

Within our inner universe, we have to be that starting point; we have to take that responsibility! The mind will always find excuses. Awareness has to be stronger. The brightness of awareness has to be given access into the deepest recesses of our being so that it reaches the shadow and embraces it as yet another version of ourselves, the version we need not choose to express.

The Native American parable about the two wolves sums it up most beautifully. While teaching his grandson about life, an old man said:

> A fight is going on inside me. It is a terrible fight and it is between two wolves. One is evil – he is anger, envy, sorrow, regret, greed, arrogance, self-pity, guilt, resentment, inferiority, lies, false pride, superiority, and ego.
>
> The other is good – he is joy, peace, love, hope, serenity, humility, kindness, benevolence, empathy, generosity, truth, compassion, and faith. The same fight is going on inside you – and inside every other person, too.
>
> His grandson then asked him, “Which wolf will win?”
>
> The old man simply replied, “The one you feed.”

What the wise elder is pointing out here is the truth that all the answers are within. The reality we live in is a direct result of our innermost beliefs. In other words, we live in the world we believe in. That is why it is important to carefully consider what we choose to believe in. Similarly, what we resist, persists. Because we resist it, we give it energy. While things beyond our control will always happen to us, it is how we respond and the perspective we adopt that ultimately determines our reality.

While my grandpa would never have chosen such a horror for his father, his reaction to that experience determined his reality. The Ustaše continued to exist in his world. It is my deepest belief that, in general, once any painful experience happens to anyone, it is up to that individual to decide how that experience will shape them. Will it pull them down into the darkness of hatred, feeding the evil wolf? Or will it serve as an inspiration to become a beacon of light for others, to help raise the awareness of others, so that something so ugly and painful would never happen again?

Unfortunately, most people look outward to try to make sense of what’s going on inside. When we feel triggered, angry, or vengeful, we feel that we cope better if we find someone else to blame. The irony here is that, in our attempt to feel more in control of the uncontrollable situations and to feel better about ourselves by pointing the finger at someone else and making them look bad, we strip ourselves of our own power. We remove our personal responsibility from the scenario. We remove our freedom of choice in how we are to approach and interpret that situation.

While blaming and hating another seems like a quick way out, it is actually the biggest trap, one that remains imprinted in our energetic structure, calling for repetition. It becomes an unconscious pattern and a point at which we stop taking sole responsibility for our own emotions in reaction to the experiences we are faced with. In this catch-22 scenario, it is our reaction that reinforces or attracts the repetition of such experiences. That is when contemplation is necessary so that we can recognize the trap and not be caught in it.

We should always remember that we are the ones who feed the wolf of our choice and that the basic ingredient that determines the overall flavor of our life are the choices we make and how these choices impact our families, communities, society, and the world at large.

During any war, the media often captures the imagination and manipulates the mindset of the people. And the more attention one gives to the media, the more power one gives away to the lobbies behind the media who seek to shape our psyche and make crucial choices for us. Attention then goes outward, not inward. Consequently, power is lost.

For example, when I was in Croatia, I remember the moment when the story of an oven-roasted baby appeared repeatedly on Croatian TV. It was the story of brutal Serbian extremists (Četniks[5]) placing a Croat baby in an oven and roasting it like a piglet. Later on, in Serbia, I heard an identical story, but the other way around – that of a Serbian baby, oven-roasted by Croatian extremists (Ustaše).

I would like to point out that no detailed historical and political analysis of the tumultuous Balkan history will be offered in this book. Volumes can be written on that topic alone. I will be focusing only on my own experiences, offering a minimum explanation of the historical and political background.

However, I do find it important to highlight that concurrent with the fall of Yugoslavia (due to the above-mentioned internal issues), there was an unraveling of a pre-planned breakup of Yugoslavia from outside of the country. In other words, Yugoslavia fell apart not only from the inside, but was also destroyed from the outside.

Aside from the Ustaše-četnik polarity, there has always been this other dimension to the conflicts in the Balkan region, one that is often underplayed or overlooked. I always remember how beautifully my grandpa summarized this second aspect within the tragic, war-plagued Balkan history dynamic. He summed it up perfectly when he said, "Our [the Balkan people's] main mistake was that we have built our home in the middle of the road." Initially, I didn't quite understand what he meant so I asked him to explain that statement further. Grandpa then spoke of the dividing line between the Eastern and Western spheres of influence over many centuries. This dividing line has always run right through the middle of post-WWII Yugoslavia!

---

5 Četniks were elite guerrillas in the Serbian royal army, part of the Yugoslav royalist and Serbian nationalist movements. To Serbs in the Partisan forces, Četniks symbolized betrayal and brutality. They fought against the Nazis and were backed by the Allies until 1943 when the tide changed and the Allies started supporting Tito's Partisans. While anti-Axis in terms of their long-term goals, with the main aim of establishing an ethnically homogenous Greater Serbian state, Četniks also engaged in tactical or selective collaboration with the Axis forces.

Četniks certainly made a big contribution when it came to exacerbating existing ethnic tensions. They were applying terror tactics against Tito's Partisans, and Croats in areas of mixed Serbian and Croatian population, as well as against the Muslim population in Bosnia & Herzegovina and Sandžak. These tactics included the killing of civilians, burning of villages, assassinations, etc.

Grandpa was referring to the 1054 AD schism between the Eastern Orthodox Church/the Byzantine Empire and the Roman Catholic Church/Roman sphere of influence.[6] He said that we tried to build our home and our nation on that dividing line, but could never enjoy stability amidst the never-ending geopolitical and religious interests at play. Those interests were additionally fueling the hatred and division between Serbs, Croats, and Bosniaks.

"We were the ground for their play and experimentation, the convenient ground for testing the waters – to see how far they could go, extending their respective spheres of influence. And considering our past, riddled with pain and violence, they didn't have to invest much effort into finding the right buttons to press," explained Grandpa.

The tool of nationalism and nationalist rhetoric, touching upon the unresolved wounds from the past, definitely was the main strategy for the breakup of former Yugoslavia. It is important to note that in the 1980s, the Yugoslav army was emerging as one of the top armies in Europe. Yugoslavia was the most powerful country in the Balkan region, on the path of becoming the most powerful country in Europe at large.

There was indeed something special in the overall power behind the united people of Yugoslavia - the talent and potential of the youth, the joy and enthusiasm of the people, the amazing humor and beauty in which unity in diversity was celebrated, and the strong drive to grow and actualize oneself in every sense. During my studies, one of my American professors shared with me that she was one of the scholars sent to former Yugoslavia to study and learn more about the "success story" of the particular type of socialism that was developing in that country, bringing forth a powerful middle class of thriving citizens.

---

6 In general, the history of the Serbs is linked to the East of Europe, while that of the Croatian people is intertwined with the fortunes of the West, mainly because of the Vatican. The Croats were first converted to Christianity by Rome, and the Serbs by the Greek missionaries Cyril and Methodius. Consequently, the Croats use the Latin alphabet, while Serbs use the Cyrillic one. Croats were historically supported by the Vatican and Germans, while Serbs were more connected with Greeks and Russians in terms of the Eastern Orthodox Church, and had historic links with the French and British due to the bravery and commitment to the Allies displayed in WWI and WWII.

This East-West divide in the Balkan region became even more obvious during the Cold War – both sides, that of the East and the West, had their interests represented on the ground of former Yugoslavia, with secret services and powerful lobbies at endless play behind the scene. The violent history and hatred between Croats, Serbs, and Bosnian Muslims were easy to stir through local and international lobbies, fueled by the media. Within the Balkan quagmire, it is often difficult to make out whether the escalation of the conflict truly came from within or was exacerbated or even staged by secret services and institutions.

Tito skillfully played the game between the East and the West. The formation of the "Non-Alignment Movement" with Nehru from India and Nasser from Egypt was one big step that Tito and the Yugoslav government took in that direction. However, that equilibrium proved to be unsustainable and started to fall apart with Tito's death. Nationalist currents, like worms in a super ripe apple, started to dig in, leading to the breakup of the entire country through the polarity of fratricidal war.

A powerful socialist Yugoslavia, which was not under the boot of the Communist Soviet Union, but also not controlled by the West, was definitely not to the liking of certain lobbies and those in the echelons of power at the larger, geopolitical level. Detailed, long-term plans were made for the breakup of Yugoslavia. One can only hope that all those schemes will be exposed by true, dedicated historians in the near future. In the end, it is the ordinary people who are manipulated, who suffer the most and carry the scars that take centuries to heal.

One could spend a lifetime studying this complexity and the various versions and interpretations of Balkan history that exist to date. At some point during my studies, I realized that the truth about Yugoslav history and the reality of what truly happened on the ground remains hidden and will most likely never enter official history books.

This is why I gave up on a career in the field of politics or diplomacy and turned my attention to that which is truly real – my inner transformation. I do hope, however, that true historians will emerge, along with the willingness of all people from former Yugoslavia to address the facts within our shared, troublesome history from the inner space of openness and compassion, not anger and prejudice. To achieve that, an elevated awareness through genuine inner work that includes meeting our shadow at the individual and collective level is necessary. Each individual has to take that responsibility. That is where I would like to add my humble contribution.

I therefore return to the initially stated focus of this book - my experience alone. My attempt at a basic introduction of the historic circumstances in the Balkan region has already consumed too many words.

So, in the early summer of 1991, with my head buzzing from the newly discovered family history (as shared by my grandpa), I witnessed day after day how the situation on the ground was worsening. Western Slavonia, the region where my family lived, was one of the areas of Croatia which was largely populated by the Serbs. Nationalistic rhetoric on both sides was followed by sporadic killings.

One day my sister and I walked to town, towards the department store where our mom had worked. On our way to the town center, we passed by the police station. Usually, there would always be two flags displayed on the flag poles in front of the police station: the Yugoslavian and Croatian flags. This was natural, with Croatia being a Republic within the country/federation of Yugoslavia. That day, while passing by the police station, Dana and I saw a group of policemen, and some other men in civilian clothes, lowering the Yugoslavian flag. We didn't think much of it because they could have been replacing it with a new one.

On our way back, while passing by the same police station, we noticed that the Yugoslav flag was no longer there. Only the Croatian flag remained on the flag pole. At the exact moment as we were passing by the police station, we saw one of the Croatian police officers holding his nose with one hand while picking the Yugoslav flag from the garbage bin with two fingers of the other hand, exclaiming sarcastically: "Yuck, it stinks!" before throwing it back into the garbage bin.

I felt chills in my body and a strong fear that these police officers somehow knew that Dana and I were Serbian, albeit newly discovered. I almost stopped breathing. Then I realized that the fear was irrational and that they couldn't possibly have known our ethnicity. Fortunately, there is no obvious distinction between Serbs and Croats that could be noticed through one's facial features. We just continued walking, but that was the day when we no longer felt safe in our own country as we realized we could no longer rely on its institutions.

However, the worst was yet to come. My entire world turned upside down and the joyous childhood that I enjoyed only days earlier now seemed like a distant memory. We were entering the twilight zone of war and there was nothing anyone could do to prevent it.

Bidding Farewell – Grandma's Smile That Hides Her Tears

Across the street and a little down the road was the house of my best friend, Sanja. It never occurred to me to enquire about the ethnicity of any of my friends, but I came to know that her mother was Croatian and her father Serbian. Mixed marriages were really common in former Yugoslavia since nationality and religion were not considered important, only Brotherhood and Unity.

During those days, word spread that one of our neighbors, who lived approximately 20 minutes by foot further down the road had joined the ranks of the ultranationalists, the resurfaced Ustaše, who were preparing to get into action. I remember him from the two big, black pit bulls that always barked horribly from his yard, and the weird vibe I used to get whenever passing through that area by foot or on my bike.

One day that summer, my best friend's father was suddenly abducted by a group of Ustaše. This came as a shock to all of us. They shoved him into a minivan and took him to some remote place, where they hung him upside down and beat him so hard that he lost consciousness. They left him hanging there. He would have surely died if it wasn't for his lovely wife who was brave enough to secretly follow the minivan and administer first aid to him as soon as the extremists left. Luckily, she was a nurse and knew what had to be done to save his life. This is how my friend's father remained alive. For a while, he became very silent and withdrawn. Most of the good people, Serbian and Croatian, just became silent and passive, ducking down and waiting to see what would happen next.

Soon after this incident, we learned that my father was next on the list. He was framed at work, something along the lines of sending goods and meat to the "četnik formations" in the woods. Of course, dad knew nothing about it, but that's exactly what was happening to most of the Serbian people in Croatia at that time, especially the men. They were losing jobs, being threatened and framed, bullied and beaten.

A family friend of ours came running over the meadow and along the brook near our house in the middle of the night, reaching our home around 5:00 a.m. to inform my father that he was next on the list. My parents decided that we had to leave Croatia that very instant. They had already discussed their options with my grandparents. "I am not going anywhere! This is our house, built with our own sweat and blood. I will defend it till my last breath. Pero and I will stay. You go to Serbia with the children until we see how things evolve," said my brave grandma.

There was no time to discuss it further. Mom woke us up and said, "Get ready fast, we will have to leave right away!" Dana and I couldn't believe our ears.

I will never forget the dawn of that summer day in August 1991, the dawn when I lost my childhood. With overflowing adrenaline, I was looking all over my room, not knowing what to take with me – which precious memory, favorite clothing item, or toy. The pain of this moment went very deep. My intuition was telling me that everything I saw around me would be lost.

To this day, I carry illogical nervousness in me when I am to leave home in a hurry, even if I am going only a short distance, not to mention international travel. It was only a year ago that I was finally made aware of my tendency to be late whenever I'm getting ready to travel. Initially, I thought it was merely a coincidence that exactly at the time when I was supposed to finish packing and leave home, something I needed suddenly went missing, or I had to sew a button, or clean or fix something at the last minute, which then took more time than anticipated. I would always blame something outside of myself for that situation, not understanding that the cause was in me.

A session of deep inner work called the Mohanji Transformation Method (MTM) was done for me in 2021. It was led by one of my friends from our special little MTM group selected by Mohanji to perform this deep cleansing by connecting to his consciousness. Through her inner vision, she saw this painful impression of leaving my home in Croatia as the cause of my delays and confusion right before travel. I was amazed that I never connected the dots and noticed this myself. This is a great example of how painful impressions work and of how, through awareness supported by the right methodology, one can come out of their grip.

Since then, I have started allocating 30 extra minutes when packing and not going to sleep until my suitcase for the next day's travel is ready. Just before traveling, I lovingly calm myself with an affirmation: "I am always on time." Just as a child enjoys being tucked in before sleep, when our inner child carries certain wounds, we need to attend to them lovingly, with extra care, especially when we find ourselves in situations that potentially trigger those painful memories. In India, such impressions are called *samskaras*. They have a huge influence on our behavior and perception of reality. It is so important to be gentle towards ourselves. In general, once the light of awareness shines onto such inner scars, they simply lose their power over us. Until then, they rule us and are like remote controls to those who want to press our buttons and throw us off balance.

Going back to the dark morning of our departure from home – my sister and I must have looked ghostly pale while packing up to leave. I remember that my father saw how stressed and scared we were so he tried to downplay the whole situation. "Oh, don't worry, we'll be back," he said. "We are just going to Serbia for two weeks or so, you know, till things calm down a bit and all goes back to normal. But we have to leave right away; otherwise, I may end up beaten up like our neighbor, or even worse."

In the end, we took only a pair of underwear and an extra set of summer clothes, toothbrushes, a couple of favorite photos, and some banknotes. We were not allowed to carry any luggage. In case we were stopped by anyone, it could not appear as if we were escaping to another country.

Grandma and Grandpa were determined to stay back and guard the house. They came outside to say goodbye and see us off, but Grandpa was overcome with emotion and quickly returned to his room. Grandma, on the other hand, stood bravely by the car. She was smiling, reassuring us that everything would be ok. She kept waving as the car pulled away. The smile on her face was certainly not genuine – she was just being strong for us.

We had already stopped waving and turned away when I felt the urge to glance back once more for a final glimpse of our beautiful home. At that moment, I saw Grandma turn her head away in pain. She couldn't hide her sobbing. I didn't even have to see it clearly, I could feel it. My intuition has always been very strong and with time I have learned to rely on it one hundred percent. Looking at my grandma, I remembered how much pain she had experienced during World War II. I knew she hoped we would never have to go through any of it. Yet, seeing the conflict brewing and intensifying, she was so eager to see us flee to safety. I could feel that she was ready to go through anything, as long as we were safe. But pain was following us like a shadow… nobody goes through a war unscarred.

Deeply shaken, I asked my parents, "Why is grandma crying so much? I just saw her. She was trying to hide her face, but I saw it."

After a bit of silence, my father did his best to fake some lightheartedness and to sound reassuring. "Oh, she is just being sentimental. We all get like that when we grow old, you know. Don't worry. Everything will be ok. As I said, we will just go to Serbia for a couple of weeks and will then come back."

As much as I wanted to believe my dad, as much as I needed to believe those words, my intuition was signaling the opposite. Deep down I knew my childhood was lost along with everything I loved about it.

That was the day when I became a refugee. We left Slatina with a heavy feeling inside. We could never imagine the horror and humiliation that was awaiting us in Serbia.

Little Branko and the Will That Creates Miracles

We drove away from our grandparents and the only home we had ever known, towards absolute uncertainty. We said goodbye to our beloved street, then Slatina, and each of the neighboring little towns and villages that we passed. Just when everything familiar seemed far behind me, I caught a glimpse of a house that gave me goosebumps – it was a majestic house with a big banner spread across the entire front balcony that read, "*Volja čini čuda*" (Will Creates Miracles). I had been to that house a couple of months earlier and the amazing details of that superbly unique experience came right back to me.

This house belonged to Branko Radunković, a.k.a. Mali Branko (Little Branko), a divinely gifted artist skilled in creating miniature plywood replicas of buildings, monasteries, churches, castles, and more. What made Branko unique in his artistic expression was the fact that the replicas were made to perfection, but without any hands. Yes, such detailed, majestic artwork was created by a man without physical hands. And that was just the beginning when it came to the mind-blowing surprises that Branko had to offer.

This artist without hands stood out in many ways. He had a booming voice and loved singing. He came across as someone truly authentic and courageous, compassionate and selfless. He also had dwarfism.

It was known that at any time of the day or night that his house was open to anyone in need of food or shelter. This was the first time in my life that I witnessed such selflessness and generosity. "Branko's Evenings" were occasions when his heartfelt hospitality would include parties open to all, with live music, dance, food, drinks, and laughter.

The first time we visited his house, we were simply passing by one evening while on our way back to Slatina. My father decided that we would drop by for a bit to see what this gallery was all about. He had not introduced the artist to us, so the entire experience was a surprise.

I will never forget the moment when we entered the yard of Branko's gallery, welcomed by the joyful sounds of a live accordion and the recognizable melody of the famous Russian song "Katyusha." Drawing closer, I realized that the beautiful, joyous, booming male voice singing that song was coming from such a small form! Out of politeness, I tried to conceal my astonishment, but it truly was a sight to behold.

Looking at Branko's head alone, with beautiful facial features and shining eyes, coupled with his confident demeanor, anyone would consider him quite handsome. However, the stumps that were holding the microphone and his small body immediately brought forth feelings of sympathy and sadness. Indeed, Branko's big smile and confident, booming voice were so opposite to his overall physical appearance. I remember my first thought at that moment: "Here is a giant in a dwarf's body!"

There was one more detail that left a deep impression on me and etched this unique scene forever in my memory. While singing, Little Branko was surrounded by a group of radiant, tall, and handsome monks with glowing eyes and long beards, dressed in long, black robes. "Who are they?" I asked my father immediately.

He replied, "Oh, these are Serbian Orthodox monks. We don't get to see them much."

I had never before seen a dwarf or a monk. In former Yugoslavia, hardly anyone went to church, and religiosity was not popular or encouraged in any way by the government. It was difficult to say who fascinated me more, Little Branko or the monks. A strange familiarity filled me with awe for reasons unknown to my logical mind. For a moment, there was no mind, only this great, expansive feeling that started radiating from my heart. I felt truly excited!

My eyes were glued to Little Branko. It did not take long to learn that he was the main artist and our host at this beautiful house and gallery. I liked him from the moment I laid my eyes on him. After singing, he offered to take all of us inside for a tour of his gallery. The contrast between his body and face was still causing amazement within me. I enjoyed looking at his radiant face, eyes, and in particular, his smile. A beautiful, tall blonde woman standing next to him turned out to be his wife! His sons were there as well, also tall and beautiful. I never even knew this was biologically possible. The whole thing was beyond amazing!

Next came the scene of many miniature replicas made out of plywood, colored and decorated to resemble the original building to perfection. At that moment, Branko held a saw between his stumps and started demonstrating how he cut the plywood to create the miniatures. The sight of him cutting the plywood by somehow holding the saw between his stumps, supported by a firm grip of his teeth, is a scene I will never forget. Cutting plywood in this way was obviously difficult for him to perform, and yet he did it with mastery. Attention to the smallest detail was evident and truly impressive.

In total, Branko crafted more than 300 such miniature replicas during his artistic career. He is the only man without hands with such an accomplishment. On the evening when we met him, ten or so miniature replicas were on display. I was especially impressed by one of them. It was the miniature replica of the Serbian Orthodox monastery Visoki Dečani, located in Kosovo & Metohija, considered the soul of the Serbian nation. There was something magical about the replica of this monastery and the monks that I saw that evening – a premonition combined with a strange feeling of familiarity. It was almost as if a deep spiritual experience that I was meant to have in that monastery nine years later had revealed itself to me through absolute time. I kept staring at it, admiring all the details.

After the plywood-cutting demo, Branko came to a painting displayed on the wall: a stunning landscape depicting a green meadow and a cow peacefully grazing on it. That's when I realized that Branko could paint as well. To demonstrate how he did his paintings, he cheerfully put a brush into his mouth and started moving his head rapidly in all directions, creating distinct strokes with the paintbrush. He could similarly type very fast on a typing machine with a miniature hammer in his mouth. I was speechless.

While roaming through his gallery, admiring his artwork, I picked up a brochure about Branko's life. When I read about his childhood, I felt as if time had stopped and the only things that moved were the tears rolling down my cheeks. In short, Branko chose to enter this world's reality at the very onset of WWII. He was born in the predominantly Serbian village Brezik near Podravska Slatina in 1941, as the sixth child in his family.

His parents faced many financial challenges and felt overwhelmed by the hardships of life, especially upon seeing their baby born with no hands. In the desperation that clouded their minds, they threw him on a pile of animal dung and left him to die in a field. Little baby Branko lay there, crying helplessly for days until nearby neighbors heard him and brought him to their home. After two weeks of wrestling with their guilty conscience, Branko's parents had a change of heart and decided to bring him back home. "If there is food for the seven of us, there will be food for one more." With these words, Branko was brought back into the Radunković family.

Even though Branko never liked to highlight this painful detail when interviewed about his life in local media, mainly out of compassion towards his parents, I do find this detail important because it speaks volumes about Branko's purity and inner strength. The sincere intention behind my sharing it hopefully justifies the freedom to do so. The image of a newborn baby with no arms, with such a painful introduction into this world, left all alone on a pile of animal dung, left a really deep impression on me, more than any fairy tale that I had ever read.

Our mind works in images, not in concepts, and this image stayed with me. Moreover, while reading Branko's biography, I felt it was divine grace that had changed the outcome of this situation. Even though I had never been to a church, nor had my parents nurtured any spiritual dimension in me, that was the first time I had a clear intuitive recognition of divine intervention in someone's life. I felt I connected with the essence of that giant in a dwarf's body; we connected at the soul level.

Not only did Branko not hold this act of abandonment against his parents, but he did his best to make them proud by supporting the family through hard work, enthusiasm, and positivity. While growing up, he was homeschooled and eager to learn, always ready to assume various responsibilities when it came to household work or work on the land, as if he had no disability of any kind. He never complained and always celebrated life. And sure enough, everyone loved their Little Branko.

He started to visit the Serbian Orthodox Church in his village frequently and with great enthusiasm. At the age of 16, he became the lead singer in the church choir and started organizing cultural and musical events, especially on religious holidays. This was not well received by the strict communist authorities of former Yugoslavia, but when someone would report him to the police, the policemen could not resist his charm. They would come and write a short report, "Organized AGAIN by Little Branko." Who could punish such a high-spirited bundle of cuteness?

At the age of 17, he started making miniature replicas of the churches, monasteries, and castles that he liked. His artwork was greatly appreciated and soon our Little Branko started traveling extensively across Europe, not only exhibiting his artwork, but also demonstrating to people how he made it. Everyone needs reminders of just how powerful we can be when we have the right attitude. After collecting sufficient donations, he built his gallery in Nova Bukovica, where I met him in the spring of 1991.

Branko was always ready to inspire and help the helpless. The power of his spirit over matter was reflected in his artwork, speeches, songs, and lifestyle. After reading his story, I loved and admired this giant even more.

As strange as it may sound, I felt that our destinies were somehow intertwined and that we originated from the same place, and the same frequency. I came to know that this is the frequency of Sirius... I will return to this topic in due time. Two decades later, Branko and I met again, in a completely different setting that we never would have imagined back in early 1991 – in a different country and under completely different life circumstances. We were able to share our stories about the ups and downs of life that we both experienced. I finally got to tell him how much he inspired me during the darkest of my refugee days in Serbia, which is a story that deserves a whole new chapter.

Chapter 2
Refugees in Serbia

The Nightmare Called Batajnica

Within a week of reaching Serbia, it became clear that full-fledged war between Serbs and Croats had already erupted in Slavonia and that we would not be returning any time soon.

"We should be grateful that we have the option of staying with your aunt in Batajnica," my dad explained. We had never met this aunt before. In fact, Dana and I did not even know she existed. My mom said that her uncle was a nice man who worked hard in Germany for many years. Upon retiring, he received a pension that provided a good living by Serbia's economic standard. After he died, his wife, son, and in-laws continued enjoying the benefit of that pension at a time when Serbia was facing inflation and a huge economic crisis.

Our aunt lived in a three-story house that she shared with her son and parents. Our cousin, who was soon to finish high school, stayed on the top floor, while our aunt and her parents enjoyed the ground floor. With just the four of them in such a big house, it seemed logical to me that our presence would not be too much of an intrusion. After all, we were family and there was plenty of space.

It was clear that our cousin was not happy to meet us, let alone share his house with us. His mother, who was also not thrilled, requested that he behave nicely, so he was polite initially. They did not want us, but they couldn't reject us either.

On the first of September, 1991, my parents enrolled me in my eighth and final year of primary school. Batajnica was a small town and my school was only 10 minutes on foot from my newly discovered aunt's house. On the other hand, Dana had to travel by city bus to her high school in the nearby city of Zemun every day. She did not mind the travel at all and found good friends there fairly quickly. Somehow I did not manage to make a single friend. Acceptance of our new life did not come easy to me.

For a week or so, my dad stayed with us in Batajnica. When the fighting intensified, he had no choice but to report himself to the authorities in Serbia for enlistment in the military. Dana and I tried to convince him not to go, but he had no choice. Even though my father was not the type of man that enjoyed holding a gun (not to mention shooting one… at someone), he was a man of duty and honor. "The only other option for me would be to hide in some basement like a rat. That would be really cowardly. I can't do that my darlings. My dignity would never allow it. Please understand."

The prevalent rhetoric in Serbia was that all male Serbian refugees from Croatia should go back to Slavonia to fight and "defend their homes." The idea was that the first men to join Serbian troops in Croatia should logically be Serbian men from Croatia. Fighting in this war was optional for Serbian men from Serbia, although many of them volunteered to join the fight to support their Serbian brothers.

We understood that he had to go, but it was extremely tough to say goodbye. The night before he was to leave, Dana and I couldn't sleep. We decided last-minute that we should give him something nice and inspirational to keep his spirit high when the going gets tough. We glued our passport-sized photos to a piece of paper. Before slipping it into a transparent plastic cover we had found, we wrote the following short poem in Serbian. It went something like this (in literal translation):

> Amidst the dark smoke,
> explosions, and whirlwinds of the war,
> may brightness come to you
> as you remember our words:
> WE LOVE YOU, DAD.

We secretly placed our gift in his pocket and put on our best brave faces while bidding farewell to our dearest dad.

Soon after he left, there was a marked change in the atmosphere around the house. We started getting daily complaints from our aunt who told us openly that her son was upset by our presence. He liked to play loud heavy metal music, have friends over, and use marijuana (and possibly more serious drugs). Now that we were in one of the rooms on his floor, we were definitely disturbing his vibe.

Since my school was nearby, I would intentionally delay my return to that house, staying at school as long as possible. It was unpleasant for me to even see my aunt and her son. I didn't feel welcome at that house. Yet, the school was not all that welcoming either. I had nowhere to go and nobody to talk to. When the weather allowed it, I would just sit on the bench in a nearby park and try to process the many thoughts that were weighing me down.

Many of the children at school were cruel to me. I could not wrap my mind around their behavior. They had their little groups, their social circles, and none of them would accept me into their circle. I had never been an outcast before.

There was only one girl, a refugee from the coastal region of Croatia, who was willing to socialize with me. As desperate as I was for any friendship, I just did not enjoy her presence. She had a village vibe and spoke in a strange accent, with a very high-pitched voice that pierced my ears. It was being propagated that all refugees from Croatia came from backward villages and that we were uneducated, stinky, and annoying. Her manner of speaking seemed to support the stereotype that refugees were peasants, low class, just barely human.

One day I accompanied her to a shop where she wanted to buy some pants. In her dialect, pants sounded like panties. The saleswoman laughed sarcastically when she understood what the girl was requesting. All in all, I felt even worse when I was around her and eventually I decided I was better off alone.

Every day I oscillated between a nightmare at school and a nightmare at the house. Some of the kids at school started addressing me using ugly slang words like *smrdulja* (the stinky refugee), *izjelica* (the one who eats everything), and *pobegulja* (the one who ran away), among others. One day a malicious boy entered the girl's restroom, stepped onto one of the toilet seats, and peaked over the stall wall while I was using the toilet. He told everyone, "I saw the stinky refugee's bum! My God, it stinks like anything." Everyone laughed and I was deeply humiliated. I remained silent, holding the shame and pain inside.

My ability to follow the curriculum was reduced by the fact that my school taught everything in Cyrillic, a completely different alphabet. I knew only the Latin alphabet that we were taught in Croatia. In other words, I could neither read nor write. Secondly, the math curriculum was quite different from the one in Croatia. For example, the Serbian children my age had already learned the Pythagorean theorem, while I was only hearing of it for the first time. Whenever they mentioned the Pythagorean theorem, I had no clue what they were talking about and the teacher couldn't be bothered to explain any of it to me or arrange additional classes.

In Croatia, I thought of myself as an extremely bright child, but in Serbia I felt intellectually disabled. I had no motivation to study because I was completely overwhelmed with emotional pain, fear, and insecurities. I couldn't even try to catch up with the rest of the class, to learn what had to be learned to follow the curriculum. With every passing day, I was sinking deeper into the darkness of depression.

My clothing was like a bad joke. Since we arrived with only one set of summer clothes, we had to get all our clothes at the Red Cross. Whenever we went there, we would find ourselves in a big hall with shelves full of clothes, but they wouldn't give us time to try any of them. Once one of the women directing the clothing distribution shouted, "Hello, this isn't a boutique! You take what is given." We quickly grabbed whatever was approximately our size and left.

My mom said, "Just make sure you don't take something too small because you won't be able to wear it. Better take something a bit bigger." All my clothes and shoes ended up way too big for me, easily two sizes too large. I felt like Dopey from *Snow White and the Seven Dwarfs*.

However, that was not as bad as my "Cinderella" nightmare with the evil stepmother whose role my aunt seemed to embody more and more each day. She would get annoyed with us for every little thing – a crumb found on the carpet or a strand of hair on her sofa. One day she dragged me into the bathroom and shouted: "What is this?! What have you done to my bathtub?" I had no idea what she was talking about. Then I noticed a thin scratch, a couple of inches long, on the side of her tub.

I apologized but explained that I had nothing to do with it. I tried to defend myself, but she had already decided that I was the guilty party. It was obvious that she was looking for an excuse to kick us out. When Mom and Dana came to investigate the commotion, my aunt's next words shook us to the core.

"That's it, we've had it with you. The three of you need to leave tomorrow. I don't care how, with whom, or where, but you have to leave this house. My son is completely annoyed by your presence. He started getting bad marks at school. He says it's because he is so frustrated that you are here. We just cannot keep you here any longer. You should find yourself some other place to live."

"But… there is no other place where we can go," my mom responded. She looked so pale and crushed in that moment. "There is no other option for us. We don't have money to pay rent anywhere."

"I don't care. All I know is that you need to leave this house," was our aunt's only reply.

We withdrew into our room and Mom immediately called my dad's sister, my dear aunt Danica, who was a refugee herself. She comforted Mom and said the two of them would go straight to the Red Cross to see if there is anything that could be done. Anything. When they arrived they were told that there was only one person who called to offer accommodation to refugees.

Mom and Danica rushed to the given address, but their initial ray of hope was extinguished as soon as they arrived. They were shocked and appalled to find that the offer to house refugees had come from an alcoholic man living in terrible conditions with his special needs son. The accommodation was a filthy, damp, and horribly smelly old house in a muddy suburb of Belgrade. My mom and aunt fled in horror. My aunt said: "There is no way you and the girls are going to end up in that mud hole with that drunkard! There must be something else. I wish there was an inch of space at the location where we are staying, but there isn't."

That same day, a divine blessing reached us in our moment of desperation. After reaching Batajnica, my mom randomly ran into a man she recognized. His name was Jovo. He was not any relative of ours, just a friend who knew my dad and visited us at our home in Slatina a few times in the past.

He barely recognized my mom. "Milena, is that you? What happened to you? You look so pale and vacant." Mom shared the entire story with him. He put his hand on her shoulder and said, "My house in Nova Pazova is only 15 minutes by bus from here. It is full of people because we have received all our relatives who were also kicked out of Croatia." And then he said something that left me speechless when Mom recounted it: "But if there is food for twenty-seven of us, there will be food for three more."

Immediately I recognized the exact sentence from Little Branko's biography. "How is it possible that this man used the same words?!" I wondered. My ears were ringing with some angelic tune and the feeling of divine grace entered my heart. "Maybe it's a sign from above that I should remember Little Branko and how tough his birth experience was. I have two arms and a tall, healthy body. I should not complain," I thought. This was my first positive thought since becoming a refugee, the very first ray of light. I noticed that I started to feel better right away. My mom agreed immediately and Jovo came with his car to pick us up that very same day.

While collecting the little luggage we had, he paused and looked deep into our aunt's eyes. With a stern voice, he said, "Shame on you! Such a big house and you have no space for them, your flesh and blood. My house is even smaller than yours, but it will house thirty people. You should be ashamed of yourself." Our aunt just looked down, waiting for us to finally disappear from her life.

That was the day we turned the page and started a new chapter in Nova Pazova. (Incidentally, *Nova* means new, so our fresh start was perfectly appropriate.) We moved into the only room left and we were grateful to get it. The room had a big, king-size bed in which the three of us slept, a chair, and a paneless window; only a thin sheet of nylon covered the opening. That bed and one chair in the corner were all the pieces of furniture we had.

Due to the number of people sharing that one home, bathing and eating were complicated. We would wait in a line to quickly wash ourselves a bit and then run to get under our blankets. Winter was coming, and it was getting cold.

We never spoke with that aunt or her family again. Later on, we came to know that her son became a full-fledged drug addict. They were not living a happy life. The energy law of karma, just like the law of gravitation on Earth, applies to all. "You shall reap as you sow," says the old proverb. I have sent them blessings many times in a meditation that I started practicing in 2007 after meeting Mohanji. Our greatest teacher is life itself. May this aunt and her family learn from their experience and grow.

Deeper into the Nightmare

I did not eat much at my aunt's house in Batajnica. The tension made me lose my appetite, but at least the option to eat was available. At our new accommodation, Jovo's wife, the lady of the house, was so overwhelmed and stressed with so many of us in the house that she quickly made some strict in-house rules. All of us refugees crowding her house had to follow them. Food options were really strict. The menu was reduced to the following: a big bucket of cabbage stew one day, followed by a big bucket of cooked beans the next day. Occasional bread on the side was a bonus. No deviation was possible unless one was ready to offer the same to all thirty people in the house.

At school, it was even worse. I was starved. Refugees were offered the same food every day – some kind of salty, greasy, deep-fried doughnut. I almost vomited the first time I tried one. I attempted to ignore the smell and just swallow, but the oil burst from the dough and flowed down my throat before I could manage to swallow the actual food, creating immediate aversion and disgust. I am not sure whether this was a reflection of my inner state, or if this food was just disgusting, but I just couldn't eat it. I found the refugee food corner and the smell and taste of the food repulsive.

During recess, I observed with a heavy heart how the other school kids were giggling, enjoying their homemade sandwiches, or happily walking to a nearby bakery to buy their favorite snacks. They were wearing Nike and Reebok shoes, looking cool. Boys and girls were exchanging glances, friends were playing and enjoying their time together. They were all enjoying their normal life.

I, on the other hand, lived in a completely different reality behind the refugee red tape. My reality was totally invisible to them. I would have given anything to taste their food and wear those cool clothes. I wanted so desperately just to laugh with them. I would have given anything to enjoy the normalcy of life which most people surely take for granted – until they lose it. Yet there I was, hungry, sad, lonely, uprooted, insecure, and utterly lost. My self-confidence was ruined by the Dopey clothes I was wearing, my lack of friends, and my inability to learn at school.

Day after day, after surviving the hours at school, I would reach our accommodation hungry and exhausted, to be welcomed by the same "beans and cabbage, cabbage and beans," our cold room, and the noisy refugees. I became really thin, with sunken cheeks and bones protruding from my *décolletage*. I had no appetite, no sign of any joy, no hope, and no willpower to do anything about my pain. I was withering away while my pain just kept increasing.

The next devastating blow came with the news that my father had been killed. We received a letter of condolences for our loss, stating that his throat had been slit on the battlefield. I remember crying incessantly for two days in my cold room. After two days of mourning, we came to know that this was some other Milan Radonić, a man with the same name, that had been killed. It was such a relief to learn that my dad was still alive, but the trauma of the experience remained.

Around that time my sister and I needed to buy some things for school. We didn't know how much money to ask for so Mom gave us her wallet with the instruction to buy only the most essential items. On the way to the shop, we stopped at a kiosk to buy something small. I remember taking the wallet out and focusing for a couple of seconds on the items when suddenly there was a strange commotion around me.

An elderly woman asked, "Did he steal something from you?" pointing at a boy who was already disappearing in the nearby crowd. The wallet! Mom's wallet was snatched in the blink of an eye and disappeared as fast as a comet. It was pointless to even try running after him. Mom's wallet was gone and my heart was crushed.

On our way to our accommodation, Dana and I were dreading the moment when we would have to stand before our mom and tell her what had happened. I tried to make an intro, to find the right words, but when I finally said what had happened, for the first time in my life I saw my mom falling apart. She was screaming and wailing in panic, tearing the hair from her scalp! Fear gripped me, a horrible fear that my mom may go insane from all that we were experiencing.

"It's all gone! It's all gone!" she screamed. "What have you done?! Now we have no money, not even one dinar. No bank checks, no Red Cross card – all is gone! We are finished!" She screamed and sobbed at the same time. My dear, beautiful mom was devastated and aging before my eyes. Pain, stress, and insecurity were eating her alive.

My sister and I decided that from that moment on, we would not tell Mom anything unpleasant, only nice things. We had to do something to comfort her. Only, there was nothing nice to share. Silence became the best option.

After surviving the shock of my almost slaughtered father and rapidly unraveling mother, I continued with my effort to simply survive each day. However, the humiliations continued. In the house where we stayed with 30 or so other refugees, there was no mirror and not much time to spend in the bathroom. I did the best I could and was generally not too bothered about my looks – until one experience that deeply wounded me.

I shared my school bench with a boy called Vojkan. Even though he was sitting right next to me, I tried not to look at him much. The multitude of pimples and blackheads on his face, combined with loads of dandruff on his shoulders and clothes were not inviting to my eyes. He also had bad breath and teeth that were growing one on top of the other, not to mention a bit of an attitude. We did converse a bit occasionally since he was not in any of the established friend circles in our classroom and he hadn't been outwardly rude to me.

He approached me one day, lifted my chin a bit, looked at my neck, and said, "Oh, so it's true."

Confused, I asked, "What is true?"

He replied, "Your neck really is dirty. I thought they were lying."

I felt dizzy from embarrassment and ran outside, looking for a toilet with a mirror. When I found one, I observed my neck carefully in the reflection. The natural creases that formed on my neck when I looked down were filled with dirt. I couldn't believe it! I felt absolutely horrible. I did not know how to go back to the classroom and face those mean classmates.

When I stepped back in, it was evident that they were making fun of me and my lack of basic hygiene. My neck was now serving as a perfect justification for the nickname "dirty refugee." For the first time, I judged myself. Of course, I had no proper mirror, there was no proper heating in the house, and my bathing was reduced to a quick washing of my highest-priority body parts, but all of that was no excuse for showing up dirty at school. Hygiene is so deeply intertwined with human dignity and this really was humiliating. I felt deeply ashamed and disappointed in myself in every sense.

After all the helplessness and despair, suddenly anger appeared. I felt indescribably angry one day when a boy at school passed another sarcastic comment. There was some outdoor activity near our school and I happened to see the house in which he lives. It was very basic and rather old and small. Yet, he was such a showoff. In answer to some provocation from his end, I suddenly told him: "You know what, my family's house in Croatia is three times bigger than yours. You have nothing to show off with."

He leaned forward to get right in my face with his rude answer. "Yeah right! All of you refugees say the same thing, how you used to live in some big, fancy houses. Or was it a castle? Yeah right! We know that all of you stinky refugees come from stinky villages. Shut your stinky mouth with your stinky sleeve and be quiet."

That was it – I had it! These mean children could make fun of my clothes, looks, accent, or whatever, but insulting the house that symbolized my happy childhood, the happiness that I lost, crossed the boundary. Deep anger arose in me. I screamed at him until I had nearly lost my voice. Yet, the more I screamed, the more powerless I felt. It was all futile. I could never prove to anyone how much more beautiful my house, my neighborhood, my school, my friends, and my entire life was. And it was pointless to compare. It was all gone anyway. All gone.

But now I had this new, uncontrollable anger that I never knew existed within me. It suddenly came to life and consumed me, all because I was unable to accept my new reality. I was unable to accept what my life had become and would continue to be from Batajnica onward. Again, I just got quiet. I walked away from this boy feeling lower than ever and utterly empty. I was a shadow of what I used to be. A pitiful victim of circumstances, a stinky refugee. I wondered, "How low can one fall?"

The Phoenix Rises

"There is no coming to consciousness without pain."—Carl Gustav Jung

Next in the sequence of my refugee nightmare experience was a game changer. It came with so much power that it literally "closed the circle" at one level of my existence and ejected me into a different reality within my inner universe. The hard shell of my ego identity was bashed so strongly that it had to crack. This experience changed me forever. The constant repetition of painful experiences snowballed into this one moment in time, my 14th birthday.

"Come my darlings," Mom said, sweetly summoning my sister and me on that lovely Sunday morning. "I will make breakfast for you today."

It was about a week or so before my birthday and she decided to begin the celebration early with an omelet for the two of us, just a sweet, simple something to bring us a little joy during our dark hour. My mouth was watering as we sat, smiling and enjoying the smell of a breakfast cooked with love. Finally, we would have something special prepared by my dear mom after what seemed an eternity. Unfortunately, that utopian scene ended very fast, before a single morsel could land on my plate. Jovo's wife stormed into the kitchen, snatched the frying pan out of mom's hands, and tossed the entire omelet through the window! She looked at my mom angrily and started scolding her.

"Don't you EVER think that you can make breakfast for only your daughters and not for all the other people in this house. I thought I made myself clear earlier," she said through her teeth. "We eat what we eat here because we cannot afford to have it any other way. So, either you make it for all thirty people, or you don't make it at all. Is that understood? And if you don't like it here, you are free to leave."

Mom nodded and kept quiet for a while. Of course, we had to obey, we had no choice. Mom turned to me and gently whispered, "Okay, we won't have any eggs or anything now, but I promise you, I'm gonna make a birthday cake for your birthday. I still don't know how, but I'm going to do it. And it will be big enough for everyone to enjoy it."

Oh, those words were like music to my ears! Finally, finally, there was something to look forward to. Finally, a bright star appeared in my endlessly dark sky! A birthday cake! How amazing. I couldn't be more excited. I honestly could not remember the last time I tasted something I enjoyed. Indeed, this was the very first joyous moment during my refugee nightmare.

For the next couple of days, I had a new coping mechanism. Whenever I got insulted at school or got sad about something, I would focus on my birthday cake. That cake was my refuge, my secret oasis. It was so much more than just a dessert. It represented hope. It represented the joy that was plucked from my life. I knew that no matter what happened, my mom would somehow make that cake.

I even started smiling. I had forgotten how it felt to smile. Day after day, I was happily awaiting that special moment when I would come back from school and taste my birthday cake. I kept visualizing and fantasizing about how the cake might look and taste. I remembered the days back in Slatina when Mom used to make a surprise cake and hide it in the freezer. Half of it was brown, the most heavenly chocolate mousse, and the other side white, with whipped cream and *petit beurre* biscuits. I wished that Mom would make that exact cake. Of course, I would be happy if she made any cake under the current circumstances, but this was the cake that appeared in my fantasy.

Finally, the day arrived. My excitement was so great that I could hardly follow anything at school. I rushed to the house in Nova Pazova as soon as I completed my classes. I burst into the house full of joy, but the scene that awaited me made me freeze on the spot.

The first scene that I saw was that of my mom's sad face at the other end of the hallway. Her face was completely dull, with dark circles around her eyes indicating recent crying. When she saw me, she attempted to hide the tears, but her face showed it all.

The next thing my eyes registered was a big black tray on a table next to her. It was full of crumbs. I paused for a moment, trying to process the abyss of pain that started to crack wide open inside me. Terrible silence and then: "Noooooo! Don't tell me this was my cake?!"

My poor mom was crying and trying to explain. "I'm so sorry… I knew you would be coming soon, so I put the cake there and… and… just quickly went to the toilet. But by the time I came back... the other refugees dug into it with their bare hands and gulped it. They ate it all! I am so sorry, my dearest."

I stood there in shock and total disbelief. I could not speak or move. At some point, I ran into our cold room and covered my head with the thick comforter of our big bed. I wished I could disappear. I wished I was gone!

Again, the pain and helplessness turned into anger. This anger was directed toward God and my former idea of a beautiful Universe which now seemed to be conspiring against me. Buried under the bed cover, I was screaming and yelling at God: "I hate you! I hate you! What? Did I ask for too much?! Huh? I asked for only one little piece of cake. And you took it away from me. Even that had to be taken away from me. I hate you! What kind of God are you? Now I really hate you!"

I was reeling in hate, desperation, and self-pity. All I could do was cry continuously for hours. My chest felt squeezed by pain as if constricted by sturdy metal claws. I was usually not the crying type, but this time… the pain was so deep, all the floodgates of the heaviest and darkest emotions within me were flung wide open. The tears simply would not stop. They flowed in a prolonged purge of all kinds of emotions and all sorts of energetic and karmic debts. The purge felt like it would never end, and even accelerated as it sped toward eternity.

I felt like I was all alone on an empty, gray battlefield – a barren, meaningless, and hopeless plane that went on forever. Everyone died and everything was annihilated. I did not try to rationalize anything, to run away, or numb the pain in any way. On the contrary, I simply let go and allowed myself to spiral downward into the deepest recesses of the darkness, to keep falling for as long as it took. Knowing what I know now, I am so happy that I allowed myself to go through this horrific purge.

Eckart Tolle and many other people who went through similar experiences refer to it as "The Dark Night of The Soul"[7], a complete collapse of one's world and everything in it, a painful catalyst that ejects or catapults one to a different reality.[8] I can only attempt to describe what it felt like.

While the world I once knew was ripping at the seams, I was left totally heartbroken, alone, disappointed, and disheartened. My ego identity had nothing to hold on to. It lost its ground and fell into the deepest darkness where my sense of "I-ness," all that I perceived myself to be till then, was cornered and utterly defeated.

"The birth of the Self is always a defeat for the ego," said the wise Carl G. Jung.

Then, like a delicate snowdrop flower finding its way through heavy, thick layers of ice and snow, a completely new dimension within me simply arose. It was incredible – so subtle and yet so powerful and tangible. This divinely delicate part of me arose from the deepest recesses of that pain and lovingly witnessed the other part of me crying.

If you ever happen to look at yourself in the mirror while crying profusely, you'll notice that something suddenly clicks in your mind and another part of you recognizes that you look quite silly (which then diffuses the crying). That is what it feels like when awareness outshines emotion.

This higher, more powerful part of me looked at the pitiful, crying version of myself for a moment, until a clear realization arose in my awareness: "I'm not this! I'm not this poor, miserable refugee! I know it exists, but I am way beyond that." My right hand formed a firm fist. I remember the

7 The very term "Dark Night of the Soul," can be traced back to a 16th-century Spanish poem by the Roman Catholic mystic Saint John of the Cross.

8 Others would insist this would be more of a Dark Night of the Mind rather than the Dark Night of the Soul, which occurs at a later stage. In this experience sharing, I prefer to avoid definitions, quotes, and frames, but am merely focusing on describing my own experience as much as I can convey it through words.

moment when my iron fist hit the bed and a deep and primordial voice proclaimed: "I am NOT a victim! I am NOT this poor, little refugee!"

This realization came from the very core of my being. It was as if this downward spiral took me to the most unapproachable cave of my inner world, only to discover that on its altar, there was the precious diamond of undefinable, powerful Divine presence that has always been there.

When we shift from the usual 3D reality, the fourth dimension will inevitably be experienced through witnessing. This loving and unbiased witnessing comes naturally, without the mind's involvement. Imagine a bird that spent years hopping on the ground suddenly fell off a cliff and started to fly. Its legs would no longer be active, because its wings, the use of which come naturally to any bird, take over. However, the legs are still there to be used again when needed. The same is true with awareness and the mind. One can never explain the vast dimensions of awareness through the limited prism of the mind. Some pointers can be given, but awareness can only be experienced.

At this point, one simple truth was revealed to me with great clarity – if I am witnessing the crying, victimized me, then… who am I? Who is this "I" that witnesses "me?" This new sense of "I" sure was completely different. It was all-encompassing and had no boundaries. It also had no personal feel to it like the previous "I." However, even though not personal, it was very intimate and very much alive.

The mind can never understand awareness. One can spend a lifetime analyzing and come to no satisfying conclusion. Similarly, if we want to run faster with our legs, some improvement can be achieved – we can build muscles, and we can improve in terms of speed and endurance, but our legs will never enable us to soar high into the vastness of the sky. Period. In the same way, awareness can only be experienced/known through awareness.

The true sense of "I" is deeper than any of our thought forms, personal stories, patterns, and all possible oscillations of the mind. It is a vast ocean (or a vast sky) from which all these thoughts arise.

Until this day, like most people, it was my mind and ego that determined my sense of I-ness, my personal, unique, and precious sense of self. The mind will always say: "I don't want to lose that precious sense of me." This is absolutely normal because the ego does not want to die. It takes a dramatic experience such as this to realize that this precious something that we feel we are is not the mind, but the very presence of consciousness.[9] That's what is precious and at some point, each little drop will become one with the ocean of consciousness.

---

9 Our true Self is essentially mindless, timeless, and formless. As long as our consciousness is entangled in the form and associated with thought patterns, memories, and stories that we hold on to, the sense of I-ness will remain limited. However, when the awareness starts to operate through our mind, without needing the mind to understand more about it, this is when all the questions will cease. The mind's activity will drop dramatically. This realization of the formless essence of who we are is called spiritual awakening or self-realization and there are certain gradation levels within that profound process, which will be discussed in due time.

When my fist hit the bed, it was like an atomic bomb that changed the face of Earth and created ripples in invisible reality. A huge power was unleashed. "I am not a victim!" This one powerful proclamation changed me. My new sense of self, the powerful Presence within, was opened to me like a hidden, hard-earned treasure that was finally revealed to its rightful owner. I was crushed to ashes of nothingness and purged of layers of heaviness that were weighing me down until this profoundly majestic "something" awoke within me.

Eventually, I learned about the mythic Phoenix, the archetypal fiery creature that rises majestically out of the ashes of its own destruction. After being burnt in its funeral pyre, the Phoenix rises as a timeless symbol of renewal, transformation, and rebirth into its higher self. I came to know that the Phoenix is typical for any Scorpio (especially the spiritual version of the same – the Eagle), my horoscope sign.

I was amazed to discover that Scorpio is the only sign in the Zodiac that has another form – the Eagle, and sometimes, the glorious Phoenix. The Eagle/Phoenix is a higher expression of Scorpio power. Once I came upon this discovery, I started being more interested in the ancient science of astrology.

I recognized myself as one who transcends from the crawling scorpion, ever-ready to give the poisonous strike, to the soaring eagle, carrying the essence of penetration and patience, clear vision, power, majesty, and freedom. The astrologers say that even though Scorpio is a water sign, it is fiery Mars that bestows its essential qualities and the immense courage to enter the flames and be transformed. They say that the Eagle will always have the basic traits of a Scorpio, but what defines an Eagle is how they use those traits. The Eagle will transmute the intense emotions of resentment or revenge into a driving force for success and higher wisdom, caring only about winning the inner battle.

The Eagle will naturally go deep and, at some point, face the darkest, deepest crevices of pain from which the mythic Phoenix arises and unravels its new reality. It is safe to conclude that this experience was "written in the stars" for me, even though one would never willingly sign up to undergo the devastation of reaching rock bottom.

Indeed, when my inner Phoenix arose, I refused to entertain the pitiful, victimized refugee version of me any longer. I realized I could choose something else. I find this strong connection between psychological turmoil and spiritual transformation fascinating. Many people have experienced it, but when it happens to us personally, it always exceeds even our wildest imagination.

When I encountered that sudden wave of overwhelming warmth, courage, and love from within, love I never knew existed, I was awestruck, awash in a fountain of endless strength, determination, and power. I sat on the bed with an erect spine and did not even feel the cold coming through the nylon window coverings. My surroundings, my life – none of it seemed so bad anymore. That warmth was coursing through my veins, my spine, indeed my entire body. (In Indian philosophy, this would be referred to as a *Kundalini* rising experience, a topic we will explore later.)

When my Phoenix arose, the new reality that I experienced was simple and clear. I just knew – yes, I had the choice. And no, I was not stuck in my old notions of victimhood. I was never really stuck in the mud of helplessness. It only appeared to be that way because I never observed the situation from the right perspective.

As per my direct experience, in moments like these, being in a state of allowance and surrender is what facilitates complete healing and transformation. When the acceptance settles in, there's no turning back – there has to be a shift in awareness, and healing is its natural byproduct.

"OK," I said to myself. "What is it that I can do to change my reality right now?" I continued thinking from that space of clarity and enthusiasm. "I don't have any money and stopping a war is not in my power." I was silent for a couple of seconds and then the clear realization came.

"Yes, of course. I can study hard. Really hard. I know I have a sharp intellect. I used to be a math champion! I used to have the best grades in my class. I can do that again. I can be the best student again. All I need to do is to apply all my willpower to studying hard. I just need to do my best. And in this way, I will restore my dignity. In this way, I will make sure I can enter the best of Universities and obtain the best of diplomas.

"And then, when I grow up, I can get the best of jobs, a really well-paid job, and earn enough money, not only for myself, but also for my family if need be. Even if another war happens and we become refugees again, my education will ensure I can get a good job wherever I go.

"We will never be hungry again. We will never be humiliated again. I can do this. I can assume responsibility for that and push until I get there."

This realization was also a promise, a pledge I made to myself at that very moment. I made a solemn vow and nothing could stop me from realizing it.

I got into action that same day. Nothing was seen as an obstacle. When my hands would begin to freeze while studying in that cold room, I would simply take a flashlight and study under the covers, imagining it is my little tent. With my inner witness (a.k.a. *sakshi*[10]) awakened, it was witnessing myself studying under the thick blankets with a flashlight. My mind would then interfere for a moment and find it all amusing.

At school, I also did my best to study as hard as I could every possible moment. I was on a mission. Very often I would come up with unique excuses that would enable me to remain in the classroom after school hours to study so that I could reduce my time studying under the blankets. All in all, my focus was on my studies alone. If any other thought came, I smashed it.

First on the list of obstacles to conquer was the Cyrillic alphabet. I got that sorted surprisingly fast. I couldn't understand why it appeared difficult earlier. Then came the math – fractions, Pythagorean theorem, geometry, all came super easily. Other subjects were even easier. Within two weeks, I

10 "In Hindu philosophy, sakshi refers to the concept of pure awareness in which the yogi witnesses the world, but does not get involved or become affected by worldly things." Source: https://www.yogapedia.com/definition/7939/sakshi

became the best student in the class. That's all it took – two short weeks. My teachers and my fellow students could not understand what was happening to me. All of a sudden, this refugee started getting top grades – left, right, and center!

None of the other students approached me to talk about my sudden transformation and I doubt they would have understood even if I tried to explain what catapulted me into this new reality. The eruption of energy that happened within me was not only about me. I felt that I tapped into something far greater. It was years later, during my postgraduate studies, when I could finally pinpoint the right words to explain this mystical experience – it was collective, ancestral, and archetypal.

Jung's Victim Archetype

> "All the most powerful ideas in history go back to archetypes. It is the function of consciousness, not only to recognize and assimilate the external world through the gateway of the senses, but to translate into visible reality the world within us."—C.G. Jung

The teachings of the legendary Swiss psychologist Carl Gustav Jung led me to the understanding of key concepts in the human psyche, like archetypes, the collective unconscious, and "the shadow" that all human beings have, whether aware of it or not.

I invite you to join me on a journey of exploration of these profound subjects. This small digression from my personal story is of great importance because it will offer us a lens through which we can observe not only the experiences shared in this book, but the overall subject of polarity in our inner and outer world.

The shadow refers to the parts of our personality that we reject out of fear, shame, ignorance, or simply a lack of self-love. While all of us carry immense divine potential within, it is important to learn what exactly is preventing our growth.

"You can't wake a person who is merely pretending to be asleep," says the famous old Navajo proverb. If we pretend that we are happy and fulfilled, if we feel that we know everything we need to know, there is no progress possible. One of the key moments on our spiritual journey is the moment of facing the shadow within us. There is no better way to open the topic of the shadow, than to refer to the words of C.G. Jung, who introduced this knowledge in the first place:

> "Unfortunately, there can be no doubt that man is, on the whole, less good than he imagines himself or wants to be. Everyone carries a shadow, and the less it is embodied in the individual's conscious life, the blacker and denser it is. If an inferiority is conscious, one always has a chance to correct it. Furthermore, it is constantly in contact with other interests, so that it is continually subjected to modifications. But if it is repressed and isolated from consciousness, it never gets corrected."[11]

---

11 "Psychology and Religion" (1938). In *CW 11: Psychology and Religion: West and East*. P.131

In other words, to truly progress spiritually, we have to embrace not only our good traits, talents, and achievements, but also our bad traits, shortcomings, and all that we find ugly and unwanted about ourselves, in the realm of the conscious and unconscious mind. And why is this so? The following was one of the key statements made by C.G. Jung that awoke my interest in this topic:

> "The repressed content must be made conscious so as to produce a tension of opposites, without which no forward movement is possible. The conscious mind is on top, the shadow underneath, and just as high always longs for low and hot for cold, so all consciousness, perhaps without being aware of it, seeks its unconscious opposite, lacking which it is doomed to stagnation, congestion, and ossification. Life is born only of the spark of opposites."[12]

The depth of this statement is immense and calls for deep contemplation about our true nature, relationships, and overall understanding of life.

I was introduced to C.G. Jung during my postgraduate studies in the United States. One day I had a vivid, exhilarating dream about a magnificent whale. I came to know about a group of Jungian psychologists who offered dream interpretation as per Jungian psychology at their humble center in a forest not far from my university. Intrigued by the power behind this dream and the deep impression it left on me, I decided to meet them and find out what it could mean.

One of the ladies from their group welcomed me warmly and we started a profound conversation that further deepened my interest in Jungian psychology and teachings. She said that the whale is one of the most powerful symbols ever, one of Jung's favorites. It symbolized the descent of the dreamer deep into the unconscious realms, in an attempt to discover the inner self. This made a lot of sense to me because I was about to complete my postgraduate studies and some key life decisions had to be made.

Interestingly enough, in mythic realms, whales are the spirits of the Deep. "The whale, originally called a fish, is found in many stories of old. The associated theme of **death** and **rebirth** with the whale is found in Japan, Vietnam, and Polynesia, all the way to Finland. Indeed, it is a story of **initiation**."[13] A powerful synchronicity happened at that time – I came across a movie called "The Whale Rider," which explores the story of a brave girl from New Zealand and the depth of her initiation as she rises to the role of a female tribal leader who renews age-old traditions. I do not recall ever crying so much while watching any movie.

I continued researching and became completely fascinated when I came across Jung's teachings about the Collective Unconscious, which he explains as the sum of all human experience from the beginning of time, the archaic heritage of humanity. I was amazed to learn how deeply interconnected all of us are! Jung taught that whatever happens to an individual or group of people, nation, etc. also affects all other human beings. This deep layer of our unconscious connects us to the whole of humankind – past, present, and future.

---

12 "The Problem of the Attitude-Type," CW 7, par. 78.

13 Source: https://www.triplemoonpsychotherapy.com/blog/whalesymbolism/.

Modern internet can connect anyone with the right gadget, but Jung refers to our "innernet" at the unconscious level. It applies to all of us because we are born with it. We all also share the potential of re-establishing a conscious innernet on planet Earth. Our pineal gland plays a key role in this process, in addition to some other special solutions, such as pyramids, which will be discussed later in this book.

Therefore, whatever happens deep within us as individuals, or whatever a group of people undergoes together, it all goes into the shared primordial mind. All of us draw from it and are connected through it, although most people are not aware of it.

Certain key archetypes arise from the collective unconscious. The most prominent are the character archetypes, which can be defined as "the core traits, values, and decision making patterns of a particular type of person."[14] They can be found everywhere, from ancient myths and fairytales (e.g. the Bad Mother Archetype is symbolized by an evil stepmother ("Cinderella") or a wicked witch ("Snowhite")) to contemporary cinema (e.g. the archetype of the Underdog Hero, Child, Victim, Leader, Caregiver, Rebel, Trickster, Professor, Bad Father, etc.).

"The Lord of the Rings" trilogy and the original "Star Wars" trilogy, some of my personal favorites, are especially rich with archetypal images and character archetypes. The hero meets the shadow and then learns to wield their power and bear the burden and responsibility of battling the dark side or carrying the ring with power that corrupts.

Examples of character archetypes in these two trilogies are Frodo Baggins as The Underdog Hero, Samwise Gamgee as The Caregiver, Gandalf as The Leader/Mentor, and Gollum as The Trickster, among others. In "Star Wars" Darth Vader is The Bad Father, Luke Skywalker is The Hero, Yoda is The Wizard, and so on.

The spiritual and archetypal depth add to the multidimensional profundity of these two legendary trilogies. The entire concept of an archetype was such a revelation to me. The more I thought about it, the more I went back to my Phoenix and "I am not a victim!" realization. I truly felt that the breakthrough during that moment was so much more than my individual experience alone. It felt archetypal, straight from the collective unconscious.

At this very moment, while sharing these words, deep inside I am aware that this book will never be read, at any point in time, by mere coincidence. At a deeper level, whoever chooses to read it is already connected to the energy frequency that brings one out of the Victim Archetype, as Jung called it, to soar into their divine potential.

I am not talking only about refugees or only people who have experienced war. Nobody goes through life without experiencing the role of a victim in one way or the other. However, the degree to which we identify ourselves with that victim essentially depends on the following choice – whether we allow the energy to flow through us or not.

14 Source: https://www.studiobinder.com/blog/character-archetypes/

In the language of the ancient science of yoga (which I deeply respect and humbly serve as a representative of the Himalayan School of Traditional Yoga since 2016), this could be expressed through the simple phrase, "Breathe through the pain." During any yoga asana (posture), instead of holding on to the tightness and blocked energy in the parts of the body where the painful impressions are stored, a yoga practitioner is instructed to be mentally fully present and breathe through the pain.

The methodology of applying one's breath and awareness exactly where the pain or discomfort is felt has a similar effect to that of ironing the fascia, a sheet of connective tissue beneath the skin. Fasciae are crystalline and therefore carry information and stored impressions. Our loving attention and breath invite the flow into the energetically blocked areas within our body. This is truly amazing and anyone practicing yoga properly can experience it.

I made this small digression into the depth of yogic knowledge to offer another angle of observation that proves the truth that essentially, it all boils down to the flow of energy. If the energy is not flowing and we hold on to the pain from the past, smothering our higher potential, there will always have to be a villain, someone or something that has done something painful or unfair to us.

Sooner or later, we would have to attract such a person and a corresponding situation. If unable to release these painful impressions, we allow them to continuously block the flow. That leads to addictions, sickness, withdrawal, self-blame or blaming of others, constant distraction or postponing, lack of responsibility, lack of creativity, and living in the past or future. This default setting will continue until we realize that the strongest villains are our negative thoughts, fears, and painful emotions and that the choice to join the flow always exists.

All in all, by not assuming responsibility for our circumstances, we also give up on the power to change them with our willpower applied to positive action. It is as simple as that.

Therefore, all we need to do is break the bubble that keeps us in the Victim Archetype, one of the main archetypes within the collective unconscious, by:

1. Accepting the given situation, no matter how painful or unfair it may be
2. Using our conscious mind and applying the willpower to engage in positive action in the present moment
3. Allowing the inner child to play as we accept ourselves the way we are and use our creativity in coming up with the right expression at that moment in time, the one that comes with the ease and flow

In spiritual terms, this is called a change in one's operating frequency, which necessarily comes in sync with acceptance. The flow and acceptance go hand in hand. And their natural byproduct is the attitude of gratitude. This is when the glass becomes half full, not half empty.

The questions that we spontaneously ask when we find ourselves in challenging situations are a clear sign of where we stand. One might ask, "What did I do to deserve this?" or "How come this always happens to me?" When we are in acceptance, the only possible question is: "What can I do now that this has happened?"

The Shadow

And finally, after looking into the collective unconscious and archetypes, let us examine more deeply the key subject at hand, the one that most strongly attracted me to Jungian psychology – The Shadow.

During my postgraduate studies, I dedicated myself with all earnestness to finding the key answers to lasting peace, in the Balkan region and the world at large. I was determined to dig deep and find the right answers. One of the key insights that I gained during my classes in Peace Studies was that the enemy in any conflict is always perceived as the "alien other." This alien other would always be so opaque and foreign that it could not be related to in any way – zero possibility of any sort of understanding or compassion. The only option would be the harshest of condemnation, leading to hatred. At the time, George W. Bush served as the 43rd president of the United States and the "War on Terror" rhetoric ruled US foreign policy. Therefore, our professors at the Kroc Institute for Peace Studies could provide a vivid example from their own country.

As I began to understand the deeper meanings in Jungian psychology, I felt like shouting from a rooftop, "Oh my god, you are projecting your own shadow onto those "terrorists." They do not exist, you are creating them, you are energizing them into existence!" Without delving into the political or military aspect of this or any previous war, every created thing exists first in its most subtle form before it grows into its physical reality. The War on Terror served as a perfect example of shadow projection onto another. Needless to say, the same was the case with the Cold War and the wars raged against the "alien other humans" as was the case with Saddam Hussein, Slobodan Milošević, etc., or in the Balkan region, between the Ustaše and Četniks.

Terrorism does not exist as a singular entity, but the shadow of terrorism affects all. To explain this further, I have to refer to Jung once again, who asserts that nothing exists alone, independent of everything else. Everything is interconnected and influences everything else. When considering how things and events come to be, we have to understand that there is always a cause and effect, a web of interrelated events (otherwise known as karma).

We are all an integral part of that tapestry, active participants in the web of cause and effect. In other words, what Jung is saying is that there is a mutual dependence between parts and a whole. Without the parts, there is no whole, without a whole, the very concept of parts makes no sense.

During the War on Terror, a true, centered, mature leader would acknowledge the fact that their leadership and the rhetoric that their government used participated in the creation of so-called terrorists. A true leader would do everything in their power to diffuse the polarity and approach The Shadow at the individual, national, and collective levels with deeper understanding.

One of the scholars I met during that time said that it looked as if Washington D.C. was on a campaign to persuade itself first, and then the rest of the USA and the world, that this war against "the bad guys who want to rule the world" is genuine and will have to continue for a long time.

Was this turmoil genuine, or did Washington require a unifying idea in the post-Cold War world, at the time when they were experiencing a threat deficit (i.e. a lack of a threat big enough to justify the role of the USA as the world's global security agent, or police officer of sorts, identified with The Savior Archetype)?

The intention here is not to single out the US, but to provide an example that all wars are man-made and they only become possible when enough people believe in an idea that justifies the war. That idea always has something to do with The Shadow. Therefore, let us look into Jung's shadow concept more deeply.

First, Jung did not claim that The Shadow was the evil in us, but that it represented everything of which we were unconscious. The Shadow is also inadequately described by words like "dark" or "black," which may be interpreted with racist connotations as well. I've learned from my African American friends just how much they had to struggle with this crucial misrepresentation of The Shadow, how much they struggled to move away from the automatic association of black or dark with evil. The idea that "black is beautiful" took a long time to make its way into the collective consciousness. Of course, African Americans could see their own beauty, but it took centuries for those who perceived them as the alien other. Barbie dolls need not be blonde and fair-skinned to be perceived as beautiful. This never would have occurred to me till I observed this situation from their perspective.

Indeed, the key word with which Jung described the unconscious was "opaque" (meaning, one cannot see through it). The Shadow is that which is opaque to the conscious mind, or not directly reachable or penetrable. That is why it requires contemplation and loving attention consistently directed inward.

The easiest way to recognize our own shadow is to observe what annoys us in other people, what triggers us and lingers in the mind so that we feel like gossiping about the person with extra zest. We should catch that moment and be aware. "I am looking at myself, everything I observe is a mirror. All those hated qualities are my own, of which I am merely unconscious." With that understanding, we need only to remember when in our own past we have acted or thought of acting in the way that triggered us.

The expansion of consciousness means that the light of our awareness encompasses both sides of the perceived opposites within our Self. We cannot destroy the negative opposite, but it is enough that we are aware and that we do not act impulsively on anything inviting our disapproval. After acknowledging The Shadow is there, we can witness it like a mother that lovingly watches all her children play, including the naughty ones.

Since The Shadow is that which we generally do not want to see or acknowledge about ourselves, it has also been described as "the blind spot" within our consciousness. Aside from the traits that we detest and intentionally keep in The Shadow, our blind spots or shadow aspects could also be positive, e.g. certain talents, gifts, or virtues that we possess that kind of scare us or are not acceptable to us for whatever reason. These could be the gifts that we possess that we are afraid to see.

I remember how scared I was of my gift of Turkish coffee reading. I had no idea where it came from and do not recall ever being trained to perform such readings. Yet, the moment someone offered me their turned cup, after having finished drinking their Turkish coffee, I would playfully stare into the little signs within the coffee sedimentation and suddenly start seeing an entire movie of events, including who said what to whom, how that person felt, etc.

I must have been 11 or 12 years old, enjoying my blissful childhood in Slatina, when this "gift" emerged out of the blue. It was fascinating and scary at the same time. It became especially disturbing when, without thinking about what I was saying, I told our next-door neighbor, "I see something eating you from inside." Two days later this man was diagnosed with cancer. I felt horrible about it, to the point that I couldn't sleep that night. Word spread and when I came back from school the next day, there was a line of people in front of our house, ready for their Turkish coffee reading. I cried and told my Mom, "No, I will never do it again!" However, at one point in my near future, this gift would actually save me from a disaster; a story I will return to in due time.

The mere existence of The Shadow and blind spots substantiate the importance of a deep, intimate relationship. Being naked (fully exposed) in front of someone whom we love deeply and trust fully, means much more than removing our clothes. When certain resistances appear in the act of exposing the fullness of ourselves to another, one can pinpoint The Shadow and say, "There it is!"

That is why all our deep, loving relationships are of enormous value. Only someone we love deeply enough to reach the desired level of surrender, someone who loves the good and bad in us, who can see us beyond our masks and defenses, only such a partner can offer priceless help in the process of meeting The Shadow.

The maturity of the partner plays a big role in that process, but there is another option, which is rare but truly precious. Since the time of Vedic India, it was known that a living Master or a Guru, i.e. the one who has mastered the mind and operates from the frequency of total selflessness and unconditional love, is best equipped for this job because not only does the Guru see The Shadow and our highest potential, but our deepest karmic patterns as well. These patterns hide in our innermost layer called "*Karana Sharira,*" the causal body. Most fascinatingly, the cleansing from the Karana Sharira starts happening in one way or the other just by being in the presence of a spiritually awakened person. However, one has to earn the blessing of meeting and recognizing a living Master. This is just a short introduction to a deep topic that will be explored in the second half of this book.

Anything that remains in the shadow of our awareness remains as unexpressed potential, something that blocks our full expression. Our "personal shadow" consists of the aspects of ourselves that are disapproved of socially and suppressed. This suppression begins in childhood because we want to please the significant people in our lives and to be accepted. Aside from the personal shadow, there is a broader "collective shadow" as well, which includes the suppressed or unprocessed ethnic, racial, and/or cultural heritage.

It is important to clarify that what is in The Shadow is also outside the view of the ego. It is what the ego finds unsightly and does not wish to include in its image of the self. The ego is our center of self-awareness, until one reaches the higher states of awareness and moves beyond its orbit, into the orbit of the Self.

The best definition of ego that I've ever come across came from Mohanji. He said that ego is "the skeleton of our personality." Its main food is praise and recognition and it identifies with our positions, possessions, and relations. When we remove position within society, possessions, and the sense of self within all our relationships, what remains is who we truly are. He said, "Man minus Ego equals God." That is why we first have to build a stable, solid ego in the process of growing up (when the unit of the family is so precious). Only then can we work further on the process of spiritual awakening and fulfillment of our divine potential. This process includes both meeting The Shadow and transcending the ego identity, a huge task indeed.

All in all, our personal unconscious is a culmination of everything we've inherited from our parents, our culture, and the belief systems in which we were raised. It encompasses the key concepts that were drilled into us by educational institutions and all the unprocessed emotions and impressions from the unknown past. We are complex beings, but genuine inner work is worth the investment of our quality time because the benefits are lasting.

The Shadow is closest to The Enemy archetype and its projections tend to become self-fulfilling prophecies. In the example of the War on Terror, all those "terrorists" who wear the cap of The Enemy Archetype represent an aspect of the self that is collectively unwelcome in the US. The concept that is Al Qaeda actually represented the path to awareness and integration of The Shadow for citizens of the US.

The Shadow is dangerous when it is collective, when an entire society or nation projects its unwanted and suppressed attributes onto another culture, the alien others. This is how xenophobia comes to life and how Hitler was successful in projecting the collective shadow on Jewish people.

The most important idea in this discussion of The Shadow is that, in order to realize the true beauty and greatness that lies within ourselves, we have to turn our attention inward and dive deep. We have to understand our individual and collective capacity for evil.

Dark and light, evil and good, hatred and love, resistance and compassionate acceptance are two sides of the same coin. One does not exist without the other. The unwanted content of the shadow has to reach our conscious mind through awareness.

One example that comes to mind brings with it a smile as I realize it is again about a US citizen. While working for the United Nations, I engaged in a conversation with a UN officer from Louisiana. We were discussing some topics related to African Americans and I was honestly shocked when I heard him utter the following words: "I ain't ever gonna allow my kids to go to the same school with the Negro children."

Hardly believing my ears, I asked him, "And why is that?"

"Well obviously because I don't want them becoming more stupid."

Some of my best friends during the UN days happened to be African Americans, so this left quite an impression on me. I thought, "How could he be working for the UN and at the same time display outright racism?"

This man is a perfect example of an explicit, self-professed racist. He did not try to hide or suppress his racism at all. In Jungian terms, his shadow contained the part of him that is not racist. Hatred, in and of itself, is not a shadow quality in the way one may think. For example, people who categorically and passionately hate others in reality hate themselves. It is their own self-loathing that is unconsciously being projected onto others. What hides in his shadow, waiting to be recognized and integrated, is non-racism and self-love.

Once such a person recognizes his self-hatred and can integrate self-love from his shadow, those projections will cease to exist. He will be able to develop empathy for himself and then extend that empathy to others. I assume this is what is meant to be achieved by the isolation criminals are forced into during imprisonment. However, I do feel that counseling with regard to the shadow would be of far greater value and would surely be more effective than mere isolation.

Until someone like this racist man can integrate self-love from his shadow, he will be violently resisting that, somewhere within himself, he harbors a love for his fellow countrymen and women, no matter their race. I believe that life is the greatest teacher and gives such people impactful lessons that eventually make them mature into higher understanding.

In conclusion, while full embracing of The Shadow is not possible, we can face it by:

1. Becoming aware of its disruptive aspects (e.g. hatred, jealousy, greed, etc.) so that we can make choices through awareness, rather than allowing said aspects life within the personality
2. Integrating aspects of one's shadow which are unrecognized positive traits, which should be a living part of the personality

This is why Jung said that facing the shadow is a moral issue. It is a personal moral struggle, not a matter of conventional morality. Real courage is facing one's shadow and becoming aware of everything that we think we are not. That is the true meaning of *Jihad* spoken of in the Islamic religion. Only after having faced our shadow can we truly say: "I love and accept myself the way I am. I know I am not perfect, but I sure am unique."

If we stand behind these words, ever ready to face the shadow, we can't be offended or triggered by others because there is no false image of ourselves to uphold, no pretense rooted in conventional morality, no continuous suppression that steals away our energy due to its high maintenance cost.

In layman's terms, facing the shadow and integrating our positive aspects leads to us becoming more whole, solid, and stable. In Mohanji's words, the true journey of our spiritual awakening, the full blossoming of our divine potential, is when "from a unit, one becomes the Universe." However, we first need to become a solid unit of consciousness, and only from the full circle of a stable, enduring, solid unit, can one undergo the quantum leap of expansion beyond all that is previously known to become the Universe.

Before concluding the topic of The Shadow, I must highlight one of the best cinematic depictions of powerfully facing The Shadow. In Star Wars, George Lucas masterfully dealt with the topic of The Shadow Archetype and collective unconscious in a compelling story of meeting The Shadow and the consequent transformation that it caused in the life and consciousness of the key characters.

Meeting The Shadow – Luke Skywalker

In "The Empire Strikes Back," Luke meets Yoda (The Wizard Archetype) who teaches him how to control his anger and consequently control his shadow, i.e. "the dark side of the force." Yoda teaches him about the importance of commitment, presence of the mind, self-control, and the use of will to both face The Shadow and allow its positive aspects to be integrated. A Jedi is trained to remain centered and observe their emotions with clarity and equanimity.

During this training, Luke faces one of his most dangerous foes – his own shadow. At one point during his training, Luke senses something dark and disturbing. While searching for the cause of that feeling, he comes across a waking dream of his own shadow. This projection takes the form of his adversary and father, Darth Vader. Luke battles him and wins. However, in this waking dream, while removing Darth Vader's mask, Luke is shocked to reveal his own face. This is when Luke realizes that he was in battle with his own shadow all along. He also understood that destroying The Shadow was not possible. As Jung would say, it is in recognizing it and being aware of it that one can control it.

In the last film, "Return of the Jedi," a huge change is noticeable in Luke's personality. He is no longer overpowered by his emotions. Instead, he has taken full control of his shadow and uses it to improve his fighting skills. At this point, Luke is reunited with Yoda. With his last breath, Yoda tells Luke that his training is complete and that he is almost a true Jedi. All he needs to do is battle his father, who represents his shadow.

This brings us to the battle between Luke Skywalker and Darth Vader. The moment is filled with symbolism and insight into human nature. The importance of suffering and sacrifice and the overall effect it can have on human conscience and spiritual development is highlighted and juxtaposed with the importance of meeting one's shadow.

I invite you to watch the film if you haven't seen it. I will refer only to the key moments during this final battle, observing it through the prism of Jung's shadow.

When Anakin was overwhelmed by anger and unbridled emotion, he succumbed to his shadow, which then started to rule him and turned him into the evil Darth Vader. Luke, on the other hand, was able to face his shadow and recognize its existence. This allowed him to develop into a powerful Jedi.

During the battle with his father, Luke's main task was to make Darth Vader find the good in himself. In line with Jung's teachings, Luke understood that someone couldn't exist with only darkness inside, similar to how it's impossible to exist with only good residing inside. The polarity of light (of consciousness) and shadow always exists.

Luke initially tried to use logic to persuade Darth Vader to acknowledge his shadow and come back to the light. However, the key moment of transformation in his father happened only after the evil Emperor (Darth Vader's superior) joined the fight. The Emperor tried to manipulate Luke's shadow and provoke his uncontrolled anger, instead Luke tossed his weapon to the side, sacrificing himself to the Emperor. Luke's bravery and suffering triggered love and compassion in Vader's shadow and Luke was saved by his father, Darth Vader. In this scene, Luke unlocked the power of nonviolence and love in his father which overpowered the negative aspects of The Shadow that were ruling over Darth Vader.

George Lucas fashioned the Star Wars films after Jung's teachings and that of his contemporary, leading mythologist Joseph Campbell. In Star Wars, Jung's archetypes were portrayed beautifully through the medium of film, bringing these insights to the everyday man. Absolutely brilliant.

One final point about meeting The Shadow is that it inevitably happens in the world, not isolated behind closed doors. We learn to deal with the shadow through our interactions with the world. Analysis and contemplation are just tools to help us recognize where the triggers are, but the real shadow work always happens within our activity and relationships. This is a subtle point, but an important one. And this is exactly how Jung lived his life.

Jung's philosophy and lifestyle were a reminder to us that to undergo self-analytic work we must above all live our lives in a balanced way. For example, he said the most important thing he had to do during his dive into the inner world of archetypes, The Shadow, etc. (while writing his famous red book) was to stay grounded. That meant staying in touch with nature, spending time with his wife and family, doing manual work outdoors, and in the midst of it all, simply overcoming the challenges of everyday life.

My final tribute to Jung is in recognition of his sense of honor, authenticity, and integrity demonstrated in his stand against Freud's sex-centered dogma in psychology. Jung consciously gave up the immense benefits and fame that he would have enjoyed in spades had he continued as his mentor's favorite, a "chosen heir to Freud's psychoanalytic process." Jung felt that "Freud's attention was too focused upon sex and its impact on behavior. Jung decided that what motivates and influences behavior is a psychic energy or life force, of which sexuality could be only one potential manifestation."[15]

After this test of standing in his truth and the consequent break with Freud came Jung's greatest period of illumination, when all the teachings discussed above were presented to humanity for the benefit of all who choose to progress on what Jung called "the path of individuation," the path of becoming complete, the path of reaching our highest potential.

I found Jung's teachings not only insightful and inspirational but saw them as a huge milestone in bridging science and spirituality in the field of psychology. I found this bridge to be of crucial

15 https://www.harleytherapy.co.uk/counselling/freud-vs-jung-similarities-differences.htm/.

importance to humankind, thus my attempt to share these important insights from the vast ocean of Jungian teachings.

A Smile Underneath the Thick Mustache

One key experience of facing my own shadow stands out very vividly in my memory. This experience was of great value in helping me become aware of some very unwelcome personality traits that I never want to integrate. A month or so after the illuminating "I am not a victim" experience, to my great surprise, arrogance, lying, and stealing emerged from my shadow.

In my new reality, all my teachers were really happy with me, but I still had no friends. From bullying and putting me down, my classmates shifted to either being jealous of me or simply ignoring me. I did not care much and remained focused on my studies. After all the suffering, I finally started feeling good about myself. I no longer felt like a victim. No matter the challenge that came my way, my attitude was, "Bring it on!"

My newfound confidence and willpower really transformed my scholastic performance, but even though my self-esteem and determination were greatly boosted, my heart was still closed. Having no friends was a clear reflection of my closed heart. I was unable to perceive that truth until another experience came that shattered my defenses. It revolved around another birthday, this time that of my little cousin Bojan, who was a refugee as well.

Indeed, it was the anger, false pride, and arrogance within my shadow that attracted this powerful triggering experience, one that I will never forget. It all started with the news that our little cousin's birthday was the next day. My sister and I were discussing what on Earth we could possibly give him as a birthday gift. We had nothing and no money to buy him even the smallest of gifts.

A dark, devious thought kept in my mind. "Oh, to hell with it! Why not go to the supermarket and steal a Toblerone chocolate bar for Bojan?" Indeed, since this unique Swiss chocolate bar is not flat like other chocolates, but has a shape of a triangular stick, it will be easy to stick it inside the sleeve of a jacket. "Life is so unfair, why play fair all the time? It's just one chocolate. And Bojan deserves to experience the taste of chocolate at least on his birthday," was the thought that became a justification for this plan.

Before that moment, I had never entertained the idea of theft. I was fed up with our situation and did not want to think about this decision much, I simply went into action. After school, Dana and I met in front of the supermarket in the very center of town. Upon entering the supermarket, we placed two Toblerone bars in our basket, plus two chewing gums. We slipped into an empty aisle where Dana placed a chocolate in the sleeve of her coat and I tucked a bar in my armpit. We put on our best calm, casual faces to hide our nervousness and proceeded to the cashier to pay for the chewing gums.

Suddenly, one of the saleswomen grabbed me by the shoulder and pulled me to the side. My heart started racing! How could she have seen us? She uttered the following words in a bitter tone: "I would also like to eat chocolates, but one has to pay for them."

I looked right at her and replied with a sour attitude, "I don't know what you are talking about."

"You know very well what I am talking about!" she shouted. "Out with the chocolates!" She began a thorough search, patting us all over. She searched my sister first and found the chocolate in her sleeve. "Ha!" she exclaimed with a vindictive tone.

She then turned to me. While she searched my arms, stomach, and legs, I kept screeching, "There is no chocolate!" Finally, she noticed that my left arm was a bit rigid. She pushed it up and from my armpit fell the chocolate, hitting the floor with a thud that made my heart skip a beat.

"Oh really, no chocolate?! And what's that? Huh?"

Her fury and spite escalated the encounter to the next level, with a fierce slap that made my cheek burn. She slapped me as hard as she could and yelled very loudly, "You goddamn refugees! We are feeding you here, suffering day after day because of all the expenses you heap upon this country, and what do you do? You are stealing from us?! Shameless!! We should put you on TV so that the whole world can see your shame!"

She hit me once more and then pushed us into a storage room. We stood in silent shock for a moment before the other four or five saleswomen suddenly burst in, screaming and shouting in a frenzy. It was really difficult to bear. I couldn't breathe. I felt like I was in a mental asylum, the only sane person surrounded by lunatics. I knew that the degree of their reaction was not normal, but since I was in a state of shock, I felt almost numb to it. Nothing seemed to surprise me anymore. These women were venting all their frustration and anger on us – a big-time shadow projection.

The women then grabbed our backpacks and began inspecting them for stolen items. Interestingly enough, a couple of days earlier, we had gone to the city of Zemun to buy some school equipment, a ruler and similar items, and one hair gel, a rare treat for our basic beautification. Even though we didn't even have a proper mirror in the house where we stayed, we decided to add this hair gel to the list of utmost necessities. A saleswoman grabbed the hair gel, shouting like crazy, "Oh! This is my handwriting on the price tag! I recognize my handwriting! Look what else they stole from here!"

At that moment, I could not keep quiet any longer. Injustice triggered the anger straight out of my shadow. "That is not true!" I shouted back. "I bought this earlier in Zemun, not here. You cannot say that this was stolen from here. I admit to stealing the chocolates, but not this. That's A LIE!" She slapped me again and started shouting and cursing. The scene was a madhouse!

One of the women spotted a police officer and screamed, "Police! Police! Over here! Take them to jail!"

Dana and I looked towards the door and there stood a tall, stern-faced police officer with a thick, black mustache. He walked in confidently, asking with a calm, deep voice, "What is happening here?"

The saleswomen were still shouting all at once about the stinky refugees, how we were a burden on the economy of Serbia, and how we were stealing everything. "Look at everything they stole from here!" the saleswoman shouted, proudly displaying her salvaged goods.

I was fuming from within but managed to keep quiet. The women demanded that we remove our coats and leave them there. "Only when your parents come to pay for all that you stole will you get your jackets back!" It was freezing outside, the height of winter. Their cruel demand filled me with anger, triggering further projection from my shadow – an unscrupulous lie that surprised me as I uttered it.

"We don't have any parents!" I exclaimed in a deep voice. "They are dead!"

The police officer decided enough was enough. "Just leave them with me now," he said. Turning to Dana and me, he continued in a very strict tone that brought great satisfaction to the saleswomen, "Put your jackets back on and follow me to the police station, RIGHT NOW!"

The police station was right next to the supermarket. While walking behind him in the snow, there was an awkward silence interrupted only by the crunching of thick, dry snow beneath our feet.

Dana started to cry. "Please forgive us," she pleaded. "We are so sorry. We will never do this again. Please don't put us in jail!" The officer just kept walking in silence.

"Keep quiet, Dana!" I said in the same deep, arrogant tone. "It would be GREAT if they put us in jail. At least we'll have a warm place to sleep and some food to eat for a change. Let them put us in jail. Who cares?!"

Once at the station, we were taken into an interrogation room. We sat at a table with a lamp shining in our faces, just like in the movies. I was prepared for anything. After all the torture and insanity we had endured, I honestly would not have batted an eyelash at a life sentence!

"First name... Last name... Date of birth... Address..." Suddenly the officer looked up from his paperwork and established eye contact with me for the first time. He looked deeply into both our eyes before revealing a big smile beneath his thick mustache. A smile!

The following words remain etched in my memory: "OK girls, I'm gonna let you go now. You haven't done anything all that bad. I just had to play the role of a serious police officer to rescue you from those women. They were a bit too excited in there. So, you're free to go now." This sudden moment of sanity, like a gust of fresh air in a suffocating room, was a lifesaver. Then, waving his forefinger in a gesture of a warning, he continued,"But if I catch you stealing anything, ever again, even chewing gum... You really will end up in jail!"

Dana and I were so happy and relieved with the sudden resolution of this nightmare episode that we hugged and cried in celebration of this unexpected end to our suffering. The drama in the Batajnica supermarket ended with our promise to never steal again. And it has honestly never occurred to me, ever again, not even at the level of the thought, to steal anything in any shop.

Life is truly the greatest teacher. Even though it is extremely challenging to go through intense pain, at some point we have to look at the overall effect of it all and ask ourselves sincerely: "Did this experience make me grow? Am I a better, stronger person because of it?"

If the answer is yes, we have to give credit to that experience of pain, observe it from a higher perspective and thus honor it as a great teacher, far greater than any book, concept, or theory. In that sense, pain is not an obstacle, because, when embraced, it makes us authentic in our vulnerability. It opens many new horizons.

I spent that evening pondering over the day's events. I was on the path of restoring my dignity and focusing on my studies, and suddenly I became a thief! What went wrong in my head? What was I thinking? Being truthful had always been a pillar of my existence. As I continued with the contemplation, I realized that, without even noticing, I allowed my newly discovered pride and confidence to turn into arrogance and I deserved this harsh lesson.

The following realization was the result of that night of contemplation. Even if starved and deprived of everything, one should always remain dignified. We have to guard the sanctity of our inner space, our innermost values, with all our heart and soul. Our core values – inner purity, truthfulness, integrity, nonviolence, love, and compassion – are of the highest importance, no matter how others may treat us. If we lose the firewall of our conscience, we lose ourselves.

I decided that come what may, I will never do anything that compromises my conscience and dignity and will do my best to express the best possible version of myself. I will be that which I expect others to be in their behavior towards me.

It was a couple of years later that I came to know about the Golden Rule that Jesus Christ shared with the world in Luke 6:31 and Matthew 7:12: "Do unto others as you would have them do unto you." Indeed, it is enough to follow just this one rule in life to experience a life filled with divine grace.

Heart Wins the Ultimate Battle

"Thank you, my pain, for liberating me from the heavy curtains of my defenses. May love lead the way to clarity. May it show me the way forward. I am now ready to *be love*." These are the words that best describe what I felt deep in my heart after going through the experience I am about to share.

This experience taught me the immense importance of creativity. I realized that one's unique creative expression stemming from an expanded heart is the best way out of trauma. It is the nature of love to expand. When creative juices start flowing, our defenses have to be lowered to allow the expansion of the heart and the light of consciousness to flow.

Darkness is synonymous with stagnant energy as light is synonymous with a flow that spreads beyond all barriers. When undergoing trauma of any sort, it is natural for us as human beings to shield our inner world. We need time to process the pain and gather the broken pieces of ourselves. We push everything away, unable to receive anything into that isolated space. Similarly, in the case of losing loved ones, we need time to isolate and mourn because unprocessed pain bounces back with revenge or reflects as physical ailments.

However, continuous separation and heavy defenses are not the right *modus vivendi* either. Unconscious identification with the Victim Archetype can be a life sentence in a self-perpetuated prison. We must eventually step out of the isolation or risk a lifetime without the sunlight of love and togetherness, the sunlight of higher meaning and divine providence.

Creative expression from an open heart stands out as one of the most powerful tools for stepping out of the Victim Archetype bubble. Once the heavy curtains are removed, not only do we receive the sunlight but we also become seen. And becoming seen and exposed means becoming vulnerable.

Summoning the courage to open our hearts AND become vulnerable is one of the most important conscious choices we will all make in life. At times like this, when coming out of trauma and victimhood, a helping hand from a loving, kind person is truly priceless.

Another important point to understand is that the way the brain processes traumatic events is mainly by storing them as images, emotions, or sensations. Creative telling and retelling of one's trauma story greatly enhances our chances of metabolizing that trauma. The key point is that trauma and victimhood damage one's ability to imagine and create. It is often said that we are not learning unless we are imagining. We "trick" our brains into learning by imagining a reality in which that information is real or the new information won't be integrated.

Without imagination, our world is reduced to what we have seen before. For any person who has undergone trauma, this means being limited to the same stale, gray, heavy world, filled with the impressions of trauma. Therefore, allowing ourselves to imagine and tapping into the unconscious through creativity is of the utmost importance in the process of healing and bringing the sunshine back.

My chance for healing through creativity came when our teacher of Serbian Language and Literature assigned an essay with a topic: "Children at War." This would be our final essay for that semester. She explained that we were free to write whatever we liked, as long as it related to the given topic. I went to my cold room, turned on the flashlight, and started writing.

I wrote whatever flowed from my heart. After all, I was a child at war. I had been holding it all within me since I became a refugee, but now, all of a sudden, I wanted to express how it felt to go through the pain I was experiencing.

Initially, I searched for the right words to convey the depth of my suffering. With a little time the right words and stories began flowing with utmost ease. The floodgates were open, the flow was restored, and the essay practically wrote itself. I just offered my hand, and my conscious and unconscious mind got to work writing in unison, held together by my expanded heart. I literally wrote my heart out.

When I submitted my essay to the teacher, she read it at home that same day. She was so touched by it that she read it to her family members right away. They all cried and spoke about it for hours. The next morning, she read it to the other teachers and staff members at school before the first classes began. They were all deeply touched and agreed unanimously that this essay simply had to be shown to the school principal.

My Serbian Language and Literature teacher knocked at the door while I was in the midst of another class and asked me to step outside. After the principal read the essay, he decided to summon me to his office. I was stunned. Upon entering the principal's office in trepidation, I saw before me a tall, handsome man with warm eyes. "Dear child," he said, "this essay is something that all the children need to read. They need to know how a child like you feels and all that you wrote in there." I couldn't believe my ears.

"Can you take this microphone into your hand? I will stop all the classes in all the classrooms right now. All the children will be asked to listen to you reading this essay out loud. Can you do that for me?"

I could feel my hands trembling and replied, "But sir, this writing is very intimate. I didn't quite expect to read it out loud to anyone. I feel that I could... you know... be overwhelmed by tears while reading it. I'm sorry, I don't think I will be able to read it fully. It's just too painful."

At that moment, this lovely man leaned forward, looked me in the eyes, and said: "Yes, you will be able to read it. I have full faith in you. I will hold your hand." He extended his hand and gestured for me to sit next to him.

His genuine expression of warmth reminded me of my beloved father, my dear dad. God knows what horrors of war he was experiencing at that very moment. It was too much to contemplate and my tears were already flowing. I realized how much I missed him... Sweet images of Dad playing with Dana and me when we were small arose in my memory. He would enter the room, and while pounding his chest like a gorilla, he would proclaim, "I am King Kong!" We would scream and laugh, running around the living room furniture, trying to escape, until he would catch one of us and lift us in the air. I felt so comforted by the strength and warmth of my dear father, by the masculine power that comes with love.

Without thinking, I sat next to the principal. This was a moment of daring to do something way beyond the usual, to do something risky, something that may not work. But in that daring, in the breaking of our self-imposed boundaries, we become truly alive.

I placed my right hand into my principal's warm palm and held the microphone in my left hand, which was already trembling. I summoned the strength of my ancestors to speak my truth, to find the courage to reveal my nakedness – the courage to open my heart in front of the children who hurt me so much.

After the initial announcement made by the principal, I started reading my essay out loud, one word at a time. There were parts where the tears made me choke and pause a bit, but the hand of my principal was reassuring. I just kept reading, reliving every word. At some point I started to feel the immense power behind the vibration of speaking my truth – it was spreading like scalar waves, cosmic and powerful beyond belief.

For a moment, the image of a whirlpool in a river came to my mind along with a story my father shared with me. While growing up, he once got caught in a whirlpool in a river. Had he resisted, the pull of the whirlpool would have exhausted him eventually and he would have drowned. Instead, he surrendered to the whirlpool and saved his breath for the moment he would be sucked into the center of the whirlpool. That was the key moment, his only chance. He allowed himself to be pulled under the water so he could push with his feet against the sandy riverbed and bounce back to the surface.

In such situations, one has to be very brave and calm, aiming for the eye of the storm, the gateway to a whole new reality, the life that exists on the other side of fear and pain. Entering the depth of pain is where the ultimate revelation of the truth happens, the truth that pain too is our God-given friend, the great giver of experience. We are here to experience, not to keep running away, not to numb anything, but on the contrary, to become truly alive. That aliveness comes only when we break our boundaries through an open heart, when the intensity of our love creates huge ripples of transformation to which other hearts immediately respond!

Once I was done reading, for a couple of seconds, the whole school was silent. I could feel the molecules of my reality being rearranged. I could feel so many hearts being lit up, like matchsticks near a big campfire, expanding the flame in all directions. The sound of the bell marked the end of that class. Perfect timing.

I will never forget the moment I came down the stairs from the principal's office and experienced that first encounter with other children. "Is this really happening?" I thought. They started coming towards me, embracing me. I was in total disbelief at what I was witnessing around me – my classmates and other children whom I did not even know, all of them were coming forward. And then it was even more difficult not to cry… (I am crying even now while writing about it, so many years later.) I was truly overwhelmed by the sudden change in my reality.

This continued for some time. So many hugs. Some children told me how deeply they were touched by my essay while others just approached me silently and held my gaze for a moment before hugging me. There were even some who said, "I am so sorry if I was one of those children who hurt you." Before my very own eyes, the stinky refugee dissolved and turned into a school star! Who would have believed something like this was possible? The microphone was my magic wand, the principal my prince, and the teacher my good fairy. All this because of one essay that opened the tap of my heart. What a tale.

That school principal… I will never forget him. His helping hand uplifted and empowered me. "May I be in a position to do this for others," was the wish I made the moment I shook his warm hand before leaving his office.

This experience was my initiation into the power of feminine vulnerability, the power of the heart. The claws of trauma, pain, and false pride rooted in victimhood could no longer disconnect me from my authenticity, vulnerability, trust, passion, and childlike playfulness. The ability to trust my creative process in which the purity of my heart leads the way in playful abandon was reinstalled within me.

I learned through this powerful experience how important it is to open up to others and not to suffer in our internal world. Just as in lovemaking, creative expression is imbued and intertwined with our vital life force energy. In the language of the chakras (the energy vortexes of our subtle body), the second chakra (sexual energy) and throat chakra (creative, authentic expression rooted in our inner truth) are deeply interconnected. The subtle interplay between sexual and creative energy is of essential importance in keeping us in the flow, in complete aliveness, with the ever-present opportunity to transmute energy into the realization of our highest potential.

The moment I opened my heart and entered the flow, I must have even started looking different. To my great amazement, the very next day I experienced something I never thought was possible – while enjoying my turn performing the role of the "duty officer" in the hallway, I couldn't believe my eyes when the famous twin brothers who enjoyed the reputation of being the most handsome teenage boys in our school, came and said hi to me. "Did the twin brothers just come to ME to say hi?! Whoa!"

I retained my celebrity status through the end of the semester.

New Life in Tovarnik

The end of this unique semester of my inner transformation in Batajnica, during which I journeyed through so many intense experiences, coincided with my father's return from the war. At some point on his journey home, he had to walk for days. He lost a lot of weight and had to remove his underwear due to a rash (one of his favorite fun facts!), but he was alive. All of us made it, and that was all that mattered.

We were worried about our grandparents back home in Slavonia. We came to know that a couple of Croatian extremists were eyeing our house as an ideal location for their headquarters. They came several times to harass my grandparents, but Grandma stood tall at the entrance to the house and told them to their faces that they can enter only over her dead body. In the end, they left them alone.

As soon as my father returned from the war, he decided to move us to a village in Eastern Slavonia. This part of Croatia was conquered by the Serbs at that time. As per the law, all Serbian refugees who were kicked out of their homes in other parts of Croatia had the right to move into empty Croatian houses in this area until they manage to sell their house or return to it. This was a temporary solution for people like us who had nowhere to go.

The name of this village was Tovarnik, located right on the border with Šid, Serbia. We moved into an empty Croatian house and my father got a managerial job in an agricultural firm (in Animal Husbandry). As a family, we got a fresh new start.

Of course, the first thing that we did when we woke up in the new house was enjoy a delicious breakfast that my mom made with all her love. I remember it well. She made scrambled eggs and a salad which tasted absolutely heavenly. It was such an amazing feeling to build our home of love once again.

It was clear to me that, as long as we were alive to love and support one another, we could recreate our home anywhere. It did feel strange to live in a house that once belonged to another family and to find someone else's photographs at the back of random drawers in the closet. However, after everything we had been through, we had learned to look at the glass as half full. We were grateful we could start a new life and this was a solid first step. Many Serbian people from Croatia did the same.

Dana and I were about the same height and weight at that time, tall and slim, with long brown hair. The word spread that two sisters who were "beautiful models" moved into Tovarnik. We found that rumor very amusing. I had never fantasized about becoming a model and striking a pose. On the contrary, only something that would allow me to be natural, wild, and unique could attract my interest. My father joked that he will have to stand guard in front of the house if too many guys start coming around to check us out.

Four years later, after the Dayton Agreement in 1996, Eastern Slavonia was returned to Croatia through a process of peaceful reintegration, which was to be supervised by the United Nations. That is how the United Nations Mission in Eastern Slavonia (UNTAES) came into existence, bringing change to many lives, including mine.

After completing high school in Šid as one of the top students, while exploring my options for attending university in Serbia, just for the fun of it, I went to Osijek, Croatia to do a written and oral test for a possible job as a Language Assistant in UNTAES. I received a notification a month later that I performed very well on the test and had gotten the job! I was thrilled to join that colorful international community and even more excited when I came to know that my salary would be a hefty $1200. I teased my father to no end. "Looks like Biba-Riba will be earning a salary four times higher than yours!" Payback for all his teasing!

Chapter 3

United Nations – Croatia

The Joyous Cosmopolitan

One fine day in late 1995, despite my assumption that a college degree or even higher qualifications were required for the job, and the fact that I had already passed the entrance exam to the University of Novi Sad, I followed my intuition to the UNTAES Language Assistant testing in Osijek. Just before embarking on my studies of English Language and Literature, I received a letter stating that I had been approved for a UNTAES Language Assistant position! My adventurous spirit immediately opted for the assistant position amid the embers of war in Eastern Slavonia. From the beautiful city lights of Novi Sad, I ventured forward with a whole new frame of mind – one of adventure and freedom.

As always, my intuition was right. At the onset of the UNTAES mission in early 1996, demand for language assistants was high and the score on the test was the only decisive factor in hiring. It turned out that, even though I was among the youngest applicants, I was also among those with the highest scores.

I loved the fact that I got my very first job entirely on my own. I had not asked for anyone's help or pulled any strings, which I had noticed was (and is) the usual way of achieving any job position in the Balkan region (and most parts of the world for that matter). I knew opportunities like this didn't come very often. It felt like a huge karmic boon after all that I had been through, and I was deeply grateful for that pleasant wind of change

Working for the UN was rewarding from day one. It took no time at all to recognize that I was a cosmopolitan at heart. While studying my astrological natal chart a couple of years later, I learned that the planet Uranus (representing the expansion of one's horizons, risk, innovation, dynamic change, and revolutionary ideas) drove my desire to embrace and enjoy the principle of *unity in diversity.* I enjoy the company of people different from me to the extent that I am excited to joyously learn from their differences. Indeed, it was fulfilling and fun to meet people from all over the world and on top of it all, I must admit this without any false modesty, to be generously paid for it.

Because Uranus is in my 10th house (that of career and ambition) and the strongest aspect in my natal chart involves Uranus, I have always felt an immense need for freedom to forge my own path. Such freedom, I felt, was the only way for me to be fulfilled and successful. Aside from that, there has always been a great eagerness in me for new, fascinating experiences, to see new places, and to encounter new ideas. I preferred to learn and grow from my own direct, authentic experiences and insights. To someone like me, to be stuck in one place my entire life was out of the question. The sense of limitlessness in me is so genuine and strong that even planet Earth at times feels too small!

While watching the Star Wars trilogy, I realized that I honestly felt completely at home with the idea that, just as we have this colorful international community on Earth, we also have a super diverse intergalactic community. It just seemed obvious to me. This kind of openness and wonder helped me fit right into the UN community.

As a Language Assistant, I was obliged to join the UN police monitoring officers wherever they went, and they in turn followed the local police officers wherever they went. The local police force was a mix of both Serbian and Croatian police officers with their respective commanders. The commanders were kind, mature, and cooperative men, so everything seemed to flow nicely.

I remember being driven to my first ever day at work by a good-natured UN Duty Driver, a man from Jordan who could barely speak English. I was headed for the police station of a picturesque little town called Ilok (which was another border town between Croatia and Serbia, only 30 minutes away by car). Ilok was a lovely, hilly town famous for Ilok Castle, established in the 15th century, with a beautiful view of the Danube river.

My day began with a morning briefing by our Swedish Station Commander, followed by coffee and chit-chat before everyone got busy with their assignments. If there was some incident, crime, or car accident happening in the municipality of Ilok, the mixed Serbo-Croatian police force would go to the scene to inspect the case. United Nations monitors would follow them in their SUV, and I would accompany them to interpret and later on translate their reports into the local language. Serbo-Croatian language used to be the official language of former Yugoslavia. After the war, there was a noticeable tendency to deliberately create differences in the language, especially in Croatia. Once in a while, I would discover a new word that popped up.

My colleagues came in all shapes and colors, with a plethora of religious and cultural backgrounds. It was great fun to learn what people in Fiji eat for breakfast, how and when couples get married in Jordan, about the habits, culture, and beliefs of people from Lithuania, Kenya, the USA, Malaysia, Ukraine, Belarus, Norway, Sweden, Egypt, you name it. The job was not at all difficult, except for the night shift duty twice a week, which was slightly challenging in terms of sleep and biorhythm.

There was a lot of time for fun, friendly discussions, lunches, and dinners, not to mention occasional parties at which I loved dancing. Sometimes I even invited my local colleagues to shock the international ones by dancing on the table – after all, we were their hosts, and we had to acquaint them with the wild and joyous Balkan spirit!

After completing my first month of employment, I received an envelope with 12 hundred-dollar bills in it. Holding that thick envelope felt truly fantastic. I remember cherishing that moment, connecting with the vibe of abundance. I was supposed to meet some friends in Novi Sad that weekend, so I took some of my newly earned money with me and decided to go to the fanciest of boutiques and treat myself to honor my new friend, Abundance.

One of the funniest memories from my UN days took place in 1997. It all began with my wild cousin Ceca, who was only one year older than me. Ceca lived in her hometown Vukovar, which had been shelled into rubble by the Yugoslav Army in 1991. I always enjoyed the humor of my cousin Ceca and her mom, Boja (my mom's younger sister). We used to joke that life on the moon would be no big deal for people from Vukovar who are now totally used to seeing craters wherever they turn. Aunt Boja survived three months of heavy shelling inside a suffocating basement, with only minimal canned food. We were now teasing her about how sexy and irresistible she looked in her black tights. Humor is a great helper in the process of healing, acceptance, and moving on after having survived trauma.

Six years later, when life in the eerie Vukovar neighborhoods (consisting of houses that were either destroyed or pock-marked with bullet and shell holes) was slowly returning to some sort of normalcy, Ceca announced she was getting married! We all celebrated Ceca's wedding with great joy, dancing non-stop all night long. Around 6:00 a.m. I concluded there was no point in going back home to Tovarnik before my morning shift, so I called the Duty Driver to pick me up from Vukovar. Sleepiness finally caught up to me after I arrived at the office, the tipping point of exhaustion happening exactly when I went to the toilet. I just leaned on the wall to rest my head for a second and fell into a deep sleep for two hours! I had never slept in a sitting position before, not to mention in a toilet, but there is a first time for everything.

Since we had only one toilet for the UN staff in our office, shared by men and women, the fact that this toilet was continuously occupied for hours caught the attention of my colleagues. One Swedish UN officer was particularly upset and began banging on the door. I woke up in shock and embarrassment, and fled, murmuring an apology.

Another UN officer from Malaysia, who had joined us recently and hardly spoke any English, approached me holding a small plastic tub in his hands. It seemed like he was trying to tell me something. The whole sequence seemed like a scene from some comedy. In a daze, with smudged mascara and dark circles under my eyes, I looked at this Malaysian man and said, "I am sorry, I don't quite get it… what are you trying to tell me? And what is that tub for?"

He was trying earnestly to explain it in words but nobody understood, so he resorted to pantomime. Leaning forward a bit, he started moving his right hand in a circular motion around his rear end.

"Oooooh! It is for washing… that! Agh, too much information, too much information!" I exclaimed. We all laughed until we were in tears. My colleagues could not decide what was funnier – the fact that I had just slept in the toilet or that the Malaysian man was demonstrating the use of his tub. We were a happy family indeed! Later on, I learned this was called "encountering a cultural bump," when cultural differences become so huge that it takes some time and effort to understand and digest them. Asian toilet hygiene habits seemed to be on the cultural bump list for us Europeans (although I must admit, I did get to appreciate them more a decade later when I started living in the steaming hot Middle East).

Along with the snow that winter, a new group of UN staff members from Fiji joined our office in Ilok. They were a merry bunch who loved their onion and garlic. They ate so much of it that their skin and sweat smelled of it big time. The entire office got a new feel, or should I say scent, to it.

When my shift ended one day, one of the new Fijian officers offered to drive me home. We passed by a large meadow that caught his attention. He asked, "And what is that white crop that you are growing there?"

Perplexed, I looked around me and of course saw no crop – it was wintertime. So I replied, "There are no crops now, only snow."

I was amazed when he replied, with the awe of a child: "Oh, so THAT is what snow looks like!" Just as I began to chuckle at this adorable and silly moment, we reached one of the steeper hills near Ilok. As we were about to go downhill, I was shocked to feel him apply the brakes fully. We started skidding sideways! I just closed my eyes, praying for my life, while he exclaimed joyfully: "Oh, dancing on the road, dancing on the road!" This is when I realized that this man had never driven in winter conditions and that it would be a miracle if I reached home in one piece.

Though the experience was very stressful, sharing the account made for some good laughs in the office the next day. "Finally," my officemates teased, "You've discovered a type of dancing that you do not enjoy."

The Flip Side of the Coin

Working with the police officers meant we were witness to many deaths and near-death experiences. This was during the time I was exploring my Scorpio nature and becoming cognizant of a strange curiosity, if not fascination, with these twilight moments when life and death meet. And sure enough, my work was full of this type of excitement from the very first day.

I remember that my first assignment with the UN Civilian Police Office in Ilok was to accompany my colleagues and translate at the site of a massive car accident. After we arrived at the scene of this accident, I watched as they pulled a man through a window of a totally smashed car. When they placed him on the ground in a seated position, a state of shock was evident on his face. One of his legs was in front of him and the other leg was completely behind, broken at the hip joint. That was my welcome to the flip side of the job coin.

Only a week later, we were called to inspect a possible death in a house very close to our police station. The neighbors were alarmed by a stench emanating from there. As we approached the home, I remembered that only a couple of days earlier, I had spotted a very old woman, around 90 years old, peeking through the window. Two local police officers, my UN colleagues from Ukraine and Malaysia, and I went inside. Entering the living room, we were welcomed by a horrible smell and two cats sitting in a mess on the floor, chewing some chicken bones. I somehow trained myself to breathe through my mouth to detach from the sense of smell. My Malaysian colleague however couldn't take it and ran out to vomit.

The police officers inspected the old lady, stating the facts. "Cause of the death is most likely natural. Occurred at least two days ago. The person is approximately 90 years old, and died in an intoxicated state with a half-empty bottle of plum brandy next to her…" I was translating all of this to my Ukrainian colleague who was managing to hold himself together until they flipped the old woman over and a liquid spilled from her mouth. It was the last sip of brandy, which had stewed in her mouth for days. The smell was so strong and terrible that by this time all of them vomited, all except for me.

Of course, I too had noticed the horrible smell, but remained calm, breathing through my mouth. At the moment of my colleagues' synchronized eruption, I was focusing my attention on something else – the wrinkled shirt that I saw when the old woman's belly was exposed. I was fascinated to realize that this was not a shirt; this was her skin! I had never seen the skin of someone that old, so that grabbed my attention more than the foul odor.

When we returned to the office, everyone commented that I was a very unusual young girl. "How come you didn't vomit when all of us did?" my Ukrainian colleague asked. I was surprised about that myself. One thing was sure – I was discovering entirely new traits about myself at this job. This was my first encounter with a dead person, and the day I earned my first UN nickname – "Young Ms. Fearless."

There was something truly fascinating about seeing a lifeless body. It had given me an entirely new perspective on life: the fact that we live our everyday life with the subconscious impression that death is something very distant, so far off that it practically does not exist. But when I saw death with my own eyes, it jerked me from that false reality. It was like an abrupt slap that brought alertness and a realization: "This could be me, at any point in time."

As unpleasant as this experience of seeing the lifeless old woman was, it was nothing in comparison to a case that we had to handle a week later. The scenario repeated itself – someone called to report a bad smell coming from their neighbor's house. "Oh boy, what awaits us now?" I thought. Another language assistant was supposed to be on duty for that task, but she asked me to fill in. I guess I had to justify my new nickname... Ready for the adventure, I joined my colleagues and the local police officers on the drive to the house. The officers said that the only information they had about the occupants was that a man with a special needs son lived there.

The scene upon entering that house was worse than anything I had witnessed till then (and I do advise the sensitive reader to skip over the next three paragraphs). The house was slightly away from the main road, which is why nobody had noticed the odor until it had become extremely strong. This was the day I received training in body decomposition. I was translating what one of the police officers was dictating to another: "A male body, approximately 50 years of age, found lying on the bed. Cause of death, most likely natural. Second stage of decomposition, at least four days from death…" I did not know till then that the human body bloats and turns purple/green before further decomposition! This man's face and entire body were bloated and purple and smelled truly horrific due to ammonia. At that point, even breathing through the mouth did not help, and the worst was still yet to come.

The most horrific scene there, something that will stay with me forever as a symbol of human helplessness and fragility, was the poor special needs boy seated on the bed next to his dead father. He was releasing some unarticulated sounds, saliva dripping from the corners of his mouth when I noticed his legs. His left leg was half rotten from gangrene, with at least a dozen maggots going in and out of the lower part of his leg! Later on, I came to know this is called "wound myiasis" which occurs as a result of egg deposition on decaying flesh with pus. This was too much even for the "Young Ms. Fearless." The special needs child was taken to an appropriate medical facility and his father to the morgue. It took all of us a while to process what we had just seen.

Another evening, just as I joined the dreaded night shift, we received a report that a local man, who must have totally flipped out during the war, was walking on the streets of Ilok carrying a "single-use disposable anti-tank launcher," a portable launch system that fires projectiles designed to combat armored vehicles like tanks or helicopters. In other words, those who came across this man and were fired upon would be 100% burnt and dead within a second.

I was unaware of all these complicated details when I came to the office, ready for the night shift. What I understood from the big fuss and furor was that some crazy, armed man was walking the streets of Ilok and that all police units had been dispatched in search of him. One of my brilliant colleagues from Fiji, who must have watched too many action movies, decided that we should drive around as well, to help with the search. The idea was, of course, that we might see this man from a distance and be the brave ones to inform the police, reaping all the glory. Since it was late at night and our Station Commander could not be contacted, we foolishly went out without his permission. After all, I was the only Language Assistant available, so I *had* to join them – to perform necessary translation.

We drove around Ilok in the middle of the night, cracking jokes and enjoying the adventure. All of a sudden, the car stopped and pin-drop silence permeated our SUV. In the middle of the road, hardly 20 meters in front of us, was a man with the anti-tank launcher on his right shoulder, pointed directly at us! For a second, we were breathless. "Reverse! F**king reveeeeeerse," we were all shouting at the Lithuanian officer behind the steering wheel. With eyes wide open, while our car was moving backward and away from the anti-tank launcher, we stared at our death... This moment seemed like an eternity. I wasn't even praying, my mind just went blank. As the car was reversing, there was this strange feeling within me, as if we were rewinding a movie reel and going back in time.

When we finally lost sight of the man and realized we were still alive, the driver turned the car around and drove back to our police station. We were all silent the entire drive. When we entered the office, we suddenly went into a post-shock delirium of sorts, shouting, laughing, hugging, and smoking cigarettes. Everyone smoked, whether they were "smokers" or not. It was just insane!

At that point, our strict Swedish Station Commander, who had come to know of our escapade, stormed into the office, furious at the UN police officers. When he heard that I had been in the car too, his shouting escalated even more. At that moment, I was like a precious damsel whose life they had put in danger. It was all very dramatic and comical really. Soon after my first time seeing the second stage of body decomposition and gangrene with maggots, I had my own near-death experience. "You gotta love it," I joked with my colleagues that night. "One thing is for sure – there is never a dull moment."

A couple of months later, I had another brush with death, this time even more ironic. There was a big event that was going to happen in Ilok, bringing a lot of excitement to our little UN Civilian Police Station. We were to be visited by the US Ambassador to Croatia, Peter W. Galbraith himself! This was the man who had brokered the entire agreement with the Croatian government, permitting a gradual peaceful reintegration of this part of the Slavonia region during the two years of the United Nations' administration. Without him, none of us would be there and further fighting between Croats and Serbs in late 1995 would have been the most likely scenario.

I was truly amazed when I was informed that I had been handpicked as the Language Assistant to translate at the main meeting between Ambassador Galbraith, our Station Commander, and Serbian and Croatian representatives, among others. Simply, wow! I felt truly gratified that my professionalism was being recognized in this way.

The main event included a relaxed visit to Ilok Castle. During a gathering in front of the castle with the Ambassador and UN officials, there was some sudden commotion. Motorolas started beeping with requests for urgent backup and before we even understood what was happening, a mob of angry protestors broke through the barricade and all layers of security protection and were running straight for us. I came to know these were Serbian men, who were very unhappy with some of the latest policies implemented.

I can't recall the exact details behind this riot, but it surely reflected the worries, insecurity, and immense frustration of Serbian people who, just like my family, were permitted to move into empty Croatian houses in eastern Slavonia until their situations were resolved. By this point in time, the Croatian government was pushing for the return of the Croatian people, and these loose solutions and policies were being redefined daily. This part of eastern Slavonia absorbed around 60,000 Serbs who were driven out of two other enclaves taken over by the Croatian Army in early 1995. I remember one Serbian man made a joke that he felt like he was stuck with a broken record continuously playing part of a popular song at that time; the line being, "Should I stay or should I go now?" that kept playing in a loop. And he was not enjoying the music.

It certainly was not pleasant for Serbian people who had received the official notification that they were permitted to return to their home in Croatia, leaving the Croatian house in which they were temporarily living, only to discover that their original home had been completely destroyed. They couldn't return to a house that no longer existed. They didn't want to rebuild but had nowhere to go and nobody to whom they could complain.

Those were only some of the issues weighing heavily on the people who gathered to complain to the US Ambassador, and tempers flared when they were not granted permission to approach him. They broke through the barricades and ran towards us with stones in their hands. At some point, tension rose and stones started flying. Along with the UN officials and members of the police, I started sprinting toward the nearby Catholic church, which had a big gate that could protect us.

"Oh, goodness," I thought, "after everything I've been through as a Serb from Croatia, it would be ironic if I was killed by another Serb in Croatia. This can't be happening." While running, I started having the feeling of being close to death, like I could hear Death's somber steps approaching.

There was a certain thickness in the air; the atmosphere around me felt more dense. I kept running, briefly turning just once to see how close the Serbian protesters were.

At that moment, in cinematic slow motion, I felt intuitively that the stone deciding my destiny was about to be thrown at my head. In one dimension, it had already happened, and in another dimension, it was about to happen. Exactly in that millisecond, I heard a male voice shouting: "Not at her! She is Milan Radonić's daughter." The density reduced and Death walked away steadily. I continued running until I reached the gate of the Catholic church. A priest opened it for us and let us in. To date, I don't know who spoke up for me, but I am 100% certain that he saved my life.

Being ethnically Serbian, I must honestly say that it felt weird to sit inside that church and be exposed to all sorts of negative comments about the Serbian people who were attacking us. Weirder still, this was the first time in my life that I had entered a Catholic church. The vibe was completely unfamiliar. It felt cold, and I suspected that the austere atmosphere stemmed from negative impressions of the Catholic Inquisition in my unknown past. In any case, I was grateful to that Catholic priest who was kind enough to let us in at that critical moment. "Destiny's practical joke" seemed like the right phrase (one of Mohanji's favorites) to describe that particular moment in time.

Dance & The Rise of the Feminine

There are no words to describe just how much I love and enjoy dancing. At any party or celebration, I find myself among the first to get up to dance, and last to sit down. I need no alcohol or stimulants to sustain my energy levels that feel inexhaustible, and I dance in playful abandon, full of only my own inner joy.

I trained initially in the folk dances of former Yugoslavia and later in Latin dances, but I love all styles of dance and can always pick up steps easily. I especially enjoyed the music of the 1980s, Latin and East Asian dances, and dances that involve hip movement in the shape of a horizontal eight (a.k.a. *lemniscata*). My intuition has always been clear about the immense importance that this kind of hip movement plays in terms of not only sexual but physical and emotional health of all people, women especially. I have always felt that hip movement during dance awakens the higher feminine qualities in me, the goddess within. This inner knowing is ingrained in my DNA and has always been alive in my body.

I feel surrendered, playful, creative, and comfortable in my own skin while dancing. I never dance to impress, and honestly don't care much whether anyone is watching. While dancing, I love to improvise my steps and have fun with the people around me, but I equally enjoy dancing alone, turning my attention within. It took me some time to understand this truth – when a woman is in touch with her own sexual and creative energy, when she feels that energy flowing through her with ease, men feel it too. Men may place a lot of importance on a woman's looks, but it's only when a woman feels in touch with her own feminine sexual energy and sensuality, juiciness, and curvy beauty, that she becomes truly attractive. That is why chubby yet confident women sometimes appear more attractive to men, than sleek models who don't feel good about themselves despite the effort they put into their forms. Attractiveness is not about how one looks, but how one feels in their own body.

In 2017, a technique called Conscious Dancing flowed through my body and consciousness while I sat in the expanded auric field of beloved Mohanji. In simple terms, I can say that I "downloaded" it. The technique involves vertical alignment in unstructured dance with attention focused within, especially along the central axis. With the addition of voice and breath modulations, the result is an amazing aliveness in every cell of the body. Since the download, I have shared the pure bliss of Conscious Dancing with other people around the globe. All in all, I cannot imagine life without dance and do not wish to. For the record, I intend to dance and celebrate life and the sacred feminine in me until my last breath.

Recently I chanced upon the YouTube channel of Dr. Kaouthar Darmoni, an amazing woman from Tunisia who lives in Europe. Watching her TEDx Talk, for a moment I felt like I saw myself in another body and another culture. Her words spoke my truth, 100%. Dr. Kaouthar eventually quit her career in academia and founded the Feminine Capital & Goddess Dance organization. I found the extent to which her words reflected the depth of inner knowing that I've always had about the essence of true feminine power and dance as the oldest sacred feminine ritual in the world to be utterly amazing. I would like to offer a summary of some of the amazing points that she made in her powerful speeches, along with my commentary.

Dr. Kaouthar shares that in ancient Mesopotamia approximately 4000 years ago, women would often gather to practice an ancient ritual, the *Dance of the Goddesses*. This beautiful, sensual dance with a lot of hip movement (combined with the occasional contraction of the pelvic floor muscles), was performed at homes and temples throughout the ages. The dance was a tool for healing and empowerment, as well as to initiate men to the feminine face of sexuality and the essence of the Divine Feminine.

Dancing indeed brings out the goddess in a woman. Admiring the beauty of a woman connected to the Sacred Feminine within and expressing those qualities through dance is equal to witnessing divine expression and beauty within a human. Hip movement following the shape of a horizontal number eight invokes the power of the womb, opening and closing "the gate" of womb energy power. Utilization of the pelvic floor muscles, movement of the shoulders, shaking and bouncing of the breasts (observable in the Balkan folk dances as well), lifting the arms, connecting the womb and the heart – all these movements bring out the essence of the feminine energy. These movements are empowering, healing, and uplifting for both men and women. Women should be free to dance in this way without fear of objectification or judgment. The dance is not about lust and should be culturally accepted and celebrated. As a woman, I resonate with this deeply and wholeheartedly.

From that brief but grand vision, let us return to reality on the ground. We shall not even look at the poverty-stricken countries without proper sanitation and education, not to mention women's rights. Let us look into the economically advanced West, where women can pursue the education and career of their choice and are supposedly free to express themselves. In reality, female sensuality and the essence of feminine beauty have been monopolized by male-dominated institutions that set the rules of the game in fashion, the corporate world, the entertainment industry, you name it. Dr. Kaouthar rightfully poses the question "Is this better or worse than what we see in the Arab world where women dance beautifully, like goddesses, all dressed up within their secluded spaces, but the moment they step out into the male-dominated outside world, they put on a veil and become silent and submissive? Their beautiful curvy, juicy sensuality is seen not only as a disturbance or a distraction for men but is even perceived as a threat, something that brings chaos."

Indeed, the harems and hamams of the Arab world can be perceived as the spaces into which women are confined, but in Tunisia, Morocco, and most of the Arab world, women at least have their secluded spaces away from the male gaze, where they can feel free and unjudged in terms of their looks, their feminine body, and sensuality. None of them would feel fat or deficient in any way, or afraid of the gaze and judgment of another woman. This is their version of the ancient "circle of women," which has always been the most powerful way of nurturing and nourishing feminine development, healing, and maturing. I have a deep connection with women's circles, way beyond this lifetime, and will share more about that later.

Dr. Kaouthar admits being deeply disappointed with the freedom that she, as a woman, found upon moving to the West. Women have no access to secluded spaces, and the main weapon used against them is time. All women are expected to be young and slim forever. Instead of the veil or burqa, Dr. Kaouthar points out, as women we have to deal with the far more cunning form of imposed humiliation, the "forever young" veil and "pornification" veil. That beauty myth makes most middle-aged women feel useless and unattractive, forced to resort to plastic surgery and similar solutions, following the example of the majority of singers, actresses, and other celebrities. The pornographic image of a female body has infiltrated fashion, visual arts, marketing, and nearly every aspect of our society. Rather than rejecting it as inappropriate, it is accepted as completely "normal." But it is definitely not normal, and not serving the highest interests of humanity.

It is important to point out that this is not about blaming men, but rather the dysfunctional patriarchal system in which we all unwittingly participate. Indeed, one key issue that lowers the frequency of present humanity is the imbalance between masculine and feminine energy. This imbalance has been the root cause of all trauma through the ages, and can eventually destroy us all if we allow it. This is precisely what needs to be healed in today's humanity, humanity that left the ancient temples of the High Priestesses to enter the modern brothels. Let us briefly zoom in on the topic of the patriarchy.

The Cunning Trap of Our Modern Patriarchy

In the patriarchy, the social system which was institutionalized approximately 10,000 years ago, power and rule are, by default, assigned to men. Ancient scriptures were interpreted and molded by this social system to suit the lust for power and dominance. It justified the public shaming, torture, and murder of women of insight and inner alchemy. Labeling such women as witches, and imposing their system's denial of sacred feminine energy, the indigenous communities of America, Europe, Australia, Asia, and Africa were destroyed. Consequently, the age-old wisdom of those indigenous communities was lost. Mother Earth was ruthlessly plundered and exploited, like a woman raped in drunken military abandon.

It was this patriarchy that also cunningly manipulated our women to rise up against it on the patriarchy's terms, not from the truth of their sacred feminine power. That is why, as Dr. Kaouthar says, "Women's emancipation turned into women's masculinization." While the basic tenets and achievements of the feminist movement (to put an end to sexism, sexist oppression and exploitation, to achieve full gender equality, freedom of education, career, reproductive rights, women's suffrage, etc.) in law and practice were certainly noble and significant, one glaring failing of the feminist movement is that it largely portrays the misery of women as men's fault or men's responsibility. I dare to disagree because that automatically places all women into the archetype of a victim. And we are not victims – we are powerful.

Indeed, as women, we too need to take responsibility for our role in the perpetuation of the patriarchy. It is women who often suppress their daughters, making them fit only for marriage and household work while at the same time supporting their sons' achievements. In sub-Saharan Africa, for example, millions of young women undergo female genital mutilation or some type of harmful procedure to the female genitalia for non-medical purposes. In many cases, these acts are performed by elder women adhering to traditional beliefs about the purity and chastity of their daughters or granddaughters. In India for example, female feticide still very much exists, and getting married off to "the highest bidder" is largely perceived as a woman's key achievement in life.

In the corporate world, on the other hand, women inevitably hit "the glass ceiling" or invisible barrier to the upper echelons, while aiming to reach executive levels in the corporate hierarchy. The key question here is whether women will come together in the spirit of feminine collaboration, or continue to mimic the old masculine ways established by the patriarchal corporate world.

Unfortunately, what we mainly see is the latter. Women proudly don business suits, unconsciously projecting the associated image of competition, elbowing, scheming, and manipulation, all under a pressure to succeed in a man's world. Women have long lost the knowledge that the true, authentic, and innate power of all women lies in the sacred womb space. It is in our curvy hips, in our movement and dance, tenderness and softness, penetrative intuition, art, wisdom, courage, kindness, and nurturing. Most of all, our feminine power is in the selflessness and purity of motherhood (whether directly through progeny or social service). And from which comes the grace of the *shakti*, the abundant feminine power of manifestation, immense courage, and grounded stability.

Tapping Into the Divine Feminine Essence

The key to tapping into the divine feminine essence is all in feminine ease and flow. To come in contact with it is to allow yourself to create, as it is found in any form of art or creative expression. In my case, it is – through dance and group meditation. Come into alignment with the aspect of you that does want to create – allow that side to flow unrestricted. If we are in the energy of resistance, we can't allow ourselves to be who we are because our energy is invested in resistance, not in our flow, ease, and happiness. Each woman is her own unique expression of the Divine Feminine and does not need to compete or compare with another or conform to another's idea. Let us explore what it takes for us as women to allow the Divine Feminine to flow through us, and to express in this physical dimension.

It has never been more critical for women to come together in the spirit of sisterhood and form women's circles. Let us relearn together what it means to be a woman, deeply and truly. This is the idea behind the red tent movement[16], or initiatives such as the Festival of Womanhood.[17] We need to open up to other women about our womanhood and its deeper meaning. Amazing things come out, and amazing energy gets released from our wombs. Within such an energetic group dynamic, any man that connects with those values is welcome too. Inclusion is one of the key qualities of feminine energy, not exclusion.

Women connected with their Sacred/Divine Feminine can hold space for others like nobody else, to create spaces where everyone feels welcome, nurtured, comforted, and loved. In 2021, I joined my dear friends from Mohanji Foundation – Jelena Fassbender, Nikolina Dragojević, and Palak Mehta – on the adventure of organizing our first-ever Festival of Womanhood within the larger, global platform of Mohanji Foundation. Words fall short of describing the energy we experienced through this festival. It was so exhilarating – like tasting the pure, divine nectar of Sacred Femininity coming from the Source. As we women joined together for the higher cause of sharing and empowering one another, we felt that we were contributing to the most important cause on Earth today – the rise of the Feminine. More will be shared about this Festival later.

I am pleased that contemporary feminism is slowly improving in terms of its alignment with our collective sacred feminine heritage. It will be my great honor to connect with many more women like Dr. Kaouthar: women who choose to embody the Sacred Feminine and lead through their own example. Dr. Kaouthar brought my attention to another amazing woman with a powerful contribution towards the modern feminine awakening into the sacred feminine – Fatema Mernissi, a Moroccan sociologist and internationally known feminist writer. I am sure there are many more similarly inspiring voices emerging around the globe and I look forward to seeing the beautiful and sacred tapestry of true femininity that we weave in this world together.

After having lived in the Middle East for ten years and being married to an Indian man, I must admit that I sometimes find myself experiencing a cultural shock in Europe, the continent on which I was born and raised. I currently live in Slovenia, a lovely EU and Schengen country, and recently walked into a mechanic's garage to get something fixed on my car. And what do I see just upon

16 A movement of women in the UK which is all about celebrating being a woman and reclaiming the power of their menstrual cycle. During monthly Red Tent gatherings, women gather to share and discuss without judgment and provide mutual emotional support. Women get to learn how to live in tune with the phases of their cycle. (There are some 60 Red Tent groups listed in the UK alone on redtentdirectory.com).

17 An annual event by the World Womanhood Project to celebrate, respect, heal, and empower women across all nationalities and females of all species (www.festivalofwomanhood.com)

entering an official garage in the city of Maribor - a calendar proudly displayed on the wall, with a pornographic image of a completely naked woman touching her genitals and pouting her lips. Aside from being shocked, I was also relieved that my 11-year-old daughter was not with me. "How can that be socially acceptable?" I thought.

During visits to my parents' home in Serbia, when the television is turned on, I was shocked to see a reality show with live scenes bordering on outright pornography, airing for hours every day. This reality show is proudly streamed on TV Pink in Serbia, with just enough emotion, spiced-up arguments, and drama to loosely maintain the appearance of normalcy and attract common people of all age groups. The magnetism is so strong that they can hardly be blamed. What they don't realize is that they are being perverted.

Whenever I see my parents watching such shows, I try not to judge. I either have to leave the room or ask them to change the channel. I rue my limited ability to convey the damage such shows can inflict on the subtle feminine power. The only way out of this trap is to raise awareness of the sacred feminine, and to create contrasting content in which feminine beauty and magnetism are celebrated; not subjected to pornification at one end of the pendulum or dogmatic suppression at the other.

And what of the sacred masculine? In this mass media culture of pornification, masculine sexuality naturally had to become dysfunctional as well. Having lost the sacred dimension of feminine sexuality, its feminine half, masculine sexuality became raw or suppressed, and oftentimes even turned into violence, sadism, perversion, etc.

On top of it all, we have scientists like Freud propping this up, propagating that small girls experience great anxiety upon the realization that they don't have a penis. This is suggestive that women are sexually inferior to men. Moreover, he was also asserting that children are not harmed by acts of sexual violence.[18] I find this to be one of the most dangerous theories of all, as it opens the doors to validation of one of the worst evils on earth – pedophilia, incest, and non-consensual sex. This is yet another reason why I feel forever grateful to Jung for standing up to Freud.

In summary, it has never been more important to revive the ancient teachings and value systems in which female sexuality was seen as active and alive, where the vaginal opening was valued as the door to the womb – referred to by ancient elders as "paradise on Earth." These teachings were passed on in the spirit of revered sisterhood, through a long line of female lineages, not only in ancient Mesopotamia, but in India, Latin American countries, Africa, China, among the Native Americans, indigenous people of Malaysia, and Australia, on the Balkan peninsula in the pre-Christian era (a separate topic that will be discussed later) and various other cultures across the globe. They are accessible to all of us through the collective unconscious, through our DNA, and most importantly, through consciousness. Recent movements such as "#MeToo" are positive

18 Florence Rush, an American certified social worker, first introduced this topic as "The Freudian Coverup" in her presentation "The Sexual Abuse of Children: A Feminist Point of View," about childhood sexual abuse and incest, at the New York Radical Feminists (NYRF) Rape Conference in 1971.

developments in the spirit of the awakening of the sacred feminine. It was moving to witness the ripple effect created by women supporting and inspiring one another to gather the courage to speak up and come out of the bubble of the Victim Archetype.

Let us not only envision but also feel a world in which a woman's sexual force is perceived and honored as a crucial part of her life force, as her source of vitality and vibrancy, rather than shame and guilt. Let us imagine: how would it feel to perceive female sexuality as active and alive instead of passive and submissive? I invite you to join me in the feminine act of holding space for this vision to become our reality today.

Let us see and feel a world in which the energy of a woman's orgasm is valued as a sacred womb blessing and channel for spiritual upliftment. Let us imagine and feel into existence a world in which grandmothers initiate their granddaughters into the art of femininity within spaces designated for such purposes. See and feel the beauty of old women with gray hair and wrinkled skin, teaching their granddaughters about authentic femininity with warmth, joy, and immense wisdom of life. Let us manifest a world that values a kind of beauty that does not age and requires no surgery because it is beyond time. That kind of direct learning through the female lineage is priceless and powerful beyond words.

Let us imagine a safety net of sisterhood with safe spaces like female temples and hamams, healing spas in which a woman of any age can be herself 100%, connect to the elements, understand the power of her womb, and construct her feminine identity freely. Imagine the revival of ancient women's circles, the key structure for nurturing and sexual education of every girl across the globe, from the sexually formative tween and teen years (nowadays even earlier) and onwards. These safe spaces completely reject the influence of the patriarchal, pornographic society and the male gazes that invoke shame or the danger of shaming. Let us imagine beautiful women of all ages performing various versions of the *Dance of the Goddesses* across the globe during any important celebration, in line with their respective cultures and yes, even within temples and holy places. Let us view such women as the true spine and anchor of stability in humanity, peace, and harmony on Earth. And most importantly, let us see women invoking and nurturing the Sacred Masculine in their beautiful men.

Finally, let us imagine the feminine qualities of compassion, intuitive guidance, vulnerability, and selflessness in our institutions, in all leadership positions in politics, finance, and the top echelons of power. We don't need to masculinize our women to have them join men in holding positions of power. Instead, we must redefine the concept of power in our world so that values like compassion, humility, selflessness, and empathy become key traits of our leaders, CEOs, directors, etc. – regardless of gender.

Let us pray together: "May sacred masculinity and femininity be re-defined and expressed in the present time, in their highest potential, through conscious couples who choose the path of intimacy and spirituality as a way of being whole and serving others, for the benefit of all. May the magic of balanced existence unfold on Earth. So be it. *Tathastu*. Amen."

My Own Magnetic Sexuality Discovered

As a merry 19-year-old woman comfortable in her own skin, with a passion and excitement for life, I was always bursting with energy. I was unaware that the UN and policemen surrounding me, men in their 30s, 40s, and 50s (very rarely did I see any UN colleagues in their 20s), perceived the energy I radiated as magnetic and sexual. On the contrary, I was very professional and responsible at work, ever-ready to learn new words, working overtime to perfect some translation, and focused to the maximum as an interpreter during meetings between local and international officials.

Soon after the event with Ambassador Galbraith, we had another VIP visit. The head of the entire UNTAES mission, Major General Jacques Paul Klein, was visiting Ilok. I wondered whether I would get the chance to translate at another important meeting. It turned out that this VIP visit left a completely different taste in my mouth.

Everyone in the office stood in line to greet the Major General and his entourage. A humble middle-aged woman walked behind him, and we understood she was his official translator. Something odd happened when he passed by me. This was the moment when I discovered the dynamic of a young woman with magnetic sexuality within our patriarchal society. The Major General smiled as he looked at me, and paused briefly to ask our Station Commander about me. My Commander replied: "She is one of the Language Assistants from our police station here in Ilok." And this Major General commented loudly, completely serious in his tone: "Oh! How come we don't have such young and good-looking Language Assistants at our headquarters?"

I was completely embarrassed, and the expression of the woman in his group soured. The Major General had disrespected his own translator and I felt he owed her an apology. Secondly, I found this comment to be rude and condescending toward me. I couldn't believe he had passed such a comment based merely on my looks, without knowing anything about my language skills, professionalism, spiritual depth, and other qualities. I was shocked even more when one of my male colleagues congratulated me on being noticed by Major General Klein. All of this was truly distasteful, but I remained silent, processing what had just happened. On the other hand, this experience taught me that I was lucky to be stationed in a town as small as Ilok and not in the headquarters, where I would have had to "swim with the sharks" and deal with these sorts of issues without being prepared for any of it.

This was my introduction to the world of men, the world of patriarchal power systems, to the trap of perceived normalcy into which a contemporary woman enters at the onset of her career, soon to discover that the way she is perceived by most men is totally disrespectful of her delicate feminine nature. This all-pervading patriarchal system crushes the beauty that we women offer to the world through the Sacred Feminine energy that we carry within.

My disappointment reached its peak a couple of years later when I discovered from a male friend in the UN that I had a secret nickname in Ilok, widely used among many of my male colleagues. I was honestly shocked and appalled when I heard that this nickname was "Walking Sex." This took some time to digest. "What?! Seriously? What walking sex? What about the quality of my translations, what about my professionalism? Did anyone bother to notice that?" I complained. No, all they saw were the curves of my body and the energy I naturally radiated when I walked, danced, or laughed, which of course was unintentional. Such energy emanates naturally from a woman in touch with the core of her femininity. Without any feminine support, preparation, and protection, I was destined to end up in trouble within this scenario – and that is exactly what followed.

The empty Croatian house that was assigned to my family happened to have an existing restaurant space on the ground floor. In 1997, my parents decided to put it to use and open a humble restaurant. I supported them in this endeavor because I noticed many UN, police, and customs officers could afford to eat in restaurants daily and were looking for a decent place nearby where they could enjoy a proper lunch cooked in hygienic conditions.

My dad had a real knack for preparing grilled meats, and my mom was an excellent cook. She paid special attention to the smallest details so her soups, salads, potatoes, cakes, etc. were always brilliant. My parents partnered with another woman who had previous experience in running a restaurant and soon we had many people coming to our place in Tovarnik. My UN job involved a lot of interaction with people, and I was happy to gently help promote my parents' newly found business a bit, so many of our patrons knew me.

Aside from the Civilian Police, within the UNTAES mission we had contingents of soldiers from different countries who had their role to play in the peacekeeping. There was a sizable contingent from Jordan, and some of those soldiers started frequenting my parents' restaurant. Their behavior was pretty odd, especially toward me. They would bother me to take a photo with them, and sometimes I would agree, just to get rid of them. While standing next to me, they would put their hand around my waist or on my shoulder and shiver, as if I was standing there naked. I sensed the most awkward sexual energy during those moments. Word spread and these Jordanian soldiers would show up for dinner just before I was to return home from work and bother our waitress to call me.

At some point, I got fed up with that and decided to say something about it to Ahmed, one of the main Jordanian police officers at our station. I told him exactly what happened, and while the men did not assault me in any way, they were bothering me with non-stop requests for photography and awkward hugs. Hearing this, Ahmed stormed off somewhere. I soon learned that he had made a big fuss about this, that a thorough investigation was conducted, and all those soldiers who came to my parents' restaurant were lined up in front of a wall as if they were to be assassinated. They were given a choice of a) getting one finger chopped off, b) renouncing two monthly salaries, or c) going back to Jordan. And Ahmed, the man who reported this, was promoted to a higher rank.

I couldn't sleep that night. Had I known how these people function, had I understood the nuances of their cultural and religious background, I would have never reported those poor soldiers. I spoke with another Jordanian police officer, Abdullah, who told me that most of these men can only fantasize about being intimate with a woman. They first have to earn enough money to build a house, and only then could they have the opportunity to marry a woman and experience intimacy. For these men, simply touching a woman's soft skin was something of which they could only dream, not to mention experience.

At this point, I came to know there was a brothel in Ilok that was getting very popular and played an important role in diffusing the sexual tension of all these men. Abdullah felt he could trust me, so he told me one day: “Sister, I am in love.” I thought that was wonderful news until I realized that he had fallen in love with a prostitute from that brothel.

I tried to explain to him, “Abdullah, brother, you can’t fall in love with a prostitute. Trust me, she won’t love you back. She is interested in your money, not your love.” But he wouldn’t listen. This was the first time that this man had experienced intimacy, even though he was in his late 20s, and he lost his head. He bought a TV for this prostitute, among other fancy gifts, and even planned to buy her a car! Luckily, at this point he started talking about their marriage, and she dumped him. Needless to say, he was heartbroken.

Every day some story related to the prostitutes and this brothel in Ilok would circulate in our office. We even had a complaint about the UN officers from Fiji. Apparently, the smell of onion and garlic exuding from their bodies was too much for the brothel women to bear, and they were demanding to be paid double if these officers stepped in there again. That caused a big commotion and endless jokes in the office. It all seemed funny until the local police made a proper investigation into the identity of these prostitutes. One of them was a ballerina from Russia who had been tricked into coming to Ilok with the promise of a career in Croatia, only to have her passport confiscated and to be forced into prostitution. I remember having a nightmare of being that woman, a helpless sex slave, desperately trying to prove to others that I was not a prostitute but a ballerina. Luckily, at some point this brothel shut down and so all the stories related to it came to an end.

Far from over were my life lessons in sexual energy. One day, upon returning home from work, I passed through the restaurant just to see if everything was under control and if any help or translation was needed by my parents or the waitress. I noticed an Egyptian UN officer seated at his usual table, with sad puppy dog eyes, listening to some music on his portable CD player. This must have been the tenth time I’d seen him sitting at that same table, all alone.

Out of compassion, or perhaps stupidity, I approached him and asked why he looked so sad. He said that he was troubled by the issues of the heart and revealed that he was listening to Whitney Houston. His name was Ayman. He had beautiful brown eyes with long lashes, and for some reason, I chose to sit and talk to him, thinking I could help him out a bit. That was a big, big mistake.

The Universe had given me one warning with that unpleasant situation with the Jordanian soldiers, but I didn’t get it. I should have understood the cultural difference right there. For some reason, I thought that this police officer was more educated and ‘normal’ in western terms, so I had a coffee with him and spoke to him for 15 min or so. Little did I know that this kind of gesture would be interpreted as my willingness to not only date him but to marry him!

The next day when I returned home, I did not pass through the restaurant. The waitress told my mom later that evening that a regular guest had been sitting for hours and had enquired about me several times. It was Ayman again. Out of politeness, I went to talk with him again, but a certain weirdness had already set in and I was becoming slightly uncomfortable. I found out from a Serbian friend from Tovarnik that his friend, who was Ayman's landlord, had spoken to him about this poor Egyptian man who was so hopelessly in love that he couldn't eat or sleep. They went shopping to buy clothes "that Serbian girls like" and also went to the hairdresser for the same purpose.

Worried about the likelihood that this man was in love with me, I decided to have a frank talk with him. The next time I found him at his usual table in the restaurant, I sat down to speak to him. Since he'd just finished drinking his Turkish coffee, out of a joke, I offered to "read his fortune" from his coffee cup. We flipped the cup around and after some time I started with the reading. I have not done this sort of coffee cup reading since my childhood days when I was freaked out by the correct prediction of the illness and death of my next-door neighbor. This time I was going to do it only because I no longer took it seriously, and thought this would be a suitable smooth intro into the uncomfortable subject of love.

I stared into the coffee cup, waiting for my eyes to go slightly out of focus, and for my intuition to gather something from the little signs in the coffee sedimentation. To my great surprise, I saw my own face! I looked pale and depressed, reacting as if I'd just been told something horrible. The next thing I saw was an entire movie unfolding in front of my eyes.

In the vision, Ayman went back home to Egypt and told his wife and mother that he was madly in love with a Serbian lady and that he wanted to marry her, to marry me! His wife was already depressed because she could not have children, which is a tough thing to swallow for a woman in a Muslim society. The very thought of divorce was something she found utterly degrading and unbearable. Since Ayman insisted that he loved someone else and demanded a divorce, she went out on a balcony and committed suicide right then and there.

The next scene was Ayman's mother running out of the house screaming to find her dear daughter-in-law dead, lying in a pool of blood. The shock of that scene resulted in an instant heart attack. Ayman buried both his wife and his mother and returned back to Croatia.

The final scene was that of Ayman asking me to marry him. My answer: "What? What makes you think I would want to marry you? We are just friends. I have never had any feelings for you." (Which was the truth!)

Seeing this entire sequence of events took only a couple of seconds. It freaked me out so much that I suddenly got up and shouted at Ayman: "I do not love you! Do you understand? I would never, ever want to be with you! Do not talk to me ever again! Do not come near me ever again. If I see you on the road, I will cross over to the other side. If you try to approach me, I will call the police. Do you understand?"

With my heart racing, I ran out of the restaurant and prayed fervently that evening that the horrible destiny I foresaw was diverted. I must say I was successful in this endeavor because Ayman never chased me again. Although I was very grateful for that divine warning disguised as a cup reading, I renewed my vow to avoid using this technique ever again.

Love Dramas Intensify

Before delving into this topic further, I would like to travel back in time to the age of 16, when I was suddenly introduced to the world of sexuality. My sister had her first boyfriend at that time and so did my cousin Ceca, so I had some discussions on this topic with them. I did not feel ready for a relationship. We must never be pushed into intimacy until we have a clear inner confirmation that we are ready. Introduction to the world of intimacy plays a very important role in the way we experience this delicate and most personal aspect of life. I learned this lesson very vividly.

I was invited to a party in Tovarnik during which I met Zlatko, a young man in his 20s who lived in one of the nearby villages. I had seen him at a coffee bar a couple of times before this party and noticed that he was interested in me. However, I was not interested in him or any other man. I simply had not reached that point in my sexual and emotional maturity. Since I was tall, rather serious, and confident, I always seemed older than my actual age.

Zlatko was determined to hook up with me that evening. He must have been very nervous about it because he got drunk on "liquid courage." At one point, he asked me to come outside with him. The entire courting was rather odd because I was avoiding his kiss due to the smell of cigarettes and alcohol from his mouth. To my great shock, he suddenly opened his car, pushed me onto the front passenger seat, and climbed on top of me. Before I knew what was happening, he started breathing very heavily and removing his clothes with one hand, while holding me strongly with his other hand. I couldn't believe what he was doing. "It can't be that I will lose my virginity by being raped in a car!" I thought. I tried fighting back but he was much stronger, and I noticed that he interpreted my resistance as my passionate interest. He clearly thought I was enjoying his outburst of passion bordering on violence. On the contrary, I was disgusted!

At some point, I changed my strategy, stopped resisting, and connected with the core of my feminine strength, which I felt was coming from my womb. Since I was not resisting, he was preparing for penetration. In the final moment of his great masculine victory, he whispered in my right ear, "I love you!"

With a deep voice, connected to my core, I replied, "If you love me, then get off of me!" This worked, it really worked! He removed himself from me and I ran! I ran as fast as I could, adjusting my clothing while running. I managed to escape and reached home traumatized.

After that, drama ensued. Zlatko knew my sister's boyfriend and pleaded that he intervene by delivering his sincere apology. I was in my room, confiding to my sister in tears when her boyfriend suddenly appeared on our balcony. He climbed the fence to the top floor like some movie character. He fulfilled his promise to Zlatko and conveyed the message. He said that Zlatko even threatened that he would kill himself if I didn't agree to be his girlfriend. "Mark my words," I replied. "No man who shows even a sign of violence will ever be my partner. There is no second chance. He showed violence and he can forget being with me, ever! You can tell him that he can hang upside down, walk on his eyelashes (a typical local expression), or do whatever he wants, but I will never be with him! Period."

That was my traumatic and dramatic introduction to the world of sexuality. This scenario of being almost raped repeated a couple of times in my life. However, in one way or the other, I would be extracted from it at the last minute. This was nothing but Divine Grace and I am immensely grateful for each one of those moments of blessings. Many other women have had to bear the weight of that horrible psychological, emotional, physical, and spiritual wound. Rape does almost irreparable damage to a woman's connection to the most delicate, most intimate, and most vulnerable part of her feminine nature. "Broken" is the word most raped women use upon describing how they feel after being raped. I understand why.

It took me more than a year to even look at another man. I became very wary of giving any signs to men, too. A year or so later, during the third year of my high school studies, I met a lovely, gentle, tall young man with soft blue eyes. His name was Boban. He was 5 or 6 years older than me and knew how to patiently wait for a girl to realize that she was interested. He knew how to approach me and was very sincere. I am grateful to Boban for being my first boyfriend and for being someone who removed the horrible first impression I had of sexual intimacy. During the two years of our relationship, he was also my best friend, and someone I could rely on in any situation.

An opportunity came for my parents to exchange the house in Slatina for another house in Serbia, in a village called Kukujevci near Šid. There were many Serbians from Croatia eager to exchange their houses to start a new life somewhere where they would not have to deal with bullying, hatred, and prejudice. Since Croatian people were not under any pressure to move out of Serbia, the supply and demand market was not in our favor. That is how we ended up exchanging our beautiful, big house in Slatina for a smaller, weird-looking, L-shaped house in some godforsaken village in Serbia.

When our grandparents arrived at our house in Kukujevci, my grandpa had some degree of a nervous breakdown. He wanted to kill himself! We had to watch him for a while. My dad tried to explain that something was better than nothing and that we simply had to decide to move on at some point. With time, Grandpa calmed down and accepted the new reality.

Since this village was only three train stations away from Šid, and the train station was not far from my high school, I would sometimes stay with my grandparents instead of going to Tovarnik. My grandma was very upset that I had a boyfriend and told Boban to his face that she did not like him. She was worried that he would intentionally impregnate me and stop me from going to university, and she knew how important higher education was to me.

One day Boban called me on the phone in Kukujevci, and Grandma answered. When Boban introduced himself and told her that he would like to speak to me, she gave him a blunt reply, in rhyme too: "*Znaš ti šta – biće mojoj Bibi Bobana i Jovana ko govana!*" which meant, "You know what – my granddaughter Biba will have as many Bobans and Jovans as poops!" Oh, Grandma!

I found this to be really funny, especially after hearing the silly question Boban posed to me right after this: "And who is Jovan?"

"Oh my god, hello! That name was only used for the rhyme," I replied while laughing.

Around that time, a weird old man who lived in the apartment building across the street from my school started stalking me. I can't remember how he managed to manipulate me to come into his apartment, under the pretense of helping me with some school project, but I soon noticed he was exuding weird energy when he would come near me or laugh. He must have been at least 65 years old, but obviously had a strong libido. That day in his apartment, at some point I noticed that he was aroused, and all the alarm bells rang in my head. He kept moving up and down the room in a restless way and I pretended I didn't see his arousal. My ruse to exit was that I suddenly remembered some important class to attend that very moment. It worked and I managed to get out, but would still have to deal with him unexpectedly popping up after school.

One day, while sitting in my room in Kukujevci doing my homework, I suddenly heard this man's voice in the yard of the house. I couldn't believe my eyes and ears! He had found out where my grandparents lived! He came with a bag full of organic apples and nicely made friends with my grandparents. They even allowed him to enter the house. There he was, in my room, starting to laugh and move around with that perverted sexual energy of his. I was totally freaked out and immediately called my grandma to make sure I was not alone with him. When he finally left, I told my grandma that this man was weird and that I had a feeling he was interested in me sexually. To my great surprise, Grandma did not believe me! She told me that he was a very sweet, old man, and "too old for such things."

I realized that he was very cunning, and was weaving his web around me. He knew how to talk to win people over. This nightmare continued for another couple of days. The old man would call me, all the time pretending that he just wanted to talk to me, to talk in person, etc.

At some point, I told Boban about this. "Don't worry," he said. "I will handle this freak." Donning a hoodie and with a plastic pistol in his pocket, Boban and his best friend paid the old man a visit. They grabbed him by the neck, pushed him against the wall and said: "If you ever come close to Biba, or try to follow her at home or at school, I will kill you." I never heard from this old man again and was endlessly grateful to Boban. He really helped me a lot.

I graduated as one of the top three students in my high school and intended to take the University entrance exam. During my preparations, the topic of my boyfriend popped up. I have to say that my parents didn't interfere with my affairs much. They never supervised my homework or bothered me about anything. I loved the fact that they always trusted my maturity, and I do believe I earned that trust from them.

They were, of course, aware of Boban and since my high school days were over, Dad asked me about my plans involving the young man. At the time, my sister was in a serious relationship with Zoran, a young man who lived in the center of Novi Sad. He was the son of a private dentist who had his own clinic. Zoran worked as a dental technician in the clinic and earned a nice living. I told my dad I was not sure, but I guessed we would probably stay together. Dear Dad then replied, "Oh, that's good. It is nice to have variety in our family. One daughter married to a city boy living a posh life, and the other married to a village boy working on the land. A nice balance. I am happy." I revolted right away.

"What do you mean? I am not staying in any village and certainly don't intend to work on the land. I intend to study."

My dad knew my psychology perfectly well, so he continued with the teasing. "Well, I don't know. This is what seems to be the situation from what I can see – Šid is pretty much a village and your Boban seems like someone who does not have any ambitions beyond Šid and agricultural work."

His words shook me. The next time I met with Boban, I planned to talk with him about his future plans more seriously. I was surprised when he told me about his plan to buy a big combine harvester and get into agricultural work, which was becoming increasingly profitable. The Uranus in my birth chart was not up for that at all! I told him about my eagerness to study, travel, and expand my horizons, and how I was certain that I could not be confined to Šid. We broke up that very day.

I met Boban and his lovely mother, who was like a dear friend to me, a couple of years later. I was flying high, living the dream abroad, and returned to Šid briefly to retrieve some documents. I ran into Boban, and he happily invited me to his home for a coffee. It felt so strange to be back in his house and see that his mom still kept my photo in their living room. Boban's mom said they were so proud of my achievements and that they would always love me. She also shared with me in confidence that Boban was deeply hurt by our breakup. In the end, he chose a girlfriend much younger than him so that they would have enough time to fall in love before her graduation.

This left a very deep impression on me, and I honestly felt bad about it. I was aware that there was a certain moral responsibility that came with the magnetism emanating from the depth and richness of my soul. After this experience, I was very careful not to hurt any man. I rarely engaged in relationships and had very high standards. That is why I did not date anyone and preferred to remain single during the first year of my work for the UN.

Despite my best efforts, there was a persistent increase in sexual magnetism, towards me and possibly also subconsciously from me. It reached a point where I was approached by men every other day. Most UN men were married and were obviously just looking for an affair. Not my cup of tea. Others lacked the intelligence, spiritual depth, and strength of character that I insisted upon in a man. No chance.

But there was one man who caught my attention, one man to whom I could talk. Once he shared with me how he rescued people from the line of fire during the worst phase of the war and the shelling of Vukovar. My inner Eagle was immediately intrigued and conversations of satisfactory depth ensued. Finally, someone had come along with the inner capacity to actually hear me. Out of respect for his privacy, I will call him my "Croatian Hero."

I must say that his nationality was of no concern to me. He could have been from Andromeda for all I cared. He was courageous, selfless, righteous, a gentleman, and a good person at heart, with tremendous depth of spirit. I never judged a person for anything other than their essential human qualities, and this fellow was truly a remarkable human. We had so much to share, and over time our conversations became incredibly profound, quenching my thirst for quality interaction of this sort.

One day, I was invited to translate at a dinner held in Ilok Castle. Our Station Commander was known to enjoy a drink or two after working hours, but this evening he was really off the hook. Once I noticed how many drinks he had, my inner alarm was ringing. By 9:00 p.m., his desire to chat was fired up. Unfortunately for him, he raised the topic of my appearance. Emboldened by alcohol, he started expressing his admiration in a really strange way. "I have to tell you Biba, you could be a wonderful model. Why don't you try to pursue that career a bit? My daughter is a model in Sweden. I could maybe help you out."

That was it for me! I had kept silent during the comments made by Major General Klein, but this time I had to give my male superiors a piece of my mind. "Thank you, but I am not interested. I do not see modeling as a serious profession nor one that would ever attract me. I find it disrespectful to women and all that a woman, in her uniqueness and beauty, has to offer in this world. Modeling reduces a young woman to a piece of flesh, to height, weight, circumference, and complete superficiality. She is starved, trimmed, and carved as per someone else's idea of beauty."

The Station Commander objected, "Oh no, my dear, it is not like that. Maybe this is how you see it in the Balkans. As I said, my daughter is a model in Sweden, and I don't see anything disrespectful in her work."

Again, I tried to convey politely that I was only there that evening to translate and that the modeling discussion was over. Unfortunately, the Commander persisted. His interests had nothing to do with work. He went right on provoking me intentionally until the atmosphere became ugly.

At some point, I got up and raised my voice. "I see a profession like modeling as one of the WORST professions for a woman, like female gladiators in a ring, only more subtle and stingy. Women are made to compete with one another based on their looks. They can't bring anything authentic of their own into their work. They are just a piece of flesh meant to please the eye. These young women develop immense complexes, often even suicidal tendencies, because of one inch more or less at the supposedly wrong part of the body. This is completely rooted in patriarchal cruelty that I never wish to support! True femininity is so much more!"

An awkward silence followed. I hadn't intended to raise my voice, but what had been brewing in me for a while had to come out. "I would like to be excused," I said, resuming my usual, polite tone. "I am working the morning shift tomorrow and need to go home."

Just as I was about to leave, agitated and filled to the brim with unpleasant emotions, my Croatian Hero appeared from nowhere with an offering of beautiful flowers and loving words. "I did not like how your boss behaved towards you this evening and kept you in there for nothing. I want you to know that not all men are like him. Some of us admire and appreciate a woman's uniqueness. These are for you." I was speechless.

The Duty Driver may have driven me home that night, but I could have wafted home on the aroma of those roses alone. I felt my heart expanding. The next day I learned from a friend that my Croatian Hero had driven across the border to a nearby city in Serbia to buy those flowers. He could have gotten into real trouble for such a risky move. His gesture was courageous and chivalrous – qualities of a Knight and Hero Archetype. I had to admit, I liked courageous Alpha men.

However, my Croatian Hero was also a married man in his 40s, so I had to do everything in my power to keep our interactions at the level of friendship. He was very charming in his expressions, jokes, and teasing, and over time we somehow sailed into relationship-related discussions as well. Before I knew what was happening, the chemistry between us grew stronger, and we ended up in a strange sort of romance.

He wrote me poems. One called "*Lepa Milanova kći*" was his version of the famous song "*Lepa Protina kći*" by Serbian music legend Djordje Balašević, a famous writer and songwriter who had been a prominent anti-war voice as well.

One night after a UN party, my Croatian Hero drove me home. The car slowed at some point in the drive, and he leaned over and kissed me. The romantic moment was interrupted by the realization that the car was still moving a bit and we were about to enter a ditch! He slammed on the brakes and we were saved at the last possible second. That moment would become the source of many inside jokes.

As our romance blossomed, my life seemed to become more and more like a movie. However, it was unclear whether it was to be a romantic comedy or espionage thriller, especially after the secret services got involved. Since we were in a post-war scenario, the fact that a Croatian police officer was frequently meeting with a Serbian girl, let alone a UN employee, did not go unnoticed. One day I stopped for a cup of tea at a coffee bar in Ilok and a middle-aged man approached me.

He wanted to talk, but I was in a hurry and tried to speed it all up, whatever it was that he wanted to discuss. He made some basic introduction and went on to say, "I am working for… you know whom. We have noticed that you have been meeting a Croatian man pretty often and that he seems interested in you. Well, he is of interest to us too, and we feel that you could extract some important information from him."

This came as quite a shock! "Ok, stop right there. Do I look like some Mata Hari to you? There is no way I would ever, ever do such work. I am incapable of doing something with a second agenda and do not wish to learn that skill either. In summary, not interested." As I got up to leave, he offered his final words, this time in a much more strict and rude tone.

"Oh really? You don't feel like doing it? And you do feel like meeting with Croatian men, do you? Just wait till you come to Serbia."

I couldn't believe he was threatening me in this way. This scene took some time to digest. In the end, I decided it would be wise for me to reduce my meetings with my Croatian Hero. He had a promising career, and I did not want trouble for anyone. I decided to share what happened with him. He laughed and said that the same thing had happened to him! He had been approached by Croatian intelligence officers, except they insisted that I was already a Serbian intelligence agent who was only using him. They had threatened him as well and suggested that he should not be seeing me. "So, what did you tell them?" I asked.

"I told them that they can go f**k themselves. We are not doing anything wrong, and even if we were, it is none of their business."

One day he took me to a nice restaurant near Ilok. He was driving us in his car when it became apparent by his behavior that we were being followed. He started speeding up, frowning, and occasionally looking at the rear window. After a while, he even gave the intelligence officers who were tailing us the middle finger salute. It all seemed very funny to me at the time. "And now we have shifted into the action movie genre," I commented. I was in the midst of my driving school experience, preparing for the final exam. I remember admiring his gear-shifting skills and joked that I was getting an advanced course in driving.

All jokes aside, I knew deep inside our relationship was not going in a good direction and that we wouldn't be laughing for long. We were experiencing the sweetness and high of a "forbidden love." We did reduce the frequency of our meetings, but because of our jobs we had to encounter each other quite often, and it was impossible not to interact.

He was so full of surprises and adorable depth of feeling and subtlety. He shared with me that he went to Slatina, my hometown, just to see the dust in which I played as a child and the house in which I lived. He went to the vineyards overlooking my house, prayed for my well-being, and buried a sacred item there in my honor. Needless to say, I was surprised and deeply touched. Never had I met any man who had such sensitivity.

One day he gifted me a nicely wrapped box of sweets. When I opened it after coming home, I noticed that something had fallen out of the wrapping. It was a piece of paper with a handwritten note on it. I picked it up and read the curious message: "I wish you all the best on the path you are walking toward success." The note was signed with a woman's name. I read it many times, trying to understand what the point was, but my intuition had more to say than my logic.

What I intuitively felt was that this was his wife, who had noticed another woman's presence in their shared energy field. She simply said, "I know you are there." I felt very uncomfortable about this and decided, "OK, that's it! I need to stop this. All I need is to have them get divorced because of me. And I am going to pursue my studies in a couple of months anyway, I do not intend to stay here. I need to be realistic."

The next day I decided to share my thoughts and my decision with my dear Croatian Hero. I told him that extramarital affairs do not align with my values and that we had gone too far. When I showed him that small piece of paper with a message from his wife, he was really upset. He tried to explain his situation to me and shared the entire story of how he got married under highly unusual circumstances. Their marriage was not based on love but had happened to help the woman out. He said they had made a deal that he would "have his freedom" regardless of the marriage.

No matter what their internal terms were, I could no longer infringe upon their marriage. I felt what his wife was saying in that message, woman to woman. I did not like it at all. He also admitted that his career prospects had been grossly reduced because of our relationship and that he was ready to move out of the country with me if I was willing. I told him I was not ready to "sail into the sunset" with anyone yet. I had pledged to myself that I would study abroad and would be unhappy if this was not fulfilled. There were years of studies ahead of me. Our timing was wrong, no matter how deep our feelings were. Our cinematic romance had turned into a drama.

One of my UN colleagues from Ukraine lovingly offered to drive me to Slatina to visit my old home on his way to do some work in that part of Croatia. I was so excited, I took the whole day off work. Upon arriving, the difference between my memory and reality was striking. I was amazed to discover how much bigger everything appears in our childhood memories. The hill to reach my house was much smaller than I remembered it to be, and the house itself was smaller and far less grand. "How is that possible?" I wondered.

My heart was beating like crazy when I entered the yard of our beloved house and stepped on the top stair with "Dana & Biba" engraved in the concrete. It was still there. I did not want to meet the new owners of the house or cause an uncomfortable scene. I was able to visit my best friend Sanja, who was now a married woman working at the school, so she could not meet me for long. Indeed, life had moved on. This experience gave me a beautiful sense of closure for which I was deeply grateful.

The entire drama with my Croatian Hero had been emotionally draining, and surely not easy for either of us. We underwent quite an inner struggle between the rational mind and emotions. All in all, it was clear to me that I needed to leave Ilok as soon as possible and begin focusing on my studies. I expedited my resignation process and started making the necessary arrangements for my studies in Belgrade.

After just a bit of research, I found one interesting option – a two-year tourism program in Belgrade, followed by two years of studies in Cyprus resulting in an international diploma. Voila! It sounded perfect. The total cost was $6,000, which was within my savings budget. I would get my international diploma, travel the world, work as a tour guide at some exotic location, and see what life would bring me. Most importantly, I would be far from war, politics, nationalism, and all this nonsense. These thoughts were comforting, and I sprang into action.

Thin Envelope, Empty Heart

My new life in Belgrade was a mere shadow of what I expected it to be. I lived with my relatives very near Belgrade and traveled to my School of Tourism by city bus. It felt so weird to be back in those noisy city buses after being chauffeured in the lovely UN vehicles for almost two years. I went through a lot of self-examination and had no problem with being out of my comfort zone in terms of my accommodation or transport. My problem was that I could not connect with anyone. The students I was meeting felt like teenagers. I could not bear to listen to their superficial conversations. I was used to interacting with mature people in their 30s, 40s, and 50s and did not realize just how much my UN job had changed me.

I craved depth, but it was nowhere to be found. Boring classes like Statistics and International Economics tested my ability to focus on something in which I was totally disinterested. Of course, I did what was needed and passed the exams, but somehow the vibe of that school did not feel right. With time I learned that some professors were taking bribes, and this harsh truth was highly disappointing. This was Serbia during Milošević – those who had money and connections could do anything. I did not like it one bit.

It was recommended to all Tourism students to engage in the practical aspect of our studies by finding a job or internship that would offer some valuable experience. My cousin had had some experience at the Hyatt Regency Hotel in Belgrade and recommended I apply there for a job or internship. Due to my fluency in English and previous working experience, I found a job as a hostess in the most luxurious restaurant within the five-star hotel hierarchy of Hyatt – *Signor Rossi.*

My job was to stand at the entrance to this fancy Italian restaurant, an imitation of some lovely 17th-century villa in Tuscany, to welcome the guests and take them to their assigned tables. It was a very lonely, monotonous job, during which my feet used to hurt from the silly high heels that I had to wear, not to mention the uniform that I hated. I became but a shadow of my former self. Just like during the refugee days, I was experiencing the famous curse, "May you have and then not have." It was tough. I always had to wear that distinctive fake hospitality industry smile, even when I was dizzy from standing. The whole thing had "so not me" written all over it.

The worst moment of all would come at the end of the month when I would receive a thin envelope with my salary in it. One hundred dollars! How ironic can life be? I couldn't digest that scene easily. Instead of 12 bills, I saw only one. So much hard work and only a hundred dollars?! Only an idiot would have left a job that paid 12 times higher… I had to congratulate myself on my stupidity. Something was totally wrong with the direction my life was taking. Everything felt off. My new life felt like a total failure. I was missing my old job, friendships, and parties, but I had to admit to myself that most of all, I was missing the beautiful deep interactions with my Croatian Hero. I was missing the way I felt when I was in his presence.

Exactly at that time, I happened to run into a Serbian girl who used to work with us in Ilok. Of course, I asked her how things were, and we laughed about some interesting stories. And then, she told me about my Croatian Hero. She had heard that he had divorced his wife and that he had been demoted, that is, moved to a lower rank position. Of course, I jumped to the conclusion that it was my fault.

The already heavy, gray life in Belgrade suddenly felt even heavier. On top of everything, I now had guilt that was eating me alive. I felt like I was carrying a pressure cooker inside of me, but alas, there was no release on my horizon. There was nobody I could confide in, nobody who could possibly understand me. Finally, I opted for writing.

I took a piece of paper and wrote my heart out. This technique helped me when I was a refugee, so I thought it would be wise to try it again. I wrote a long letter to my Croatian Hero, explaining how miserable I felt and how sorry I was for his divorce, lower rank, and everything he had to endure because of me. None of it was my intention. I wanted him to know that I really did have feelings for him and that I fought them hard… I wrote two pages of everything I felt and I did feel a bit better, a bit more relieved. Of course, I knew better than to send that letter by mail. I knew it would have traveled through the hands of the secret service before ever reaching him, if at all. I never sent it, but in the end, that letter exploded like a bomb.

Two days later, my relatives somehow found the letter in my drawer and summoned my parents. I received the worst shaming of my life. My parents were quiet and visibly ashamed, but those relatives just went for it. One whip after another, words that cut into me. They had lost their home during the war, and all their hatred towards Croats was triggered by my actions. There was some serious shadow projection on me and some wild accusations, that included me spying for the Croats.

Their final words were, "You were with a married man! How could you?" I was asked to move out of their home right away. Ashamed and broken, I quickly packed all my things, sat in the car, and drove off to Novi Sad with my parents. At this point, our new house in Novi Sad was being built. My parents had sold the village house in Kukujevci, saved up some money from the restaurant business, and built a brand-new house in Novi Sad. I could stay there until I found new accommodation in Belgrade.

There was dead silence in the car, and I just kept crying silently, sinking lower and lower into the back seat. My world had fallen apart and I was in total darkness. I never thought I would be slut-shamed by my own family. The destructiveness of slut-shaming is beyond what one can bear, and most women who go through such an ordeal become suicidal. Not only was I shamed for my presumed sexual activity, but for engaging in a relationship with a married man, who was on top of that a Croat and for whom I was supposedly spying, betraying my own family. Ages of an ancestral slut-shaming load fell on my head. Punishment from my parents was the final blow, and I was awaiting it like a lamb awaiting its slaughter.

At last, my dad pulled over, turned toward me, and said words I will never forget: "You know what – what you did was not good, but you are our daughter and we love you nevertheless." Oh my god! I had never heard more beautiful words. They were my lifesaver. My dear, dear Dad – he understood the shadow projection and did not want to argue with my relatives because he understood them as well. They had lost everything and my love for a Croat was not something they could ever comprehend. But my parents had met my Croatian Hero several times and they knew he was a good man. They could also tell right away that the accusation of spying was ridiculous. Though I had made a mess within our family, Mom and Dad both said this was a big lesson for me for the future.

After a couple of days, I went back to Belgrade, found some accommodation via the Yellow Pages, and moved in with an old woman from New Belgrade who suffered from severe asthma. She was a bit of an energy vampire as well, intentionally creating drama to get attention. She would start breathing very heavily and wheezing very loudly in the middle of the night so that I would shoot out of bed to call an ambulance in a panic, but in the end, they would just bring her back. So my lovely new life moved in a circle between a dying landlady, boring studies, no friends, and a boring job.

It was the winter of 1998, and in those cold winds and gray days, I lost myself in the meaninglessness of my new life. My mind was still digesting the entire story with my Croatian Hero, and at some point, a powerful self-destructive mechanism was activated within me. In astrological terms, the Scorpio had turned its poisonous tail against itself. I suddenly had a powerful inner enemy from which there was no escape. I was my own worst judge. "You are a horrible person," my inner enemy was telling me every day. "You care only about yourself and destroy people around you.

That poor Croatian man is divorced, and his children and wife must have suffered a lot, all because of your selfishness. People like you don't deserve to live." I didn't know what to do with myself or how to escape from that inner judge that turned me into the darkest person on Earth. The verdict had already been declared. I was the worst. I saw nothing but darkness.

Samadhi, the Blessing of St. Paraskeva

With every passing cold winter day, I kept sinking lower and lower. I did not care whether I would continue living or simply die and vanish somewhere. I lost my inner compass and, even worse, my self-respect and my will to live. During the refugee days, the darkness that engulfed me was that of victimhood, but it was not as destructive as this merciless guilt that made me turn against myself. I was the one to blame, so there was no anger toward God or anything that could be perceived as external. The darkness was inside me and everything seemed totally pointless.

I started aimlessly roaming around Kalemegdan park one day. I did not care that the ruthless, freezing cold Košava wind was, as we say in Serbia, *blowing through my bones*. At some point, I felt the pull to go down the old, snow-covered Kalemegdan fortress stairs. I saw a cute little building there and allowed the magnetic pull to bring me inside.

After seeing the beautiful frescos that completely covered the interior walls, I realized the building was a church. Everything about it was a surprise to me. I was not even aware of how I had stumbled upon it. The magnetic force that brought me there was the loving presence of a mighty saint.

This was a church dedicated to Saint Paraskeva, a.k.a. St. Petka in Serbian. "*Petak*" in Serbian and "*paraskeva*" in Greek both mean "Friday." The Church of St. Petka is a true place of power with amazing energy. It is located within the historic Kalemegdan park (a.k.a. Belgrade fortress), the largest park and most important historical monument in Belgrade.

The powerful presence of this saint oozes grace on all who visit her humble church. The whole area around the church and the little hilltop nearby also had an amazing vibration – whoever went there felt refreshed, uplifted, and cleansed, whether aware of St. Petka or not.

Moreover, there was a miraculous spring of water that appeared at the exact location of this church with her blessings. This water had special healing properties – small bottles with this healing water were always distributed in the church.

Before sharing my experience, I would like to share some basic facts from the life of this amazing saint. St. Petka is considered "the protector of women, the sick and the poor. She was born in the 10th century in Epivat, near the city of Kalikratia in Asia Minor, and according to the Serbian Orthodox Church of Saint Sava in London, she was of Serbian origin. Her parents were wealthy and devout Christians."[19]

19 Source: https://tekdeeps.com/who-was-saint-petka-life/ The article has been translated based on the content of Dnevni list Danas by www.danas.rs.

I was born on a Friday, and it has always been my favorite day of the week – this beautiful synchronicity could also be a hint of a subtle connection with this amazing saint. I was also happy to learn that St. Petka's life story had been portrayed in a movie. The Serbian-Jordanian movie "Sveta Petka – Cross in the Desert" was based on her true story and the novel "Petkana" by Ljiljana Habjanović Đurović. It was officially screened in Serbia in September of 2022. The film told the story of "how the pious girl Paraskeva, leaving her life among people in the city of Constantinople and after a pilgrimage to Jerusalem, goes to the Jordanian desert where she spends the next 40 years of her life fighting temptations, sins and inner demons. It follows her journey from an ordinary girl to the most beloved and respected saint of Orthodoxy."[20]

The story of the journey of St. Petka's relics (holy remains) is also truly fascinating. They kept changing their location and in "1396, Empress Milica begged Sultan Bayazit for the relics of the saint and transferred them to Serbia. Thus, the relics of Saint Petka were transferred to Belgrade on Kalemegdan, near the spring of miraculous water, where a chapel was built that still exists today."[21]

Without knowing any of this, I blindly followed where Mother Paraskeva, with the powerful magnet of her Grace, was bringing me – to pray at the time when my own inner demons were tearing me apart.

Because St. Petka's church was very popular and often frequented by visitors, it was such an amazing blessing that there was nobody present inside the church on that fateful winter day. I was guided to enter St. Petka's holy space for a private moment. Surrounded by beautiful frescos that cover the church walls and its ceiling, I was soaking in the beautiful vibe of the loving divine intimacy that I immediately sensed in that space.

At one moment I noticed a painting of a gentle female saint with a compassionate expression in her eyes, dressed in the black clothes of a renunciate. I approached what seemed like the sanctum sanctorum of this church and the altar of the chapel (the actual source of the healing water). With a soft step, I came closer to a painting depicting St. Petka. I stared into her eyes, mesmerized by their intensity and compassionate expression.

Since nobody was there, and the heavy load on my heart was unbearable, I started whispering my prayer. That whisper soon broke into loud sobbing. "Please help me! I can't take this guilt. I can't take this horrible heaviness within my heart. I hate myself. Please help me to come out of this feeling. Save me from this darkness!" As I was praying, tears were pouring down my cheeks.

---

20 Source: https://tekdeeps.com/who-was-saint-petka-life/ The article has been translated based on the content of Dnevni list Danas by www.danas.rs.

21 The relics rested there until 1521 when Suleiman the Magnificent II captured Belgrade. After many other tumultuous events, the relics were finally settled in Iasi, Romania, where they remain today.

Source: https://tekdeeps.com/who-was-saint-petka-life/ The article has been translated based on the content of Dnevni list Danas by www.danas.rs.

I also remember pleading to St. Petka to help me start loving myself again, to take me out of the grip of darkness. My eyes were continuously filling up with tears and thus my vision could have been slightly blurred, but at one moment I became breathless upon realizing that, somehow, her eyes BECAME ALIVE. Just like living human eyes that move a bit while gazing intensely, these living eyes were right there in front of me. I will never forget the intense compassion these eyes were radiating. Like a fountain of bliss, St. Petka's eyes flooded my inner space with the loving energy that melted all the negativities within me.

At some point, all the crying stopped and I witnessed an inner shift. I could not pinpoint what that was, because my analytical mind had simply stopped functioning. I enjoyed the incredibly expanded and vibrant state I was in, without interference from the mind or judgment. I was energized and flooded with immense love, totally blissful. There was no trace of pain, and there were no thoughts. I just existed in the blissful state of expanded awareness, the pure joy of being. My breathing was very, very slow, and I was not even blinking. My awareness was spread all around me and there was a sense of oneness with all that is, with the entire creation.

At one point I moved towards the door – like a queen with a big flowing gown, except that a gown was not behind me, but all around me. I walked slowly and gracefully towards the door. It was a strange feeling passing through the door, or aiming for the door and squeezing through it because I was so expanded. It was even more strange when I started climbing the stairs covered with snow. A part of me was climbing the stairs, while another part of me was witnessing me climbing the stairs and noticing the fact that my legs were moving on their own. I could not feel my leg muscles being utilized – quadriceps muscles, knees, calf muscles, I felt none of them. My legs were moving and I was climbing, but not like a human being with a physical body. I felt like a cloud of consciousness floating up the stairs. The feeling of lightness and bliss was that overwhelming.

Outside, the piercing cold Košava wind was blowing with equal intensity. My hair was flowing in the wind, but I could not feel any cold on my face or anywhere else. Nothing at all! It was as if I was surrounded by a huge transparent shield in the shape of a big bubble filled with pure bliss! I floated in this manner through the entire Kalemegdan park, not feeling my muscles, the cold, wind, or anything - just holding the thread of the uninterrupted blissful awareness and moving along with a smile. I witnessed that whoever passed by me would turn. "Wow, what is going on with this person?" was their thought. I could hear those thoughts. Just as I was noticing them with my side vision, after they would pass me by, I could also sense/see them behind me. I could see that they would inevitably turn around and stare at me in wonder. I was aware of everything.

This blissful floating continued for the entire walk through the park and it was only when I entered busy Knez Mihajlova Street, buzzing with people, noise, coffee bars, and restaurants, that my transparent shield suddenly disappeared. The cold Košava wind made its presence known right away. I started blinking and breathing normally again. I placed my palms on my cheeks that now felt the cold wind, and just stood there, filled with awe and excitement.

"Wow, what just happened?" I thought. It took me a while to digest the experience, but there was no confusion. On the contrary, I had crystal-clear clarity that no trace remained of my previous self-hatred or any negative feeling. I felt great! So enthusiastic, so grateful, so happy. My logical mind could not explain this, but deep within I knew that St. Petka had transferred some powerful energy into me, and uplifted me in a way I never knew was possible.

Years later in India, I came to know that powerful saints and Masters can perform *Shaktipat*, the transfer of divine energy, by touching someone's higher chakras or simply through the eyes. I believe that St. Petka transferred divine energy through her living eyes into my being, and she took me into an elevated state of consciousness. This state is known as *Samadhi*. There are different levels of the Samadhi state, each offering the direct experience of a whole new dimension of being. The one I experienced can only be described as a superbly deep, blissful, intensely soundless state of breathlessness and bliss, a state in which super consciousness took over and none of the rules of the mind from the 3D world applied. This state of intense inner absorption and purity of being simply happened to me, not out of my own doing but out of the Grace of St. Petka. It was like being sucked into the depth of my being all of a sudden, but simultaneously witnessing the physical world as well, without identifying with it.

This was my introduction to the wondrous dimensions of consciousness. I find it amazing that this very first experience happened in my own country, as a result of an immense blessing of a female saint from the Balkan region. What was the Divine telling me? It certainly was not a coincidence that I was born in this tumultuous region, and yet soon was to discover such a deep connection with Vedic India.

In the language of the Christian Church, St. Petka is a saint, while in spiritual terms one could also say that she is a great Master who operates from higher realms of consciousness and continues to shower her blessings on those who connect with her with faith and surrender, as an "empty cup" ready to receive.

She gave me my life back! I was ready to flow through it all, dance through it all, but sure enough, new challenges were just around the corner.

Chapter 4

NATO Bombing & UN in Kosovo

Dance Me To the End of Bombing

After the fall of former Yugoslavia, the last remnant of Yugoslav unity was Serbia & Montenegro, now renamed the Federal Republic of Yugoslavia. Feeling at heart that I belonged to and understood the international community, I was 100% sure that the threat of NATO bombing in my country was a total bluff used for diplomatic negotiations. I was wrong.

On March 24th, 1999, the first civil defense sirens sounded at 7:45 p.m., and all television and radio channels broadcast the same warning: "Attention, attention! This is an air raid warning. Turn off the electricity, turn off the gas and open your windows. Collect your prepared supplies and slowly proceed to the nearest shelter."

At 8:00 p.m. sharp, the North Atlantic Treaty Organization deployed its powerful stealth bombers. I was stunned at the extent of the bombing that followed; the aftermath was totally surreal. The sights, sounds, and terrible consequences of bombardment became a part of daily existence for the next 78 days.

I attempted to follow both Serbian and western media coverage of the bombing, but their narratives regarding the military intervention were polar opposites. The power of the media in shaping public perception is truly immense. Unsure what to believe, at the time I felt that listening to both the opposing media perspectives would make me schizophrenic. NATO called their military action "Noble Anvil," but in Serbia it was called "Merciful Angel."[22] What was termed "NATO aggression" in Serbia was at the same time called a "NATO bombing campaign" in the western media.

"Campaign" certainly was a deceptive and diplomatic choice of word for a military intervention during which millions of innocent civilians were traumatized. Of course, many such civilians, myself included, had never voted for Milošević or approved of his leadership. Still, thousands of innocents were killed or wounded, especially during the famous "Oops, we missed!" moments when NATO stealth bombers would hit civilian infrastructure that had absolutely nothing to do with the military. Examples were many, and every other day a new disaster was reported either on TV or would happen in the neighborhood – the bombing of a school and residential area in Surdulica where 11 children were killed, the shelling of the Chinese Embassy in Belgrade (where

22 https://www.rts.rs/page/stories/sr/story/9/politika/52258/poreklo-imena-milosrdni-andjeo.html

three Chinese journalists and the son of the ambassador were killed, a huge international incident), and the neurology department of Dr. Dragiša Mišović Hospital in Belgrade (wherein four babies were being born, two expectant mothers injured), etc.

This bombing was essentially illegal, not adhering to the rules of international law. It was done under the guise of humanitarian intervention, without the endorsement of the UN Security Council. This military intervention by NATO set a very dangerous precedent, and the legitimacy of this intervention is still debatable. Another painful topic is the use of depleted uranium, which was consequently proven by a UN Environmental Programme[23] study to have horrific health consequences, including cancer, that people in my country experience to this day.

I prefer not to go into an analysis of "morality vs. legality" regarding the justification of this military intervention, nor to delve into any other historic or political details. In the spirit of this autobiography, I will stick to narration of my own standout experiences from this period.

I had moved to Novi Sad to be with my family, but one of the first decisions I made was that hiding in an underground shelter or basement was out of the question. My Aunt Boja, who had survived three months of heavy shelling in one such underground shelter, shared with us a vivid description of the experience. Part of the basement she was in collapsed, and everyone hiding started to suffocate, essentially buried alive. They were saved at the last moment, but their hearts were crushed, watching the despair and panic of a woman whose baby's little lungs were the first to stop working due to the lack of oxygen. All of them watched in agony as the baby suffocated.

After hearing that story, that was it for me – no underground shelters. "I would prefer to experience my last breath out in the fresh air, thank you very much." In 1941 the Nazis had wiped out entire neighborhoods during their bombing of Belgrade, but the current bombing was selective. This bombing was focused on selected military targets (apart from the occasional misses). All in all, my intuition passed the verdict that staying in a basement was not worth it.

I do believe that we attract what we fear and that a positive attitude in any circumstance is a sign of one's maturity, something that ought to be nurtured. Instead of going to a shelter, I hopped on my bike and went to the nearest Latin dance school in Novi Sad. The famous song by Leonard Cohen, "Dance Me to the End of Love" (with a playful twist on the lyrics) would be the theme song of my life during the NATO bombing of my country.

The main dance instructor, also the owner of the studio, was stunned to see me. "This is fascinating. All my students dispersed when the bombing started, and you have shown up here looking for

23 "Detailed laboratory analyses of soil samples revealed low levels of widespread depleted uranium (DU) contamination at five of the six study sites. This indicates that during the conflict, DU dust was widely dispersed into the environment following the explosion of a DU round." (UN Environment Programme, Depleted uranium in Serbia and Montenegro: post-conflict assessment in the Federal Republic of Yugoslavia, https://wedocs.unep.org/xmlui/handle/20.500.11822/8251)

a dance instructor? ! I must say, I am amazed." He refused to charge me; instead, we agreed to exchange dance for English lessons, which was a perfect arrangement.

We trained every day, and I loved it. In addition to Salsa, I also learned the Cha-Cha, Samba, Rumba, Paso Doble, Jive, and Argentinian Tango. After about a month of training together, my teacher said something that surprised me. "I have to tell you, if we continue training like this on a daily basis, we could start preparing for the Olympics. Your talent is amazing. I see that you have it in you. We could totally do this."

I was flattered, but also overwhelmed. I honestly did not expect anything that serious. "I will think about it," I replied diplomatically. However, deep in my heart I was certain that competitive dancing was not my path. I loved dancing for the sake of dancing, not as a profession. More than anything, I was eager to continue with my studies and fulfill my solemn pledge to myself of completing higher education. Anything that distracted me from my goal would make me unhappy.

I was fine with staying away from TV stations and focusing on my dance and future education plans. NATO's missiles did not frighten me. I even saw once a tomahawk cruise missile hitting a bridge, which caused immense pressure in my ears and head. It was our daily reality to hear the sirens wailing, followed by the sounds and tremors of bombardment. Even while riding my bicycle, I would just continue pedaling along, unfazed. It was only when I watched the news, CNN especially, that I got upset.

Civilians were dying, damage to the infrastructure was immense, and there was nothing that could be done. When someone would lose a child and it was chalked up to "collateral damage" or "an unintended consequence" on some news channel, it only made matters worse. No matter the reasons or Kosovo-related justifications for the bombing of my country, everyone in Serbia & Montenegro felt that it was all absurd and unjust. The feeling of helplessness and the inability to fight back against such a large and sophisticated military force didn't last long.

"Crazy Serbs" was an epithet given to Serbian people throughout history, and I must admit, we have justified it time and again. In all that hopelessness, while bombs and missiles whizzed over our heads, we witnessed the awakening of the famous Serbian defiance – *inat,* a word with multiple connotations that cannot be adequately translated into another language. It can be only explained as a persistence in doing something stubbornly, out of pride, even though this action or attitude could be pointless or even contrary to common sense. The satisfaction one gets from inat may not be deemed reasonable by someone else either. As far as I was concerned, it was better than victimhood. It was inat running through our DNA that made thousands of people, myself included, put printed target signs on our chests and stand on the bridges of Belgrade and Novi Sad as human shields.

Get the F**k Off That Bridge

It was shocking and highly revolting to everyone in Serbia that NATO kept bombing our beautiful bridges. When the bombing of the bridges in the city of Novi Sad began, I could not stand by idly.

I remember passing by one of the bridges on my bicycle and seeing a group of people, including Serbian Orthodox monks, standing on the bridge. Reminded of the monks I'd met in front of Little Branko's gallery in Croatia in 1991, I felt an immediate pull to join them.

We stood together on the bridge, singing, joking, and sending out into the ether a prayer of hope for understanding, peace, and justice. In my prayerful gazing across the Danube river, my Motorola StarTAC cell phone (which I had bought just before leaving the UN) rang. It was an unknown number, but the voice was familiar. I recognized right away one of my American friends from my international community.

"Biba," he shouted, "get the f**k off that bridge! Have you lost your mind? !"

"How on earth do you know I am on a bridge right now?" I asked in amazement.

"Because your face is all over goddamn CNN live!"

I turned to find a CNN camera in the distance. "Oh my goodness!" I thought. "They are recording and broadcasting live!" This funny moment stayed with me. The contrasting realities of my international community and my isolated and bombed country had converged, and in that brief moment, I was the bridge between two worlds. I also found it funny that in my astrological chart, my Moon (representing my inner nature) in Leo was attracting cameras even in the most absurd situations.

There I was, one of the Crazy Serbs, dancing in the face of bombardment instead of hiding in the shelters. The spirit of my ancestors was alive in me, our resounding message being: "You can conquer us, but we will never be defeated." Even though we could have been blasted away with the push of a tiny red button, there was no fear or victimhood on the bridge. I do like to believe our defiant strategy had some effect and that we did protect those bridges with our bodies.

When the NATO bombing campaign finally ended, I began contemplating my next step. Finding the propaganda techniques of Milošević's regime outrageous, I felt that staying in Serbia long-term was not in my best interest. I consulted the highest authority that had never failed me – my own intuition. Regardless of my feelings toward NATO, my destiny was intertwined with the colorful international community, with the many amazing people from all over the globe, and the options that blossomed from that diversity. There were so many good people out there and overall, I felt that the international community was my friend, not my enemy. My astrological Uranus happily raised the anchor once again, and I started packing for my new adventure - the only UN job available at the time – in Macedonia.

As expected, when I informed my dance instructor of my decision at what would be our final lesson, he did not like it one bit. He demanded that I explain why I would reject this God-given opportunity to compete at the Olympics for some silly job with the UN. "Is it about the money? Huh? Well, I'll give you the money!" he shouted. He bent over and took out a stash of thousands of dollars from – get this – his sock!

That was the final straw. I'd had enough. My final words to him were: "Look, I am not under any contract here. I was simply doing something constructive and positive with my time during the bombing. I do not see dancing as my career and you can't force me to make that choice. Education is very important to me, much more than you could even imagine. I will not explain myself to you. Good luck with your dancing career, and goodbye!" It was that swift. With equal speed and determination, I disassociated myself from the School of Tourism in Belgrade. I concluded it had been a total waste of a year of my life. In just 24 hours, I was ready to travel.

Right after the NATO bombing, there was a strong international presence in Macedonia, and of course in Kosovo. There was the UN, NATO, the Organization for Security and Co-operation in Europe (OSCE), various non-profits, and non-governmental organizations, you name it. With a hunch that it would be easy for me to land a job there, off I went to try my luck.

Reaching Skopje, the capital of Macedonia, I went straight to the UN and OSCE building to enquire about the HR department. To my great surprise, the moment I stepped into their HR office, I was met by the familiar face of a lovely blonde from Sweden who used to work for the UN in Ilok.

"Oh my god, Lena Larsson! What are you doing here?"

"I am the head of the Human Resources Division," she said as we exchanged hugs and smiles. It was all too perfect. I did not need to hear anything else to know that my next UN job was guaranteed.

After catching up for a few minutes, she realized, "You know what, you could be my Personal Assistant. I need someone reliable and responsible." How amazing was that? ! It was simply my destiny to effortlessly get a job with the UN.

I immediately started planning my educational strategy, counting my savings and noting the funds still needed for the high-quality international education of my dreams. While one thousand dollars was a lot in Serbia, it wasn't all that much in the west. The cost of the education I wanted was in the tens of thousands of dollars. I would have to work hard and save up for quite some time for that kind of tuition. In any case, I was determined and felt so energized, as if I was finally on the right track!

Hardly two weeks into my new position, Lena approached me with an unpleasant update. "Biba, I have some not-so-good news for you. Looks like this entire office in Skopje will be shutting down and all of us will be moving to Priština, Kosovo. I'm sorry, I know this is quite dangerous for you, but that's what the situation is. Let me know what you'd like to do."

I had to withdraw a bit and give this some serious thought. Kosovo was the most hostile and dangerous place for Serbian people at that time. However, I had no opportunities whatsoever in Serbia, and my parents would never be able to come up with the money I needed either. "Oh, to hell with it," I decided. "I'm just gonna go to Kosovo. Whatever the Universe puts on my path, I will handle it. What could possibly happen to me? I don't hate anyone." I was convinced that when

Kosovo Albanians got to know me, they would realize that I don't hate them and that I don't mean any harm to anybody. I was convinced that somehow, everything would work out. I was so naive. I packed my bags and boarded a minibus to Priština.

Entering the Twilight Zone Called Kosovo

> "Run from what's comfortable. Forget safety. Live where you fear to live. Destroy your reputation. Be notorious. I have tried prudent planning long enough. From now on I'll be mad."—Rumi

Entering Kosovo was entering the twilight zone. The long lines of tractors and cars full of Serbian people leaving Kosovo left a dramatic impression on me, the single Crazy Serb going in the opposite direction. The sight sent a chill through my spine, a hint of what awaited me.

When I reached Priština, as agreed, I joined the HR Office of Lena Larsson in the main UN building, with OSCE on the ground floor. My top priority was securing housing with the Accommodation Unit which was staffed by a young Kosovo Albanian woman.

When I introduced myself, she hesitated for a moment before explaining, "I'm so sorry, I really can't help you with your accommodation. Frankly, I'm afraid of the KLA (Kosovo Liberation Army[24]). I find it simply too risky to look for accommodation for you. I'm sorry, you'll have to manage that on your own." The fact that Kosovo Albanians feared their own liberation army was shocking news to me.

I asked in reply, "How do you think I'll manage on my own? I've never been here in my whole life. I don't know anybody in Priština."

Her reply was abrupt. "Well, I don't know, but good luck!"

That day I also met a Kosovo Albanian man in his late 50s who was working for the UN as well. He was intrigued by the sight of me and struck up a conversation with me straight away. He said that he'd always had many Serbian friends and could immediately tell from my facial features that I was one. (I guess there was no point in pretending to be a foreigner as it would not work anyway.) This man just couldn't believe that a young Serbian woman would show up in Priština, right after the war, just like that. "You're either a spy, or you're crazy," he said.

I laughed and replied, "Well, I'm not a spy, so it must be that I'm crazy."

We both laughed, but then his tone suddenly changed. "You have no idea what you just got yourself into, what can happen to you here. I don't know what you were thinking, coming here."

24 Designated as a terrorist group by Serbian authorities since the onset of their activities in the 1990s, the KLA was an ethnic Albanian separatist militia that sought the separation of Kosovo from the former Federal Republic of Yugoslavia and the formation of a Greater Albania.

I appreciated his concern, but I was not afraid. I had my sights set on a goal, and I was on a mission to fulfill it. "I don't know," I replied. "I simply have faith. This is where life has brought me, and there is no turning back now. I will just have to deal with whatever comes my way, one day at a time."

As much as I had surrendered to and accepted the situation, I must admit that, for the first time in my life, I lied to my parents about my whereabouts. I simply could not tell them that I had moved to Priština. I felt this would be too much for them; they would stay glued to the TV in panic every day. I had no doubt this white lie was for their highest good. As far as they were concerned, I was still working for the UN in Skopje. Luckily, they did not have enough insight into country codes and such matters, so even when I would call or message them from Kosovo, it was easy for me to perpetuate the lie.

I mentioned my search for accommodation to some of my new friends in the UN. Among them was Don, a tall, handsome African American man who was kind-hearted, refined, and always eager to help. Considering how caring and approachable he was, I was surprised to learn that he was working as the UN Deputy Police Commissioner in Priština. Don shared that he had recently stayed in a Serbian apartment building nearby, called *Bela Ladja* (White Sailboat). Many of its Serbian residents had simply locked their apartments and escaped to Serbia, some managed to rent them out, while others arranged to have their Albanian friends move in. Don said though he had really liked the apartment, he'd found a place more suitable for him.

It was only a 10-15 minute walk from the office, so I went to check it out right away. When I met with the Serbian landlady, she was thrilled to have me move in. "You can move in this very day, absolutely no problem!" she said with a big smile. She seemed relieved that she could finally leave Kosovo to find refuge in Serbia. She'd had enough stress and pressure to stay any longer, which should have been a warning sign to me.

I naively and happily moved into this apartment, thinking I'd gotten a good deal. What the landlady did not tell me was that all Serbian apartments were on the KLA extremists' "Break In" list. The most extreme and bitter among them were KLA men from the Drenica region of Kosovo, men who killed without hesitation. It was only a matter of time before they would appear at my door.

While working for the UN, I befriended several kind-hearted Kosovo Albanians. At the time, I was totally ignorant of the history and turbulent relations between the Serbian and Kosovo Albanian inhabitants of Kosovo & Metohija. During my year in Kosovo, we engaged in many discussions about their life and history, and I would like to relay a couple of important points shared with me, without referring to any official history books or citing sources.

It was explained to me that the ordinary citizens of Kosovo were all afraid of the KLA. Some Kosovo Albanians were accused of collaborating with the Serbs, or being sympathetic towards Serbs, causing them to be seriously harassed, if not killed by the KLA. That would explain why many local Kosovo Albanian UN staff members were not too eager to talk with me.

My new Kosovo Albanian friends shared that hatred between the Serbian and Kosovo Albanian population had been prevailing for a long time, especially after the massacre of thousands of

Kosovo Albanians in the Balkan wars of 1912-1913. I was told that the only good period Kosovo Albanians ever enjoyed in former Yugoslavia, in terms of quality of life, fair treatment, and acknowledgment of their rights, was from 1966-1980, ending with Tito's death. Everything before or after was filled with struggle and injustice. After the start of Milošević's rule in 1989, they started feeling increased humiliation, provocation, and denial of rights. NATO's intervention was the last straw that resulted in an attempted mass exodus.

While visiting the nearby Gračanica monastery, I spoke with a group of Serbian people who shared their version of the story at length. They shared that Serbian people have been systematically persecuted and expelled from Kosovo throughout history. In 1901 Serbs were massacred by Kosovo Albanians in what was then Kosovo Vilayet of the Ottoman Empire, and during WWII the Albanian Nazi troops launched a widespread terror attack against the Serbian population (similar to that of the Ustaše in Croatia).

Tito gave them many privileges and since it was normal for Muslim people to have many children, ten per family on average, their subtle strategy was to overtake Kosovo through their population growth. I was told that, out of the ten children, at least one would be working abroad, and very often in connection with the well-established Albanian mafia. "That's why they have the youngest population in Europe – more than half of Kosovo Albanians are younger than 25," one man said. Later, I researched to cross-check his statement and learned it was true.

However, Kosovo's relevance in the hearts of Serbian people had nothing to do with the percentages and population. Kosovo & Metohija was the religious, political, and cultural core of the medieval Serbian state, the cradle and soul of Serbian civilization. The monasteries that had endured to that day were testimonies to the depth of that cultural and religious lineage (although more than 150 churches had been destroyed during the Kosovo war, and those that remained were there thanks to the Kosovo Force (KFOR), a NATO-led international peacekeeping force).

These Serbian men insisted that the province be referred to by its actual name – Kosovo & Metohija (or Kosmet). They said *Metoh* translated to "church estate," an important word that spoke for itself. Approximately half of Metohija belonged to these historic church estates which had been overtaken by or given to Kosovo Albanians during communist rule. This, too, was completely new to me. I thought the use of "Kosovo" alone was only for brevity in communication, but the omission of "Metohija" now seemed deliberate. Most prominent Serbian Orthodox monasteries such as Dečani, Patriarchy of Peć, and Gračanica were indeed the jewels of Serbian heritage that need to be protected at any cost because they were the soul of the Serbian nation.

The words of these men left a deep impression on me. I started visiting those monasteries, and for the first time in my life, I experienced a tangible, indescribably beautiful divine energy within those historic, medieval walls. This energy touched the core of my being, awakening a wish in me to connect more deeply to my religious and ethnic roots.

While passing by Gazimestan, the historic location of the Battle of Kosovo in 1389, I fell into deep thought about this crucial moment in my ancestral history during which all Serbian men who could fight, went to the battlefield and died. Being there made it all come to life in my imagination and heart. One of my Serbian friends from Kosovo who loved studying history shared with me that our Serbian ancestors knew they would be grossly outnumbered (the Ottoman army was more than two times bigger). I also came to know that heavy rain had fallen the previous day, and mud made the movement of the horses more difficult, while the Ottomans mainly attacked from the hills.

Regardless of all this, my ancestors fought bravely till their last breath, consciously choosing to sacrifice their lives to defend their country and the whole of Europe from the Ottoman invaders. Five hundred years of horrific Ottoman rule ensued. Turks used to harass Serbian civilians to no end, and the worst of all taxes they imposed was the dreaded "blood tax." Turks would storm the villages and take Serbian male children aged eight or above, snatching them from the desperate embrace of their parents. They would then take them to Constantinople or some other military headquarters, and bring them up as Turkish soldiers. The boys were made to forget their roots and eventually fight their own people. This was a cause of immense heartache among Serbian people, and many hauntingly sad folk songs were written on that theme. Out of desperation, some parents would opt to maim their sons (by cutting off a finger on their right hand) so that they wouldn't be of use to the Ottoman military and would not be taken away, but most could not bear to do that. The loss of the Battle of Kosovo marked the beginning of five centuries of suffering.

In terms of the depth of emotional and religious connection, Kosovo & Metohija to Serbians is like Jerusalem to the Jews, Palestinians, and Christians - a very sacred place filled with rich and painful history, the soul of the nation, and a source of endless conflict with Kosovo Albanians.

Over centuries of Ottoman rule, and later on in former Yugoslavia, Kosovo grew predominantly Albanian, and every year this disparity in numbers continued to grow in favor of the Albanians. Some of the Serbs from Gračanica shared their own experiences of how it felt to live in such conditions, witnessing their Serbian neighbors succumb to pressure and bribes, eventually abandoning Kosovo. This too was news to me. They gave the following example which left a vivid impression.

"One of my friends lived on a street with three Serbian houses in a row, surrounded by Kosovo Albanian houses. My friend's house was the middle of the three. Whenever his son would go out to play, there would inevitably be some problem or incident with the Kosovo Albanian children. This is just a small example of the overall atmosphere in which these Serbian families lived. They were so frustrated that, at some point, they considered moving away. The Albanians offered a huge amount of money to buy the house, a really hefty offer, but only to my friend in the middle house. This offer was too tempting to refuse. The sum would end his family's struggles and allow them to live super comfortably in Serbia. He took the offer, betrayed his neighbors, and betrayed his Kosovo. He is only one of many who did that. Once that Serbian family left, the other two would find it too difficult to remain in such a neighborhood, and would eventually leave on their own.

"So, one by one, many Serbian families began to gradually leave Kosovo. Some faced violence and death in their families, others just couldn't take the overall pressure. Only the communities around the monasteries, such as ours, and some other areas like the northern part of Kosovo, around Mitrovica city, which was predominantly Serbian, remained intact. What we saw in 1999, when the conflict happened in Kosovo, was that the vast majority of the population of Kosovo & Metohija (around 90%) were indeed Kosovo-Albanians (around two million). So realistically speaking, Serbs did not stand a chance. That's why Milošević tried some extreme measures, which included sending paramilitary units to Kosovo."

This was my first insight into the Drenica region, and why the men of that region were so bloodthirsty. I came to know that Milošević's paramilitary units committed serious atrocities in the Drenica region of Kosovo. The men deployed to the area were either released from prison for this purpose or were already sufficiently hardened on the battlefields of Croatia or Bosnia, so they had no problem committing the required atrocities. On the other hand, the official Yugoslav army was largely deemed very professional. I was told the same thing several times, not only by locals but by members of the International Community as well.

I found out that the horrors perpetrated in the Drenica region included the killing of entire Kosovo Albanian families, women and children as well, to create a panic that would expel Albanians from Kosovo. There was a perceived "window of opportunity" for changing the demographic of Kosovo & Metohija that Milošević sought to exploit. However, Kosovo Albanians had their own allies and lobbyists on their side, as well as the bad reputation that Serbian leadership already enjoyed after all the killings in Bosnia.

Milošević's plan of a large-scale exodus of people in the middle of Europe was not happening as easily as he anticipated. By the end of the war in June of 1999, a vast majority of the Kosovo Albanian population had been displaced by the conflict, the NATO Bombing, and the violence they feared and/or experienced at the hands of Serbian armed forces.

After all this, Kosovo Albanians eventually returned. It was time for their revenge, and many Serbian families felt forced to flee Kosovo. This was the situation on the ground when I arrived in Priština, literally while the smoke was still rising. I have to admit that I was ignorant of just how bad the overall situation in Kosovo was until I was right in the middle of it.

Since Milošević declared that all Serbian people working for the international institutions in Kosovo were nothing but traitors, my chances of education or employment in Serbia went down to zero. Staying in Kosovo was my only option. I realized I might as well put the song "I Will Survive" at the top of my daily music playlist and just go with the flow.

Sailing into a Near-Death Experience

Of all the connotations that the name White Sailboat could have invoked, sailing into the zone between life and death was not one I would have ever imagined. And yet, less than two months after I moved in, that was exactly the kind of journey on which I was taken.

One day, just as I was reaching my apartment building, I saw my neighbor's child screaming and running, all in tears. I had met this boy, his mother Fljora, and some of her other kids only a couple of days prior when we had tea together and chatted a bit. I explained to Fljora that I was originally from Croatia, that my family was forced to move to Serbia during the war in 1991, and that I work for the UN. She briefly told me that the Serbian owners of her apartment were friends who asked her to move in with her five children to guard their apartment as a favor. She agreed because her family was poor and their living conditions were not that great. She warned me, "You should be really careful. You're in big danger here. Even us, Kosovo Albanians, are afraid of the KLA."

Seeing her little boy crying, I was immediately curious about what could be the matter. I saw some KFOR[25] soldiers standing nearby and asked them to accompany me as I went to check on the well-being of my neighbors. I explained to them that though I couldn't understand what the boy was saying in Albanian, I would translate to them from the Serbian language once we found his mother.

When I knocked at her door, I noticed that the door handle looked a bit off, but had no time to process the damage because Fljora quickly opened the door. It was immediately apparent that something was wrong. Her wide eyes, ringed with dark circles, darted around as she spoke. She did her best to appear normal but spoke in an unusually formal way. "Yes, how can I help you?"

"Fljora, is everything ok with you? We got some information that there is some problem happening. That's why the KFOR guys are with me." We spoke in Serbian.

At that moment, a strange man with intense, aggressive eyes popped out behind her. In a strict tone, with a typical Albanian accent, he blurted out, "What is the problem?"

I was stupid enough to continue speaking in Serbian. "Sir, no problem at all, we are just talking to Fljora, because we got the information that she had some problem."

"There is no problem here, you can leave now," he insisted. The look in his eyes was so crude, it was unpleasant for me to look at him. I didn't know whether he was her husband or not, but there was no point in continuing this conversation. I went straight to my apartment, the KFOR soldiers went outside, and Fljora closed her door.

I had a peculiar sense of disquiet; there was something wrong with this story. To make myself feel better and to try to relax after a busy day, I removed my clothes to have a shower. Suddenly I heard some commotion in the hallway. I could identify at least ten male voices. They were all shouting at the same time in Albanian and before I knew what was happening, they were attempting to break into my apartment. I was horrified that only a door separated my naked body from those men.

I grabbed an orange summer dress and put it on as fast as I could. I needed to calm down to think about what could be done. These men must have been in Fljora's apartment all along.

25 Each region of Kosovo was under the jurisdiction of different NATO Kosovo Forces battalions. For Priština it was British KFOR.

They were those extremists I had been warned about. I was just trying to help but had only drawn attention to myself, plus I had spoken in Serbian... I was stupid and now they were after me. I ran to my handbag for the Motorola that every UN staff member was assigned. All I needed to do was to call security and survive for a couple of minutes until they arrived. That was the promise I had been given back in my UN office. They had said, "We cannot assign you a bodyguard, but with this Motorola, you will be safe because we will come immediately if you call us."

I will never forget the desperation and panic with which I kept searching through my big handbag. My Motorola was nowhere to be found. With a big knot in my stomach, I realized, "Oh my God! I forgot it in the office. That's it, I'm dead! This is where my life ends."

I stormed into the kitchen and opened the cutlery drawer, hoping there would be at least one big knife in there. Ironically, all I had were normal butter knives. "Oh well," I thought. "Even if I had a bigger knife, what use would it be? There are at least ten men out there."

The enraged Albanian men kept pounding on the door. The sound, "Bam! Bam! Bam!" was louder than my thoughts. At that moment I realized, "I will be gang raped."

My next thought came with a firm decision. "Forget it, I'd rather die! I will sit on the window frame with one leg out. The moment they break in, I jump."

I quickly opened the window. I was on the third floor with concrete below me. I doubted I would survive the fall. I sat on the window frame, with my right leg already out. Left leg and right palm were on the window frame, ready for the fatal push. My full attention was on the door and that door handle that was getting looser with every hit of their elbows and shoulders. Only one thought made me sad at that moment, that of my parents. I regretted lying to them. I thought about how shocked, disappointed, and devastated they would be when they found out about my death in Kosovo. That was my last thought.

I accepted that my life was over and I was at peace. "We all have to die someday, and now my time has come," I thought. My focus on the door handle was so intense that I even stopped breathing. My heartbeat merged with the rhythmic, drum-like "BAM! BAM! BAM!" Nothing else existed, only that sound. After some time, I realized that the sound was slowly becoming more and more distant. I started to feel lighter and lighter, as if I was gently floating up and away, blissfully detached from everything. Sometimes when I travel by airplane and watch through the window as the city lights slowly disappear below me, there is this beautiful feeling of detachment from all the noises, all those people and their dramas. This feeling was somewhat similar. I felt no connection to my physical body as I surrendered to the beautiful lightness that overwhelmed me. Awareness in 360 degrees now became my natural state. I could no longer hear the aggressive banging. Along with the lightness, all I could feel was a beautiful expansion from within.

Time was no longer linear. In a flash, I saw the scene of my body on the concrete floor with a pool of blood around my head, but there was no way of telling whether that had already happened or was yet to happen. In the end, it didn't matter. I was no longer attached to that body anyway; I was much more than that.

My brain capacity expanded into amazing multipoint awareness as if all the dormant centers of my brain had lit up like a Christmas tree. I was able to see and follow many little movies all around me, at least 20 or so. It was revealed to me that these were scenes from my life, possibly key lessons of my life, and I was going through the final summary. Some specific lessons I had passed, while others indicated I had more learning to do. The new sense of self was as the "objective observer" in the middle who was smoothly gliding through this entire setup, simultaneously watching all those movies that were spread out in a semicircle around "me." Through these little movies, I was gathering the essence of my soul's experience – what I learned and gained through all those experiences. This is when it was revealed to me that there is a little camera within our consciousness, recording everything. Whenever we engage in an act of unconditional expression of love, it doesn't matter whether anyone saw that or not, thanked us or not, it was recorded and added to our inner wealth – the only wealth that truly matters. This was a really powerful insight.

There was no sadness and no analysis. It was just a simple witnessing, with my expanded sense of Self flowing through it all in complete acceptance and surrender. Was my soul moving or were the scenes moving around me? If you've ever sat in a train that stopped and then another train started passing by yours, at that moment there is that strange feeling when you can't tell which train is moving. This was the same feeling. For the sake of convenience, let us say that my objective observer was passing through the middle of what felt like a tunnel made out of all those movies and impressions from my life.

The lessons that I was learning were sometimes connected to this life alone, but sometimes they were connected to some other lifetime as well. I could tell that certain lessons were crossing the boundaries of only one identity. I kept flowing through it all, and the more I glided through this tunnel, the more relaxed and equanimous I became. There was no craving to go back to my physical body. The sense of "I" was no longer connected with the identity of Biba. It was far more expanded, far grander now. The further I went in the tunnel, the more I started noticing a vibrant, living light at its end.

I will never forget just how exhilarating it was to see and feel this light! There was a deep longing from the bottom of my soul to merge into that light. That merging and dissolution in the light was the true sense of returning home. This living, pulsating light was so filled with love. It was the essence of all Light and the essence of all Love that ran this and all universes, in all dimensions, and all times. This was the one and only divine light of the Source.

I recognized how much my essence thirsted to merge into that light. Such a strong, beautiful, and most intimate pull. I kept floating towards the Light, and the closer I drew, the more I was expanding, opening, eager to merge with it. Every cell of my body was awash in that high-frequency light. I can now say in all honesty that intimacy with the Divine is the highest form of intimacy, unmatched by anything we get to enjoy in physical terms. It was just so powerful, so beautiful, and so exhilarating to disappear in that light.

Just before reaching and becoming one with the light, I felt an invisible barrier was reached. Some invisible force stopped me. I could hear or sense a voice coming from the living light. It was a crystal-clear telepathic message: "It's not your time yet, you have not fulfilled your mission, and your mission is to serve the Unity."

There was no angelic being, Master, or anyone with a shape or form conveying that message. There was nothing but the living Light from which all shapes and forms originate. From that expanded state and brightness, I started contracting and moving backward. I continued to recede until I suddenly realized that I was back in my body and my old identity of Biba. I must concede that my first feeling was that of disappointment. Not because I didn't value life, but because I felt reduced to that small version of me. I remember looking at my right hand. I started moving my fingers and that was a clear confirmation that I was indeed back in my body. I have no words to describe how small and restricted that felt in comparison to my expanded state of awareness in 360 degrees and that living, majestic Light.

My logical mind was back, and I started gathering what had happened to me. My physical body was still seated on that window frame. It was pitch dark outside and I saw a KFOR helicopter flying in the distance. I pulled my freezing leg inside the window and sat down on the floor. My entire body was shivering so I grabbed a blanket to cover myself. I looked at my watch and saw that it was 10:30 p.m. Four hours had elapsed since those men were breaking down my door!

"Oh, the door handle!" I thought. It was dark in the apartment, but I could just make out that the door handle was still there. It was rather loose, almost hanging, but it still held on.

"Nobody got in. What on earth has happened? !" I was thinking out loud. Fljora could probably give me the answer, but there was no way I would ever have the courage to step out of my apartment in that situation.

Still shivering, I pulled the landline rotary phone next to me and decided to call my African American friend Rob[26] who was in Skopje and about to move to Priština. He was the first person I felt like calling. Rob was in his late 50s and had a really good heart. He was very protective of women and on the whole someone I could rely on at any point in time. He was a kind of father figure and a best friend at the same time. I kept dialing on that rotating circle for more than an hour until I finally got through to Rob. I briefly explained what had happened. I was still shivering and digesting all that I experienced. I told him, "I don't know where these men are, so I can't move."

Rob said, "Biba, just hang in there, I'm coming!" He got in his car immediately and sped for hours until he reached my apartment.

"Damn it, girl. I am so sorry you had to go through this," he said as he hugged me. "I can't even imagine how I would have felt if you were killed! Ok, I'm going to get this sorted. You can't stay in this apartment anymore. You'll move in with us. There is a big house on Dragodan hill where a couple of American buddies and I are staying. Please just move in with us. To hell with this!

26 Name changed out of respect for privacy.

There is no way you should stay alone anywhere in Kosovo. It is too dangerous for you." I packed immediately and left the apartment early that morning.

Through some contacts, Rob arranged for a paper from the KLA to be posted on the door of that apartment, stating: "This apartment is under the protection of the KLA." This was probably the only Serbian apartment in the history of Priština that was protected by the KLA – another one of destiny's practical jokes that really made me laugh.

I met with Fljora a couple of days later. I was even more amazed by my near-death experience (NDE) after she told me her side of what happened that evening.

"I was heavy-hearted when you knocked on my door that evening. I knew straight away you would be in great danger. Those extremists were all in my apartment, harassing me about moving into that Serbian apartment. I tried to explain to them that the owners were my friends, but they didn't like that. When you and KFOR showed up at the door, I thought I was going to die from stress. They had a shotgun pointed at the head of my other son to ensure I would not reveal their presence to KFOR.

"After you left, they couldn't wait to get you. I was choking back tears watching them at your door, breaking in. My entire body was trembling. And then, something really strange and unexpected happened. I still don't know how to explain it. All of a sudden, I felt very stable, strong, and confident. As if some energy entered me, I wiped off my tears, lifted my chin, and stepped into the hallway. Next thing I know, a confident voice came through my mouth: 'What are you doing? What is this? Leave that girl alone! She is Croatian. She works for the UN. Leave her alone. Get going! Now!'

"The way in which I spoke was very mysterious and strange. I had never spoken like that before. And what's even more strange, the way they reacted was as if they were hypnotized by my words. Their facial expressions changed, and they seemed kind of dazed or confused. Some murmured: 'Oh, she is Croatian. UN…' and then they just left. Can you believe it? Just like that. I have no idea where that courage came from. I am still amazed whenever I recall this experience. But I am so happy you are okay."

Whoa! I was blown away by Fljora's story. It was clear to me that she was an instrument in some sort of divine intervention. I never knew such a thing was possible. My faith in God increased a million times over. I felt truly, truly blessed.

The Hill-Top View

The villa on Dragodan hill marked a new chapter of my life in Kosovo, one with a higher perspective and an upward trajectory. I was a changed woman, freed from the fear of death. With great joy, I started jogging outdoors, cautiously of course, aware that I was pretty much a walking target in that city. No longer naive and with renewed courage, I also began going to the gym, feeling centered and confident.

I had my own direct experience of the living light of the Divine! Whenever I see a sunrise or a sunset, I always remember that radiant, living Light. To this day, the memory of that experience remains super sharp and vivid. It cannot be compared to any dream. On the contrary, it was a part of my reality that has remained alive in my consciousness and changed me from the inside out. Not only did I experience the existence of God, but I experienced with all my heart that God loves me. I experienced that God's love cuts across all boundaries, including life and death, time and space, mind and spirit. It cuts across everything and permeates everything. It became clear that no matter what life brought me, the worst thing that could happen would be to lose my body and end up in that beautiful living light again. So, what reason could I ever have to be afraid?

It is only when we are about to lose our life that we realize how much more alive, joyous, loving, giving, fearless, and adventurous we could have been. We realize how many people we could have forgiven, helped, or inspired. It was made clear to me that my life was a precious gift, and that every present moment was a precious "present" from the infinite love of the Divine. "I shall use my present wisely," was my firm decision.

I also decided that I would henceforth approach all challenges as gifts. If they didn't feel that way, it only meant that I was still learning; that the lesson I was meant to learn was not over. Indeed, once we close the circle with any challenge, we will view it as a gift, simply because we realize how much we progressed because of it. I grew so much from my near-death experience. While entry into that experience was terrifying, it was so worth it. Sometimes when I would lie down to sleep, I would try to invoke that feeling of 360-degree awareness. I longed to be back in that expanded state. I longed to explode in the light.

Two decades later, a friend gifted me an amazing book, Dying To Be Me by Anita Moorjani from Hong Kong. In this book, Anita shared the details of her powerful near-death experience. Not only did she leave the state of blissful expansion to return to the constricted physical world, but she also returned to a painful body with open wounds, a body in the last stage of lymphoma cancer. However, she knew her body would heal because she understood what had caused her cancer. Though to others it would seem delusional, Anita knew beyond any doubt that she could heal just through self-love and awareness. And she did it! In front of the astounded eyes of the doctors, Anita healed herself in a mere five days. Her cancer was 70% gone by listening to ABBA and enjoying ice cream! In other words, she healed by loving herself and changing her frequency. After five weeks, she was completely cancer-free. What a powerful story!

This was my first time reading about someone else's near-death experience. I saw so many similarities to my own experience and knew exactly what she was talking about. Something that caught my attention in that book was that, just like me, Anita was struggling to find the right words to describe the state of consciousness and the expansion that she had experienced. No matter how much one tries, that state and how it feels is always so much more than what can be understood within the limited frame of our mind. Words are simply ineffective in communicating consciousness.

Anita did make one beautiful metaphor in particular which caused an immediate, gigantic "YES" in me. I would like to share that example from what I recall but recommend you read the book or listen to Anita's talks on YouTube.

Anita asked her readers to imagine themselves in a completely dark, pitch-black warehouse. It would be natural to feel afraid of that dark and unknown space, or at least to be very uncomfortable. We were then to imagine navigating our way through the dark with a flashlight, in that warehouse full of all sorts of things, some familiar, and some completely foreign and strange. In absolute darkness, it is only possible to see what the beam of the flashlight illuminates. Seeing something completely new takes some time to accept, especially with the intense darkness all around, and no clues about what else might be hidden within.

Next, we imagine a huge central light switching on, illuminating the entire warehouse. For the first time, everything is visible, the entire big picture. We become aware of just how big the warehouse is, full of a truly wide variety of things. Some things are so extraordinary, they exceed our wildest imagination, filling us with awe and appreciation. (A good example of such remarkable and unprecedented variety would be the flora and fauna shown in the movie "Avatar.")

The light is switched back off and the small beam of the flashlight is once again our only way to navigate the warehouse. However, now that everything in the warehouse has been revealed, there isn't the same fear or discomfort as before, nor any need for hesitation. We are now aware that so much more exists beyond the limited picture that the flashlight provides. And now we know that, just because we haven't seen something within our flashlight's tiny scope, just because something has not been revealed within our limited awareness, that doesn't imply that it does not exist.

"Yes, she nailed it!" was my immediate reaction. She had found such a good metaphor to explain the inexplicable. The same metaphor applies to the fear of death. We fear it because it is something unknown. However, in the case of those of us who have been blessed to undergo a near-death experience, and/or people who are fully awakened in consciousness, that fear is no longer holding us in its grip. Everything is revealed in the full Light of the Divine, dispelling the fear of the dark unknown. We are left with the realization that what is known is so little and so limited, while what truly exists is worthy of only our awe and gratitude.

I have to admit that after this experience, I started feeling awkward regarding tears and grief at funerals. Not only did I no longer feel sad for the person that transcended this realm (death seems like an inappropriate word because it connotes ending), but I felt like saying, "Lucky fellow, he is in that amazing state of being now." The only thing to regret is that he (or she) could no longer work out their pending karma and unburden themselves from certain impressions, karmic mistakes, or debts that create a sense of weight. (I will return to this topic in a later chapter of this book.)

My near-death experience was a true blessing, but brushes with death are not required for such a realization. We are all deeply interconnected through a living, limitless consciousness. What connects us the most within that field of consciousness is love. So, dear reader, what I learned from this experience is that to feel plugged in, all you need to do is just be you. That's all you need to do. Be the loving, truthful, authentic, fearless you. Be comfortable in your own skin. Share your gifts and at the same time, receive the gifts rooted in love from others. Be in the flow, in the acceptance of everything with grace and with utmost faith that everything happens for a reason and your highest good. Your world will open up beyond all the boundaries of the mind. This is when the true magic and magnificence of life will reveal itself to you. After my NDE, that is exactly how life transformed for me in dusty Priština. I knew the truth of who I was and could then live my life fully and fearlessly.

Shortly thereafter, I went through an experience that further revealed my new state of awareness: attempted slut-shaming. One day I brought a small photo album of mine to share with some colleagues at work. I had forgotten that there was one rather inappropriate photo in there, hidden beneath the other work-safe photos. It had been taken the previous summer when, after getting super tanned, my cousin had jokingly asked me to pose for a "sexy photo." She and I had a good laugh after I posed with legs wide open and slightly pouty lips, wearing shorts and a bikini top. Just innocent fun between cousin-sisters. I did not know that some of my Albanian colleagues discovered the photo, scanned it, and sent it to all the printers in the UN building.

I was in the tea room when an older Albanian gentleman (the same one who told me I must be either crazy or a spy) suddenly ran in, gasping for air.

"Oh, thank goodness, you are OK. I thought you were caught by KLA or someone and forced to strip!"

How confusing. "What made you think that?" I asked.

That's when he told me, "A strange photo of you half-naked is all over the place, coming out of every printing machine in the building!"

I was shocked, but I have to admit that it didn't shake me all that much. Previously I would have felt embarrassed and humiliated, but after my NDE, I was far more detached. At the subtle level of existence, I was constantly integrating a higher awareness and felt some sort of a buffer from all the unnecessary emotions and ego-related silliness. I brushed this embarrassment off like dust from the shoulder. If anyone asked me about that silly photo, I would tell them, "Oh, it's a prank." Period. I was not interested in explaining myself to anyone, nor in giving my attention and energy to such a story. I had become less attached to my egoic personality and more drawn toward deeper spiritual exploration. I had a new perspective and was more interested in that which was REAL and truly relevant, and not what others may or may not have thought of me based on some photo.

I soon realized that it was fairly easy to change jobs within the United Nations Mission in Kosovo (UNMIK), so I hopped over to another building and started working as a Legal Translator for my dear friend Don. These translations were far more elaborate, and I had to refer to the dictionary much more, but at least I was hidden from the view of others and far safer. At the same time, this was a rather lonely and monotonous job. It was quite depressing to sit alone all day long in the office and translate a pile of documents, especially because I had absolutely no friends. The local

Kosovo Albanian staff were not willing to let me enter their social circle, apart from a couple of them whom I would meet randomly. There was hardly anyone willing to become my friend, even though I had a really friendly disposition toward everyone. I found those days to be really tough in terms of loneliness. This was nothing like my UN experience in Croatia. The only time I could talk to anybody was when I would come back to the house where I was staying and would start joking with Rob and the American friends.

I must say I was particularly fond of African Americans because of their sense of humor and "chill" demeanor. They had been the underdogs in America, just as I had been the underdog. There were so many similarities in our personal and ancestral traumas that we could very easily connect at a deeper level. Rob used to tease me, "You Serbs, you are the niggers of Europe. Yeah, don't laugh. That's exactly how all these white folks perceive you. Especially thanks to your buddy Milošević. But that's OK - we feel you, we understand where you come from. You're just crazy. You are just off the hook – like we are!"

Rob was hilarious. He would always make me laugh. Sometimes I would tease him with a "Nigga' please!" – a common phrase they would use while joking amongst each other. If I would say it, they would immediately change their expression and start warning me how it was not appropriate. I understood that, I understood how packed with violent history that one word was, but loved to tease them nevertheless, pretending I did not get it.

Don, my new boss, was far more formal than Rob, but very kind and respectful. One day Don saw me smoking during tea break. Everybody smoked in Kosovo, so I started smoking as well, probably from all the stress. It was normal to see everyone smoking and drinking coffee, so those habits rubbed off on me as well. When Don saw me with a cigarette in my hand one day, his eyes were filled with sadness.

"I can't tell you how much it hurts me to see a beautiful young lady like you, smoking," he said.

I replied half-jokingly: "Oh Don, is it really that bad?"

"You have no idea, it's a horrible addiction, one that is really bad for your health. I have to tell you, my father had lung cancer, and I'm positive he got it because of chain smoking over the years. That addiction was so strong in him, that even when he got lung cancer, even when he could only breathe through a little hole that they drilled in his throat, he would ask me to put a cigarette in that hole so that he could take another puff. It hurts my heart to say that this is exactly how he died. That was his last puff of deadly smoke. And now when I see you smoking, I honestly just can't bear the sight of it."

I felt so bad after he shared that story that I immediately put my cigarette down. I reduced my smoking and whenever I saw Don I would not think of holding a cigarette in front of him.

There was one other story involving Don that has stayed with me. He was a very elegant, dignified, and well-educated African American man who had known immense suffering in life. He told me one day how, at the onset of his career in the USA, he got into his big SUV and was reversing down his driveway, when he suddenly felt that he ran over some kind of bump.

He had not noticed that his three-year-old granddaughter was in the yard, busy picking flowers. His heart was torn into a thousand pieces when he came out of the car and realized that it was her tiny body that he ran over. She was dead on the spot. The guilt and remorse, that unending pain was something he could never erase from his heart. It took him years to recover enough to function. I couldn't even begin to imagine that kind of pain and told him that this was one of the most horrendous stories I'd ever heard. It was amazing that he could even find some sense of normalcy after that and continue working. I knew how destructive guilt could be. The entire episode with my Croatian Hero had taught me that, so I truly respected Don.

I realized just how much people suffer, and how many things can go wrong in our lives. During my long, lonely hours in the office, I started contemplating my true calling. I had stayed alive because of divine grace. I had a mission to "serve the Unity," but in which way? What did this phrase "serve the Unity" even mean? I realized that I had not done much since coming back to my body after the NDE, to be of any help to anyone apart from several instances of delivering food to a poor Serbian community in Gračanica.

I started seeking within for something more that I could do to serve the Unity. One image kept appearing in my inner vision, and that was golden light – sometimes it came as a golden thread that would unite all the hearts, sometimes as a golden light that would emanate from the hearts of many people, breaking through all possible barriers of human prejudice and hatred that create wars, bitterness, violence, and anger. Maybe there was something that I could do to break all such barriers that came my way. Still, that entire notion was pretty vague, until the great teacher called "life" presented me with another powerful lesson.

The Golden Ball That Saved My Life

A couple of days later, I was walking down the main street in Priština wearing one of my favorite pieces of clothing – a beautiful blue dress. It was a nice sunny day, and I was in a good mood, about to join a friend in a restaurant for lunch. Suddenly, out of the blue, I noticed an Albanian man coming directly at me. His face was contorted in anger, his eyes brimming with hatred and rage. I'd never seen him before and could only assume that he was one of those Albanian men who had suffered at the hands of Serbian paramilitaries or whoever. I had a feeling that he knew I was Serbian. Regardless, it was more than obvious that he was after me.

He was approximately five meters in front of me when his body language began to indicate that he was definitely about to attack me. He was saying something in Albanian that sounded horrible. I do not speak one word of that language, but it was all too clear from the tone of his voice that he was cursing, and about to assault me right there in the middle of the street. At that very second, there was no question of calling UN security for help using my Motorola – I was all alone and it was all happening right there. He would be in my face, in a couple of seconds.

At that moment, my mind went blank. Puff! Just like that. The clouds of all thoughts and worries disappeared, and I was left with a clear sky on which a surprising divine insight appeared with great clarity in the shape of a golden globe. It came telepathically - a golden ball with an instant download of detailed instructions. I was guided to visualize a golden ball in this man's chest, representing the purest divine love in a human. I was to feel the same golden ball in my heart and just focus on sending all the love I could muster at his golden ball. My entire attention and thoughts like: "I love you, you are Divine, your heart is so beautiful, you are amazing, we are one in that golden light, we are love!" were aimed at the golden ball.

Within three or four seconds, he was right next to me. Even though I was not looking at his face, I could sense how his energy had changed. He just passed me by like the wind. We both continued walking. Nothing happened. In my blue dress, I looked up at the vast blue sky and beautiful sun and sent out a massive "Thank you" to God.

The transformation in this man was so drastic and obvious that I was left speechless. "Wow, that was simply wow!" I thought. To my mind came the memory of my grandma and her moment with the guard at the concentration camp. Well, this was my moment and it was just magnificent! I too had found a way to break the barrier of hatred and allow the flow of love to take over. I knew it; I had always known this was possible. I knew that the power of our hearts could transform reality. And I knew we could all shift from fear to love in an instant. This experience was beyond powerful, and it has inspired me in many ways.

Two decades later in 2020, while casually massaging Mohanji's calf muscles as he was resting, I had another instant download that had something to do with the golden ball. This is when the guided spiritual process that I named "The Light Beyond," manifested in my consciousness. It came as my humble contribution to our collective consciousness at the time when the Covid lockdown was at its height, and mass media was stirring up fear in people, blocking their ability to dream, imagine, and project a beautiful new reality for all of us.

Trauma kills our creativity and ability to dream, while it is exactly this childlike quality that is essential for our growth. We can create different scenarios and different timelines of possibilities for ourselves and others, if we create them through open, expanded hearts, with the purest of intentions. This is not merely my belief, but my inner knowing.

At that moment, Mohanji's calf muscle suddenly became hard like a stone. That was when I had a sudden, clear vision (and inner sensation) of a huge transparent crystal in front of me, with a gentle turquoise and white glow around it. I intuitively knew that it represented the heart of Mother Earth. This is when I heard (or sensed) the words, "Sanctity of life."

Indeed, to our Mother Earth, every life is sacred – be it human, animal, or any other, yet there is so much insensitivity and violence on Earth. Through "The Light Beyond" process, we open our hearts, energize the central axis, activate our pineal glands, align with the purest love frequency of transformative light originating from the Great Central Sun (our galactic Mother Sun), and then help bring that energy to Mother Earth while she births a new reality for all of us.

This beautiful process was initiated on that day in Kosovo with the golden ball, and manifested two decades later within linear time, in the powerful presence of Mohanji. God knows what else may come out of it at some other moment in time, through me or someone else connecting with the same energy frequency.

Nearly Kidnapped by KLA

Kosovo kept treating me with powerful experiences that strengthened my faith and surrender. Next on the list of such experiences happened a month or so later. I happened to travel to another region of Kosovo & Metohija and visited the Patriarchate of Peć, a stunning medieval monastery and the seat of Serbian Orthodox patriarchs throughout the centuries.

This region was under the protection of the Italian KFOR. Italian soldiers would occasionally come to check on the nuns and the one lovely, cheerful monk that resided there - Father Peter. He was tall with long blonde hair, hinting at a bit of gray, and beautiful blue eyes. He used to train in martial arts so he was very quick, agile, and incredibly youthful. He spoke just a bit of English, but not enough to converse properly.

The Patriarchate of Peć was like a rare Serbian oasis, surrounded by angry Kosovo Albanians. Some of them could be found hanging around the hills that surrounded the monastery, often throwing stones, eggs, or trash at the nuns, along with a juicy variety of curse words. Neither the Italian KFOR, local police, military, nor governmental support could ensure safety in the post-war scenario in which over 150 Serbian Orthodox churches were destroyed or desecrated. The same threat loomed over the Patriarchate, along with the trash and curses.

When I met Father Peter he told me that someone from the UN, KFOR, or other members of the International Community would come to speak to him very often. He was eager to share their current living conditions, history, and relevance, but most of the time there was no translator available. I felt an instant calling in my heart to make a positive contribution and offer to volunteer as a translator.

I immediately explored my leave options at work. The only solution was to take an unpaid leave in early April of 2000 so that I could volunteer at the monastery for two weeks. And this is exactly what I did. Soon after I reached the Patriarchate, a meeting was organized with a group of people who wanted to record a documentary about the monastery.

We all met at a coffee bar in Peć. The filming crew included a nice young man from Macedonia, who was a UN translator like me. He was ethnically Albanian but spoke pretty good Serbian as well. Father Peter, the Macedonian translator, a couple of UN staff members, a couple of film crew guys, and I all sat around a table. We mainly spoke in English, but occasionally I lowered my voice to speak in Serbian with the Macedonian gentleman.

The topic of Stari Račak, the location where 45 Albanian civilians were massacred, as per the official narrative, by Serbian police, came up during the meeting. This is my recollection of that conversation in my own words.

One of the UN gentlemen at our table commented that he knew several witnesses from OSCE that had shared what really happened at Stari Račak. It became the final tipping point and the final outrage dramatic enough to justify NATO bombing of the then-Federal Republic of Yugoslavia. He said at least 15 OSCE cars with OSCE monitors, and some French members of the press were present at the site when the conflict between Serbian police and KLA members took place. This was an armed conflict with the KLA, not with any civilians. That night, the KLA got into action, and some dead bodies were brought from another location. There was a lot of fuss, and proper investigation and access to the site were obstructed for two days, mainly by William Walker and his team. Serbian and Ukrainian forensics teams were repeatedly denied access no matter how much they tried.

Then the official statement came out that this was an outrageous massacre of civilians, with a huge media outcry meant to mobilize otherwise weak public support in the USA for NATO bombing of then-Yugoslavia. Those who thought otherwise knew their lives would be at great risk if they raised their voices. Stari Račak was a KLA stronghold, a village fortified with trenches. There were no civilians even living there. It was a classic setup by KLA, supported by NATO.

In the end, the full weight of this incident fell on the shoulders of the Finnish woman, Dr. Helena Ranta, who was the head of EU Forensic Experts Team (EU-FET) and was leading the Finnish forensic team that investigated the killings. She was put under some serious pressure to endorse the official story about the massacre of 45 civilians.

I was speechless when I heard all of this. I felt immense pressure in my head and my heart was racing. I could tell this man was really sincere. When someone speaks the truth, the vibration that this person exudes is easy to tell, at least for me. The Macedonian translator who was of Albanian origin and another UN staff member corroborated his story in very matter-of-fact tones. I had heard this already in Serbian media, but there was a lot of propaganda circulating as well, so it had not hit me as deeply as this discussion did. This was the moment when my perception of international politics changed.

Over the years, I kept returning to Dr. Helena Ranta, following her statements in the media. I could make out just how much she had been pressured to follow the official narrative.

> [P]ressure was high, specifically in the investigation over Račak. That pressure also came from the media. According to Ranta, in the winter of 1999 William Walker, the head of the OSCE Kosovo monitoring mission, broke a pencil in two and threw the pieces at her when she was not willing to use sufficiently strong language about the Serbs. Helena Ranta has worked in the Balkans and Iraq, and has investigated the victims of the sinking of the Estonia and the victims of the 2004 tsunami in Thailand.[27]
>
> The full report by the Finnish pathologists remains under lock and key to this day. An interview broadcast by one of Germany's main television channels with Dr. Helena Ranta indicates the pressure placed on her at the time to go along with charges that a 'crime against humanity' had taken place. She told ARD that she was conscious that one could say that the whole scene in this small valley was arranged. Because this is actually a possibility. This conclusion was included in our first investigation report, and also in our later forensic investigations, which we made in November 1999 directly in Racak. And we passed on this conclusion directly to the Court of Justice in The Hague. [OSCE representative] Walker

27 http://www.kosovocompromise.com/cms/item/analysis/en.html?view=story&id=1456&sectionId=2

> came to Racak on Saturday, and it was his personal decision to speak about a 'massacre'. I systematically avoided using this word.
>
> Racak was at that time a stronghold of the KLA. I am convinced that there is enough information in order to establish that armed engagements between the Serbian army and the KLA took place there. There is no doubt about this. Moreover, I was told, and I was also able to read the information myself about the fact that KLA fighters were killed there on this day.[28]

"What a great injustice!" I thought. I remembered what my grandpa had said about East and West, and us in the middle. And now we have a NATO base in Kosovo, a big step forward toward Russia. As always, it has never been just about the people of the Balkans.

Coming back to the coffee bar in Peć, I continued whispering about this with the Macedonian translator and we spontaneously shifted our language to Serbian. This was unwise, it is only natural that sometimes one feels like conveying something important in one's native language. Even though we were whispering, I had a feeling that the Albanian waiter heard us while changing the ashtrays. For a moment, I caught his facial expression, just before he disappeared behind the counter.

Right then, I had the clear intuition that I should leave that coffee bar right away! It was as clear as if someone had poked me in the butt, and it came with a sense of urgency. I jumped up and told Father Peter, "We have to leave right now!"

Father Peter was confused because we had not finished discussing what we came there to discuss. "But why?" he asked.

"We have to leave! I have a strong feeling. Please." Father Peter got up right away and two of us left for the Patriarchate of Peć, while the others remained seated at the table. A minute later, just as we left, a white minivan full of armed KLA men arrived at the coffee bar. It was months later that I got the full story from the Macedonian translator.

"Five or six KLA soldiers with big shotguns jumped out of this minivan, stormed into the coffee bar, and yelled: 'Where's the Serbian girl? !' We replied calmly, 'There is no Serbian girl here!' The other UN guy said, 'There was a girl here, but she left already.' Suddenly, they grabbed me by the neck and shouted, 'So, you like talking to Serbs, huh? !' The Albanian waiter obviously had tipped them off that I was speaking to you in Serbian. I was super scared and said politely, 'I'm sorry, I just met this girl now, I don't know her. I'm from Macedonia and I work for the UN.' In the end, they let me go and did not harm me but I was scared like never before in my life."

I came to know a couple of years later that one of the main tasks of this special white minivan was to collect Serbian women and take them to a specific location. While visiting my parents once in Novi Sad, something on the TV caught my attention. The obscured face of a Serbian lady from Kosovo was sharing her painful story of being gang raped for months at that location in Kosovo.

---

28 https://www.wsws.org/en/articles/2001/02/yugo-f12.html

Her face was blurred to protect her identity, but she was filmed live and the vibration of her authentic experience was evident. I stopped everything I was doing and was glued to the screen. I kept feeling chills throughout my body.

She shared her story of how one day she was walking on the streets of Priština, headed for a restaurant. Nobody was around her and it was around mid-day. Suddenly, a white minivan stopped next to her. Before she knew what was happening, KLA soldiers with shotguns came out and grabbed her by her hair. They put a sack on her head and shoved her inside the van and took her to a location in Kosovo where they were holding at least 60 Serbian women. She was able to get away somehow, but the trauma of that experience was so heavy that she couldn't function in life.

I was stunned. I rarely ever watched TV yet happened to run into this. "Oh my God, this could have been me that day," was my first thought. This could have been my destiny. It had happened once again that I was protected and saved by my intuition. Thanks to this woman, I came to realize the fate from which I was saved. It had never dawned on me before. From that moment onward, I have trusted my intuition with my very life. I spent that day in silent gratitude to the Divine for all the love and protection I had been given.

Regarding Stari Račak, I do hope that I will live to see a proper international investigation, especially considering the magnitude of this incident. Perhaps it is naive, but my faith in justice is not based on a system or people – it is based on my faith in the Divine operating through those institutions and people. At some point in time, there will be people who will feel a higher calling to dig into this matter, collect all the evidence, interview the eyewitnesses and present the truth. I have shared my own experience and must say that this information has weighed on me heavily. I can only imagine how I would have felt if I were one of the actual eyewitnesses who had to keep quiet as the entire machinery of NATO and international politics dominated the narrative.

While reading about Dr. Helena Ranta, I pondered what it would have felt like to be in her shoes in March of 1999. On one side, there was her professionalism and a rich international career in the field of forensics and pathology. On the other, an immense pressure to follow the official narrative. Where does one draw the line when it comes to the moral responsibility of telling the truth? How is one to stand by the truth in a situation with such massive, multi-level repercussions, a situation in which key global military decisions made by the big players can be based on the simple practice of stating the truth?

The role that Dr. Ranta was pushed into and the burden that she had to bear was immense. Yet, that was her destiny. Just like Apostle Peter, some people's internal dilemmas and tests of courage to stand by the truth at a specific, crucial moment in time, can become collective, if not even archetypal. May Dr. Ranta be blessed on her soul's journey.

Similarly, one man's terrorist is another man's freedom fighter. It's all a matter of perspective. I had full respect for that, but my issue was with the intentional manipulation of data. How many Kosovo Albanians got expelled from Kosovo due to NATO bombing, and how many due to violence by the

Yugoslav military and other Serbian armed units? In the end, we were served with statistics that were blurring this line with the intentional negative portrayal of Serbian people. Denial of violence is very harmful, but at the same time, it is important to set the record straight about how statistics can be presented, emphasized, or tweaked in one way or another. The only question is, to whose benefit? Nobody knows that better than the Balkan people living on the dividing line between East and West.

All in all, Kosovo gave me so much insight and dispersed the clouds of my youthful idealism. At the same time, it strengthened my faith. I learned to judge less and do more – more of what feels right to me deep within, and more of that which comes from the purest space of my heart.

In Service of His Holiness Patriarch Pavle

Due to my religiously neutral upbringing, I was not even aware that Easter, the greatest Orthodox Christian holiday, was nearly upon us. It was April of 2000, and the few days I'd spent in the Patriarchate had already been so eventful. Little did I know that on Easter, His Holiness Patriarch Pavle, the highest-ranking individual within the Serbian Orthodox Church, would be visiting the Patriarchate of Peć. This is called "being at the right place at the right time." I also feel this was a reward from the Divine for my choice of selfless service. I had no idea what a great honor awaited me.

Patriarch Pavle was a frail old man physically, but a giant spiritually. This was the first time I ever met a saintly person from my own religion (even though newly discovered) and my own nation. There was a deep sense of humility and sincerity that I felt within the Serbian Orthodox Church, which vibed with me especially when it came to monks and monasteries.

I once visited a monastery called Crna Reka (Black River) in Serbia where I met and spoke with a monk of immense wisdom. He shared with me the details of his own near-death experience, and how much he enjoyed the silence of the monastery after that. He looked deep into my eyes at one moment and saw something. I could feel it. He blessed me that day by putting his hand on top of my head. I still remember how deeply touched and incredibly blessed I felt afterward. His sincerity touched me to the point that I pondered life in monastic silence. I wanted to spend some time in a monastery to simply observe myself in that environment and see how it resonated with me.

The first time I glimpsed His Holiness was from my little monastic room on the first floor. I woke up early in the morning, around 5:00 a.m. Looking out the window, I saw a sweet, humble, tiny man dressed in a long black robe. He was seated on a bench very peacefully reading a book. The yard of the Patriarchate of Peć was incredibly beautiful and scenic. I kept looking at this peaceful, old man; that idyllic scene was engraved in my memory. After my NDE, I had grown in sensitivity to subtle energies, and could almost see (or sense) an aura of Divine presence, peaceful and yet so powerful. It was very rare that one sees it, but it was definitely there around this amazing old man.

It did not take me long to realize that this was Patriarch Pavle himself! Like a warm tide, a wave of loving energy arose in my heart. It was almost as if my ancestors were rejoicing through me.

There he was, at this super historic location, seated in the vicinity of the mulberry tree planted by Archbishop Sava the Second, the nephew of St. Sava himself. After around eight centuries of tumultuous history, this black mulberry tree[29] (*Morus Nigra*), believed to be the oldest such tree in Europe, was still offering its sweet fruits and loving shade to all who came into its energy field. And it was around this tree that Arsenije čarnojević, Serbian Patriarch in the 17th century, gathered Serbian people from around this region to initiate The First Great Migration to the north (to the present Vojvodina, where my parents built our new house). This was due to the unbearable living conditions under Ottoman rule.

What I found fascinating about this tree was that it split in half after being struck by lightning during a storm in the mid-20th century. One branch ended up facing east, the other west. The two halves of the tree trunk remained laying on the ground but instead of rotting, they began to support new growth, and thus two new trees emerged from the split branches.[30] The official symbolism assigned to this phenomenon was that of schism in the Christian Church into Eastern and Western.

When Mohanji visited the Kosovo monasteries with me and a group of 60 other pilgrims in 2021, I remember the moment when the two of us got to stand beneath this tree. I was having continuous goosebumps all over my body. We took a photo with the sacred tree, which remains one of my most cherished photos ever. At this moment, I closed my eyes and prayed to the Divine to bless us with a new, additional symbolism that we could assign to this special tree. I prayed that it be the symbol of unity between the essential spiritual teachings of the East and West, the unity for which I was brought back from the NDE, to serve. At the core of my being and feminine nature, I knew that Love always finds its way, just like water flowing through the most inhospitable cracks in a rock eventually finds its way to the ocean.

The spirit of Easter was in the air at the Patriarchate of Peć. I felt blessed to be in the presence of His Holiness Patriarch Pavle at a location brimming with the soul and essence of Serbian history. This was the first time that I understood the unimaginable power and blessing of selfless service. This is when the Divine gives us back so much more than we could ever imagine. We often pray for silly things that the mind perceives as important. But when we serve others selflessly, the Divine gives us what we truly need. From then on, whenever I felt that inner pull to serve and express love purely for the sake of love, and no other reason, I would make it my number one priority. I know now that the rewards of such selflessness are immeasurable.

So there I was, joining a table at which top-level officials had gathered to meet His Holiness on Serbian Orthodox Easter. There were official representatives from NATO/KFOR, UN, OSCE, the US State Department, etc. I had never imagined this would be such a big, truly historic event. I made sure not to apply any makeup or wear clothes appropriate for the monastery.

---

29 It is also called the Sham mulberry tree, because Archbishop Sava the Second brought that seed from the Sham province, today's Syria.

30 Source: https://digitalna.nb.rs/, "Politika" daily newspaper, 22. August 1938, p.11

The seat reserved for me was right next to His Holiness. The meeting was about to start, and I was ready to translate when His Holiness looked at me with his incredibly deep, penetrating eyes and asked, "And where are you from, my child?" Oh, his voice was so sweet and his energy so calm and soothing that my heart melted instantly. Indeed, his energy was like a lifeboat in the sea of restless minds that I was sensing in the room.

Gazing into those divine eyes filled with peace, I said, "I'm originally from Slavonia, from Podravska Slatina. We were refugees in 1991."

I saw an instant warm reaction on his face. He started asking me several other questions. I had no idea that His Holiness was also from the same part of Croatia, maybe one hour or so by car from my hometown! And just like me, he had faced the horrors of war while growing up, but in his case, it was World War II. I was melting while talking to him. It felt like we had entered a special energy bubble and had a reality of our own in that room full of people. I was truly honored by the undivided attention, genuine care, and love that he displayed.

At one moment, I caught a peek at the other people in the room. I noticed how restless our international VIP's around the table had become. Their body language said it all. They were tapping the table with their fingertips, frequently looking at their wristwatches, sighing, etc. There was something comical about this situation. The energy frequency of these people and that of His Holiness were poles apart. They were dismayed and just couldn't understand what on earth this Patriarch had to say to this interpreter in Serbian, while all of them, the really important people, were made to wait. This would have never happened in their world. Out of politeness, they kept quiet.

Luckily, this awkward situation did not last long and the meeting soon commenced. I translated with full concentration and poise, in a smooth flow. I could tell how impressed the members of the international community were with all that was spoken by His Holiness, Father Peter, and by several other prominent people from the Serbian monasteries in Kosovo. For the first time, they were hearing the perspectives of exceptional people from the Serbian Orthodox Church, as well as from long-time Serbian residents of Kosovo & Metohija. The overall impression was beyond positive. I too received quite a few compliments on my translation and felt so grateful for this opportunity.

Over the next couple of days, I got to translate for Father Peter during several other meetings between him and other UN and KFOR officials. He shared some powerful details from his daily reality in Kosovo. Narratives of various injustices and misinterpretations of truth were presented factually and humbly, without any tone of hatred towards Kosovo Albanians. There was a lot that I learned as well. I was so happy to see these officials leave the monastery feeling truly impressed with its historic power and its sacred energy, and with Father Peter and his purity and wisdom. And I in turn was deeply satisfied to contribute in this way. I started feeling at home within the sacred energy of the monastery.

Italian Romanticism in Kosovo

Italians are known for their love for women, flirting, and romance. It simply runs in their blood. Father Peter was the first to notice this.

"What a strange thing. These KFOR soldiers hardly ever come here. Since you came, they have been showing up every day," he said. "I find this odd."

I didn't know what to say in reply, so I simply smiled. Little did I know that my destiny was soon to be linked with Italy and this could have been a small wink from the Divine. A moment later, we had a visit from the main Italian KFOR commander and a couple of his men, plus some other UN staff members who entered the monastic yard.

The commander was an older man in his 60s. He came towards us with a big smile. He saluted Father Peter politely and then turned to me. He greeted me with a polite kiss on my hand, but continued to hold it and then started caressing it with his other hand, saying, "We Italians, we like to looooooove our women."

With Father Peter standing next to me, I thought I was going to sink into the ground from embarrassment. A UN man standing behind the Italian commander found this really amusing and decided to throw a joke as a cherry on top.

"Let me ask you something," he said. "Do you know why a nun is called a nun?"

Luckily, before I even considered translating this, I waited to hear the full joke. That was when he replied in laughter, "Because she doesn't get none!"

"Oh my God! I'm definitely not translating that," I thought.

Father Peter noticed the laughter and asked, "What is happening here? What are they saying?"

I did my best to diffuse the situation. "Nothing, nothing, it's all ok. They are just talking about some irrelevant stuff."

These jokes were such a contrast to the sacred energy of the monastery, but the experience itself demonstrated different dimensions of real life that all people are exposed to. I somehow extricated myself from the company of these men and ran inside the monastery, but giggled to myself, "I'm obviously not monastery material."

The Mother Mary Moment

Soon after this, there was another even more awkward moment, this time within the monastic walls. I was talking to Father Peter, discussing our adventure from the day before. He had taken me to some area near Peć to rescue an important fresco of the martyr brothers Cosmas and Damian from the ruins of one of the many Serbian Orthodox churches, burned to the ground by Kosovo Albanians. I was also aghast at seeing desecrated and destroyed Serbian cemeteries in the Peć area. The opening of graves, destruction of coffins, and to top it all off, the scattering of bones represents the height of insanity by the Kosovo Albanians in their attempts to erase every trace of Serbian presence in Kosovo.

People who performed such acts had no appreciation of the powerful role of the monasteries of Kosovo & Metohija in the collective consciousness of the Serbian people. Over the centuries, the monasteries have reached the status of representing the very soul of the Serbian nation. I used to think these were exaggerations, but after having experienced that energy, after having spent time in Kosovo & Metohija, I started to truly comprehend what the Serbian men in Gračanica had been telling me for a while.

The soul itself, at the individual or collective level, can never be destroyed. The soul is presence, and presence belongs to the realm of the Divine. It simply makes itself felt. Unfortunately for the Serbian people, these most sacred monasteries were inconveniently located on territory that over the centuries changed completely in terms of its demographic. I do hope and pray that Serbian and Kosovo Albanian people will eventually find a harmonious modus vivendi in Kosovo & Metohija regardless of the highly turbulent past.

Even though the desecrated graves that I witnessed in the Peć area that day made my stomach turn, somehow any situation in Father Peter's joyous presence would become something cheerful. His childlike simplicity, and "Oh, no problem" style, made everything appear so light. We were joyously walking toward the ruins and chatting when a kind Albanian man yelled out, "I do hope you are aware that you are walking on a minefield!"

Father Peter walked about another two meters, grabbed the fresco, made a sign of the cross, and off we went returning the same way we had come through the minefield. Later while recalling this experience, he teased me that I was tip-toeing back, as if that was going to save me. "Well, at least my chances of stepping on a mine were a bit smaller!" We were laughing about it for a while, grateful to God that we made it with all body parts intact.

Suddenly Father Peter paused as if sensing something, then asked, "Can you put a scarf over your head? There is something I saw once when you wore a scarf. I would like to see whether it will come again."

When I put the scarf on, he went to fetch his camera and said, "I would like to catch this on camera if possible. You know, when I see you with a scarf on, I sometimes get this beautiful vibration and feeling of Mother Mary."

It just so happened that we were standing behind a door when our unique monastic photo shoot began. At that exact moment, the Mother Superior of the monastery suddenly opened the door. She peeked in and said with a big frown, "What are you two doing in here? !" I felt uncomfortable since she sounded as if she had caught us doing something indecent.

My next thought was, "Okay, I think it's time for me to leave this monastery. This is not going in a good direction. I'm obviously not cut out for monasteries."

On top of everything, I engaged in a conversation with one of the nuns – a conversation that did not go all that well. I asked her about something I could not quite understand – what was the need or requirement of fearing God, of being a "God-fearing" Christian? She was explaining all about fear as a friend keeping us from harm, just like the fear of getting burned will help us not to touch a hot surface. However, when it comes to God, I was not able to connect with that idea. I could not understand how I was to reach intimacy and oneness with God if I had fear of God. My own near-death experience was still fresh in my memory, and there was no room for fear when it came to my deep sense of merging into oneness with the Divine.

"I have to say that I disagree." I said, "When it comes to God, you are safe because you are loved, not because you fear something. Love keeps you much safer than fear. For example, when you love someone, you naturally keep them out of harm's way, and they do the same for you. It is through Love that we connect to God, not through fear. Similarly, very mischievous children need some scolding, and fear is often used as a tool in that case. But well-behaved children need no such reprimanding; we just need to love them and they will blossom. Just like the children in this example, we are not all the same." She did not like me presenting my theories, and insisted we are all sinners who need to fear God. In the end, I realized that I would never fit into the monastic setup in which one is just supposed to blindly follow the strict rules.

I also realized I could never live with restrictions on expressions of joy, humor, and laughter, nor could I give up dancing. I observed that is what little children do all the time. Joy, love, fearlessness, playfulness, awe of life – all of us had it as kids, and yet most of us lost it as we grew up. I wanted to discover that which makes me feel true joy. I honestly felt joy was my number one spiritual goal. To me, life was a gift.

After this conversation, I suddenly gained more clarity about what I wanted from life and mentally thanked that nun. My two weeks at the Patriarchate were almost over. "I did what I came here to do, offered my contribution, learned a lot, plus had some wild adventures and lovely conversations with Father Peter," was my conclusion. It was time to leave.

Divine Presence at the Dečani Monastery

Just before ending my two-week monastic adventure, I joined Father Peter on a visit to the Dečani monastery. I was looking forward to that experience from the day I first saw the miniature replica of the same monastery in Little Branko's gallery in Croatia. And now I finally had the blessing of visiting this monastery in person.

Dečani is the largest medieval monastery in Kosovo and thus its name, Visoki (Tall) Dečani. This monastery is resplendent with wonderfully preserved frescoes of Byzantine style throughout the interior. They are truly stunning, and the frescos alone make this monastery worth the visit. But what makes Dečani monastery truly special are its remarkable monks. Their purity, dedication, and spiritual depth, combined with their plethora of talents and the true spirit of brotherhood that they express, is something that leaves a very deep impression. Father Sava (later on promoted to Archimandrite and the Abbot of the monastery) for example is fluent in six languages, amazingly talented, smart, and yet so pure and humble. The then Abbot (now Bishop) Teodosije had such a soothing presence, and a face with such Christ-like purity, that one feels drawn to gaze at him continuously.

Other monks contributed to the monastery and the larger community through their icon painting, wood carving, cooking superbly tasty food while praying, wine production, beekeeping and production of their famous chestnut honey, preparation of written works for publishing, translation of holy texts, and use of modern technology. Decani.org remains one of the most beautiful multilingual websites from Kosovo, which was at one point considered one of the most reliable sources of news from the region. This was all largely due to the amazing Father Sava, whom they called "cyber monk." The photo library on this website is a true treat and offers the best possible view of the profound beauty of this stunning monastery.

However, the pinnacle of monastic life in Dečani is the liturgy and all the divine services that the monks perform with all their heart and soul. I have never seen anything like it, and will never forget the Sunday liturgy they performed that day. Just as they commenced with the liturgy, I was mesmerized by the view of the famous Dečani choros, a massive round chandelier hanging from extremely long chains. Standing underneath the Dečani choros offers a beatific vista of the dome, with Christ the Pantocrator showering blessings upon all present from that impressive height.

When the liturgy started, these beautiful, tall monks with Christ-like expressions on their faces, shifted their gaze upward to the Heavens. Their eyes were beaming with light, their hearts were invoking Divine presence with immense intensity and they were chanting with such sincerity that a real downpour of purest Divine energy was inevitable. Sensitized to subtle energy after my NDE, I could immediately recognize that powerful, indescribable Presence as it descended upon us.

I would usually close my eyes during powerful spiritual experiences to focus on the feeling within, but what I was seeing with my physical eyes brought forth tears of gratitude. It was so grand that I was forced to remain with my eyes open. Aside from the beatific faces of the monks in graceful white robes, I was soaking in the beauty of Divine rays of light that were penetrating the stunning windows of the tall monastery and caressing the glorious frescos. At that moment, I saw something that made me rub my eyes to ensure I was not imagining – the famous Dečani choros, a massive round chandelier, started moving on its own! It was moving in circles. I watched this breathlessly as tears poured down my face.

Later on, I was told by the monks that while this was rare, it had occurred several times in the past when Divine energy during liturgy became very high. Oh wow! I was so blessed to be able to see what I saw with my own eyes, and to feel what I did, with my heart and soul. Dečani remains my favorite monastery in the whole world. I did have an intuition about it when I first saw the miniature relic by Little Branko, but the experience was so much more than I could have ever imagined.

In 2021, my heart was brimming with love and gratitude when Mohanji and 60 or so of our friends who joined us on this special pilgrimage to Kosovo & Metohija, visited this monastery. I broke two metatarsal bones on my right foot just two days before the pilgrimage, but nothing could stop me from coming to Kosovo at that time. I was hopping around on crutches, while two of my friends would sometimes carry me around like a princess. When we entered this monastery, I knew all of them would feel it as deeply as I did. Unfortunately, we did not come at the time of the liturgy and could not meet Father Sava that day, but the experience was beyond grand nevertheless.

One of the monks agreed to make an exception for us and open the sarcophagus with the holy relics of St. Stefan Dečanski (King Stefan Uroš III of Dečani, who constructed this monastery and died as a martyr in 1331. His body was buried at the Dečani monastery). However, that was not how the story ended. As the monk explained to us that day in fluent English, in 1343 the abbot of the monastery had a vision of St. Stefan who ordered that his body be exhumed. All witnessed the miracle of his dead body being found "intact and fragrant" 12 years after his physical death. The first miracle connected with St. Stefan happened just before his coronation as king. He had been blinded, but his eyes were healed through St. Nicholas, the Miracle Worker. The second miracle was the discovery of his preserved body. Since the 14th century, his holy relics have been made available for viewing on specific days (usually on Thursday).

It was so special for all of us to receive a blessing on the forehead by the consecrated oil through the hands of a humble, Christ-like Dečani monk, and then climb the stepladder to view the relics of St. Stefan Dečanski. One by one, we offered our prostrations and bent down to kiss the sarcophagus just above the hand of St. Stefan. This part of his holy relic that is uncovered and visible strikes a spiritual chord in one's being. It was right there before our very eyes: the hand that crosses the boundaries of time, the boundaries of life and death. It is a direct proof and celebration of eternal consciousness.

The scent of St. Stefan's relics, the presence, the immense history and spirit of the ancestors and all the sacrifices they went through – all of it snowballed together within my heart and brought out so many tears. This time I wept so much more, as if a seal had broken. All the emotions that I had accumulated over a long period just flowed out through those tears. Even Mohanji's Personal Assistant from the UK, who knew nothing about any of this, cried out loud. He said it wasn't logical, but he felt it deep in his heart.

All of us were deeply touched beyond words. Together with Mohanji, I have visited many tombs and samadhi places of saints in India and other countries, but this was so much more special to me because it came from the soul of my ancestry. I feel so grateful that I could share that precious heritage with Mohanji and my friends from various countries. This is a true treasure that needs to be honored and shared. I do hope we will have a chance to go there again, although the situation in Kosovo is worsening, especially for the Serbian community.

Saved From Rape

Upon my return to Priština, I found it even more difficult to adjust to the heavy vibration of the city. The noise and the dust only added to the hostility and burden of the pressure I was feeling as a walking target every day. I tried to make things easier for myself by changing jobs within the UN system.

For a couple of months, I worked at the newly established Police Academy. I was translating for the very first generation of mixed Serbian and Kosovo Albanian police officers who were being trained together. That helped me to interact more with people and to make friendships, and not be stuck in the office all the time. At their graduation, in the big hall full of 99% Albanian people, I saw for the first time some of the main KLA leaders.

Chills ran down my spine when one by one the police officers came up on stage to receive their diplomas. Kosovo Albanian police officers would receive a huge round of applause and cheering, but when a Serbian police graduate would come on stage, there would be dead silence. It was so awkward and unpleasant. After I had enough of the Police Academy, I shifted to the headquarters and worked as the Personal Assistant for the Head of the Finance Office.

Just as my intuition told me during my UN days in Ilok, working at the HQ meant being exposed to all sorts of gazes from the patriarchal hierarchy. There were many awkward situations in that regard, and I was also fed up with the UN parties during which married men were constantly after me. Overall, I didn't feel comfortable in this place. There was nothing that attracted me to Priština, and with every passing day, I started to feel more and more suffocated.

For some time, I did not attend any parties, but boredom and loneliness soon began to set in. One evening there was a farewell party happening at the UN headquarters around eight o'clock in the evening which I was eager to attend. The driver who promised to pick me up never showed up, and Rob and my American friends were not home.

I was all dressed up and ready to go but was kept waiting for the driver to arrive. After an hour or so, I got stubborn and decided, "Oh, to hell with it! I'm just gonna walk there." It would not take me more than 20 minutes to go down Dragodan hill and reach the desired location, but it was not safe, especially in the dark.

I took pepper spray as an additional safety measure in case of any attack and started walking down the hill. After a couple of minutes, I noticed a car continuously following me. I got seriously annoyed seeing the face of some Kosovo Albanian villager with half of his teeth missing, opening his window and telling me something in Albanian. I kept quiet and continued walking, but he wouldn't stop. Eventually, he was driving right next to me with his window open. I reached a point when I could no longer tolerate his actions. "Ok, you asked for it!" I thought. Full of confidence, I took the pepper spray from my handbag, leaned over, and pressed the red button right in front of his face. But alas, nothing happened! Unfortunately, I had forgotten there was a security lock on it.

Before I knew what was happening, he grabbed my hand and head and violently dragged me inside the car through the window. He shoved me onto the back seat and climbed on top of me. He started moving his nasty tongue and drooling his saliva all over my neck, breathing heavily, and trying to remove my clothes. "Oh no, another rape on a car seat!" I thought. This felt so horrible that I was in a state of total shock and disgust. I couldn't believe this was happening to me with this stinky, filthy man. I tried saying something in English, but it was obvious that he did not understand any of it, just like I did not understand his Albanian.

I connected with my core feminine womb power and, without thinking about the consequences that could be even worse, I suddenly spoke to him in Serbian. I spoke with a deep voice, through my teeth. “You have no idea who you’re messing with!”

Again, it was just my divine intuition that I should say that in Serbian with a very deep and serious voice. He could have raped me with an even greater zeal after coming to know that I was Serbian. However, my intuition was correct as always, and my words caused the right reaction. The man was visibly shocked and confused. He did not want to take his chances and simply lifted himself off of me for a moment. I immediately pulled myself out of the car and ran. This was an incredibly similar parallel to the scenario with Zlatko when I was 16.

I ran and ran as fast as my legs could carry me until I reached the house. I locked myself inside and kept calling one of my colleagues from the UN until I managed to get through to him. This colleague, originally from Bosnia, came to get me and took me to the party. After we spoke and I calmed down, I even managed to dance that evening. Nevertheless, this experience stayed with me as yet another instance of Divine blessing through my intuition, the blessing that saved me from getting scarred for life in the most horrible way.

Dance as a Peacemaker

There was one really interesting experience from this period involving dance. One handsome Kosovo Albanian man, whose father used to serve as a Minister during Tito’s days in former Yugoslavia, was getting married. We met at some smaller party and I shared some of my experiences with him, including my recent sexual assault. He wanted to change my perception of Kosovo Albanians and invited me to his wedding party. I was surprised when he added, “And please do feel free to speak in Serbian when you come to my wedding party. If anyone has a problem with it, they will have to deal with me.”

His attitude impressed me. I decided to go and asked Rob to accompany me. We both dressed all in white. When a crazy Serb and big, chubby African American dressed in white walked into this wedding party, I do imagine we made quite an entrance. All heads turned, especially when the groom intentionally spoke in loud Serbian, “Oh, Biba, welcome!” Suddenly, I felt so many eyes on me. These eyes were like arrows. One man stood there on crutches, with only one leg. His eyes were fixed on me, emanating hatred.

Rob and I were seated at a table and soon their local music started. A dozen people got up to dance. They danced in a circle, moving their feet rapidly. I immediately noticed that this dance was quite similar to our kolo (circular Serbian folk dance). There were some minor differences, but nothing I could not catch. The moment I figured out the steps, I got up and joined them.

The music was uplifting and the dancing took us into a different vibration altogether. I forgot about the hateful gazes that had been directed at me only a couple of minutes ago. When the dance was over, I noticed a complete shift in the room’s energy. I was accepted! Nobody gave me any strange looks. People were joyous, loud, laughing, and having a great time. “Oh wow,” I thought, “I never knew dance could be used as a diplomatic tool for peacebuilding.”

I realized that evening just how powerful dance was in terms of shifting energy, making me love it even more.

The Only Way Out

My days in Kosovo grew increasingly heavy. Being a walking target and exposed to potential danger every day eventually did start to get to me. I could feel myself sinking and withdrawing. I felt a certain heaviness in my heart upon realizing that I would have to stay in the hostile, dusty Priština for years to earn sufficient money for a proper university abroad.

It was Rob who inspired me to open up to a different approach to fulfilling my dream. He said there are many kind-hearted people out there who provide donations and scholarships. I just need to open myself up to such an idea. “Wow, that’s true. Why not believe that I can get a scholarship?” I thought. That idea had never even occurred to me; I always assumed I had to earn every penny myself. From that moment, I started praying for the right scholarship to come my way. I called upon the feeling with which I declared “I am NOT a victim!” This was not the time to give up on my dream.

One day I was surfing the net and noticed something that left me breathless: “The Balkan Presidential Scholarship.” My intuition lit up at the sight of this and I started reading about it fervently. This was a scholarship for the Undergraduate Studies of International Affairs at the prestigious private American University called John Cabot University (JCU), located in Trastevere, the heart of Rome.

I had goosebumps upon reading that James Creagan, who served as the President of that university, was suddenly inspired, considering all the wars and human suffering that were happening in the nearby Balkan region, to offer a scholarship to a deserving student who had the experience of war but also demonstrated academic excellence and service to the community. Such a student would have a lot to contribute to the classroom in terms of their experience and insight.

The moment I saw that my instant reaction was, “That’s me! This scholarship manifested for me. I can feel it. It was the Divine that put that thought in the JCU President’s mind in answer to my prayers.” I was sure that competition would be stiff since any student from the entire Balkan region could apply for this scholarship, but deep inside I felt it was exactly meant for me.

Without any delay, I sat down to write my heart out. I recalled how my reality had changed after I wrote my heart out during my refugee days. Just as in my middle school essay, and even in this very book, I wrote with no exaggeration, only that which had truly transpired, and expressed it all from the deep, sacred space of my heart. I described how I had set my goal for higher education abroad during my refugee days, what my reality was like in Kosovo, and the fact that Milošević had declared people like me as traitors, so my prospects in Serbia were not good. In summary, I could not stay in Priština and I could not go back to Serbia. “You are my last chance in fulfilling my dream,” is what I expressed in that application.

After a couple of weeks, I received a letter from JCU. I opened the envelope with great excitement. My heart could barely take it. And then I jumped in the air and screamed when I read the first sentence: "Congratulations! We are pleased to inform you that you have been awarded the Balkan Presidential Scholarship for the studies of International Affairs at the John Cabot University in Rome." Oh my goodness! I had to pinch myself! Four years of studies covered by a $40,000 scholarship had just landed on my lap. At that moment, I was the happiest person on earth!

I never stopped believing that my dream would come true. I did everything I could, including risking my life, to fulfill my dream step by step. I did not have any Plan B and returning to my old life was not possible. However, it was only when, after doing my best, I surrendered the rest to the Divine that the result came. I opened my heart and allowed Divine Love to manifest through the unconditional love and goodness of humanity. It was only then that the actual blessing manifested in full.

I was so very grateful to Rob for his loving support through all the thick and thin moments in Kosovo, but I surely had many naysayers as well, even after I won the scholarship. I remembered the words of a relative of mine, the one who accused me of spying for Croats earlier. When I told him that I had been awarded the $40,000 scholarship, he said in a sarcastic tone that I live in the clouds and that those types of scholarships always come with some catch to them. Well, that was his truth, not mine. In my world, human goodness was real. Nobody asked me to spy for Americans or whoever, and nobody asked me to do anything in return for this scholarship. All I had to do was to demonstrate my seriousness as a student by achieving a reasonably high academic score, which I would have done anyway.

It was time to sail into a completely different reality. The Uranus in my astrological chart was ready to lift anchor once again. With a wide smile and fervent joy, I said to myself, "Goodbye, dusty Priština. Sunny Rome awaits me with open arms!"

Chapter 5

University Days in Rome

True Love Blossoming at Flower Square

Before reaching sunny Rome, I hopped over to Zagreb, the capital of Croatia, to get my student visa stamped in my passport. I planned to be in and out, only staying at a friend's place for one night. When I reached the Embassy, my perfect plans were immediately disrupted by technical difficulties, a two-day delay. What was I supposed to do in Zagreb for another two days?

It was August 8, 2000, and this minor inconvenience could spoil neither my mood nor the gorgeous weather. I decided to explore Zagreb a bit and go for a walk in the spirit of adventure. While passing by a jewelry shop, I noticed a bracelet with a hook clasp in the shape of a horizontal figure eight. My mind overflowed with thoughts and ideas of circles and eights. A circle is the fullness of an individual that becomes a perfect unit of consciousness – stable, authentic, and aware, with no need to steal energy from someone else. This gave a whole new perspective to horizontal figure 8. When two such circles/conscious individuals join at one point, they automatically enter into a perfect flow of the energy of union, while remaining in their own authentic, stable energy.

"Wow, such flow is perfect and eternal, just like true love. This must be why this is the symbol of eternity as well. This is truly amazing. How come I never thought of this before? I can't think of a better symbol of the energy flow within a perfect relationship of two conscious individuals. It must be the eights and the zeros of today's date that made me think of this. Amazing synchronicity!"

I had no idea where all this came from. It had nothing to do with my student visa, plans, or previous thoughts. At that very moment, I lifted my head and noticed a young man and woman talking. Intuitively I felt it was safe to talk to them, so I approached them with a silly question that I posed in my awkward-sounding, long-forgotten Croatian. "Excuse me, is there any museum nearby?"

The young man was approximately my age, perhaps a bit older. He lifted his head and I noticed his amazingly deep blue eyes and long eyelashes. He smiled and said, "Sure. There are many. Which one are you interested in?"

"I don't know. The biggest one, I guess," I said with a smile.

I made note of his directions, thanked him, and started walking. I felt like a bird released from a cage, so light and happy, finally free to fly. I was 23 and ready to conquer the world with my love. In a couple of days, the biggest dream of my life would manifest in my physical reality at last. I'd never felt this happy before and I simply felt great in my own skin. I was wearing my favorite white suit (the same suit in which I danced at the Albanian wedding) that accentuated my curvy waistline and had bell-bottom trousers. The look was punctuated by my long black hair flowing in the warm summer breeze.

From the corner of my right eye, I spotted the young man walking beside me. As he moved to pass me, he smiled and casually commented, “You are Serbian, aren't you?”

Although I attempted my best, rusty Croatian just to be safe in the post-war scenario, this guy still figured me out. Since he was so cute and smiling, I dropped my fake Croatian accent straight away and replied in Serbian.

“Well, indeed, I am. Is that a problem?”

His reply surprised me. “You know what, I am also Serbian.”

“How is that even possible? You have a typical Zagreb accent.”

“Of course I do. I was born here and have been living here all my life. This is exactly where I live, right on this Flower Square. Are you in a hurry to go to that museum? Maybe we could have a coffee or juice together?”

I agreed happily. There was something special about this fellow. Talking to him felt surprisingly comfortable and joyous as if we had known each other for a very long time. In other words, I did not feel a need for any introduction or to hold anything back.

We sat, started talking, and four hours disappeared on us! The conversation was so interesting that we just couldn't get enough of exchanging our energy and experiences. I noticed right away that he was extremely intelligent, spiritual, mysterious, and complex. His IQ was exceptionally high. He was like a living encyclopedia, but without showing off in any way. I could tell that he was completely natural – it was completely normal for him to read a book in one day and also gauge whether he wanted to read a book just by feeling its energy. I just loved exploring his reality and also enjoyed sharing my many adventures with him.

I found it amazing that he liked everything I liked, but took it to a whole new level. For example, I liked Salsa – he loved dancing and even organized Salsa dance evenings in Zagreb. I liked martial arts – he trained for many years in multiple techniques, a black belt in one of them. I liked spirituality and mystery – he had been studying various esoteric teachings since childhood and had his own spiritual group that met regularly. He meditated on a dot at the center of a circle and had been recognized as advanced within certain mystical circles. I liked the Star Wars trilogy, myths, and legends – he conducted an in-depth study of it and could remember every mythological story, with all the original names. I liked energy healing modalities – he already had a modality of his own. I liked astrology – he studied it in-depth until he mastered it fully.

He started asking me deeper questions about my horoscope, like my Ascendant, etc. Since I had no clue what the Ascendant even meant, he asked for the place and time of my birth and – get this – calculated it in his head, right there in front of me. He was looking up, sorting things out in his brain, and said, “Oh, yes, that makes sense, your Ascendant is in Capricorn.”

I was truly amazed, impressed, and intrigued by him, to say the least. However, this was not all. My intuition was skyrocketing while I was in his presence. I did not need any Turkish coffee sedimentation. While listening to him I would look at him with a steady gaze. At times my vision blurred and I would see or sense things with my inner vision. When he spoke about some really tough times that he went through as a Serb in the center of Zagreb in the early 1990s, I suddenly had a vision of him being surrounded by a group of men and using his martial arts skills to fight them off. I saw that, at some point, they got to him, beating him and breaking his front teeth.

Without thinking, I shared that with him. It came out awkwardly when I asked him out of the blue: "Were your upper front teeth broken in a street fight in which you got surrounded by men? Have these teeth been replaced with porcelain ones?"

He went very quiet and murmured, "Yes. Strange – nobody ever noticed that before." Soon after that, he excused himself, saying he had somewhere to go. He promised to be back soon if I would care to wait.

He was back after less than an hour. He rejoined our table with a big smile and said, "I'm sorry, but I had to use my sources to check on you. I was suddenly seized by a doubt that you were some kind of a sinister agent, sent to seduce me. I had a disturbing thought that you were not real, you know. But now I know that all you said about your past, UN and all, is true. I'm just amazed that you got this part about my teeth exactly right as if you had witnessed it!"

I smiled and said, "Well, Sinke [this was the nickname I gave him], I have my secret talents as well."

My autobiography would not be authentic if I skipped the story of Sinke. Luckily, I have a husband who transcended lower frequency emotions such as jealousy a long time ago, which makes me free to share the story of my first true love from the heart. Not many married women enjoy such a privilege. In the spirit of the famous Italian song by Enrico Ruggeri "*Il primo amore non si scorda mai*" (First Love is Never Forgotten).

I honor this experience because it changed me in so many ways. Any situation in which we move beyond the boundaries of reality defined by our mind and all our spirit-dulling comfort zones is a blessing that enables us to reveal the hidden parts of ourselves, to ourselves. Loss of control within the powerful chemistry of love surely comes as a shock – we can't even recognize our former selves. Many people dream about something like that happening to them, but it never does. I went through a lot of turbulence due to this relationship, but I still consider it a rare blessing and have no regrets.

I continued talking to Sinke and, at some point, I realized that I just could not imagine moving away from him. The magnetism between us was unlike anything I have experienced till then! I did not need to eat or sleep. The energy was through the roof! All I wanted was to be one with him. Almost all of those two nights and days were spent intensely and completely with Sinke. The rest of the world did not exist. What I experienced with him went so deep that it occupied my heart for the next seven years. For the first time, I lost my head. I wonder which nickname my UN friends would have given me this time. "Walking Sex" would surely be replaced by something more suitable

– perhaps "A Floating Longing." That this kind of intensity of feeling and craziness was even possible for a person like me was hard to fathom.

I was at the height of my adventurous youth – living in the heart of Rome, surrounded by romantic bridges and cafés, and yet unable to be with any other man throughout my studies. One specific moment from the height of our intimacy at Flower Square kept coming back to me as a faithful companion. This was the moment when Sinke's eyes slowly gazed upwards and I saw them fixated at the brightness, reflecting an intense, glorious vision of the Divine. His eyes reflected at me the way I felt during my NDE when I was about to dissolve in the brightness. That went straight into the very core of my being and kept returning to me again and again as a most cherished memory.

What transpired between Sinke and me was way beyond physical. This was like some material for Osho's book, *Vigyan Bhairav Tantra.* I gained my first insight that the Divine indeed dwells in the deep intimacy between a man and woman who truly love one another. After this life-altering weekend in Zagreb, it was not our fate to experience intimacy ever again. There were certain complications... Yet, Sinke was with me all the time for many years to come. My mind was helpless in these deep waters of the heart and was ill-equipped to handle anything within that realm. There was no space for logic, self-control, or calculation based on personal benefit. None whatsoever. I was hopelessly, madly in love. I understood what the great poets were talking about in their love songs. Olivia Newton-John's song from the movie "Grease" comes to mind:

> I know I'm just a fool who's willing
> To sit around and wait for you
> But baby, can't you see there's nothing else for me to do?
> I'm hopelessly devoted to you.

Never in my wildest dreams could I have envisioned such a romance happening to me. And what timing! The greatest dream of my life was on the verge of fulfillment. Sometimes I would feel something bordering on panic, thinking: "How on earth am I to focus on my studies now? I can't see any books properly, forget about studying from them with these rose-colored glasses on. This is something that should have happened to me when I was in high school, not now. I need to gather myself. I need to focus." I fought, I fought so hard, but just like a puppy running after a treat, I ran to my University's computer lab every day in anticipation of Sinke's next email. And when I would see it in my inbox, my heart would almost jump out of my chest. It was tough to keep all this abnormal intensity inside of me. I was a truly hopeless case.

From Priština to Hollywood

Upon reaching John Cabot University, I realized just how perfect my new university was for me. Very near the River *Tevere* (Tiber), located in the heart of Rome and in the ancient area called Trastevere, this scenic, elegant University was everything I dreamed of and more. There were even moments in which I felt it was all too beautiful, so vastly different from the harshness of my previous years.

I must admit that living in danger, hostility, and insecurity for more than a year had scarred me. I could not just shift to the new super happy and merry life. It was all too perfect for a wretch like me. I felt like an alien from a different planet, one filled with immense pain and struggle, who had landed in a place where nobody had to deal with any real hardships in life. I did not find it appropriate that I bother anyone with my heavy stuff that they could never relate to or begin to understand. I had nobody to talk to about my past and yet could not adjust to the new world so easily.

Later on, I realized that at some point during my life and work in Kosovo that I had already started to sink in a quagmire of despondency. My scholarship came just in time to preserve my sanity, like a lifeline to a drowning person. In addition to the beautiful ambiance of their lovely classrooms and terraces, and the incredibly kind professors and administrative staff (and here I would like to especially highlight our lovely Dean Franco Pavoncello and Francesca Gleason from the Registry Office), John Cabot University gave me love, support, and the perfect measure of discipline to slowly bring me out of that mud, restoring me to my true, balanced self.

I was glad that I arrived more than a week early, to have enough time to settle down and explore my new surroundings with gusto. After completing all the formalities at the Registrar's Office, I was invited to join a group of students on a trip to Cinecitta, the largest film studio in Europe. This is where Hollywood movie shoots often take place. At that time, the movie "Gangsters of New York" happened to be filming at Cinecitta, and our university arranged to even meet some of the movie crew.

It was truly fascinating to see entire streets constructed as a replica of 19th-century New York. I was smiling and thinking to myself, "I just arrived from Priština, barely surviving so many dangers, fell madly in love over the weekend, and now I am in a 19th-century New York scenario. My life is more surreal than the script of any Hollywood movie."

At that moment, a young man from Romania approached me. He was a member of the film crew tasked with conducting a short tour for our jolly John Cabot University group. We started chatting casually and at one point he asked out of the blue, "Hey, if you are free tomorrow evening, you are welcome to join me at the birthday party of Leonardo di Caprio. I have one ticket, and it is for two people, so... Would you like to come with me? No strings attached." He caught me off-guard. I did not see that coming at all.

"I would love to, but, you see, it's not like I have any Armani or Versace clothing items in my student wardrobe," I said.

"Oh, no problem at all. This will be totally casual. Leonardo said we can come in jeans for all that he cares. He is not too fond of formalities from what I can see," he replied. I was so excited and of course ready for the adventure.

That day at Cinecitta, I met a lovely girl from Serbia who turned out to be in my JCU class. Her name was Marija Govedarica. She was even taller than me and incredibly sweet, straightforward, friendly, and witty. I loved the depth and clarity in her big, brown eyes and her wide, super sincere smile. We soon became best friends forever. This is how Marija described to me her impression of our very first encounter:

"I noticed a girl who stood out from the rest through her very presence. You were dressed differently and radiated differently, a certain royal vibe. I could feel your clothing and posture, with a straight back and head slightly up, were not a show-off different, but authentic different. I somehow knew right away you were from Serbia. When I heard you speak, I could make out by the accent that my intuition was correct. So, I approached you right away."

That day marked the beginning of a friendship that truly enriched my life. I did not realize just how much I needed it. Marija was someone who could "hear" me and love me for who I was. So, on top of all the blessings, I got a BFF as well.

The next evening, I was all set for fun. I was open to whatever that night might bring. Upon arriving at the venue, I met my new Romanian friend and joined a sea of people dancing on a podium near the bar. The DJ introduced the latest song by Madonna and soon we were all dancing to the cool tunes of the song "Music." I was dancing right next to a young man with shoulder-length dark blond hair, a cap turned backward, and wide-leg jeans. After a minute or so he lifted his head a bit and I got to see the blue eyes that connected with so many girls, including myself while watching the movie "Titanic."

"Oh my god, that's Leonardo di Caprio, dancing with me!" He'd built more muscle since "Titanic," grown his hair, and his real-life persona had a totally different vibe than his onscreen characters. I was super excited and soaked in every second of this experience. Smiling internally, I thought to myself: "This is totally surreal. If he only knew where I just came from and what I've been through."

Indeed, this looked like a moment in which two people from parallel realities converged at the same place. If someone told me a week ago, while in Priština, that I would be experiencing this, I would have never believed it! "I love my life!" was the only thought that came to me. I did not feel like bothering Leonardo with a boring formality such as an autograph – dancing the entire "Music" song with him was more than enough. I couldn't wait to share this with Marija!

"Šeša, tell me how it went. I love it when my day starts with your famous line, 'Marijice (my dear Marija), you won't believe what just happened!' Come, I want to hear every detail," said my dear Marija in her loving tone. She had a gift for coining unique terms of endearment. The word Šeša (pronounced Shesha) was one of my favorite of her creations. This word, embedded with immense cuteness, softness, and love, was given to all those whom she loved a lot, including her ginger cat. I was her favorite Šeša in Rome.

Marija was the only person on Earth who called me *Biljka* (pronounced Bilyka, meaning "herb." Everyone else called me Biba or Biljana). This nickname instantly cued the expansion of my heart. The moment I heard Marija's warm and long "Biiiiiiiiiljka," I was engulfed in a wave of pure joy. She made me feel so loved and special. Such was Marija's nature.

Whenever I shared anything, she listened ever so deeply and devotedly, noticing each tiny detail, and mining each story with me for deeper aspects of truth. From the authenticity and peace in Marija's eyes to the joy in her mouth-wide-open, hearty laughter – Marija was utterly unique in her inner and outer beauty and inimitable in her warmth.

Marija was my best friend and Maid-of-Honor when I married Mohanji in 2010. While the bond we continue to share is beyond words, here is my humble attempt to convey my love for my dearest Marija, her incomparable beauty, and most of all, her striking purity of heart which will never be forgotten, even though she is no longer with us physically.

I loved nothing more than meeting my dearest Marija for a cappuccino in one of the many beautiful cafés near my university to discuss our number one topic – Spirituality & Sinke. These small, in-between moments are the real beauty of life. It is an illusion that big events mark our lives. No, it's the small moments that we cherish. In the USA, people pay a lot of money for psychiatrists, but the blessing of having a true friend that can hear you deeply and truly is as good or better than any therapy. It is so deeply fulfilling.

Marija and I loved to talk about spiritual teachings, real-life issues, challenges on the soul's journey, astrology, depth of love and pain, spiritual awakening, and the essence of life. I couldn't wait for lectures to end so that we could sit together in a super cute Trastevere café, restaurant, or park. Sometimes we would walk along the River Tevere, enjoying the sight of the ancient bridges, and discuss something from the menu of our favorite topics. Very often, the most striking topic would be the latest message from Sinke and the realization related to the same.

I would greet her, brimming with excitement: "Šešo, you won't believe what happened!" Her sparkling eyes would lock on mine. She would sit so breathlessly still, so deeply engrossed, and listen to my intense stories. I have never met such a great listener. Her empathy was endless and her focus on herself and her own needs so incredibly small. I don't think I will ever find the words to describe just how special and precious Marija was to me – and how much I miss her loving presence...

It was divine providence that Marija and I, two polar opposites, were matched so perfectly and brought together as friends. Marija was fond of astrology and the two of us loved dissecting the 120-page astrological analysis of mine done by Sinke's father Zdravko whom we met in Serbia that year. Soon, he did one for her as well. While dissecting it to pieces, we often joked about my Moon in Leo (which is why I always had to have puffed hair and a striking presence, like a proud lion). My dear Šeša's Sun in Leo didn't have the same effect. Unlike me, she was quite introverted, mainly wore jeans, and paid minimal attention to hair styling or make-up. She was completely natural, casual, and profoundly beautiful in her simplicity.

One day I received a deeply mystical message from Sinke which touched a really deep chord in me and caused endless discussions and interpretations by Marija and me. This is what he said (as far as I remember):

"And so I came before the Creator, who greeted me with heart-melting words: 'Come my son, it is time for you to assume your rightful place. You have done well.

And I reply: 'Thank you most beloved Father. I am saying this in all awareness that even the thoughts that we think are ours actually come from you: I am grateful for your love and recognition, and the award surely is tempting. But I choose to go back dear Father, to go back into the darkness and density on Earth to bring more light. You know I am not afraid to fight. But I request only one thing this time. Aside from the wish for the fight to be fair, may I please have one true co-fighter.' And the Father replies: 'Oh my son, but I have given her to you. From the beginning of all time. Search for her and you shall find her.'"

There were no other words in this email, only this powerful bomb of a message. It has a life of its own in my heart and mind. It caused a lot of contemplation, imagination, and inspiration.

Sinke was always ahead of me. He knew my full psychological profile based on my natal chart and sometimes I felt that he understood my deepest driving force more than I did, at the level of awareness I was on at that time. He shared with me some stories about the history of the Knights Templars, the order he belonged to. I did not know anything about any of it, so he sent me the book *The Hiram Key* by Christopher Knight and Robert Lomas.

Both of the authors were Freemasons and in this book, they presented a theory of the origins of Freemasonry and unravel many other mysteries, such as Friday the 13th (the day when many noble Knights Templars were killed in France), their own version of the historical Jesus, and the original Jerusalem Church. It was intense to read this kind of content seated right in front of the historic Porta Settimiana, the gate of the Aurelian walls from third-century Rome, the only gate that remained in its original form and location throughout the centuries.

John Cabot University is located right next to Porta Settimiana, at the beginning of Via della Lungara which leads straight to the Vatican. There I was, surrounded by ancient history, only ten minutes by foot from the Vatican and reading about some serious conspiracies that involved its secret circles. Seated in my favorite Massi Café near Porta Settimiana, my inner Eagle was busy with all the book's mysteries of past, present, and future.

Cigarettes were part of my daily reality, up until one fine day when I had another spiritual experience that made me love Sinke even more. In one of his messages, he asked me whether I would like him to help me stop smoking and I agreed. I did not ask any additional questions. A couple of days later, right after I enjoyed my regular morning cappuccino with cornetto (a croissant, my favorite being one with a bit of honey at the middle) fresh from the oven, and a cigarette, I noticed that the smell of that cigarette suddenly seemed rather intense and really ugly. I still finished it and after having extinguished it in an ashtray, I continued sensing that ugly scent of the ashtray on me. I felt the pull to smell my right hand's middle finger, against which I always held the cigarette (so much so that it even turned a bit yellow – smokers can surely relate to this). When I did that, I almost vomited! It smelled so bad that I had to go to my apartment and wash it several times with soap and hot water until I was satisfied that the smell was gone.

That was the moment when something just clicked in my head and I could not even imagine smoking ever again. My sense of smell was not only back, but it was increased! This was a real game-changer. I did not even feel like going into cafés in which people smoked. If I went out dancing and someone smoked in that space, I would have to wash my hair that same evening. I could not go to sleep with that ugly smell of smoke in my hair.

"He did something, some long-distance energy work, just as he said he would. I can no longer feel any attraction to cigarettes. On the contrary, the smell is repelling!" I concluded.

I messaged Sinke and he replied: "Oh, good, so it worked." This was a real 180-degree change. Marija was super happy because she never liked me smoking. To this day, I find it unbearable to have someone smoking next to me. I politely remove myself from that space, even though I understand smokers because I used to be one for years.

My energetic frequency was changing and around that time my food choices started changing as well. Being surrounded by many local grocery shops with organic vegetables, various types of pizzas and pastas, etc., I found it easy to shift to a vegetarian diet. There was something about meat and the violence behind it that I suddenly found truly repulsive. I first dropped red meat, then chicken, and finally seafood. I'd never had eggs alone for breakfast but could tolerate them as an ingredient in dishes like pasta.

A subtle change in energy was evident within, a process that resulted in all these outward changes. At the same time, I was also very focused and responsible at the university. I volunteered at the Computer Lab and Library and was also part of the Student Government. I had only the best grades and in this way demonstrated my gratitude to my wonderful university.

The Dean saw me once walking around with a book on Kabbalah in my hands. Being of Jewish origin, he couldn't help but comment with a smile: "Biljana, what are you doing with that book in your hands? It's not something one reads casually in a café? These are very deep, esoteric teachings that usually people in their 40s or older delve into." I replied that studying such topics in coffee bars, over the low buzz of background conversations, was exactly what I loved to do. I can only imagine how weird that looked to my dean.

Of all my professors, my Visual Arts professor was a real character. After a lecture by a traveling scholar about the fall of former Yugoslavia and I was interested in speaking with this scholar in more detail. A group of us met with the scholar to discuss the topic of war in former Yugoslavia in the seriousness that it deserved. During the discussion, the scholar, who had been staring at me for a while, suddenly proclaimed: "I finally figured out what it is about Biljana's face that makes it so harmonious and proportional. My dear, you have a perfectly straight nose!"

I thought I was going to sink under the table out of embarrassment. That was so uncalled for. He went on talking about the Greek profile and how rare such straight noses are. Finally, we managed to drop the nose topic and return to our discussion, but this was something that finally gave me clarity. I was frequently told I looked like someone else. It still happens to me a lot, at least a couple of times per year. Somebody stares at me and says, "It is incredible how much you look like [so and so]."

I was also told that I resembled the Romanian actress Ramona Badescu who was quite famous in Italy. People would stop me on the street and enquire about my next movie. They were 100% sure I was her. I once even got a free haircut from a hairdresser who thought I was her. What can I say, life is great fun!

After some time I decided that enough was enough regarding my constant preoccupation with Sinke and his messages, the daydreaming about us together, etc. I decided that my studies had to be my number one priority and that all these emails with Sinke, mystical topics, and philosophies need to wait until I finished my studies. I wrote to him one day with a sincere request: "Can you please help me out here and stop all communication with me? I really need to focus on my studies. I do hope you understand. Please don't write to me or call me again." To my great amazement, he honored my request, like a real knight.

Then reality hit me. Life became so dry and empty without him that it was unbearable. I felt as if part of my body was missing. It was *that* unnatural and painful not to have Sinke in my world. I managed to endure that feeling of awkward emptiness for two weeks before writing to him again: "I was thinking, could we still keep in touch, as friends...?"

His reply came back within five seconds and it made me blush. "Are you sure this friendship won't turn into a romance?" There was nothing I could say that he did not already know.

Striking the right balance with Sinke resulted in a marked improvement in my concentration and focus on my studies. The scale tipped to 60 – 40 in favor of studies. Then came the month of November, my birthday just days away on the fourth. Exactly on that day, a professor handed out group assignments, saying we would be graded together as a group. We had to do the research and PowerPoint presentation all together. This assignment was due the next day and I was not happy with how the other members of my group took it. They were too relaxed about it, completely casual. Most of them were from rich families and to them, grades were of no relevance. They just needed to pass. I knew our group grade would be bad unless I did something about it. I decided not to tell anyone it was my birthday, but to invite them to my place and spearhead the completion of the project.

We were at it for hours and it was getting dark. At around 7:00 p.m., I received a text from an unknown Italian number with the message, "*Buon compleanno*." I glanced at it, and wondered for a moment who that might be, but did not want to be distracted. So, I ignored it completely. At around 9:00 p.m., the same message came from the same number, but we were still finishing the project and I ignored it again. As the night wore on, I was exhausted from the group effort resting entirely on my shoulders. I would have done it faster and better on my own but had no choice.

The next morning, I was walking along Via della Scala towards my university. It rained a bit the previous night and I just observed the overall vibe of Trastevere in a relaxed way when a sudden, crystal-clear intuitive message hit me: "Sinke was here! He was walking here, on this very road yesterday evening. Oh no! It must have been him who sent that message twice!" My heart was beating fast during this flurry of intuitive messages and I texted him straight away.

He replied, "Yes, I was there. I drove to Rome to be with you on your birthday, but you did not reply. I figured you didn't want to see me. I am now driving back, almost reaching Croatia."

Oh, what could I say... My heart sank. I was so deeply filled with regret. Never have I wished to turn back the clock as much as I did at that moment. It took me a while to get rid of the pointless "I should have..." thoughts.

Several months later, Sinke proposed we meet halfway in Venice. He would drive from Zagreb and I could go to Venice by train or plane. Delighted to have a second chance, I bought an airplane ticket and eagerly awaited the day. However, something unimaginable happened exactly on the day I was to leave for the airport. I suddenly got the most painful abdominal cramps.

"What on earth is this now?!" I thought. It felt like someone was stabbing me with a knife. I could not even move from the bed, not to mention travel. I am fortunate to never have cramps or any discomfort during my monthly cycle so I simply had no idea where this came from. I had no choice but to cancel my flight. With a heavy heart, I informed Sinke that I wasn't coming. "What is the Universe telling me here?" I wondered. It seemed like there was some invisible force that kept us apart intentionally.

During my visit to Serbia during one of the holidays, Sinke agreed to meet me at his father's home. Sinke's parents were divorced when he was a child and his father moved to Serbia where he married a lovely, spiritual lady. This meeting was the weirdest of all experiences. Sinke revealed to me that he could no longer wait for me. Our long-distance relationship was too emotionally draining and he had gotten back together with his former long-term girlfriend Helena.

Since I was the one who pleaded to be left alone to focus on my studies, I could not complain. However, my love for him was still the same. This girl also happened to be one of his best friends since childhood. He was in a relationship with her even when we met, but when the tsunami of our powerful chemistry and feelings swept us both off our feet, he decided to break up with her. I laughed internally upon realizing that, when we met at Flower Square, it did not even occur to me to ask him if he was already in a relationship. My brain was obviously gone for a toss!

Zdravko enjoyed the privilege of teasing Sinke in front of me. I sensed a bit of rivalry between them, but they also clearly loved each other. They would speak in their special astrology language and analyze everything through the planetary squares, trigons, conjunctions, etc. The only thing I could gather from that discussion was that Zdravko claimed that Helena was too similar to Sinke, which is why they were great as friends, but the attraction and chemistry were highly questionable.

As I stepped away for a moment, I heard Zdravko yelling at Sinke in a rather offensive tone: "That is not you! Don't you get it? You are not at all at that level. Keep dreaming!" It was years later that I understood. My astrological Jupiter was exactly in the house of marriage, I could only marry my ultimate spiritual authority, meaning, my Guru (represented by the planet Jupiter). And considering the depth and spiritual predispositions of my Eagle, that had to be someone at a high level of spiritual mastery. In other words, it had to be a Spiritual Master. What Zdravko was telling Sinke was that he did not consider him to be at that level. He was referring to some examples of uncontrolled anger from the past, things that Sinke had never spoken to me about.

That night we slept in the same room by default. Sinke tried to get another room for me, but Zdravko insisted that nothing was cleaned and ready, that as two grown-ups, we ought to handle it. My feeling was that Zdravko was kind of hoping we would get back together. There were some highly romantic moments between us that night, as the insanely strong chemistry between us was fully back on. However, Sinke obviously fought it with all the self-control he could muster.

He did not speak much, but at one point murmured something along the lines of, "It wouldn't be fair to Helena." My pride did not allow me to push for anything and I somehow managed to fall asleep in the end, regardless of the inner fire and insane magnetic attraction between us. When I woke up in the morning, I found him doing push-ups next to the bed. He admitted that he was awake all night. I found him adorable in his sincerity. I respected Sinke's determination to stick to certain moral rules. This was the last time that we ever shared a room.

That night I dreamt of him walking through a fog. He turned towards me and I saw that his eyes were red! He spoke and behaved differently and was even smoking! He looked like he was possessed by some evil spirit. This dream was so vivid, it gave me the creeps. I also had to admit that I did not connect with the path of Freemasonry. I did not know much about it and had no idea what Sinke did and to which group he belonged. I trusted that his group (or Lodge, as they would call it) would be on the side of Light, but whenever I thought about Freemasons, I could intuitively feel some resistance from within. Though my communication with Sinke continued, along with my feelings for him, something changed that day.

One more powerful experience happened during this trip to Serbia. I visited Ljubica Spasenović, an amazing woman who was excellent in Non-Hypnotic Regression. I came to know about her from Dr. Ljubiša Stojanović, from whom I purchased a pendant for the harmonization of one's energetic field. Dr. Stojanović happened to be present when I was buying the pendant and we engaged in a conversation that included his experience from India. He shared with me the moment when he visited a great Master known as Sathya Sai Baba. "I never saw a man whose aura was like a Sun – so huge, expanded, and golden. As someone who can see the human aura with the naked eye, which is related to my work and research, I found his auric field to be so majestic, so resplendent, that I could never forget it. I felt like telling people – you are standing in the presence of a golden sun! You have no idea what a blessing that is!" said Dr. Stojanović.

These words left a really deep impression on me for some reason and my intuition went through the roof! I realized how eager I was to meet true, living Masters. I became aware of my powerful inner connection with ancient India and my deep inner longing to travel there. I asked Dr. Stojanović if he knew anyone in Novi Sad who did Past Life Regression. I felt like it was time for me to undergo one such session and get some answers. He recommended Ljubica to me and gave me her number. I was at her home the very next day.

Guidance From my Higher Self

The experience that I had with my higher self during the session conducted by lovely Ljubica remains a source of inspiration and insight to this day. It was unlike anything I have experienced before. I came to Ljubica's humble house in Novi Sad during a heavy thunderstorm. It was pouring rain outside, but inside her home was complete peace. I did not know till then that Ljubica was a quadriplegic. She suffered a spine injury during a massive car accident when she was in her 20s. When we met, I first listened to her amazing story, with the added dramatic soundtrack of heavy rain and thunder outside.

"When I woke up in the hospital without feeling in my legs or my hands, I did not want to continue living. I was into sports, a sexy, tall, dynamic young woman, and then this nightmare happened.

I broke up with my fiancé right away. I did not want anyone's pity and I wanted him to move on with his life.

"Every day, for ten years, I contemplated the method by which I would commit suicide. I was on the edge of doing it, but something always kept me alive. It felt horrible to live in a prison of one's paralyzed body. The only solace I found was in reading spiritual books. At that time not much spiritual literature was available in Serbia, but my friends helped me get some books from Osho. I lived and breathed those books. They saved me. That's when I started discovering my interest in communing with one's higher self through the modality of Non-Hypnotic Regression. This was something completely new in former Yugoslavia at that time, but I was persistent.

"I have been doing this for many years and really enjoy it. I discovered my higher calling and it restored my faith in life and the higher meaning behind all our experiences, no matter how painful they may feel. I also realized that I had died by suicide to escape from this burden in many past lives. In this life, I finally managed to overcome that trap. There is no greater mistake than to take one's own life. Nothing is resolved and the karmic lessons become even more harsh."

While Ljubica was talking, my vision spontaneously blurred and I saw her face change right in front of me seven or eight times. I told her that I saw the face of each of the embodiments that were ended by her own hand. I was so happy that she found her higher calling and felt truly honored to experience my first ever Non-Hypnotic Regression with someone like her. I also felt that I knew her from before – that familiar feeling when no introduction was needed, as with Sinke, Marija, and many other people whom I met later on, especially Mohanji.

Once we were ready to start the session, I got into a cozy and warm sleeping bag on the floor. I could hear Ljubica's voice from her propped-up position on the bed. She guided me through an induction process during which I eventually found myself in a lovely garden and I was asked to begin describing what I saw. I answered her prompts without any effort or thought. Even though a part of me was aware that I was lying down on the floor, 90% of me was engaged in a different reality. At some point, I felt the pull to step up on a garden bench and sit on the backrest. After that, the next clear intuitive guidance that came made no sense to the logical mind, but that was no obstruction in this so-called alpha state of mind. I was asked to surrender and push against the bench with my feet to roll back into the unknown. A huge leap of faith was needed to do this. It was an incredible test of surrender, something one would normally never do. But I did it. Instead of hitting the ground, I was falling. I kept falling in complete surrender.

At some point, I felt that I landed gradually and gracefully on a hilltop. I could not see my body but felt that my presence was expanded and very radiant. I felt how magnetic my presence was and realized that the radiance I was emanating was golden in color. I could feel in 360 degrees around me how many people, from all directions, were moving towards me, slowly climbing that hill. There were hundreds, if not thousands of people. I could feel all of them within me. I could feel their essence. This state of oneness and pure love was beautiful beyond words. It's not that I felt love, I was BEING Love.

Only when the first person came in front of me and looked at me, a beautiful woman with brown eyes, did I realize what my task was. I simply stood there in my super high frequency of purest love and whoever looked into my eyes would suddenly experience the "A-ha!" moment, their eyes would light up even more and they would remember everything. After that, they would pass through me into the Light. The joy, the bliss of oneness that I was experiencing, was beyond words. I was so expanded, sensitive, and loving that all of these people felt like a part of me. There was no separation. It was as if different parts of me were coming to me, remembering the truth of their being, and then passing through into the Light. This went on and on. There was no question of getting tired of the ever-new joy with each soul finding its way back into the remembrance, truth, awareness, and bliss of their being.

A man came before me, but I saw no reflection of my golden light in his eyes. He could not see me! My frequency was too high for him, or shall I say, his frequency was too low, too gross. The heaviness of guilt and hatred that he carried inside blinded him. Blind to my brightness and deaf to my telepathic guidance, he started moving away from me to my right. I realized that there was a camouflaged cliff in that direction. An absent-minded person could easily miss seeing the precipice until it was too late. I could also feel the presence of dark spirits luring people to the edge of that cliff. It took me only a fraction of a second to become aware of all this and to start emanating the strongest possible telepathic warning signals. "No! Don't go there! It's a trap! Can't you see me? I am right here! Don't go there!" But it was all in vain.

The pain of that experience was unlike anything I had ever experienced before. In that state of utmost sensitivity, my usual defense mechanisms failed. When I loved, I gave all I had, and when I experienced pain, it was infinitely deep. It was unbearable to get torn apart like that. This man was like a part of me that was now being torn away. Endless tears flowed like rivers, wetting my hair and filling up my ears. My sobbing and gestures of pain signaled to Ljubica the agony I was experiencing in my physical body. She tried guiding me to return to my post, to focus on my mission, since there were so many other people who desperately needed me.

Eventually, I managed to gather myself and restore my inner balance. My golden, expanded presence continued with its divine task and, one after another, souls were experiencing remembrance and bliss, passing through me into the Light of their highest potential – until another person who could not see me appeared. The same scenario repeated and I was being torn apart with unbearable pain. The only comparable pain would be that which women experience in natural childbirth when the pubic bones separate to allow the infant to pass through the birth canal. That pain was multiplied many times over and felt through the entire body, especially the heart.

When Ljubica saw me entering that horrific pain zone again, she opted to slowly pull me out of that experience and close the session. At some point, I opened my eyes and noticed how wet my hair and ears were. I had never wept this much in my entire life. "What on earth was that?!" I asked Ljubica. I had expected to see some past lives.

Ljubica replied that this was a very important message from my higher self. She said that I was predisposed to reach very high states of consciousness, and through those states, hold space for people to enter into elevated states of consciousness, remembering their essence at the soul level, way beyond the mind. Such powerful presence cannot be remembered unless it already happened before and/or is destined to happen in this lifetime. However, to operate at such a level, there was no room for sympathy, only empathy. There was no room for trying hard to "save" or persuade someone who was not ready or who was yet to work out some karma through certain painful experiences. Ljubica said that understanding of higher karmic laws was required to accomplish my highest calling. Maturity and equanimity were a must. This is what my higher self was showing me.

Words fall short in describing what that experience meant to me and how much it changed me. Indeed, it was far more meaningful than any visions of past lives. I revisited the feeling of this expanded state many times. What I experienced in this profound process of Non-Hypnotic Regression remains ever-fresh and vivid. It is not like some dream or fantasy that slowly fades away. This is a direct, powerful experience that remains like a bright lighthouse during any dark, stormy night of life. Ever since then, whenever I caught myself trying to save someone not ready to grasp deeper spiritual topics, I would immediately be reminded of the essence of the message from this experience. Whenever I felt I had a real treasure to share, something that would help the person in front of me, I learned to first see whether that person was genuinely interested. In other words, I understood what Jesus Christ meant when He said, "Cast not pearls before swine."

It is also this experience that I connect to and invoke whenever I conduct group meditative processes. Recalling that state and serving as an instrument of that sacred energy began in 2017. When I enter such an expanded state with the purest of intentions for all participating within the group energy, I must admit that this is where I truly feel "home." This is where the real me shines forth. Conducting group meditative processes such as Group Mai-Tri blessed by Mohanji, Awakening Yoga Nidra, The Light Beyond, Awaken the Goddess in You Yoga Nidra, etc. gives me tremendous joy and brings me in alignment with my highest mission on Earth.

Similarly, when someone doesn't see me, doesn't understand me, or even talks badly about me, I don't attach much importance to it. I just recognize that it is not their time yet. I never chase people to subscribe to my version of the best path to God. On the contrary, I hold space for the Unity of all paths, especially in terms of their respective value for those specific souls who vibrate with that particular path. In other words, when someone is truly and fully on their path, I feel happy for them. I rest in the simple awareness that the brightest of all the lights is at the top of the sacred mountain of all our spiritual endeavors and longing. That brightness on top is the One, the Source that is the same for all – God, Allah, Parabrahma, whatever name human minds choose. Our destination is the same, only our paths and the speed with which we progress vary.

I realized over time that the crucial phase of travel along any path commences only after there has been a period of consistent connection with the Source. This is when the travel shifts to cosmic speed and progress happens without movement, without doing, in complete surrender of pure beingness. It is then that one grows in leaps and bounds. The role of a Guru, an elder, a guide, an accomplished one, whatever the name for one's ultimate guide may be – this is where such a role becomes invaluable and most precious. I shall return to that topic later.

Coming back to Rome, I spent many days discussing these newly discovered dimensions of reality with my beloved Marija. I soon realized that the powerful experience during this Non-Hypnotic Regression was a loving preparation for a massive experience yet to come.

Conscious Astral Body Travel

Certain experiences happen only when the time is right. Such is the dynamic of Grace. The inner expansion that I experienced with the blessing of St. Petka, plus the expansion during my near-death experience and non-hypnotic regression, were a mere preparation for what happened toward the end of that eventful year 2000, during my studies in Rome. This experience was so deep and powerful that it changed my life. It moved me, changed me, and re-wired me from within to the point that my entire life orientation became drastically different. The effect of that massive change became evident over time.

This entire experience started with a mere thought, a clear inner prompting that simply appeared in my mind one evening – to stare at the candlelight in a specific way. I did not know where this thought originated, but I had complete clarity that I was to place a candle in front of me at the height of my eyes and continuously gaze at it for as long as I could without blinking. Life had already trained me to listen to my intuition, so I didn't question it much. In any case, I loved staring at candlelight ever since my NDE.

When I felt that my eyes needed some rest, I would close them without losing focus on the candle. After staring at any brightness, it is normal that we see it in some color (green, pink, white, golden, etc.) when the eyes are closed. The point was to keep continuous attention on the light, eyes open or closed. Another thought came: while slowly inhaling and looking at the candle, I was to imagine that the energy of the candle's brightness was being inhaled straight into the center of my forehead. With my eyes closed, I would allow the light to settle within my third eye for a couple of seconds, then, on the exhale, I would feel as if I was exhaling that energy from my forehead back into the candle.

This beautiful cycle combining brightness and breath went on and on, for at least 30 minutes. I would open my eyes just a bit to see the light and inhale it into my forehead. Then, with eyes closed, I would feel the energy on the forehead and exhale it back into the candle through my third eye. It was already getting late, so I decided to lie down on my back and continue the process from my pillow. I was consumed by the blissful energy on my forehead, where I sensed a really strong vibration. As I continued gazing at the candle in the same way, at some point I remained with the brightness even though my eyes were continuously closed. The brightness took over and something powerful happened. I drifted into a blissful floating state up and out of my body. Later on, I learned that the right term for this experience would be astral projection or conscious astral body travel. At that time, I didn't even know that I had an astral body, let alone the ability to travel in it consciously.

I felt exactly the same as always – my identity, memories, everything remained, everything except the physical body. This state was different from the near-death experience, where I was just witnessing what was happening to me and slowly started detaching from all my memories, all the ties to my physical life. In this experience, I was not detached from anything but my physical body, which was somewhere below in a suspended state.

There was nothing scary about this floating state. I felt adventurous and curious, but very peaceful as well. Mind chatter was minimal and there was absolutely no insecurity. I simply found myself soaring like an eagle, way up in the air above a huge white surface. It was marvelous to fly like that. That was when I began to figure out how my "flying equipment" actually worked – it was being directed by my thoughts. When I thought, "I want to go up," my invisible vehicle would take me up without delay. When I thought, "I want to go faster," my being would respond instantly and go faster. I have no words to explain how liberating this felt! The spiritual version of my horoscope sign became my reality – I was soaring high like a majestic eagle.

After some time of enjoying this newly discovered state, there came a point at which I looked down and realized that the whitish surface I was flying above was a huge desert. Even though I'd flown incredibly high, I could see or sense a tiny dot on that whitish sand that somehow attracted me. I felt some sort of a magnetic pull to direct myself toward this dot. That was super easy. All I had to do was to think "down" and within a couple of seconds, I found myself landing on this beautiful, whitish sand. This may have been the Gobi Desert, but I can't say that with certainty. I just know that the sand was really beautiful, clean, and smooth and that it was an actual location on Earth.

What I saw upon landing was the most beautiful sight I have ever seen to this very day, one I will never forget: a majestic, bare-chested young yogi with a beautiful slim waist. His profoundly peaceful and radiant face was adorned with long, shining, dark brown hair. Even though he was seated on a royal chair embedded with many precious stones of different colors (ruby, sapphire, emerald, etc.), the beauty of his face, body, and overall presence surpassed any precious stone or luxury furniture item on Earth. This radiant, spiritually royal-looking yogi was seated in a lotus pose (*Padmasana*). His right palm was facing up and resting on the left, while the tips of the thumbs were touching (what is called *Dhyana Mudra)*.

It would have been understandable for the logical mind to start analyzing at that point. Surely it would have been normal to ponder the appearance of a yogi seated on a throne in the middle of nowhere, but my mind was blank. In the powerful presence of this yogi, oscillations of the mind could not exist.

I was simply mesmerized by the beauty of this yogi and kept staring at him in a blissful, thoughtless state. He was absorbed within himself and emanating the subtlest, incredibly loving energy. I was in total awe of his radiance and simply couldn't stop looking. I was absorbing his energy more and more, feeling increasingly peaceful and fulfilled. Along with the bliss and lightness, I also noticed a steady sense of expansion from within. With so much love in the heart, it was natural to expand. Essentially, it is love's nature to expand. What I felt was the most purified love. This was devotion, the love towards the Divine, the highest of love, which engulfed and overwhelmed me completely.

This young yogi seemed so familiar, but my mind could not reach that point in the unknown past. I was only certain that I knew him. After some time of simply enjoying his presence, a thought emerged from the ocean of my mind's stillness. The thought sounded like an eruption after all that perfect silence. "If I could only see his eyes." Deep inside I knew that the unique expression, the unique sparkle in one's eyes remained the same through all our lifetimes. So, the justification behind this thought was, "If I ever get the blessing of meeting this yogi again, at any point in time, even if in a different physical form, if I could only see his eyes, then I could be certain. I will always be able to recognize him by his eyes."

Immediately after that thought arose, he suddenly opened his eyes! Oh wow... I lost my breath upon seeing the unfathomable depth in his blissfully penetrating eyes. In this breathless state, I was absorbed into the universe of regal beauty within his eyes – the universe of compassion and unity consciousness, the universe of majestic presence. What I saw and felt in those eyes were universes, galaxies, and multidimensional realities, all gloriously flowing in eternal, harmonious motion. It was impossible to behold such a glorious vision and remain the same. The more I looked, the stronger my inner sense of expansion became.

This expansion picked up speed and intensity to the point that the balloon that was my previous state of existence was about to burst. I could either burst and dissolve into the unknown or stop the expansion and remain in the known sense of self. Later on, I was amazed to hear another spiritual seeker's description of their encounter with this yogi, in which he said the same thing: "When you look into [his] eyes, you can either become that or you have to stop looking because it's so powerful." That dazzling light and immense cosmic presence could not be contained within the boundaries of the ego.

Had I only known at that time what I know now, I would have never stopped at that threshold. This was my chance for dissolution, a stage beyond enlightenment. I could have gotten it right there, but it wasn't my time. I was not ready to withstand the intensity and power of that experience. Most importantly, I was not able to surrender fully to the powerful presence of this great yogi to endure the death of the ego.

What happened next was a clear telepathic message from the yogi, powerful words I will always remember.

"What are you doing here? You are not ready yet."

Yet! This beautiful word, so full of promise, became my favorite word and the powerful inspiration for my spiritual practice.

Zapped by this experience, I was not in a position to think or respond in any coherent way. My mind was too still for that. I simply held his gaze until I sensed a kind of farewell smile. The next thing I noticed was a sense of contraction from that vast, expanded state. I started contracting and moving backward until I landed back into my physical body.

My body started shaking and bouncing off the bed. My arms, legs, torso, head, my entire body was bouncing in some sort of energetic recalibration. After about a minute the shaking and bouncing stopped and my relaxed body sank into the softness of the bed. I was knocked out for at least 12 hours after that. My body needed to readjust after experiencing such intense, high-frequency energy. I remember that I totally missed the morning lecture and barely made it for an exam around 11:00 a.m.

It was challenging to shift back into the same old university life. I was blown away by this experience, but sadly had no one to share it with who could provide me with guidance or explanation. I could talk to Marija at least and that was comforting. This experience was worthy of my famous line, "Marijice, you won't believe what just happened!"

I was bursting with eagerness to understand what happened to me that evening. It was clear that this was not a dream. More than anything, I was intensely longing to discover the true identity of that youthful, royal yogi, and learn why he had summoned me.

My intuition told me that it was he who had arranged this meeting in the desert. I could not have reached such a state on my own, it was all his grace. It was a blessing just to be in his presence. I felt intuitively that the technique of staring into the candlelight came from him as well. I was so eager to understand what all of this meant, but the time was not right. Somehow I managed to refocus on my studies, but deep inside I felt I was no longer the same.

Another Life-Changing Scholarship

My blissful years of studies at JCU passed at rocket speed. By utilizing their summer sessions and transferring a couple of courses from my School of Tourism, I was able to graduate in three years instead of four.

While surfing the net during one of my long volunteer shifts in the Computer Lab, I casually glanced at some link advertising a full scholarship ($40,000) for a Master's Degree at the Kroc Institute for Peace Studies at the famous University of Notre Dame in Indiana, USA. I felt the inner pull to read more about it and had goosebumps all over when I read my own description within the list of the prerequisites for this scholarship!

"This can't be real," I thought. I felt that this scholarship was being served to me on a platter. I fulfilled all the criteria: experience of war (preferred), volunteering, work experience within the international community, excellent grades, etc. The only missing requirements were the GRE (The Graduate Record Examinations, a standardized admissions requirement test for many graduate schools, especially in the US) and a recommendation from a higher-level official or any respectable member of the international community. This information had my brain spinning. I was eager to complete my undergraduate studies and finally unite with Sinke, but on the other hand, this opportunity was so amazing that I needed to see it through.

That day, while enjoying a cappuccino at the Massi Café, I happened to speak to David, a lovely JCU student from the USA. I shared my discovery with him and one concern that I had. "I regret not making any effort to stay in touch with some of the higher-ranking members from the international community with whom I worked in Kosovo. I have no idea whom to approach about this recommendation."

David's reply came with a big smile, "Oh dear Biba, you need not worry about that at all. Our JCU President, Mr. James F. Creagan, is a Notre Dame Alumni himself, plus he used to serve as the U.S. Ambassador in Honduras, among other diplomatic roles. You can't get a better recommendation than from a respectable alumnus of that very university. Trust me on that one."

I could not believe my ears. I knew I was going to get that scholarship. I approached our lovely JCU President the same day and he said he would be delighted to write that letter for me.

Over the next two months, I studied as intensely as possible. I suffered a sore neck from constant studying in preparation for the GRE, on top of all my regular studies. It wasn't easy to have all of this squeezed into the final days of my last undergraduate year, but I did it. I passed the GRE successfully, submitted all the documents, and awaited the final reply.

My joy knew no bounds when I finally received a response. It was *déjà vu* of the first time I was awarded $40,000 three years earlier, except that this scholarship was for only one year of studies. (In fact, it was a year and a half condensed into one. A serious tempo of studying was to be expected.) My parents were delighted with the news and my father made an interesting remark. "You could have built a really big house just from the money you received in scholarships."

I understood where he was coming from. I understood how much the act of building one's own house meant to them, to the point that this was a measuring tool of worth in his mind. This was when I told him that, to me, this money was worth much more than any property. It was the money that came as empowerment directly from the Divine. This money was the wind beneath my wings, a confirmation of God's powerful support and love for me. My faith was strengthened a million times over.

I started researching more about the Kroc Institute for International Peace Studies and came to know that this scholarship came from an extraordinary woman. It was a part of $50 million, the single largest gift in the history of the University of Notre Dame, given by philanthropist Joan B. Kroc:

> Joan B. Kroc, widow of McDonald's Corp. founder Ray Kroc, was a passionate advocate of peace and a generous benefactor of the University of Notre Dame. From 1985 until her death in 2003, she contributed a total of $69.1 million to establish and support the Kroc Institute for International Peace Studies. [...]
>
> The Kroc Institute for International Peace Studies was inspired by the vision of Rev. Theodore M. Hesburgh, C.S.C., and philanthropist Joan B. Kroc of a world free from the threat of nuclear holocaust. During his 35 years as president of Notre Dame, Father Ted was a leading national voice for civil and human rights and the abolition of nuclear weapons. Joan Kroc was deeply concerned about the nuclear arms race and committed to world peace.
>
> Founded at the University of Notre Dame in 1986, the Kroc Institute focuses on research on a wide range of issues relating to peace and justice and the causes of violent conflict.[31]

31 https://kroc.nd.edu/about-us/history/

I couldn't wait to spread my wings at Notre Dame, but at the same time, a part of me was sad that my life with Sinke would be delayed once again. I did not tell him about the scholarship until I won it. Finally, I made the decision to present my options to him and let him decide what was best to do in this situation. My heart was filled with warmth when I received his reply. "Don't be silly," he said. "You can't possibly miss this kind of opportunity! It will not come again. Go and complete these studies as well. If we are meant to be together, it will happen after this additional year as well. I would never want you to miss such an opportunity because of me. Congrats! You are amazing."

Surreal Graduation Moments

There were only a couple of exams left before my undergraduate studies would be over. A lovely graduation event was planned by our university and I decided to invite my parents to come to Rome. To them, this was like flying to the Moon! They had endless questions for me. They had never traveled by airplane before, spoke no English or Italian, and were not sure what was to be done after going through customs. I was relieved to learn that the parents of a classmate from Montenegro were traveling on the same flight. Our parents would surely help each other navigate their grand adventure.

I remember sharing some basic words with my father who wrote them down to memorize.

Grazie - Thank You
Prego - Please
Buongiorno - Good Morning/Day
Buona sera - Good Evening

I could not welcome them at the airport because I had stayed up late studying for the final exam and was too tired to wake up early that morning. After my exam, I went straight to their hotel near the Vatican. I do not recall ever laughing as much when my dad recounted his experience at the hotel:

"We left our bags in the room and while walking toward the hotel's restaurant, I saw someone coming in our direction. It was the hotel maid. My mind was racing and I was thinking of the words on the list you gave me. When she came near, I bowed to her politely and said *Bonaparte*. But she gave me a really weird look."

I couldn't believe my ears! "Oh my god, Dad! That's not Italian for anything, that's Napoleon's last name, for goodness sake. And nobody usually bows in salute to hotel maids."

I shared this joke with all my friends and laughed about it a million times. It remains one of my favorite "Dad" jokes of all time. I love my dad, in all his innocent silliness. I told him, "Well, hats off to you, Dad. This one beats even the 'Mother and Child' recital moment from your childhood – by far!"

My graduation ceremony was conducted in an elegant Roman villa. It was so majestic and memorable that some moments were surreal. I did not know until the last day whether I would be lauded as Valedictorian and get to perform the speech or not. In the end, an Austrian girl turned out to be the best student in our class. Her final score was higher than mine by only 0.6%. I was grateful for this experience because it made me reflect deeply upon the very principle of competition. I realized that I did not mind at all being the second best. I studied hard to show gratitude for the generous scholarship I had been awarded by JCU. I needed no other recognition from them.

All in all, the graduation event looked and felt truly grand. My life turned a majestic circle and my diploma meant so much more than just proof that I had completed my studies. It was proof that my intention was pure and intense and that it was supported from above. The moment when JCU President James Creagan shook my hand, followed by Dean Pavoncello, with my beloved parents in the audience applauding, was truly memorable and deeply touching. No amount of gratitude could ever be enough for these two amazing men, the institution they represented, and their life-saving scholarship.

It was also wonderful to see Mom and Dad in the audience. Dad's head was held so high that he stood out from the audience. It looked as if he was following everything super intently, but I knew that he did not understand one word that was spoken. He was just being proud. And my Mom, my dearest Mom, had tears in her eyes. To pursue higher studies had been her greatest dream, a dream she never got to fulfill because her parents were not able to support her. Her father was overwhelmed by the difficulties and pressures of life and unfortunately committed suicide, while her mother resorted to alcohol. My dearest Mom had a tough childhood filled with many dreams she could not fulfill, even though she was very bright, disciplined, and hard-working. Tears welled in my eyes when I saw her face in the audience that day because I felt that she had fulfilled her dream through me. I felt truly happy I could serve as an instrument for that sense of satisfaction within her.

It was such an honor to make my parents proud. But more than anything, it was a privilege to hold the torch of hope and faith for all those who, like me, came from the shadows of victimhood and pain and simply started walking, started believing, and started co-creating a new reality.

Twenty years later, I had the magical experience of visiting John Cabot University once again. This was in September of 2022 and the occasion was the 50th anniversary of JCU (and nearly the 20th anniversary of my graduation from the beautiful university that changed my life). With great joy, I met some of the students from my generation and one of my professors (Diana Rich). I especially enjoyed meeting my dear Dean Pavoncello who became the new President of JCU.

I was amazed to see how much the University had expanded over the years. It was really sweet and truly surprising to hear from the then Dean and now President of JCU, Franco Pavoncello, that he was aware of what was happening in my life. "Yes, I follow you on Facebook," he said. I did not expect that a man of his generation would be active on social media, but that goes to say how different our reality has become. Moreover, he invited Mohanji and me to visit JCU and conduct a lecture for the current JCU students, when time permitted. Indeed, that will be such a beautiful way of closing the circle.

Returning to 2003, my next adventure would take me across the ocean to the USA. The University of Notre Dame University beckoned and the Eagle was ready to fly once again.

Chapter 6

Postgraduate Studies in the USA

Mother Mary Wider Than the Heavens

It was really interesting that, in all my research about the postgraduate program at the campus of the University of Notre Dame in Indiana, USA, I had somehow missed key information – the actual meaning of the French words *"Notre Dame."* It had never occurred to me that the campus was named after "Our Lady." The only explanation was the play of the Divine. Perhaps that was the most effective way to reveal to me the Grace behind this scholarship. Our Divine Father/ Mother knows that all children love surprises!

I arrived at the Kroc Institute for International Peace Studies in August 2003. After registration, the first thing I did was to go for a long, peaceful walk to familiarize myself with my new surroundings and imbibe its spirit. I soon came to realize why Notre Dame is ranked in the top 25 institutions of higher learning in the entire USA.

Wherever I looked, I saw breathtaking vistas – from Gothic architecture to stunning landscapes, greenery, sculptures, and state-of-the-art academic and student life facilities. It had a beautiful traditional feel to it, with a modern touch and student liveliness. At some point, I arrived at the famous Golden Dome, the symbol of the university. Though I had previously seen photos of the Golden Dome, standing below it *in vivo*, with rays of sunlight dancing on the golden aura of the statue of Mother Mary and the vast blue sky above it, had me gasping in awe.

Suddenly, a long-forgotten memory of a powerful spiritual experience around the end of my high school days sprang back to life very vividly in my mind and heart. This had been my first ever profound spiritual experience, but I had nobody to share it with and somehow it faded from memory. It was meant to resurface exactly at this time.

We were on a short high school excursion, exploring our cultural heritage, including some of the Serbian monasteries in central and south Serbia. I can't even remember the exact Serbian Orthodox monastery it was that we visited when this powerful experience knocked me off my feet.

While exploring the monastery, I left our group and intuitively felt drawn towards an area wherein I suddenly entered some sort of a strange spiritual state. I can only describe it as a zone in which sound became muffled and time stretched. Everything seemed to be happening in slow motion. My eyes registered an old nun in a long black robe and a beautiful, joyous five or six-year-old girl standing in front of her with a cute dress and a bow in her hair. I was admiring the encounter of two generations and two worlds meeting in a monastery. The nun was smiling at the girl and then turned her gaze toward me. She looked at me intensely and then slowly gestured “this way” with her hand toward a passage into an area that was most likely designated as restricted access.

I had no questions or any thoughts in my mind, I simply followed her cue. Led by my intuition, I bent down to protect my head as I passed through the low, cave-like passage. At its end was a special chamber emanating sacred energy. There were many glowing candles and frescoes painted all over the walls.

I will never forget the moment when I took a deep breath in, straightened my back, and simultaneously lifted my head. As I suddenly looked up, I beheld the most amazing view of a dome with a fresco of Divine Mother with arms wide open. In the Eastern Orthodox Church, this depiction is called *Bogorodica šira od nebesa* (Mother Mary Wider Than the Heavens)[32]. I have a feeling that the old nun could foresee that I was to have a divine vision of the Mother or perhaps even blessed me with that experience.

All I can say is that it felt like my entire being flew up and expanded in the embrace of Divine Mother’s open arms. I saw her as brightness spread over the entire sky, wider than the heavens. The hemispherical shape of the dome only enhanced the effect of expansion. When one bows down in humility while entering this chamber and then looks up toward this glorious image of the Mother, the feeling is equal to that of a dove being released from a cage. I felt instant expansion of not only my heart center but my entire being. This expansion was continuing and taking me into an indescribably blissful state.

My mouth remained open in the awe of the vision I beheld and endless tears flowed from my eyes. Tears were flowing, but I was not crying. This was the strangest of all the experiences. I never knew this was possible. It was unlike anything that had ever happened to me. Whenever we cry, be it out of sadness or gratitude, we have a bit of a runny nose and a specific inner sense of squeezing or pressure that brings out the tears. Or perhaps there is an emotion that touches us deeply and triggers the crying. But here, there was none of that. I was empty and had no thoughts. I simply raised my head and my being expanded as wide as Mother’s expanded arms. This state of expansion and rivers of tears continued for some time as I beheld the glory of the Mother, who is “wider than the Heavens” because her holy womb holds the one who in turn holds the entire universe.

This long-forgotten memory appeared exactly as I stood below the golden dome at Notre Dame, with the statue of Mother Mary in her luminescent glory. The same feeling came back!

---

32 Source: https://orthodoxwiki.org/Panagia_Platytera

“Panagia Platytera (Greek: Πλατυτέρα; ‘wider’ or ‘more spacious’) is an icon of the Theotokos, facing the viewer directly, usually depicted with her hands in the ‘orans’ position, and with the image of Christ as a child in front of her chest, also facing the viewer directly. Sometimes the image of Christ is contained within a medallion. Poetically, by containing the Creator of the Universe in her womb, Mary has become *Platytera ton ouranon*, which means ‘wider/more spacious than the heavens.’ This type is sometimes called the ‘Virgin of the Sign’ or ‘Our Lady of the Sign.’”

"Oh my god! Well of course – *Notre Dame* is French for Our Lady. How come I didn't get that before?! It was her, it was her all along, whose motherly love and blessing had protected me from assault, death, and all sorts of danger in Kosovo. It was she who had led me to the fulfillment of my greatest refugee dream and ensured the scholarships. And I now finally stand before the Holy Mother in all her eternal, golden glory."

These thoughts came with many tears of gratitude. I suddenly realized just how much I loved Divine Mother and how alive she was in my heart and consciousness. I stood there in awe of the blessings on my journey and the beauty into which it had led me. I was ready for the challenges ahead of me, aware of Mother's protection and blessing. Enjoying the sight of the Golden Dome would be a daily reminder of her blessings.

Down Came the Black Bird

Just as my UN experience in Kosovo was much more work and far less fun in comparison to the one in Croatia, my postgraduate studies at Notre Dame were a completely different ballgame than my undergraduate studies in sunny Rome. My days of long cappuccino breaks, socializing, and student fun were over. It was easy to be one of the top students at JCU. However, only the best of the best were present at the Kroc Institute for International Peace Studies. Out of many hundreds of applicants, only the most outstanding students won this super prestigious scholarship gifted by the noble Joan B. Kroc. And I was one of them. This was a merit-based tuition scholarship that also included a stipend for housing and living expenses, so all of our expenses were covered.

Aware of just how rare and prestigious such scholarships were, all of us arrived at the University of Notre Dame geared up for a great academic challenge. There were 21 of us and our countries of origin spanned the globe. Most were from countries riddled by conflict, bloodshed, and unrest like Rwanda, Cambodia, the State of Palestine, the Kashmir region in India, etc. I was the only student from former Yugoslavia. We also had outstanding students from other countries such as the Philippines, Mexico, Sri Lanka, Kenya, USA, Canada, Ukraine, Turkey, Kazakhstan, Thailand, etc. These students had significant professional or volunteer experience in a global setting, either in war zones or within institutions directly or remotely related to peacebuilding, global affairs, peace, justice, etc.

We were on a joint mission of studying peace. Peace Studies were the next level of Conflict Resolution, the studies of top-down, bottom-up, and every other possible approach to peacebuilding, to address global problems with an integrated mindset. We called ourselves "The Peace Bunch." We sure were a colorful bunch, stemming from so many diverse religious, secular, and philosophical traditions.

"Our mission is not to bestow dignity on others; it is to work tirelessly to provide everyone with the means to achieve a material and spiritual life that matches the dignity they already possess."[33] This was one of the key messages from Scott Appleby, who then served as the Dean of the Kroc

33 Source: https://keough.nd.edu/integra-human-development/

Institute for International Peace Studies. This message beautifully encapsulates the ethos of this institution that truly enriched our lives.

I remember that year as the time I challenged myself intellectually like never before, but I also had other life-altering insights and experiences. I spent many hours of continuous studying and endless research and essay writing at the main library. Yet, I must say that I learned the most from my fellow students and some truly exceptional professors. I would like to share one precious memory in that regard. This was the moment when the energy shifted within our little Peace Bunch, the moment when we opened up to one another and became deeply connected, like a real academic family.

This crucial moment happened within the depth of feminine vulnerability and the act of holding space for deepest pain to emerge within a safe, intimate setting. None of us saw that coming within a classroom. The trigger for this experience was a movie that we were asked to watch during our Gender and Violence class. The name of this movie was "Down Came a Black Bird." Our professor of Gender and Violence, Dr. Cynthia Mahmood, an authority in the anthropology of violence, an accomplished author, and a true hero of peacebuilding, shared with us that she would have to leave the room at one point during this movie. There was a part that was personally too disturbing to watch due to her own painful past experiences. However, she invited us to watch it in full concentration because we would have a thorough discussion of the film afterward. That raised our curiosity about this intriguing movie and we were soon fully engrossed in it.

The movie was about victims of torture from different parts of the world trying to put their lives together again with the help of a psychiatrist, herself a former victim of the Nazis (the brilliant Vanessa Redgrave). She was now running a refuge for torture survivors and people with Post Traumatic Stress Disorder Syndrome in Canada. She created a safe space for these traumatized people to come out of the victimhood bubble and open up within a space deemed safe for the casting out of their pain. Some of the scenes and stories shared are truly upsetting. What I found to be most interesting was that this shocking tale at some point came across as very real and surprisingly close to reality. Indeed, this movie is a tough, super intense, emotional roller coaster that can have a profound impact, especially on those who have trauma from torture or assault in their past.

At the end of the movie, we were left simply speechless, with teary eyes, still digesting the emotions that had overwhelmed us completely. This was when the real "movie" began. Our amazing professor, Dr. Cynthia started our own little session of casting out our innermost pain and trauma by sharing her story first, the assaults that she survived as a woman. Still emotional after the movie, all of us wept and were deeply touched, especially by how she eventually picked herself up and came out of the victimhood loop by teaching this amazing class on Gender and Violence, volunteering at a shelter for assaulted women, and expressing herself creatively through her books. She not only shared with us her pain but showed us the most effective way out. I have no words to describe what a deep impression her story had on me.

Her courage to step into such a deep space of vulnerability triggered the same in each of us. One by one, we started sharing our own stories. One student from Turkey shared how he had been tortured in prison. He said, "They hanged me upside down, with rope wrapped around my ankles. Then they beat me so badly... [He cried for a moment and all of us cried with him, before continuing] ...so badly that I can now say with certainty that I will never be able to have children."

Students from Cambodia and the State of Palestine touched us very deeply as well, but the details shared by the student from Rwanda, who was a survivor of the most horrendous slaughter of his people, the Tutsi minority (as well as the moderate Hutu citizens), by the majority Hutu soldiers, police, and militia, rocked us to the core. He shared vivid details of the Rwandan genocide of 1994. The unforeseen scale of brutality sent ripples of shock around the globe, but no country and no international institution bothered to provide timely intervention to stop the slaughter of civilians.

We sobbed as we listened to his story about finding his entire family within a roadside canal. Their bodies were dumped along with hundreds of other bodies. Entire families were killed most brutally in front of each other, on the spot, by machetes and rifles in the hands of their neighbors. Hutu gangs even searched out victims hiding in churches and school buildings, dragged them out, and killed them.

This was the first time that I realized how lucky I had been during all the wars and conflicts that ravaged the former Yugoslavia. "Oh, I could have been scarred so much more," I realized. Spontaneously, a healing session ensued after all of us had shared our stories and insights. We shared, cried, and hugged, opening up to the healing process by bringing back into wholeness those scattered parts of ourselves associated with the most painful memories. In the end, we felt truly amazing and blessed to be there and to have the opportunity to grow together in such a special academic environment.

When our professor Cynthia spoke about her healing process and how being of service to others is the only way to rise above the pain, it resonated with me very deeply and continues to inspire me today. She said that she thought she was healed after undergoing therapy for some time and that resuming her job meant she was back to normal. But from deep within, the dark shadow of victimhood continued to haunt her, attracting another similar experience. Beneath the surface of the conscious mind, which we know is only the tip of the iceberg, she was attracting the same frequency energy because that was something that still gripped her, something that she feared the most. In Jungian terms, that pain was still unintegrated, still in her shadow. This is why girls who, for example, are sexually assaulted by their fathers, very often by default and unconsciously, attract a partner who turns out to be abusive.

However, when therapy is effective in bringing this deep pain into the light of one's awareness, the patient finally starts to radiate a different energetic frequency. That is where the real work of maintaining the newly achieved frequency starts. The best way to do this long-term is to be there for others dealing with the same trauma. In other words, there is no better way to heal long-term than to help others by sharing our own traumatic experiences, volunteering, and serving others selflessly. This one moment of deep inner connection remains the most precious diamond from my postgraduate studies, something that translated into my present life.

Along with Carl Gustav Jung and his teachings about the Shadow, Dr. Cynthia Mahmood remains one of the people who has inspired me the most by sharing her journey from being broken by abuse to becoming a powerful advocate of women's rights through academia and volunteering. I am so grateful to finally thank her for inspiring me to immerse myself in the exploration of the most effective healing modalities and to combine them with group meditative processes and long-term humanitarian work.

This is exactly the pinnacle of my current work within the Mohanji Foundation, combined with hands-on selfless service through our ACT Foundation. I am excited to share more about this in a later chapter.

The Man Who Talks to Christ

One day during my postgraduate studies, a super powerful, deeply transformative experience happened most unexpectedly. I became friends with a young man (with an exceptionally high IQ) doing his Ph.D. at Notre Dame who was deeply intrigued by my war stories and experience sharing. He said, "I also receive deep intuitive messages at times. As a matter of fact, I have received one right now. I feel you should meet my special friend. His name is Ferdinand Roccanti. Have you heard of him?"

I shook my head, waiting to hear more about this man. My friend then shared with me the strangest of all the life stories I have ever heard, a journey that brought this man Ferdinand to the point of communing with Christ. Intrigued, I asked to be introduced to him. I never expected that this strange encounter would bring me to the point of closing the circle with one of the most powerful experiences from my past. I will let you guess which experience that would be as I share the story of meeting Ferdinand.

It was close to Catholic Christmas time when I was invited to this extraordinary man's home for dinner. My friend was amazed that Ferdinand, who hardly ever agrees to meet random people, welcomed me not just for a brief visit, but also for dinner. He confided, "This is very rare. Something huge is going to happen. I can't wait to hear all about it."

Arriving at Ferdinand's home address in the late afternoon, I was greeted by a very sweet and childlike man with gray hair and joyous blue eyes. Ferdinand's beautiful wife Barbara, slightly taller than him, stood by his side. As someone who enjoys seeing spiritual couples, loving partners who support one another through all the ups and downs on the path, I felt great joy upon seeing the two of them welcoming me at the entrance to their beautiful home. I could feel their purity and warmth straight away. When I entered the house, I was captivated by Ferdinand's paintings of Jesus, Mother Mary, the Holy Spirit, and similar subjects adorning the walls of their home. Though my friend had already told me that Ferdinand was a painter, I did not expect to see that many paintings. This was the first time for me to socialize with truly religious and also spiritual Catholics, so unique in many ways.

I loved the fact that Ferdinand was completely informal, and I especially enjoyed his childlike lightness. He played a nice tune for me on the piano and welcomed my spontaneous exploration of his beautifully decorated house. I was mesmerized by the paintings of Jesus Christ. After looking at them for a while, I told him, “Ferdinand, I noticed that Jesus was depicted with blue eyes in all the paintings except this one, where I see him with brown eyes. Can you please comment on that?” (In the Serbian Orthodox Church Jesus is always depicted with brown eyes and brown hair.)

Ferdinand replied with a childlike giggle, “A-ha! An excellent observation. Nobody ever noticed that before. I knew you were special!”

He then explained how Jesus once told him that people are too preoccupied with his appearance, the real importance was the consciousness that he embodied and the message to humanity that he brought forth. That is why Ferdinand was instructed to paint him with brown eyes as well, which is not common in the Catholic Church. The message behind that instruction was that eye color did not matter and should never be a point of division between different religious groups. However, nobody had ever noticed the brown color of his eyes in that particular painting, so he had never spoken about it – until then.

I was satisfied with that answer. I knew very well that every soul has a unique sparkle, a unique expression in the eyes. Our eye color, hair color, race, height, weight, etc. are all irrelevant details in the long run. They are impermanent. But the expression in the eyes remains the same. And in that sense, eye color does not play any big role. I could tell that something was going on and that Ferdinand was eager to hear my story, but whenever I asked him something, I noticed that he also enjoyed sharing his story.

Before engaging in a longer conversation, he showed me a special anointed oil of Mother Mary which he rarely shares with anyone. However, he said that, if I would like, he would be happy to apply it to the center of my forehead. He said that not many people can withstand that energy and there have been some who have even fainted in the past, so he would have Barbara stand behind me just in case. I thanked him and said I would be honored to be blessed through Mother’s consecrated oil.

Its fragrance was truly beautiful and noticeable the instant he opened the little glass bottle. When he touched my forehead with that oil, for a moment I became breathless and had a glimpse of the profound experience of expansion that I had in the past when I looked at the fresco of Mother Mary Wider Than the Heavens in that monastery in Serbia. This time the same vision came but from within, as if I looked up from within and sensed/saw her loving presence and brightness. It did not last for long but felt very beautiful.

When I opened my eyes, I noticed Ferdinand was smiling and observing me in a very curious way. He was happy that I could “absorb” that powerful energy so easily. I briefly shared with him what I had seen and experienced a decade ago at the Serbian Orthodox monastery. I also shared with him how amazing it felt to have tears flow like two rivers from my eyes without me crying. When I said that, his eyes started to beam with joy! He was even jumping a bit and clapping, saying: “Yes, yes, I have had the same experience! This is the first time I have met someone who experienced it as well. I even painted Mother Mary with this stream of tears flowing from her eyes and then the sacred oil flowed from this painting – look!”

He then showed me one of his paintings of Mother Mary and gifted me a card with that image. I was amazed and felt the same childlike joy and excitement in my heart. It was contagious! It was wondrous that we had the same experience even though we were not of the same religion.

We sat down and I asked him how he had learned to paint so beautifully. He smiled and said, "I didn't. I don't paint." He then shared his powerful story that left a deep impression on me. I will share it the way I remember it, but many of his testimonials and sermons can be found online as well.

Ferdinand said that he used to work as a car dealer in Florida because that was one of the rare jobs he could pull off without anyone noticing that he could not read. Things went downhill at some point and he spiraled into a Dark Night of the Soul experience during which he started contemplating suicide. As he sat in his car, he suddenly heard a heavenly, most loving woman's voice whispering, "Ferdinand! Ferdinand!" Glancing in the side mirror, he saw Mother Mary in white brightness, floating in the air.

"Unique. What else is possible?" I wondered. She consoled him and blessed him, gently bringing him into a state of complete stillness and bliss (similar to my experience with St. Petka) in which all the dark thoughts were wiped away. With Divine Mother's blessing, he then developed a knack for selling cars and miraculously amassed a fortune of five million dollars.

Blessed and prosperous, Ferdinand and his wife Barbara traveled to Croatia, to Medjugorje, attracted by the stories of apparitions of Mother Mary. I have to admit that while I had heard these Medjugorje stories, I never really believed they were authentic. It is natural for human minds to assume exotic and powerful experiences happen only in faraway places, not in their own country or community, or even in their own lives.

Secondly, the religious divide went hand-in-hand with the ethnic divide between Serbs and Croats, so as a Serb I did not feel much attraction to anything coming from post-war Croats and the Catholic Church. Because my soul's mission is unity, that barrier had to be broken at some point through a profound experience. And this is where Ferdinand came in. What this man shared with me was authentic and came with a powerful message for me to refrain from judgement and to always respect the faith coming from people's pure hearts, regardless of the frame of their religion or chosen spiritual path. This was a powerful lesson.

Ferdinand went up the Apparition Hill in Medjugorje and knelt by the pile of rocks where Mother Mary was said to have first appeared. After he sat for a while, palms joined and head bowed in prayer, he felt a very soft and delicate hand under his chin, gently lifting his head. As he raised his head, he saw the heavens open up. He beheld Mother Mary in bright whiteness, as big as the heavens. As he was describing his experience, it sounded like the description of my own experience in the Serbian monastery! I understood then why I was reminded of it when he had anointed my forehead with consecrated oil. Just like me, he couldn't talk, move or take his eyes off of her mesmerizing holy effulgence.

And then he said, "Tears were flowing down my cheeks, but I was not crying. They were flowing on their own." This powerful confirmation of the authenticity of my own unique experience, one that

I had never shared with others, touched me deeply. He said that Barbara shared the same vision of Mother Mary's luminous face, enormous, as big as the heavens, sort of transparent, white and bright with heaven's light. Only one more pilgrim saw it that day, all the others saw nothing, simply feeling a pleasant energy.

Ever since then, Barbara and Ferdinand started practicing sitting in silence for two hours every day. They would start praying to the Mother of God, repeating the same prayer again and again, until the mind was no longer involved (the same principle as mantra chanting in India) and silence took over. They also said that something immeasurable and indescribable had happened deep in their heart and soul that day that had changed them completely. (Mohanji has a beautiful contemporary term for that – "a software change.")

I have no words to explain how overjoyed I was to hear about Ferdinand and Barbara's experience. I could relate to it so deeply and felt so blessed to meet them. I felt we were " birds of the same flock." This is when Ferdinand's story went up a couple of notches higher in terms of the intensity and drama associated with real tests of faith.

One fine day in the early 1990s, Ferdinand heard Christ's voice in his head, followed by three most curious and shocking questions that left him speechless.

"Ferdinand, would you be blind for my sake?" Ferdinand did not know what to say to such a shocking question and simply cried like a child. He couldn't say no to Jesus, but at the same time, he could not muster the strength to say yes either.

"Ferdinand, would you be an invalid for my sake?" At this point, Ferdinand was weeping.

Finally, "Ferdinand, would you give away all your money for my sake?" All that poor Ferdinand could do was cry. He said, "I was crying like a person who just lost his whole family." His mother was next to him and she was already hysterical, really worried that her son would die from the stress and shock he was in.

At that moment, Ferdinand felt the presence of Mother Mary who came and said, "Take a tear and touch your mother's arm." After he did that, his mother became calm. The same was done for his sister and Barbara. They all became calm and relaxed. Mother Mary then said, **"**Little Ferdinand, I'm giving you my heart."

Ferdinand felt greatly empowered. He could say with confidence, "Jesus, do with me what You want."

That very second, he was stricken with a horrible neuromuscular disease. From a successful millionaire, he was reduced to a blind man in a wheelchair. This happened in 1994, approximately ten years before I met him. Jesus and Mother Mary would speak to him and tell him to which individual, church, or institution to donate money. His millions slowly started disappearing.

One day Jesus told him, "Ferdinand, go buy a canvas, paint brushes, and paint." Ferdinand did not ask why, but certainly was wondering what a blind man could do with those materials. After acquiring everything on his list, Jesus told him to hold a paintbrush and touch it to the canvas. The moment Ferdinand complied, he witnessed a miracle he could have never imagined – his eyesight returned fully and his hand was moving on its own, painting on its own. This is how all the paintings in his house came into existence. When a painting was finished and Ferdinand put down the brush, his eyesight would disappear again. This went on for quite some time. Eventually, his health improved and he returned to normal.

Ferdinand's inner guidance from Jesus continued. He said that for a long time, Barbara and he traveled, living out of the trunk of their car and fulfilling their divine tasks assigned by Christ's voice in his head. His only income, after giving away all his millions, would be from the sale of his inspirational, miraculous paintings.

All these stories were so interesting and touching that time simply flew by and Barbara was reminding us that dinner would be cold if we didn't gather at the dinner table. She had prepared a really beautiful dinner which we were all eager to enjoy.

Ferdinand added just one more point before the dinner. "The fun thing is that the instructions I would receive from Jesus and Mother Mary often did not make any sense to me whatsoever. But they surely made sense to the recipient of the holy message.

"For example, one time we were seated in an airplane and the voice told me to unbuckle and go to the woman two rows ahead, seated on the aisle seat, and tell her that her son is taken care of and will return home in two days. It was not always pleasant to do this. I never knew how the person would react to me as a stranger, but my faith had become strong and blind – I asked no questions, I just did as I was told. Every time I did that, the recipient of the message would cry a lot and feel moved in a way that only the Divine can move us."

Ferdinand looked deep into my eyes and said, "Well, my dear, this goes to say that I got one such instruction from Jesus for you, too. That is why we invited you for dinner."

My heart started beating fast and I asked shyly, "I am not sure I understood the message from what was said thus far. Is it yet to come, or…?"

And that moment, Ferdinand's blue eyes shone brighter and he raised his voice in a playful tone. "Barbara, dear, you can bring it in."

Before I knew what was happening, I saw his wife coming from another room with a big smile, carrying a cake in her hands. (I am catching myself crying while typing this.) She was not carrying just any cake, but *the exact cake* that I had dreamed my mom would make for me on my 14th birthday, at the height of my refugee sufferings – half brown fudge and half white whipped cream.

Ferdinand and Barbara were smiling and I was sobbing with tears of gratitude. I was honestly in total disbelief – never in a million years could I have imagined something like this happening to me twelve years later, on the other side of the globe. Like a curious child, Ferdinand clapped and said, "We can't wait to hear the story. It's OK dear, you take your time to calm down."

After I had shared my cake story with them, Ferdinand remarked: "Oh wow, Jesus and Mother Mary never cease to amaze me. I am blessed to hear so many amazing stories like this. Well, my dear, I hope you understood what Jesus conveyed here for you. He wanted you to know that the Divine hand never left you, even at the height of your sufferings. There is Divine Providence behind all our experiences, no matter how painful they may seem at times. You should always remember that you are a child of the Divine and that you are greatly loved. Do share that message with other people as well."

It was already late at night when I stepped out of their gracious home. Ferdinand and Barbara had many beautiful Christmas decorations in front of their home, with colorful bulbs in the shape of reindeer, Santa, and whatnot. Though there was deep snow outside, my heart was aglow with so much warmth and joy that I did not feel any cold. I felt incredibly grateful to Ferdinand and Barbara, two beautiful instruments of the Divine, for this unprecedented blessing. This experience truly expanded my horizons and strengthened not only my faith but my feeling of intimacy with the Divine as well.

Native American Spirits & the Blessing of Martha

A couple of months later, not far from the Notre Dame campus, I was destined to receive another blessing from a blind person in a wheelchair.

It all started with a complex essay assignment that kept me in the university's main library till 4:00 a.m. Several books were open around me and I was stubbornly writing away until the essay was complete. At that hour I was all alone in the library and at times I felt a strange cool breeze. Though I noticed it, I did not pay much attention because I was so focused on my essay.

At some point, I heard someone crying and sniffling. This went on for a couple of minutes, so I decided to investigate. After searching for a minute or so, I discovered an African American cleaning lady seated on the ground sobbing, her broom off to the side, with a computer screen in front of her. Placing my hand on her shoulder, I asked, "Are you OK? Can I help you with anything?"

She was surprised to see me at this odd hour and said, "Oh, I am sorry. Some evil spirit attacked me. It came from this screen. I know this sounds strange and I am sorry to bother you. But, you know, I am half Native American and I can sense spirits. I would prefer not to have this gift, but I can't do much about it. I am usually OK with them, but this particular one was mean."

I smiled and told her, "Don't worry. I have seen many strange things during my life, much more than you can even imagine. All I can tell you is that you are strong, you are powerful and the Divine essence is in you. You need not fear any spirit. For what? That spirit doesn't even have a body. Just realize how strong you are and brush it all aside."

She was staring at me as I spoke, and said at some point, "I see your energy. You are beautiful. The evil spirit ran off the moment you came here and started speaking. You are right, spirits can't do anything to us, but I was rather down due to some financial and marital problems, so he did get to me because I was low in energy. But I am OK now, thanks to you. I'm sure you felt all these spirits tonight. I can see your pupils are dilated. That means they were near you. But you are strong, so they couldn't get to you."

Intrigued by what she said, I went to the restroom to look at my face in the mirror. I was amazed to see that my eyes were almost black – my pupils were that dilated! I'd never heard of this before. When I came back to the lady, we chatted a bit more until she said, "I would like to thank you by introducing you to my mother. Her name is Martha. She is a very special soul, and you will enjoy talking to her. She became clairvoyant after her near-death experience. Would you like to meet her?"

I have always had a special fondness for Native Americans, but never had a chance to meet one. Feeling the pull to meet Martha, the two of us decided where to meet the next day so she could take me to her mother. I was very excited!

I was surprised to see that Martha lived in a very old mobile home. It looked more like a temporary housing solution than a home. It was obvious that they were poor. The moment I stepped into Martha's room, her eyes grew wide and with a glowing smile, she exclaimed, "I know you – you are the one with the long white hair and the slim waist!"

I did have long hair during my studies at Notre Dame and my waistline was always rather slim, because of my hourglass body shape. But it was clear to me that she was referring to me in a different life or different reality.

Before my mind had time to analyze what this could mean, she gestured for me to come closer to her and then pulled me into a most beautiful, long hug – that of dearest friends meeting after a long time. I was speechless, absorbed in instant love for Martha.

Her heart was overflowing and, as she kept gazing at/through me with her clairvoyant eyes, it was obvious that she was seeing so many things, so much so that her verbal expressions couldn't keep up.

In sheer excitement, she started clapping and screaming in a high-pitched voice. "Oooooh! Oooooh! You are going to be sooooo loved. You are a blessed soul! Oooooh! You will live in something like a castle. Ooooh, these palms of yours – they are a magnet for money. Sooooo much money will flow through them. This will not be your own money, it will be for some higher causes of humanity. You will not be attached to it and will never feel that you lack anything. Many shall benefit from it. So much love! What a light! Divine! Divine!" Martha's eyes were half closed, but her inner vision was full on.

I was completely dazzled by this unexpected outpouring and, after regaining my composure, managed to say, "And when will all of this be happening, Martha?"

Tears of joy were streaming down her face as the invisible slideshow of my future continued before her inner vision. She said, "God is going to guide you, my dear. You just focus now on completing your studies. As soon as that is over, just surrender, open your heart and follow the guidance. All will happen, God will guide you. Oh, you will be so loved – he, the one with a pure soul, will be there for you at every step, to love and protect you. You will melt in his love and will bear his child. He is a great soul, a golden being. You are blessed!"

She was so sweet, clapping and rejoicing about my future. I have to admit, I was intrigued by her prophetic words and they remain etched in my mind. I was not only deeply touched by Martha's words but also felt an instant connection with her at the soul level.

I thanked Martha and promised her that I will surely remember her when all this great money starts pouring in. No matter how far I may be, I would help her to come out of her financial challenges. She and her family became my family. I did my best to support them, volunteer for them, and be of help in any way that I could.

There was another lady from their community, a poverty-stricken former drug addict, coping with the challenges of being HIV-positive, uneducated, and poor. This lady, nevertheless, had the willpower to study for her final high school exam at the age of 45. It was an honor for me to help her achieve this noble goal. I always enjoyed helping people and now I found the right opportunity. I asked Martha to promise me that she would come for my graduation at the end of my studies, and she agreed. This most unusual trio would attend the dinner and final ceremony as my family members.

Ever since then, I began to notice that spirits were in fact present on the Notre Dame campus. I spoke with one lady from the Kroc Institute and she said that unfortunately, many of the buildings on the campus were built on unmarked graves of Native Americans, which was pretty common in South Bend, Indiana.

I researched a bit about Native American history and learned that the US government adopted a policy in the 19th century of forced displacement of self-governing tribes of Native Americans from their ancestral homelands in the eastern United States to designated Indian Territory west of the Mississippi River. This was called The Indian Removal Act. As a former refugee, I read with deep empathy about the forced displacement and ethnic cleansing of Native Americans during the "Trail of Tears," when thousands of Native Americans suffered from disease and starvation en route to their newly designated Indian reservations.

Thousands died from disease before even reaching their destinations, or shortly after. I came to know that 90% of Native Americans died from exposure to smallpox, measles, or flu and that they were deliberately given blankets that had covered people suffering from smallpox or measles. I pray that the injustice suffered by Native Americans, not to mention the former African American slaves, in the USA be acknowledged and rectified through sincere, organized governmental efforts.

At the Kroc Institute for International Peace Studies, there is an official acknowledgment that I appreciated at least as a gesture:

> We acknowledge the Kroc Institute's presence on the traditional homelands of Native peoples, particularly the Pokagon Potawatomi, who have been using this land for thousands of years and continue to do so. We recognize our own place in the history and practices

of colonialism and understand that our responsibilities extend beyond this gesture of land acknowledgment. We must also reflect on the University of Notre Dame's past, present, and future relationship with the original stewards of this land and actively pursue ways to amend this troubled relationship.

We also note that a land acknowledgment alone could be meaningless if it is not accompanied by active work to address the structural injustice and violence perpetrated against Indigenous people around the globe, both historically and currently. The Kroc Institute is committed to working to address these harms and to find ways to contribute to constructive transformation through our teaching, research, and peacebuilding efforts.[34]

Time Stops

My dear Marija wrote to me that she had met with Zdravko, our favorite astrologer. While they were chatting, she came to know that Sinke's girlfriend was pregnant. "I am sorry Biljka, I had to tell you this. I couldn't keep silent about it."

I checked with Sinke and he confirmed the news. It was not planned, but it happened, so he would soon be a father. This weighed heavily on me, but I could not say that I decided to break every connection with Sinke. Our bond was so strong that nothing seemed to break it.

I tried to ignore the situation and focus on my studies, which were so intense that I had no time for anything else. My only "me time" was Salsa dancing every Saturday evening at a nearby Mexican club. I loved to go there and dance for hours, even though all the local Mexican men were very short for me. They were up to my chest or neck, which made quite an odd pairing. However, they were such great dancers with intense joy in their eyes, that none of that mattered.

We occasionally had parties in one of the apartments in the building designated for our Peace Bunch. I was delighted to discover that one of the students from our group, Mirak from Sri Lanka, was trained in Latin Dance and was very good at it. I was so happy to have a dance partner! We had some fun parties, although very rarely because we were mainly focused on our studies.

I also discovered a great Korean Sensei in Taekwondo around this time and went to his martial arts classes three times a week. This training was super intense. I realized how much exercise helped me in improving my concentration and overall performance. I am really happy I made the time to stay active.

One day as I was walking toward the nice coffee bar within the bookstore near Kroc Institute, I saw a man holding a baby against his chest. The baby's head could be seen just a bit above his right shoulder. As this man passed me by, the strangest mystical experience overwhelmed me. This baby suddenly looked straight into my eyes and poof – everything disappeared!

34 Source: https://kroc.nd.edu/about-us/

That such an experience was even possible had never crossed my mind. I was baffled. Time stopped and everything around me was white as if I had entered a thick white cloud. All I could see were the intense eyes of this baby and the white fog. I could not breathe, blink, or move, and felt as if time was suspended.

Finally, a notification on my mobile phone interrupted this experience. The white fog dispersed and my reality was normal again. I took out my phone and was shocked to see a message from Sinke. The message read, "I am at the hospital. My son was just born!"

I had no idea how to explain this experience to myself except that it was a sign of some deeper soul connection with Sinke's son. The experience was way too strange and it was pointless to analyze it, so I just dropped it. Years later, while talking with a friend from Serbia who had visited a great Master from India called Sathya Sai Baba, I came to know that he had had a similar experience – everything around him suddenly became white like a thick fog and time stopped when Sathya Sai Baba glanced at him. I was happy to hear that someone else had such an experience. It surely left a deep impression. The issue was the interpretation of it, a topic I shall return to later.

My Talks in South Bend

Considering my "colorful" past, which many American people found exotic, I was invited to speak at a couple of events. There were many Catholic Churches in South Bend with a wide variety of names connected to Christ (Christ Saves, Holy Cross Church, Christ The King Church, etc.) that organized regular meetings and discussions that were attended in great numbers. I was invited to speak at a couple of those meetings. After my experience with Ferdinand Roccanti, I decided to cultivate openness to receive blessings from the Divine regardless of the religious institution. We visited a Sikh Gurudwara, The Church of Jesus Christ of Latter-day Saints and community, Amish and Mennonite communities, Baptist churches with great gospel music, Quaker gatherings, etc.

I was especially impressed with the experience at the Quaker gathering. They also had a church but instead of the benches like in Catholic churches, the seating arrangement was circular. All of us sat in a circle and shared our most intimate and most cherished experiences of Divine Love. Quakers believe that no particular ritual is needed to get in touch with God. I shared with them my experience of the golden ball in the heart, and how it had saved my life back in Kosovo. I was surprised to see that they seemed familiar with it, saying that this was something that all Quakers are aware of as it is part of their teachings. How amazing was that?

Another time I was invited to one of those Christian Churches to conduct a talk related to my experience of war in former Yugoslavia. This happened to be a day commemorating something important regarding NATO. I was amazed that the speaker before me was a pilot who flew the NATO stealth bombers over Serbia! "What an amazing synchronicity," I thought. I listened to him sharing his experience of sadness as he was bidding farewell to his wife and small child before he sat in that stealth bomber, not knowing whether he would remain alive or ever see them again.

Right after the round of applause that he received for his courage in service of a great cause, it was my time to speak. I was respectful but conveyed straight away that I happened to be at the receiving end of the bombs this man was releasing above Serbia in March of 1999. He looked at me in complete shock. I said that it surely took courage to fly a stealth bomber, but the Yugoslav Army could not target those sophisticated NATO aircrafts and that the real danger was on the ground for ordinary citizens like myself. I shared some of my experiences during the NATO bombing and my inner drive to serve the cause of peace. In the end, I received a standing ovation and felt happy I could convey a different perspective that touched their hearts. It was clear to me at that moment, I was an ambassador for my own country and it was a noble task indeed.

I loved the fact that people in America were generally very informal and open. Sometimes they surprised me with how little they seemed to know about Europe. For example, they could not distinguish between Serbia and Siberia, which I found really funny. One man was even amazed that I could speak more than one language. His amazement about this was so intense that it made me laugh.

In moments like that, I realized how many American citizens never left the USA and don't even own a passport. It's almost as if they live in a different reality than people outside of the USA. On the other hand, people from all over the world come to study and work (or visit) the USA to experience a truly superb multicultural environment. I also had the pleasure of meeting some exceptional scholars and, especially at the Kroc Institute, there were plenty of opportunities for personal growth through academia and a multicultural environment.

One day at the Kroc Institute we were visited by Archbishop Desmond Tutu himself, one of South Africa's most well-known human rights activists. He won the 1984 Nobel Peace Prize for his efforts in resolving and ending apartheid. He gave an amazing speech in the biggest hall on campus and the next morning our Peace Bunch had the immense pleasure and privilege of meeting him in private over breakfast. This informal meeting was beyond special. We spoke about some deep topics, drawing from his rich life experience.

During our Q&A session with him, I asked him about the meaning of suffering. He answered that suffering can play a big role in raising one's spiritual awareness. Even though one would never want to intentionally call for suffering to happen, when it does, it should be used to reach the naked truth about our own essence. He spoke about Nelson Mandela's 27 years of suffering in prison and how that suffering brought him to the inner truth, maturity, and courage needed to rise above hatred and the need for revenge or to blame anyone. His suffering ultimately led him to become his country's first black head of state and a spiritual inspiration to many.

I was especially touched by his personal experiences with The Truth and Reconciliation Commission. This was a truly innovative and brilliant restorative justice body that played the role of a court, but in a unique way. It was assembled in South Africa in 1996 after the end of the apartheid. It was chaired by Desmond Tutu himself, who played a key role in this spiritually healing setup meant not to punish, but to naturally bring out truth, forgiveness, and reconciliation. The Commission invited witnesses who were identified as victims of horrific human rights violations to give statements about their experiences during this public hearing. Perpetrators of violence were in the same room and they were also given the right to testify, as well as to request amnesty from prosecution.

One such sharing stayed with me. Desmond Tutu offered a detailed description of one of those cases from The Truth and Reconciliation Commission. He said that they invited a victim of violence to speak first. A brave South African woman shared the painful details of the torture inflicted upon her while looking into the eyes of the perpetrator of the crime. She shared how he assaulted her sexually and at one moment even placed her breast into a wooden drawer and kept opening and closing this drawer violently while she screamed in pain.

Desmond Tutu said that, while witnessing this scene, he prayed to God for a change of heart to happen. At some point, he looked at the face of the perpetrator and saw immense remorse. It was evident that this man was ashamed and that he regretted performing those violent acts. The victim's detailed sharing of all that he had done, in the presence of Desmond Tutu and all those people in the audience, really had a transformative effect. Darkness was released and humanness could be restored. In the end, with eyes full of tears, the woman looked at him and said, "I have now reached a point when I can say in all honesty – I forgive you." The man started sobbing and all of the people present in the hall had tears in their eyes. His transformation was evident and Desmond Tutu's prayer for change was answered.

"Wow, this methodology of restorative justice would do wonders in the Balkans," I thought. I felt truly inspired. Indeed, the South African example of breaking cycles of violence through spiritual transformation is a great learning experience for all humanity.

The Living Book That Changed My Life

Amid my daily essay writing, book reading, lecture attendance, etc. I managed to find the time to watch one exceptional movie called "The Whale Rider." I have never watched a movie that touched me more deeply. It is the story of a 12-year-old Maori girl from New Zealand whose ambition was to become the chief of her tribe and restore its glory. However, her grandfather, the tribal leader, was convinced that only a male child could perform this role. The depth of her connection with the whales and her readiness to dive into the zone between life and death stirred something deep within me. Ever since my vivid dream of a whale, there seemed to be some deeper connection.

After the film, I walked over to the bookstore cafe near the Kroc Institute. As I passed by some rows of bookshelves, I felt some sort of tickle on my arm. It was so strange that I simply had to stop and look into this. With my palm, I started following the source of this tickling sensation, slowly moving closer to its origin. My palm rested over a book with an orange cover. I took it from the shelf, to see the beautiful, radiant face of a yogi unknown to me, smiling from the book cover. *Autobiography of a Yogi*[35] was the name of this book and the author adorning the cover, with his childlike smile and glowing eyes, was Paramahansa Yogananda. Intrigued by the entire

35 The e-book version of the *Autobiography of a Yogi* can be found as a free PDF download online, but I recommend buying the actual paper copy and holding it in your hands so that you can really honor it. I also

experience, I was tempted to open the book to browse through the contents a bit, even though I had barely any time to read something just for fun with all my daily assignments.

Never in my wildest dreams could I have imagined what awaited me at that moment. As I opened the book casually, right there, on the left-hand side, I saw an image that I so longed to see for the last three years, ever since my conscious astral travel experience. There he was, my royal-looking yogi from the desert – in the same lotus pose, with the same slim waistline and long, glossy hair. His eyes were pointed upward in this image, but I could remember the expression in those eyes instantly. I remembered every detail of my astral experience, especially his eyes. I was so surprised and thrilled by this discovery that I lost my breath. Then came the wave of sheer joy and excitement, "Finally! Finally! I have found him. Or rather, he found me, in his unique way."

I finally got to see his name – "Mahavatar Babaji" was written at the bottom of his image. Everything slipped away – the cafe, the Kroc Institute, where I was, and what I was to do – nothing existed but my royal yogi and the joy of this discovery. I ran to the counter to purchase this book right away. I hugged it and held it close to my heart for a while. I was as happy as I could be.

A student from my group mentioned being stressed about the looming big exam, upon us in three days. This jerked me out of my joyous reality, and I decided to apply the brakes. Summoning all my self-control, I decided to hold off reading the book just until the exam was over. This was so incredibly tough considering how great my thirst was to discover everything about this yogi.

Three days finally passed and a week-long spring break was ahead of us. I politely refused the offers made by my Peace Bunch friends to join them for some fun travel to Chicago, New York, and other destinations. I told them I needed some time alone. I started walking around the campus in an attempt to find the perfect location for relishing my special book in total seclusion. I found a scenic lake. "This will do," I thought.

I do not recall ever feeling such great excitement and anticipation. I was so deeply and immediately engrossed in the book that I couldn't tell if I was breathing. I came to know more about Paramahansa Yogananda and his journey. I was amazed to discover that he lived the last 32 years of his life in America. One amazing synchronicity happened at that moment. Just as I was reading about the meaning of the word *Paramahansa* (The Supreme Swan), an actual white swan was blissfully gliding across the lake toward me. I had goosebumps all over my body as I felt my reality begin to merge with the book.

Yogananda explained that *hansa* literally means "swan," and the white swan is mythologically represented as the vehicle of Brahma the Creator. Since Sanskrit is an incredibly rich language with layers of multiple meanings, there is always more to the story. Yogananda explained that the sacred hansa is said to have the power of extracting only milk from a mixture of milk and water, which is why it symbolizes spiritual discrimination. Yogananda also revealed another meaning

recommend taking the time to read it very slowly, with full focus, just as I did over those seven days at Notre Dame.

of hansa (this time pronounced as *hong-sau*) which literally means "I am that." The actual, super powerful Hong-Sau technique for raising one's spiritual awareness (my favorite shorter spiritual technique), reached me more than a decade later under truly amazing circumstances, which I will share later in this book.

Paramahansa is a supreme celestial swan that hatches in the air and learns how to fly before ever touching the surface of the earth. This connotes a young yogi who reaches the highest states of consciousness before reaching the age of sexual maturity. Such a yogi is a fully realized soul, completely liberated from all bonds of this world. He has no worldly obligations and no likes or dislikes. He is also without any needs because he is completely immersed in God. These topics opened up a whole new dimension of possibilities in the human experience, of dimension that is rooted in consciousness. I was in awe.

Insights and revelations were offered one after another through this living book. Many stories finally made sense to me, like Yogananda's explanation of the deeper symbolism of the Adam and Eve story. I would not like to quote from it, but to inspire you, my dear reader, to read this book in its entirety. Indeed, this book is as special as it can be. Years later after I met Mohanji, he told me, "This book is a Guru. It has been blessed by the Masters and endowed with the living vibration and grace of Guru Tattva (the Guru Principle). It will enrich and transform the lives of all those who read it with an open mind and heart, just like the presence of a Guru does."

When I finally reached the chapter about Babaji, I couldn't hold back my tears. I was especially touched by the scene when Lahiri Mahasaya met Babaji. Just like me, when he met him, he did not recognize him, but could feel something deep inside, some sense of familiarity and awe. In the case of Lahiri Mahasaya, Babaji asked him to sit in a cave and then asked him, "Don't you recognize this cave? You used to sit here in meditation many times."

Lahiri Mahasaya's memory of past lives was gone, as is the case with most of us. So, he was just looking around and had to admit, "No, I don't remember."

Babaji then gently tapped him on his forehead to bring the memory back into his awareness. Babaji's next words were the most loving words that went straight to the soul, "I watched you over the ocean of space and time. I watched you entering your mother's womb. I watched you going through your childhood, your teenage days, and your married life. All this time I waited; I waited until I could see that you were ready to receive me."

I couldn't stop crying after having read that moment of most intimate sharing from a yogi's soul journey. I was touched beyond words and blown away. And then, my mind started bothering me with thoughts like, "Is it possible that you met this supreme, intergalactic Master? Yogananda and Lahiri Mahasaya are great yogis, but what could *you* have possibly done to deserve this kind of blessing?"

These humiliating thoughts and doubts were tormenting me. On the other hand, the knowledge that I gained from this book caused a deep shift within me. Something momentous had happened and I felt reprogrammed. After the astral experience, when the change happened at a deeper level, it was this book that brought it all to the level of the conscious mind, and closed the circle of that powerful, life-altering astral experience.

I had some discussions with our career advisor at Notre Dame a couple of days before spring break, but had now lost all interest in that kind of career. There were some job interviews already lined up for me in Chicago with some prestigious companies. I told the career advisor that I had changed my mind and just wanted to return to Europe. I did not want to elaborate further and tell her that I was now eager to go to India to learn the ancient science of yoga. My goal was now to be initiated into Kriya, described by Yogananda as a profound technique that speeds up one's karma and directs one's inner compass toward spiritual liberation.

After having read Yogananda's autobiography, I knew it then and there – my REAL journey had begun!

The mystical way in which this book entered my reality symbolized my new path in life – a path rarely walked upon, the path of aloneness on the way to our inner spiritual pinnacle. This is the path of self-realization, of full blossoming in all aspects, and the path of liberation from all the veils of illusion.

Indeed, this book was more alive to me than most people I had met in my life. I tried to share my immense joy about this book with some of my friends from the Peace Bunch, but I realized right away they would not understand me. There was no receptivity, no frequency match. Remembering the key lesson conveyed to me by my Higher Self during my hypnotherapy session with Ljubica from Novi Sad, I knew not to insist on conveying the depth of knowledge within this book to anyone who did not show keen interest from their end. This was my own profound experience and my own path. I learned to keep quiet and contain my excitement about the quenching of my divine thirst.

As I was going through the pages of Yogananda's book, many long-awaited answers finally reached me. Each time that click happened, I was deeply touched, overjoyed, and even ecstatic. I have to admit that, when this "click" happened within me, it fascinated and frightened me at the same time – the challenge had been recognized and now there was no turning back.

One particular insight from this book was instrumental in the formation of THE dream of my life – Paramahamsa Yogananda said that, aside from our sincere spiritual practice and selfless service to humanity, the fastest and most safe way to grow by leaps and bounds on the path of self-realization was to be in PHYSICAL PROXIMITY OF A MASTER. He said that, when we are continuously present near a spiritually awakened being, our aura (energy field) starts attuning to those vibrations, and the subtle impressions in the Master's muscle memory start to transfer onto us. This inner exchange at the subtle level, not to mention receiving direct answers to one's most burning questions, is the most effective and most transforming. Indeed, he said, blessed are those who can be in the *satsang* (company) of a Master daily – that indeed is one of the highest blessings one can receive in life.

Moreover, through this book, I learned of the great ocean of inner faculties that our Creator has endowed us with and, at least intellectually, I received an understanding of what it meant to "master the mind" and establish oneself at the apex of purest Truth, Love, Bliss, and Surrender.

Armed with the insights from this book, I was finally able to grasp what happened to me that evening in Rome when I hovered above a desert – that I was blessed to be in the direct presence of none other but the greatest of the Yogis – the immortal Himalayan Master, Mahavatar Babaji.

I allowed the goosebumps, tears, emotions, sensations of inner expansion, and whatever else came to just flow as I devoured the pages of this living book, oblivious to time, space, and physical needs. It was then that I understood the greatness of the astral experience that I had. To meet a Master of Mahavatar Babaji's stature is close to impossible. It was this experience that encouraged me to DREAM BIG, to ask for the impossible. The life experiences of the Masters depicted in Yogananda's autobiography gave me something new to aspire for, something TRULY WORTH IT – the full flowering of our inner potential, the fulfillment of a soul's ultimate quest – SPIRITUAL AWAKENING and liberation from all bondage related to the earthly experience!

I knew then and there that no other worldly goal could ever come close to this – once we bask in the glory of a majestic sunrise, the light of a lamp looks so sadly feeble. Fulbright scholars were lecturing at Notre Dame, my fellow students were dreaming of doctoral studies at Harvard and the like, and I suddenly became an alien among them, so not interested.

This book opened my eyes. I suddenly saw reality differently. I saw slavery to Ego all around me. I attended the lecture of some famous Fulbright scholar who had come to Notre Dame and saw the entire show. All of a sudden, I felt like I was seeing through him. He used humor to break the ice, then quoted Aristotle or some other great thinker from the past to demonstrate his erudition, and then used some impressive words to demonstrate his eloquence. However, in the end, there was nothing of his own that he could contribute, nothing that came from the depth of his heart and arrived fresh as a unique expression presented from the depth of his awareness.

At that moment, I gained clarity about what my goal in life was – to find the right spiritual practice and the right guidance to take me to the point when I would be able to move my ego to the side whenever I wanted and download knowledge or guidance directly from the Source. I aimed to deliver unique, authentic, pure expressions for the benefit of all, devoid of any second agenda. The moment such thoughts arrived, I felt immense excitement which caused high energy states and endless joy for no reason.

I did not even attempt to explain to my career counselor anything about my newly discovered ambitions. I knew she could never understand what had happened in my inner space after reading this book. My whole life suddenly made so much more sense to me and that was all that mattered. Yes, I knew then that THIS was the reason I had come to this world, this was the reason I survived all the obstacles of life including that of a near-death experience in 2000. I knew that I had found my next step, and I was ready.

On the other hand, I also understood the immense challenges associated with this journey – all the fears, inhibitions, wrong habits, confusions, mental constructs, social conditionings, and notions of identity and separation that stood in the way of self-realization. And yet, each one of us longs from deep within to somehow break through all the inner blockages and find our way to the "top of the mountain." I did not know how, but I knew that one day, I would walk with the Masters, the

Self-Realized ones. I would vibrate at their most subtle, most loving frequency and would serve as their instrument on Earth, expressing my love unconditionally.

My graduation from Kroc Institute for International Peace Studies finally arrived and as promised earlier, Martha, her daughter, and the woman I tutored joined me for my big day. It was truly touching when they arrived in a state of amazement. Martha's daughter told me, "We have been living here for many years, passed by this Institute many times, but it never occurred to us that we could ever enter inside, let alone be invited for a fancy ceremony like this. Thank you so much."

Mirak and I choreographed a nice Salsa to add a bit of spice to the event. Martha and the ladies were clapping very loudly and even whistling, which caused some polite, slightly reserved heads to turn. It was great to have my Native American family with me for my graduation. My heart was full. I left Notre Dame with a great sense of fulfillment. The tempo of my studies had been tough, but I learned a lot and experienced so much. I was truly grateful for this tremendous blessing.

My only regret was that our Peace Bunch, generation 2003-2004, never got to thank Joan B. Kroc in person. She died from cancer a couple of months after our program began. May my sincere prayers of gratitude to this extraordinary, generous woman reach the spirit realm as the light that takes her ever higher into eternal bliss.

Chapter 7

New Life in the New York of the Middle East

Disillusionment

The spiritual high of graduating from Notre Dame and discovering *Autobiography of a Yogi* did not last long. Martha's prophecy amazed me, but she had said nothing about the thorns on the path of roses. Their first pricks came as soon as I returned to my "new home country," now called Serbia & Montenegro, as the name Yugoslavia had been completely discarded. After all the intense experiences I had during my studies in Italy and the US, it felt strange to be back in Serbia. I went to live with my parents and grandparents who were fully settled in Novi Sad. Within a week, I became completely disillusioned.

My love life was a disaster. Four years of undefined, long-distance love with Sinke had started to weigh heavily on me. Whenever we spoke on the phone, I realized how preoccupied he was with his newborn child, which was understandable. He shared with me how he and Helena had hardly slept since their son's birth, and he even arranged for me to speak to Helena a bit in an attempt to initiate a friendship. All of it felt very odd, no matter how open-minded I was. I could not come to terms with the fact that he was now a package deal, three for the love of one.

In my wishful thinking, I projected all that Martha had said about my special partner onto Sinke, and it hurt terribly that our relationship was now crumbling. In the way that I had discovered the pitfalls of my own fortune-telling, this experience too was revealing yet another danger of fortune-telling, and I lost my taste for it.

Any clairvoyant, no matter how clear their inner vision may be, can see only one option of our future and one possible timeline. Still, our destinies are not written in stone and the interpretation of the vision could be wrong. What's more, predictions about our future can increase expectations, and enslave us to our minds. Instead of living in the present and making the most of it, our attention and energy are fixated on the future in anticipation of the desired experience.

Martha had never specified when my life with that special man who would "looooove me so much" would happen. It was I who had projected that prophecy onto Sinke. I was sure he was that *one and only* super special man, but the big balloon of my fantasies and expectations burst without any warning. I felt completely shattered.

My professional life was also in shambles. I went for a couple of job interviews but realized that my fancy Master's Degree from the USA did not mean anything back home, especially without connections. I became bitter, wondering why I even bothered to study so hard when I could not get a proper job in Serbia based on my merits alone.

Evidently, certain life lessons of great importance simply have to be learned the hard way. To get my mind off my idealized and unrealized love from Zagreb, a love that turned platonic, I embarked on another relationship in Belgrade. Needless to say, since I entered that relationship for all the wrong reasons, while the bond with Sinke was still very strong, it quickly led to an unfavorable ending. This was a mistake not to be repeated. After all, who could compare to my great knight Sinke?

I knew the relationship was over the moment this fellow proudly exclaimed: "What meditation means to you, marijuana means to me. Essentially, it is the same thing – we are both looking for some sort of deep relaxation and a way out of the pressures of life. And I better not see you doing that outside, sitting under the tree like some Buddha looney. I don't even want to imagine what would happen if any of my friends saw you!"

The aggression that I sensed in this was ringing all my alarm bells. It did not take long to realize that we were "perfectly incompatible" and I ended this relationship before it even started properly.

I decided to mention this experience because, after two decades on the spiritual path, I have noticed this strange dynamic in couples. When the frequency of one partner (usually the woman) rises significantly due to a healthy lifestyle, spiritual practice, and social service, her partner may be inspired to follow along, and they support each other on the path. This is beautiful to witness. However, it unfortunately also happens that the partner not only rejects the spiritual path but develops arrogance and even aggression in the presence of her higher frequency. It is as if his ego is provoked by her new sense of purity and annoyed by her higher purpose. Her new, more refined frequency triggers his anger, and he then does his level best to prove that she is not so "spiritually advanced" after all. Things get even worse if the husband has issues with alcohol or substance abuse. There comes a point at which such relationships cannot be maintained. The woman feels they are no longer compatible and, culture permitting, opts for a divorce. That surely would have been my destiny with this man, had I even considered continuing with that relationship.

That silly escapade made things even worse for me emotionally and, in my desperation, I returned to entertaining the thought of traveling to Zagreb and giving it a try with Sinke, Helena, and their son. "After all, it's just for a couple of days, just to see how that would feel," I thought.

This is when I met a woman who played a huge role in my life. She was truly an instrument of Sai Baba during critical crossroads and challenges on my path when very important decisions were to be made. I always called her Dr. Maja (pronounced "Maya"), even though her full name was Andjelka Majić. She was an amazing spiritualist who had survived many challenges in life (including leaving a toxic marriage with a partner whose ego was triggered as described above, a marriage in which she almost lost her life), and eventually excelled in holistic healing.

Beginning in her teens, she had astral experiences through which she received the most loving guidance from a great living Master from India called Sathya Sai Baba. She then wanted to become a Catholic nun, but he guided her to study the world's religions and expand her horizons first. She remained his sincere devotee all her life. Until then, I had never met anyone as "real" as Dr. Maya. She truly lived what she preached, and her very presence was powerful.

Dr. Maja was an expert in Homeopathy, Radionics, and Marine Biology. She played an instrumental role in healing more than 30 women from breast cancer and helped many other people to overcome their health challenges through awareness and homeopathy. My sister Dana was one of the people who benefited immensely from Dr. Maja's help. After a year of suffering and loads of allopathic pills, she was finally healed from a horrible bacterial infection through Dr. Maja's treatment.

Dr. Maja's gift was to look a person straight in the eyes, listen intently to their story, and identify key stumbling blocks at the root of their health problems. Her own troubled life and high spiritual sensitivity had turned her into a well-centered empath, able to guide people back to their center.

Intrigued and inspired by Dana's healing story, I decided to meet Dr. Maja in Belgrade, and join her at a spiritual occasion, an exuberant Peace Pole Planting ceremony in Belgrade. Peace Poles are planted at various locations on Mother Earth in a way similar to acupuncture at the planetary level, to awaken and uplift human consciousness. This movement aims to spread the Universal Message of Peace, *May Peace Prevail On Earth.*

While Dr. Maja and I enjoyed tea together in the divine afterglow of the event, the topic of my troubled relationships arose. When I shared my plan of giving it a try with Sinke and his family, she looked me straight in the eyes and said: "My dear, in the triangle of a man and woman at the base and a child at the top, the child draws its vital energy and stability from both parents. Where do you fit in? That child has its mother and father. Why are you meddling in there?"

This succinct appraisal triggered something in my inner space. Clouds dispersed, and it became suddenly clear how ridiculous it was to even entertain the thought of going to Sinke. I decided to move on.

Dr. Maja opened my eyes to many truths. The story of her divorce from the father of her children who had turned into a vicious enemy was sobering. Our lives can be altered, positively or negatively, through our relationships. We should choose our partners wisely, and only after connecting with and understanding ourselves at a deeper level.

When Sinke and I were still messaging, I mentioned to him about Sathya Sai Baba and a devotee of his whom I had recently met, and who had impressed me greatly. I was dismayed by what he wrote: "Oh, Yogananda is ok, but Sathya Sai Baba – absolutely not. He is a demon, trust me. He has his demonic army on the astral plane. Stay away from him."

His message was hard to digest. Sinke's words didn't match up with what I heard about Baba from Dr. Stojanović, or what I learned from Dr. Maja, whose life had been completely uplifted and transformed by Baba, and most importantly, my own intuition. My heart sank, and I had a sinking feeling in the pit of my stomach. For the first time, I questioned Sinke as my spiritual authority.

One day I even had a vision that he would force me to subscribe to his truth and his path, hindering my spiritual growth. My essence would attempt to escape such a scenario, but the intensity of our connection would not allow me to leave Sinke. My soul would not want to waste time, and a terminal illness would have to develop in my body to make a hasty exit. This vision disturbed me, but this is what I intuitively felt after Sinke spoke those dark words about a great Master and embodiment of purest love.

Indeed, Sathya means Truth, and He is That. It is tough to face the truth, but it is the bitter pill that saves one's life. Several times in my life, the test of truth, be it related to a person or an important life decision, was somehow connected to Sathya Sai Baba. Was the situation before me aligned with my highest truth? Dr. Maya taught me to listen carefully and await the inner response. There should be a resounding YES at all levels of my being. There should be five yeses, not just the one from a mind ruled by desires.

I was pondering my path in life, just as in Kosovo, when my special African American friend Rob entered the scene to play a big role once again. He called to check on me one day, asking about my life after graduation. I told him the truth – that I was miserable and utterly lost. Teasing me in his usual witty style, he suggested I go to Dubai, "the New York of the Middle East," and try my luck there. He had a buddy there who needed an administrator or office manager.

When I found out that Dubai was not too far, only a two-hour flight, from India, I was ready to accept. I would take any decent position in Dubai just to get out of that rut and move even a tiny step closer to the fulfillment of my dream.

Living La Vida Loca in Dubai

My relocation to the New York of the Middle East was exactly the boost I needed. My cosmopolitan spirit of adventure was back, and it felt so good. I had a new goal as well – I was on the lookout for Kriya, a Guru, and a spiritual practice that would raise me to higher consciousness. Only a couple of days after I arrived in Dubai, my spiritual journey began with a spiritual technique called Sudarshan Kriya.

I was not aware at that time just how many different Kriyas were available on the spiritual market. This was the onset of my three-year-long journey with the worldwide spiritual movement called The Art of Living (AOL). I became very involved with their activities in Dubai, attending every possible meditation course, and fun *kirtan* (musical worship) events with *bhajans* (devotional songs). And I traveled as often as possible to AOL's main *ashram* (spiritual center) in Bangalore, India, steeping myself in India's ancient spiritual wisdom.

During an event in one of Dubai's many tall buildings, I met an American named Henry who used to work for the State Department before starting his own logistics company. He said, "Wait a minute. Aren't you the woman who translated the meeting with the Serbian Orthodox Patriarch a couple of years ago in Kosovo?"

I was astonished that he remembered me. Of course, I recognized him as the State Department representative at that meeting. It turned out that Henry was the friend with whom Rob had discussed setting up an office in Dubai, casually mentioning that I was a Notre Dame graduate. "Well, we sure need an office manager. Working for a startup is challenging, but you are welcome to join us."

I was thrilled! Of course, I was not afraid to work and loved the challenge. The company grew fast and all the new employees were joining the company through me. In the end, when the villa in which this company operated was furnished and ready, and a dozen new employees had joined our team, by default I was promoted to Director of Administration. I was earning my highest salary ever, with full freedom to employ whomever I wanted. I brought in my dear Marija – I knew she was smart and diligent, as well as my sister Dana. She was feeling stuck in Serbia after years of a marriage that did not go anywhere and needed a fresh start. I even arranged an amazing job interview for her then-husband, but he did not feel ready to leave the comfort zone of his family's business in Serbia. In the end, they divorced. A friend of Marija, Aleksandra (Belka) from Belgrade also joined our merry group.

Rob had leased a huge residential villa not far from Jumeirah Beach, and the four of us stayed with him. Rob was always introverted. He suffered from sleep apnea and since he never slept properly, he would often doze off in front of the TV. Since we were very informal and accepting, our cheerful Serbian mentality and youthful spirit suited him. He also knew it would make me happy to have my best friend and sister with me. We did perform our job to the best of our abilities and were professional at work, but with Americans, Rob especially, it was all so casual and relaxed that we never felt the burden of the corporate world.

For almost two years, our joyous group of Serbian ladies and an African American friend lived in that villa by the sea in Dubai. We traveled to India several times for various spiritual courses and training. Dana and I completed a scuba diving course. Marija and I went salsa dancing. We walked and meditated at the beach together, trained Tae Kwan Do together, and shared many unforgettable experiences that deepened our friendship and bond of love many times over. This was our time to enjoy being financially independent and open to all the fun of life. We were so blessed to live and work together, embracing the infinite possibilities and experiences of life with openness and gratitude.

The Sathya

At the time, The Art of Living played a big role in all our lives, but deep inside I sensed something was missing. My many fun activities kept me too busy to sincerely look within and admit my true feelings. It wasn't until May 2006 that the opening into real experiences appeared. This opening was spearheaded by Dr. Maja and the energy of Sathya (the Truth) that emanates from her being.

Dr. Maja arrived in Dubai in April 2006 as our guest and brought with her what was at that time one of the latest discoveries in the field of holistic medicine – the Gas Discharge Visualization (GDV) Aura Camera (next-level technology from Kirlian Photography). Through mere fingerprints, this electronic wonder was able to show just about everything about a person who undergoes the screening – past, present, and signs of future health challenges, where one gets stuck emotionally or mentally; all of these are nicely imprinted within the layers of the human aura. Having a knowledgeable holistic doctor such as Dr. Maja to interpret the complex GDV readings was invaluable.

My aura scan was a real eye-opener. I realized that our standard allopathic medicine was merely patchwork – it never treated the root cause of illness, and most of the diagnosing could be reduced to guesswork. (However, if one breaks a bone, allopathy surely does come in handy. One has to respect that.)

How our emotions and outlook on life impacted our health fascinated me. Dr. Maja was able to identify the link between one patch of cellulite on my left outer thigh and my painful emotions during my refugee days. She also warned me about my thyroid.

"Right now, your thyroid is still fine, but if you continue like this, within six years you will most likely develop hypofunction of the gland. You have to examine yourself. Where is it that you are not living your truth? Where are you not fully authentic and aligned with your truth? Identify that and dare to make the necessary changes. Otherwise, your body will not be 'in ease,' which leads to disease. That imbalance will remind you of the changes you did not make and the truth you do not live."

Whoa! This diagnosis landed like a bomb. While I was comfortable with my job and happy about my income, I could not really say that this was what I had dreamed of becoming in life. After hearing what Dr. Maja had to say, I increased my introspection. I was not yet living my highest truth, but I was already attending Yoga Teacher Training within The Art of Living's system and equipping myself with powerful tools and breathing techniques.

I will never forget the moment when I brought Dr. Maja to our office to scan the auras of some of my colleagues. That day, Henry happened to be present at work, though he was usually traveling. Introducing Dr. Maja to Henry, I was once again the bridge between two worlds. Dr. Maja stared into his eyes without blinking, seeing God knows what, as they shook hands. Henry smiled and said, "And where are you from?"

Continuing to stare into his eyes, Dr. Maya replied dramatically, "From God!" Oh goodness! This was not going in the direction I expected.

Henry replied, "Mm, right. OK." and found an excuse to disappear.

Dr. Maja could not be controlled. She didn't care about exchanging pleasantries or engaging in any type of superficial conversation. She was a free bird, living her truth and doing what she loved. I was not in the same position. It was not easy to connect her with the meat-eating, beer-drinking Americans in my office, so I realized it was better not to linger there.

Of Rob, she said, "Be assured, he is not doing you any favor by having you girls stay with him in that villa. He is feeding off your youthful shakti energy. I could feel that straight away. Change your accommodation and you will see that you will feel much lighter and much more energetic than now." While I knew there was some truth in what she was saying, I was glad she did not say this to Rob in person.

Aside from her aura screening and holistic healing work during her stay in Dubai, Dr. Maja had another adventure in mind – to go to India and screen the auras of several enlightened Masters.

Her goal was to compile enough scientific material for a book through which she would explain and depict the changes that the human aura undergoes as a person evolves spiritually.

Naturally, I was fascinated with the project from the moment she started talking about it. Returning to my office job groove after my inspiring conversations with Dr. Maja was a real challenge. A few days later she startled me with the following suggestion: "Why don't you take two weeks off from work and join me for this trip to India? I need someone to help me carry all the equipment, take the notes, and most of all, share the fun."

I was speechless – but what a blessing! I jumped at the opportunity! There were no obstacles on the path – my leave from work was approved (Rob was forthcoming as always), the visa was acquired, etc. Everything was resolved so smoothly that I knew without an iota of a doubt that, yes, I was destined to go with Dr. Maja! "Enlightened Masters of India – here I come!" My joy knew no bounds.

The Indian Adventure

The first Master we met was Hira Ratan Manek from Calicut, Kerala, who practices what is called Sun Gazing, done within one hour of sunrise or sunset. Hira Ratan Manek was the first Yogi to agree to undergo testing by NASA scientists to prove that he indeed lived off only the sun's energy and required no food whatsoever. They tested him for three months, collecting readings from electrodes attached to his body 24/7.

He was a mighty presence – a tall and sturdy man, with a striking resemblance to a Native American tribal chief. A man one had to see to believe. I was dazzled and speechless, especially when I realized his entire family relied on the sun alone for sustenance. Nevertheless, our kind hosts prepared some snacks just for us. They were very sweet and showed us how they only drink a glass or two of water per day, but this is energized water, exposed to the sun on their terrace and kept in a big glass container.

While Dr. Maja was doing Hira Ratan Manek's aura scanning, I explored the apartment a bit. I was drawn to a framed image hanging on the wall of Hira's living room, a peculiar image of a yogi with a golden ball on top of his head and eyes that were rolled upward. There was another golden ball next to that golden ball, which could have been the moon. "These are either two moons or two golden balls, but only one is exactly above his head as if emerging out of his crown. How mysterious," I thought.

The more I looked, the more I noticed certain odd details – the yogi's fingernails and toenails were more than an inch long. He had been in a deep meditative state for a very long time, considering the length of his nails and hair. He was very thin and his ribs were protruding. His belly was drawn in, and his long hair and beard were curling up and intertwining with the bushes, leaves, and roots around him. He was seated in *Padmasana* (Lotus pose). I kept getting the vibe of Mahavatar Babaji. "Oh my God, could this be him?"

Just as the thought crossed my mind, Hira Ratan Manek came toward me and said, "Oh, do you like it? Who do you think that is?"

I replied, "I feel it is Mahavatar Babaji because thinking, in this case, leads nowhere. There is nothing logical about this mystical image."

Hira smiled and said, "I am really happy to see that you have recognized the great Babaji even under such disguise. I don't think any of my visitors ever recognized him from this image."

I was humbled and asked, "But why are there two moons there?"

Hira then explained how this image came to life. A man walking through the forest in the Himalayas saw two full moons with his own eyes. Since this defied logic, he decided to take a photo of it. When he returned home to develop the photo, he was amazed to see the image of this great yogi.

I took a photo of this image with my phone's camera. Hira also shared with me that it was Babaji who had imparted to him the technique of Sun Gazing, telling him that many people could benefit from it, especially those starving and dying from hunger in Africa every day. If they only knew that all they needed was the sun to be completely healthy and balanced!

Hira said that the technique is very easy: one is to stand before the rising sun (or the setting sun, but rising is best) when the sun's rays are diffused through the atmosphere and are not harmful to the eyes. The feet should be on the ground or sand, not on concrete, and not in shoes. The eyes should be rolled up in *Shambhavi Mudra* (as if looking toward the third eye) so that the white part of the eye absorbs the sunlight. Every day the length of time spent Sun Gazing should be increased a bit. When one can sustain 42 minutes, the body will no longer require any food. It will obtain all nutrients from the sun to function in a balanced way – no food or supplementation is required.

"This is mind-blowing. Indeed, so many people are dying from hunger and malnutrition, while the greatest source of nutrition is right there before their very eyes," I commented. I wanted to share with Hira how much my experience with Babaji had changed my life, but there was no time because the discussion went back to aura scanning.

Upon bidding farewell to Dr. Maja and me, Hira Ratan Manek gifted me *Divine Romance*, another book by Paramahamsa Yogananda – as if he knew what Yogananda's first book meant to me! I took this as a subtle sign, a confirmation that the Masters were bringing me closer to them. My heart was full!

It was no coincidence that the next extraordinary spiritual person we met was Sri M, a yogi and spiritual guide who was also active in the field of education and social reform. It was wonderful meeting Sri M. I was overjoyed when he mentioned some of his experiences with Mahavatar Babaji and his direct disciple Babaji Maheshwarnath (who was mentioned in *Autobiography of a Yogi* as the one who guided Lahiri Mahasaya to a golden palace materialized by Babaji, to help him overcome certain cravings related to gold and wealth).

Sri M was writing his autobiography at that time and said that some of his spiritual experiences were so surreal that he was not sure he could even include them in the book. Yet, he knew that he would be guided to the right words and right timing for the book. When he bid us farewell, he waved his hand, smiled, and rolled his eyes up, an image that remains etched in my memory.

I could feel the vibe of beloved Babaji and felt so grateful. Indeed, I felt as if I was following some invisible trail set by Babaji himself – it was such a joy and privilege to explore Mother India in this way. I felt truly at home.

After a few more adventures, we embraced the long-awaited peak experience – we headed towards Brindavan, the summer camp of Sathya Sai Baba (on the outskirts of Bangalore), the only location where he spent time apart from his official abode Puttaparthi. Dr. Maja was not sure whether she would be granted the opportunity to screen Baba's aura, but she said one thing was for sure – in His presence, everything would speed up, the right things would happen and the right people would come into her life...

Divine Play in Brindavan

We arrived at Brindavan, Sathya Sai Baba's summer camp near Whitefield, Bangalore, in a chaotic quagmire of noisy rickshaws. Rain had just begun to fall, simultaneously stirring up dust and turning the overcrowded streets to mud. A sea of people moved all around us and I almost didn't want to step out of the taxi!

I had no idea how or where to find decent accommodation, but Dr. Maja knew the drill. "Just watch," she said, then confidently exclaimed: "Baba – room! NOW!"

Before I had time to analyze, Dr. Maja ran out of the car and started marching through the rain like a little girl who had no idea where she was going. Within a few seconds, a Croatian devotee of Sai Baba suddenly appeared from around a corner. "Maja! What are you doing here?!" this middle-aged lady excitedly inquired. "Hey, are you looking for a room? There's a vacant room next to ours. Come quickly before it's taken. It's a madhouse here!"

Dr. Maya reeled with victorious joy, jumping and giggling, and declared with a radiant smile, "You see – it works! Instant gratification! You know, Baba always says: 'Why fear when I am here.'"

I so admired Dr. Maja's faith, courage, intelligence, discipline, loving heart, and child-like lightness. In many ways, she was my role model and this quality time with her meant receiving the blessing of her wisdom through her divine experience sharing. Of course, Sai Baba provided the perfect room to fulfill his child's need; cute and simply ideal for the two of us, the first of his miracles during our visit.

The next morning at 4:30 a.m. we joined the throng of Baba's devotees in the main Darshan Hall, eager to finally get to see Baba. After the ordeal of long lines, big crowds, and almost two hours of waiting, we welcomed Baba with great love and excitement.

He was so tiny and cute, I could not believe my eyes! In the photos I had seen, he had appeared a bit chubbier, but in person, he was somehow completely different. Loving energy surged within me as I stared at yet another giant in a tiny body. I fell in love on the spot, like a mother falling instantly in love with her newborn baby. We are helpless to react in only the most loving ways to Divine Presence because that which is pure and child-like within us responds spontaneously.

Dr. Stojanović's description of Sathya Sai Baba's huge golden aura came to mind. As the energy blazed within and around me, I knew for sure that what Dr. Stojanović had said was true – I could not see the aura, but I could feel it. I was amazed to see some people falling asleep during *Darshan* (the moment one's eyes see Divinity). Later on, Dr. Maja explained that those people were unable to withstand Baba's high energy because their energy meridians were full of blockages, and their minds were too active. They fell asleep to allow the system to integrate the energy and readjust. During those ten days with Baba, I too experienced drowsiness several times in the middle of the day. Dr. Maja just laughed and teased (in reference to my martial arts and yoga training), "And you thought you were in shape, huh?"

Each fun-filled Self-learning experience in Baba's energy field was supremely enriching, and I could not get enough. They were all necessary confirmations to my still-doubting mind that Baba knew my every thought and was there to guide me, cleanse me, and eradicate all the "viruses" that were slowing my "inner software" and preventing me from living my life with full vibrancy and joy. Whatever question I had would miraculously be answered through situations, experiences, dreams, or people that Baba used as his instruments. The whole *leela* (divine play) was a perfect combination of loving discipline and SHEER FUN!

Meeting Devi Amma

One blissful day in Baba's energy, Dr. Maja and I decided to visit Devi Amma, a great saint who lived near Baba's summer ashram. As we traveled to her accommodation, a mere ten minutes away by *tuk tuk* (rickshaw), Dr. Maja explained that Devi Amma had access to the Akashic records, the grand cosmic library holding the full compendium of all universal events. She knew my past, present, and future. Dr. Maja advised me to think deeply about what I wanted to ask her so that we did not waste her time on trivial matters.

While waiting for our private meeting with Devi Amma, I basked in the images of great saints and masters displayed on her huge altar. Overwhelmed with love, I closed my eyes, relaxed my head onto Dr. Maja's shoulder, and shed a tear of gratitude. At that moment, she quietly took a photo of the two of us in the reflection of Mahavatar Babaji's framed picture on Devi Amma's altar. In that highly symbolic picture, an image I will treasure forever, it looked like I was leaning on Babaji's shoulder.

I was overwhelmed with Devi Amma's simplicity and love when we finally got to meet her. In the precious time spent with her, she shared some details of her life, including her parents' reactions to her spiritual pursuits. From the time she was a child, she would cover herself with a "golden blanket" at bedtime, before falling into a bliss-filled sleep. She thought that everyone had this golden blanket until she realized in her teen years that she alone enjoyed that privilege.

Devi Amma's parents were actively planning her marriage, which was something she never wanted. When this issue escalated, she invoked the presence of a deity who manifested in the room in which she and her parents were seated. Her parents finally understood their child's divine mission and the marriage plans were halted by Divine intervention.

Devi Amma can travel to any location through consciousness, so she does not feel compelled to leave her home. Instead, multitudes come to her for blessings and guidance, and she attends to all of them with endless love and patience. She has no personal agenda, no expectations, holds no judgement, and welcomes all with an open heart as a pure instrument of the Divine, absorbed in Divine consciousness 24/7. Meeting someone who is completely self-sufficient and needs nothing from this world was utterly inspiring.

Both times that I met with Devi Amma (in 2006 and 2022), she was exactly the same, delivering herself unconditionally to the world. She has sat for decades in the same room showing no signs of boredom. On the contrary, she exuded ever-new freshness with her beaming smile, passing on the divine warmth in her palms, and offering heart-melting chants in her beautiful voice. She welcomes and blesses one and all who come to sit in her divine presence. Devi Amma, simple and pure, is nothing less than a Saint.

Devi Amma's main spiritual guide has always been Sage Agastya, the first of the 18 *Siddhas* (Perfect Ones). Agastya is considered the father of Siddha medicine and is held in very high esteem in India. He is a famous *Saptarishi* (the seven mind-born sons of Lord Brahma, led by Sage Vashishtha, the guru of Lord Rama) and one of the most revered *rishis* (Revealers of Divine Knowledge) in India. His name is mentioned in many sacred texts of Sanatana Dharma (the Eternal Truth) such as *Ramayana*. His lineage includes the Sage Patanjali (the originator of Yoga) and Valmiki (the author of the *Ramayana* epic). Agastya and his beautiful wife Lopamudra are also the celebrated authors of some hymns in the *Rigveda* and other Vedic literature.

It blew my mind to meet a Saint so deeply connected with Sage Agastya. As a devoted disciple, Devi Amma communes with him regularly. Their connection began when she was fifteen. He appeared before her when she was enduring a lot of suffering on the earthly plane and simultaneously great bliss and infinite consciousness on the spiritual plane. She shared with us how challenging it was to have one leg in this world, and the other on much higher planes of consciousness. Such a delicate balancing act was not easy to sustain. With the help and guidance of the great Sage Agastya, Devi Amma eventually managed to settle into the body properly and function in full harmony, sharing the nectar of higher consciousness and pure love with everyone.

I had no questions for Devi Amma; I simply wanted to soak in her loving presence. As she caressed my palms lovingly, Devi Amma surprised me with the revelation that I had healing power in my hands, and it was only a matter of time before I would begin using it. At one point, a question emerged about my great love from Croatia, Sinke, and whether I had any duty to his son. I couldn't shake the feeling that I was connected to the child ever since my time-stopping experience at Notre Dame. She replied adamantly, "No. That child has his mother. You have no duty or obligation to him."

I then relayed to Devi Amma how heavily that relationship weighed on me and how defeated I felt in terms of my love life. She looked at me intently, and smiling mysteriously, said something that amazed me: "My child, the Masters have somebody special for you..."

She said nothing more, but those words were enough for me to finally blow the clouds of Sinke-idealization from my inner sky. Something deep within me clicked, and I finally created space and opened myself up to higher possibilities. If that was all that Devi Amma ever did for me in my life, it would have been enough for me to love her forever.

Sai Baba's Astral Visit

One evening Dr. Maja and I ventured more deeply into her intimate spiritual experiences from the past, whispering in our room until late at night. I was deeply touched by all her experiences and admired her even more. That day we bought a lovely CD called "Gayatri Mantra" (one of the most powerful mantras of the *Rig Veda*), chanted by Baba himself, with the sound of birds and flowing water in the background – simply awesome! His voice had such a distinct color and clarity – I never knew Baba could sing so beautifully.

We fell asleep immersed in the sounds of Gayatri Mantra. That night I dreamt about a spiritual man I had met in Dubai (in my waking life) and whose company I enjoyed. Although married, he developed a strong affection for me and grew eager to spend private time with me. We walked together along Sheikh Zayed road with eyes semi-closed, holding hands, focusing on our spines, and breathing in *Ujjayi* breath (a technique of elongating the breath by constraining the passage of air through the throat). This kind of walking, with awareness on the spine and breath, was very blissful.

Being single, I was free to spend my time with whoever I pleased, and I enjoyed my long walks with him in Dubai's warm evening air. He was mature, gentle, and subtle – someone with whom I could talk about spirituality. Deep inside, though I knew where our occasional walks and talks could potentially lead, I did not do anything about it. And now, in Baba's energy field, all my unconscious and wrongful acts were surfacing. He was like a loving parent, asking us to see ourselves in the mirror and become better individuals.

That evening in my vivid dream of this man, he had returned to India from his business trip to Dubai (during which he enjoyed a loving walk and interaction with me) and lied to his wife, saying that he preferred to sleep alone due to his spiritual practice and active inner world, with no mention of the feelings he was harboring for a certain someone in Dubai. She was a very dedicated housewife and seeing all this, I suddenly saw him in a completely different light. I realized it was wrong to allow anything more than spiritual discussions and friendship to exist between us.

I was suddenly jerked from this vision by Dr. Maja shaking my arm, exclaiming: "Wake up! Baba was here just now in his astral body! He illuminated the entire room! Didn't you see it? Without thinking, I just jumped with my astral body into his ocean of Light! It was amazing! I can't believe you slept through it."

I got up in shock, goosebumps all over my body, seeing with my own eyes that the whole room was still vibrating/glittering with energy. Sadly, that is all I saw from Baba's visit to our room. I felt miserable, but I understood right away – I was not yet eligible to see him. His light would have been too bright for me. My inner space needed further cleansing. Moreover, I understood that I needed to work on my purity in relationships.

While discussing this with Dr. Maja, I said, "You know, ever since I moved to Dubai, I have been quite pleased with my life in all dimensions except one – my love life, i.e. relationships. Somehow I'm just not able to find the right person for me. I'm not even searching. Or maybe I am just expecting too much."

It was then that Dr. Maja gave me the most important advice of my life. "You can create him, but you need to have clarity. Especially now, while in Baba's energy field, you can manifest just about anything if you have clarity on what you want. Sit down right now, and write down in bullet points what you want in the right person. Create him here and now. And then submit that request to Baba humbly during the next Darshan. Once you read it out to him in your mind, have full faith that he will bring exactly that special someone into your life. Have no doubts, ask no questions like how, when, or where. When you plant your seed into the ground, if you keep on digging it out to check on it, it will never sprout. Just let it be – have full faith in Baba, and enjoy your life. I assure you from my own experience – it will happen!"

Planting the Seed of My Highest Dream

I followed Dr. Maja's advice and, after deep introspection, wrote the following on a piece of paper before we left for the Darshan:

Dear Baba, I would like my life partner to be:

- ★ Highly evolved spiritually, like a Master, but unassuming. Zero pretense, please.
- ★ I don't care much about the looks, but he shouldn't be clumsy – slightly sporty, skilled in everything he does, and a natural leader (after all, I am from the Balkans, and we tend to like strong men).
- ★ Our relationship would be for the HIGHER CAUSE of selfless service, not mere human needs.
- ★ We are to touch many people's lives, empower them, and help them grow.

It felt so good to submit this to Baba – I bowed humbly and prayed deeply, handing over this paper to him mentally, covered with my tears. I felt great relief and knew that the "seed" of my "Prince on the White Horse" had just been planted.

As advised by Dr. Maja, I dropped all doubts and questions about this matter and allowed the Universe to work on it while I focused on cleansing my inner space further. After some time, I completely forgot about it. Since I aspired to become a yoga teacher, I decided to drop my Salsa and Martial Arts classes and focus my full attention on yoga. My office work and Yoga Teacher Training preparation filled up my schedule.

The Mighty Spiral

Spending time in the expanded presence of Sathya Sai Baba was truly wonderful, but little did I know that this would change my life completely. As soon as I returned to Dubai, everything in my life that was not built on higher truth started to fall away. With time, I understood that, unlike the physical journey which is linear, the spiritual journey is a spiral.

When one meets a powerful Master, let alone an Avatar (the Divine Incarnate) of the stature of Sathya Sai Baba, life can never be the same again. Karma speeds up, and the spirals on our path grow smaller. The frequency and intensity of karmic lessons increase, along with the speed of spiritual progress. On the level of worldly comforts, that is not good news. To many people who visited Sathya Sai Baba, that kind of purification showed up as turmoil in their lives. But from the level of higher awareness, the speeding up of karma and coming closer to spiritual liberation is a rare blessing.

The spiritual path brings the highest joy and opens one up to the mystery of life and to blessings that exceed any expectation our minds can produce. Counter to the spiritual path is the comfort zone, where no spiritual progress is possible, period. We crave comfort, but once we get it, comfort/routine dulls the spirit and no progress is made. Boredom settles in, especially if there is no selfless service on the horizon. Along with boredom, there is lethargy and escapism that opens the door to addictions. I have observed this truth in my own life and the lives of many other people.

Soon after I returned from Sathya Sai's abode, I entered a tornado of events that caught me off-guard. The company I was working for started to sink into bankruptcy. Because I trusted Rob and Henry, I was there to help them out in any way, including the purchase of some airfares on my personal credit card. We stopped receiving our salaries but were told, "Nothing to worry about, all will be paid eventually."

I fully trusted and believed my friend and my colleague, without a moment of doubt. However, after six months without a salary, we came to know that Henry had fled to the US, the company did indeed go bankrupt, and Rob even was in jail briefly until all the pending utility bills were paid! This came as a real shock. I was not even halfway through my monthly car payments, and the bank was calling me every month about my credit card debt. The bomb called "bankruptcy" destroyed our comfortable life in Dubai in a flash.

I applied for various jobs, but nothing was coming through. I surrendered my problem to Divine in desperation and resolved to do social service for a few days. On the third day, a friend from The Art of Living told me that he knew of an Australian landscape architect who urgently needed an administrative manager. I went for an interview and landed the job on the spot, invited to join the office the very next day. "Wow, just like that!" I thought. I realized once again the power of social service. When we serve without asking for anything in return, by default we enter into the frequency of abundance and leave all victimhood behind. The grace reflects in our physical reality in only a matter of days. This has been my direct experience.

My new job paid less than my previous position, which was to be expected, but I was very grateful that I had a stable job and a fresh new start.

The Life-Changing Yoga Teaching Experience

While people across the globe were celebrating New Year's Eve 2007, I was preparing for the yoga teacher's exam at The Art of Living Ashram in India. Yoga asanas were no problem for me, but the Latin anatomical and physiological terms and Sanskrit asana names made my head spin. My teachers demanded excellence and in the end, only a third of my class passed. I was elated to make the cut after more than 30 days of intense training. I was a certified Yoga Teacher at last!

I returned to Dubai eager for rest and relaxation after my program's wild tempo, but that was not to be. My cell phone rang the moment I landed – it was one of my friends from The Art of Living. "Biba, I heard you passed the test. Congratulations! Your timing is perfect! Two days from now, for the first time in the history of Dubai, we'll hold a Mega Yoga Course at the Shangri-La Hotel. One man donated the money to rent a big hall. We are aiming at 350-500 people in attendance. You must be one of the five teachers conducting the course."

My exhaustion vanished with this amazing news and without even unpacking my suitcase, I got straight to marketing and organizing the event. The preparations for this massive gathering were incredibly hectic, especially in addition to my day job at the office. Thankfully, my excitement and enthusiasm kept me energized and able to give my best.

The beginning of our event was glorious. A senior Yoga teacher from the US arrived to lead the program, doing all the talking while I demonstrated the postures on stage. Occasionally I would move through the crowd to correct postures when and where necessary. While mingling with the crowd of about 350 participants, exactly when I expected it the least, an exceedingly pleasant energy caught my attention. The feeling was hard to pinpoint, but I found that just being near one specific individual was... perfectly enjoyable. He seemed completely absorbed in what he was doing; the happenings around him could not distract his singular focus. Every now and then, our group paused briefly to meditate and deepen the experience of asanas. At each meditation, it turned out that I would find myself near this man again, basking in his energetic field.

While at work the next day, one of my Indian colleagues who was participating in our event, asked if I could give him a ride to the Shangri-La Hotel after work. On our way to the hotel, I shared a few apprehensions I had developed about The Art of Living over time:

"I enjoyed and benefited from all the AOL courses, but I feel one thing is missing. I don't get to do real *seva* (selfless service) – what they call seva amounts to marketing work for AOL, distributing the flyers and volunteering during workshops. I want to experience real, hands-on seva. I want to truly serve the needy, the poor, and the helpless people."

My colleague said, "Well, there is one man I thoroughly admire, who has a charity foundation called Ammucare. He is doing exactly what you're looking for. His name is Mohanji. I can introduce you to him tonight if you'd like."

I spent most of that evening demonstrating postures on stage and forgot to approach my friend about the introduction to his role-model Mohanji. I remembered the next day and decided to learn about this man Mohanji and his charity foundation on my own. The very instant I clicked on

Ammucare's website, my cell phone started ringing. I looked at the screen, but nobody was calling me! I was perplexed – it was ringing continuously, but nobody was calling. How could that be?! I was surprised to realize that the background music of the Ammucare website was identical to my ringtone: "Lady of Dreams" by Kitaro. "Impossible! This Japanese composer Kitaro is not all that famous, and he composed more than a hundred songs. This man Mohanji chose the same obscure melody for his website?! That's just too much of a coincidence!"

That evening was the final session of our Yoga workshop but there was no way I would forget to meet Mohanji this time. I was intrigued, big time. As soon as the final meditation was over, I approached my colleague to inquire about that introduction to Mohanji. To my great surprise, my friend brought me to HIM – the man to whom I had been vibrationally drawn on the first day! My mind was racing as he shook my hand gently and said with a clear deep voice: "Mohan."

Silence. I became breathless. I felt that his eyes went right through me, like a scanner – in and out. There was something most unusual about those penetrating eyes – they looked straight into my soul. It felt as if, for the first time ever, I saw a reflection of myself.

His eyes revealed immense inner depth. It was clear to me that his appearance in the illusory physical world was but a small part of Him. His inner stature and presence in the subtler realms were gigantic.

I was completely vulnerable in the power of those eyes. There was a sense of nakedness without shame, like someone who, after a long time of hiding behind multiple veils, had been suddenly revealed – disarmed and a bit shaken, but so happy and free. I felt like a drop of river water suddenly exposed to a mighty ocean. My studies of Jung's psychology had given me enough insight to understand the following: this was a glimpse of reality beyond the confines of the ego, the mask, and the false and limited notion of the self. This happened by default in the presence of One who had already crossed that threshold, who operated at the level of higher consciousness. Indeed, it was electrifying to experience such a presence behind Mohanji's eyes.

I was treading unknown territory but felt no fear. Mohanji's hand was so incredibly soft and warm, and his smile so reassuring. We basked in a silent void for eternity.

"It's a real pleasure meeting you." The physical world reappeared at the sound of my voice. "I read about your life from the Ammucare website and was deeply touched." I could feel his continuous scanning as I spoke. "I was so happy that your sufferings led you to spirituality and not depression. In that sense we are somewhat similar – war, nearly dying, and many other experiences have set me on the spiritual path to seek with utmost sincerity the Truth of our existence."

Mohanji handed me his business card. A few seconds later, his deep voice reached my ears and my joy knew no bounds. "We shall meet again."

I immediately saved his number in my contacts. I used to always add some explanation of each person in the entry field of their name. Without thinking, I instinctively typed: "Mohan – *srodna duša*" (Mohan – the soul mate, or familiar soul). I did not have any interest in him aside from friendship and spiritual guidance. I only felt a great familiarity with that magnificent soul and knew intuitively that he would play an important role in my life.

Further exploration of the Ammucare website revealed the podcast (internet radio program), "Mohan's World." There were many links to free recordings of interviews which I (and many people across the globe, especially in the US and China) found to be extremely interesting. Mohanji casually interviewed people about their spiritual experiences – my favorite topic! It was all spontaneous, but so profound. After a few days, I decided to give him a call, just to tell him how much I enjoyed his podcast. I also told him that his booming voice has a certain power – I called it "the mountain voice." He laughed and said: "As a matter of fact, I wanted to ask you whether you'd like me to do one such interview with you – about your near-death experience." I was surprised but agreed instantly. We planned to meet the following day at the "Wellbeing Show," a big event at the grand Convention Center, where I was to do my AOL marketing seva and demonstrate a few yoga asanas on stage.

Taking the Plunge

The energy of my next meeting with Mohanji was like a flooding river – there was no holding it back. We met at the Wellbeing Show as agreed, and decided to go for tea at an organic restaurant. I was in my chirpy, bubbly mode, which meant that I would be talking most of the time – I couldn't wait to share with Mohanji all my spiritual experiences. I finally felt free to share my most intimate experience of all – the astral encounter with Mahavatar Babaji. Before beginning my tale, I asked him whether he had had any experience with this great Yogi. What followed was such a profound sharing from his side that I didn't feel like opening my mouth again. I listened intently, soaking in the bliss of his experiences, absorbing them as if they were happening to me then and there. I was spellbound, amazed by his humility and sincerity and the spiritual depth he had reached.

His words were like instant beautiful imprints in my inner space, and I wanted to hear and feel more and more. Even though it was time to go, it was really hard to part from him. We decided to meet again, and then again, and again… It felt natural; it felt great. I had made many friends and met many people in my life, but there had been no one with whom I was able to share my deepest truths, no one who could understand my most complex and most intimate issues so effortlessly – until now.

While all of this was going on, I must admit that I still did not consider Mohanji to be my potential life partner. I did not harbor any fantasies about him or feel attracted to him as a man. I was happy being a yoga teacher, and since my "free bird" lifestyle had become a kind of comfort zone, I was not seeking a relationship. I had even forgotten about "the seed" I planted almost nine months prior at Sathya Sai Baba's summer camp in Brindavan.

A few days later, Mohanji invited me to join him at a cozy little studio near the beach where he conducted his "Mohan's World" interviews. As always, he humbly and casually welcomed his guest with his booming voice. Before he commenced the interview, he shared a quote from Dr. Brian Weiss's book, *Only Love Is Real*. The beautiful passage he read about souls reconnecting through lifetimes, and how "soulmates" recognize each other, went a bit over my head at that time. I did not see how this introduction connected to my interview on the topics of war, my near-death experience, yoga, etc. However, as soon as the interview began, I forgot all about the quote and started my narration.

A few days later, another surprise from Mohanji awaited me – he had purchased a Ford Explorer and asked me to join him for the auspicious occasion of its inaugural drive. When I asked why, he smiled and said, "Just like that." Again, I did not quite see the bigger picture. Why would he select me of all people? Nevertheless, I agreed to go. I felt a bit shy but happily checked out his new car. I did at least understand his invitation to be a subtle expression of companionship from his side.

While dropping me off at the office, he made a phone call to India, to ask a Swami about our spiritual connection. We thought that was a fun thing to do. What ensued was surprising – this Swami said, "She has been connected with you right from Jesus's time – it's a deep connection through many lifetimes."

This statement left a deep impression on me, so much so that I couldn't sleep that night... It was so true – whenever I thought of Mohanji, I felt as if I had lost him somewhere and now experienced this great joy of finding him again. There was so much familiarity, belongingness, and joy. (A small digression – even though I come from a Christian background, the concept of reincarnation has always intrigued me. My curiosity was satisfied and my awareness expanded after reading *Autobiography of a Yogi* and two lovely books from Dr. Brian Weiss – *Many Lives Many Masters* and *Same Soul, Many Bodies.)* However, I would not like to impose my opinion on others – it is, in the end, our free will to believe whatever resonates with us, while being nonjudgmental and open to receiving knowledge in life. As always, I am simply sharing my experience.)

The next day was February 14th, Valentine's Day. Mohanji called me while I was at work and said that my podcast interview had been uploaded. While listening to his introduction about soulmates a second time, I finally understood the message. His subtlety and the refined way in which he was operating impressed me. The idea that he could be more than a friend and spiritual guide began to blossom in my heart and mind.

I accepted his invitation to join him for dinner and a walk by the beach that evening. Between the warm breeze, the smell of the sea, and the romantic lights, the ambiance was such that we felt like holding hands and walking together as a couple. While chatting casually, I mentioned to him how miserable my love life had been for so many years and that I had even stopped looking for a relationship.

All my previous relationships had shown the same pattern. At the onset, I would open up and get very close to the person before gradually realizing that he could not follow where I was going spiritually. I would outgrow them and leave. Sinke had walked with me for the longest time, but even he was not destined to see me through to my highest spiritual self. I never wanted to be the stronger or the superior one. I wanted to be equal, only just a small step behind. I wanted to be fascinated by my partner, proud and inspired by him. I never wanted someone "ordinary" who wanted to lead a routine life, enjoying material comforts and/or worldly fame. Without the spiritual dimension, all that glittered in the physical realm looked so boring to me. So, I remained single.

Mohanji then commenced sharing his relationship experience. It was completely different, but also very disheartening. After the experience of an arranged, loveless marriage (common in India), and especially after losing his four-year-old daughter in a road accident in 2000 and divorcing, he decided to stay away from all women. He was happy with his spiritual progress and once the telepathic communions with the Masters began, and profound inner experiences became a part of his daily life, he never longed for companionship or felt any sense of lacking. "However, after I met you, that changed."

His statement had my heart pounding. Looking into my eyes, he continued, "There is a higher, much higher purpose in our meeting. The Masters have brought us together."

He then revealed what one such Master had told him a few years ago. "You will get married again in this life."

Mohanji then pleaded, "Can it be avoided, please?"

The Master said, "No, because you should not take another birth just for getting married. Karma also means unfulfilled desire at a subtle level. You were a renunciate in many lives, and the experience of a deeply fulfilling, loving marriage and a child or children is still pending in your karmic agenda. Exhaust your karma, Mohanji, and be liberated in this life."

I was amazed. I had never understood the concept of karma from that perspective – what profound truth! We can exhaust/transcend our deep desires only through direct experiences (or higher awareness), not through suppression, pretension, or fantasy.

Mohanji and I parted for the evening having left all our cards on the table. I remained awake till late that night, contemplating all that we discussed and experienced. I felt that everything was moving a bit too fast. I was confused and needed some time to digest all these elevated matters.

The moment my eyes opened the following morning, my cell phone rang. It was Mohanji. "Good morning!" he greeted me. There was a childlike smile apparent in his voice, and his energy felt very bubbly and innocent.

Astounded, I asked, "How did you know that I woke up this very second?!"

Mohanji replied, "We have now connected astrally. You are within my consciousness, so I just know. It is actually very simple once you reach a certain level of evolution."

This was Mohanji's usual style – to downplay all matters related to the higher spiritual levels he had attained. What he said next surprised me even more. He continued in his casual tone, "Actually, I called to tell you that this morning while I was shaving in the bathroom, Baba told me telepathically: 'Poor girl, she is so confused, she doesn't know who you are.'"

By then I was fully awake – "What?! Baba talks to you just like that? And he said this about me?" That was a bit too much – I never thought Masters would be involved in my intimate life. I mean, it was flattering, but just so startling! My idea of receiving a telepathic message meant sitting in a meditative posture, not shaving in the bathroom!

From that day on, Baba was telling Mohanji one thing or another about the two of us. He could see that we were both still hesitant to enter a relationship. But when Baba got involved, everything progressed rapidly and was upgraded to the next level of fun!

The "icing on the cake" came a couple of days later when Mohanji received another wake-up-call-worthy telepathic message. This time Baba said, "I had no choice, I had to give her you. There was no one else, no one else could fulfill her conditions."

Mohanji said that this message made no sense to him. I was silent. That message was the final confirmation that Mohanji was indeed that special someone I had requested from Baba. "Highly spiritually evolved, like a Master, but unassuming." (Mind you, I had never told Mohanji about my forgotten letter to Baba.)

I had to pinch myself. My seed had sprouted! Baba's blessing had finally arrived! I felt like telling Mohanji: "You know what? I created you at the abode of Sai Baba." But I was too shy, thank god. "Hey, I ordered you on spiritual Amazon.com!" Horrific. I had to find the right way in which to tell him about that experience.

I went to meet him again that evening, determined to tell him everything – about the prayer request I humbly surrendered to Sathya Sai Baba, and truly everything about my past. I had to make sure he was not idealizing me before we proceed any further. I told him that I had had a few relationships in the past (which was normal in Europe) and that I had been deeply in love with one young man from Croatia for four years until he deeply hurt and disappointed me in 2004. Even though it became a platonic relationship, I genuinely believed for years that he was the special "one" for me and it was still not easy to remove him from the "throne of my heart."

Mohanji's response was profound and surprising as always – he already knew everything!! He said that he was already fully aware of my past because my soul had gone to him the other night and narrated everything. I was shocked and thought to myself, "What?! My soul went to him and 'spilled the beans' behind my back?! Unheard of!" I never knew that was possible.

From what he told me, my soul felt that, in terms of purity, it was not sure whether I was eligible to be with a person like Mohanji. It felt inferior to his stature. It kept repeating to him: "I am not pure enough to match your spiritual stature."

However, Mohanji reassured me that he didn't care at all about my past. My life experiences were my spiritual training and all a part of my soul's evolution. It was so beautiful to hear that from him, and such a relief!

What he told me then was truly profound and will remain my heart's treasure forever. He told me this in person in a sentence or two, but that evening he also sent an email. I cherished this message and felt that, after this, I needed no worldly marriage vows. He said it all in one go, in his inimitable style:

> My path is clear, Biba. It's spiritual. I might increasingly become a misfit in the gross external world and I might tend to belong more to the subtle internal world. It's a great possibility.

The transition that happened before I met you was the increase in communion with Baba, Babaji, and other Masters from different planes of existence. That will change further to explicit display of Divinity after some time.

Will you be able to be with me through all terrains, all seasons, all dualities, beyond all barriers? Will you be able to accept me as I am, with all my strengths and weaknesses? Will you be able to cease from judging me for what's obvious and understand the inner principle? Will you be able to love unconditionally and hold my hand at all times?

I promise you all that. I love you the way you are. You must not change an inch for me. All I need is your whole-hearted, true and undivided love. All I need is your total support.

I will never stop loving you. As evolution gains momentum, we may not utter our love, but we will exist in it more than before.

Our existence will not be usual since the whole world is my arena. I want to spread the Ammucare concept of unconditional love and service into the whole world. This would be my mission. Baba and all the Masters are with me in this. It goes without saying that all that I have is yours too if you are with me. I do not own anything. Everything belongs to the Almighty and is kept only temporarily by me.

You are a pure soul, Biba. I love you for what you are.

I just stood there, in awe, witnessing the dream I had treasured for so many years, unfolding before my very eyes. I could not withstand this feeling of unbearable love. Tears of joy came to my rescue, releasing a pressure that was dissolving me from the inside. I felt (and do feel to this very day) that meeting Mohanji was the greatest happening, the greatest blessing of my life.

Full Circle with Mahavatar Babaji

Aside from my work and yoga practice, all my free time was devoted to Mohanji. The area of Dubai where he lived was not too far from mine, plus his landlady was very nice, so I would happily drop by his apartment every now and then. One such evening I felt particularly energized and joyous to the point of ecstasy while driving to his apartment. Before reaching his apartment, I sent him the text: "I'll drop by in a few minutes. Are you in your body? Ha ha." I found this joke to be so incredibly funny because the usual question, for non-freaks like us, would be, "Are you home?"

I received no response. I thought maybe he didn't get the joke. After a few minutes, he called me, saying in a very serious tone, "Come upstairs."

The scene that awaited me in his room exceeded my wildest dreams. Mohanji was lying on the bed, staring at the wall without blinking, his face shining with the most incredible GOLDEN GLOW; his eyelids were especially bright. His whole body was radiant and he could not move an inch. Picking up the phone to tell me to come upstairs was a very difficult task for him.

I observed his state in silence for some time, completely motionless. Finally, he managed to say, "Mahavatar Babaji is here."

My heart was racing. "What do you mean? Where?" I asked.

"Within me," he said. "I am talking to him right now."

I was stupefied, immediately asking, "Oh my god, can I stay? Can I talk to him?"

"Yes," Mohanji whispered. "He is saying that you are allowed. It was he who brought you here. He was showering you with golden and blue light while you were driving – did you feel it on top of your head? That was Babaji navigating you through the city."

I was overwhelmed and utterly excited. "Yes, I felt it! My God, I didn't know that was him. It felt so great! I *was* driving kind of intuitively, without thinking, as if being navigated through my crown. I felt constant vibration until I reached your address. Now I know why."

I paused for a moment, noticing my mind was blank. I already knew from my previous astral experience with Babaji during my studies in Rome that the mind stopped working in the presence of the high frequency of his Divine presence. There I was, finally allowed to ask Babaji questions, but my mind was so blank that I didn't have any – except one, related to my astral experience with him.

I happened to share the story of my astral experience with Dr. Maja and her opinion was that the yogi in the desert was most likely a symbol of my Higher Self and not Babaji after all. While I greatly respected Dr. Maja and her opinions, I was confident that I recognized the same yogi right away, when I first saw the drawing of Mahavatar Babaji in the Autobiography *of a Yogi*. In any case, doubts remained.

Here was my chance to confirm my experience. Even though I felt timid asking such a silly question, I would not waste this opportunity for clarification. I asked him, "Was it really you, dear Babaji, in the desert, who brought me there in my astral body?"

There was only silence for a while, during which I waited with bated breath. Mahavatar Babaji finally whispered through Mohanji, "Do you feel the answer in your heart?"

At that point, tears poured from my eyes and I managed to say, "Yes, my heart always said it was you, but..."

And he then asked, "Then why do you doubt?"

This was it; it was all the confirmation I needed. Later on, Mohanji told me that Mahavatar Babaji talks in that way, in a very crisp, commanding, "no nonsense" manner. He is also most loving. His stature is amazing. Our minds cannot even comprehend the complete form or the powers of such a great, intergalactic Master.

Mahavatar Babaji went on to share a lot about Mohanji and me and our path together. I recall that he said, "Yours is the royal path. You belong to the Golden Tradition." I understood later that he was referring to the path of *Raja* (Royal) Yoga, with elements of *Bhakti* (devotion) Yoga, Karma (social service/duty) Yoga, and *Jnana* (knowledge) Yoga. "Royal" did not refer to life as a king or queen, but to the state in which one feels that they lack nothing, possessing within themselves every needed thing, and requiring nothing from the outside world.

In Mohanji's words, "The Royal Path is one of mindlessness. When you are mindless, you are the Emperor of your own life. You are above everything and are totally free. The Golden Tradition is one of total dissolution, not just enlightenment. You go beyond enlightenment and totally dissolve. You no longer exist, even as a drop. You become Shiva, the pure consciousness. You and Shiva are one."

I remember that I wrote an entire A4-size page of notes on everything that Mahavatar Babaji was revealing to us. I folded it nicely and put it into my handbag like the precious treasure it was.

Mohanji remained in that trancelike state for more than six hours that day, lying in the same position, with eyes fixated and open, and without moving an inch. It was such an amazing and unexpected experience bringing a most-fulfilling new dimension to my existence. Moreover, it made me see Mohanji in a completely different light. I began to understand his spiritual stature and kept feeling so incredibly blessed that I had found him. I knew this could never have happened without the support, guidance, and blessing of the Masters.

Deep inside, I knew that Mohanji was a true ascetic, evolving rapidly on the spiritual path. At that time, his evolution was hidden from the public eye and he managed to mask his spirituality effectively. Only those whose "third eye" (the seat of inner vision) was fully open or those who were very subtle and intuitive could recognize his spiritual stature... And I was blessed to be one of those people, blessed to be right there, next to him, witnessing so many divine occurrences that one could not even imagine.

The next time I sat in my office, I opened my handbag to read my notes and bask in the memory of that surreal blessing. However, the paper was missing. I was perplexed. I knew for sure that I placed it inside a specific part of my handbag. I remembered putting something in my desk drawer when I came to work, so I checked for the paper in there. Nope. It had simply disappeared. Dissolved. I messaged Mohanji to share the mystery of the missing notes with him. He said, "Babaji dematerialized it. It's OK; the experience is what matters. You remembered what you were supposed to remember."

I must admit, I was saddened to lose such a priceless memento, but I knew I had no choice but to accept and move on.

No Graduation Without Examination – New Life with Mohanji

During my time in Brindavan, I noticed a famous quote by Sathya Sai Baba on a poster: "No graduation without examination." Its meaning became crystal clear to me after meeting Mohanji. It was indeed logical – those who decide to pursue the highest studies (Doctor of Philosophy, Ph.D.) have to be willing to push themselves and undergo many trials and tribulations culminating in a test. The same applied to a request as lofty as a spiritual Master for a life partner – I had to prove to the Universe that I was "up to the mark." The testing was inevitable – but alas, sooner than I thought.

The first test came only a few days later. The General Manager of the Australian company I was working for at the time told me that their profits had reduced a lot. They were therefore forced to downsize – in other words, they could not afford me any longer. However, he said that he had found an even better job for me, one more in sync with my profession and background. It involved Program Management in the field of Sustainable Development, which would have me working closely with NGOs in Africa, etc. But to get that job I would have to move to their branch office in the Netherlands.

I was shocked. This was the best job offer I had received since my graduation from Notre Dame, but leaving Dubai after meeting Mohanji was simply not an option I would consider. Between my career and Mohanji – the choice was immediate. I declined the offer politely and, sure enough, within two weeks I was jobless.

Mohanji had a skin condition that became increasingly severe around that time. He had developed acute skin dryness after the shock of seeing the dead body of his most-beloved four-year-old daughter. For some time, the itching was bearable but was getting much worse. Certain portions of his skin looked like that of an elephant. It was scaling and falling off, and he could not sleep due to the itching. All in all, it was horrible. I was happy to care for him, applying creams and medications to his body. Even though his condition was unsightly, it made me love him even more. Later on, Mohanji told me that moment in our relationship was a test – Baba wanted to see whether my love for Mohanji was real or superficial. I passed the test, proving my love was indeed real and transcendental.

My physical beauty also received a strong hit at that time. I suddenly started getting acne on my face. After receiving the wrong homeopathic treatment, my skin became even worse. A randomly selected practitioner of homeopathy that I visited showed their incompetence by mistakenly giving me pills for rashes and allergies, causing me to then suffer from rashes, allergies, and acne. I did not know whether I looked better or worse when I applied makeup to my red, bumpy face.

My condition lasted for a few months, during which I trained myself to still say, "I love you," to my reflection, and "I am not the body, I just have a body" whenever I looked in the mirror. Now and then someone would ask me, "Gosh, what happened to you?" This crushing of my ego and the release of vanity was not easy at all.

In the end, we finally visited an expert in homeopathy, the father of one of my friends from The Art of Living, who offered free medical check-ups and homeopathic treatment. My friend told me that Mohanji and I were welcome to come to their home and consult with her father. We were all so hopeful that he would be able to help us with our skin issues.

When we met this man, we immediately noticed his purity and spiritual stature. He interviewed us individually to understand more closely the deeper causes behind our skin issues and then gave us small homeopathic sugar pills with instructions on how to take them. Before we left that day, he whispered something to Mohanji that indicated he was an advanced Kriya yogi. His treatments were his seva, offering his immense homeopathic knowledge free of cost before he left the body.

Less than a month later, Mohanji told me that the old man had left his body. He said, "I saw it. He left this world through the crown – which means he won't be coming back. He is liberated. We were among his last patients."

Once again, I was amazed. I checked with my friend and she confirmed it – her father was no more. She never knew he was practicing Babaji's Kriya or that there was such a great soul sharing her home. His seva was so deeply touching. With his blessing flowing through his homeopathic medicines, both of us recovered from our skin issues within a matter of weeks. We were deeply grateful.

The Financial Nightmare Test

The loss of my office job would not have been that big of a problem had I not acquired a huge debt on my credit card due to the bankruptcy of my previous employer (my American bosses still owed me five paychecks). After two years of a lavish lifestyle in a posh area of Dubai, living in a villa near the beach, I was not mentally prepared to suddenly shift into a scenario of lack and poverty.

Rob was silent, and I had nothing to say to him either. I knew the bankruptcy was not his fault, and that he would never intentionally hurt me, my sister, or our friends, but all of us were facing severe financial crises.

Mohanji's job was at stake as well. He was working as the General Manager of a shipping company in Dubai, but jealousy and continuous backstabbing from one of his superiors left his position hanging by a thread.

Mohanji was somehow managing to effectively conceal his rich inner world while juggling his deep spiritual evolution and his harsh commercial life. He prioritized his inner world, saying, "My spirituality is priceless and definitely not for sale." To those who sought and "found" him, he gave priceless spiritual experiences, free of cost.

One day, Baba asked Mohanji to shift his residence. He simply said, "Time to move." Thus Mohanji shifted into a more affordable apartment in a more remote area of Dubai called Rashidiya, not far from the Dubai airport. At the same time, the lease on Rob's villa was also expiring so I had to leave my accommodation too. What effective pre-planning and perfect timing!!! The very moment I needed accommodation, Mohanji's doors were open and ready to take me in.

Frankly speaking, it was rather embarrassing to move in with someone for such reasons, but I decided to take the plunge. After living in luxury, dining in expensive restaurants, and spending all my free time having fun, exercising, and taking care of only my own needs – this was a shocking plunge indeed!

I did my best to learn Indian vegetarian cooking and did all the necessary cleaning, washing, and ironing. This new "Biba the Housewife" would have been a hilarious sight for all my American friends, but I loved serving Mohanji wholeheartedly. With loving care, I made our modest new accommodation look and feel delightfully cozy. The warm golden light of our Himalayan lamp reflected off the wooden walls making it feel even more beautiful. The only issue with our new home was that the kitchen was shared with the other tenants, none of whom were vegetarian. I was often greeted by revolting smells when I entered the kitchen. Yet, because of the love we felt for each other, no amount of discomfort could bother us.

Mohanji and I enjoyed every moment together. Even though our financial issues were pressing, our spiritual progress was happening at a very high pace! The experiences were out of this world! Masters would frequently visit our room in their subtle forms and somehow I even learned to distinguish between them – Shirdi Sai, Sathya Sai, Jesus, Mahavatar Babaji – they each had a unique divine vibration.

Cosmic Agenda versus Karmic Agenda

While I was busy with my worldly activities, consumed by restlessness and tension due to financial instability, Mohanji's spiritual evolution was happening by leaps and bounds. He was shifting more and more to the level of simply "being." His inner world became even more active, and communion with the Masters seemed near constant. Sometimes he would just get up from bed and start typing at very high speed without pausing for a second. Whenever I read what he wrote, I would be astounded – what profundity, what intensity of expression! He was an empty vessel being filled with *Amrit* (nectar of immortality) from the highest realms of consciousness.

His inner beauty was increasing every day – sometimes I would just look at him and could not get enough of that indescribable something that touches the heart. His expression would be similar to that of small babies – when their eyes close, one can feel their inner bliss. His spiritual powers were increasing yet he would not demonstrate them, preferring to remain his quiet, introverted self, as humble and childlike as always.

One day in May 2007, early in the morning around 4:00 a.m., Mohanji got up and began his frenzied typing. A beautiful meditation was being "downloaded" from the higher realms of consciousness under the guidance of Shirdi Sai Baba (a supreme Master for whom Mohanji has great respect, and with whom I started developing great closeness).

Shirdi Sai Baba lived in the 19th-early 20th century and was the first Indian Master to appeal to both Hindus and Muslims, as well as people from all other religions. (Sathya Sai Baba carries his consciousness in contemporary times, although his expressions are softer and rather different.) The download that Mohanji received included every detail, even instructions on the background music, the number of candles that should be in the room, etc. Mohanji was told that he was to teach this meditation across the globe, free of charge. Delivered unconditionally and with utmost purity, the technique Mohanji had just downloaded would have a great cleansing effect, speeding up a person's spiritual evolution manifold.

Upon receiving this meditation, Mohanji was not too thrilled with the idea, as his very nature was that of an introvert who prefers to remain silent and away from the limelight. He complained to the Masters, "How am I, an introvert, to teach such meditation to people?"

The reply came: "That is not your problem. People will come to you. When they do, understand that we sent them. Do your duty without expectations."

It was only later that I understood the real "cosmic agenda" of an extroverted, bubbly person like myself coming into Mohanji's life – I was to prepare the ground and nudge him into action. (Baba also said that I would be his shield. I am yet to see what exactly he meant by that.) And that is exactly what I did, feeling immediately that what he had received was so precious that it had to be shared with the people.

I began spreading the word about this meditation. I spoke to a few people in Dubai about the possibility of a venue, and finally, four months later, our first meditation took place. At that time it was called "Bless The World Meditation." If not for that meditation, I do not doubt that Mohanji would have withdrawn into a full-blown ascetic life by now. He would have shunned worldly life completely. After the meditation, he allowed time for *satsang* (meaning "in the company of Truth," a spiritual discourse or sacred gathering in the company of a Master) in the form of a beautiful "Question & Answer" session, which program attendees loved.

Our spiritual lives were spectacular, but our existence on the physical plane was going from bad to worse. Mohanji eventually lost his job as well, and slowly but surely we sank further into debt, especially after Mohanji decided to borrow some money from his friends, and open his own company. He thought it was a good idea that would not only make us independent but also take care of our visa residency requirements. Unfortunately, the new business did not prosper, and we dropped it eventually.

My income situation was even worse. After unsuccessful job interviews for an office manager and personal assistant position, I decided to try my luck at leading a few yoga and salsa classes in different parts of Dubai, while also doing a part-time job in event management. It was all quite experimental, and this initially seemed like a wonderful idea. However, since I didn't have the funds for proper marketing of my classes, the overall attendance was really poor; at times, the fees I earned would not even cover the expense of renting the hall. I felt exasperated from running around all over the place to conduct yoga classes, wasting my energy in Dubai traffic, and not earning enough to even cover food expenses.

My part-time job in event management was another disaster. My employer offered so many empty promises and excuses that at the end of the day, I was working hard, but was not getting paid.

On top of all that, we soon had to leave even that most-humble rental house due to a strange government regulation, causing us to temporarily move into a friend's apartment. It became immediately clear that we were unwelcome guests there. And yet, out of our financial helplessness, we had to force ourselves on him.

This saga continued for quite some time – no matter how hard I worked, I was either getting grossly underpaid, used, or not paid at all. In the midst of it all, I was silly enough to invite a spiritual teacher from India (who propagates a scientific approach to spirituality) to come to Dubai and allow me to organize his first-ever workshop outside of India. I soon learned that convincing people to pay money for a workshop conducted by a person they had never heard of, was quite a challenge. I worked 20 hours per day, every day, for a month or so.

I never expected this workshop to be the most challenging and stressful event management experience of my life. We did not know how many people would turn up, and whether we would even cover the basic expenses of the venue and catering, until the last day. Mohanji was in India at that time and there was no one I could call on to help me.

The drama that ensued surpassed anything I had ever seen in movies. One day before the workshop was to begin, Mohanji's friend who had allowed us to stay in his apartment for a while free of cost, asked me to leave immediately. He said that his landlord was complaining, and he didn't want to risk losing his apartment.

I woke up that morning with enormous stress and anxiety – my body shivered and my stomach was completely upset. I had nowhere to go, I did not even have money for food, and I was too proud to even consider asking my parents to send me some money. I was completely helpless, a feeling I recognized very well from 16 years before when I suddenly became a refugee. I felt that I could handle anything… just not this. My very first reaction was, "No, I cannot handle such humiliation again."

However, after a bit more introspection, I felt that this time around, after all my training in yoga and acceptance, and my deeper understanding that "all that happens, happens for a reason," I was better equipped to deal with the situation. I had already experienced the presence of the Masters and knew that I was not alone. I took a break from my packing, and rather than falling into despair, I started praying sincerely. I was ready to live out of my car for a while and cope with each day as it came.

Within the next hour, I received a phone call from a friend, a practitioner of homeopathy, who had found that a friend of hers, Dr. Samata, could host me for ten days or so, just until her husband returned from a trip. Surely the Masters could not contain their amusement at my reaction when it was revealed to me where Dr. Samata's apartment was located. It was in the most luxurious area of Dubai – the Dubai Marina! I was overwhelmed when I arrived at her apartment on the 46th floor, dropping off my bags in a room covered with windows, offering the most stupendous view of the city!!! Oh, the unimaginable ups and downs of this life!

That same day, another friend got in touch with me to say that she knew of a young millionaire who would like to take a few private early-morning yoga classes. She recommended me to him, adding jokingly that a private session with me would cost $100 – and he accepted!!! I called my new prospective client immediately, and almost fainted when he told me his address – his luxury apartment was not only in Dubai Marina but was in the skyscraper right across the street from the one in which I was staying. I could almost see his apartment from my window. My heart melted in gratitude to the Masters – that day I surely must have been the happiest yoga teacher in the world!

I remember looking through the window, enjoying the view of Dubai Marina, and crying for joy as I listened to the song, "Amazing grace, how sweet the sound… I was blind but now I see…" I was overcome with gratitude and marveled at this sweet reward.

The workshop I worked on so hard not only happened successfully but was the best spiritual workshop I have ever seen. All my efforts paid off as I tasted the sweet nectar of Divine Grace and felt so blessed, so empowered. However, that was just a temporary relief, like an oasis in a big desert that I still had to cross all alone. The tests continued...

For another year or so, I could not get a proper job. In Mohanji's case, things worked out a bit better. As soon as he returned from India, he got a very good job offer in Oman and within a month became the General Manager of a shipping company in Muscat, the capital of Oman. I tried getting a job in Muscat as well and went for several job interviews, but each time my work visa was rejected. I felt really angry when I came to know the reason – I was told my visa was rejected because I was "young and beautiful," meaning a potential prostitute from Eastern Europe. There were many times in which similar patriarchal sentiments were obstacles on my path.

Back before the American company I worked for went bankrupt, I had been hit by a wild taxi driver from Pakistan while driving my car. I went to the police, awaiting their report of the incident. They kept me there for four hours, only to tell me, "Pink is for you. You are a lady, pink suits you." I do not recall ever being so angry. The pink form meant that the accident was caused by me and I had to pay for the damage. I came to know that the Pakistani taxi driver would have lost his license if they filed the correct report. After a quick chat in Arabic, they all agreed it was my fault. This was really tough to swallow.

In the end, while Mohanji lived and worked in Oman, I had no choice but to remain alone in Dubai, exasperating myself with yoga and salsa lessons that very few people attended, running around like a headless chicken, all for small bucks.

It was at this time that something surprising came my way, something that made my experience even more ironic. Through a strange series of events, I got the main role in a regional (Marathi) movie in India but got paid only peanuts. The producer made the excuse that the reason for my low pay was that they did not know I could act so well. I was told that I was still paid "much more" than any of the other actors (which may have been true, but the standard of life in India and the UAE differed greatly). Financial issues aside, filming the movie was a really fun experience. Surely it fulfilled something within my karmic agenda or it wouldn't have happened. In the end, I considered it a blessing.

The "Foreignchi Patlin" Movie Heroine

During my tumultuous life in Dubai, never in a million years could I have imagined that someone would offer me a leading role in a movie. When I first met Ms. Sanjivani Gawai, the producer of "Foreignchi Patlin," she had just finished her postgraduate studies and was contemplating making a Marathi movie that would be truly different from the run-of-the-mill movies.

It was mid-2007 when Mohanji and I went on one of our first outings together – we intended to take a romantic Dhow Cruise on the glittering Dubai Creek, but ended up sharing a not-so-enjoyable dinner (along with not-so-enjoyable entertainment) on a boat from which, unfortunately, one could not escape until the two-hour tour was finished. We tried to make the best of the situation and somehow managed to survive all the noise, smells, and other stimuli assailing our senses.

Little did I know that this boat ride had a much larger purpose in my life. Throughout the evening, Ms. Sanjivani had been secretly eyeing me for a role in her latest film. She was looking for someone able to carry the role of the heroine in her movie – an innocent, bubbly westerner who could be transformed into a proper Indian wife.

That evening I was wearing something semi-Indian, semi-Western, and kept talking about my yoga training and deep appreciation of the spiritual richness of India. Since I was in a relationship with an Indian and traveled frequently to India, she thought I had the exact qualities she had been looking for.

Later on, she organized a proper casting in India and considered several western ladies already involved in Bollywood, but none of them fit the role. Finally, she contacted me through her father who lived in Dubai and knew of Mohanji. The most unusual "casting" followed.

Sanjivani and Pradeep Ghonsikar, the movie's director, decided to entrust her father (who used to work with Mohanji) with the task of buying an Indian sari and recording me with his Sony camcorder. Donning the sari, I read the few lines they had prepared in Marathi. Without taking it too seriously, I fulfilled the task simply for fun.

Soon enough, I was informed that the entire film crew agreed, with great enthusiasm, that I was THE ONE for the role of Jennifer, the heroine of their movie "Foreignchi Patlin." They thought that my Marathi pronunciation and the way I looked in the sari were just perfect. To say that I was surprised would be an understatement. I reminded Sanjivani that I had never, ever acted in any movie in my entire life, not even in a school play, and that this was not just any role they were offering me, but the MAIN role. "How can you be sure that I will do well?" I asked.

She replied, "I don't know, it is my intuition."

Even though I only had a part-time job in Dubai at that time, I had to ask my employer in that event management company for a month-long leave. When I told her about this most unusual offer, she told me, "Don't even think about getting into some low-budget movie in the villages of Maharashtra. They'll probably do some sloppy shooting and won't even be able to release it. You will just waste your time and end up not getting paid."

I thought about the whole thing carefully and consulted with my dearest Mohanji whose faculties of deeper insight I trusted fully – his words matched my intuition: "It's not a coincidence that this has come to you. Why not take the challenge? You have nothing to lose." The payment I was to receive for this movie was equal to a cleaning lady's salary in Dubai, but not all in life is about money. The experience was worth it.

So there I was, on my way to India, ready for my experience "out of the comfort zone." The entire movie was to be finished in 25 days, before the end of December 2007. I'll never forget the moment when I landed in the minuscule "airport" in the middle of a corn field, near Kolhapur village in Maharashtra. I knew that very second – the adventure was on! Mr. Gawai and a few other members of the crew welcomed me with a big bouquet and recorded the arrival of "the star" on the same Sony camcorder. The entire scene was comical, but I decided to enjoy the adventure.

The newly arrived "village heroine" surely stood out – all eyes were on me. We went straight to the shooting location, a shanty village house where they had already started filming the scenes that did not involve Jennifer (my role). I was happy to meet my co-actors and the entire crew – all were very sweet, witty, and natural. I had time to rest and would begin filming my scenes the next day.

We had an early start at 6:00 a.m. (which would be my standard call time for the next month of shooting), and we wrapped up filming at midnight almost every day. While in the car on the way to the shooting site, Sanjivani would give me my script in Marathi, read it out to me in Marathi, translate it into English, and then emote it. I would write the pronunciation in English and start memorizing the words and corresponding emotions/expressions.

All in all, it was tough – especially when they sometimes, five minutes before the shooting, decided to suddenly change a few words, or decided that Sanjivani's version of Marathi was not fully correct. It became evident to me that in India, nobody speaks their regional language 100% correctly! It was equally challenging when they decided to replace a scene with another one for which I did not receive the script in advance.

Sometimes I would be envious of the other actors. Unlike me, they were not appearing in all the scenes and had a lot of time to rest and joke around, not to mention that memorizing the script in their native language was a piece of cake for them. I was the only one who was puffing and sweating all the time – either memorizing the lines or changing costumes and makeup.

However, those issues were nothing in comparison to my biggest problem – the toilet issue. When I first saw the toilet they were using, I did not even realize that it was a toilet! A hole in the corner of the floor, with a stone in the middle on which one is to stand (or maybe sit?!). That was a real shock (a "cultural bump," as Americans would say)! Sometimes we had a better version of it, but a hole in the corner was mainly it.

Moreover, when I was to wear the traditional Marathi saree (called Nauvari Saree – the fabric of which is wrapped around each leg, making me feel like a sausage), I would inevitably get dehydrated. Since dressing and makeup for shooting would take at least three hours, using a toilet in this sari was not an option as it had to be completely removed to relieve myself.

The most memorable "toilet experience" happened during the shooting of the windmill scene, set in a hilly area. There was nothing but barren hills and windmills all around us. The breakfast I had that morning didn't sit well with me, and my stomach was giving me alarm signals. I asked Sanjivani to take me to a toilet ASAP. She said, "Oh. We'll have to drive down to the nearby village and ask someone to allow us the use of their private toilet – that's all we can do." That was a real test of my endurance.

When we finally reached the village and started walking down the street, deciding on whose door we might knock upon to ask for this mighty favor, I felt truly embarrassed. We first picked one house that seemed decent, but all they had was a hole in the floor. I didn't know whether to laugh or cry! I ran out and told Sanjivani, "This won't work for me. Please, I need a proper toilet – with a flush!" We continued our search immediately, Sanjivani explaining my predicament to all the neighbors. Finally, we found one such toilet. I was overjoyed – agh, what a relief! I still laugh when I think of the "hole in the floor" scene, one of the strongest impressions I carried with me from filming. It is amazing what kind of conditions some people live in, while still managing to be happy and grateful. That is a big lesson that Indian villages taught me.

In terms of movie shooting and acting, my greatest challenges were:

- ★ Not looking at the camera lens during the shooting but at the CORNER of the camera, which felt very unnatural
- ★ The crying scenes. I rarely cry in real life. I'm just not the type. Crying in front of a camera was naturally even more difficult. My co-actors explained that I should swallow saliva, raise my eyebrows, remember some deeply painful moments from my real life to trigger the tears, and then get into the role fully. I was amazed – it worked! When my first natural tears came and the scene was over, there was a big round of applause! I soon gained confidence and most of the scenes were done with one rehearsal and one take on film, which was, as the director told me, *"how the professional actors do it."* I was very happy!
- ★ The awkward moments when they would shoot only dramatic facial expressions in reaction to a group discussion (being shocked, surprised, angry, happy, etc.). They seldom had the time to translate what each actor was saying, so I felt a bit idiotic as I could only guess what my reaction should be.
- ★ Long monologues for which I had to memorize several sentences in Marathi in one go. That was really tough. Two such scenes were my greatest challenge.

Aside from those few issues, it all flowed with utmost ease. There was a fight scene as well, before which I saw that the director, Mr. Pradeep, was completely upset. I asked what was disturbing him and he replied, "The stunt person who is supposed to do the fighting scene is late, and is probably not coming. This will disturb our complete shooting schedule."

When I understood that the stunt person was supposed to do my bit in a fight against several thieves stealing a golden statue from the temple, I smiled and told the Director, "That's not a problem at all. I can fight. I'm almost a black belt in Tae Kwan Do." His face brightened up instantly and we started shooting then and there.

The scene was a lot of fun and they could see that I enjoyed the "fight" thoroughly. I always loved my martial arts training but was not sure whether the skills would ever be of any use in life. It was so fulfilling to see my training utilized!

When the whole movie was complete, I realized it was as if this role was tailor-made for me. The story and character of Jennifer resembled my real life quite a lot (accepting the challenges of life and choosing to live out of the comfort zone, remaining dignified despite experiencing lack after a life of abundance, etc.), and acting the part was not at all difficult.

However, the hectic shooting schedule and lack of sleep got to me in the end – no amount of makeup could hide the dark circles around my eyes. The songs were done last and were the greatest challenge. I was to run through the field enacting great joy and bubbliness, while my skin was itching from the leaves touching my arms, while sweat was pouring down my spine. A real blessing was that the dance choreographer noticed I could dance and therefore suggested that I improvise some of my dancing scenes. This prevented us from wasting a lot of time rehearsing under the harsh sun (not to mention that some of his choreography, alas, belonged to ANOTHER ERA). Thank God I could improvise!

All in all, the experience was great fun! After the hectic schedule, Sanjivani and a few of her family members offered to take me to Shirdi to pay gratitude at the samadhi tomb of Shirdi Sai Baba, a Great Master whose presence, and direct guidance and blessings, continue to touch the lives of thousands of people across the globe.

Already exhausted, I nevertheless agreed to a full-night jeep ride on bumpy village roads just to reach Shirdi in time for the morning *arati* (devotional offering of light, usually with candles or lamps) at 4:30 a.m.

The car was packed, the driver wild (especially with the brake pedal), and I sat at the very back, on top of the luggage. By the time we reached Shirdi, my legs were red and swollen due to the many merciless bites of bed bugs (my first ever encounter with these cruel creatures) – ugh...

However, irritating itching and supreme tiredness were all forgotten the moment I entered Shirdi Baba's magical abode. The vibrations around his samadhi tomb immediately expanded my heart. This is something one can only experience, it cannot be described in words...

The moment I reached his *murti* (the big white marble statue alive with his consciousness, directly above his samadhi), it became completely clear to me that this movie had been entirely his *Leela* (divine play). I noticed that most of the"Foreignchi Patlin" film crew members were Baba's devotees and that the movie even started with his image! (I was soon to find out the real reason why Baba brought me to Maharashtra to act in this movie – a story yet to be told.)

And finally, 15 months later, the greatest surprise of all came my way – I received a phone call from Sanjivani who said that I should come to the famous Dadar Hall in Mumbai for a movie award ceremony organized by the government of Maharashtra – to receive their Best Actress Award! I had to pay for my own ticket to go to Mumbai and collect the award, but hey, it would have been a pity to miss this unique moment of glory.

Even though "Foreignchi Patlin" is an emotional drama with only a few elements of comedy, Sanjivani also received the award for "Best Comedy." Furthermore, I was amazed to learn that "Foreignchi Patlin" was screened in Kolaphur's main cinema for more than 100 days in a row and each showing was packed! (Which meant that many people must have seen it several times. I heard some saw it as many as six times!) It did very well in other theaters across Maharashtra and the songs became very popular on Marathi channels. "Foreignchi Patlin" made history as the first Marathi movie with a foreign actress in the leading role, acting in Marathi language no less.

All in all, I can't but conclude that the success born of a conscious choice to follow one's intuition (against all the odds) is so incredibly sweet because it opens the door to a new, magical dimension of life – surrender…

The Test Called "Taking For Granted That What We Have"

Even though the depth of spiritual experiences I had with Mohanji was incomparable to anything I had experienced before, I still had to learn that a student can have only one Master. I had the tendency to thirst after other spiritual workshops and still became highly impressed with other spiritual teachers that were more sensational, i.e. had more clout. After some time, I always became highly disappointed in the other teachers and their methods, leading me to understand and appreciate Mohanji even more. I simply had to go through this process.

As all of this wavering was happening, Mohanji never gave up on me, knowing that I would recognize him sooner or later. It took me more than two years to reach this point. I am so grateful to him for allowing me to go through these experiences because nothing except experiential learning would have taught me this lesson.

Since I had learned several different Kriyas all attributed to Babaji and claiming to be his original Kriya, I was not sure which one to practice. One of them created a powerful effect in me, especially the first time I did it, and the man who taught it insisted that visualization should never be present in Kriya or in any of my other meditations. He said that he saw great potential in me and could teach me how to attain abundance by promoting his profound technique, but in order to do so, I would have to cease any other practice that included visualization.

"That's not a problem," I said. "I don't practice any visualization anyway." At that moment, I remembered a part in Mohanji's "Power of Purity" meditation wherein one is guided to "visualize your father and mother coming in front of you, blessing you…"

I told this to the man and he said, "Well then, you will have to drop that."

When I met Mohanji that day, I felt confused and heavy. I told him what had happened, and he first said, "You are free to make your own choices." He appeared to look off into the distance a bit, and I noticed that he was in communion with someone. With a bit of a frown on his face, he said: "Shirdi Baba just spoke to me and said, 'Oh, she is a hopeless case. Just leave her.'"

My heart sank instantly. I was greatly disturbed by this and tears came to my eyes straight away. I told Mohanji (and Baba), "I did not say I would do it! I just told you what he told me. There is no way I will not do Power of Purity meditation. I know that it came from Baba. I witnessed it all. I will say no to this man."

That was a powerful lesson in integrity. I knew I had to stand behind my experiences and never be swayed by tempting offers that could knock me off my path. At that time, I was still unaware that Mohanji was my Guru and the ultimate blessing. I definitely deserved a shake-up and scolding from Baba. I can't say that I was searching elsewhere, but I still had a fascination with other amazing experiences, while taking Mohanji for granted. The mind's traps are indeed endless.

Profound Insights from a Past Life Regression

In September 2007, Mohanji and I happened to travel to New Delhi. He mentioned that Dr. Yogesh Choudhary, one of the world's greatest past life regressionists, lived in that city. He was a direct disciple of Dr. Sunny Satin, founder of the Californian Institute of Hypnotherapy and author of the much-acclaimed book *The Shift,* which explains all about the shift in consciousness we are collectively undergoing at this time. Dr. Sunny Satin meticulously collected data from hundreds of people whose Higher Self spoke about the different aspects of the shift – from fear and greed to unconditional love – and how it will inevitably reflect on all aspects of life and demolish rigid structures that no longer serve us. In short, the shift started in 2012 but is gaining full momentum as the rays of the Great Central Sun now reach us directly through our sun. In short, the Shift will have a positive effect in raising the awareness of human beings, and in causing changes in the perception and understanding of our history (including the role of extraterrestrial beings in it throughout the millennia), the banking and finance system, education, the energy industry, and our overall relationship with Mother Earth, etc. For all other details, I highly recommend reading the book.

I was really happy to meet Dr. Choudhary and had that feeling of instant familiarity the moment I entered his room. Since I had tried regressing to past lives two times before and failed, I did not have any expectations. I only went because I trusted Mohanji's judgement. During my session, my Higher Self said that Dr. Choudhary had been my grandfather in one of my past lives, which confirmed the familiarity and the love behind this session. I have to admit that I never felt the need to dive into past lives again after this session. It gave me all I needed and my focus was now fully on my spiritual growth in this life, the contribution I could make to humanity through my very existence, and the truth that I stood behind authentically, with all my heart. This is the main motive behind all that I do, including this autobiography.

Dr. Choudhary made it very clear that he was not interested in entertaining superficial curiosity and being fully booked for the next six months, he had made an exception by receiving me, that too only because he respected Mohanji a lot. I told him that the reason I wanted to do the regression was to see my stumbling blocks in the lives in which I had spiritually progressed the most so that they could not trip me up in this life. Most importantly, I wanted to find out more about my soul connection with Mohanji, and why I feel such a deep connection with Mother India...

The regression was three hours long. I experienced myself vividly in several different lives; I was hopping in a second from one century into another, rewinding and fast-forwarding with utmost ease. Most interestingly, my Higher Self described me as "she" and came across as incredibly wise, loving, and rather authoritative (everything was recorded, of which I have a full transcription that I treasure still).

I successfully underwent an induction process in the alpha state of mind. Dr. Choudhary had some equipment that showed him my brain waves and pulse which, combined with eye movement below the eyelids and breath, could give a clear indication of whether I had entered the desired state or not. I first went into a life at the time of Jesus Christ (i.e. Jeshua ben Joseph) when I lived on the Mount of Olives as a healer. This confirmed that what the Swami from South India had said earlier about my connection with Mohanji, was correct.

When I entered that lifetime through past life regression, I was in my early twenties and my name was Antya (I had never heard of such a name in this life). It was amazing to first see my unusual shoes (wrapped with thin leather strings around my ankles) and to answer Dr. Choudhary's questions with utmost ease and no hesitation. I could not see my face because I was in that body, but shoes certainly left an impression.

I was fed up with a routine life with my parents who owned a flour mill, and ran off to Jerusalem in search of a mystical circle of women who used crystals, essential oils, herbs, and energy to heal people. I was very eager to find them, but they kept moving and were very secretive. One woman told me that the only way to find them was to mentally address them from the purest space in my heart. If I was eligible, they would allow me to find them. One day, I finally found them on the Mount of Olives and they accepted me into their fold.

It was my dream to become a healer and I was very happy with them. I devoted my life to the healing of helpless people and eventually moved into a leper's colony. There I served the people in desperate need of help till the time I left the body.

I enjoyed a very profound, telepathic, heart-to-heart connection with Jesus and Mother Mary, and the spiritual connection remained after Jesus's crucifixion and Mother Mary's exile. I also had a deep admiration and love for Mary Magdalene and felt that great injustice was done to her over the centuries by depicting her as a prostitute. From what I saw, she came from a well-off, respectable family and was highly spiritually evolved. There is no way she could have been a prostitute. This must have come out of jealousy or the cunningness of patriarchal agendas.

I invite the reader to derive the right conclusion about her spiritual stature from the actual excerpt from my regression, which also offers the authentic feel of communication with the Higher Self. This deep past life regression is called "non-hypnotic" because one is partly aware that the physical body is lying on the bed and that another person is guiding the session but for me, 90% of my attention was on the inner visions and vivid experiences.

It was not an easy decision to share this, being aware of the religious sensitivity behind this topic. My calling is to share the truth of my experience. I have great respect for all who do that because humanity grows through the telling of Truth. We rely on insights shared for the benefit of all.

This is exactly what Dr. Brian Weiss did. He was a renowned scholar and therapist from Yale. As a Catholic, he did not subscribe to any possibility of reincarnation. However, he started working with patients and regressing them to their childhood to find the root cause of certain phobias and blockages. At some point, his patients began referring to another life. The authenticity of their experiences could not be doubted because everything made perfect sense and healing would happen after they revisited that painful experience through awareness. Dr. Weiss even received confirmations from his past-life friends or other souls to which he was deeply connected. He gathered all the strength he had and shared the truth of his findings in his exceptional books, like

Many Lives, Many Masters and *Only Love is Real*. I can't but offer my deepest gratitude to heroes of modern academia such as Dr. Brian Weiss and Carl Gustav Jung. Hats off.

I now invite the reader to join me on the journey through one of my past lives. I am sharing only one interesting excerpt from the transcription of my session from the lifetime on the Mount of Olives.

> Dr. Choudhary: I'm gonna count to three and you are going to move forward in the same lifetime as Antya and reach that place where the inner circle of women lives and you are about to join them. One, two, three, and you are there now.
>
> Biljana: Very strange. They have many baskets with different grains, and seeds, and stones – I never thought this was so complicated, there was a lot to learn. Different spices, some are for healing, some for food. There are some special stones for healing also, like minerals for balancing the energy centers. They say that women have known this for many years, this is old knowledge. I feel very blessed that I am with them because I don't want to enter into my adult life without being initiated properly.
>
> Dr. C.: What are these women called, is there a name for them?
>
> B.: Some kind of "White Circle," White Circle of Women.
>
> Dr. C.: And who guides them, who's the head lady who manages and admits people and checks them out? Is there any particular lady like that?
>
> B.: It's not like some kind of institution. It simply goes on and if someone is about to deliver a baby, or some lady is pregnant for example, they teach her how to connect with the soul of the child, guiding her through the delivery. They always connect intuitively. There's no need for formal meetings and all that – they function on a telepathic level. I am so deeply impressed with all that, because I somehow had a feeling that, as a woman, I want to have a more serious role, as if I have not been taken seriously till then.
>
> Dr. C.: OK, and all these women, do they live in this place as a group?
>
> B: Mainly nobody knows what they do, it's not public. Sometimes when we meet in a bigger gathering, we just nod to each other – it's very secretive.
>
> Dr. C.: Now when I count to three, you move forward in time, in some time when you connect with Mother Mary, Jesus's mother. One, two, three and now.
>
> B: She doesn't talk much.
>
> Dr. C.: Is she part of the White Circle?
>
> B: She's much beyond any of that. All the things she does are in the background. She doesn't want anything out in the open. And she always hugs me (crying a bit). Whenever I see her, I don't feel like talking, simply that love is there. And she would caress the top of my head with her left palm, like when she hugs me she would touch the top of my head with her palm, and I would always cry out of immense love…

Dr. C.: You live near her?

B.: There's a beautiful small house made of stone and wooden columns, and grass and flowers around. It's very homey and very humble – she doesn't want to make it much distinct from other houses, but the energy is very, very good.

Dr. C.: Are you with her now?

B: Yeah.

Dr. C.: So what have you come to her for?

B: She is telling me about the future, and that I would forget her (crying…) and there would be many lives when I would not remember her, but she would be with me always. She says "*You have to learn to go very deep. Don't lose your depth in your daily life. When you are deep within, I am always there with you*."

Dr. C.: I will take you backward in time and you will go to the time when you have met Mother Mary for the first time, and you will see what was the reason for your acquaintance.

B: Mmm, one day as I was walking, I FELT this lady walking towards me. She was so special. You can feel that she is merging with everything, flowing, like the light blue color and sky and water when they merge. That's the kind of sensation that I would get. So, I was thinking "Wow, I would like to be like that," you know. And then, just when I had that thought, she looked at me and smiled. That's when I felt that I am connected with her. But I didn't speak, it was simply intuitive, like an inner recognition.

Dr. C.: So move forward in time to the time when you visited her first.

B: There's a wooden table in the yard, flowers around. First day when I came we spoke. And she said, "Do you think this is the first time you are around [alive]?" I think she was referring to reincarnation, which I was not aware of. I said that I never really thought about it, but I'd say that it is possible that it's not my first time to be on this planet. And she said, "Good, just stay with the wonder."

Dr. C.: How did you find where she lived?

B: It was a friend who told me that she is very special and very pleasant. And at that time she was very lonely, I think this was the time when her son Jeshua was not there, gone somewhere, to some other country. So, she was missing him a lot, and at the same time, she knew it had to be like that. So, I came to her. Even though I was much younger, we became good friends. I was able to discuss many things with her. Like deeper topics about life, and then she would say that I need to remember not just previous lives, but that feeling of Union, that we know before we come to this separation, polarity of space and time. I felt that she was praising me a lot, that she was addressing some higher me, that I wasn't really there, at that stage… Maybe she was talking for the future, but I was hoping that I could live up to that expectation, I mean, to that praise. I love the expression in her eyes when her eyebrows go a little bit up and that softness is there.

Dr. C.: Are any of her children around, apart from Jesus?

B: Right now, no. I think her husband is doing some work with wood, but she... She holds so many secrets. It's like an ocean, every time I come, I am so deeply impressed. And her silent ways, the way in which she works – she is so able to touch people's hearts, directly, she connects immediately.

Dr. C.: I'll move a bit forward in time when Jesus is at home, and you are visiting Mother Mary. One, two, three and now.

B: When I come he would also be doing some work, and I used to tease him about how it doesn't suit him. And he would laugh: "Even I work, everybody works." And I would say, "But still, it doesn't suit you," you know, some funny conversation like that.

Dr. C.: How old is he and how old are you?

B: He's around 30, and I'm slightly younger, 26 I believe. He has a shirt of beige color, more tight around the wrist, some kind of design like that. He doesn't wear that very often. There is some turbulence. He's going to some meetings slightly political in nature – there are some issues that are being discussed and I'm not really informed about what is going on, but I feel that he is in slight distress. When I come, he prefers me to joke around with him, because too many of these things are going on and I bring a lot of lightness, so it's better to laugh.

Dr. C.: How does he look like?

B: He has a bit longer brown hair, split in the middle. Usually he wears some earthy beige colors. He is taller than me, and I can always see his collar bone (near the neck), he is slightly slim. I also feel that he is slightly bent, his upper back is not completely straight. And I like to observe him from the back and that moment when he turns his head, that brightness comes. I used to love those moments, I would just observe. When he turns, there is like a shift in energy and like the Sun is shining. That's how it would feel.

[There is a photo of Jesus Christ materialized by Shirdi Sai Baba. On it, one can see the image of Jesus Christ healing a young woman lying on the bed. This is the first time I got direct confirmation that this detail with slightly bent upper back was true. This photo also shows the beauty of Jesus's compassionate expression and an authentic door from those days. It is truly precious. I have included it in this book.]

Dr. C.: You are really enjoying this, I see the glow on your face. Do you feel his presence now, is he there now? It is really wonderful, being with Jesus in such an informal way, isn't it?

B: There would also be meetings in some kind of a garden. It's like, covered with leaves and greenery. Men and women would get together informally, those would be like some kind of healing sessions, but with so much positive energy, it's so beautiful. Like regular people could never possibly understand what's going on in there, cause it's some unusual way of healing.

Dr. C.: Can you describe a healing session with Jesus?

B: Yeah, he kind of plays. For him it takes only a second, you know. The other ones, it takes them longer to achieve the same result. And nothing is hard and impossible, everything can be done. Even in the most complicated cases of people who come, he would joke like "Well bring us some bigger challenge, this is peanuts." And when all these patients leave, we all stay together, we joke around, we sing – it's just such a great crowd, of 15-20 people all together.

Dr. C.: Was this held secretly, without the knowledge of other people, the Jewish priests?

B: No, there were no priests, it was very informal.

Dr. C.: But is it done away from the knowledge from the priests of the Temple of Jerusalem?

B: Yeah, yeah, it's more like a "folk thing," of the people, not any institution. It's being close to nature, to animals and minerals, observing everything, feeling the vibrations, being attuned.

Dr. C.: And he's imparting the knowledge of this manner of healing to other people?

B: Yeah, yeah. He doesn't come every time. He's rarely gracing our sessions. But Mary Magdalene is essential in these gatherings. We are meeting in her place actually. She is like the main one.

Dr. C.: You met Mary Magdalene also here, or you met her at Mother Mary's house?

B: I met Mary Magdalene at some other part of the city. She lives on Mount of Olives. Jesus says that the most beautiful energy is there, and that is why we do the healings there. She is very attuned for healing. She awakens the heart chakra especially and people get very deep, deep experiences. Lots of love comes out, some even get into ecstatic states. It's as if he is the most advanced among the men, and she is the most advanced among the women.

Dr. C.: Who taught Mary Magdalene?

B: I think he did. Because she was sooo thirsty for knowledge, a pure heart…

Dr. C.: Is there any special relationship between two of them?

B: There is something that only two of them know, like a deeper connection. And it's very visible, I mean, they communicate via telepathy and, they just, I think nobody can reach THAT what they have. I thought that if every couple could be like that, our world would be really amazing. But I don't think they are together sexually, it is simply that depth of relationship. I mean her face is not like all that beautiful. I saw so many other ladies with more beautiful facial features, but that radiance of hers, the way she walks, her beautiful hair and grace… You can tell that when she's present, the atmosphere is immediately charged.

Dr. C.: That's very beautiful that you have observed that. Did Jesus teach any methods for people to evolve spiritually so that they can come to that level of generating that radiance? Did he teach any special, what you call, meditations?

B: Not many were able to do that, so what he could mainly do was perform miracles and healings, because not many asked for higher. They only asked for healing on the physical level. It's just like that – if the cup is not open, how will you pour into it?

Dr. C.: And he had a pretty good following. He was only 30.

B: I think that was like the height of the good times.

Dr. C.: Did you attend any of his other meetings, which were more political?

B: It was very challenging for them. There are some people in the desert area who are mainly organizing this kind of rebellion. Their meetings are like that of partisan groups. They are riding donkeys, not equipped with any weapons. And then there are some politicians who are also on their side – it's like these people in the desert, they infiltrate people in all levels of society, and it's more of a secretive thing, spiritual connection and secretive.

Dr. C.: Have you heard of people called Kaloos of that time, teachers of the Essenes?

B: I think they are the ones with wooden sticks. They walk with wooden sticks and are quite rigid, in a sense of being very strict in teaching. It's not easy, this path. Because lots of challenges are there to overcome, you know.

Dr. C.: It's really nice to know the cheerful side of Jesus.

B: Yeah.

Dr. C.: Thank you very much. Now we will move forward in time and come to some significant event in your life as Antya.

B: I think I left everything, I became involved in more of a monastic life... I went inward, because these high times of happiness, it's all gone now. I turned inward, more into meditation, more the inner than the outer. I think both Mother Mary and Mary Magdalene are gone, they are not in Jerusalem anymore. I am in my 50s.

Dr. C.: They are gone?

B: I mean physically they traveled somewhere. It was not possible for them to stay.

Dr. C.: OK, so they traveled somewhere else. That was after Jesus's crucifixion?

B: Yes. I feel like I am much older. I am 50, but I feel that I am much, much older. I am teaching something, kind of keeping myself busy. Outer world is less of an interest to me now.

Dr. C.: OK. When I count backward from three to one, you will go back in time to time when Jesus was still alive. See what is happening politically, can we get some more information on that?

B: It's a very tough place, very, very cruel. Those big walls, steel, tools for torture, and such a contrast to the Mount of Olives where we used to meet, Gethsemane Garden and the olive trees... It's like two realities – the greenery and those walls.

Dr. C.: What are those walls?

B: Like forts where the authorities are. I don't even want to go there. They are always selling animals in the market, and blood, and noise – I just don't fit in there, I hardly ever mingle. So many raw and primitive people, very low level of consciousness. Just mixing with that vibration is already enough, not to mention anything else. I admired Jesus, how come he could love all of them, even those. I was not like that. If I feel those raw vibrations, then I get repelled and cannot bridge it, I cannot reach out to their essence easily. But with those who are at least a little bit more refined, then it's easier for me. Or those who are suffering, and then the compassion comes, but just seeing all those raw ones, arrogant soldiers or those poor people who are in that illusion that they are just that lowly being…

Dr. C.: What about the time when Jesus got captured, in case you heard of that?

B: He knew in advance everything that was going to happen, there was no surprise. [crying] And then he said goodbye to us in our last meeting in the green yard, at Mary Magdalene's. On one side he knew it had to happen, and then on the other side it was hard, cause he knew what was getting ready to happen. [crying] That sensation of shrinking in my heart chakra is always there when I remember, and I… and that ugly moment when the soldiers from the fortress came to our green area and they took him from there.

Dr. C.: Oh, so you were there at the time when he was taken away by the soldiers?

B: I was awake that night. I was not really present, but I could hear the sounds. It's like they came to, what I considered, our territory. They never come there because by vibration they are not attracted, you know. But this was a special order, it just had to happen, and it was like the twilight zone had started, that was the feeling – like sinking.

Dr. C.: Did you know about his crucifixion, did you go?

B: Oh, it is so ugly…. It's like when you see those people who made him undergo those sufferings, they are like caged animals, completely raw. And then he, with his vibration, he is so beautiful [crying]….You don't even wanna see him stand next to them, not to mention that they would hurt him. And in my heart I kept asking "How can you do it? How can you be so blind"… Sometimes I felt [crying] that these people can never be awakened because they are so blind. And then there were those who were oscillating between feeling him and not feeling him, but a very small number of people. Majority were just like zombies.

Dr. C.: Did you move to the place of crucifixion?

B: I knew what was going to happen.

Dr. C.: So you didn't go?

B: I was feeling it all happening. In the end, I knew that Mary Magdalene was going to help… I wish I could have done something, but I had no strength, it was too painful. But she carried it all, she carried the whole thing energetically [held the space].

Dr. C.: And now when I count to three, you will move forward in time, to the day prior to death in that lifetime. See what you are doing, where you are.

B: I'm actually lying down. I knew it was coming. I think I was applying some techniques I was taught. So when it happened, it was the end of breathing and then as if I was sucked in by something, and I was gone. I wasn't suffering in any way.

Dr. C.: So now that you are in spirit, just look at your body, can you see it? Where can you see it from?

B: From up, and I can choose, it can also be from around.

Dr. C.: The spirit is all-knowing of the complete lifetime of Antya and the purpose of the life you lived as Antya. So I would like to ask the spirit of Antya, what was the purpose of that life?

B: Well, the purpose was clearly to see life from a higher perspective. To detach from the daily experiences and seek the ways to bring more light, no matter how difficult the material plane seems.

Dr. C.: And did you learn that purpose?

B: I did quite well, but I felt that I could have done much more. That sense of full completion was not there. Like, I haven't gone as far as I could have. I think I just… I could not fully do what Christ said, the forgiveness. I could not penetrate the walls of those people who were too raw. I knew that I could have been more compassionate. Like, some I liked, some I didn't like. And I knew I should like all of them, that full love was not expressed, but it went quite far…

[…]

Dr. C.: [addressing my Higher Self] I am sure she will benefit from this information. I really thank you very much. You already showed her connection with Mother Mary.

B: You know, the olive trees are still there. Biljana went to Jerusalem and she saw them. They are protected from tourists, yet there are many imprints in them, in their consciousness. So those who are sensitive and can meditate there, they should. She should go there and spend more time on the Mount of Olives.

I was deeply touched by this experience and am forever grateful to Dr. Choudhary. Mohanji prefers not to reveal anything about his past lifetimes, so all I can say is that he and I did meet during that lifetime, just as that Swami from South India once said.

Mohanji's basic personality traits in that life were identical to this life – a leader, highly organized, specialized in logistics, meticulous in pre-planning and execution, serious, reliable, and loving. I noticed that the facial features were somewhat similar, but I recognized him fully through his eyes. As mentioned earlier, the expression in the eyes remains the same throughout all lives and that is how one's identity can be easily recognized, through past life regressions or after the soul leaves the body – as I saw during my NDE. (Indeed, "eyes are the window to the soul," is so very true.) In short, Mohanji and I were good friends, but were both devoted to service and had no time to deepen the relationship.

In that lifetime, I served for many years in a leper colony a couple of hours away from Jerusalem. I served the outcast and sick with all my heart, and applied all the knowledge I had to wash their wounds and rotten flesh. I gave them my loving attention with utmost sincerity. (This could be the explanation why the encounter with dead bodies in Ilok did not make me vomit.) This social service created a lot of good karma, but I couldn't forgive the people who hurt and crucified Jesus. I saw them as more primitive and crude than any animal.

I found it amazing that one or two years before this session with Dr. Choudhary, I had traveled to Jerusalem on my own. The Kroc Institute organized a Peace Panel attended by Jewish and Palestinian representatives (one of them had to crawl through mud to cross the barricades between Palestine Authority territory and Jerusalem to get to that meeting).

I got to see how harsh the living conditions of the Palestinian people were when I went over to their side with our little group of mainly American scholars. We were stopped by Israeli military authorities around noon and were held without explanation for two hours. Our journey was worthwhile because we got to go to the Nativity Church in Bethlehem when there were no tourists and spend quality time in silence there. It was a beautiful experience, and the energy was so sacred, especially at the lower area marked as the birthplace of Jesus. I could feel that special energy that my essence remembers, and felt deeply fulfilled.

However, at some point, I began to feel that I should not visit churches that were erected centuries after the people or events that they were built to honor. There are sometimes big questions about their authenticity and/or the motivation behind their construction. My time there was limited and precious and, at some point, I felt a strong pull to go to the Mount of Olives, just like that, on my own.

One man told me that it could be dangerous and that it was better to stick to the group, but I did not listen. I trusted my intuition. As I walked up the Mount of Olives, at some point I suddenly got a very strong feeling of familiarity. It was the same as going to the vineyards near my home in Slatina or any other location from my childhood. I just knew that area. I sat there in silence and simply observed around me and meditated. There was something that interrupted my meditation, some presence. I opened my eyes and saw in front of me two white horses looking at me with their big, beautiful eyes. They had no bridle, no owners. They were just there – two free-roaming white horses, which was highly unusual. There was something so mystical about them, and to me, they felt like deliverers of a blessing.

During my trip to Jerusalem in 2006 I also visited the two original olive trees from the time of Jesus. They were magnificent. I managed to touch them and stayed in their energy field for as long as I could. Tourists were there, so meditation was not possible. I do hope to go there again and get some quiet time with these powerful trees, especially since this was something that my Higher Self suggested during the session with Dr. Choudhary: "[...] there are many imprints in them [the two olive trees in Gethsemane Garden], in their consciousness. So those who are sensitive and can meditate there, they should. She should go there and spend more time on the Mount of Olives."

Of the reason I had to be born in a war-torn country, my Higher Self said:

B.: Mmm. Like in her mind, that war area of former Yugoslavia is like those fortresses of Jerusalem. The raw people. She has to face them. She has to carry that task of approaching even those who are like animals. That is why it's so hard because she is repelled by them. It's easier to do peace work in any other country, but that one is too hard to deal with, cause that wall has to be penetrated. It's like this – there are certain souls that were supposed to be benefited by her in the time of Jesus. But she didn't get to them, didn't save them. And now they come again.

[My experience with the Kosovo Albanian man and the moment with the golden ball comes to mind.]

Dr. C.: So for that she needs to go back to her country and give this help to those people?

B: Yeah. You know, those who do mass graves, those really most terrible ones that everybody would lock like a beast into a cage, she can get to them.

Dr. C.: She is able to do that because she is full of love.

B: Yeah, nobody would even think that anything related to love could even reach them. But actually that's not true. Everybody has it inside. But with some there are so many brick walls around the heart, and it takes an exceptional spiritual person who can penetrate that. That's what she actually longs to do, to go deep, deep inside.

Dr. C.: So she will have to live in Yugoslavia?

B: Maybe she won't really have to live there like all the time, but there will be some kind of sessions, maybe she can go to places like prisons, or... She will find the way. But she has to be ready for it, it's very hard indeed.

Dr. C.: OK. Any particular method that she needs to adopt to go deeper, to do her service to humanity, what she is supposed to do in this life, towards her own Moksha?

B: Hmm, more of silence and... more of seeing herself as light within, because she thought that she needs to look at the candle [referring to the astral experience with Babaji]. There are many techniques, but seeing yourself as light from within and expanding – that expansion and light, full circle, that is the key. And presence of the Masters. That will do the job.

Dr. C.: Will she achieve Moksha in this life?

B: Yeah, but that final step has to be made, to penetrate all levels, so being ready to conquer any hint of arrogance within, any trace of separation, polarity. Penetration through all the levels and heart full of compassion and love, no judgment, no criticism, focus on the feeling. And it's possible – the feeling of love and light can carry you through. The only obstacles are the notions like, "I'm at the higher level, others are at the lower level." That is, ego – spiritual

> ego is very hard to combat. That is why that hard test will be given, reaching those who are very raw, very low in vibration – it's only a test, to see how far you get…"

There was another amazing life that I visited in this past life regression with dear Dr. Choudhary, the one that explained why I now feel so at home in India and so deeply connected to Shirdi Sai Baba. This was the story of my immediate past life in the state of Maharashtra, India. However, this story deserves a separate chapter.

Mohanji and Devi, 1st trip to India, March 2007, Enhanced by Marko Milović

The signs of light on the forehead, Devi and Mohanji, 2007

Devi's Mother Mary moment, Dubai, 2007

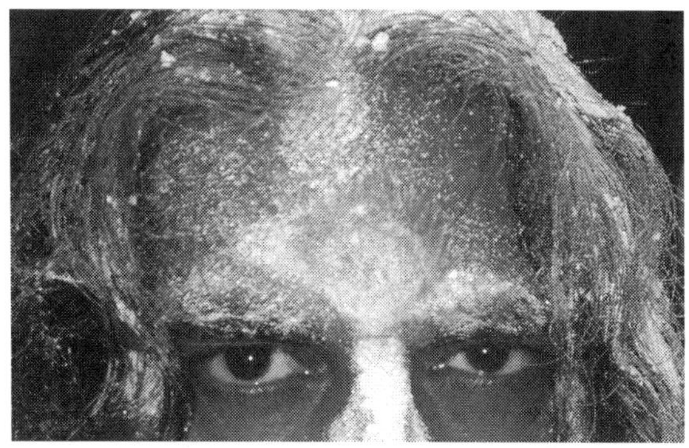

Third eye with vibhuti and cobra on top of it, 2008

First larger meditation in Dubai, Dec 2008

Miracle of Baba's appearance, Muscat, 2010, Photo by Dr. Deepali Jaju

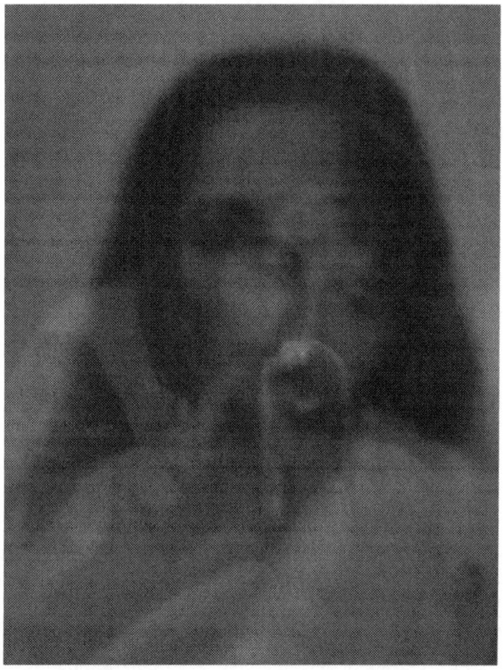

Devi on the shoulder of Babaji, photo by Dr. Andjelka Majić.

Babaji and the Two Moons, enhanced by Marko

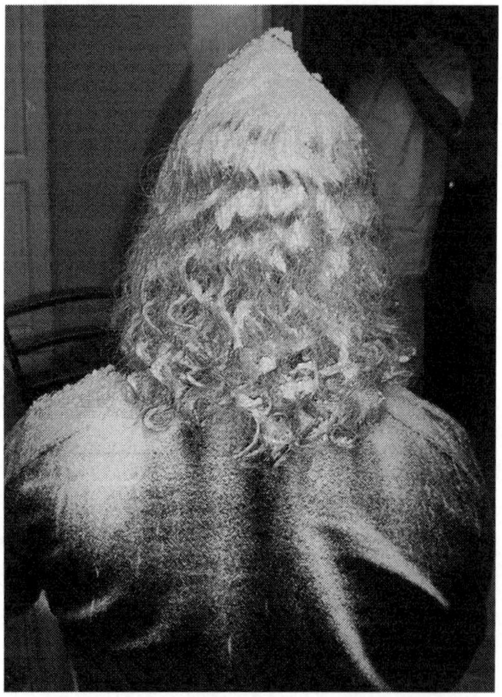

Mohanji - Kailash of vibhuti, 2008

Shridi Sai Baba as a young sadhu. (sourced from the net, enhanced by Marko M.)

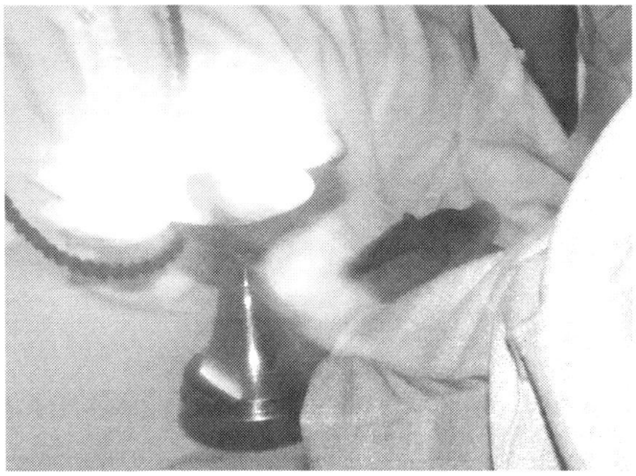

Baby's profile (nose & forehead) visible, Muscat 2010, Photo by Dr. Deepali Jaju

Original Shirdi Sai Baba photo, enhanced by Marko Milović

M family 2013

Taking Mila out to play after work, Muscat, 2013

Ganeshananda Giri with Mohanji and Mila, Shirdi, 2014

Orb in Shirdi, morning food seva, 2015

Devi in the Movie 'Foreignchi Patlin', 2008

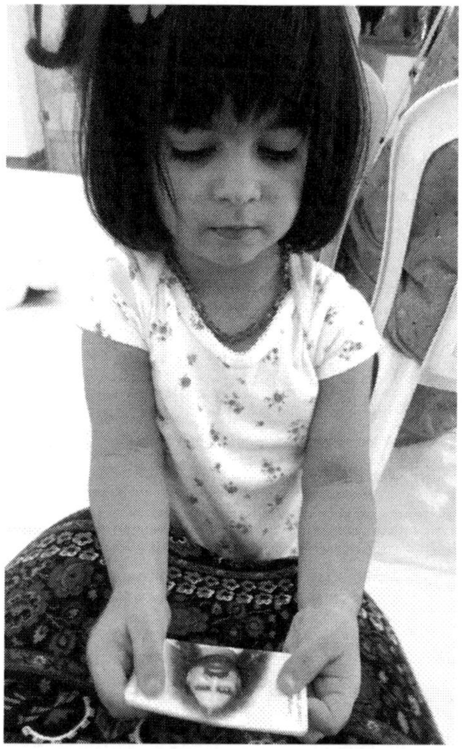

Small Mila seriously looking at her Papa's card on Mama's lap, Durban 2013

Devi and Mila on the stage right after Mila's fall, Nov 2013

Mansarover Lake 2014, imprint on the forehead, photo by Sumit P. Gupta

Devi shaking hands with dignitaries after her speech at the PoWR, Toronto, 2018

Devi in Kriya-induced Samadhi, Bosnian Pyramids Tunnel, 2018, photo by George O.

Mohanji, Devi and Devi Amma, India, Gurupurnima 2019

Devi and Mila Mohan meet Indian President Ram Nath Kovind in Slovenia, 2019

M family at the Nandi temple, India, 2022, photo by Tea Klincov

Mila with Mohanji's parents Acchan and Amma, Bangalore, 2022

Chapter 8
Living With Mohanji in Dubai

Profound Connection with Shirdi Sai Revealed

It was during the past life regression that I finally understood why I felt such a deep connection with Sathya Sai Baba, especially his previous incarnation – the Sai Baba of Shirdi, a.k.a. Shirdi Sai Baba. For the reader unfamiliar with this great Master and Avatar, one of the greatest who walked the Earth, I would like to offer a small introduction.

It is not known where or when Shirdi Baba was born, only that he arrived at the village of Shirdi in the state of Maharashtra, India when he was about sixteen years old. He was found seated under a neem tree. He stayed in Shirdi for three years, disappeared for a year, and then returned to Shirdi permanently around 1858, which is where he attained *mahasamadhi* (the state a yogi enters upon making a conscious decision to leave his body) and left the earthly plane (only in terms of physical existence) on October 15, 1918.

It is said in India that leaving one's body in mahasamadhi is only possible after one has "already achieved God realization, or *nirvikalpa samadhi*, in which the yogi recognizes and experiences his true oneness and unity with God."[36]

As always, Mohanji makes it all clear using simple words:

> Sai Baba was expanded as Supreme Consciousness while He was in his body and stayed expanded even after He left His physical body. Life is the union of the gross (body) and the subtle (energies). When one identifies himself only with the subtle, he becomes liberated from the birth and death cycle. When he sheds the gross, his subtle, which is already expanded to a universal state, stays the same. Then, the form is just an identification for devotees to connect and concentrate. Sai Baba was indeed Supreme Consciousness, and will always remain as that.

When this young yogi first arrived in Shirdi, he was noticed as a simple young man who led an ascetic life, sitting motionless in meditation under a neem tree, not minding heat or cold. It was evident to all the villagers that he needed nothing from the outside world and was not afraid of anything. He had long, dark hair and was lean and muscled. (A photo of Shirdi Sai Baba as a young sadhu (sage or ascetic) is included in the photo section in this autobiography. The photo

36 Source: Yogapedia (https://www.yogapedia.com/definition/5825/mahasamadhi)

has been enhanced by software utilized by my friend Marko Milovic from Novi Sad, Serbia, and offers a unique glimpse into the facial expression of a young sadhu whose eyes are fixated on the Divine - the eyes of a young Shirdi Sai Baba.)

After a year of absence and subsequent return to Shirdi, he lived in a dilapidated mosque (called Dwarkamai) with no protection from heat and rain, not to mention the multitudes of people who started coming to him asking for relief from their sufferings and life problems. He used a stone as his pillow. No comforts of any sort, and no privacy. He was often seen levitating while sleeping. Whatever donations he received from people during the day (after some time, this grew to millions of rupees), he would distribute to the poor before the day's end. He chose to live as a beggar, although he was a true king. He was a perfect example of an *avadhoota*, one who needs nothing from the outside world and has everything within himself.

Over the years, the many stories and testimonials of people who lived with Shirdi Baba or experienced his blessings were piling up. He was the first Master who attracted Hindus and Muslims equally, and later on Christians, Parsis (Zoroastrian people living in India), and people from many other religious backgrounds. Baba used to say, "All human beings are one. Our religion is humanity." He also demonstrated that truth with how he lived.

The famous book *Sri Sai Satcharitra* is a tale of common people's experiences with Baba and the various miracles that he displayed, such as levitation, bilocation, mind-reading, materialization, etc. He lit oil lamps with water, cured the terminally sick with sacred ash or a piece of a fruit he blessed, appeared to many people in their dreams, rescued countless devotees from dangerous, life-threatening situations, and displayed unimaginably advanced yogic powers such as the advanced form of *dhauti kriya* (in Chapter Seven of Sri Sai Satcharitra it was described that Baba was seen throwing up his intestines, cleaning them inside out, and placing them on a tree for drying) and *khanda yoga* (Baba removed the limbs of his body then "reassembled" them). Yet, his greatest power was that of unconditional divine love towards all who approached him with a pure heart and an open mind. No such person left Baba empty-handed.

Sri Sai Satcharitra is one of those powerful, living books that change people's lives. It is recommended to read it in exactly seven days (two to three hours of reading per day), starting on a Thursday. This is called a *Parayan* or *Saptah*[37] and can include a wish one makes, a blessing one asks for from Baba before commencing the reading. On the last day, upon completion of reading this book, one is to perform any act of selfless service (e.g. feeding the homeless).

As one of the greatest yogis, Shirdi Baba's life's message is so powerful that it expands the modern notion of yoga. Here are some examples:

> Sai Baba used to separate all the limbs from his body and put them in different places in the mosque. One night, a devotee saw this and feared that someone might have killed Baba. He

37 Source: http://www.saibabaofindia.com/all_about_sri_sai_satcharitra_parayan.htm

> wanted to report this matter to the village *munsif*, but later he kept quiet fearing that as he would be the first to complain, the authorities would think that he had something to do with it. Unable to suppress his curiosity, he went to the mosque early in the morning and to his astonishment found Baba sitting there as usual. Then he prostrated before him. The act of separation of all the limbs of the body is called "Khanda Yoga."
>
> Similarly, he once treated some nervous ailment in the right leg, by removing the flesh over that part, rectified the affected nerves and again put back the flesh which he had cut. Perhaps, Sai Baba used to wear the long shirt covering his entire body, with a view not to exhibit such things on his body.
>
> He used to practice all kinds of "Yogas" from his younger days. But he had never exhibited them before anyone publicly. Now and then, piercing light rays used to emanate from his eyes and hand (*abhaya hastha*). These light rays were very powerful and capable of curing all ailments.[38]

Most could not understand the Great Sai while he was alive physically, as is commonly the case with human beings. Mohanji expressed this beautifully during one of his talks:

> Today, Shirdi temple is rolling in wealth. When Baba was living, he lived as a poor man. People even denied him oil to burn his lamp. He hardly had shelter from rain or sunshine. We always tend to glorify the gurus of the pure White Path after their death and we shower riches on their tombs because we cannot deny the truth. Truth must be appreciated sooner or later!

The same applies to Sathya Sai Baba, who said, "My life is my message." And indeed it was. Even the most prestigious heart surgeons from around the world would come to Baba's abode in Puttaparthi and perform complicated heart surgeries free of cost out of gratitude and devotion to Baba. Such was the power with which he inspired people to serve. But many were stuck with the "physical frame" of Shirdi Sai and could not connect with the consciousness of Sathya Sai Baba, a different manifestation of the same Avatar. This is human nature. Devi Amma once told me, "Even some saints don't understand or recognize Sathya Sai Baba, it's OK." If one could simply connect with purest Love and evaluate everything with the same, all problems and conflicts would disappear.

In my own experience with Shirdi Sai Baba, he was mainly very playful toward me just like Jesus, with the occasional scolding when I did something really silly. Because I underwent my past life regression before the movie acting experience, I could connect the dots and realize that this entire movie acting experience was a *leela* (divine play) of Shirdi Sai Baba. I giggled when someone from the film crew commented that it was amazing that a European like me could walk with such ease in the traditional Marathi Nauvari sari. I was no longer surprised about anything connected to this movie and assigned it all to Baba's playing behind the scenes.

38 Source: http://www.saibaba.org/lhossb/lhossb8.html

When we traveled for a Kailash *yatra* (pilgrimage) in 2014, I met a group of Marathi people on the China border. It was amusing to be recognized as the "Foreignchi Patlin" heroine and to be asked for photos at such a remote location. During the COVID lockdown, Sulakhe Maharaj, the chief priest of Shirdi got sick at some point, and for the first time in years actually watched TV. He came across "Foreignchi Patlin" and told me soon afterward, "I noticed a familiar face on TV. At first, I wasn't sure, then I realized 'Of course, this is Mohanji's wife Devi! ' I watched the entire movie and really loved it." Whenever I hear such things, I smile and within my heart say, "Oh Baba, you always play with me."

What I saw in my past life regression was that I had spent most of that life as a yoga teacher in Shirdi, performing selfless service (mainly to children) and enjoying the mighty presence of beloved Shirdi Sai Baba. In that life as in the present one, I completed my postgraduate studies first, and then suddenly the "spiritual bug" bit me and all worldly aspirations went for a toss. My parents in that life were quite well-off. My father was a Muslim and my mother a European, which was rather unusual. They could not dissuade me from joining Baba in Shirdi – at some point, I dropped all career options and wealth to move to Shirdi, where I spent most of my life.

Mohanji was a very dear friend in that life as well. He was dedicated one hundred percent to selfless service, and deeply connected with Shirdi Baba. In that life too, he was a renunciate. I had the pleasure of meeting him almost daily and greatly enjoyed his guidance and beautiful energy, and after some time I started developing deeper feelings for him... However, I could not pursue those feelings. I knew he had taken a vow of celibacy and devoted his life fully to Baba. At times I felt sad about it, but since I didn't want to be with anyone else but him, I too decided to stay celibate. Baba knew of my deep wish to be in a relationship with "his son" (Baba calls Mohanji *mere beta* (my son) in this life as well), but could not fulfill it at that time. However, Baba smiled and blessed me... I accepted that "verdict" eventually and learned to enjoy my life the way it was.

Here is an excerpt from my past life regression by Dr. Choudhary, the part related to Shirdi Sai Baba:

Dr. Choudhary: Thank you [addressing my Higher Self]. She had some information from somebody that she was living in the time of Shirdi Baba and was doing yoga teaching. Could you throw some light on this information?

Biljana: Shirdi Baba, such a great Master... And he teaches everybody in a unique way. Somebody is scolded, somebody praised, somebody hugged. But yes, she was teaching yoga. There was one particular place where lessons were held. There would also be gatherings around the fire, like music, bhajans, with Baba's presence and so many miracles.

Dr. C.: I am asking the subconscious to give some flashes of some of the moments of the time spent with Baba, so that she can feel it, remember it, and be confident of her role in this life.

B: She once spoke to Baba, and... she used to love his chest, for some reason. He would sometimes keep his shirt open and you could see part of his chest. And then he allowed her to touch his heart with the palm of her right hand once. And that was like touching a magnet or something, like "whooof! " - a woofer effect [most likely referring to a deep thump of the sound with a heavy bass]. He basically blessed, whatever she was doing, he blessed. Whoever does service, he would bless. And he didn't say that one way of service was better than the other, we all have our ways and what we can do.

Dr. C.: Was she there with him for a long time?

B: There were some gaps, there were years spent away, and then she went back there for good.

Dr. C.: Was she an Indian, or did she come from abroad?

B: She was Indian, but the family was not approving her visits to Baba and Yoga teaching. Muslim background. Father was Muslim and was a little bit skeptical, and because of her higher education, this Yoga teaching in some village Shirdi was like running away from regular life. But she was doing something deeply spiritual and profound, doing service with village people and teaching them yoga, and most importantly being with Baba. She knew that those village people were the most blessed ones. You can't get more blessed than that, being with Baba and living that simple life.

Dr. C.: Was it similar to the feeling she had on the Mount of Olives, with Jesus?

B: Well, Baba had much stronger energy. Jesus was more subtle, and Baba was very intense... Sometimes he would suddenly hit the floor with his stick or shout at someone. But she always smiled. She could never be intimidated by anything he did. She was understanding he was doing something for some people to scare them off, or scare some evil spirits off, or something like that. He would sit on any dirt or rock, but he was so clean and bright – that was why he was wearing those white clothes, because any other color would simply DISSOLVE from his brightness. Only white could be there. And then his beard became white and his hair white, so beautiful. But his skin was young. That's exactly why she liked to look at his chest – it's like, his chest was of a young man, and then that white beard would contrast it. That contrast was so beautiful and spoke volumes.

[I would like to add here that I noticed something similar with Mohanji. Even though his skin would sometimes get a bit dry, the skin along his spine was always so incredibly soft, like the skin of a baby. I always enjoyed touching the skin blessed by his powerful Kundalini energy. I had the same experience one time when we visited Ganeshpuri, and I got the blessing to touch the *murti* (statue) of Bhagawan Nityananda. When I touched the spine area, I felt the same warm, soft baby skin as on Mohanji's spine. That reminded me of Shirdi Baba's baby skin and the feeling I had that time when he allowed me to touch his chest. I would immediately cry out from the sheer grace of that experience.]

Dr. C.: I really, really thank you so much for giving us all this information. I really feel very grateful, and I'm sure Biljana feels the same. I hope you will give us more opportunities to interact with you.

B: Sure.

Dr. C.: And give her the chance to get more confidence, more clarity, and maybe achieve what she came to do in this life. One more question. Could you tell us what is Mohan's relationship with Biljana?

B: Only love. (soft smile)

During past-life regression, I especially enjoyed seeing/re-experiencing how I died in that life. Since that life had been so filled with love and purity due to constant selfless service and deep connection with Baba, when it came time for my soul to leave the body, it floated upwards most peacefully and connected with the Light so smoothly and spontaneously that it was truly blissful to witness. It was a really beautiful experience – it made me realize how powerful a connection to a living Master truly is and that, indeed, I am eternal.

Moreover, it made me respect my amazing, wise, old soul which has seen so much, experienced so much, and always somehow had the blessing of connecting with the self-realized Masters. I could now finally understand the intensity and depth of my seeking, especially after that astral encounter with Babaji, which reignited that longing. I understood why in this life Baba has brought Mohanji and me together in a scenario that would allow us to experience the dimension of an intimate relationship and life partnership devoted to a higher purpose. What an amazing, GRAND scenario!

Shirdi Sai Satcharitra Highlights

I cannot close the subject of Shirdi Baba's life without mentioning some of the experiences shared in the most amazing living book *Sri Sai Satcharitra*, which is equal to an experience-based gospel of Shirdi Baba's life. I hope to inspire those of you who have not read this book to do so in order to expand your horizons, connect with this Love, and experience first-hand miracles in your daily life. No matter how many experience-sharing stories one may read, one's relationship with the Divine is ultimately individual, soul to soul, and can be established only through direct experiences.

Many people claim they can connect with "God," the formless, omnipresent Absolute, through their prayers as per the directions/conditionings of their faith. However, I do believe that the experience of Divine Consciousness associated with a form is incomparable to any other blessings. It is of great help to first connect to that form through deep experiences and iron-strong faith before one can develop faith in the Formless and see it as One. In critical times, especially during the harshest tests, this generalized notion of faith mainly fails us. The Divine in human form brings us closer to the realization of the formless Absolute/the Father/Allah/Parabrahma, whichever name one opts to use...

Sai Baba's *Satcharitra* is a book filled with special energy and blessings which simply overwhelm one's heart as one reads about the life-transforming experiences of people living with the Great Sai Baba in the small village of Shirdi a century and a half ago. From all the experiences described in *Sai Satcharitra*, the following two touched my heart as they speak volumes about Baba and the depth of his Love.

> In the year 1910 A.D., Baba was sitting near the *Dhuni* [sacred fire] on Diwali [the Hindu Festival of Lights] holiday and warming Himself. He was pushing firewood into the Dhuni, which was brightly burning. A little later, instead of pushing logs of wood, Baba pushed His arm into the Dhuni; the arm was scorched and burnt immediately. This was noticed by the

servant Madhava, and also by Madhavrao Deshpande (Shama). They at once ran to Baba and Madhavarao clasped Baba by His waist from behind, dragged Him forcibly backward and asked, "Deva, for what have You done this?"

Then Baba came to His senses and replied, "The wife of a blacksmith at some distant place, was working the bellows of a furnace; her husband called her. Forgetting that her child was on her waist, she ran hastily and the child slipped into the furnace. I immediately thrust My hand into the furnace and saved the child. I do not mind My arm being burnt, but I am glad that the life of the child is saved."

I have never heard a story of such great mastery and selflessness exhibited in such a pure way. This story lived with me for long after I read it and would always cause an instant expansion of the heart. I would like to highlight how this story ends because that beautifully explains Baba's operating level, the deeper meaning of all his words and actions, as well as the unimaginable depth of his Love.

On hearing the news of Baba's hand being burnt from (Shama) Madhavrao Deshpande, Mr. Nanasaheb Chandorkar, accompanied by the famous Doctor Parmanand of Bombay with his medical outfit consisting of ointments, lint and bandage etc. rushed to Shirdi, and requested Baba to allow Dr. Parmanand to examine the arm, and dress the wound caused by the burn. This was refused. Ever since the burn, the arm was dressed by the leper devotee, Bhagoji Shinde.

His treatment consisted in massaging the burnt part with ghee and then placing a leaf over it and bandaging it tightly with Pattis (bandages). Mr. Nanasaheb Chandorkar solicited Baba many a time to unfasten the Pattis and get the wound examined and dressed and treated by Dr. Parmanand, with the object that it may be speedily healed. Dr. Parmanand himself made similar requests, but Baba postponed saying that Allah was His Doctor; and did not allow His arm to be examined. Dr. Paramanand's medicines were not exposed to the air of Shirdi, as they remained intact, but he had the good fortune of getting a darshan of Baba. Bhagoji was allowed to treat the hand daily. After some days, the arm healed and all were happy. Still, we do not know whether any trace of pain was left or not. Every morning, Bhagoji went through his programme of loosening the Pattis, massaging the arm with ghee and tightly bandaging it again. This went on till Sai Baba's Samadhi (death).

Sai Baba, a perfect Siddha, as He was, did not really want this treatment, but out of love for His devotee, He allowed the 'Upasana' – service of Bhagoji, to go on un-interrupted all along. When Baba started for Lendi, Bhagoji held an umbrella over Him and accompanied Him. Every morning, when Baba sat near the post close to the Dhuni, Bhagoji was present and started his service. Bhagoji was a sinner in his past birth. He was suffering from leprosy, his fingers had shrunk, his body was full of pus and smelling badly. Though outwardly he seemed so unfortunate, he was really very lucky and happy, for he was the premier servant of Baba, and got the benefit of His company.[39]

39 Source: http://www.saibabaofindia.com/shirdisai.htm

First Experiences with Shirdi Sai Baba – in This Lifetime

A couple of weeks after I met Mohanji, when I first visited him at his accommodation, he gave me *Shaktipat* (transmission of spiritual energy). Mohanji and I were talking when he said, "Baba is here." He then placed the tip of his thumb on my forehead and his other fingers on my crown while staring at me intently. I closed my eyes and felt a very strong transfer of energy happening. Mohanji said (in fact, Baba said through him) something I would never forget.

"The highest version of you is Mother Mary." These words came as a shock to me, stirring something deep within. This had happened ten months before my past life regression and invoked something in me, a distant memory of Grace. I just wept silently, deeply touched.

Eight years later, when I decided to change my name to Devi, this was one of my main inspirations – to continuously invoke the highest version of me through my very name. One could say that the word Devi corresponds to Mother Mary as per Sanatana Dharma, connoting the Divine Mother aspect. (However, the very term Devi has much wider connotation than Mother Mary as the Virgin Mary and historical figure. Devi includes all aspects of the Divine Mother, including a fierce one that can destroy all negativity. I shall return to this topic at a later point.) Baba gave me the blessing to look beyond ego identification, beyond the lures of worldly life, into the highest of my potential. This is a very tall order though. I do my best in my everyday life to move in that direction, through selflessness, pure intentions, thoughts, words, and actions.

The second experience of Shirdi Baba happened very soon thereafter. A *homa* (Vedic fire ritual involving mantra chanting and offerings made to the fire for purification) was organized in an apartment of Mohanji's friends in Dubai. They were not close friends, but we were invited along with a select group of 15 or so people. All we knew was that there would be a homa and that some special guest from India closely connected to Shirdi Baba would be attending. I did not quite understand that the homa would be going on the whole night.

At the time, I was still working for an Australian company. I knew it would not be easy for me to remain awake the whole night and then go to work in the morning, but I joyously accepted the challenge and what I saw as a spiritual adventure.

As we all gathered in that friend's apartment, we were introduced to a sweet, humble old man from India who said that he prayed to Baba for years to serve him effectively and once got the blessing to materialize a *lingam.* (The lingam is the first shape of creation because it can hold the most energy – as explained by Mohanji, "The supreme unmanifested is represented by the Shiva linga, the egg-shaped material which contains the whole universe or which represents the whole universe. The first form is an egg shape, and Shiva linga can contain the maximum possible energy and that is why all the atomic reservoirs of the world are in the form of Shiva linga.")[40]

40 Source: https://mohanji.org/blogs/satsangs/2014/11/19/shiva-state-of-consciousness-an-aspiration-of-every-yogi/

Sathya Sai Baba was seen manifesting lingam, even a golden one, so though I was familiar with that concept, I never imagined this would be something I would be seeing in person. I also did not know it was painful, but if a large-ish marble were to form in the area of the heart chakra and then pass through the chest and throat to finally emerge, I do imagine it would hurt a lot.

This sweet, old man went into the bathroom, and all of us waited for the holy sighting of a materialized lingam. I somehow ended up being the one to hold a metal tray into which the lingam would be placed after being manifested, so I had to stand right before the bathroom door. It all sounded very nice, but then the old man started wailing and moaning in the bathroom and I could feel his pain. This was not pleasant at all, and I kept reminding myself that it was he who had asked for this, and that each time he manifests a lingam, a lot of karmic cleansing happens in his life through that pain.

Finally, he opened the bathroom door. Exhausted, he briefly looked at me holding the tray, opened his mouth, and leaned a bit forward. Nothing happened for a few seconds until I could see the unforgettable sight of a black lingam emerging from his throat, and then – "Bah! " He catapulted the lingam onto the tray. When the black lingam banged on the metal tray, I was stunned to see that it came from a completely dry throat filled with *vibhuti* (sacred ash). I was in a state of shock! Vibhuti from his throat and mouth splashed over my face and chest when the lingam landed on the tray. It took me some time to digest this intense experience while everyone was clapping and saying "Jai Sai!" This was one of those moments when all logic fails us and we behold the realm of the Divine expressed in action on this material plane. "What else is possible?" I thought.

The next blessing our chosen group of fifteen was to be showered with, was to have a private meeting with this man who would no longer be himself – Baba was to take over his form. This was part of the humble old man's "service package" if I may describe it in this way – to materialize a lingam and channel Baba so that the devotees could talk to him one on one. When our turn came, Mohanji and I entered the room and immediately noticed Baba's intense, palpable presence and divine fragrance, as well as a different expression in the old man's eyes. It looked like vibhuti was freshly materialized and randomly sprinkled onto the *Sri Sai Satcharitra* book that Mohanji had previously left for blessing, with a *rudraksha mala*[41] inside of it. Everything was covered with vibhuti. Baba said that we have his full blessing. I cannot remember whether we asked him anything else that evening, or simply bowed down and surrendered all our issues and challenges to him.

Finally, what awaited us towards the end of this blessed evening was the homa. I had no idea how long it would go on, but the very notion of linear time disappeared after some time. It was a beautiful experience. After all the miracles that I had seen, my silly mind still harbored worries that the fire and smoke would cause the fire alarm to go off in that apartment building. But they opened the windows and it all worked out. After everything I saw, lighting a fire in one's apartment was no big deal.

41 Rudraksha is the name of a special seed that absorbs energy very well. A mala is a beaded prayer necklace that usually consists of 108 beads.

There was a lot of smoke and their entire apartment would obviously have to be repainted afterward, but they did not care. It was quite a powerful fire, to which we were offering different seeds, ghee (clarified butter), flowers, chanted mantras, etc. That was my first homa in this lifetime, and I must say that it was very, very intense. I remember that I was amazed when I noticed at some point that I did not feel sleepy at all throughout the night. There was a lot of heat in my spine, and some beautiful meditative experiences were happening that entire night. The homa finished around 5:00 a.m. They said they would be doing this for three days in a row, and that we are welcome the next day as well.

I noticed a big change in my life straight away. The truth came out and it wasn't pleasant, but it brought much-needed clarity into my life, especially in terms of my troubled area of relationships. After the American company went bankrupt, I continued staying in the villa by the sea with Rob, my sister, Marija, and Belka for a while longer until the lease for that villa expired. I found a new job in Dubai, Marija and Belka were soon to return to Belgrade jobless and penniless, while my sister found a job as a spa manager in a hotel in Nepal.

Rob was in a bad mood all the time and did not want to be asked about the money the company owed us for the last six months of work. All of a sudden, it was nobody's responsibility that we did not get paid, and we were just expected to "move on." This was not all that easy due to my massive credit card debt, which was acquired in service of the company.

When I returned to the villa around 5:30 a.m., with the smell of smoke in my hair and clothing, I found that the entrance gate was locked. I knew this must have been done deliberately by Rob because we never used to lock the entrance gate, only the door to the villa (to which I had a key). When I called Rob and the girls, nobody answered the phone. In the end, I had no choice but to sit in my car for another two hours and go to work smelling like a smoked turkey, without even having brushed my teeth. I was not happy, and I knew that a serious discussion with Rob was awaiting me when I got back from work.

As I rightly guessed, it was he who had locked the entrance gate door. He was angry as he had figured out that I was seeing someone. I told him briefly about Mohanji and he was not happy. When I complained about the gate being locked and how I was forced to go to work without even brushing my teeth, he said something along the lines of, "Your new man should have taken care of you." This was the first time it became evident to me that Rob expected I would never find the man I was looking for, or that I would realize that Rob had been the right man for me all along. Rob was at least 20 years older than me, but he was obviously hoping that I would eventually realize that he was *the one*. He once teased me that I was like an immature girl, dreaming about some *prince on a white horse*. He was certain that the kind of person I wanted did not exist in reality.

When I started living with Mohanji, and when I witnessed the ease with which he downloaded profound pearls of wisdom, wrote truly amazing texts, created and conducted meditations, served society so selflessly, empowered the people with whom he worked, faced all dangers and fears head on, etc., I had a deep sense of satisfaction that what I was looking for was real, and not any prince from a fantasy land. What I had asked from the deepest space of purity of my heart was for a partner who was in coherence with my highest purpose. No words suffice to describe the depth of satisfaction I felt after finally meeting Mohanji. Of course, without Baba's intervention and blessing, I surely would not have found him or would not have recognized him. I know very well that it all happened only because of my beloved Sai Baba...

Rob's locked gate made me realize how naïve I had been, believing all along that Rob was always supporting me unconditionally. He once shared with me the story of a young woman from a poor community in Africa whom he had helped get a nursing education and move abroad. She started earning a good salary, etc. He really was keen to empower women and had a deep connection with his own mother who suffered a lot in life. This was something he loved and I know it came from his heart. I thought that, as with that African woman, he recognized a special potential in me and was happy to support me during my studies in Italy (when my scholarship did not cover the accommodation and living expenses) and whenever I found myself in a financially tight situation as a student. I once told him, "I don't want it to appear to anyone that I am using you."

He laughed about it and said, "Oh please, you can never use me. I am helping you because I want to. Do you think I care about all this money I am earning?"

I chose to believe him and considered myself truly blessed for having such loving, unconditional support. At some point during my studies in Rome, it was Sinke who warned me that I was incurring karmic debt by allowing Rob to cover some of my expenses. He said, "You will see that, sooner or later, you will feel that you owe him something."

After this rude awakening with the gate door, it was clear to me that Rob's support came with the hope that I would actually fall in love with him, regardless of our age difference. I realized that I would never get back the money for my last five salaries because that was my "karmic payback," the price I would have to pay for my freedom and independence.

Karmic lessons are never easy, and this money situation came exactly when I was not only at rock bottom financially, but "in the red" as they say. That was not an easy realization to accept. I appreciated Rob in many ways, as he was the one I turned to after my NDE, he was the one who inspired me to look for a scholarship online before Rome, and the one I could count on in case of any emergency in life. However, this one night orchestrated by Sai Baba simply burst the bubble. It was time to be fully independent and handle my issues maturely, on my own.

I decided to take the challenge, and the blows kept coming. Very soon, I lost that job in the Australian company and was left like a leaf in the wind. Yet, I did not feel lost because Mohanji was in my life. I was not even ashamed. I did not feel a need to hide anything from him because I knew that he meant it when he said, "I love you for who you are." This was all that I needed.

After all the luxuries of Dubai, trips, training, nightlife, salsa dancing, lunches and dinners in fancy restaurants, I knew that was not where true happiness was to be found. The day when I lost my job in the Australian company, soon after this incident with Rob, I spoke with Mohanji and he suggested "Why don't we move in together then? We are both jobless now and need to save money. We will support one another through this transition. I am sure Baba will take care of this too, nothing to worry about."

I agreed with Mohanji completely and was truly overjoyed. I moved in with Mohanji understanding that nothing was a coincidence. I could feel Baba's gentle nudge speeding up this entire karmic cleansing scenario, ensuring the two of us finally got together and started living together.

Before sharing the journey further, I would like to revisit the three-day-long leela by Baba wherein the old man acted as his instrument. A huge change happened after only the first homa, and there were two more ahead of us. Mohanji asked me on the second evening, "Should we go there again? We already took the space last night and got the blessings. So many other people are eagerly waiting… Maybe we should be considerate toward others."

Overall, we had felt fulfilled on the first day and thought that maybe we should let somebody else have the experience. So, we decided to go to the cinema instead. This was the first time we would be going to see a film together.

We assumed our seats in the theater and the movie was about to start. All of a sudden Mohanji asked me, "Do you smell vibhuti?"

I was stunned. After a couple of seconds, I said, "Hmm. Now that you pointed it out, I do smell that specific scent of Baba's sacred ash." Both of us could clearly smell vibhuti all around us.

Mohanji became very quiet and was looking into the distance. I figured he must be receiving a telepathic message. He then said, "Baba is scolding us."

I whispered, "Oh goodness. What is He saying?"

Mohanji replied, "He said, 'You cannot not attend when I'm working on you. You have to be there. Why didn't you come for the homa?"

After receiving our first scolding as a couple that evening, we immediately got up, left the theater during the movie, and went back to the homa. Those three days were very special. We certainly needed the powerful cleansing that we received, for so many other challenges awaited us as a couple.

Baba's Leela and the Cloud of Mosquitoes

Even though I love visiting magical "Mother India," there is one serious problem that bothers me a lot. It's the mosquitoes. Mohanji once made me laugh to tears when he shared a joke that the mosquito was India's "national bird." No matter what mosquito repellent I use, I always get bitten mercilessly.

Soon after Mohanji and I moved in together, we traveled to India to attend the wedding of Vanamali Amma's son. Mohanji considered Vanamali Amma his spiritual mother and we could not refuse this invitation. After the wedding, we visited an ashram. We were chatting with a friend outside when I suddenly noticed a bunch of mosquitoes flying above Mohanji's head. It was really odd that they were sticking together and forming a ball-like shape. I was perplexed and wondered what could be the cause of this most unusual gathering.

"Oh my gosh! There are so many mosquitoes flying exactly above your head! " I found this to be very funny as Mohanji reminded me of the cartoon character Winnie the Pooh who always had honey bees circling above his head.

Mohanji smiled and said, "I know how much you complain about mosquitoes whenever you come to India, so I pulled them all above my *sahasrara* (crown chakra) to protect you. It's very simple, I just increase 'the light' in that area and they get attracted."

I was speechless. And so it happened again – Mohanji somehow managed to surprise me beyond imagination, no matter how much I thought I knew him. It was only later that I realized that this experience was just an intro to what was yet to come.

I had just finished my acting experience in "Foreignchi Patlin." Mohanji and I were both penniless, and with our last dime, we somehow managed to reach Puttaparthi, the abode of Sathya Sai Baba.

I had visited Puttaparthi two times earlier on my own, and based on those two experiences I was mentally prepared for lots of out-of-the-comfort-zone drilling and ego bashing like before. I will make a small digression and share these experiences first, to give the reader an idea of how Baba operates and imparts knowledge.

Ego Bashing Moments in Puttaparthi

During my first visit to Puttaparthi, Baba's abode had been super crowded throughout and no single room was available anywhere, so I ended up sharing a room with ten Russian women. They were very loud and, if I may say, pretty raw. In short, they were totally inconsiderate toward others. It never occurred to me then that this was deliberately designed by Baba to show me where my buttons get pressed and where my ego reacted with judgement. (After all the insights from my past life regression, I should have known that I had some karma to work out with the "raw" people.)

On top of all of the noise in the Russian language, I had to cope with the frequent loss of electricity, which meant that the fan wouldn't work and I would feel too hot to cover myself. Unfortunately, since there were many mosquitos, if I didn't cover myself, mosquitoes would devour me. If I did cover, I would sweat and not be able to sleep at all. The Russian ladies' waking noises turned into loud snoring. Combined with the heat and mosquitoes, the entire setup made sure I didn't get any sleep. I was desperate for some rest and even cried at some point, but it was not meant to be. In the end, I waited, dead tired, for the clock to strike 3:30 a.m. so that I could get away from that snoring orchestra in preparation for the long lines for Sathya Sai Baba's darshan. Cleansing in combo with ego bashing was definitely the hallmark of this visit.

I noticed that by the end of that day, I was feeling much lighter and that my meditation was deeper, even though I was supposed to be tired due to the complete lack of sleep. I sure was pushed out of my comfort zone big time. There were some really beautiful experiences as well during that visit, deep enough to make me want to visit Puttaparthi again.

During the second visit, I had some really funny experiences – I giggle whenever I think about them and really can't believe how silly my mind can be. The first one happened at the western canteen (a dining area for western people, with separate men's and women's areas, serving wonderful *sattvic* (balanced) food for a nominal price). I volunteered to help with cleaning at that canteen after noticing how crowded it was and how much the ladies who were cooking and serving, actually struggled to keep up with the pace. Cleaning was the last thing they had time for and volunteers were needed.

I was really happy to have the opportunity to do seva in Baba's abode. I was mopping the floors in both the women's and men's canteen. While cleaning the men's area, I suddenly noticed a plate with sweets. There was one sweet that especially caught my eye, one I really liked but did not see served in the women's canteen. Nobody was around and, without thinking, I took the sweet (it was a small, round ball, made out of cocoa, nuts, and coconut). I continued mopping and chewing my treat when the voice of my conscience spoke. I could actually hear it. "I can't believe you just stole that sweet, that too in Baba's sacred abode. Aren't you embarrassed? You know very well you promised yourself and that police officer in Batajnica that you would never steal again, not even one chewing gum. Shame on you."

As if someone had poked me in the butt, I stopped mopping and gave this act serious thought. "Oh my god! It's true. What was I thinking – stealing this sweet from the canteen?"

The next day when I arrived at the canteen, I was thinking about how to rectify the situation. I would have just given money for the sweet to the cashier (I know it would be something ridiculous, like ten cents or even less), but I did not know how much it would cost or how to explain to the cashier why I insisted on giving more money.

While passing by the sweets area, I couldn't believe my eyes when I saw a pile of different sweets and only one such small coconut-covered ball among them, awaiting me. I looked at Baba's smiling picture and was smiling as well. "Baba, you are amazing, I have no words." I took that sweet, went to the cashier, and asked, "Excuse me, how much does this cost?"

When I got the answer, I replied, "Wonderful. I would like to pay for two such balls because yesterday I accidentally took one and did not pay for it." The cashier lady smiled and said, "Ok, whatever." I left the canteen that evening content and grateful to Baba for teaching his child a lesson.

The next day, I experienced another, even more ridiculous scenario. There were many books available to purchase in Puttaparthi and I chose a small booklet about Shirdi Sai and Sathya Sai – it was like a booklet for beginners. I thought its size was convenient to carry with me to read while waiting for hours in the darshan line (sometimes a two or three-hour wait). I wanted to utilize the time wisely and thought this booklet was a good idea.

I was told that no items, including mobiles and books, were allowed. One should come empty-handed and water would be served. (A bottle of water would be passed along the line of people seated and waiting for darshan. I thought it was disgusting for everyone to be drinking from the same bottle. But then I saw they were drinking it "the Indian way," pouring the water from a height of a couple of inches, with the lower jaw protruding slightly forward – it was really practical. I learned it then and still drink water that way.)

Even though I was aware of the rules, I still decided to bring this booklet with me. I had a justification in my mind, "Oh well, this is not a real book. It is small. And it is about Baba – what is the problem there?"

I tried to hide it, but at the entry to the Darshan Hall, the guards (volunteers called "Seva Dals") discovered it and told me very strictly, "This is not allowed." Since a yoga mat or pillow is allowed as a support for the lower back, the next time I came I wrapped the book into a rolled yoga mat. The previous time I came with the yoga mat, they did not open it to check it, but this time, as if they knew, they opened the yoga mat and the booklet fell out of it. It turned out to be the same woman who had scolded me previously, and she came forward to give me one more scolding. I couldn't believe it!

The third time I went, as stubborn as I am, I decided to put the booklet in my underwear. "This is where they surely won't touch! " I thought. Whenever they check us, they gently tap the sides of the body, definitely not the genitals.

While waiting in line and coming closer to my turn, I started sweating. I saw the same woman from the Seva Dal who had caught me last two times, standing nearby. I suddenly had a thought, "Oh come on Biba, is this really worth it? What if they find it again?"

At the last moment, I came out of the line and hid the booklet in a nearby bush. I re-entered the line and when my turn came, the Seva Dal checked me and, get this – looked me straight in the eyes and gently touched my pubic bone. At this moment, it dawned on me that all these Seva Dal people were being telepathically guided by Sai Baba. I understood my lesson and quietly sat on the floor in the hall, digesting this experience. I realized the reason why Baba did not allow any books was that we were supposed to witness our busy minds and learn how to calm them. We needed to create space so that He could work on us. I was amazed by just how silly I was and apologized to Baba for this act of utmost immaturity and disobedience.

I learned that day that one should never question the rules or orders of spiritual Masters. However, such blind faith and devotion took time to develop. We always start with questioning; this is how human nature is. Whenever I remember this experience, I always smile. "What would have happened had I kept the booklet in my underwear?" I think. They would probably kick me out of the Darshan Hall.

I did not leave a good first impression on Mohanji's spiritual father with all this immature behavior, but then again, he knows me better than I know myself. I am not at all embarrassed to share my ludicrous moments here because I sometimes like to remember them and joke about them on my own account – this is how we grow, so it's all good.

Eye to Eye with Baba

Coming back to my experience in Puttaparthi with Mohanji – I felt it was really good that I had these previous experiences so that I could notice the huge difference between going to the same location with and without Mohanji. This time, with Mohanji around, it was not only different, but

I felt like I had come to a different place or as if somebody had given me a VIP ticket to heaven! The experience of Baba's abode was superb and truly unforgettable. The moment we reached the super crowded hotel, the receptionist welcomed us with a big smile and said, "Welcome! We are fully booked, but one room just became available so you are lucky. Just wait for ten minutes till they change the bed sheets and clean up. It is room number nine." (Number nine represents completion and is considered "Baba's number," so in spiritual terms, this was the Presidential Suite in the hotel.) Mohanji and I looked at each other and smiled.

From the moment we reached Puttaparthi, Baba was continuously engaging in telepathic communication with Mohanji. He spoke to him with so much warmth, like a father receiving his beloved son after a long time of travel abroad. Mohanji was in a complete bliss state, his eyes were glowing and I could tell that his communion with Baba was happening more or less all the time.

Baba was enquiring lovingly whether Mohanji liked the hotel room, whether this or that was OK. At one point, I went to the toilet and when I came out I had a real sight to behold – Mohanji removed all his clothes (he told me he couldn't bear to have anything on his body because the energy was so high) and was blissfully staring at one point. His body language was similar to the time when Mahavatar Babaji had entered his body, so I had a pretty good idea of what was happening. He did not have to tell me, "Baba is here," it was all clear to me. I just stood there humbly, waiting to see what would happen next.

Then suddenly, to my great surprise, Baba said, "Show me the photos." He asked in his succinct way, through Mohanji, to see the photos from my Marathi movie. I had a stack of fresh movie photos with me. However, I was baffled and so overwhelmed at that moment, that I didn't quite understand that I was supposed to give the photos to Mohanji and that Baba would look at them through Mohanji's eyes. Then he cleared that fog from my brain and I suddenly got it. I must have looked really funny standing there all breathless, next to Mohanji (whose body language and expression in the eyes were now completely different), while he (i.e. Baba) was flipping through the movie photos and smiling upon seeing some of them. Needless to say, I was so deeply honored that I didn't know what to do!

Then, to my great surprise, Baba conveyed lovingly through Mohanji the words I will never forget. I feel like printing them in big, golden letters and framing them. He said, "In your life in Shirdi, there were some wishes I could not fulfill. In this life, I'm going to fulfill them all! "

I understood that it was Shirdi Sai (or probably Shirdi and Sathya Sai together) speaking through Mohanji. (Please note that many people greatly respect and worship Shirdi Sai Baba, but cannot believe that Sathya Sai Baba embodies his consciousness in our contemporary time. I never had this doubt, especially not after having a darshan of Baba in vivo and having so many experiences that confirmed this connection. However, this exact experience confirmed to me the truth of Shirdi Sai and Sathya Sai being one.)

I lost my breath at that moment, and tears were falling. This was a huge statement. Not only was this direct proof to me that the same consciousness works through Shirdi Baba and Satya Sai

Baba, but that there was also something really grand for me. Mohanji has explained to me that karma also means unfulfilled desires. Karma is not just the result of good or bad deeds. It also corresponds to all the items on our life agenda's "shopping list," mainly desires that are yet to be fulfilled either through direct experience or by transcending them through higher awareness. So, when Baba said that he was going to fulfill them all, for me, this was a huge statement. I'm still grasping the meaning, but dare to conclude that Baba said he will ensure that I am left with no desires to fulfill, which means no reason/pull to return to Earth. When Masters speak, it's very cryptic. One has to contemplate for some time to grasp what the Master truly means. But this one statement was filled with overwhelming grace and landed in my lap as a bomb!

After all the tears and goosebumps, I also intuited that the movie experience must have been one of my past life wishes. Moreover, it was explained to me that, during my life in Shirdi, I was not eligible to receive a spiritual name because I had asked for it in the wrong way, i.e. opted for celibacy out of resentment because I could not be with "Baba's son," i.e. Mohanji. However, that same special someone has been given to me in this life, and the spiritual name requirement got fulfilled as well when I eventually changed my name to Devi (only in the light of this experience do I understand why I felt it was so important to change my name). I did not make this connection in my mind at all until Mohanji pointed it out to me during the name-changing ceremony (which will be covered later). He said it all in a couple of words, "Baba always keeps his promises…" I was overwhelmed and couldn't gather myself – how the Divine works is indeed truly unfathomable.

Miraculous Glasses and New Mosquito Clouds

While we were in Puttaparthi, Baba's showering of love continued. Since one glass from Mohanji's specs somehow fell out of the frame and was lost on our way to Puttaparthi, he was peeking through one eye like a pirate and had to buy new specs urgently. This was not all that easy as there was no proper optician in that rural area. He bought whatever they gave him in the small optical store, but it was not perfectly attuned and he already detected a mild headache.

While waiting for the new glasses at the small store, we chatted with a friend of Mohanji's who worked at Baba's Hospital. Mohanji gave this man the old glasses as a souvenir and he kept them in his shirt pocket for no reason. The next morning the old man called us, euphoric with excitement: "Mohanji, you won't believe this. When I woke up this morning, I came across your broken specs in my pocket – Baba fixed them! BOTH GLASSES are there now, they look brand new. The materialized glass is still warm! "

Mohanji was overwhelmed and said, "Indeed, Baba gave me the right vision." We were both bursting with joy.

Furthermore, that evening, after Baba's darshan, I felt like being alone for a while and simply went for a walk in that beautiful energy. I had learned that there was a particular building in which Sathya Sai resided and devotees were allowed to walk below his window and pray there quietly for a minute or two after darshan. That was exactly what I did that evening. I just felt like thanking Baba for bringing Mohanji into my life, for fulfilling my wishes across lifetimes, and for guiding me so lovingly. At that moment, I also couldn't help but request that Baba fulfill one more wish of mine and allow me to see him at least for a second... I stared at his window, hoping he would appear behind the curtain. I remember that my heart was beating so fast, tears were flowing and, at one point, I noticed something really strange – a big, weird-looking CLOUD OF MOSQUITOES (in an egg-shaped circle, more than one and a half meters in diameter) formed in front of Baba's window out of the blue. I was bewildered as it slowly floated in my direction.

It is interesting – when the human mind registers something never seen before, there is a strange blankness inside as it is not able to "frame" the experience into anything known to it from the past. So I just stared at this "mosquito cloud," feeling rather confused. The next thing I registered was the immense upheaval of 50+ birds that were hiding in a nearby tree. They all started flapping their wings and creating a lot of noise as if they had gone mad. The whole tree was shaking! I still stood there in a daze, not knowing where to look first – the tree overcome by birds or the cloud of mosquitoes. I really did not know what to think of the whole incident.

It was only when I met Mohanji later that evening and recounted the whole experience that my idiocy became strikingly evident. He told me, "How come you didn't figure it out? That was Sathya Sai Baba, right there in front of you! He came towards you in his astral body, and since you were obviously not able to see him, he attracted all the mosquitoes from that area into his aura. Since I did something similar just a couple of days back, he thought you would have connected the two incidents and thus recognized him. Anyhow, the birds did so and that's why they were so excited. They love Baba."

I was shocked and kind of embarrassed to have missed the whole thing and not connect the obvious clues only a few days after that scene with Mohanji and the mosquitoes. That's what they call "an educated idiot."

"This is just great – first I missed seeing him when he came to the room I shared with Dr. Maja, and now I have missed seeing him right in front of my nose." I thought to myself. "Oh well, I just hope that, after missing Baba's astral presence twice, I will get the chance to experience the *treća sreća* ("third luck" in the Balkans), and be more attuned and aware the next time around..."

Experiencing the Miracles with Mohanji

As I got to know Mohanji better (in this life, that is), I noticed one thing about him that I admire a lot – even in the greatest of pain and distress, or in the midst of a financial crisis, he would not ask anything for himself from the Masters. When I once asked him why he doesn't use his third eye to seek their help in such situations, he answered, "I know that Masters are with me all the time and I surrender to their will fully. If I am to go through some experiences for the purpose of karmic cleansing, so be it. Otherwise, what surrender are we talking about?"

This statement was so clear and powerful that I never thought of asking him this question again. He was right. It was my direct experience that whenever we reached a dead end, Masters would unfailingly offer their loving helping hand, but usually at the last moment... That was the experience I had already witnessed numerous times.

There were so many indescribably sweet and unforgettable moments when an explicit display of divinity was visible through Mohanji, followed by his child-like smile, shining cheeks, and sweet playfulness. I have witnessed him displaying spiritual powers and performing miracles so many times, but not only would he not brag about any of them – he would even downplay them by making them seem normal or simply smiling about them without giving them any big importance. "Highly evolved but unassuming" – just like "I" created him...

The following are a few such unforgettable experiences from our early days together in Dubai.

Mystical Defogging

It was a few days after Mohanji and I had moved in together that one weekend, early in the morning, we decided to go for a yoga class. It was very humid outside and, unlike ever before, my car's windshield and all the windows were fully fogged up. I could not see anything. I tried everything – all the possible options with AC, opening the window, using the windshield wipers, etc. but to no avail. When we had somehow reached the main road, I didn't know whether it would be worse to turn back or continue driving ahead. I told Mohanji, "We are guaranteed to have a car accident in this scenario. I can't see anything! " I was just catching glimpses of where we were as the wiper would do the job and the fogging would immediately undo it.

Mohanji kept quiet, but at one point just said, "Pull over. Let me drive."

I looked at him as if he was crazy, "What?! Your vision is much worse than mine. And can't you see how much I'm straining my eyes to see anything?" I was visibly upset with this entire situation. He ignored me and repeated the same sentence like a programmed robot. I then said, slightly annoyed, "OK, YOU handle it." I stepped out of the car and swapped seats with him.

The moment he sat down and touched the steering wheel, the fogging on the windshield started clearing. I was completely confused and started laughing, saying, "How on earth did you do that?"

Mohanji just smiled in his typical, sweet way. Soon I shifted from anger to laughter and we really enjoyed the morning.

The Fire Incident and Mystical Healing

The first miracle I experienced with Mohanji happened a few weeks after we met. It was time for me to take my annual leave and visit my family in Serbia. Unfortunately, Mohanji could not accompany me for this trip, so I came to his apartment to say goodbye and was to leave from there for the airport early in the morning.

By the time I packed my bag and arrived, it was already late at night and Mohanji was sleeping. I just entered quietly, lit one candle to have some light in the room, and slipped softly into the bed. The candle I lit was my gift to him a few days prior – it had some nice Christmas-y decorations around the outside of the tea candle. It was late, and my intellect was not really "switched on" – I didn't think much of the fact that the candle was placed on top of the TV...

We both went into a deep sleep when suddenly, in the middle of the night, the smell of SMOKE woke me up – it was a huge shock to see FIRE on top of the TV which was already in flames as well. (I had failed to notice that there was some paper money Mohanji had left next to that candle decoration, and the AC was on, so the flame must have caught it.) We both jumped up, and before I could think of anything, I was doubly shocked when I saw Mohanji extinguishing the fire with his bare hands.

Since the fire had already reached the glass portion of the TV, I was really scared that it could explode and all that glass would pierce our bodies. The whole thing was terrifying, like standing before a time bomb. However, with Mohanji's swift action, the fire was extinguished within ten seconds or so. After the adrenaline rush was over, we noticed how bad his palms were looking – with burns all over, blisters already forming, and pieces of dark plastic mixed with the burnt skin. Needless to say, I felt very bad and guilty for causing him this pain and material damage. I knew it must have hurt a lot because burns cause a high degree of pain, and these were not small burns.

Instead of shouting and blaming me, to my great surprise, Mohanji just asked me to sprinkle some vibhuti (the sacred ash from Sai Baba, which works as a cure for everything, provided one has faith). This incident happened around 1:30 a.m. so we still had another two hours before it would be time to head for my flight. Mohanji said, "We'll just lie down and calm down a little bit before we get up to go to the airport." We were both very tired and slept. His palms were facing upwards and were covered with Baba's vibhuti.

When we got up, we looked at the palms immediately and a huge change was clearly visible. The burns were about 80 percent healed! There were still remnants of some of the burns, some dead skin and all, but there was a huge difference. "Wow! Look at your palms! They look much better! " I said.

"Yes. I told you not to worry," Mohanji said. "Baba will take care."

I then asked: "Should I call a taxi now? Your hands are better but burns are still there."

He was so sweet when he insisted: "No, no. I'm gonna drive you."

Mohanji was so quiet that I could not make out whether he was in pain or not. I remember that when he was driving me, he was holding the steering wheel mainly with his wrists, but still had to use his palms when turning the steering wheel. Whenever he did that, there were some pieces of the skin from his palms falling off here and there, visible on the black rubber of the steering wheel. I felt terrible. Never had I seen anything like this before.

I told him, "I'm sorry! " I must have said "sorry" 50 times until we reached the airport. Upon returning to his apartment, he applied vibhuti again and went back to sleep. Within the next two days, no sign of burns remained and his palms looked the same as before (which was IMPOSSIBLE with burns of that degree). That left a strong impression on me, and my love for Mohanji grew even deeper.

My Aunt Seeing Mohanji's Astral Form

Upon reaching Serbia, all I could talk about with my family members was Mohanji. I showed them the photos, and nobody except my Aunt Danica, who writes poems and prays a lot, had the subtlety to notice anything special about Mohanji in those photos.

The following day, I decided to mark Christmas Eve in a special way and go with Aunt Danica and Mom to an old monastery near Novi Sad. While we were attending the religious ceremony there, my aunt suddenly told me, "Biba, this is amazing. I just saw your Mohanji! My eyes were closed as I was praying, but I saw him! He was playful and kind of just peeked in, checking whether everything was OK. He smiled at me and then disappeared. He was wearing some kind of long maroon shirt."

I was dumbfounded! That was the same *kurta* (Indian wear, a bit longer than western shirts) that he had been wearing when we parted. I was happy there was at least someone in my family with whom I could share my most unusual new life with Mohanji.

And I have to confess, I was a bit jealous that I could not see him, and she did. (I was feeling really cold in that monastery and had a bit of stomach pain, so that could have reduced my awareness level. Or, it could be that my aunt was more attuned to the subtle world than me.) In any case, it was a groundbreaking experience that showed me yet another dimension of Mohanji. Before going to sleep, I texted Mohanji and said, "My aunt spotted you."

That was his first introduction to my family. I just felt so proud – and strangely excited, like a high school girl. I truly felt that my life had become magical!

Miracles of Healing of my Family Members

My trip to Serbia was just a preparation, laying the groundwork for my family to meet Mohanji. It was a couple of months later in 2008 when the two of us got to travel to Serbia together. After one year of the two of us being together, I finally got the chance to introduce my "most special someone" to my parents and relatives. I tried not to be nervous about it but knew, especially with my dad around, that something funny and crazy was to be expected.

Mohanji wore his usual jeans and T-shirt and was acting normal. He was very quiet, only speaking in response to a direct question. By that time, the popularity of Mohanji's Power of Purity meditation was rising. I translated it into Serbian and recorded it in a studio in Dubai. Both versions were available on the Internet, and people around the world had started connecting with Mohanji. I spoke to my family about what we were doing, and about some beautiful meetings taking place with Mohanji's first devotees-to-be. Since it all looked very casual, my parents understood none of it. Considering him just a normal person, they were asking questions like, "What's his education?"

Dad thought it was good that both Mohanji and I had Master's degrees because he was worried I could have been more educated than Mohanji. In his opinion, that would not reflect well on our relationship. He then asked, "What is his job in the shipping industry?"

I explained to them that he was about to start a new job in Muscat as the CEO of a shipping company. They were happy. It was all a bit unusual for them because he was not European, had a different skin color, and came from a different culture and religion. My parents also couldn't speak English and therefore could not communicate with him without me translating.

Even though I informed my parents beforehand that Mohanji did not eat meat, my dad thought it was good manners to offer him some meat nevertheless. After Dad offered it, Mohanji just said, "I don't eat meat, thank you."

Dad then offered some plum brandy to raise a toast, but Mohanji said, "Oh, thank you, I don't drink."

I was giggling as I could read my dad's thought, "Gosh! What do I offer this man?"

So I told him, "Don't worry. We are on a spiritual path and we don't consume all this, but there are no formalities, you know. It's all okay."

During our stay in Novi Sad, we managed to organize a small meditation gathering and as always for such events, Mohanji decided to wear his white *dhoti* (a typical Indian garment consisting of a piece of material tied around the waist and extending to the ankles) and kurta. When he wore those clothes for the first time, my father was in a state of shock. He couldn't believe his eyes. I intentionally did not want to tell him anything because I wanted to have fun seeing his reaction.

Dad asked, "What is he wearing?"

I said, "Well, it's some typical Indian clothes, you know. The long shirt is called a kurta, and below that is a dhoti."

He said, "Oh, I thought he forgot some of his trousers, so he borrowed our bed sheet."

I was laughing hard for minutes and simply couldn't stop. I can picture my dad sharing these jokes with his buddies over a cup of plum brandy. These were the initial cultural bumps that we overcame pretty fast. It was all very sweet in fact.

When we were about to leave, my other aunt from Croatia, my mom's elder sister Mara, happened to come for a visit. The topic changed to physical pain the moment my father suddenly complained about continuous pain in his right shoulder. Mohanji looked at me and whispered into my ear, "It's from one of his past lives. He was stabbed through his shoulder by a spear or something. It's one of those deep *samskaras* (painful impressions) which stay in the muscle memory in the next life as well. But don't tell him that. He's not going to be able to understand that."

Mohanji then said very humbly, "Well, maybe I can help you. Can I just hold your wrist for some time [as if to check his pulse] and I'll see if I can help you?"

My father said, "Okay, sure."

Mohanji held his wrist and closed his eyes. My dad was quiet like a little schoolboy, waiting to hear the doctor's diagnosis. This was the first time I saw Mohanji holding someone's wrist similar to how ayurvedic doctors do pulse diagnosis. I knew that he just needed an excuse to transfer the energy and wanted to downplay all of it. After a minute of silence, it was finished. Before we knew what happened, my father started to lift his arm at the shoulder and shouted with joy, "Look! See that?! Oh my god, I can lift it all the way up! Look! I can even make a circle! "

He got so excited that he kissed Mohanji, and then the whole family got excited. My aunt Mara was standing next to Dad and said: "Well, Biba, can you please ask Mohanji about my arm? I had a car accident and I broke my arm. There were multiple fractures. It still hurts, even though they fixed the bone a year ago."

After translation, Mohanji just held her wrist for a minute or two and when he opened his eyes, her face lit up as she realized that the pain was gone. "Yes! The pain is gone! " she said, also super excited. The atmosphere in our living room was all charged up, but when I looked at the watch I realized it was time for us to leave for the airport.

We had to rush, so we just hugged everyone and bid them farewell. As we sat in the car, everybody came out to see us off and my grandparents waved from their window. They lived one floor above and had eventually come down to participate in the experience-sharing. My Mom shared with me later on how funny it was to see my grandfather's reaction. Upon hearing about the healings, he said angrily: "I cannot believe it! Nobody told me this on time! Do you know how many pains I have?! "

Everybody found this really funny and my mom told me over the phone, "You left just at the right time; otherwise, you would have missed your flight."

Mohanji left quite an impression and all of it was just so incredibly sweet. A couple of years later, he told me, "Healings are Masters' calling cards. Masters are not meant to do that but are here for something far more important. However, hardly anyone thirsts for the highest." That is so true.

I hope I can convey just how normal all these healings, meditations, and telepathic communications looked around Mohanji. He was always downplaying everything. If he did something extraordinary and I asked him, "So how did you do that?", he would usually say, "It's all just happening, flowing. It's very easy."

Being around him was always an ever-new joy, and full of fun with an abundance of love that made everyone feel fulfilled.

My First Miraculous Cooking Experience

When we moved into our affordable accommodation in Rashidiya, just behind Dubai Airport, I realized I was one of the rare women who, at the age of 31, had never really lived with a man. I'd not yet had the chance to serve a male life partner, cooking and cleaning, and everything else. I had been too preoccupied with my studies and then lived in a villa where we all earned so well that we mainly ate out or ordered something in. I had never really cooked proper full meals before. I remember when Rob once told me, "Promise me, you will never end up with some Balkan man who shoves you in the kitchen, and you just end up cooking all your life."

However, when I started living with Mohanji, I saw it was actually such a great joy to make someone you love happy, through food or any small thing a woman can do. I was so happy to have our modern "YouTube University" available at any time. I used it for cooking instructions. I began following tutorials and exploring recipes. I loved discovering how to make something and then surprising Mohanji with a new dish. We really enjoyed those most-special months in Rashidiya before Mohanji got that job in Muscat. It was our most cozy and pleasant time together. After that, we never had such time completely to ourselves.

One time a friend of Mohanji's decided to visit us in this new accommodation. This was a first. Mohanji told me, "My friend Kannan is coming in one or two hours. Can you quickly cook something because it will be lunchtime?"

I was thinking of making *dal* (lentils), but I hadn't made it for three people before – I would have to guess at the measurements, ingredients, and spices for better taste, etc. I was nervous but tried to hide that from Mohanji. At that time, I closed the door of the kitchen and started praying to Baba earnestly, "Baba, please help me, you know I have no idea how to make this! "

Then, in a hurry, I quickly started to chop some vegetables, boiled the rice, and eventually, my hands seemed to be selecting spices on their own (I didn't even see which ones). Something strange was going on and before I could think or analyze anything, the pot was full of lentils and vegetables and it all came out perfectly tasty. When I served the food, Kannan said, "Very good! It is very tasty."

I was so happy and was thinking, "I never thought I would be bothering Masters to help me with my cooking."

Middle of the Oil Lamp Turning Into Lava

When we started living together, we did a lot of *sadhana* (spiritual practices) and it was especially beautiful when we would do it around 4:30 or 5:00 a.m. Our makeshift altar was a big cardboard box. We always maintained the flame of an oil lamp with a wick in the middle. Often when Mohanji would chant, I could see immediate changes in the flame of the oil lamp. It would inevitably become taller. Sometimes the presence of the Masters was felt, and the flame would become really tall. I remember one time when Mohanji chanted the powerful Shiva Tandava chant that the flame of the oil lamp grew more than 5 inches tall and the middle part of the *diya* (oil lamp) which is metal with a hole in the middle for the wick, became red like lava! At that point, I got really worried that we were going to burn the house down. The cardboard around the altar, wooden flooring, and furniture in our room could easily catch fire.

Many intense experiences were happening and I loved them all! This was my dream coming true, and I relished every second of it. In those Rashidiya days, I was gently nudged into the understanding of Mohanji's consciousness. He was always very humble about all of it. He was not displaying anything. One time when we were practicing something we learned from Babaji's techniques, Babaji himself told Mohanji telepathically, "Do it like this, not like that."

Mohanji conveyed this to me, and we then laughed about the fact that we had gone elsewhere to learn some supposed techniques of Babaji when we had the Source within us. That was hilarious!

Mohanji was always very quiet and introverted, for that was his nature. Even if something that could be called a miracle would happen, he would not make a big deal out of it. So, naturally, I too was just flowing through it all, but I was deeply touched and transformed by each one of those experiences. I will share a few more.

A Dimensional Shift – Experience of Being a Whale

While living in our "nest" in Rashidiya, with the wooden walls reflecting all the golden and orange colors of our love and warmth, there were so many other beautiful experiences that took place. One of them was a dimensional shift into a different state of existence. I can't describe it any other way.

One day, Mohanji was in a deep meditative state. I was just observing him and soaking in the energy. I could make out that he was in a sort of communion or that something deep was happening. I sat next to him, and after a while, I asked him what was happening in his inner space. He said, "I'm in communion with a whale."

That was quite a surprise! He was communing with a whale telepathically. That was awesome. I loved whales, especially after I had dreamt of one during my postgraduate studies.

I just sat there quietly when he surprised me with a question, "Would you like to experience it?"

I replied joyously, "Yes, I would love to! "

He asked me to touch a part of his body and guided me on exactly how to do it. It all looked very simple. I touched him and then retreated to sit down. He was lying down and became immovable. As I sat in meditation, not only did I suddenly connect with a whale, but I became one! I experienced a grand, super-fast movement through the ocean waters – going up and down. I was this massive being, so free in the vast waters. After flying in my astral body like an eagle (back in Rome), this was my second most powerful experience of freedom through movement. The speed with which this mighty whale moved was great. It came with a feeling of the great power that whales carry, power beyond the physical realm. I could feel their power was in their connection with the unity consciousness.

I don't think that as human beings we understand the first thing about these grand beings, whales and dolphins – just how connected and attuned they are, and what a blessing it is to have them on our planet. When I was within that whale I embodied the whale's consciousness at that moment. I will never forget this. It was beyond powerful to experience this. I didn't know who Devi was. I was fully immersed in the whale experience for some time. Then when I came back into the feeling of my body and my identity, I just sat there awestruck and it took me a bit of time to come out of the depth that I felt. I hugged Mohanji and thanked him because this was one experience that I will always remember with immense gratitude. I never knew such an experience was even possible!

Knocked Out For Hours

After a couple of days, I saw Mohanji in a deep state again. Sometimes I would just enter the room and see him like that. I would not know what was happening, but I could feel that it was something big. I would just sit there humbly and quietly, not wanting to disturb the energy with movement, sounds, or even my thoughts. At some point during his meditation, I got the idea to ask him, "Could you possibly, give me Shaktipat and, kind of, include me in the experience…?"

He replied, "You can't. You're not going to be able to take it."

My ego would not permit me to believe that. I said, "No, it's okay, trust me. I can take it. After all the yoga training and everything I've been through, I can take it."

Just because I asked once again and was already bothering him, at some point he briefly touched me. He just touched my shoulder; there was no Shaktipat on higher chakras.

What I remember next is that there was a huge surge of energy and I felt the need to lie down. Not only did I lie down on my stomach, but I also squished my face into the bed, and in that squished state I remained, immovable for three or four hours. I was knocked out! I don't even know how I even managed to breathe through my squashed nose. After this incident, I came to trust Mohanji's words regarding my eligibility to receive such intense energy.

Mohanji smiled and decided to share one story with me. He said that in the time of Shirdi Sai Baba, one man used to keep asking Him to give him enlightenment. Baba said, "You can't handle it." And then at some point, because he was pestering Baba, Baba finally gave him the Shaktipat he asked for and gave him the experience. This man started running around Shirdi like a madman. He had no control over his body, thoughts, or emotions. He was probably making sounds and running around like an insane person. At some point, other people begged Baba to make him normal again.

This is when Baba took it back. Once this man regained his old consciousness, he understood. We cannot ask for higher consciousness states, or enlightenment experience – it all has to happen organically, from within. There is no skipping possible. Through the Grace of the Guru, one avoids sidetracks and can speed up the process, but only to some degree. We still have to walk the path. This is very important to understand. Otherwise, we are not able to cope with the energy - the *nadis* (the subtle energy meridians of our aura) are still too blocked to handle the strong current gushing through the subtle body and physical body. Most importantly, our entire system has to be properly aligned. So, working on the alignment, opening the heart, purifying, surrendering, all of this is very important for us to experience the highest of states. In summary, no skipping of lessons. That was the lesson of that experience.

Eye to Eye With Death

As our blissful days in Rashidiya were passing by, both of us were sending our résumés to different companies. I decided to go to downtown Dubai for a possible job interview but was hesitant to leave Mohanji because he was not looking well. He did not have a fever but was coughing frequently. He was definitely sick.

When I woke up that morning, I had an unpleasant intuitive feeling, but could not pinpoint what it was. I was in an early morning daze. There was just some heaviness and sadness. I told Mohanji, "I have to go to this meeting now. Are you sure it is wise for me to leave you?"

He was lying in bed and just nodded. After I left and was driving toward the venue of the meeting, Mohanji suddenly had an intense choking experience. He coughed incessantly and couldn't catch his breath.

He told me later on that he choked. There was no air going through and there was nothing he could do. It was all completely blocked. At that moment he left his body. The next thing that happened was that he floated above the body. That was when he saw his late daughter, Ammu, standing in the golden light, extending her hand to Mohanji. She was welcoming him to the other world, and he was so happy to see her!

He started moving in her direction. Ammu kept looking at him with utmost love. She smiled and told him telepathically, while also pointing with her eyes, "Look down, look down! "

Then he said, he looked down from that realm, and saw me with my arms up, crying and pleading, "Come back, come back! "

Ammu told him telepathically, "There's somebody there for you now. You should go back. You have a different life to live and so much to express."

He looked at me and decided to return. He was able to break through an invisible barrier and finally take a breath.

Now, the strangest thing is that I was not there physically, but with my light body I was involved in this whole story – this was what I had been feeling that whole morning. The understanding just did not trickle down to the point of my conscious mind fully.

At that point, my sister Dana called me. I was amazed when she told me, "My dear sis, I was meditating and suddenly I had a vision of Mohanji leaving his body." She recounted the exact same story of his daughter welcoming him, him looking down, me calling him to come back, etc. She described the whole thing exactly as it had happened.

From my NDE, I knew exactly how it felt to be back in the body after such an experience and was so happy to be next to Mohanji, so grateful that it all worked out. That was his new life. He was sent back to the body, and we were able to continue with the blessing of our life together.

Masters Appearing Through Mohanji's Body

I had started to witness a change in Mohanji's body shape and/or size, depending on which Master was communing with Him telepathically. This was happening quite often after we started living together, once a month on average. The change in Mohanji's body was always obvious to me. I could even discern the Master with whom Mohanji was working or interacting, by catching those subtle changes of his body features or the special "flavor" of the energy.

Sometimes they would enter the room in their light bodies. Sometimes they would work, speak, or radiate energy through Mohanji's body. For example, one time I was driving him to the venue where he was conducting the Power of Purity meditation, followed by a Satsang and Shaktipat in Dubai. I glanced at him casually and I noticed that his foot had become much longer. I knew immediately – it was Shirdi Baba. Also, the way He spoke was very firm, and his voice was deeper and a bit more coarse.

One other time, I noticed that he had suddenly started typing a blog. I entered the room, and from the back I could see him seated with his spine straight, typing something very fast. He was wearing only his dhoti, his upper body bare. I was especially drawn to stare at his waistline because I recognized the youthful, slim body of Mahavatar Babaji. At that moment, Mohanji was writing his famous blog, "Babaji Beyond Definitions." These are precious experiences. I always had to pinch myself. My dream from the days of reading *Autobiography of a Yogi* had now turned into reality. The presence of Masters in my life was an immense blessing, all thanks to Mohanji.

The presence and guidance of enlightened Masters from higher planes of consciousness is an indescribable blessing. Their sole purpose is to lead us to liberation, inspire us to seek more earnestly, and point us in the right direction when we get sidetracked. Masters are like road signs – at the right time, the right Master appears to guide the seeker.

Moreover, those who are blessed by experiences with enlightened Masters know that, with them, the love that a human being can experience matures to a whole new level – one gets to experience the depth of devotion and loving intimacy with the Divine which is not only beyond the physical but beyond the barriers of life and death too.

The magnetic bond of love becomes so strong that even death cannot break it. Our vulnerability becomes even higher as we surrender more, and can say with all earnestness, "Let it be Thy will, not mine," allowing the Master to work on the ego aspect and "shake our reality" fully. Again and again, over lifetimes, when the time is right, the right Master appears in our life to help us fulfill our soul's ultimate agenda. They give us the boost at the crucial time when the seed is ready to venture out of its comfort zone, tread unknown territory to reach the surface, and sprout in the grand sunlight, celebrating its uniqueness.

In my case, before meeting Mohanji, I already had had several previously described profound experiences that confirmed this beyond-life-and-death connection with Mahavatar Babaji and Shirdi Sai/Sathya Sai Baba. However, when Mohanji entered my life, it all kind of consolidated and was reinforced. His very presence changed my life completely.

Mohanji explained this point to me once so beautifully: "By expressing compassion and unconditional love through thoughts, words, and actions of selfless service, we serve the soul's purpose of relieving itself from the density of multiple incarnations, and finally arrive 'Home.'"

In this process of shedding density while on Earth, denser souls catch hold of the lighter souls to help them elevate themselves – just like a basket that, when connected to a balloon (which is of lesser density) filled with helium, gets to float up.

That explains the importance of being in the presence of elevated beings, the Masters. Among the Masters currently present on Earth, there are differences. Some are like balloons with helium, but some are like rockets! Anything is possible. As Mohanji says, "We get the Master we deserve, not the Master we desire. Thus, work on increasing your eligibility to experience the highest."

After numerous experiences like the scene with "the cloud of mosquitoes" happened, I started to realize what an enormous blessing it was to be in the continuous physical presence of someone through whom so many great Masters communicated, imparted experiences, offered their loving guidance, and performed much-needed cleansing of *samskaras* (subtle impressions from the past that add to the "baggage" we carry). Finally, finally, this realization started to dawn on me. Thanks to Mohanji, I have understood that each Master, in their own way, works on a different aspect of our spiritual journey.

Moreover, I understood that among true Masters, there can't be any conflict of agenda because they operate from the super-conscious level of Oneness and Unconditional Love, and their sole purpose is our liberation. It is so fulfilling and so deeply touching to see how great Masters work in unity, and with deep respect and genuine love towards each other because they are indeed One.

Chapter 9

Dubai Without Mohanji – Testing Time

An Abundance of Tests, Lessons, and Blessings

When Mohanji left Dubai to begin working in Muscat, the capital of the nearby Sultanate of Oman, I was left alone in a tiny rented room, with the burden of my tens of thousands in credit card debt and no proper income. I would occasionally dine at cheap Indian restaurants but mostly survived off of fruits as I did not have any sort of kitchen. I slept on a mattress on the floor. Though determined to at least cover my living expenses, I could barely make ends meet. It felt like I was a fish out of water, struggling for life. Big cities can seem so cruel when one has no money. The glitter and glam of Dubai – truthfully the dazzling lights of any city, had lost their appeal, and my perspective shifted away from the fascination with *maya* (the illusory world). To this day, my eye is more drawn to people, nature, love, community, and compassion. This was a big lesson.

Nevertheless, I will always have love and gratitude for Dubai, the city where it all happened. It was in Dubai that the perfect circumstances culminated for me to meet Mohanji, and it was Dubai where ACT Foundation outside of India was founded in 2003. Subsequently, many beautiful charitable initiatives were initiated, conducted, or coordinated in other countries.

Dubai was also our home when another key spiritual experience happened – Mohanji called it "the Shiva experience" to avoid the frames of enlightenment. He never cared for titles and the only change to which he would agree was adding "ji" (denoting respect) to his name, Mohan. This is how Mohanji described this powerful experience:

> It was February 24, a day after my birthday in 2007. I was with my parents and decided to celebrate my birthday at a nearby ashram. I usually celebrate my birthday by feeding the poor children. However, that day, since morning, I was feeling dizzy. My head was spinning. I was feeling very uncomfortable and was also having a bit of nausea. I reached the ashram by evening. When I reached there, I was almost helpless as even my eyesight was blurred. I could not see people clearly. But, I behaved as natural as I could, to avoid unnecessary questions and explanations. That morning, I had a deep urge to buy the book "Shiva Sutras," without any particular reason. [...] All I could remember was reaching one house within the ashram complex, entering the hall and sitting down on a chair near a table.
>
> Sacred Ash started coming out through the top of my head and then slowly falling down my body. (Sacred Ash sprouting out of Sahasrara is a sign of burnt karmas. When the last

remnants of karmas are getting exhausted, like a volcano, with high intensity, they are burnt and expelled through the Sahasrara. This is typical of Dattatreya Tradition.) My body was transparent, and a huge bright light was glowing from within. My eyelids became golden. The light penetrated my clothes and was radiating to the outside world. I was expanded beyond description. Everything was within me. Mohan did not exist.

Vibuthi kept flowing... There was no time or space. There were no *gunas* (attributes) such as *Sattwa*, *Rajas*, or *Tamas*; there were no identities. Everything got erased in a split second. The need to return or come back was also not there... I do not know how much time I existed in that state. All I heard after some time was the voice of Swami shouting to other ashramites: "Shiva is here! Come fast....Bring the camera." I slowly started regaining my body awareness, but that took some time. I became aware that many people were around me. I became aware of the flash bulbs. Then, at one point, I opened my eyes.

I saw a lot of people in front of me. The first photo caught a slight glimpse of the brightness that was coming out from inside my body. Swami said that the brightness was so strong that initially, he couldn't allow anyone to enter as they (their nerve endings especially) would not be able to withstand this level of energy. The later photos just caught my physical frame with the Vibhuti and the state after the experience. As it is said, "Images can speak much more than words." So, do enjoy the photos. [The original image from Mohanji's Shiva Experience is included in the photo section.]

That experience tilted my consciousness. My awareness level changed. As of then, I started shifting to different awareness levels effortlessly.

When a seeker becomes the sought, his limited entity dissolves into that of unlimited nature. He becomes all pervading, completely lucid and transparent, vibrant, shining, subtly dynamic, and exists in complete awareness. The momentary sourcing of data from the higher realms becomes effortless and continuous.

This is what I wrote soon after the Shiva experience:

When we touch the realms of Shiva, the Supreme, everything dissolves. Everything merges into one. It's only a vast, expanded brightness, absolutely peaceful, and all-knowing. All the planets, various suns, stars, and various spheres of existence, become simply parts of the vast existence of Shiva, the Supreme. It is all contained within the infinite brightness which has supreme awareness. That was my experience on Feb 24th, 2007. That state can be called the state of the Father, or Allah, or Parabramha, it's all the same. All one needs is to understand that effect.

When the limited entity called Mohan became Shiva, at first, there was only the bliss, indescribable bliss that encompassed me. The bliss of infiniteness. The bliss of liberation. The bliss of bodylessness. Existing in that expanded state, I became one with all the beings of the Universe. Limited awareness of Mohan merged with the entire cosmos and became one with both, the limited and unlimited existence. In that expanded state, one can only express Love, our very nature. I became every being, and every being became me.

> Human intellect cannot comprehend the state of Shiva. Humans can experience that state only when they cease to become humans. They need to get out of their body, mind, intellect, ego, and every other aspect and become empty and pure. Shiva's state is that of extreme purity. Human intellect has limitations and its data bank, the subconscious, is usually filled with stored memories and their attached emotions, and this is what it can refer from. The state of Shiva can never be stored and extracted this way. It can only be experienced and that too, when we can effectively transcend our "humanness."
>
> Whenever intellect tries to comprehend, humans miss the Shiva aspect. Humans cannot achieve the state of Shiva by "doing." Be it of physical or intellectual nature, "doing" amounts to action and movement. Action is an expression of duality. Duality is dilution of the true state of Shiva which is all-encompassing and exists as non-duality. The state of Shiva is truly that of Oneness. They can achieve the Shiva state only through "beingness," being in the state of Shiva.
>
> In that state of complete bliss and love, the transformed entity will choose to lead many more souls to His stature – that of the Supreme. This is a pure act formed out of love and compassion. By doing this, he is guiding himself; because everything is part of himself. It is as if some part of the body gets dirty, we wash and clean it. Just the same, when some souls search in the darkness, liberated souls, with full understanding and awareness that those souls in darkness are essentially a part of themselves, lead them to light. By doing this, they are becoming more complete…[42]

I must say, I was sad that I missed being in Mohanji's presence when this key spiritual experience took place, but I know that I am blessed with the full benefits of the same, provided that I connect with his consciousness.

I am very grateful that I was present when he received the Power of Purity meditation. I return to this key moment once again because, in terms of the entire Mohanji platform that we see in the world today, present in more than 90 countries with registered, active centers in 17 (and counting), the milestone that marked the beginning of it all was the moment when Mohanji received the Power of Purity meditation (available free of cost on www.mohanji.org). It has since been translated into many languages by the volunteers whose lives it has touched.

Since this was such a powerful moment in our lives, I would like to share Mohanji's experience of this most sacred milestone:

> Three months after the Shiva experience, at about 4:00 a.m., I was woken up and immediately sensed very high energy, within me and around me. The Power of Purity meditation was given to me by Baba. (I consider all Masters as BABA, because there is no importance to name or identities in the other realms. All work in unison, under the guidance of the Supreme. This is my experience.) So, when I was woken up and asked to write the meditation, I was

42 Source: https://brahmarishimohanji.wordpress.com/2010/07/28/babaji-beyond-definitions-part-3/

not aware of what I am supposed to do with it. I had no idea what I was going to write. I was not even aware of the content.

As it was being delivered, it took only about 10 minutes for me to type the meditation using my laptop. It was like Baba was making my fingers move. Everything was crystal clear. When I realized that it was a full-fledged meditation, I asked Baba: "What am I supposed to do with it? Am I supposed to meditate?" He said: "No. You must teach." Immediately the introvert in me objected: "No Baba, I am not cut out for such a thing. You know that I am an introvert. I cannot go around and tell people – Hey, come here, I will teach you meditation. Moreover, I am not Guru material. I am an ordinary man, with all the strengths and weaknesses of normal human beings." Immediately the answer came: "That's not your problem. We will send people to you. Understand that those who come to you are sent by us. Others will not reach you. Nor will they understand you. Your strength is your subtlety. You are empowered. You will represent our tradition." Again, my logical mind objected: "I need people to assist me in this, especially if the mission that you are entrusting me is so big." The answer was: "That is not your problem either. We will make things happen at the appropriate time. Just be." I realized that my holidays were over and I was about to embark on a much larger mission. The journey had begun!!!

I recorded the meditation in a studio quite effortlessly because, at that time, I was doing the radio show called Mohan's World, which was reasonably popular amongst the spiritual circles. Just as Baba said, our meditation took off in Dubai. It started spreading wider and wider to the stage that we have reached now. What had I done to achieve this? Nothing. This is Divine play. All my Question & Answers sessions and blogs are also similar. I never read or prepare. Appropriate answers happen at the appropriate time. Our path is so pure and simple. No expectations, no conditions. Only two pillars. Purity and Faith. We operate on the ground of unconditional love, beyond all man-made barriers such as caste, creed, country, community, culture, and color.

Even though I received the meditation in May 2007, I did not conduct any classes nor did I attempt to record it till September.

Biba saw the entire text, right after I received it telepathically, and told me: "It is amazing. You should spread it." A crystal clear answer appeared in my awareness:

"I will do it free of cost, as a service to society. This would be the next dimension of what I am doing through the Ammucare Charity Foundation. Through Ammucare, we are physically helping the poor and helpless of society. Through Bless The World (BTW) Meditations [the initial common name for all the meditations received telepathically and shared with the world by Mohanji], we shall work on unburdening the helpless karmic entities called Human Beings. Unburdening/cleansing of the conditionings that one carries forward through lifetimes, definitely will take time. If change from the cycle of birth & death is a necessity, then commitment and patience is a must. Faith is a must because the cleansing that happened may not be tangible. Yet, it will be effective for sure.

> In October 2007, Biba took the initiative and organized the first-ever meditation session in Dubai that I myself conducted. Then, every week, the sessions happened. People experienced heavy cleansing. Some experienced communions with the Masters. Some got answers to their questions without even asking them. Some had certain miraculous experiences. Thus, all have their own experience and are getting results. As always, some are consistent and committed. Some just come to see. Some to test. Some to taste. Some appreciate. Some criticize. Some ridicule. Some praise. This is nothing unusual. This is the way the world operates. We conduct the sessions free of cost and voluntary donations are used for expenses of the premises and charity activities. So many people, love incarnates, came together and made this happen. They are carrying it forward. Slowly, BTW meditations spread to other countries, as people shared their impressions and experiences with others. We did no campaigning or marketing. Baba's words always ring in my ears: "Understand that those who come to you, are sent by us."[43]

I was deeply touched and so grateful that Mohanji was in my life. With his inimitable humility, acting as if what he was doing was completely normal, he covered my most urgent monthly installments for the brand-new Ford Focus car that I had bought earlier (when I took my stable income for granted) along with my monthly credit card payments. Without his support, I would have had to hide from the financial police or go to jail. He had his debts to pay but never said one word about paying mine as well. His selflessness touched my heart, and his loving presence was greatly missed.

My yoga and "Fitness Salsa" sessions had very poor attendance and the distances I had to cover within Dubai were huge, not to mention the traffic. I met Ihsan, a kind man from Pakistan, who allowed me to work at his landscape architecture company doing part-time administrative tasks for a while, just to survive. I was very grateful.

One day rashes appeared all over my body. I recognized the itching that I experienced when I traveled to Shirdi with the "Foreignchi Patlin" crew – bed bugs! They were incredibly difficult to get rid of, and on top of everything, I had to throw away half of my clothes, keep my mattress in the sun, etc. I was in a state that can only be described as agony.

On our life's journey, testing times are usually only realized in retrospection. While we are in the experience, we can't see the forest for the trees. I certainly never received any warning: "The test is coming," or "This is a test." On the contrary, I was so immersed in the experience that this kind of conclusion only arrived later, after the experience was over. I'm just very happy that I always follow my intuition and listen to my heart. That was the only way forward for me during the testing times.

The Luring Offers

In the midst of my agonies, I chatted online with a friend of Rob's who had continued working for the United Nations, at that time in Jordan. He told me, "If Dubai is not working out for you, why

43 Source: https://brahmarishimohanji.wordpress.com/2010/07/28/babaji-beyond-definitions-part-3/

don't you come to Jordan? Send me your CV. I can put in a good word for you, and surely you'll be able to get in based on your education and your previous UN experience."

I was happy to hear this but my intuition told me, "No! After all my years of searching, I have finally found my special someone, and this relationship would not stand a chance if I moved to another country. If living together is not possible, I at least have to be near him."

At the time, all Dubai had to offer me was agony and bed bugs, but I decided straight away I would not give up all that easily on my dream of living with Mohanji and serving humanity. I told this friend, "Thank you, but I prefer to stay here."

I was also aware of what some called, "UN syndrome" – the tendency to become accustomed to a super-high salary and relatively easy job which involved a lot of travel, sacrificing any semblance of family life. I realized that I had finally met a man with whom I could imagine myself living and, if it is given, even forming a family. I knew I would not be happy living a UN life. I was in my early 30s, and I felt ready to commit to such an exceptional man and experience a different life, the life of my dreams!

However, more tests were to come. I once met a chubby clairvoyant woman from the UK who came to Dubai to conduct some workshops. She was dressed in black (probably for its slimming effect) and led some meditative process in the desert, where I felt the presence of many spirits and actually did not enjoy myself at all. She liked me, and in the end, offered me a one-to-one session free of cost. I shared my financial predicament with her and she started explaining to me the importance of "assuming responsibility for my reality," etc. At one point she told me, "So, this boyfriend of yours, this Mohanji, is he much older than you?"

I said, "Well, he is 12 years older, but that really doesn't matter – he has exactly what I have always been looking for, and that does not belong to the realm of physicality in any sense."

She replied, "Hm, I knew it. I am not sure that he is really the best option for you. I see someone much closer to your age, maybe two or three years older than you, someone from Europe. Why don't you go back to Europe? Why do you have to stay here and suffer? Think out of the box." I got really confused and said that I once had a relationship with a man two years older than me (Sinke), which did not work out.

To my great surprise, she started shivering, exhaling like an aroused person, bouncing off the chair and whatnot. And then she said something that really hit me.

"I knew it! I knew it! That Sinke – he is your Twin Flame! My main mission in life is to bring Twin Flames together. You have no idea – Twin Flames will do anything for one another. You don't know the story behind his decisions. He would have sacrificed himself for you any time. He would always do what is best for you..."

At some point, I stopped hearing what she was saying. My head was bursting and I had to get out of there. This was the last thing I needed. I felt like I was being fried in the scorching sun. All my weak points – the poverty of my refugee days and my unresolved feelings for Sinke, were thrown in my face. Everything seemed to be conspiring against me, testing the decision I had made to stay with Mohanji NO MATTER WHAT. At some point, I made a firm decision – there was no way I was going to believe her more than my own direct experiences with Mohanji and all the confirmations I had received from Baba. When it comes to clairvoyant (or so-called clairvoyant) people or any external opinion for that matter, one should always trust their innermost feelings and intuition and stand firmly in the truth of their direct experiences. This woman's vision was far from my reality. Had I followed her advice, I would have ended up in greater confusion, if not trauma. In the end, I chose my own truth over her words, ignoring her and moving on.

What would be my final communication with Sinke had happened only a few months earlier. We ended our relationship elegantly when he called me all of a sudden after a long time. I made it clear to him, "I am not alone (anymore)." The following day, he sent me an email and wished me all the best on my path. He said something about ending the relationship cleanly. That was the end of our seven year relationship, a connection across space and time that was truly stranger than fiction. I wished him all the best on his path as well, and we both moved on. I appreciated the fact that he always honored his word and allowed me to live my new life freely.

A couple of days after the experience with the British woman, I had a job interview with a huge construction company in Dubai. They were looking for an administrative manager and liked my CV. "Oh, finally," I thought. The interview went very well and I could tell that they liked me. I was to wait for the final confirmation for another couple of days. Five days later, I got a call from their HR office. The lady who interviewed me said, "Ms. Biljana, I was about to congratulate you on getting the job with us because we really liked you and thought you fulfilled all our conditions, but today it just so happened that a young woman from Palestine came for an interview. She had all the qualifications like you, literally identical, but also speaks Arabic. We all assumed that, considering her background, she would be in really grave need of a job, you know, and that we are doing a good deed by giving her this position. I hope you understand."

Hearing that, I was devastated. Nothing, absolutely nothing was working, and only hardship seemed to come my way. When a decent job seemed finally within my grasp, it would slip through my fingers. For most other jobs, I was "overqualified," and I could not get a visa to Oman because I was "young and beautiful" – I felt like shouting so that the entire Universe could hear me: "What nonsense is that?!"

There was one more big test that I would like to share. It had all started a year or two earlier, before I even met Mohanji, when Sri M (whom I mentioned earlier when describing my trip to India in 2006 with Dr. Maja) came to Dubai. I was happy to meet him, and I must say that I continue to have profound respect for Sri M as an authentic spiritual Master. I requested a one-on-one audience with him, and at that point shared the story of my astral encounter with Mahavatar Babaji. We spoke very briefly because there were many people in the hallway waiting for their turn and he told me I was welcome at his center and meditation hall in Madanapalli, India any time, to receive initiation into Babaji's Kriya. My sister Dana and best friend Marija were invited as well.

When I came out into the hallway, one of the organizers of this gathering asked me about my experience. When I briefly shared that it was really nice and that I had been invited for the initiation, his reaction astounded me. He was totally dumbfounded and just couldn't digest that some jolly European girl like me had received approval for initiation "just like that," while so many people waited for years to get it and kept being told to come back again after being given some preparatory breathing techniques, etc. I had no idea about any of this, but was grateful and knew this was a blessing from Babaji.

The entire experience with the initiation was really beautiful and sacred. After all the many Kriyas I had learned by that point, this felt like the real deal. I could feel its energy deep within. There was one interesting moment during the initiation itself. It was 5:00 a.m. and all of us initiates had been waiting for Sri M in the meditation hall for almost an hour. Sri M was late because of a disagreement, a telepathic argument of sorts, with Babaji. (This is actually Maheshwarnath Babaji, a great Master from Mahavatar Babaji's fold, mentioned in the "Autobiography of a Yogi" as well, who had guided Sri M through his initiation, his Kundalini awakening, and his path of serving humanity.) He told me that Babaji had asked to give me a higher number of rounds of Kriya, which was not common, and Sri M was worried that this would be too much for me. I have no words to describe how deeply honored I was by this special blessing. After all the years of waiting and searching, I felt that I had finally received THE Kriya blessed by beloved Babaji. I made sure that I respected it by practicing the Kriya diligently. I never revealed the details of this Kriya to anyone, including Mohanji as I took my sacred vows most seriously. All of this occurred just before I met Mohanji and went on into the time when we had only just met. At the time of my Kriya initiation, I was convinced that Sri M was my Guru.

On the same day, we visited Sri M's future Peepal Grove School, a wonderful educational institution which left a deep impression on me. Sri M said that we were the first to be photographed in it because they had just brought in the school benches. It was all truly joyous, and we were overwhelmed by the entire experience. However, something else happened that day. We happened to meet a dignified, old woman who was introduced to us as the generous person who had donated the land for this school. I spoke with her a bit and noticed the meditative depth in her eyes. She told me that she was Sathya Sai Baba's devotee. While Sri M had great respect for Shirdi Sai Baba and his photo was present at the entrance to the sacred place where initiation was given, he did not recognize Sathya Sai. A hint of that was given to me that day through a passing comment of his about Sathya Sai Baba, which I chose to ignore at the time.

Over time, especially after I had my own powerful experiences in Puttaparthi with Mohanji and after other comments that Sri M made about Sathya Sai Baba reached me, a strange pain occurred within my heart. I could not comprehend how a Master of Sri M's stature, of which I was convinced, did not recognize Sathya Sai Baba. My own experience and deep conviction with regard to Sathya Sai Baba did not match his words and this created an immense inner conflict.

I remembered a story that Dr. Maja shared with me. She once traveled to Tamil Nadu and spoke with some prominent Kriya yogis from Mahavatar Babaji's lineage. He offered to take her to a highly confidential location that only very few people, mainly Kriya Yoga practitioners of an advanced level, could visit and therein meditate. As they walked toward that location, the man enquired with Dr. Maja about the practice that had helped her achieve her spiritual depth. She of course mentioned Sathya Sai Baba, who had been her true spiritual Master all along. This man stopped and did not attempt to hide his disgust, "Don't tell me that an educated, spiritually evolved woman like you falls for the magic tricks of that man. We have such fakirs on every street of India." At this moment, Dr. Maja simply remained silent but she stood by her truth. She thanked this man, and walked straight away in the opposite direction. I really appreciated her dignified ability to stand by her truth in all circumstances.

At some point, I had to make my choice as well and it was not easy. I remembered all the thirsting, searching, and seeking that I had been through, especially after reading the *Autobiography of a Yogi.* I finally got the Kriya I was looking for, and it was priceless to me. I could truly feel this Kriya and knew it was genuine. I loved going to Jumeirah beach at 5:00 a.m. to do the Kriya at sunrise and then listening to the sound of waves and the chirping of birds whose songs would begin exactly as the sun rose. This was truly magical – the real present of the present moment with Mother Nature.

And yet, just like Dr. Maja, I came to a point when I had to face this unpleasant issue. Everything was 99% there, but this 1% issue of inner conflict with my own truth regarding Sathya Sai Baba was like a grain of sand in my eye. It meant that Sri M was not my Guru after all. If that was true, the ultimate spiritual practice like the Kriya could not be my ultimate practice either. This really hurt.

After I started living with Mohanji, I decided on my own one day that I need to give up on this precious Kriya by Sri M. I decided this on my own, without Mohanji ever interfering into this matter in any way. This was a tough decision to make, but to me there was no compromise with the truth. I prayed to Babaji and Baba for guidance and surrendered this issue at their feet. I was comforted by Devi Amma who told me, "It's OK my child, even some saints don't recognize Sathya Sai. His leelas are endless. I saw this happening. Just stay with your truth." Through simple, loving words, Devi Amma created a bridge that helped me move into acceptance and the feeling of inner resolution of this matter. I was finally able to leave this behind me. I still feel a lot of love in my heart when I run into a video or story about Sri M. Even though my mind cannot understand his motives behind his disapproval of Sathya Sai Baba, I do not judge him from the mind level. I just know that while that love and respect is still there, Sri M just couldn't be my ultimate Guru. When I realized that Jupiter was in the house of marriage in my horoscope, implying that I was meant to marry my Guru, this made a lot of sense because Sri M had a wife and family already and indeed, Mohanji was the only great soul that could fulfill all my impossible criteria, just as Baba said.

Through this experience and many others over the years, I have learned that when it comes to the Guru and Disciple relationship, one has to take the time to understand all the deep nuances and to await the final inner confirmation of the Guru and the path in all earnestness. This is a very sacred, very powerful relationship. It transcends the boundaries of life and death and indeed, I see it as the most important relationship that a human being can enter. It should never be taken lightly. After a testing phase, which should take as long as one feels necessary, if the relationship really "clicks" with a big, resounding YES at all levels, and the inner recognition of the Guru is fully there, then there should not be any turning back, for then comes the depth, intensity, and tests of a different kind - tests of consistency and commitment. I was not afraid of any of it, but could never live with myself if I was not in the truth.

I share this experience with the utmost respect for Sri M. I was really happy to see that his autobiography was published (just as he announced when we first met in 2006) and created some powerful ripples in the collective consciousness, just as I knew it would. He is a Master who has a lot to give. At the same time, I know he doesn't hide his disapproval of Sathya Sai Baba, so I am not revealing any secrets in this sharing. I only hope that through this sincere experience sharing, all of us can learn and grow through the understanding that the spiritual path is always INDIVIDUAL. All of us come with a complex history and really need to dig deep to find and recognize our true path. Sri M could not be my Guru, but he was the perfect Guru for many others. I would also like to say that one has the right to like or dislike a path or a Master, but one's focus should always be on what is right for oneself, not on criticizing others (especially the Masters, who cannot be fully comprehended because their operating level is beyond the mind – one cannot measure an ocean with a small glass).

What I learned from Mohanji is that through the defamation of selfless beings like Masters, one accumulates karma and will have to deal with it sooner or later. This is a principle and guideline that I follow in my own life: if I don't like something or someone (including a Guru), I just leave that path and focus on that which I do like. I need not judge and criticize, only acknowledge that "this is not for me." It is very simple. Unless one is in a manipulative sect that binds people through fear and dark energies, leaving should always be easy.

Mohanji explained this beautifully during one powerful satsang in Serbia:

> Traditions are interconnected**.** Why Traditions are different outside is because you have a different orientation. Each person has a different orientation. We talk about the path of devotion, path of knowledge, path of activity, and path of dissolution. All these paths are suitable for somebody. So every path has value. Every Master has value. Every Master is delivering something unique. Never compare. All Masters are valuable. Every Master is sent. And who is the right Master for you? As per your orientation, what you can do and who guides you, that's the right one for you.
>
> [*Holds up a glass of water.*] What is the strength of this glass? The space. This is exactly the strength of a disciple. If you are empty, you are eligible. If you're filled with concepts, filled with fears, filled with ideas, filled with prejudices, you have no space for any Master to give you anything. As I said, I had no clue what to ask any Master. This was my biggest strength because if I had asked for something small, I would have probably gotten it – some siddhis [spiritual powers], for example. Actually this is one of the things which Babaji told me in my second communion with him.
>
> Those days I was meditating a lot, from 3:00 a.m. to 8:00 a.m. every day, without fail. I was working as well. During those days when I looked at a person I could see through that person instantly - all the past lives, future lives. I could see everything. And I had no idea what to do with this information. Should I tell this person? A couple of times I tried telling, and it became a disaster. I was a general manager of a company at that time. They started asking, "Are you some kind of an astrologer? What are you talking about?" Then I had to explain too much and I thought: "This is not good – better keep quiet."

When I had the second communion with Babaji, Babaji said, "You can tell the future of everybody and sit in one corner and everybody will come to hear about their future out of insecurity. Is this what you want to do or would you like to take people to Liberation?"

I said, "Definitely I would like to take people to Liberation if I can." Then he said, "*Tathaastu.* [So be it.] Drop the siddhis. You don't need them. Drop them."

I have never checked if I have any powers afterward, because I realize having powers is easy but to have the maturity to maintain them is very difficult. Sometimes you get carried away – oh, I know all these things so I can probably do something. That is a trap. The moment you start using any power, it becomes your trap. People may appreciate you because you're extraordinary but that again is a trap. If you're walking the path of Liberation, everything is a trap. So you might as well be empty – nothing. And the highest feeling you get when you reach a certain stage is that you know nothing. Then you are home. Then you are fine. If you feel you know something, the mind is involved. If you feel you know nothing – empty – good enough, you are fine.[44]

Astral Closure With My Previous Masters

After three years with The Art of Living, I felt it was time for me to leave. I learned a lot from The Art of Living and still respected Sri Sri Ravi Shankar, but I was following the pull I felt toward Baba and Babaji, and loved the completely different vibe in my life, especially after I started living with Mohanji. In late 2007, I experienced the most beautiful closure with Sri Sri, as most people lovingly call him. (The name "Sri Ravi Shankar" was already taken by a famous Indian musician, so there was some confusion and complaints. He laughed and just added another Sri – I loved that!) He came to me astrally and shared an important message through the following conscious astral encounter:

I saw myself in a beautiful garden and noticed that Sri Sri was there. He was usually surrounded by people, but since we were alone I took the opportunity to strike up a conversation. I bowed down in reverence and then joined him for a light walk. He spoke with his melodic, higher-pitched voice: "See, you should just observe what is happening in The Art of Living, how the organization is functioning because one day you will have something like this of your own."

In shock, I said, "Who, me?! I really find that hard to believe." This happened at the time when Mohanji and I were in the midst of our financial crisis and heavy tests. There was no inkling of Mohanji Foundation as a global platform at that time. And yet, over the years, I understood what Sri Sri meant and still remember every second of that vivid astral experience.

I would hereby like to extend my deepest gratitude to The Art of Living and all the friends I made through AOL during those three years. I had so much fun and gained many sattvic habits from them, which had a really positive influence on my life. I am still in touch with some of my AOL

44 Source: https://qawithmohanji.wordpress.com/2018/05/02/babaji-is-in-every-tradition/

friends and maintain a deep respect for them. Now that we have our own volunteer-run events and often face challenges within that dynamic, I fully understand Sri Sri's loving advice.

Another powerful astral experience with another Master took place somewhere around this time and deserves to be mentioned. This was my experience with Paramahansa Nithyananda. I went to his ashram called Nithyananda Dhyanapeetam in 2008, right after the "Foreignchi Patlin" movie shoot. I was trained in their version of hatha yoga, which was conducted by one of the best yoga teachers I have ever met – Rahi Santhanam (whom I lovingly call Rahi Ma). The two of us remain in contact to this day, and it is always such a special treat to meet with her. I learned from Rahi Ma how important it is to speak from the belly and allow the voice to carry the subtle vibration, especially while conducting yoga sessions. Her feminine depth really touched my heart.

A couple of months after I was in that ashram, there was an attack on Nithyananda, a huge incident that happened at his ashram. I would not like to delve into that topic. I would just like to share my own experience and say that, at the time when I was there, I had nothing but profound and blissful experiences that really expanded my horizons. Nithyananda encouraged me to search for the right path by following my heart. I felt immense depth and sincerity. I even had a full-fledged samadhi experience under the famous banyan tree at their ashram (similar to the samadhi experience I had in Belgrade, with the blessing of St. Petka).

This powerful tree with a super wide trunk (in which a Master from the past attained Samadhi), whose branches reach the ground and become roots, was a tree that appeared in a vision of young Nithyananda, compelling him to search for it all over India. In the end, an old man felt an inner prompting to donate the land of this ashram to Nithyananda. When he came to see the land, he found the banyan tree… That is how it became the centerpiece of all spiritual practices at that ashram. This tree has amazing, sacred healing energy and is considered one of the portals to Shamballa…

At the end of our yoga training, we traveled to Tiruvannamalai with the task of walking barefoot around the holy Arunachala mountain, which had played a special role in young Nithyananda's life. He called this holy mountain "the incubator of Masters," and shared some truly unforgettable stories from his childhood when his spiritual awakening started. I cherished those moments. We started the circumambulation of the mountain around 4:00 a.m. and after an hour or so I had a sudden sharp pain in the area of my second chakra, from the back. It was truly unbearable. At that exact moment, somebody from their team said, "Please note that there is no turning back. I know you are not used to walking barefoot, but whatever happens, just keep going. There is no option of going back at this point."

I had no idea how I was going to continue walking, let alone endure such pain, and my mind was also busy trying to understand the reason for the pain. At that moment, I prayed to Nithyananda to help me. Within less than a minute, he appeared in a car, smiled, extended his blessings to everyone casually, and poof – the pain was gone. I shared this experience with Mohanji later on and he said, "Nithyananda removed a painful impression of rape from your system, ensuring you don't attract it to your life subconsciously again. It was a big blessing."

I could share many such stories with Paramahansa Nithyananda because my days in his ashram were packed with wonderful experiences, but will just highlight that in the end, when I had the opportunity, I asked him for a blessing to enter into a serious relationship and (most likely) a marriage with Mohanji. He smiled and said, "Go ahead, Ma. But know, it's not going to be easy." His words echoed in my mind over the years.

In my astral experience with Nithyananda, we met on a majestic hilltop. He was wearing some western clothes and I found that surprising because I always saw him wearing nothing but his formal Guru attire. He noticed my surprise and said in his witty style, "Oh, I will be conducting a program in the West and have to dress accordingly for the occasion, you know." He then invited me to come to the edge of that tall hill with him. Pointing toward something in the distance that looked like huge, transparent, etheric bubbles, he said, "See Ma, Masters from all these different *ghotras* [meaning clan or lineage] are now imparting knowledge to Mohanji. He is precious. Stay with him Ma, no matter what, for one day he will impart that knowledge to you and to the world."

I was deeply touched by this astral experience and Nithyananda's sincerity. What's funny is that I was aware during that experience that I had no clue what the word "ghotra" meant. Too embarrassed to ask Nithyananda, I just kept quiet. When I shared this with Mohanji, he immediately explained the context of lineage and said that he, for example, belongs to the Bharadwaja gotra, the same gotra to which most Masters from Datta Tradition belong, including Sripada Sri Vallabha, Narasimha Saraswati, Shirdi Sai Baba (even though it was not explicitly), Sathya Sai Baba, etc. Mohanji said that all the people who are married to his consciousness, without distractions and delusions (beyond all barriers and doubts, beyond the need to search any further) spontaneously come under the umbrella of Bharadwaja ghotra. That is why marriage is a big deal because through marriage the woman is officiated into her husband's gotra. The child enters the ghotra by birth and requires no initiation. During all the Vedic marriage rituals, such as homa, the priest will ask for one's *nakshatra* (birth star) and gotra. I was amazed to learn all that and felt truly privileged, truly blessed.

In summary, after all these experiences, I made a commitment to myself that I would always stand by my own truth, no matter how inconvenient it may be, and that I will never criticize other Masters, other religions, or spiritual paths, for they all benefit someone and ultimately all lead to the same One. Respect for one's free will and choice, rooted in one's inner truth, is the key. All spiritual and religious paths should honor that key principle. Otherwise, one cannot be on the path with full sincerity and remain on it with love, complete dedication, commitment, and devotion to the Divine.

Sirius Connection Revealed

In the midst of all the tests I was enduring in Dubai while Mohanji was in Muscat, I met a dear friend of mine, a humble Indian man called Ramduji. Ramduji had once organized a spiritual workshop in his company that I conducted, eliciting Ramduji's earnest prayers for my success. He was very sweet and sincere. At this point, he told me that he had a powerful communion (telepathic, not physical) with Murali Krishna Swamiji (now known as Sharavana Baba), a Guru from South India who visited Dubai quite often, and he had something important to share with me.

I had actually met Murali Krishna Swamiji myself once when he visited Dubai and really enjoyed sitting and meditating in his presence. He then met Mohanji and me during his other visit to Dubai and immediately recognized Mohanji's spiritual stature. I remember the moment when he said powerful words about Mohanji, words that stayed with me: "Mohanji is pure gold. He is now lying in the mud of the treacherous business world. Gold can be thrown into the mud and be completely covered, but gold always remains gold. It never decays or wears out, but always remains pure and bright, despite the mud that may get stuck on the outside. One day the rain will fall and wash away the mud — he will shine forth and dazzle the world. It is only a matter of time before his full brilliance will be revealed to the world. Mohanji is Lord Dakshinamurti [the one who imparts knowledge through silence]. He will work silently. His presence will transform people even if his actions may not be that visible. The transformation in people will be visible." (The great Master called Tyagananda shared the same message about Mohanji later on.)

Murali Krishna Swami's amazing telepathic message as relayed by Ramduji began with a real shocker: "Swamiji told me that you as a soul originate from Sirius."

I had instantaneous goosebumps all over my body, and my jaw dropped! I know this topic may be a bit "over the top" for some readers, but this was my experience and in the spirit of deep and intimate sharing, I have decided to share this aspect of myself as well. However, I do understand why most people would decide not to share something that intimate. Opinions and judgements are many when topics of this sort emerge. I am simply sharing what I experienced, in all honesty.

"He said it was many lifetimes ago that you came to Earth, not out of karma, but because of your compassion and sincere wish to help people on Earth. However, you were not prepared for the density of vibration on Earth, and that pulled you down completely, so you have been incarnating as a human since then.

"He also said this will be the first lifetime, after many, many past lives, that you will have a chance to wake up in that body as well, which is still there in a dormant state. (Something similar was shown in the movie "Avatar.") In this life, you will have a chance to remember your Self from Sirius and all the bliss you always enjoyed there. He said your parents were highly evolved, like Masters, and their Guru is Mahavatar Babaji. I simply had to tell you what was conveyed to me. I felt it was important."

This was another "bomb" that landed in my lap and shook my reality. Never in a million years could I have ever imagined hearing something like this! This was literally mind-blowing. Yet, deep inside, Ramduji's words immediately stirred some powerful feelings, and they did not feel untrue at all. On the contrary, it all felt like someone was telling me something from the time of my childhood, something that sounded very familiar, but I couldn't quite remember it fully.

As shocking as this information was to the logical mind, it made a lot of sense when juxtaposed with my previous experiences. Firstly, it explained how I earned the grace of a direct astral encounter with Mahavatar Babaji – we obviously go back a long way. Secondly, I immediately remembered the profound experience I had as a baby when those two beings with a golden hue and big, compassionate eyes floated into my room while I was crying in my crib in complete darkness. I somehow knew they were my parents, but none of it made any sense and I kind of ignored this experience throughout my life – until this moment. However, I could not explain to myself how it was possible that I could remember something from such an early stage in life. And now I realized that just like then, amid my "darkness" in Dubai, my parents from Sirius had come to me in the form of this breakthrough information to bring me some light and comfort.

After a couple of days, Ramduji, Berislava (the spiritual artist), and I met and spoke about this. Berislava proposed to do some healing process of her own and, if it was possible, she would telepathically address my parents from Sirius. I did not expect much from that session, but I recognized both of them as pure souls and decided to give it a try. In the end, this turned out to be amazingly powerful.

I was lying down on my back with my eyes closed and Berislava did some energetic process, removing some heavy energy from my stomach. At some point during this session, Ramduji was asked to hold my right hand on behalf of my father and Berislava my left hand on behalf of my mother from Sirius. I could feel their most loving presence through my palms, and especially in my heart. I cried a lot and have no words to describe how much love I felt in that moment. I felt like a child that had longed for her parents for countless years and finally got to feel their presence and energetic embrace. They comforted me during that session and simply filled me with love. They blessed my relationship with Mohanji and said that I needed to "hold on, just a couple more months until some karmas are cleansed." I would have preferred to hear days instead of months, but I had no choice but to accept all that was happening.

While addressing the topic of Sirius, I will make a small digression and fast-forward in time a bit, to the time when I started my training in Non-Hypnotic Regression with Dr. Choudhary in Delhi. It was my wish to be able to conduct these amazing sessions for other people, and I managed to complete Level 1 of his beautiful training (unfortunately, I could not continue after that due to my busy life). In Level 1, I learned to conduct deep Yoga Nidra (meditation that accesses the state of consciousness that lies between waking and sleeping) in the alpha state of mind, but this was still not sufficient for the complete induction into the deep theta brainwave state required to access past lives.

During that training, Dr. Choudhary asked for a volunteer who would like to act as a client for a brief demonstration of induction into the deep theta state, and I was happy to volunteer for that. This was the occasion when I regressed to that exact scene from my childhood – I re-lived those precious moments with my beautiful, most loving parents from Sirius. I still remember their eyes and their blissful faces, their slim waists, long necks, unusual head shape, and more than anything, the love they radiated. This was all the confirmation I needed.

A couple of years later, I had another powerful experience related to Sirius. I visited Vanja[45], a lady from Serbia with deep regard for Mohanji. Vanja started connecting with Mohanji's consciousness

45 Name changed out of respect for privacy.

and was conducting some truly deep spiritual sessions of her own. She would rarely meet him in person, but the clarity of her clairvoyance was truly impressive. During her session, which consisted of her continuous clairvoyant viewing while I simply listened and felt the energy, she confirmed all the information I had received about my parents from Sirius and added something more. During that session, she shared with me the full story of how I came to Earth.

She kept seeing me with my head bent down, like someone in deep regret or shame. She said I was deeply ashamed that I had not listened to my parents from Sirius when they advised me that going to Earth was unwise. She could hear my thoughts: "I don't deserve blessings from the Masters. I did not listen to my wise parents when I should have. I was so naïve!"

She said that I was only 17 or 18 years old at the time when I developed my interest in Earth and was very eager to go to Earth to help, unaware of what that truly entailed. My parents warned me several times, but I did not pay heed. After I repeated for the third time that I wanted to go to Earth, Vanja said my father knew that this desire had already become my karma. They had to let me go.

It was revealed to me that Sinke was from Sirius as well. When it was my time to go, we were sent together. He was my knight. (How interesting is that?!) He was sent to accompany me and protect me. We came with a noble purpose but were ambushed by the dark forces that exist at lower frequencies on Earth, and were eventually killed. This was when we both began the cycle of reincarnation on Earth.

I was amazed by everything Vanja said, and finally understood the depth of my connection with Sinke. In this most unexpected way I learned yet another reason why he could not be my ultimate spiritual authority. Through each incarnation, I connected more with the spiritual Masters from India while his soul chose different journeys which brought him to the Knights Templars and his present secretive lifestyle. Even the fact that we both loved the Star Wars Trilogy made a lot more sense in light of these exciting revelations.

At the end of this session, Vanja did a special process to ask for forgiveness from my parents. This was really touching and, just like in Dubai, I clearly felt their presence. Vanja said my attitude of self-loathing was not at all necessary and was blocking the blessings of not only my parents from Sirius but also from other Masters. This was truly pointless and had to be ended. I am deeply grateful to Vanja for that powerful session that cleared a lot of blockages and helped me connect to myself and the elevated frequency of Sirius much better.

To close this topic, I would like to mention a lovely man called Prema, whom Mohanji and I met when we visited Puttaparthi. (Prema was actually mentioned in Mohanji's famous blog series "Babaji Beyond Definitions" and Mohanji met him once again, years later, at Devi Amma's house. He is deeply connected with Babaji and Mohanji as well.) Aside from his powerful experiences and communions with Mahavatar Babaji, Prema shared something else with us that stayed with me. While still in California, he happened to get abducted by Pleiadeans, a spiritually advanced civilization that had been helping humanity on Earth for millennia (Mohanji once said that Nikola Tesla, the renowned, most revolutionary scientist (a Serb from Croatia, like me, if I may add) was originally from Pleiades). I was eager to learn more about Prema's experience, but he was shy to talk about it. He certainly would have gone through a lot of ridicule in regard to this topic in the past, which must have made him decide to keep the experience to himself.

However, he did tell me, "You can surely find all you need to know about Pleiadians and several other civilizations active on Earth in a special book called *Alcheringa* by Valerie Barrow. Sathya Sai Baba blessed this book. I think this is the only book on this topic that got Baba's direct blessing."

I was intrigued by that information and went to the small bookstore in Puttaparthi as soon as I could. An old man with blissful eyes worked there. I asked him about this book and he said he was doubtful they had any copies left, but went to check. After two minutes, he re-emerged from behind the counter and said with a big smile, "Here you go dear. This is our last copy."

I was super-thrilled and read this book in one breath. It is truly fascinating, and the civilizations of Pleiades and Sirius are mentioned as the ones that supported people on Earth the most in terms of scientific, spiritual, and any other advancement. I highly recommend this intriguing book.

It is interesting to note that the Dogon tribe from west Africa still carries the knowledge of the advanced civilization from Sirius through their mythology and customs. This includes knowledge of the role played by the elevated beings from Sirius in the development of consciousness and overall human advancement on planet Earth through the millennia. In 2021 I noticed some amazing speakers on the Gaia platform (www.gaia.com) who spoke volumes on these topics. I was especially impressed by the video "The Fall of Atlantis" (yet another lifetime from which I carry deeply imprinted memories) from the powerful video series called "Initiation" by Matias de Stefano, a brilliant young man from Argentina.

All of this is a sign that the veil that clouded our awareness and knowledge over thousands of years is now slowly being lifted, which is why I have decided to give my humble contribution in terms of these still controversial topics, no matter how private and personal all of this information truly felt to me.

Sirius is the brightest star in our sky and the chief star in the constellation Canis Major, the Big Dog. In India, since the ancient days, Sirius was known as Svana, the dog of Prince Yudhisthira, who joined the Prince and his four brothers "on a long and arduous journey to find the kingdom of heaven. However, one by one the brothers all abandoned the search until only Yudhisthira and his dog, Svana, were left. At long last, they came to the gates of heaven. The gatekeeper, Indra, welcomed the prince but denied Svana entrance. Yudhisthira was aghast and told Indra that he could not forsake his good and faithful servant and friend. His brothers, Yudhisthira said, had abandoned the journey to heaven to follow their hearts' desires. But Svana, who had given his heart freely, chose to follow none but Yudhisthira. The prince said that, without his dog, he would forsake even heaven. This is what Indra had wanted to hear, and then he welcomed both the prince and the dog through the gates of heaven."[46]

46 Source: https://earthsky.org/brightest-stars/sirius-the-brightest-star/

In reality, all of us are multidimensional beings, but limitations in our awareness prevent us from realizing that. I suddenly remembered my experience of the past-life regression with Ljubica when my Higher Self showed me that powerful, expanded state in 360 degrees, with incredible depth of feeling and golden light that brought people into remembrance at the soul level. I knew right away – THIS is a natural state on Sirius.

I learned a lot about "the Shift" in awareness on planet Earth from Dr. Sunny Satin's book *Incredibly Believable!,* which covers the topic of the Shift on planet Earth in detail. It includes the accounts of the Higher Self from hundreds of people, compiled most diligently by this amazing man, through which it is said that we are now on a steady trajectory into the light of remembrance. There will be many more people like Matias de Stefano, especially among the newer generations, who will, like him, realize at an early age that their sole purpose is "to remember" knowledge that is already there and bring in more light.

Mohanji was a special child like that as well, who loved being alone, and who started remembering. But nobody understood him and there was no support, except for his grandfather, a wise man, and great astrologer. He foretold that one day, the whole world would know about Mohanji. Masters like Mohanji are working hard, on multiple levels, to help the Shift and rescue beings that are stuck here on Earth. Mohanji has told me many times that there are people of various frequencies existing simultaneously on Earth at this time. The aim of Masters on Earth and Masters from higher dimensions is to bring all those people who are stuck to their original frequency and empower them to reach the higher dimensions. The method is Ahimsa (non-violence), kindness, selflessness, goodness, compassion, righteousness, etc. In Mohanji's case, I see him doing it individually (for example through Mai-Tri Method and Mohanji Transformation Method sessions done one on one), collectively (sessions done in large groups - in person or on distance) and also multi-dimensionally and intergalactically (what some people have seen and conveyed). Even though most of Mohanji's work is silent, one can feel (if looking close enough) that on each of these dimensions there is positive action by Mohanji.

The existing educational system filled with dry memorization and meaningless competition among children will certainly have to be adapted for such souls – and there are, and will be many of them. Sirius is also called The Great Central Sun, or Mother Sun, which has aligned with our sun in 2012. The knowledge of *yugas* or different ages that human beings on Earth go through in cycles over tens (if not hundreds) of thousands of years, has been preserved in India. Whenever planet Earth starts entering the brightness of the Great Central Sun and aligning with it, a shift in awareness occurs on Earth and reaches its peak during the Golden Age (Sathya Yuga). We are truly blessed to be in exactly that process now. I have never heard a better presentation about the yugas, with a profound depth of knowledge and immense clarity, than the one delivered by Mohanji in 2021, in what has now become his signature course – "Empowered." I will not be covering such topics in this autobiography because they require deep immersion into the subject, but I recommend a sincere dive into this profoundly transformative material.

In summary, as of 2012, we have started moving at an accelerated pace out of the darkest of ages toward the Golden Age; from an existence based on fear and greed, into an existence based on unconditional love and far higher awareness. This change will be gradual but strikingly evident. We can already see just how great of a change the internet has brought. As our entire world changes before our eyes, our idea of our very nature, our true history, and our great potential as human beings will change completely. Our "junk DNA" will no longer be perceived as junk but as proof of expanded awareness and much higher potential that we once had, and will have again.

The system of "innernet" will be restored on Earth, and the grand pyramids will resume their original roles, not as any tombs, but as powerful generators of energy that sustain higher awareness on Earth, of which the "innernet connection" is but one feature. What are considered higher yogic (or "paranormal") powers now (telepathy, teleportation, levitation, telekinesis, etc.) will become our second nature. The time of free energy envisioned by the amazing Nikola Tesla will finally come. Manipulations of sacred scriptures and ancient knowledge by the Reptilian race that has been wreaking havoc on Earth since the time of Atlantis, through Babylon and all the wars and traumatic events on Earth, will be revealed and overcome.

One of the grand disclosures that awaits us all is about the role that the advanced extraterrestrial races have played on Earth and just how many souls on Earth, like mine, originate from elsewhere. Hollywood scripts of little E.T. or depictions of dangerous aliens about to take over the Earth will be replaced by more realistic accounts of our true status among the beings of much higher awareness. I believe it was in Dr. Sunny Satin's book that I read about a comparison between a tribal village from Africa applying for membership status to the UN, and that of human beings from Earth wondering why we are not members of the Great Galactic Federation. We still have a long way to go.

Just how low we fare is visible from the simple fact that we have not even been capable of establishing peace on Earth for millennia. Greedy elites and their corrupted servants from higher social strata have ruled our media and infiltrated every pore of our society, relentlessly abusing all possible systems created on Earth, extracting natural resources mercilessly to their benefit and blocking progress that would serve the whole of humanity (such as free energy). This is the reason why people with higher awareness and higher subtlety also have higher responsibility and even more work to do. As per Dr. Sunny Satin, the greatest change on Earth will happen when "crystal children" of higher awareness assume the positions of political and governmental power.

In the current time of challenges, there is no place for an ungrounded world of daydreaming – spirituality means selfless contribution to others. It means tireless work without asking anything in return, and the even higher responsibility to bring in as much light as one can, in different walks of life, through our own presence, our higher talents, and our blessed existence on Mother Earth.

When I was a student in Rome, I once woke up around 5:00 a.m. and received a super clear telepathic message, "Purify yourself. The Great White Brotherhood is waiting on you." I initially thought that this was some kind of organization, some Great White Lodge or something of the sort, and could not understand this message. However, after learning about my origin beyond Earth, and after all the experiences with Babaji, I understood where the message came from. I currently serve as a Global Ambassador of Mohanji Foundation and sometimes like to joke about my career, "I am very ambitious and actually aim for the position of the Intergalactic Ambassador."

Jokes aside, I simply offer myself to the Masters as an empty flute and pray to be able to serve as a pure instrument...

More Blessings Pouring In – In 360 Degrees

After delving into all these higher topics, I would like to return to full grounding and my life lessons in Dubai. I must say that I am most grateful, that regardless of all the challenges, I held on and stayed on the path to eventually recognize who Mohanji is beyond his physical presence. Living away from Mohanji for almost a year was an eye-opener. I learned to recognize Mohanji in the dimension of consciousness, which was and is available to me (and anyone else who chooses to connect to it) regardless of distance. Indeed, there is no distance in consciousness and no boundaries imposed by the mind. I learned how the connection to the consciousness aspect feels, and what power and grace it brings. I cannot say that I understand all about it 100% because it sure is an ocean, but I am gaining evermore insight, as the Masters give it. This knowledge is not something that one can find in books or even learn directly from another person. It has to happen from within, as an inner recognition, and a conviction that can then pass any test of fire. Tests are difficult but so beneficial because that is when we get to see just how much we only believe, and what we actually know. Tests reaffirm our convictions and make us strong.

A huge blessing from Baba came at this time, through his devotees and Mohanji's friends Madhumita and Anup Shivaraman, who lived in another part of Dubai called Deira. After Ammu left this world in such a tragic way, Mohanji moved to Anup's house, joined by another friend Sundar (who was the main chef at The Art of Living ashram during my yoga teacher training and I really loved his cooking). Just like Mohanji was welcomed to their home at the most difficult time, I was given the same blessing of their warm hospitality. I can't describe how relieved I was after receiving their loving invitation to move into their home. I even got a room with Sai Baba's big picture. I unpacked my bags, sat, and wept from joy, feeling so immensely grateful. I knew that the worst phase was over. I continued applying for jobs and doing my best with my ad hoc lessons and part-time options, but overall, I felt that the fog of blocked energy was finally clearing.

My Sacred Initiation – Done Remotely

I knew that shaktipat was one of the key blessings on our path. It helps speed up a person's spiritual evolution many times over. What is normally achieved through spiritual practice is greatly accelerated and yet it is completely safe because one can receive only as per one's capacity.

When Mohanji started delivering shaktipat at the end of his meditations and satsangs, people started experiencing great transformation. He was permitted by the Masters to initiate others. He even gave part of his own consciousness to people who were initiated in those days (this is the highest of initiations called Shivapat – initiating others through his own consciousness, implanting part of his consciousness in them). Mohanji's Shaktipat is alignment, not activation. It also includes removal of unnecessary junk, enabling the recipient to subsequently deliver pure energy. Mohanji was not activating Kundalini shakti because for that one needed supervision. Unless one is living within a stable ashram setup, Mohanji insisted that this was not a wise thing to do. A Master called Tyagananda met Mohanji once and warned him: "Don't do this. No Master does this. If you initiate others into shaktipat through you, you are giving a part of yourself and this can backfire on you. This could be done only to the closest, most selected disciples, not to 20 or 30 people [as was the case then]. If the person is not pure enough, he or she could use it in the wrong way." The truth of Tyagananda's words was proven later when some of the people who were initiated by Mohanji in this way turned against him or even scandalized or ridiculed him. That ingratitude was something we regrettably had to witness.

However, at the time Mohanji opted to do it anyway. One person got initiated in Dubai and when I heard that, I deeply desired to get this blessing as well. When it comes to such things, I always feel shy to ask for myself. I could not imagine myself asking Mohanji: "Can I also get it?" It just didn't feel right. So I kept quiet. Yet, I did start praying for it, even though Mohanji was already in Oman and I thought this could only be done in person.

A few days after I started praying to be initiated, one evening while I was reading something in my new accommodation in Deira, I suddenly got a message from Mohanji: "Wear your pajamas, brush your teeth, and lie down on your bed. Baba said that he is working on you." I was really surprised to hear that. I did as he instructed me to do.

As I lay down on my back, I could feel a sudden surge of energy that started flowing through my body, especially through the spine, feet, palms, and crown. It was all flowing. Then the entire body felt like rising and descending, just like when one floats on their back in the ocean waves, blissfully surrendering and feeling that pleasant and gentle upward and downward movement. I felt like a baby in the arms of the ocean of consciousness, being gently lulled into loving surrender. This feeling was so beautiful that I felt I could remain in that state for the rest of my life. I lost the sense of horizontal time but I am sure this went on for a couple of hours, with huge energy gushing through my body. And with that, I eventually fell asleep.

There was no frame or name for this experience known to my mind. The next day I came to know that this was "Baba working on me." That's all I knew. Mohanji said nothing else, in his usual style of downplaying things. The next day, in the afternoon, I was to conduct the Power of Purity meditation in the conference room of the "Focus Direct" office in Bur Dubai, invited by our friend Jenny.

Early in the afternoon, I felt a similar energy surge and the need to lie down. The moment I did that, the waves were back on! Mohanji did not need to call me, I just immersed myself in this blissful experience. I thought, "Hmm, maybe I'll just lie down for a sec and enjoy these blissful waves." They were very strong and the amplitude of the descending and ascending waves was even greater than the previous day. This went on for another couple of hours and when I looked at my watch, I realized the meditation was in only 30 minutes, exactly the amount of time I needed to get there. Unfortunately, parking would usually take an additional amount of time. I got up immediately, grabbed the meditation CD, went to my car, and just started driving. I took it for granted that I would just snap out of that state the moment I got up, but this was not the case. As I started driving, I realized that I was not in the usual state of mind and that something was very different.

First of all, I was driving the car but I was not able to see anything, as if everything around me was blurred. It was as if I had become cross-eyed, feeling constant and intense vibrations on my forehead. I was driving, and everything was blurred, but instead of seeing everything, I was SENSING everything around me.

When there was a car on my right side, left side, or behind me, I could feel those cars within my aura, so I didn't have to see them *per se*. That meant I was operating from expanded awareness. I recognized a similar state after the blessing of St. Petka and under the banyan tree of Nithyananda, but this time I was driving through busy traffic and that was a whole new ballgame! The issue of not seeing the traffic lights was resolved by the fact that I could feel all the other cars and simply moved when they moved. When others stopped, I would stop as well and simply be in that beautiful, thoughtless state of immense inner fullness.

At some point, I joined an even bigger road with several lanes in each direction (similar to a highway) which could have been potentially dangerous, but I have to admit that I had no fear, not for a single moment. That's the benefit of having no thoughts. I simply relaxed and drove. All went smoothly until the point when I felt that the energy started becoming stronger and stronger. I was already nearing my destination, when I felt this immense heat, especially in my spine. The heat within my body rose so much that I thought I was going to burn. It was unbearable and I became jittery. (I could possibly compare it to the feeling I had in Babaji's presence in the desert, the feeling of being jittery before the balloon bursts. At that time it had been the expansion – now it was the heat that exceeded all my limits.)

Somehow I managed to pick up my phone. I can't remember whether I messaged Mohanji, or called him in the midst of my blurred vision and burning sensation. I just told Him: "Please help me! I'm burning from this energy. I'm burning big time. I can't take it."

He messaged me back right away and said in his typically cool tone: "It's okay. You'll be fine. Just buy yourself an ice cream."

I couldn't believe what he said to me amid this burning crisis. "What? An ice cream?!" I thought he was joking and said: "Look, this is not a joke, I'm burning right here!"

He said: "Yeah, yeah. You'll be fine. Just get ice cream." This was one of those frustrating moments with Mohanji when I couldn't tell whether he was joking or not. I really thought he was taking it all much too lightly.

Somehow, I managed to reach the building where the Focus Direct office was. Usually, this entire area was packed with cars and one can never find parking, but that day there was one spot – right in front of the building and conveniently located next to a small grocery store on the ground floor of the building. I had one minute left before the meditation was to start. I parked, went inside the shop, bought the ice cream, paid, came out, and started devouring the ice cream (there was no time for slow savoring and casual licking – I was desperate). I was literally swallowing chunks of this ice cream and moving towards the elevator when I noticed that, while the heat was still there, it had become a bit more manageable.

I could handle it. Something had changed as if I had become more grounded by it, and was able to handle it from a different level. It was a bit funny to enter a room full of people with "business as usual" facial expressions, while I had just gone to another Universe and back. I managed to put the CD into the CD player with my hands still trembling. That's when I received the message from Mohanji: "Today you can give Shaktipat during the Power of Purity meditation. You have been initiated."

I was joyous like a child. "Wow! So that's what this was – my shaktipat initiation!" I could have never imagined it would happen from a distance, and in such a dramatic way. I never even knew one could receive a long-distance initiation, otherwise, I would have prayed for it.

During the initial part of the Power of Purity meditation, there is a part with slow breathing. That was when I finally managed to calm down and digest all the Grace that had just been showered upon me. I realized how everything was perfectly timed and positioned – the second when I woke up after blissful waves, the drive, the empty parking slot, the grocery store right there at the entrance, the ice cream that I swallowed in the hallway, and then a change in my state and me entering the meditation room exactly at 7:00 p.m.! I would call this "divine precision."

I will never, ever forget this experience. It was so beautiful to connect with that superb, hot energy through the spine and pass it on to people. I could feel their soft crown, the point where the soul entered the body (the fontanelle), and when I placed the tip of my fingers on the forehead chakra, I could feel a slight pulsation and then knew they were receiving the energy. With long-term meditators, whose *agnya* (forehead chakra) was more active, I could feel as if my finger was sinking into their forehead as if passing through soft clay and entering inside the head! With time, I even started getting some intuitive messages about the people, especially when I imagined Mohanji's third eye on my forehead. The connection was instant. Familiar heat would appear in the spine and on the palms, vibration on the forehead, and I was ready for the shaktipat. I always enjoyed being an instrument of this powerful, sacred energy, and would feel immense love embracing all of them – as if all those people had become my own children.

A dozen of other people received shaktipat initiation from Mohanji over the next couple of years, and each person had his or her own reaction – some vomited, some got so energized they couldn't sleep, some had visions, etc. but mine was pretty dramatic and super awesome! As my friend Jenny used to say, "What else is possible?" – one of the greatest questions and expressions of wonder, opening us to ever new possibilities. It sure has been a wonder of wonders to experience all this and without any preparation, or any prior tip being given to me. I was simply just thrown into the water and learned how to swim on the way. That was how things worked out for me most of the time.

It is important to note that, when Mohanji transfers energy, imparts knowledge, and gives people great experiences that may include the so-called miracles, he always plays it down. This is because very often, people don't have the maturity to handle it. I've seen examples of that. When he started giving these shaktipat initiations there was a danger of boosting the ego, especially for someone who was not fully on the path with Mohanji.

There was one man who, after receiving shaktipat initiation from Mohanji, retained the imprint of Mohanji's finger on his forehead, resembling a little flame. Whoever saw it would comment, "What's that flame on your forehead?" This attention boosted his spiritual ego. People noticed that the clarity with which he spoke was greater, and his yoga sessions and lectures were more efficient and of higher quality. He attributed all these improvements to himself. He started feeling special, feeling that he could now even become a Guru. He was carried away with it, not understanding that the power that came to him through this experience was not from himself and his intellectual knowledge, but from Grace that he received through shaktipat.

However, this process of initiation was bound to evolve. A couple of years later one Master from India warned Mohanji: "You should not call it shaktipat, only Masters give shaktipat." After giving it a second thought, Mohanji decided to change the name to Mohanji Energy Transfer (MET) and stopped giving direct initiations but only through our own Sadhana Team, with a specific process of mantra chanting and connecting with Mohanji's consciousness before the energy is passed on through the palms and fingertips. There are more than 170 people, beautiful souls from around the globe, who serve as instruments of MET at present. The experiences people have had, and the speeding up of their evolution is the realm of Grace that is truly beyond the mind's reach.

It is amazing to see how effectively one can connect with the consciousness of a Spiritual Master like Mohanji who is connected to the Source. Mohanji was first drilled and bashed big time until he became sufficiently emptied so that Grace could fill in and full expansion could happen. It is such an amazing feeling to have a living human being in our midst who has undergone this entire process and dissolved in consciousness, the consciousness that is alive and vibrant and finds its way to other people through our palms and fingertips, through meditations and processes, through a mere gaze, through a dream or astral encounter – in a myriad of ways. Such is the love of the Divine.

A Double Divorce

Sometimes in order to get to know more clearly who we are, we have to experience that which we are not. Some people appear to mirror such unpleasant things to us. When Mohanji first began his position in Muscat as a CEO, he faced quite a lot of jealousy as well and ended up going through, what we called, a "double divorce."

First of all, he had decided to officially finalize the divorce from his previous wife. She had a serious health issue, a mental health issue even before the marriage. There was a Swami from South India (mentioned earlier) whom Mohanji loved a lot and connected with for years, much before I met him. This Swami recognized who Mohanji was, and the predictions of some astrologers confirmed it. These astrologers said that Mohanji would be known to the entire world. However, the intentions of this Swami were not pure. He wanted to keep Mohanji within his ashram, and did all that he could to keep Mohanji and myself apart. I will call him the Seeming Swami because he does not deserve the title of a swami.

When Mohanji was in his jobless phase, Seeming Swami was scheming to keep Mohanji with him. When I came to the ashram of Seeming Swami, Mohanji introduced me to him and I noticed that he was not too happy and occasionally passed some sarcastic comments. He saw me as an obstacle to realizing his plan of keeping Mohanji within his ashram and having him work there.

When Mohanji and I moved in together in Rashidiya, he tried his level best to persuade us not to live together and that this was bad karma because of Mohanji's unresolved marriage status. That didn't work. Then later on, he tried to play a silly card of making me feel jealous. He tried to make me believe that Mohanji was seeing one beautiful actress from India. But, he didn't know that I had met this actress in Dubai. Mohanji had introduced us, and I could see that she was not interested in Mohanji. She was more of a sisterly friend, advising Mohanji not to wear black clothing and hide, but to expose himself to the world. Their friendship dated back to 2001 and there was no trace of attraction between them. All women, especially when in a relationship with a man, have that extra sense to feel when someone else is attempting to encroach on their intimate space. She was totally not like that and I liked her. I could see that she was just a friend of Mohanji, and I too became her friend. So when Seeming Swami was trying to pull this trick on me, I was thinking "What is he trying and why?" It was all a bit silly.

Things got much worse with time when Mohanji and I learned that Seeming Swami had also played a major game in manipulating a lawyer who was handling Mohanji's divorce case to cause it to fail. It was in 2003 (three years after he physically separated from his wife) that Mohanji first thought about filing for divorce. Seeming Swami immediately proposed his own lawyer to handle the case and Mohanji naively accepted. He could not understand why his divorce proceedings took so many years, but was not pushing for it because he was not planning to get married again anyway. He was not interested in relationships at all. But now that Baba had brought me into his life, all of that changed and this pending divorce became a big obstacle for our marriage.

There were court expenses and fees to be paid. Mohanji and I definitely could not get married until he divorced his first wife. At that point, he hadn't even seen her for more than ten years. I was shocked to learn what Seeming Swami did. To control the situation, Seeming Swami first made sure that the lawyer submitted the proper papers requesting the divorce for several valid reasons. Mohanji approved those forms. Then Seeming Swami, playing the card of trust, asked Mohanji to give this lawyer authorization to act as his agent and submit some other papers if need be because Mohanji was not living in India at that time. They would "handle everything." Mohanji agreed, trusting his friend blindly. Seeming Swami and his puppet lawyer then secretly submitted another letter which was completely contradictory to the first letter, saying that Mohanji's wife ran away and he wanted her back.

Seeming Swami was deliberately attempting to disrupt the proceedings, in a way that would make a mockery of the court, knowing this would upset the judge. Had those papers remained with the court for long, Mohanji could have been arrested the next time he came to India. That was the masterplan behind the whole grand deception. Luckily, Mohanji casually spoke about this to some other friend who visited Dubai. His friend asked, "It's been many years now, why is your divorce not over yet?"

This friend was a lawyer so Mohanji asked him to check on his case. When he came to know about these contradictory papers that were filed, he told Mohanji, "My friend, you are in serious trouble. Your head is in a lion's mouth! This is so bad that you could even get arrested next time you go to India." Had that really happened, Mohanji would get a black mark on his record and then Seeming Swami could easily keep him in his ashram, as planned. That was clearly the idea, to pull Mohanji down and trap him.

Without marrying Mohanji, I could not live with him in Oman. The Middle East was the last location in the world where a man and a woman could live together without formalizing the relationship. There were so many things legally linked to one another. On the verge of being arrested, Mohanji immediately retained a new lawyer and did everything possible to salvage the situation. He managed to do that literally at the very last minute. This was when the issue with this Seeming Swami, whom Mohanji considered his best friend till then, was revealed. The truth about his hidden agendas came into Mohanji's awareness. Seeming Swami opposed the new lawyer, who even came to know that Seeming Swami told the family of Mohanji's ex-wife, "He has a lot of money. You should not settle for anything small." In other words, "Rip him off." This is why the family of Mohanji's ex-wife tried to extort money sufficient for building a shopping mall (unbelievable!) which she could then rent and have sufficient income for the rest of her life.

Mohanji had trusted Seeming Swami to the point that he wrote blank checks and left them with him (and he sure wiped Mohanji's account clean by withdrawing more than $5000 from it). Mohanji had full faith and trust in him at that time. That was mainly because of the selfless service that he did. Mohanji used to go to his ashram and feed the hungry people himself and do other seva (social service). Mohanji never considered the Seeming Swami as a Guru, but as a friend, someone he really liked because he was doing extensive seva at that time. Seeming Swami even denied taking the $5000 from Mohanji's account and had the audacity to say that Mohanji owed him money. In the end, when Mohanji's court case was finally over and he was legally divorced from his ex-wife, he also divorced his best friend.

It was extremely difficult to bear the heaviness of such betrayal and go though this entire deceit-filled process. The trust was really at the highest level and the betrayal was bitter, especially because he was no ordinary person but a spiritual person supposedly deeply devoted to Sai Baba and selfless service.

Seeming Swami was a perfect example of the phrase "Dark Light," a phrase that describes a kind of darkness that is always there, close to the truth, but tweaking it, perverting it. What we learned through this direct experience was that there are people who pretend to be like Sathya Sai Baba, and use people's fascination behind the materializations of various pendants and items to the point when one cannot make out whether they are seeing magic or an actual materialization. It all looks very authentic.

When the astrologer told this Seeming Swami that one day Mohanji would obtain global recognition, this caused jealousy in him. His behavior changed from then on. I never knew how powerful negativity caused by jealousy could be, even among people who have attained higher levels of spiritual awareness (but have obviously not yet transcended the ego and mind games). I saw that through this example. He extorted money from the people Mohanji introduced to him, and since those people thought Mohanji had something to do with it, they left Mohanji. Mohanji once traveled to Qatar to conduct a meditation, and that entire group of people left him because the Seeming Swami asked for money from them by manipulating their trust in Mohanji.

Mohanji had some deeper spiritual experiences at Seeming Swami's ashram because he liked being in a space where continuous selfless service was done along with regular aarti to Shirdi Baba (with movement of light in a clockwise direction around the statue of Shirdi Baba for cleansing, protection, and strengthening of the connection with the consciousness). However, those experiences had happened because of Mohanji's purity, sadhana, eligibility, and communion with the highest of Masters such as Baba, along with their blessings, not because of the Seeming Swami.

Mohanji was happy to help Seeming Swami in any possible way and even recorded a shorter meditation for him in English so that he could sell those CDs. However, at some point in time, Mohanji understood it was all a farce – the social service that Seeming Swami was doing was only to show it to the public in order to exploit that visibility to make money. During those years he constructed a big ashram and built all sorts of facilities around it with such money.

Once Mohanji got to know how the divorce issue had been manipulated for six long years and finally separated from Seeming Swami, all sorts of rumors started to circulate in that area, including the preposterous one that Mohanji took the Power of Purity meditation from him, i.e. that Power of Purity is a copy of Seeming Swami's meditation. That was too much! When I heard that, I got up and told Mohanji, "Well, I am a living witness of the Power of Purity meditation. We can go to court and they can use a lie detector! I can surely prove it."

Of course, I would be ready to do that if need be. I was there when Mohanji gave a copy of the newly recorded Power of Purity meditation to Seeming Swami, but he hardly even looked at it. He was not interested. Instead, he asked, "Can you record a meditation for me?" Mohanji said: "Sure. I can do that." At his usual amazing speed, Mohanji recorded a new meditation for him. He scripted and voiced it, put music to it, and released it. Mohanji also acted in a video about this meditation which they shot together at this ashram. He even arranged for people to film it. I remember how odd all of this felt, but I did not want to say anything. I considered all of it as seva. Mohanji was committed to his work because when he is committed, he is 100% present.

Seeming Swami was not fluent in English but he started traveling, took that meditation to various countries, and made money from it. Mohanji, on the other hand, never sold Power of Purity – it has always been free. The claim that POP was a copy of Seeming Swami's meditation did not fly because Mohanji recorded many other beautiful meditations after Power of Purity, with equal ease and special Grace behind them, which is something that money certainly cannot buy. People can see the truth for themselves. It is rightfully said, "You can fool some people for some time, but not all the people all the time." The truth always comes out.

I must say that such treacherous acts did hurt because they exist as a mockery of everything Mohanji, supported by myself and all other people who connect to him, have been doing from the purest space of our hearts. It is unfortunate that many people still fall prey to the manipulations of the Seeming Swami, but then again, there must be some karmic agenda behind it. Mohanji came out of it after years of being manipulated and shared this as a powerful lesson for us when it comes to blind trust.

I would like to conclude this unpleasant subject on a happy note and share one story that demonstrates how beloved Baba broke the bubble and conveyed a powerful message related to this topic at the right time. His love gives meaning to all our experiences, and his timing is always perfect...

This is a story about a man who served as a Seva Dal (dedicated volunteer) in Puttaparthi. He was planning to request a private meeting with Sathya Sai Baba at one point in time and had written a letter about Mohanji, simply out of love, in case he got lucky and got to talk to Baba in person.

In that letter, this man wrote the entire list of losses that Mohanji endured – the loss of his daughter, possessions, money, job, health, etc. He then asked Mohanji to pray to Sai Baba that he gets the blessing of that private meeting. Mohanji was surprised by his request – this man, who worked as the Seva Dal in Baba's ashram, certainly must have known Baba much more than Mohanji, who had never even met Baba in person. This man then said: "I know I work there, but I don't know why, I feel Sai Baba will listen to you."

Mohanji then agreed to pray and mentally conveyed, "Baba, if it is your will, do see him privately."

Later on this Seva Dal person shared with Mohanji that not only did he get the private meeting, but Sathya Sai Baba called him personally and took only Mohanji's letter out of many other letters in the pile. And then, the best part – Baba put the unopened letter on his lap and started tapping on it with his right hand, while saying: "You have written about Mohan to me in this letter. I know him very well. I gave him enough tests in life. Anyone else in his position would have committed suicide. I took away everything he had. I emptied him. He never complained. He never fought back. He never developed self-pity. He never accepted sympathy. Now I will walk with him. Now I will be with him. Every step he takes, I will be there."

All these things were happening in parallel while Mohanji was connected to this Seeming Swami. This is why I strongly feel that we can, in the end, thank the Seeming Swami for playing his role in Mohanji's cleansing process – for there is Divine Providence behind all our experiences, pleasant or painful.

Chapter 10

Life With Mohanji in Muscat

Mercedes-Benz

During my second yoga teacher training in 2008 in the ashram of Paramahansa Nithyananda, I was introduced to an Indian gentleman called Sudeep Basu. Much to my surprise, he contacted me a year later to deliver a most unexpected blessing.

"Hey Biba, just wanted to let you know that I got the General Manager position at Zawawi Trading Company in Muscat, the authorized dealer for Mercedes-Benz in Oman. Are you still looking for a job?"

The moment I saw this message – I knew it. That was my chance! Since a job and visa were not coming through in any other way, the Divine had intervened with a perfect opportunity. Sudeep said he was allowed to hire a personal assistant of his choice, and I knew that this job had my name written all over it. I had never imagined working for Mercedes-Benz, but hey, life is always a mystery, and that's the fun part!

Even after I got the job, I had to wait for another couple of months until my visa went through, and that "almost there" situation was a real test of my faith and patience. I would pray to Baba saying, "I see you are really working on my *shraddha* and *saburi,* dear Baba."

I traveled to Muscat every other weekend just to soak in the embrace of my beloved Mohanji. Each time I arrived at the bus station, Mohanji and his driver, Firoz, would welcome me with overflowing love and positivity and loads of laughs. Firoz was a chubby Muslim man from India with whom Mohanji loved to joke. Mohanji said, "Did you hear? A couple of days ago, there were tremors in Oman. Yes, people thought it was an earthquake."

I was surprised. "Really? So what happened?" He replied, "It was Firoz – jumping into the sea from the rock. A big tremor!" We laughed heartily.

"But nothing to worry about," Mohanji continued. "Firoz is on a diet now; he will lose weight. He went to a dietician the other day and got a paper listing which foods he should eat each day. He then asked, 'Oh, so this is what I am supposed to eat. Is that before or after the meal?'" We were laughing till we reached Mohanji's accommodation. And Firoz loved it. He would do anything for Mohanji.

When I mentioned that my visa had not gone through after almost two months of waiting, Firoz commented that everything was delayed during Ramadan. I was still concerned that this job would turn out like the previous scenarios wherein I was awarded the position, but then at the last minute, something would go wrong. Firoz placed a warm hand on my shoulder and said so sincerely, like an innocent child, "It will be OK. I will pray for you – every day." Firoz was a great support.

In the end, I mentioned something about the visa to Mohanji and he smiled mysteriously and said, "Let us see." Two days later, I received the visa.

I was so excited about my new life, and the day when I finally moved to Oman was amazing. The Mercedes-Benz showroom was stunning, perfectly polished, and luxurious, and my new job was not difficult at all. Sudeep was more of a friend than a boss. He loved to talk about spiritual topics (sometimes even too much), and my colleagues were wonderful, so there was never a dull minute at work.

I loved my new life – Baba took care of everything! Since accommodation was part of my compensation package, we began looking for a nice place near the office. One of my colleagues mentioned that a staff member was leaving Oman, and the house he had occupied for nearly two decades would soon become available. It was barely a five-minute commute to the office, and when we went to see it, I was delighted – the house had a huge open living and dining room, perfect for satsangs and meditations. I just said, "Jai Sai! We'll take it."

Mohanji and I had an agreement that my salary would be used for our living expenses, and his entire salary would go toward the payment of our debts. After a couple of years of doing exactly that, we managed to escape the chokehold of the debt acquired in Dubai and Mohanji's huge divorce proceeding fees. Once we were freed from our debts, it was finally time to leave the corporate world and begin working on our mission.

The Ghostbuster Phase

My boss Sudeep was given lovely accommodation – a fancy villa by the sea. There was only the small issue of ghosts. His Indian housemaid was terrified. Every night they would hear phantom footsteps and other odd sounds, an object would move by the power of an invisible hand, etc. None of their efforts to resolve the problem had succeeded.

At that time, our weekly gatherings in the living room of our new house had already begun. The gatherings included the Power of Purity (POP) meditation with Mohanji Energy Transfer, Shirdi Sai Baba's aarti, and a light dinner. We had a lovely group of people, and profound spiritual experiences occurred regularly. During our very first POP meditation in the new house, when Mohanji's voice in the recording said, "See your parents, your father and mother, coming in front of you, blessing you," Firoz had an amazing experience.

For the first time, Firoz saw his parents coming to him and blessing him. He had lost his parents in childhood, and sorely missed them all his life. They said to him, "We love you, son. We hear your prayers in the mosque every day. You need to know how proud we are to see what a man you have become. With regards to the registry papers of the house in India, we know you lost them and could not sell that house. The document is there, but it fell behind the top drawer of the old closet. Look for it and you will find it."

After the meditation was over, Firoz quietly stepped out of the house to gather his impressions. He called his brother in India, asking him to quickly check behind the top drawer of the old closet. He then returned to the room to share his experience. While we were having dinner afterward, his brother phoned to say, "I found it! It was exactly where you said it would be!" All of us rejoiced, hugging and celebrating. Our spiritual work in service of others was truly underway.

Sudeep was then encouraged to seek the resolution of his haunted-house problem as well. When he asked Mohanji for help, Mohanji looked into the distance for a couple of seconds and then said: "Ok, print a large photo of me, like A3 size or bigger. I will work through the picture. Light the oil lamp in front of it and let it burn continuously night and day. Just keep adding oil, making sure to maintain the flame of that lamp."

That was the first time I had heard Mohanji say to someone that he would work through his photo. Sudeep followed his instructions diligently, continuously maintaining the flame and presence of Mohanji, and the ghost simply vanished. Sudeep and his maid could scarcely believe it.

People were connecting effortlessly and having deep experiences with Mohanji not only through the Power of Purity meditation and 360 Degrees meditation, but also by merely gazing at a photo of Mohanji's eyes. Mohanji could handle complex issues which had completely stumped the world of official professions. Doctors and lawyers were helpless when it came to energetic issues, strange blockages, mysterious illnesses, etc. Only someone at the required level of subtlety could handle such things.

Another friend who lived in a big villa in Dubai had an issue with disturbing spirits or entities. Things around the house would move inexplicably, frightening this lady and her family. One night, the spirits managed to knock down a large, full-length mirror with gilded frame off the wall, breaking it. She became desperate and asked Mohanji for help. He checked on the situation through his third eye and told her: "The ground on which this house was built contained several graves. That is why these spirits were upset. They feel this was their territory, and you just barged in. They are trying to scare you so that you move away."

Then Mohanji went into a diplomatic negotiation of sorts. (As a Peace Studies graduate, I found this very entertaining – perhaps there could be a new elective course at my US university called "Spirit Mediation.") Mohanji spoke with the spirits, telling them: "Look here, you have to learn how to live with the owners of this villa. They live here now, and you live here too. They will respect you; you respect them. But you'll have to learn to live together. This is the only way."

Once Mohanji put his foot down and explained to them how things will be, they accepted it and became quiet. That was the beginning of, in diplomatic jargon, their peaceful coexistence.

Mohanji, the Astral Humanitarian

One rather dramatic event occurred while Mohanji and I were sleeping. Mohanji's astral body suddenly went to his parental home in Palakkad, Kerala. This is how he described this experience to me: "As I was sleeping, I suddenly became aware that I was taken to my home in Kerala. There was this huge horrible being with a deformed, giant-sized body and a very ugly head. I don't even know how to describe it, but it certainly was not very pleasant to look at. This entity was trying to enter the house of my parents to harm them. So, Baba summoned my astral body there."

One moment he was asleep, and the next moment he found himself on his back, with his knees to his chest, the bottom of his feet facing upward. He saw that strange entity and that very second, like a reflex reaction, he pushed it away with both feet. With that strong kick from Mohanji, the being went flying and was gone. I told him, "Oh wow. That's not a very pleasant way of being jerked from sleep. But thank God you could save Amma and Acchan [our terms of endearment for his parents] from such danger. Baba is amazing."

This was my introduction to Mohanji's work on the subtle plane – the invisible work that he does every day (and night). No one knows of such work except for the people who are helped, who then write to him. Nowadays, so many such messages pour in that Mohanji's personal secretary and office team have to handle the calls and requests. We also have more than 300 Mai-Tri practitioners and a few of us do work with deeper issues involving spirits, entities, heavy blockages or curses through ancestral karma, etc.

But when it all started, it was only because I had been sleeping next to Mohanji that I could observe him closely. I became aware that he does not sleep the way other people do. From his breathing pattern, I could clearly make out when he was sleeping and when he was traveling astrally. We all breathe in a specific way when we sleep – producing a slightly prolonged, relaxed exhalation. When Mohanji is in conscious astral travel, I can barely hear any breathing at all. It's so soft and subtle and then I know: "Oh, he's gone. He is traveling."

Remembering how intense my own conscious astral travel experiences were (to this day, I can vividly remember every little detail), at one point I asked Mohanji, "What is it that you do every night? I'm observing that you are not in your body most of the time?" Mohanji said that on the astral plane, many souls are a bit lost and need help. He said: "Imagine you have come to a hugely crowded airport and are seeing people running around desperately, not knowing where their gate is. I just direct them, comfort them, etc."

He told me that sometimes I automatically accompany him. Hearing that was so inspiring! As per his instruction, I would focus on an intention before I went to sleep. "May my astral body travel with Mohanji and do the required seva on the astral plane." I found this to be such an amazing use of my time – working even while sleeping.

Once, Mohanji woke up with really strong muscles, as if he had gone to the gym consistently for a month. I noticed this and asked him: "Goodness, what happened with your body? Look at all these muscles now!" He said that when he had been on the astral plane the previous night, he encountered horrific entities who looked like huge predators. They were approaching an innocent, helpless being that did not stand a chance. "So I went and fought with all of them to save this being, to help this soul go further into the light."

Mohanji inspired me to offer myself for even greater service on the astral plane, whatever it may be, just so I could be of any help. Sometimes people would tell me that they had seen me in a vision with him, or had a "dream" in which they saw us both, then I would know that was a glimpse of the astral experience. Though I did not receive the blessing to participate in these astral journeys consciously, as it had happened in the experience with Mahavatar Babaji, a couple of times I had glimpses and clear recollections of myself with him. Usually, these glimpses would be in 360-degree awareness, where I could feel everything around, in front, and behind me equally (the state that I experienced during my NDE and Shaktipat initiation).

One needs to develop the courage to "swim in those waters" and occasionally deal with frightening, demonic entities as well. They are not to be underestimated, and one certainly has to conquer all fear and have complete faith and surrender in order to handle such sightings. Babaji's words come to mind – "You are not ready YET." I trust that Mohanji knows my capabilities and potential better than I know myself (not to mention that there is plenty to be done on Earth physically). As he once beautifully stated, "All you need to do is to just make yourself available. Have pure intentions and surrender. The Masters will take care of the rest."

At one point, I was overcome with gratitude for being able to witness and experience so much with Mohanji, and for so many amazing experiences that had opened my eyes. I was blessed with the opportunity to understand how the Masters work; the huge responsibility they have, and the massive burden they carry – not for themselves, but primarily always for everyone else. It's a huge responsibility requiring continuous vigilance, like walking on a razor-sharp edge. It is the responsibility to handle duality in the best possible way while always continuing to be an instrument of the highest of consciousness and purest of love. It's an enormous blessing to witness this with someone physically alive, available in the physical body.

What I have always loved about Mohanji is his simplicity, and the way in which he would allow people to connect to him the way they were, in whatever way came as most natural to them – some through the business world, some as a friend, and some in other ways as well. Many people saw him as their son, naturally feeling that parental kind of love and care toward him. People connect with him in whichever way they feel most comfortable. I realized then just how unique Mohanji's contribution really is. His education, the hard work he put into building his corporate career, his successes and failures, his previous marriage and the pain of losing his child, his humanitarian work, and even our relationship – he had gone through all these worldly experiences to relate to everyone and offer practical advice relating to both the physical and spiritual world. He is not a Master who lives in celibacy or in a cave, removed from people. He was given the task to be among the people and still bear that torch of higher consciousness to show that it is possible to be *in this world but not of this world*, to be the silence of consciousness among the worldly noise.

Marriage on the Go

My closeness with Mohanji being so deep, and our true union existing so far beyond this lifetime, I honestly felt our earthly marriage was just a superficial formality. We wanted to keep it as simple as possible and not involve any religion or traditions. We would have been fine skipping the formalities altogether, but we lived in the Middle East, and as mentioned earlier, it was literally illegal for me to live with Mohanji unless we were married.

I have to admit that I always feel a bit odd introducing Mohanji to someone from non-spiritual circles as "my husband." After everything we have been through together, I can only say that to me, Mohanji is primarily vast consciousness, truly beyond barriers, open and universal. He cannot be bound. If anyone tries to bind him (and some have tried), he or she will lose him forever. He is like the wind. You can never bind wind.

Mohanji once told me, "We are terrestrially married. But, many people are married to my consciousness. All are inseparably connected. All are one!" These are not just mere words but something we have experienced as true, time and again.

It is wonderful to belong to our fast-growing global family. I have been a proud member from the onset, and it gives me tremendous fulfillment. I have seen this family grow organically, from within, relying on nothing but the time and talent people have invested out of their own free will and unconditional love. And I wouldn't want it any other way. Some tried to bribe Mohanji with expensive media campaigns, but he never fell for it. There was even one member of a government who recognized "great potential" in Mohanji and secretly offered a deal – their lobby would support him through an indirect, world-class media boost, and he would occasionally support their causes in return. Of course, it did not work! Nobody can bribe or buy Mohanji, and this is why I love him so much. He has utmost, uncompromising purity.

His initial website (created by a loving devotee) was an embarrassing display of flowers, bubbles, and butterflies in all colors, and his first videos were done without professional cameras, lighting, or sound. Yet his message reached those it was meant to reach, and with time, all the technical aspects gradually improved.

I feel so privileged that I was able to witness this journey from its very beginnings, and will forever hold space for our ever-growing family of souls serving the same higher purpose. Some people joined this mission with full dedication, while some just tested the waters and took time to connect. Some left and were never asked why. From our end, free will has always been honored and nobody is judged for the choices they make.

Concerning the depth of my connection with Mohanji, I must say that I am among the least jealous members of our global family, as I know that many people may be even more deeply connected to Mohanji's consciousness than I am. I do not hold any privileged position in the realm of consciousness – there is no reserved seat for anyone. It is all based on merit and eligibility. Any comparison is silly because we are all one consciousness. No one can own consciousness – we can only choose to "plug in" or not.

Back to the topic of our marriage, it was April 2010, and we had traveled to my parental home in Novi Sad, Serbia to get the wedding sorted and out of the way. My natal chart's Uranus showed up in my rebellious choice of a subtle green dress (the color of the heart chakra), rather than the typical white gown. I was a 32-year-old adult woman, ready to stand for what I felt was right. I thought, "After all, it is my wedding, and I should be wearing something I truly enjoy."

The same applied to the choice of the wedding ring. I never enjoyed wearing a ring on the ring finger, always preferring the middle one. Moreover, the shape of the typical golden wedding ring never appealed to me. It somehow always reminded me of a golden chain, and I had seen plenty of marriages that were nothing but bondage. Then I came across a platinum ring (the only one in the entire jewelry shop) that truly symbolizes our union – two hearts in *lemniscata* (a horizontal eight or infinity symbol) connected in an eternal flow of energy, celebrating Love with no hooks, Love beyond all barriers, Love pure and eternal...

I was deeply touched when I learned that my beloved Sirius is associated with the number eight. I also remembered the moment when this thought had first emerged in my awareness, of a higher union and purpose-based relationship symbolized by the horizontal number eight. It had been in Zagreb, on the eighth day of the eighth month of the year 2000, when I met Sinke, who turned out to be my knight from Sirius from many lifetimes ago. I had come a long way since then and was finally ready to answer the calling of marriage to consciousness. Sinke and I had walked in parallel for some time, but our paths diverged. Sinke did not pass the test of Sathya, the test of truth given by Baba, who revealed a truly special path for me. I was aiming for the top of the mountain.

When one of my friends saw my choice of wedding gown and ring, she smiled and said, "Biba, you are a bit of a rebel, aren't you?" The word "rebel" calls for a small digression from the narrative. Interestingly enough, while I was still in Dubai and struggling to make ends meet, I had once been interviewed by a sweet Indian lady (about my life, yoga teaching, and movie acting experience) who then published an article called "Rebel With a Cause" (the title an obvious play on words in reference to the famous movie with James Dean, "Rebel Without a Cause"). That was my first appearance in the print media.

I was intrigued by the title the journalist chose based on my interview, since I had never said anything remotely rebellious in that interview. However, the more I thought about it, the more it vibed with me. I am a rebel, but I don't invest my energy into being AGAINST anything – my path is to serve through my own example and show what is possible, beyond the usual frames imposed by society and our own minds. Indeed, I am *a rebel with a cause*, a rebel with a mission of celebrating the unconditionality of love, liberation from all bondage, and unity in diversity – through the golden thread that connects all of us, which again is Love, the path and the destination.

When I decided to marry Mohanji, I knew very well that I was marrying uncertainty. Those were his exact words (not most people's idea of romance, if I may note). "By marrying me, you are marrying uncertainty." I knew there would be no structured living. And I have to admit that the regular, clock-work married life was never my cup of tea anyway. I liked challenges, and we surely had plenty.

Mohanji and I were married at the marriage registrar's office at noon, and the whole event could well have been from a Bollywood script. The registrar was really confused when she realized that Mohanji's first name was my married last name. She said, "This can't be." I did my best to explain with the utmost politeness, "In South India, it is common that the husband's name becomes the wife's last name. My husband's name is Mohan Pathirisseri Kesavan. Unlike the family names in Europe, his family name means parental home, paternal grandfather and father. I cannot marry his grandfather or father, so my last name can only be Mohan. I hope you understand."

She kept scratching her head, and finally decided that the only option would be for me to change my name through a legal procedure (which would involve loads of paperwork, court filings, and take more than a month), and I had no choice but to agree. I decided to leave that to some other point in time when I would be in Serbia for a longer period.

After sweating over this slight complication, all the rest went very smoothly. My closest family was present at the wedding, including Dr. Maja who joined this special event with her daughter Petra, my sister Dana who flew from India with her new life partner Ranvir, and my best friend Marija who stood by my side as my maid-of-honor. Dana's friend Klara stood with Mohanji.

My grandparents were very excited and I must admit that the moment of entering one's signature into the registry book does feel very special. I was yet to change my name, but that very moment of signing the registry book evoked the feeling of entering the Bharadwaja gotra and coming closer to the fulfillment of my dream of being in the company of the Masters.

Once the official part was over, it was time to go home and celebrate a bit with my family. My mom made sure there was a table with vegetarian food, and that all the meat (prepared as per the usual custom) was served at another table. Everyone was in a jolly mood, regardless of how unusual all of this seemed to some of my family members, especially when Dr. Maja first arrived at the event and greeted Mohanji by placing her forehead/third eye on his third eye. My aunt Boja asked, "Is she kissing him, or what?" I found all of it really funny and mumbled something about a forehead-to-forehead salute!

Everyone fell silent when my dad raised his wine glass to offer a short speech. Seeing the tears welling up in his eyes before he even started speaking, I thought, "I hope the speech does not end up like the 'Mother and the child' recital from his childhood." His words were really beautiful and touching and before we knew it, music was playing and people were already forming a circle. My grandma joined in, inviting Mohanji to follow her. This was when tears finally came to my eyes – the sight of them hugging and moving in that circle was simply too sweet.

After about three hours, which was the time we had secretly allocated to this entire event, it was time for us to leave for Belgrade because a hundred or so people were eagerly awaiting Mohanji in a hall where he was scheduled to conduct the Power of Purity meditation. I had not mentioned this to my relatives because I thought the lunch would be over by then anyway. In the end, I had to stand up and say, "I am sorry, but my husband and I will have to leave now. We have a meditation to conduct in Belgrade. But please continue, take your time." My aunts from Croatia were especially shocked, "What do you mean you are leaving – this is your wedding!" Everyone at the "vegetarian table" laughed because this was something that sounded like us, while the "non-veg" side was in visible shock after this announcement.

I will never forget this funny moment that marked our most unusual marriage. I knew I was marrying fluidity, flexibility, out-of-the-comfort-zone challenges, and liberation. Again, this was fully in line with my rebellious nature and was completely ok as long as it felt right to me, as long as it had the stamp of approval from my unmistakable intuition.

The meditation in Belgrade was truly amazing and very special as well. This was the only time when not only I but everyone present, felt the presence of Jesus Christ during meditation and through Mohanji's words when he spoke during the satsang afterward. When we later saw a photo of Mohanji taken that evening, an etheric layer of different expression could be seen, as if merging with his face. The words he spoke were very powerful and everyone's heart expanded. I took that as the blessing of Jesus Christ on my wedding day and wept out of gratitude.

Seven years later, Avadhoota Nadananda, who found it amazing that a spiritual Master from India coming from the family of Namboodiri Brahmins, had married a woman from Europe, decided to conduct a special ceremony of his own, with the guidance of Divine Mother. We had narrated to him the full story of our wedding and he wished to fulfill the spiritual aspect of a wedding in India. That was really nice of him.

Mohanji's parents and our daughter Mila were present. We started with me doing aarti to Amma, Mohanji's mother. The energy during this ceremony was amazing, and Amma said that she really felt like Devi (Divine Mother). The energy was so powerful that she could not open her eyes. With Devi's blessing, we spiritually crowned the marriage as well, in India. This was really unexpected but very sacred and beautiful.

Limited Understanding Causes Judgement

Some people expected that nothing but blissful, sweet words were ever exchanged between Mohanji and me. Normally, people judge a situation using their mind's limited faculties. Sometimes Mohanji would scold me in front of others, and inevitably there would be someone who would ask me: "Why is he so abrupt and rude with you?" or "Does Mohanji ever even spend time with you? Does he talk to you with love, kindness, and consideration?" I would like to address this issue briefly, just to set the record straight.

Mohanji is objective and totally impartial. He grants me no special favors, nothing more than anyone else receives. I also never expect any special favors because I know his heart and I know his dedication to the higher purpose that he lives for. He is, as he says, "purpose-bound." I see that purposefulness happening all the time. He is like a mirror, reflecting what people bring to him. If one approaches him with anger and a hatred-filled mind, he responds in the same way with laser-sharp definiteness in order to blast it off that person that very instant. The same principle applies to me in those moments when he scolds me. If you bring love, however, he is love, and he melts... The mirror called Mohanji sincerely and objectively reflects people's individual constitutions.

Whenever he has uttered sharp words to anyone, I have clearly seen almost immediate changes in them. His presence always transforms and heals. Many people, however, come with expectations. Those people will also leave with complaints. Expectations never work with Mohanji. He never caters to such desires. He always says, “I never intercept or interfere with anyone’s karma. All I do is remove blockages so that they can move on effectively in evolution.”

Those who complain have clearly not understood him. When I once told him that his straightforward approach may be taken as rude behavior, he said: “What have I got to do with people? I never do anything for myself. I do it for their own good. I do it out of love and compassion and the need to shake them up, to wake them up from their deep slumber of routine habitual ignorant patterns. I am doing it out of love, not hatred. When someone scolds another out of anger and hatred, it is not good for either party. What I do is not out of anger or hatred for the person. It is out of love. That makes my responses pure and clear. If someone does not understand that and thus decides to leave me, how can I help it?” Indeed, the crucial difference here is in the intention. Is the occasional scolding based on love or hatred? This should be clearly understood.

The Blessing of Scolding

Typically, scolding creates the sensation of the heart chakra shrinking, the painful emotional scarring which is often remembered long after, but I never felt that with Mohanji. On the contrary, I always felt something was being removed from me. Some blockage would be cleared, followed by an inner shift, bringing a sense of relief, clarity, and blissful lightness.

What’s even more interesting is that I do not even remember any of his past scoldings. I honestly cannot remember a single one. And he too does not remember what he told me or anyone else after the incident unless someone reminds him. He always operates in the present, sliding to the next, and next event effortlessly. Nothing stays on his canvas as he glides through life. Nothing can hold him beyond the specific time. This, I must say, is the unique quality of a Master – if a Master cannot scold his disciple and prick the balloon of his/her ego, then he is no Master.

Sugar-coated words due to second agendas are the quality of politicians, not spiritual Masters. Every true disciple should recognize the value of a scolding by an awakened being and accept it with gratitude, for only a Master can fight the in-built ego mechanism. In my case, the situation is unique and slightly more challenging because my Master is also my husband and when disagreements happen, all wives like to be right – at least sometimes. That dynamic is pretty limited in our case because Mohanji is my Guru as well. In those situations, I remind myself that this union was my conscious choice. As Nithyananda Swami said, “But know: it’s not going to be easy.”

The number of people coming to Mohanji has increased manifold over the last fifteen years, making his private time increasingly precious and limited. He never complains. He only requests discipline and understanding from people. At the same time, Mila and I are not just brushed aside. He never misses even the minutest detail and always ensures that we are taken care of and protected. He attends to us, wherever he is, in one way or the other, if not himself then through someone else from our closest team. All I know is that, in the end, our problems get solved. Bear in mind, he does the same with almost everyone connected to him. From that perspective, imagine the size of his workload in this world (not to mention the astral plane and other dimensions).

The numerous testimonials coming out each day through emails and blogs are a true reflection of what Mohanji is to the world. I can only say that I share his devotees' love and admiration for him. He means the world to me. He means the world to many other people across the globe and has touched many lives over the years. Many people have come to stay, and at the same time, some have been disappointed and have left him.

It is usually those who come with many expectations or those who entertain certain fancies of the mind that leave disillusioned. When such a person would come to him, Mohanji would sometimes tell me: "This person will not stay. He has come with expectations. I cannot fulfill his desires. This is against his karma. I will not do anything against his karma."

Mohanji always stays with the truth and ethics of spirituality. I have seen him doing things that even compromise his health, leaving him sick and bedridden. People have come to him with serious problems and out of sheer compassion, he would remove their affliction and bring it onto himself, leaving them liberated. I saw him reduce the effect of a car accident with my very own eyes.

While traveling to a beach famous for snorkeling, not far from Dubai, my sister Dana and I were in the back seat and Mohanji was sitting in the passenger seat next to the driver. The road was full of curves and at one point I had a sudden premonition that we were going to be in an accident. I even told the driver to be careful. Dana mentioned the same feeling. We all became silent and went through a strange experience of literally awaiting the accident – our intuition about it was that strong. However, after a minute or so, this feeling disappeared and a small cut on Mohanji's hand (which had not moved from the grab handle, colloquially called the "panic bar") appeared from nowhere. I knew right away that he had prevented the accident and taken that karma onto himself. He could reduce it but not remove it fully. A small cut thus appeared on his hand. I asked him about it and he confirmed it was true. Dana and I were deeply touched. Love overwhelmed my heart...

Many people have written blogs, testimonials, and books about Mohanji's presence in their lives and the transformation they have experienced. On the other hand, many others who have benefited from his presence have chosen to ignore it, calling it a coincidence. I sincerely feel pity when one cannot fully cherish the grace with which they are blessed. Mohanji always keeps on delivering in whatever form he chooses. He has never expected anything from anyone or cared if someone chose to criticize him. He just made himself available and kept on delivering.

But if there is one thing that Mohanji dislikes, it is artificiality, masks, and pretension. Without naming anyone in particular, he would sometimes say, "These people need nothing from me. They will get nothing. They do not care for liberation. They are wasting my time – I can give them nothing. They came to share with me their pretensions and insecurities. Some of them have come to compare me with others. I have nothing to do with it. They wasted my time and theirs."

He also never liked superficiality on the spiritual path. I once heard him say, "Oh, that person has nothing to do with God realization. She is just after some spiritual sensations. I am the wrong person for that. My path is that of annihilation of everything and merger with the Supreme. All she needs for spiritual elevation, if that is her true choice, is a conscious shedding of her pretensions. She can reach the highest only by shedding her masks."

Betrayals

Soon after our wedding, Mohanji was nearing the point when all our debts would be paid and he could then focus only on his spiritual calling. He planned to leave all his contacts from years in the shipping industry, as well as his vast business knowledge (in the form of advice) with one of his best and most trusted friends who worked in the same industry. The plan was that, by leaving it all to him, Mohanji would still get regular basic income from the company, and all of his programs would be conducted free of charge. He could then dedicate himself fully to selfless work and his spiritual mission.

Yet, that was not to be. Mohanji experienced a massive betrayal from this friend, who scandalized Mohanji and simply took over everything. No one saw this betrayal coming. Even more unexpected was the deeper reason behind this unpleasant experience, which was revealed years later in the UK.

Years later, when we went to Skanda Vale ashram in the UK, we came to know more about the life of another amazing Master, Guru Subramanium. Swami Surya, one of his main disciples, shared with us how the Skanda Vale ashram in the UK came into existence. (The swamis from this ashram serve humanity with utmost dedication and have a deep connection with Mohanji as well. This is where Mohanji installed the *murti* (statue) of Lord Dattatreya, the first such murti in Europe. He plans to install a Shirdi Baba murti in June 2023.)

We learned how Guru Subramanium intended to leave the flower business he ran with his partner and dedicate himself to the ashram and their spiritual work. He attempted to make an arrangement through which he would still receive his basic income from the flower business. However, his partner betrayed him, did not honor their agreement, and simply took over the whole thing. Mohanji and I looked at each other and smiled saying, "Yep, the story sounds familiar."

From another perspective, when something grand, pure, and selfless is to commence, there is a sort of removal that takes place. Perhaps through such betrayal, some karma or an obstacle was removed. Or he simply had to enter into the new life of complete service without any secure income option, without anything to hold on to except faith. I just knew that hearing this story was not a coincidence but a higher message for us. Yet another experience from which we have grown.

The Price of Betrayal

Before continuing further, I would briefly like to touch upon the price of betrayal, just to put it into perspective. When we betray someone, when we do something that is actually immoral, there is a huge price to be paid. Very often people are unaware of it. Even if we betray a "normal," average human being, somebody who is dedicated to his family, his income, his desires, and pleasures (let alone a Master), there are karmic consequences to be paid. But when we do this to someone who is operating from a completely different level, who doesn't even operate from the mind, but the substratum of the mind, someone who doesn't operate from the level of fulfilling his own desires, but is completely selfless and dedicated to serving others, then when we betray someone like that, the price that has to be paid is enormous. It doesn't affect just the person who committed the act of betrayal, but affects their family too - the ancestors, the present generation, and the future generations.

Just as we inherit wealth from our forefathers or some debt from our immediate family members, we are interlinked within our family at the energetic and karmic levels as well. If one goes into bad-mouthing, betrayals at various levels, or even into black magic, dark energy work, etc., the consequences and huge karmic debt could take lifetimes to pay.

I remember one fascinating encounter I had during one of my visits to Puttaparthi. While waiting for Sathya Sai Baba to arrive at the Darshan Hall, I noticed an older lady from Croatia swathed in a blanket next to me. She said that she lived at the ashram. She had been there for more than a year at that time. I noticed that she looked a bit strange because, even though it was really hot, she was wearing a sweater and a blanket. At some point, I asked her: "Aren't you feeling hot?"

She said: "No, I'm freezing. I have some kind of illness or disorder, where I'm continuously shivering and freezing." I didn't know that was possible. She continued: "It's not just a mere physical ailment, it's a karmic thing. With the help of Baba, I became aware of what I did. I did black magic on people in my past life. Now I'm paying the price. And, while I'm in the presence of Baba, the effect is significantly reduced. I can still bear it. When I go away, once that umbrella of His grace is gone, it's unbearable. It's a continuous torment that I'm going through because nobody can help me. It's not something I can resolve by taking any medicine, and no matter how many clothes I wear, even with the layers on top, I am continuously shivering and freezing." That was an eye-opener for me. That sounded like a description of hell and was a perfect example of the consequences of our thoughts, words, actions, and intentions.

Maha Kumbh Mela Fun in 2010

In February 2010, I joined Mohanji for a super fun trip to Haridwar. We joined a huge gathering of 50 million people by the river Ganges, honoring the Kumbh Mela tradition of meeting the Masters who make themselves available at this special gathering, the tradition dating back to the 8th century and the great Adi Shankaracharya.

There were many profound spiritual experiences and special encounters with Masters and Avadhootas. There was one especially funny moment, something that Mohanji loves to tease me about when I "got him into trouble."

During one of Mohanji's most beautiful satsangs so far, which happened in Zemun, Serbia in 2017, Mohanji shared the stage with Sun Yogi Umashankar. I was next to him, translating and laughing like never before. The atmosphere was superb. Mohanji spoke with endless humor and depth that enthralled the audience. I would like to share an excerpt from the transcription of that speech which covers the funny scene with Swami Paramananda Giri, a great Master who comes to Haridwar only for Kumbh Mela.

Mohanji spoke, and I laughed and translated in front of an audience of 300+ people:

> You know, Devi comes with me to certain programs, like Kumbh Mela, etc., and puts me in the soup. One time, it was in 2010, we were standing together outside and suddenly we saw a saint. He resembled Osho very much. I went to him and said, "You look like Osho." And he started laughing. With his beard and everything, he was really looking like Osho and I couldn't resist it.
>
> Then he said, "I came here with my Guru. My Guru is here in the neighborhood." I replied, "Oh, you have a Guru."
>
> Then he said, "He's a very great Master. He's one of the key Masters of the Kumbh Melas. So if you would like to meet him, I'll take you."
>
> I said, "Definitely, I'd like to." So we went, both of us. And you know, I normally don't open my mouth in front of Gurus. *She* talks. [*Laughter*]
>
> So when we went, we saw him lying down on a bed on the stage – he's a 90-year-old man. And this 'Osho' took us straight to him and asked us to sit next to him. When we sat down, the Guru sat up.
>
> He asked, "Who are you?" I didn't say anything. I just bowed down. She said, "He teaches meditation." He was looking at me. "What meditation are you teaching?" I said, "Nothing."
>
> Then he started asking me questions, one by one, throwing them at me like bullets. He was testing me, whether I knew something. And he was asking those questions in front of everyone, in Hindi – my quota of Hindi is very limited. I answered in Hindi. He asked six questions. I answered six questions. Then he smiled, tapped me on the head, and said, "Good, you have arrived. Eat from my ashram. Go. Take them. Give them food."
>
> Then I told Devi, "Never, ever, say things like this in front of any Guru because we have no clue what they're going to ask then." And she was sitting quietly, enjoying this game. [Laughter] The moral of the story is never to put your head in a lion's den.
>
> One question he asked, I remember, was: what is your purpose? Not exactly what is the purpose of life – he asked me, "In spirituality, what is your benchmark? What have you set for yourself?"
>
> I said, "My presence should be more powerful than my teaching. If that is not happening, I'm not worth it. My energy and presence should be powerful enough to transform."
>
> Then the last question in Hindi that he asked was: "So what would you like to teach the world?" "Nothing," I said. That he liked. He laughed, actually.
>
> He said, "This is the right path. Don't think that people need to learn something. They already know. All you have to do is, with just your emptiness, allow them to reveal it to themselves."

Miraculous Pregnancy

Whenever I think of my pregnancy, I still feel an urge to go back in time to try to demystify just how I got pregnant in 2010. However, that is pointless and all I can do is simply share the story. I always conclude, "After everything I have seen around Mohanji and Baba, why am I even surprised?" My pregnancy story is intriguing and may raise some eyebrows, but it is just another one of my authentic experiences that expanded the realm of possibilities within the perceived reality.

One night in July 2010, I woke up in the middle of the night and couldn't get back to sleep. This rarely happens to me as I have always been blessed with deep, sound, uninterrupted sleep. That night I simply got up, feeling the urge to sit in front of the altar in our bedroom and meditate. For the first time, the picture of Ammu (Mohanji's daughter who was killed at the age of four) stood out with some special energy. I had never meditated on the image of Ammu, but that night her eyes caught my attention, and I felt a deep connection with her angelic essence. I was aware of just how deeply involved she was in Mohanji's entire mission and what a huge role she played in his spiritual awakening.

I looked deep into her eyes for longer than I ever had before. With tears welling in my eyes, I whispered sincerely, "Dearest Ammu, I would be so blessed if you would come into my womb and be my daughter. You know, I would love you with all my heart, with all that I've got." After releasing that prayer like a dove from my heart, I meditated some more and then went back to bed.

Approximately two weeks later, during our weekly Power of Purity meditation, it was the turn for Dr. Deepali to deliver Mohanji Energy Transfer (at that time it was still called shaktipat) to all present, including me. I enjoyed receiving that pleasant, warm surge of loving energy through my top two chakras and went very deep into meditation. As soon as the meditation was over, Dr. Deepali came to me and stunned me with the following statement, "Biba, guess what – while giving you shaktipat, I clearly saw that you are pregnant. Baba told me. The Masters went even further, giving me instructions on how I, as a doctor, should help you and ensure that everything goes well with the pregnancy." I was stunned by this statement, to say the least.

I told her, "That's amazing, but I find it hard to believe because, you see, it's been a while since Mohanji and I were intimate… He had some serious lower back issues and underwent treatment over the last two months, so sometimes he even had to sleep on the floor. But thanks, that surely was interesting information."

The next day, I could not stop pondering Dr. Deepali's intriguing statements. "What if I am pregnant?" I thought. I was not even sure when I was supposed to get my period. I did not count the days properly because there was no need. I was preoccupied with my office work, our charitable work, my spiritual practice, etc. After all, we had been married only a couple of months earlier, and had not yet reached the point of actively working on this aspect as some couples do.

Just to appease my mind, I decided to go to the pharmacy to buy a pregnancy test. I took the test and, lo and behold, a PLUS SIGN appeared! I rubbed my eyes to see again, and double-checked the instructions on the box – yep, I was pregnant! I couldn't believe it! I shared the amazing news with Mohanji and he just pressed his palms together, thanked Baba, and then hugged me. We were going to be parents! How amazing was that?! This was one of the biggest surprises of my life and I strongly feel it was none other than Baba behind it.

Dreadful Pregnancy Challenges

The new life growing within my womb was a truly wondrous feeling. Ladies who are mothers will know all about that special soft and exciting feeling that cannot be fully expressed in words. I sailed bravely through all the phases of the pregnancy while working for Mercedes-Benz and diligently participating in our weekly meditations with aarti to Shirdi Baba. As per Mohanji's instructions, I stopped performing shaktipat and was only at the receiving end, enjoying Mohanji's meditations and aarti in an entirely new way. I was continuously aware that the new being within me was feeling what I was feeling, listening to my thoughts, and benefiting from any meditation that I did. I felt more emotional and sensitive but was hardly ever cranky. I was determined to "handle" anything that pregnancy brought with no fuss. Frequent healthy snacking helped prevent sickness and vomiting. All in all, I was able to cope just fine.

Before I got pregnant, I was quite regular with my morning gym exercises, yoga, and meditation. Mohanji and I had a good deal with a nearby Crowne Plaza hotel and paid for annual membership to their gym. Due to the immense heat in Muscat, especially during summer, this was the only place where one could possibly do any exercise. I loved caring for and connecting to my physical body in that way and did not want to give it up. I have to admit that I was also worried that I may gain a lot of weight during pregnancy as some women do, so I was all the more eager to continue being physically active, only carefully reducing it to longer walks on the treadmill and mild exercises suitable for the prenatal phase.

I was therefore really not happy when Mohanji told me one day, "It's ok that you walk outside when it's not dark, but don't go to the gym now that you are pregnant. Some silly thoughts may come to you, and you may do something you will regret."

I couldn't believe what he was telling me! "This is not logical at all," I thought. Walking outside was fine (in suffocating, sauna-like temperatures and humidity), but walking on the treadmill (in a nice, air-conditioned gym for which we already paid) was not. I brushed aside his advice and simply would not listen. A rebellious, disobedient aspect of my ego reared its ugly head. To this day, I feel this is one of the most difficult aspects of my ego that occasionally stands as a roadblock, truly as a massive obstacle to full surrender. Despite my determination to conquer this roadblock through higher awareness, I still cannot say that it is fully behind me. The danger of this rebellious attitude was revealed by the predicament that ensued when I refused to listen and continued going to the gym.

A week or so later, when I went to the gym, I noticed a nice movie (it was the movie "Australia" with Nicole Kidman) on the TV screen above the treadmill. I put on the headphones and walked along, immersed in the movie. I did not notice that this movie was longer than most movies, almost three hours long! After an hour or so, it was time for me to stop walking because pregnant women should never exert too much, but I was too keen to see how the movie ended. I assumed it would end soon because I had been watching it for more than an hour, so I ignored my body's signs of fatigue. The gym started to get a bit crowded at that point and I noticed that some people were waiting to use the treadmill, so, as if hypnotized, I shifted to the stepper to continue watching the film. I could not just stand there and stare at the TV, I had to move to the stepper to justify remaining at the gym, and to begin stepping to justify occupying the machine. I just wasn't thinking properly… I just had to see the end of the movie! Only when the movie finally finished did I realize just how tired and exhausted I was, prompting me to quickly return home.

The next morning, a sudden, sharp pain in my abdomen awoke me from sleep around 6:30 a.m. I had never felt such pain before – it felt like someone was stabbing me with a knife. This pain scared me. I did not know what to do. I tried some deep belly breathing, but nothing helped. The pain would come in cycles – pain, a pause for a minute or two, and then pain again. During the pause, I messaged my gynecologist and she replied right away, "Well, this is definitely not normal." This is when the fear crept in. I knew she did not want to scare me, but I could feel what was in the subtext of her message. I realized that I had overexerted myself in the gym the previous day and the words "losing the baby" appeared on my inner screen. "Oh no! This can't be happening!" I thought. Dark thoughts followed the piercing pain, and I started judging myself for overexerting. I especially judged myself for not listening to Mohanji who had given me a clear warning a week or so prior.

Mohanji was in the bathroom, getting ready for work. At this point, I was already panicking. Complete darkness overtook me as I sank into the abyss of horrible fear, pain, and self-loathing. I called Mohanji near, and told him what was happening. He had a very serious expression on his face and walked to the altar, stood in front of it with pressed palms, and stared at Baba's big photo. After a couple of seconds, he told me lovingly, "Baba said you should swallow the entire pack of Shirdi Sai Vibhuti. Here it is. I will have to go now because we have a meeting with someone from the Royal office. It will be very short and I will return as soon as I can. Just do what he said. Everything will be ok." He kissed me and left.

At this point, I was in the most horrible phase of miscarriage. The stabbing pain was unbearable, the pauses were shorter and the emotional pain and fear that gripped me were even worse. I was sobbing and squirming on the bed. I tried to swallow that Vibhuti, but couldn't get to it because the pauses were so short that I could barely regain my breath before the most horrible pain would start again.

After 40 minutes of such torment, I gathered all my strength and willpower to lift myself up and swallow the entire package of vibhuti. The moment I did that, as if I had been touched with a magic wand, my contractions disappeared. I had to pinch myself to believe this was really happening. I went to the toilet, washed away my tears, and decided to get dressed quickly, just in case my contractions returned. I had not developed faith in Baba's vibhuti because I had never really needed it before. I saw it more as something kind of symbolic rather than something in which I fully believed. It was then that I finally got to experience for myself what a difference that small package of Grace in the form of sacred ash could make. Baba saved our baby.

Mohanji came back shortly after that and we went straight to the hospital to see whether everything was ok with the baby. The doctor simply said, "I see traces of muscle contraction on the walls of the uterus, but the baby is completely fine, nothing to worry about."

From that moment onward, I took Mohanji's words of caution much more seriously, and my faith in Baba increased manifold. I don't know how I would have lived with myself had I lost my baby through a miscarriage that day due to my silliness. Later on, Mohanji told me that this was exactly what he saw in the vision – dark entities luring me into watching TV. I was not fully conscious and alert, as if drunk with such an obsession for that movie that all bodily signs would be ignored. This was a huge lesson.

Only a week or so later, there was one more dreadful experience, which could have been even more dangerous. Mohanji told me specifically not to go outside after dark. He said, "This is a crucial time when the soul is getting fully anchored into the fetus. Some dark forces may try to prevent that. Do not go outside when it is dark. If you are in the house and shielded here by my energy, nothing bad can happen." This time I followed the instructions diligently, but one night I woke up around 2:00 a.m. due to heartburn and just couldn't fall back asleep. The heartburn gave me a feeling of suffocation. I was tired, irritated, and annoyed.

Mohanji appeared to be sleeping, but when I observed more closely, I realized his breathing was barely audible, which meant he was traveling astrally. I did not want to disturb him with my issues, but I just did not know what to do – I felt like I couldn't breathe properly. I needed some fresh air. A thought came, "Maybe I should open the window, just to see whether I will feel better." Because I was so tired and not alert and aware, I did not realize this was not *my* thought. It was imposed upon my mind by a foreign entity. It was not even logical – during the summers there, it is so hot outside that opening a window definitely does not bring any freshness. I was dreaming of the day when I would be able to open the window in the morning, see some greenery and sunlight, and inhale fresh air. This is something that people in Europe take for granted, but while living in the Middle East, this was one of my greatest fantasies.

That night, I craved that feeling of opening the window and inhaling cool, fresh air. I opened the window, and inhaled deeply, but felt nothing. There was no freshness. Another thought came. "Maybe if I just protrude my head through the window a bit, maybe some fresh air will come then."

I was just about to lean forward through the window when Mohanji made a moaning sound and then somehow managed to say, although in a hoarse voice, "Close that window right now!"

Taken aback, I looked at Mohanji in wonder. I closed the window and went closer to him. I noticed that he looked exhausted. It took him some time to be able to speak properly. Then he told me, "Those entities wanted to lure you into putting your head outside. Then they would hook on to you and aim for the baby. I had told you to be careful. I warned you about going outside in the dark."

I was really confused and said, "I'm sorry, I did not think that protruding my head through the window to get some air would fall into the category of going outside." What Mohanji said next really shook me.

"I was high above us with my astral body and from that height, I saw a couple of entities luring you to put your head through the window so that they could attack the baby. There was no time to return to my body properly, so I had to crash-land. I am not feeling well right now, and will have to rest."

The next day one of our friends who went into deep meditative states told me, "You have no idea how dangerous this was for Mohanji. I saw him crash-landing. I saw it through my third eye. He risked his life for you and the baby. It's pretty much the same as crash-landing with a helicopter. Only a very few lucky ones can survive that. Please, please, never do that again. This nearly killed him."

This entire incident took some time to digest. This was my introduction to the world of dark energies and entities, a world one surely doesn't want to know. Whenever there is a greater potential for light to make a true difference, the dark side will try to prevent it. My pregnancy now came with a heavy load of responsibility to be constantly vigilant. I was determined not to fall into the trap of dark energies again. I began meditating more and following all the rules set by Mohanji. Our weekly meditations and Baba's aarti helped. I felt so much lighter afterward and I kept surrendering everything to Baba. However, another, even bigger blow came a month or so later.

This time the full weight of the attack was on Mohanji. He was attacked by Dark Light like never before. They hit his main pillar – his spine. Suddenly, Mohanji's spine was no longer straight but had the shape of the letter S. I just couldn't believe my eyes when I saw that. It was such a ghastly sight to behold. Mohanji could hardly function, and I felt so sad and so helpless. For the next couple of days, we tried all sorts of things to help him with his back, but we knew this was not a physical issue. We knew it was an attack.

When our regular group gathered for meditation, we sat and discussed what was to be done. The conclusion was that we could all do aarti to Mohanji with a sincere prayer to Baba to remove this dark burden from him and bring his spine back to normal. We proposed this to Mohanji, and he immediately agreed. He sat on the sofa, with both palms facing out in the blessing position. We lit up the pancha-aarti (five flames) lamp and started the worship.

The energy was truly special, and all of us had teary eyes from our earnest prayer. Mohanji noticed that he felt much lighter and withdrew to our bedroom to rest. The next morning, he felt completely fine and our joy knew no bounds. That afternoon, Dr. Deepali ran to our home after work and said she had a special surprise, something we had never seen before. We were all incredibly curious. She came to show us the photos she had taken the previous evening when we did aarti to Mohanji, and we immediately noticed something truly stunning. We saw a man with gray hair, all covered in white, doing aarti to Mohanji. "This is impossible," we concluded. "We were all wearing colorful clothes. How is it possible that nobody noticed this person among us? Who was it? And what kind of strange white sack is he wearing?"

Since the photo was in high resolution, taken with Dr. Deepali's professional camera, we enlarged it and tried to make sense of it. The man's hands were not visible; only a small portion of the temples and some gray hairs could be seen. The rest was the white cloth he was wearing, which was very unusual; nobody dressed like that.

At that moment, Dr. Deepali (originally from Maharashtra) noticed the double stitch on the part of the cloth covering the man's head, and that rang a bell. She suddenly exclaimed, "Oh my god! I just realized that in the olden days in Maharashtra, like in the 19th century or so, this double stitch was considered to be typical for that region. It's very obvious now – this was Shirdi Sai Baba."

Excited, all of us started discussing and sharing impressions, but I still felt the pull to stare at the photo. "Something else is there," I felt intuitively. I was especially drawn to a round, brownish-yellowish "something" that looked like it emerged from the light of the pancha-aarti lamp. As I looked, I suddenly realized, "Oh my god, the brown part is a profile of a baby, with the head covered with a dark yellow cloth. I can see the nose, eye with eyebrow, and lips. The forehead is small and round." When Mila was born, she looked exactly like that. This was the first time I saw her – coming from the light of the lamp in Baba's hands while she was still growing in my womb.

This special, historic photo that truly expands the boundaries of the realm of possibilities has been included in this book's photo section, now published in public for the first time with the full background story. The photo did appear in some blogs, but only some of our closest friends knew the full story. In all his humility, Mohanji was hesitant to show a photo in which Shirdi Baba is doing aarti to him, as some Baba devotees may find it offensive. However, this was Baba's divine intervention to save Mohanji in the midst of an attack and should be seen in that light. One thing is for sure – there are no formalities when it comes to Baba. He loves, blesses, and gives full-on.

Sacred Entry Into Motherhood

The rest of the pregnancy went smoothly, but some unexpected turbulence awaited me at work. One day, my assistant position at Zawawi Trading Company suddenly disappeared. The owner decided to dismantle the general manager's position, and my friend-turned-boss Sudeep was gone. I remained in the company in a floating administrative position, feeling really uncomfortable. Since I was pregnant and my belly was very visible, there was no question of looking for another job.

A week or so later, I happened to run into the new CEO of the Automotive Division, an Australian gentleman called Craig Hardie. He was a bit strict but very professional. He came to know that I was "floating" within the company, and after inquiring about my experience, he mentioned that he wouldn't mind having me join his division as his Personal Assistant. That was an amazing, super timely blessing. I was far busier than before but enjoyed the professionalism. Being halfway through the pregnancy and having faced all those challenges with the dark energies, I needed stability and focus.

I used all my free time for spiritual practice and preparation for the moment when the special soul I was carrying inside my womb would see the light of day. I signed up for prenatal yoga classes with a lovely South African lady who was also a doula (spiritual midwife). I liked her energy and learned quite a lot from her. I did not know that contractions of the pelvic floor muscles done in two yogic positions were far more effective than the usual Kegel exercises. I enjoyed doing yoga with other future moms in addition to the socializing and mutual comforting. This was my first glimpse in this lifetime into the beauty of women's circles. In all stages of life, women should support one another as sisters, especially during pregnancy and after delivery. It is my dream to see women's circles blossoming around the world, circles within which women share knowledge, insights, joy, and pain in a free flow, as unconditional support for one another.

My South African prenatal yoga teacher was also trained in hypnotherapy. One day I stayed a bit longer after class chatting with her, exploring the possibility of doing her version of a session of this sort. This was not a real regression and was done in the alpha state of mind, more like a deep Yoga Nidra, but the point was to establish communication with the baby and support one another during the process of delivery. This idea of communicating with the baby and adopting the attitude of "We're in this together, and we've got this!" sounded exciting and I agreed to give it a try.

I came open-minded, not expecting anything, which is why I ended up being amazed by the whole story of symbols that appeared in my mind as brief but very clear visions. The first thing that I saw was an umbrella. This umbrella was kind of floating upwards slowly, and the handle of this umbrella was connected with my heart. Then I saw the small head of the baby and a twinkling star on top of it. After the session, we discussed the meaning of the symbols and my South African teacher said that, as per her experience, my baby was conveying the following through this symbolism: "In this lifetime you are progressing spiritually from the heart chakra and moving upward (with life lessons corresponding to heart and higher chakras). However, in my case, I am already at the crown." Considering all I had experienced till then, that sounded very true.

The second vision with symbolism proved to be even more important. I saw a feather, a very light, beautiful feather which was slowly falling down, moving like a pendulum – right and left, right and left... At some point, somebody tried to make it fall faster by blowing on it. That only disturbed the flow and the feather moved in a hectic way, all over the place, eventually re-assuming its natural falling speed. Nothing was achieved by rushing it, and the height from which it was falling was even greater than before. The conclusion was – don't disturb the flow and don't try to speed anything up, just connect with the flow. I did not need much explanation for this as I understood that the feather was the baby, and falling is the progression through the birth canal during delivery. I was very grateful to my South African friend and wished she could have been my doula, but the decision was already made that I would deliver my baby in Serbia. I really couldn't deal with the paperwork nonsense of delivering the baby elsewhere, plus I was eager to change my last name before our baby was born, and that was certainly going to take time. This was my perfect opportunity to resolve this matter before the baby was born.

I was shocked to learn that mothers-to-be in the Middle East get only 40 days of paid pregnancy leave. I had to take two months of unpaid leave before the delivery (as airlines would not let women fly after the seventh month of pregnancy), and planned to use that shortest-ever maternity leave after the baby was born. There was no point in making comparisons with Europe. Since many Muslim women get pregnant soon after getting married and then keep getting pregnant (as one of the major purposes of marriage in Islam is procreation and contraception doesn't seem to be very popular), employers will not give more than 40 days of maternity leave, period. I was grateful that I could be with Mohanji, and I needed this job, so I kept quiet. I could not imagine how it would feel to show up at work 40 days after childbirth, but I knew I would survive as always.

Immediately after reaching Serbia, I submitted all the necessary papers to the police and court to initiate the legal procedure for the name change. It must have been a funny scene seeing a pregnant woman running around every day with her big belly in the midst of the cold and snowy month of February. I went to all the possible offices with the mission of making Mohan my last name. That was only one of my activities. I was busy with our Ammucare charitable work, in terms of coordination and writing of texts, and with direct action as well. I managed to conduct several humanitarian initiatives in shelters and similar locations. In fact, I noticed that, as my baby kept growing in my womb, I had increasingly more energy and no *tamas* (lethargy and procrastination).

After changing the name in my Serbian passport and ID card in February 2011, it was early March when I finally got the new Serbian passport and was ready to start the procedure for legal name change in my Croatian documents as well (many people from former Yugoslavia had dual citizenship – one based on permanent residency and one on their location of birth). I was not happy when I came to know that I would have to go all the way to Virovitica, the city in which I was born, to submit the necessary documentation. There was no one to help me with this or to drive me to Virovitica and back. There was no way that I would be going on a long bus journey all by myself in the eighth month of pregnancy.

I suddenly remembered my Croatian Hero. At first, I thought contacting him was a bad idea, but then I just went ahead and messaged him on Facebook. I explained the situation briefly and he agreed to help me. I was so happy I did that. Twelve years had passed since our romance and the drama in Ilok, and both of us had matured and moved on in life.

I loved talking to him during our pleasant drive to Virovitica. When we reached the required office, they were just about to close, which was a bit stressful for me. “Oh, it’s the 8th of March, Women’s Day, so we are closing early. Apologies. Please come again tomorrow.”

I requested politely that they reconsider. I had come all the way from Novi Sad in the eighth month of pregnancy, blah blah blah, but they did not care. My dear Croatian Hero stepped in and said in a polite but stern way, “Yes, it is the 8th of March, and this lady here is a woman as well, that too a pregnant one, about to deliver. You can’t tell me that you will shut the door in her face! I know you can do better than that.”

The two ladies in the office looked at each other and decided to serve me after all. I was really glad that I had followed my intuition and called my Croatian Hero – he was definitely the right person for the job. We have not been in touch since then, and I love the fact that we were given such wonderful closure after our intense emotional rollercoaster of a relationship. I thanked him for all his loving support, and shared with him the unimaginable blessing I got from St. Petka thanks to the drama in which he had played the main role. It all worked out so beautifully in the end.

A week before my due date, I finally had both Serbian and Croatian passports in my hand with the name of Biljana Mohan. Mission accomplished. My next focus was on preparations for the delivery. I was eager to deliver my baby in water. There were numerous benefits of water delivery; the shock of exiting the blissful, dark womb of the mother into the bright lights of the hospital, where some unknown giants lift you in the air, is more traumatic for the baby than one might think. Gradual transit from water to water is far less traumatic. I had already done thorough research and learned that there was only one place in Serbia offering the option of water delivery – in the area of Belgrade called Zvezdara (*zvezda* means star).

My intuition said this was the place for me. I visited my cousin Bojan who lived in Zvezdara and went to the hospital to enquire. A lovely woman who had worked as a midwife there for more than 20 years explained the full procedure to me. The moment I saw her, my intuition confirmed that she was the one for me. We made a secret deal that she would handle my case when my contractions started. She told me, "Nothing to worry about dear, that tub is always available. It is no secret that we have the tub, but hardly anyone uses it."

I shared a bit more about my background with her and expressed a sincere desire to place the baby on my chest after delivery, as well as not to have the umbilical cord cut right away, to keep the stem cells and nutrients flowing for a couple of minutes, as long as a strong pulsation in the cord could be felt. My second request was to be told the exact SECOND of the birth of my child, not some approximate timing. I explained that my husband requested that I ensure this as it is important in astrology. My lovely midwife said, "No issue at all."

I was really happy and over the next 2-3 weeks, focusing on charity and taking long walks to Kalemegdan (where I had received the blessing from St. Petka) and back to Zvezdara. I loved the vibe of spring and the fresh air and greenery that I missed so much after years of living in the sauna-like air of the Middle East. I felt great and had a lot of energy. I started conducting regular Power of Purity meditations in a small center run by a lovely spiritual couple. One of our long-term Mohanji Foundation volunteers, Dragan Vučenović, once shared with me his impressions from his first POP meditation.

"I was really amazed seeing this super bubbly pregnant woman with a big belly joyously sharing some incredible stories from her life with an Indian man. She was conducting meditation, running up and down, as if the big belly and everything that the last stage of pregnancy brings, was no burden at all. 'This is definitely not normal,' I thought. Meditation itself was super powerful, but seeing such an effect on a pregnant woman really left a deep impression. I knew it at that moment – this is right for me."

On the night of April 5th, I was determined to complete a blog I created about our charitable work and Mohanji's meditations. I was writing this blog until 1:00 a.m. and then finally went to sleep. Around 4:00 a.m., I woke up with slight pain in my belly. I tried to get more sleep, but it was not easy. By 10:00 a.m., the pain of contractions hit me with full intensity. I felt it from the back side, not the front. It hurt so much that I vomited from the shock I felt. It is said that the pain of contractions, on a scale of 1 to 10 is beyond 10. My aunt told me, "It will always hurt much more than you think it possibly could." Well, that was true.

I did not want to inform my mom of my contractions because I worried she would be too stressed. I called my aunt Danica and she came right away. When the contractions would hit, I discovered that it helped when she rubbed my lower back and tailbone with one palm and held my forehead with the other. I was told not to go to the hospital until the contractions become very frequent and the pauses in between much shorter.

In my wishful thinking, I thought around noon that it was time to go. However, when they checked my dilation, I was only halfway there. This was not good news. I was already feeling terribly exhausted. With no proper sleep, no food, and constant pain, I was really worried about whether I would have the strength to endure this painful ordeal. My aunt looked so pale that one nurse wanted to first attend to her, leaving me to sit there on my own. I think that my aunt, aside from being worried about me, was reliving some traumas from her own days of delivering Bojan in a hostile environment. The nurse said, “I am not worried about you, you have a long way to go before you deliver. This woman looks like she will faint.”

After changing my clothes and being taken through the standard procedure including an enema, I finally got to meet my lovely midwife. With her calming voice, she said, “Don’t worry dear, it looks horrible now but know that you will endure. I have seen and assisted with countless deliveries over the years, I am here for you. My shift will be finishing soon, but I will stay as long as it takes to help you. Let me check about the tub.”

I felt blessed to have met such wonderful, selfless people. After some time, she came back, but this time her face was less serene. She told me, “I have some not-so-good news for you. I am shocked – this never happens. One blonde woman just asked for the tub. She has been here for hours and will most likely deliver soon, so this is the perfect timing for her. You, however, are still at only five centimeters of dilation (out of ten), so it would probably be too early to have you go to the tub now. The tub is best when you are at eight or nine centimeters. You let me know what you want to do now. If we let her use the tub, it will take hours to first finish with her, then wash and sterilize the tub – most likely you will have delivered by then.” I immediately decided to go into the tub and see how it went from there.

While I was soaking in the warm water and contractions would hit, I noticed that the pain was reduced by at least half. Such was the power of the water. I was really amazed. It felt good to enjoy a little relief from full pain. However, after one hour they rechecked my dilation and said I was just wasting time and postponing the delivery. Sadly, I was still at five centimeters. When they took me out of the tub, I could feel my heart sinking. It was my dream to deliver my child in the water and I had done everything possible to make it happen, but it was not given. And now my strength was completely gone. While I was passing through the room with several other women going through the same process as me, I noticed the blonde and knew she must have been the one who wanted the tub. She had just started with the actual delivery and was trying to push. Her screams were horrible and I could feel her pain. At that moment, something happened to me, as if I had entered some dark, hopeless place from which there is no way out. Dark thoughts began to arise suddenly: “I will die here tonight. I cannot do this. There is no more strength left in me, I am finished. Hopefully, they will save the baby, but I will not survive this horror.”

Later on, I came to know that most women pass through this zone of darkness during delivery. It just doesn’t seem humanly possible to endure that kind of pain. Humanly it may not be, but the divine hand is there in every delivery. They tied me to a bed, hooking me up to monitoring machines with all sorts of wires, measuring my blood pressure, heartbeat and whatnot. The contractions were like sharp knives being stabbed into my lower back. It was such torture to undergo this, and I was truly desperate.

At some point, I started praying to Baba, "Dear Baba, why have you forgotten me? Please help me. I cannot endure this." The pain continued for another minute or so, but then, in the midst of the agonizing darkness, the light of one single thought appeared – the feather. I remembered what my baby and I had agreed upon during the session with the South African doula/yoga teacher – we would do this together, the feather, the flow… Those thoughts led me to another thought, which went centuries back to the White Circle of Women and probably the collective unconscious of all women of all times – I was led to stand up and start moving my hips, right and left, just like the falling feather. This was the way to enter the flow during the pain of contractions. I called my midwife right away and pleaded, "Please, please, help me get off of this bed. I need to stand and move my hips." My midwife was really surprised and said, "My dear, are you sure you have any strength in you to stand?" I said, "I just know I can't remain in this bed, all tied up. I feel like I am on some torture device from the middle ages. I have to try this."

She removed all the wires and electrodes from me and, at some point, quietly left the room. She was sensitive and knew that I needed to be alone. An immense sense of relief and freedom overtook me the moment I stood up. I allowed my intuition to lead the way as always, and as I started to move my hips, with soft knees, soft neck, and wobbly head, the vision of the cyclical movement of galaxies appeared, along with the highest degree of surrender and vulnerability that I have ever felt. I stopped resisting the pain of the contractions and continued moving the hips in a soft, circular motion similar to the spinning galaxies (or the spiral observed on snail shells). I never knew how powerful this shape was and this was the moment when the power behind it was revealed to me.

When the sharp knives of contractions would hit me, I would keep moving my hips and would exhale through that pain, which sometimes felt like moving through a wormhole and traveling through time and space. After the pain was over, I felt as if I had reached another galaxy and another dimension. The depth of this altered state was immense. The entire experience can be described only as a cosmic flow. Finally, I did it, I entered the flow.

My lovely midwife came to check on me after twenty minutes. She had a feeling she should double-check my dilation. She was dumbfounded when she discovered that twenty minutes of my hip movement had done more than the previous ten hours of contractions – I was there, ten centimeters. "Oh wow, in all the twenty years of my working experience, I have never seen something like this. Your technique worked – you are ready! You can start pushing."

What followed next was very intense. My intuition was that I should not be horizontal but stay vertical so that the pressure of the baby's weight would support a quick exit from the birth canal. The moment I started pushing, I did it with all my strength, feeling like the veins and capillaries in my head would pop and burst. It was a horrible feeling to push so hard but not feel much progress. I was just about to tell my midwife that I would like to try to do this part in a vertical position or to be on the floor in a tabletop position. However, this was a public hospital where such unorthodox improvisations would not be received well (I was really lucky that I could even do the hip movements, which was possibly solely thanks to my midwife). Exactly at that moment, the main doctor appeared (even though I would have preferred it to have only my midwife, who was essentially a doula, so sensitive and experienced) and spoiled the whole thing.

I knew there was no point in suggesting changing the position now that the doctor had arrived. I simply had to follow their standard methods and keep quiet. He even scared me by saying, "Push harder. This is not a joke. Your baby's head is stuck – this is very dangerous for her." Of course, I was pushing as hard as I could, but the more nervous I got, the more the pressure went into my head and not where it was supposed to be. At some point, he pressed against my upper belly with his elbow and underarm and this helped – my baby started to come out and her head cleared the birth canal. This was such a relief and at that moment I suddenly remembered that Mohanji told me to check the exact time. I had even bought a special waterproof wristwatch and kept it on, thinking I would be able to see the time. I tried checking the time on my wristwatch, but with all the pressure, sweat, and tears, my vision was blurred. I mumbled something about the time to my midwife and she and the doctor shouted at the same time, "F*ck the time, push!"

This was another comic moment that marked my delivery. Yet, the sweet midwife tapped me on the shoulder and gave me a nonverbal sign which amounted to: "Don't worry, I got the time part covered, just focus."

In less than a minute, just before 6:00 p.m. on April 6, 2011, our beloved Mila entered horizontal space and time with a loud cry. She was still all purple and slimy, but I noticed the same small, round forehead that I had stared at so much in the miraculous photo with Shirdi Baba performing aarti to Mohanji, when her little profile was made visible to me for the very first time. I also noticed the same long, elegant fingers as Mohanji and my heart simply exploded. An indescribable wave of happiness overtook me. This was the height of bliss after an abyss of pain, the bliss that only mothers are blessed to experience. Our Creator endowed us with the blessing to experience the intensity and depth of bliss so grand that it makes the entire agony of birth and the challenges of pregnancy so minuscule and irrelevant, like an old file in a dusty basement. Selflessness and the depth of unconditional love make the heart blossom into a galaxy of ever-expanding love. Mothers are blessed to behold the grandeur of divine creation through the most intimate moment of their child's delivery.

The most special moment, one that I will cherish forever, was the moment when the midwife placed my precious daughter on my chest. She recognized my heartbeat and was immediately consoled. After another milder cry, she calmed down completely and blissfully surrendered to the love she had felt within my womb. Whenever I recall this moment, I cry. This was it – the Universe of Love within my heart. My heart became one with the never-ending Source of Love. I could feel the pulsations of the umbilical cord and was grateful to my midwife that she honored every part of our secret agreement. Indeed, the sacredness and joy of these special moments when Mila was lying on my chest and the cord still physically connected us could never be explained in words.

After they had cut the cord, they took Mila away to wash her, and finished the procedure with me. I couldn't wait to call Mohanji and share my joy with him. He was just about to board a flight to Serbia. I spoke to him in English, to my mom and dad in Serbian, then one friend happened to call at that exact moment and we briefly spoke in Italian – I felt like sharing my joy with the entire Universe, in all languages possible. Funnily enough, I heard a voice from behind a curtain, "Oh shut up, will you!" This was another young woman who was yet to deliver. I was not even aware that someone else was there! She was crying and saying that she felt she would not survive her ordeal. Switching to the role of a comforting roommate, I started telling her, "Oh, I've been through all of that just now. Please just hold on, have faith – you will see what joy awaits you soon."

After sharing the spiritual dimension of my experience, I would like to share what medical science says about the flooding of the happiness hormones that create this effect during delivery, as well as the importance of being relaxed during delivery, not stressed and scared. Let us briefly examine the bliss that a woman experiences and what it consists of:

> "Oxytocin is the love hormone, which is why it's released during sex, orgasm, birth, and breastfeeding (Odent, 1999; Buckley, 2002). Oxytocin will make you feel more affectionate and selfless, and its main function in labour is to bring on contractions. You'll get a surge of oxytocin in the final stage, so if you're having a vaginal birth it will help you along with pushing. Oxytocin reduces stress, calms you down and helps with pain during labour.
>
> Beta-endorphins or the pleasure hormones:
>
> Endorphins are naturally occurring opiates, similar to morphine and heroin. Like oxytocin, they mostly appear during sex, pregnancy, birth and breastfeeding. If you're stressed during labour, that can make you release excessive beta-endorphins, which may inhibit oxytocin and slow things down. That's why keeping things as calm as possible is a great thing in labour.[47]

Spiritual Dimension of Childbirth

This brings me to another important topic – the spiritual dimension of childbirth and the importance of providing the right conditions for a woman so that she can excrete oxytocin properly. I have met several women who have opted for a natural delivery at home, in a small pool, with their husbands by their side (provided they are sufficiently prepared and can handle it). When we went to Peru on a pilgrimage to Machu Picchu, I met the lovely wife of our spiritual tour guide who shared the details of her orgasmic delivery of their first child. She said it loud enough for the entire minibus to hear, and sure enough, all heads turned when she said the big O word, "I had a beautiful orgasm while delivering my first child at home. It was so amazing that I was really eager to have more children." This was really sweet.

We are yet to reach the point of introducing the spiritual dimension into childbirth within mainstream medical institutions. Unfortunately, what we still see is a lot of misuse within the

47 Source: https://www.nct.org.uk/labour-birth/your-guide-labour/hormones-labour-oxytocin-and-others-how-they-work

medical establishment. This was my experience as well. When I arrived in Serbia and went to the right medical office to report that I will be delivering my child in Serbia, the main doctor was pretty rude and condescending, telling me, "Oh, you are quite old – already 33 and having your first child? [I do think this has changed by now. I see a lot of women delivering their first child in their 30s and 40s.] I would highly recommend the C-section. I can schedule it for you right now. I wouldn't take the risk of being completely torn down there. Aside from being painful, it will definitely affect your sex life – your husband won't be happy, you know."

I couldn't believe what I was hearing. Applying all my yogic knowledge and calming myself through breath to respond and not react, very well aware that they get paid for performing C-sections but not for a natural delivery, I told him, "Thank you, but I would like to try my luck with the natural, vaginal birth."

After I delivered Mila and was sent to the room where mothers await their babies, there were two other young mothers in there and neither could sit up due to their painful stitches. I enquired a bit later on from my midwife and came to know that I was the only woman on the entire floor of Zvezdara hospital's Maternal and Newborn Care department who did not have any issues with the pain and stitches after episiotomy. I do believe this was mainly because of my prenatal yoga, and the effective exercises for strengthening the pelvic floor muscles (aside from the blessings of Baba and Mohanji).

This entire experience inspired me to enroll in a yoga teacher training course in prenatal yoga. I did that years later when I returned to Serbia and was blessed to be taught by one of the best spiritual midwives and prenatal yoga instructors in Serbia – Divna Miljković. I could write volumes of all that I learned from this course. In some of the books we were guided to read, I learned about the deeper connection that babies feel with the placenta. This was a huge eye-opener. It is perceived as a most loving friend or sibling. Separation from the placenta is painful for every baby. I was amazed to learn about the depth of the spiritual midwives from the Philippines from the pre-Christian era, who knew that, if a woman bleeds during delivery, all that is needed is to give her a small piece of the placenta to swallow. No medicine is needed. This brings the system into balance and the bleeding stops. They even had a heartfelt ritual of placenta's burial with special prayers. This just goes to show how respected the placenta was in their culture.

Considering my past life history with the White Circle of Women, it was evident to me why I felt such a deep connection to this ancient knowledge. During my prenatal yoga training, I came across an image of a woman standing in a knee-depth creek, with two other women (possibly doulas) bracing her under the arms. It was explained that connection with the water element, a vertical body position, circular movement from the hips, and loving support of other women was considered the optimal, most natural way of delivery of the child. I had goosebumps when I read this and the instant, "I knew it!" feeling from deep within. It is my sincere wish and prayer that these profound ancient practices are given back to women of our contemporary world plagued by artificiality disguised as advanced science.

I hope that the experience shared above will inspire many young women to opt for a natural delivery (preferably without the neon lights and the usual hospital setup) and the most memorable divine experience behind it. With proper breathing, mental and spiritual preparation, plus a good doula, childbirth can be one of the most spiritually profound experiences a woman can have.

I once read a text about the deeper reasons behind the entire process of a baby's passage through the birth canal. I learned about this from a text I found online written by Sergey Nikolaevich Lazarev, a famous Russian parapsychologist and writer who communicates with a lot of spiritual depth. He generally gives a lot of importance to the diagnosis of karma, which he recognizes as the cause-and-effect dynamic behind all events occurring in a person's life. My intuition responded deeply to the words of Lazarev when he said that babies who pass through the birth canal, aside from all the regular benefits of natural childbirth (including the exposure to all the right bacteria that prepare the immune system, the natural process of squeezing out the amniotic fluid from baby's lungs so that she or he can breathe better upon entering the world and have fewer respiratory problems), carry far less of a load of heavy karmas from the ancestors. He said that this was yet another profound mechanism given to us by our Creator as part of natural childbirth.

Years later, I gained one important insight from Mohanji which I would like to share. He said, "Every pregnancy is a contract. If it's not completed, it becomes a pending matter. The appointed soul could hang on like a purposeless entity." It was only in 2020 when I got trained in an advanced method of deep energy work called Mohanji Transformation Method (MTM – first given to Ivana Kalinić from Serbia, who then trained five close devotees of Mohanji, including myself) that all six of us started noticing the pattern of issues that women who opted for abortion (or happened to have a miscarriage) displayed.

I saw that when a woman aborted a child and then any time later got pregnant again, that child faced certain traumas in the womb. It mainly happened that the spirit of the aborted child would disturb the new child in the womb because it felt its place was being taken. During MTM, we would connect to the consciousness of Mohanji and then witness how he would first help the spirit of the aborted child to go into the light (several times I also saw him handing the child over into the golden, effulgent arms of Divine Mother) and then work on reducing the trauma of the child that was in the womb. To sort out the karmic debt incurred by the soul of the aborted baby, the mother (and her partner in that pregnancy) was asked to do a charitable act at some orphanage or in any way help children without parents or children that felt abandoned and unloved. I have decided to share this with utmost humility and no judgement toward mothers who have opted for abortion due to various complex circumstances of life. I honor everyone's free will and choices in life. It is a great benefit that the morning-after pill has been included in contraceptive measures of the contemporary world and that contraception in general has improved. In the spirit of this biography, I share the insights with the purest of intentions, insights that I find to be of value to people. I hope this sharing is understood in that light.

Chapter 11

Tests During Motherhood and New Life

Baby Mila Changing Lives

Mohanji arrived at Zvezdara Hospital on a windy spring day, walking through the door with his shoulder-length hair flying in the wind. My midwife happened to see him, sharing with me a bit later (referring to Mila's thick, black, two-inch-long hair, which was certainly unusual for a newborn in Europe), "I see where the hair comes from!" Indeed, Mila did take after her father in many ways, and it was so sweet and wonderful for the three of us to finally be together.

After another two days, my aunt Danica and uncle Stevo brought us to Novi Sad where my whole family awaited us. It was very windy that day, and we carried Mila in a bassinet which was removable from her stroller. She was so tiny, like a loaf of bread being carried in a basket – our most precious bundle of joy.

My mom, dad, and grandparents all had teary eyes. The warmth of joy and tenderness filled our happy home. My best friend Marija was there, and Dana arrived a day later. The entire house was filled with love, and Mila was the center of attention as the very first grandchild in the immediate family. A couple of days later, Mohanji left and I remained in Novi Sad for another month, aiming to gather my strength during the short forty days of maternity leave.

This was the time when I got back in touch with a man who had inspired me so much, the great Little Branko. He visited our home with his wife and blessed Mila and me with his loving presence. I shared with him my story from the refugee days and how many times I had remembered him and his unimaginable challenges in life during my toughest days. This was a beautiful time of joy and togetherness.

When the time came to fly to Muscat, I was amazed to see how comfortable Mila was with all of it. She loved being breastfed, and her tiny palm would always be on my chest, connecting with my heartbeat and the love my heart showered upon her. I enjoyed every single moment of our sacred bond and continued breastfeeding her for another two-and-a-half years.

I also practiced the approach to parenting called Attachment Parenting – I kept her close to my body and next to me (in a kangaroo-style baby carrier) whenever I could during the day and night. When the time came for her to go to kindergarten, she was not crying at all as some children did. This goes to show that children who are nourished with love, touch, and attention at the time when they need it the most, children who are not left alone in a separate room to cry themselves to sleep, grow up into more independent and more stable individuals. I do believe in the benefits of this approach and recommend it with all my heart, as I have witnessed the truth behind it as a mother.

The moment we arrived in Muscat, and Mohanji's parents first saw Mila was one of the most touching moments I have ever experienced. I was aware of just how deeply shaken and lost Mohanji's parents, beloved Amma and Acchan, were when they lost Ammu in that tragic accident in 2000. Acchan had worked as an orthopedic surgeon till then and simply stopped working after the accident. Amma, devastated and unable to recover, had turned into a recluse. When we arrived at the airport, and Amma saw Mila in my arms, she broke down, sobbing as she went straight for Mila. She took her into her arms and brought her close to her heart, crying uncontrollably. This was a moment of healing for the entire family, especially Amma and Acchan. Mila brought the joy back into their lives. The meaning and immense Grace that only the Divine could give them was delivered through Mila's precious presence.

Just before Ammu left her body, Mohanji happened to travel to Shirdi and had a profound experience of meeting Shirdi Sai Baba in Dwarkamai. During that experience, Baba was holding a child in his arms. It was soon after that Ammu left this world. Mohanji could not understand the full meaning of his encounter with Baba at the time, but later, he understood that Ammu had been with Baba all along. Ammu played a pivotal role in changing Mohanji's track completely, from materialistic business life to a completely spiritual life. Her influence continues as the foremost participant in Mohanji's spiritual mission.

The tiny, round, and rather prominent foreheads of Ammu and Mila were identical, to the point that I could not make out whether the tiny face I saw emerging from the pancha-aarti lamp (held by Baba in the miraculous photo we were blessed to see in 2010) was that of Ammu or Mila. I have always felt that Baba brought Ammu back as Mila after I prayed to Ammu sincerely. After a couple of years, I noticed that Mila was aware of the minutest details of Ammu's death and spirit journey, as she shared all the details about it with me one day in 2016 (I shall return to that experience at a later point).

Upon my return to work, I was promoted to Marketing Manager. Though I would have been thrilled otherwise, as a breastfeeding mother, this was far more challenging than I could have imagined. I had to take longer lunch breaks to be able to both eat and nurse Mila in a relaxed manner. Because of that, I had to work overtime and hardly ever reached home before 8:00 p.m. Mila would eagerly await my arrival and would demand all my attention. I was lucky to get five hours of sleep on a working day. My working, mothering, and breastfeeding schedule was exhausting, especially with the intensity and increased responsibilities of my new position. It all started to wear me down.

When Mohanji left the corporate world in 2012 and focused on his spiritual mission, I felt left out, since either breastfeeding or my work would separate me from all the exciting discussions and plans. Dr. Deepali and her family were in charge. People started calling Mohanji "Father" and Dr. Deepali "Mother." Sometimes I wondered what my role was. When all of them left for the Kailash yatra (which was my dream), I sank into a depression of sorts. My aura was weakened, and for the first time ever, I experienced being cut off from Mohanji's consciousness and being intruded upon by spiritual entities. Thanks to an amazing couple from Canada (former students of Dr. Choudhary), I managed to have them removed through a remote session and immediately experienced the familiar heat in the spine and vibration on the forehead (which I always feel when I connect to Mohanji in consciousness). I could feel what he felt at Kailash (even sharing in some physical sensations) and was deeply fulfilled. This experience with entities helped me relate to others struggling with this issue in my own energy work later on.

Mila and Baba Connection

One fine weekend in late 2012 when Mila was almost one and she and I were dozing off together, I had a vivid dream with Shirdi Sai Baba that was filled with intense emotions. I still remember every detail of it. I had had sufficient prior experience with astral projections to know this was no ordinary dream. During this astral encounter, Mila and I arrived at a location in India that could have easily been 19th-century Shirdi. Baba walked towards us, with his intense, deeply compassionate eyes fixed on me and baby Mila. He had short gray hair and his head was uncovered (unlike the usual images and Baba murtis). Interestingly enough, soon after that, one of Mohanji's friends who was a Baba devotee living in Sharjah near Dubai, shared with us a rare original photo of Shirdi Baba that very few people had seen. For the purpose of this book, I requested my friend Marko from Novi Sad to enhance its resolution using the latest software, and have included it in the photo section of this book. I am happy to share it with you and must say, this is exactly how Baba looked in this astral encounter of ours in 2012.

When he arrived right in front of me, Baba smiled at Mila lovingly and took her into his arms. I gave her to him and stood there spellbound. He walked away with her, climbed some stairs and disappeared from my sight. I stood there for a while and began getting worried. I did not know what to do or what this act of taking Mila away meant. Seeing some people sitting on the nearby bench, who were speaking Marathi, I approached them to ask whether they had seen where the old man (Baba) with a child had gone, but I could not remember Marathi and they could not understand me at all. I started crying and praying to Baba to return.

I then saw him in the distance, walking towards me with Mila still in his arms. He was smiling at me with endless compassion. The moment he handed Mila back to me, he gave me shaktipat through the eyes and I had the most unforgettable experience. I started levitating just a bit. The big toe of my left foot remained on the ground and then I slowly started spinning clockwise. I was still able to see Baba until the speed of my spinning increased. I could hear his familiar deep and slightly raspy voice, first slowly and then faster and faster, saying: "Baaaa – baaa – baa – ba ba ba ba..."

I was jerked out of that blissful state when I suddenly woke up. I could still feel the intense vibration of *prana* (vital energy). Mila, who was by my chest as always, woke up at precisely at the same moment. She looked me straight in the eyes and – get this – with her sweet voice said the same words: "Ba ba ba ba ba!" She had just started speaking a week or so prior, and sure enough, her sweet, adorable voice confirmed the authenticity of this experience and the fact that she too had seen and felt it all.

The very first words Mila spoke were not Mama or Papa, but Baba. I was not surprised and covered her with kisses the moment I heard it. Whenever she heard "Allahu Akbar," the Muslim call to prayer from the nearby mosque, she would immediately say with her super sweet, melodious voice, "Babaaaaaa Bab!" Baba surely dominated Mila's world. Like every parent, I saw her as the most adorable child ever, and the greatest blessing in our lives.

Mohanji shared with me one day that ever since Ammu left this world, he had always felt her subtle presence in the form of an energy sensation on his shoulder. After Mila was born, that feeling was no longer there. Our experience with Mila was a confirmation that if we really wanted something, we would get it, provided there was eligibility. A birth is always connected to the larger purpose, which is to be fulfilled. This purpose can transcend individual karma. We have now seen that such a possibility exists. Having Mila return the grace and loving presence of Ammu into the lives of Mohanji, his parents, and family, and bless me as her mother, is proof of such divine possibility.

Pada Puja With Mohanji

The second time that I experienced something grand directly from Mohanji took place two months after I returned to Muscat with Mila. This happened on Guru Purnima (a full-moon festival dedicated to the Guru) in July 2011. Our small group proposed to perform Pada Puja (worship of the feet of the Guru) to Mohanji for the first time ever, and he agreed.

My friend Gabriela from Romania, Peter from the US, and I were the only non-Indians present at this event that took place in our living room. Needless to say, we had no clue what was to be done. There were so many different steps in preparation for it, including the placement of flowers petals near Mohanji, along with powders of various colors, different leaves, water, ghee, and the many other materials needed for this sacred ceremony during which the ego bows down to the consciousness of Guru Tattva, symbolized by the feet of the Guru.

The three of us were total outsiders, just looking around, not knowing the purpose or meaning of all the little items being offered. With a bit of childlike innocence, I peeked into a small package made out of newspapers to see what was inside, briefly touching one of the items. At that moment, one of Mohanji's Indian devotees yelled: "Don't touch it! What are you doing? You touched it, and now it's dirty!"

He said there were some flower buds in the paper which were to be offered in the puja and because I had touched them, they were now spoiled and unfit for offering. His contempt and disgust were like cold water poured all over the enthusiasm I had for this worship, taking me completely out of the blissful energy of the puja. I withdrew a bit, allowing the devotees to lead the way. Only later did I understand that this unpleasant experience was perfectly timed ego-bashing which created needed space within me for incoming Grace.

One by one, devotees would come to Mohanji's feet, offering the flowers and other items in accordance with the ritual. At the end of their offering, they would bow down to Mohanji's feet and then step aside for the next person to make an offering. Toward the end of this pada puja, there was some whispering: "Should Devi do it or not? She is his wife, and the child is here..." I did not understand what their objection to my participation might have been, but I followed my intuition which suddenly became very strong – I should do it.

I went to Mohanji and asked: "May I do it as well? I would really like to do it." Mohanji granted my request so I put a white scarf on my head, and came into a beautiful loving space within. I copied what the others had done with all the materials given. At the very end, while bowing down, I unintentionally touched the middle of my forehead to Mohanji's big toe, led by my intuition.

At that moment, there was a huge transmission of energy from Mohanji's big toe into my *ajna* (third eye) chakra. It was very intense. When I slowly lifted my head back, I was a bit dizzy and could not open my eyes. I somehow wobbled toward a couch and sat there. The moment I sat, that was it. I went into an indescribably beautiful intense state of withdrawal, a complete absorption into the space within. The familiar state of samadhi that I had experienced a couple of times already, sucked me into that most blissful, pure, and intense presence within. Mohanji says: "This is our home, the home within." It truly felt beyond beautiful.

There are no words to explain the comfort and fullness of that home. I felt as if a big glass cylinder was placed around me. Within that glass cylinder, I had optimal air, and there was no noise or oscillation of the mind, only the most beautiful energy, silence, and bliss. I was aware that there were people around, but I was completely absorbed within, cradled in a beautiful energy. In that inner space, there was complete silence and bliss. Indeed, this was being home, in our natural state beyond ego identity. Indescribable Love filled this home. It felt timeless and eternal. Pure beingness.

My isolation in the vacuum of bliss went on for an hour or more. I was frozen in time, and could not move my body at all. Even if I wanted to, even if the thought to move out of the state arose, there was no movement. I don't know whether I was even breathing in that perfect stillness.

It took quite a while to emerge from that state. First, I just moved one finger, then after another minute or so, another finger. Then I slowly managed to move one hand, then the other hand. As I regained connection with my physical body, I only remember being so grateful for yet another samadhi experience.

At that moment, I had a glimpse of the state from which Mohanji operates. In that state, there is only Love. Even if one were offended, humiliated, and betrayed a thousand times, when one is in that space, the physical body is perceived as nothing but an instrument, and there is no mind and ego to take offense. There is only love for everyone, even the betrayer. There's just that immense beingness and love. Operating from that space, there is no second agenda, there is no hatred, there is no revenge, and there is no personal need to prove anything or to grab or grasp for anything because it's all already there. The fullness is there. For me, this was one of the most unexpected and memorable experiences ever.

Later on, Mohanji said: "Whenever we have a deep experience, we should not expect it to happen again in the same or similar circumstances. This is the play of the mind. Experiences with a spiritual Master are always new, always fresh, and very often unexpected."

I felt grateful for the scene with the flower buds as that small ego-bashing may have prepared me to surrender fully when I bowed down at Mohanji's feet. On the spiritual path, a higher meaning can always be found in any situation. In the case of the man who betrayed Mohanji by taking over his company, he removed something from Mohanji that allowed him to begin his mission grandly, and set himself fully on the path of service to humanity. In the end, it was all good.

Consciousness Kriya

Another immense blessing I experienced while living in Oman happened during a trip to Dubai in 2014. I remember Mohanji had been experiencing another attack by Dark Light at that time. There were people spreading malicious gossip and rumors about him, and all the lies and negativity behind it came as a complete shock to us. We kept wondering why something like this would happen and how people close to us could say such things.

We were staying overnight at a friend's place. That morning when we woke early, we saw an apple next to a vase filled with other apples. The lone apple had something engraved on its side as if someone had taken a toothpick or something sharp and engraved a circular message. Mohanji read slowly, "Just… be… love." The signature below: "Baba." Seeing this miracle filled us with love and brought immense bliss. This was typical of Baba – never ceasing to amaze us. Mohanji commented on how effectively Baba said, "Don't pay attention to any of the lies when you know your truth. Do not energize negativity in any way. Just ignore it. It's not worth it. Just be love." Mohanji then said, "Let's cut this apple into several slices, and everybody can take one piece as prasad (consecrated food)." Mila and our hosts thus also got a piece.

After sharing that special apple, and eating our slices with utmost gratitude, we went back into our room around 5:00 a.m. We sat on the bed and Mohanji became withdrawn. Suddenly he told me with great seriousness, "Bring me a pen and a piece of paper." I could feel something important was happening, and quickly brought the items he requested. He started writing something; it was obvious to me that he was channeling ("downloading") something important. The energy was superb. I just said there, waiting in meditation. When he had stopped writing, I could not believe my eyes – the title of the text was Kriya.

I have already shared how I had given up Sri M's kriya, and surrendered my desire for an ultimate spiritual practice for liberation, to Babaji. Once I stopped all my previous Kriyas and practices, I never thought about them again. Seeing the word Kriya, my heart exploded in immeasurable joy. I was simply overwhelmed as I knew at that very moment that my ultimate desire was fulfilled – my Guru, my beloved Mohanji, received the Kriya from Babaji! I had to pinch myself. This was what I had been waiting on for years.

When we actually went through it, I was amazed even more. Mohanji named it the Consciousness Kriya. The first initiation happened only a couple of days later. A few people were invited from our closer circle, and Mohanji explained what he had received. I was the only one who knew that this Kriya had two similarities with Sri M's Kriya. As mentioned before, though I never revealed its content to anyone and never would, I couldn't help but notice this synchronicity. And yet, there was so much more to Consciousness Kriya. It felt like all the pieces of the puzzle had finally come together to reveal the full picture. With this final piece, I could actually understand the multi-dimensional profundity of the Kriya.

The Kriya that Mohanji received had several preparatory elements and then the key part which is the actual heart of Kriya. Preparatory parts are also very important. It's like a journey in a full circle. You start the circle with a technique that signifies the womb of consciousness from which all of us emerge as souls; then the soul enters the mother's womb. For this phase, there is a particular way of breathing and one other process after which we enter horizontal time and space. In the end, we journey vertically back to the womb of consciousness, which is the key part of Consciousness Kriya. That's how we close the circle.

One could say that each Kriya reduces our karmic debt by one lifetime. It imitates the journey of the soul and actually helps us cut across karma, with *moksha* (liberation) as the ultimate aim. Needless to say, this is a very profound technique and Mohanji said, "If you are being initiated into this Kriya, be clear that this becomes your number one practice." For this Kriya, you simply have to find the time, about half an hour per day. Mohanji said that Kriya used to be eight hours in the past (in the olden days). I found it truly profound and had many experiences with it. My search was definitely over. I am forever grateful to Babaji and Mohanji for the most precious gift of Consciousness Kriya.

There is a team of people within Mohanji Foundation responsible for the approval of the applications for Consciousness Kriya. They are very strict. Mohanji was also guided to give a special Shaktipat as part of the final initiation into Kriya. This Shaktipat is given with both hands, and its purpose is to align the three main *nadis* (energy meridians) to ensure that once the Kundalini rises, it rises through the proper central meridian, not through any of the other two (which is very unpleasant and can happen to people due to wrong practices or attempts to manipulate the process). This initiation comes only from the Master (Mohanji). Because there is great interest from people around the world, we now have a group of people (including myself) who have been trained to actually teach the Kriya as a method and prepare the ground for the final initiation by Mohanji.

Babaji's Confirmation Through Baba Nataraja

During our trip to the US in 2014, we met a lovely Master called Baba Nataraja for the first time. I remember how interesting it was for me to meet this Indian sadhu with an American accent. He definitely looked like he did not belong in the US.

At some point, he shared with us his experience of leaving Mahavatar Babaji's fold and being sucked into the womb of his physical mother. He said that he felt a pull as if a big vacuum cleaner just sucked him into the dark womb. He was aware of everything. He could feel and hear the thoughts and feelings of his mother. He then said something of great significance – that he was blissfully levitating in his mother's womb, feeling a golden ball moving up and down his spine, which was a process of energetic breathing of sorts.

I remember exchanging glances with Mohanji and smiling from within – I knew this was a powerful confirmation by the great, beloved Babaji because the golden ball plays a big role in the Consciousness Kriya that Mohanji received from Mahavatar Babaji. I suddenly remembered the golden ball that came to me during my encounter with the violent Albanian man in Kosovo and was amazed to make the connection with Babaji.

We then mentioned to Baba Nataraja that the golden ball is already part of the Kriya that Mohanji had received, and he said: "Yes, Kriya is sacred and secret. What is sacred is secret, and secret is sacred." Again, these were the exact same words that Mohanji was already using while introducing Kriya to people. We smiled again, knowing beyond any doubt that these amazing synchronicities were nothing but confirmations from Babaji.

To crown this topic with yet another experience, in December 2019, I traveled to the sacred city of Kashi or Varanasi as the Global Ambassador of Mohanji Foundation to attend an event organized by Unity Earth. I never expected to experience anything related to Babaji Kriya there, but I did, and it was a huge blessing.

I discovered that the home of the great Lahiri Mahasaya was in Varanasi, only ten minutes away. *Autobiography of a Yogi* shares that Lahiri Mahasaya was the very first disciple of Babaji who revived the Kriya lineage in modern times. He lived in the 19th century and attained samadhi (as well as his son and grandson – the whole lineage) at that home. I knew nothing about any of this.

When I reached the house, there was a very nice, humble man at the entrance who permitted me, along with some others, to go inside. I had intended to meditate there and do my Kriya. Not knowing what to expect, I was surprised to see the murtis of Lahiri Mahasaya and his descendants. Standing there at the entrance, I was feeling a powerful pull, a brightness of sorts. I followed the pull to find a majestic white marble statue of Mahavatar Babaji, with a huge image of Kailash behind it. It was beautiful, and the energy that hit me at that moment was overwhelming. I knew right away this was where I was to do my Kriya.

I was about to sit down to meditate when a woman appeared and started scolding me, "What are you doing? This place is closed, go outside! It's closed now."

I couldn't even speak. I was so in awe of what I had just seen that I simply walked out like a dazed person without even being able to say anything. On my way out, I met the same humble man who was now cleaning the hallway. He said, "You want to meditate?" I could only nod. "Okay, you go sit there and meditate. No worries, I will tell that lady to leave you alone."

I was astonished but knew right away that Babaji had arranged this for me. Sitting down before his stunning murti, I started doing the main part of the Consciousness Kriya. At some point, I received additional guidance from Babaji about one part of the Kriya where I was to add a minor but powerful detail involving rolling the eyes up to focus on the center of the forehead (Shambhavi mudra). Doing that, I entered a very deep state, the depth of which was proven to me soon in a really funny way.

There were many mosquitos in the room, but for the first time in my life, I was able to remain seated and allow mosquitoes to bite me without being bothered at all. There was one bite that I could really feel. This was the first time I experienced a mosquito bite in an altered state of consciousness. When the mosquito bit me, I felt the prick in very slow motion. Then I felt a circle of heated energy forming around the bite, but there was no itching sensation as if I was under some sort of anesthesia. I felt just a bit of warmth, but my body was in a different vibration. There was no way I could move my body, and the mosquito was completely irrelevant. It was like the experience of a mosquito bite from another dimension. I would always joke that when I go into deep meditation, I could handle anything (noise, heat, cold), but mosquitoes always manage to disrupt it and create annoyance. So this was an important experience for me and my "mosquito karma." I couldn't have received a better confirmation of the depth of the state I was in.

At some point, time stopped or possibly slowed down, bringing forth immense stillness, and freshness. The sacred presence brought tears – they flowed down my face, but I was not crying. The tears kept flowing by themselves. If the reader recalls, this happened to me once before, during an experience with the Divine Mother in a Serbian Orthodox monastery. This was the second time I recognized the ultimate grace of divine blessing that transcends all frames. I stayed there in the timeless bliss of Kriya for almost two hours. After this experience, I started feeling the blissful waves (sensation of ascending and descending, as if floating on waves) after Kriya. All thanks to my beloved Babaji...

Kailash Yatra 2014 & New Life

It was in 2014 that I finally had the guts to leave my job with Mercedes-Benz and live my dream, that of serving the world together with my beloved Mohanji, shifting from karma to *dharma* (sacred duty). Even though Mohanji had taken that crucial step in 2012, it took me another two years to gather the strength and make that leap. A Kailash *yatra* (pilgrimage to the abode of Shiva) was always planned in the month of July (or August at the latest) because otherwise, no visibility of the sacred Mount Kailash would be possible due to clouds and snow. However, Ramadan fell in the month of July that year, and that happened to be when most Omani people would buy their cars. I would have never gotten leave from Mercedes-Benz at this most crucial time for sales and marketing. I decided to go before our new British CEO and announce: "I am resigning from my position as Marketing Manager. I have a different calling in life. I want to go to Tibet for the Kailash yatra, circumambulation of the holy mountain Kailash."

The new CEO surprised me by saying: "Well, I've been going through your file. I feel that considering the quality of your work and your performance, you have been grossly underpaid so I would like to offer you double your salary. You can resume your work after this journey."

The offer of double the salary came as a test, just as the offer of a position with the United Nations in Jordan had appeared in the past, at a key moment to tempt me from my path with the promise of ease, comfort, and familiarity. And, yet again, I stood my ground with a resolute, "No, thank you! I have made up my mind and I'm going for good."

With that, we first shifted to Dharamshala where Mohanji had rented a house, and Mohanji's parents and his friend Firoz were left in charge of Mila for the duration of our pilgrimage.

The year 2014 was particularly special because it was the year of Deva Kumbh wherein it is said that one circumambulation of Kailash was equal to twelve circumambulations. Those who go to Kailash in that year, have the right to travel a route closer to mount Kailash called the Inner Kora, which one is otherwise eligible to do only after completing 12 yatras. Naturally, it was very special. Deva Kumbh also means the special year when gods and celestial beings come to bathe in Manasarovar Lake, a celestial lake in the vicinity of Mount Kailash, from which you can have its darshan.

The experience of Kailash yatra can never be fully explained in words, but this humble attempt will hopefully be an inspiration for those who read it to strive to reach this majestic "crown chakra of Mother Earth" and achieve their own experience. I will share only two key experiences but urge the reader to explore the many beautiful accounts of Kailash yatra shared in the book *Kailash With Mohanji: The Inner Kora*.

The greatest blessing our colorful international group of 80+ pilgrims received was the opportunity to undergo this experience in the physical presence of Mohanji. When dealing with matters beyond the mind, only those who have mastered the mind can provide precious guidance at the right moment when transformation either happens or is missed.

Mohanji had prepared us mentally that the journey to Kailash would be tough – a true test of our faith and surrender. He said that during the Kailash yatra, "Grace is more essential than oxygen." However, my mind could not quite grasp the true meaning of those words until the great teacher Experience appeared.

The energy of Kailash, just like the consciousness of a Master, is like a mirror – when approached with ego, expectations, concepts, and doubts, it will reflect back to us just how small and fragile we are. It is when we truly surrender, empty ourselves, and with utmost humility allow ourselves to simply experience/feel Kailash beyond any of our existing concepts, that we can behold Kailash in its grandeur and allow its energy to work on us deeply. As Mohanji said, "Nobody leaves Kailash empty-handed," but the depth of the experience depends on one's receptivity and eligibility. One must ask themselves the crucial question – am I ready to face the mirror?

I must admit that I was dreading the experience of Manasarovar Lake. We were in the Himalayas in our winter jackets with several layers of clothing, and altitude sickness was creeping in. It was not all that easy for me to believe I could just blissfully enter the ice-cold water for nine or more dips without any consequences to my health. During the long bus ride on the way to the lake, my mind bombarded me with fearful thoughts like, "If I get an ovary inflammation due to that ice-cold water, the whole yatra is gone for a toss. Is it really worth the risk? Maybe I should come up with an excuse and skip it."

At one point, I got tired of these thoughts and decided to share my concerns with Mohanji. He immediately reassured me that I would be just fine. He said there is no way I could miss this opportunity of a lifetime – the cleansing at Manasarovar lake is too powerful; it penetrates and removes the negativities of many lifetimes, for myself and my ancestors.

When we reached Manasarovar, its surreal beauty left us in awe. While admiring its azure green shades and the divine sparkles of sunlight reflecting on the water, I suddenly saw a bright flash from the clouds. It was just like a camera flash only a couple of meters away from my face – except that this was coming from the faraway clouds. I kept looking intently through the window of our bus but could not see anything after that strong flash. There was a strong intuitive feeling within me that this was something important.

While wondering what it was, a couple of minutes later, Spomenka, my friend from Serbia, shared with me photos she had snapped with her cellphone, pointing at two balls of light that were visible in a dozen of the photos. Two golden balls of light had another smaller orb of light behind them. The balls of light appeared in different locations (in the clouds, near the lake, near a house, etc.). I was blank for a while, and suddenly a thought came, "The two balls are my parents from Sirius and I am that small puff!" I suddenly had goosebumps all over. The celestial beings had already made their presence known to us. I was getting more and more excited about our Manasarovar dip!

When we reached the beach and the bus door opened, my joy was spoiled by many huge mosquitoes (at least three times bigger than the usual ones) that instantly surrounded us. Apparently, my mosquito karma still needed to be exhausted. I kept waving my hands in distress until one of the tour organizers said with a smile, "Nothing to worry about, these are vegetarian mosquitoes. They don't bite."

I was not quite sure whether he was joking but soon realized that they were indeed not biting us. The idea of "vegetarian mosquitos" amazed me and elicited a hearty laugh.

The overall feel at the lakeshore that day was surprisingly great. The weather was sunny and a perfectly pleasant 70°F. We all rushed to remove our sweaters and trousers to enter the water. I scrambled to get in line for my turn in one of the two small tents allocated for the ladies to change their clothes. This took some time, and I was growing worried that I would be very late.

At first, Kailash was hidden by clouds but then, as if in Divine theater, its mighty base was revealed beneath the white clouds, with an unmistakable small "m" clearly written all over it in snow. What a beautiful welcome for Mohanji and all of us! After some time, the clouds parted, and our joy knew no bounds as we beheld both Manasarovar and Kailash with our physical eyes.

I finally got to enter the holy Manasarovar – the cold water was strangely energizing and the feeling of diving into it and then looking at Kailash in between each dip was truly grand. After taking ice-cold dips for Mohanji, Mila, our Masters, and our immediate family, I suddenly remembered my ancestors. I first remembered my beloved grandma and prayed for her and the souls of the 17 babies she was forced to abort (as they could not afford to have more children) to be released into the light. This was a horribly high number of abortions. I also remembered a horrific story she had shared with me from her experience in WWII:

[I would like to warn younger or very sensitive readers that the content until the next subtitle could be very disturbing.]

"One time we were being bombed from the air. My sisters and I were running as fast as we could across the field while they were shooting at us from the air. One of my sisters was pregnant. It was horrible to watch her stomach being cut by the shrapnel to the point that her intestines were falling out. That moment of us running, bombs falling, and her intestines starting to fall out will always stay with me. I was desperately trying to collect her intestines while running. I tried to help her, but it was already too late. I had to give up. Both she and the baby died."

I took a dip for Grandma's sister and her unborn child.

Then I remembered my Grandfather and the most horrific experience that he shared with me in 1991:

"I was only 17 when WWII erupted in 1941. That same year, the biggest trauma of my life happened. I was on my way back home when I saw a group of Ustaše (the Nazi-backing Croatian ultranationalists) in front of our house. There was a lot of cursing and shouting and then they dragged my father out of the house. I was hiding behind a nearby concrete pillar. There was nothing I could have done. My body froze and I could hardly breathe while listening to my father's horrific screams. There was no justified reason why they would do this to him. He was not involved in politics, the army, or anything of the sort. They just started torturing him in the most hideous ways.

"One of the Ustaše took out a big, sharp knife and started plucking my father's eyes out. First, they plucked out one eye, then another eye… I can still hear those screams. I can still feel that paralyzing feeling of helplessness. I lost my breath when they proceeded with the ears and felt like vomiting. Then, in the end, only after all the torture was over, they finished him off by piercing his heart. What remained of my father in the pool of blood in front of our house was barely recognizable."

I prayed sincerely that no such violence and pain be experienced within my family ever again, and that the soul of my grandfather and great-grandfather be elevated in the brightness of the greatest peace.

I also prayed for my maternal grandfather, who committed suicide. All these painful instances from my ancestral karma flashed before my eyes in a second, and I took a dip for each one of them to wash it all away. I recognized and fulfilled my higher calling to do this for my family.

The Greatest of Blessings on My Forehead

I remember shivering violently from the freezing cold and the huge energy encompassing us all. While doing the dips, I suddenly felt a strong desire to touch Mohanji's feet in the holy Manasarovar water. I turned around and saw Mohanji. He had already been in the water for much longer than me and was moving to get out of the lake. I waved and said, "Wait! Wait for me!"

Spomenka and Sumit, another of Mohanji's devotees, also shouted: "Wait Mohanji! Biba is coming!" (At that time, my name was still Biba.)

Some strange excitement overwhelmed me and my heart was beating like crazy! I briefly saw Mohanji's eyes and understood immediately that he was in an expanded state – the expression in his almost red eyes was that of Shiva, very intense and powerful! I tried with all my strength to run through the water. When I was finally close enough, I took a dive straight for his feet. I touched his feet, and when I came out of the water, I performed an *abhishek* (the ritual bathing of a deity) upon him by sprinkling water on his head.

Then Mohanji took some water with his hand and poured it on my head, but strangely enough, energetically it felt like a mighty slap, as if the water had fallen from the top of a mountain. Bam! I have no idea how to explain this in a logical way. The pressure was that of a waterfall. I was not ready for that totally unexpected blow that almost knocked me out. I was squatting in the water, barely managing to press my palms together in a prayer position, when – Bam! Another "hit" came, so strong that it felt like it literally peeled a layer of skin from my face and body. These were the strangest of sensations. There was no time to think, pray, breathe, or even remotely try to understand what was happening. I was sobbing and in a state of shock. With eyes full of water and tears, I looked at mighty Kailash in the distance, and then – Bam! Another splash of water fell on me, and another layer-peeling sensation. I cried and laughed in total delirious gratitude! The next thing I recall is Mohanji leaving the lake, supported by Sumit and one more person. I followed, helped by dear Spomenka.

I have still not fully digested this experience, nor do I know what to name it. Baptism by Shiva? Astral operation in lake Manasarovar? Whatever it was, I am forever grateful to Mohanji, to Shiva, for granting me the blessing I could not have even prayed for because I never knew it was possible…

Sumit, who was the nearest to us in the lake, fortuitously had his phone with him. It was amazing that somebody had brought a phone into the lake! My heart skipped a beat when browsing through the photos in his phone's gallery, I came across a photo that has become one of the most precious photos of my life. He had captured the moment perfectly. In the photo I was crying and, in my furrowed brow, one can see the mark of Shiva upon my forehead – a circle representing the third eye and the *tripundra* (three lines, representing the three gunas). The symbol was not a shadow but appeared as if permanently branded on my skin. That photo (included in the photo section) is a lasting reminder of that profound supernatural experience.

Gauri Kund and Mother's Blessing

The toughest part of Kailash yatra was climbing the mighty Dolma La, a steep pass over the rough, merciless mountains (not to mention the helplessness one feels due to altitude sickness). Once we reached the top of the hill, I suddenly came across Mohanji. My joy knew no bounds upon seeing the familiar glossy eyes full of love, the eyes that my soul had been connected with through lifetimes. Deep gratitude overwhelmed me. I knew he was watching over me, over all of us, and that the inner transformation was all due to his Grace. When I told him I would like to go to Gauri Kund, the lake of Mother Parvati, his smile and gentle nod were all the confirmation I needed.

I walked a bit further until my eyes could finally behold the majestic Gauri Kund, which revealed itself before me like an azure green jewel. It was even more beautiful than what I had seen in the photos! I then noticed the big sharp stones and steep decline that led to the lake. Mohanji explained Gauri Kund's strategic location – it is right after the extremely tough climb up the Dolma La Pass when most people can not even think of another climb. He also said that most of the time Gauri Kund is covered with clouds to hide it from undeserving seekers. The stones around the lake are often wet and slippery to further deter unwanted visitors.

Indeed, had there been even a drizzle, the wet and slippery stones would have been too big of an obstacle. But that day, the sun was shining, and I felt the path to Gauri Kund was open. In my heart, I felt I was invited... I walked for only a couple of meters and already felt breathless. For a split second, there was a hint of fear that I wouldn't be able to make it, but the fear wasn't nearly as strong as my desire to keep moving. At that moment, I made up my mind that I would go to Gauri Kund even if I died there – and I meant it!

Sumit, Hein (from South Africa), Vijay (from the UK), and one of the sherpas joined me on the journey across many big, sharp stones toward sublime Gauri Kund. Great excitement overwhelmed me, and my legs surprised me with their sudden speed and strength – it was as if they walked on their own.

The moment when I touched and tasted the water of Gauri Kund will remain forever etched in my mind and heart. It was like a long-awaited flower that finally bloomed from my energy blueprint. I have never felt such a sensation – this water carried secret codes far beyond this plane of existence. Its purity was indescribable, its sparkle divine, its taste sublime – the purest mountain spring would bow to it in awe. While washing my face with this water and placing some of it on my crown chakra and third eye, I felt nothing but pure bliss as I witnessed the thirst for intense purification, a thirst from beyond this lifetime that was now being quenched...

I looked up, and on the mountain that was facing Gauri Kund, I suddenly saw many faces of sages, mainly with long beards and expressions of profound depth. More than seeing, it was the inner sensation of utmost sanctity and purity that overwhelmed me. The lake and that moment in time indeed felt unearthly...

More than the beauty of nature, it was the vibration of the purity of Goddess Parvati that resonated most deeply within me. She performed unimaginable penance in order to reach Lord Shiva – hunger, heat, cold, nothing could deter her. Out of her pure heart and deep compassion, she pleaded with him to share his wisdom with humanity. She was humanity's bridge to Lord Shiva, whose energy and presence were too powerful to be accessed by humanity alone. As our sweet Rima Yadav said during one of our conversations, "In our family life too, when children want something, and cannot approach a strict and authoritative father, they always go through the mother."

I recalled lines from Guru Gita that I enjoy listening to on YouTube, describing the grand historical moment of eternal beauty embedded in the collective subconscious of humanity, the moment when Goddess Parvati bowed to mighty Shiva, addressing with a plea to initiate her into the knowledge of the Guru. Shiva answered, with words brimming with immense depth and Love:

"O Goddess, you are My very Self. I speak out of My love for you. This question, which is a boon to uplift the world, has not been asked before by anyone. [...] Listen, I will reveal it to you. The Absolute is not different from the Guru. [...] The Guru is not different from the conscious Self. This is true, this is true, there is no doubt. Therefore, a wise one should indeed make an effort to attain the Guru. [...] He by whose light the true knowledge arises is known as 'Guru.' The Guru who reveals THAT [...] who illuminates like the flame of the lamp, the Guru whose feet are the visible form of the imperishable – one should meditate on that all-pervasive, eternal Guru."[48]

48 Source: YouTube video "Shree Guru Gita" with English translation, sung by Kumuda

While all of this was happening in my inner space, Mohanji stood above, overlooking all of us who had descended to Gauri Kund. I felt his presence, and my heart melted as my mind acknowledged the miracle of everything that was happening in my life, all those unimaginable blessings… Indeed, the blessing of a physical presence of a Guru in the life of one who yearns for Liberation is truly the greatest blessing one can be granted in a lifetime.

In the midst of my bliss, Sumit approached me with the most loving request – with endless devotion, he held prasad from Vaishno Devi temple in his hands and asked me to offer it to Goddess Parvati. He really touched my heart – what a beautiful gesture and what an honor it was for me to make that offering from one aspect of Mother Divine to another. All of us present prayed together. I prayed for the purity and selflessness of Mother Divine to become so deeply established in my heart that nothing can ever taint it... This powerful experience prepared me for the ultimate, most heavy tests that were to follow.

Vision of Mohanji Liberating Many Souls

I later learned what had actually happened in Manasarovar Lake, and far more had happened than what I had experienced. Mohanji was in that huge, exalted state and the work that he was doing at that time was tremendous. We received a testimonial from a woman, a devotee of Sai Baba, about a vision she had while cooking in her kitchen back in Europe. Her visions were almost like movies on a screen. She was able to see not just glimpses, but an entire actual event as it was happening. She received a vision while we were all in the lake, about which she wrote to Mohanji and his team.

The vision was that of Mohanji and around 100 people, traveling in buses toward a huge lake. Many other souls were traveling along outside of the bus, like a cloud of mosquitoes following it closely. The souls flying along sensed the time was coming for their dip in the divine lake in the presence of Mohanji, which meant a chance for liberation.

As Mohanji entered the lake, all the souls followed in stages, one group after another. They went in for a dip and came out freed from the weight that had held them down. They could go on into the white light, to liberation. This was going on and on as there were so many. They were like waves of souls. Mohanji did not put any restrictions – whoever came, he allowed. This is exactly how He operates. He never measures. He never says, "I'll take you to level one, level two, level three." No. He just gives because that is his nature. As long as he was present there, all the souls that came received liberation.

In the woman's vision, she suddenly saw a couple of huge, dark beings, most-horrendous entities that were very angry. They were outraged that Mohanji was helping so many souls. The woman felt that the vision was not going in a good direction, and she expected the worst. She then heard the voice of Shirdi Sai Baba. "Mohan's life is in danger. His life will end now." The woman was shocked to hear that. She said to Baba: "Baba, please help Mohanji. The world needs Him. We have to do something. Please help Him."

Baba was quiet for a while and then said: "I can save his physical body, but he will have a different type of death. His character will be assassinated."

The force of those dark entities was incredibly strong, so even though Baba intervened, there had to be some effect. Even Baba could not entirely remove the total effect, but he diminished it, saving Mohanji from physical death. Mohanji's death at the age of 49 had been prophesied, but as Baba said, destiny was changed and his life saved, at the expense of his reputation.

The Character Assassination of Mohanji

Hence, soon after the Kailash yatra, Mohanji's character assassination began. It was orchestrated by people from whom we least expected that betrayal. The stories that came up against Mohanji were just utterly ridiculous. As with most instances of malicious gossip, they were either about money or sex. These are the two topics that can destroy someone's reputation, and all kinds of such ridiculous stories started floating around.

This nightmare reached its crescendo when we traveled to the US for back-to-back programs. I was performing all the tasks that a team of people currently performs (selecting and ironing Mohanji's clothes, answering the phone, getting his hair dried and ready, conducting intro talks, taking photos, making posts on social media, etc.) – in addition to dealing with exhaustion and jet lag, putting Mila to sleep, etc. Mila was three, so there were constant tasks associated with having a small child as well. In short, I was swamped – perfect timing for the first wave of attacks. There were just so many negativities and so much weight from the emotional response of other people. In addition to the attack on Mohanji's character, there were comments by a woman who kept serving us spicy food that neither Mila nor I could eat. Apparently, she perceived my inability to eat her food as an insult, and therefore it was her opinion that I was not living Mohanji's teaching and unfit to be his wife. I was honestly greatly offended and deeply hurt by it all.

I remember a trip planned for us to go into some old forest where there were giant trees that were hundreds and hundreds of years old. Whenever there was an attack, it would inevitably involve an attempt to split our family and separate me from Mohanji. This has always been the topmost agenda of the Dark Light.

Emails had begun flying around filled with ridiculous accusations, and people connected with Mohanji were believing the stories, without even giving him the benefit of the doubt or asking him if the accusations were true. They just blindly believed the lies and disconnected from him. Some people even joined the bandwagon, assisting in spreading the rumors. This was quite a shock to experience, especially after having served with these people and given everything we had, from the heart. To see them turn from us so quickly was quite a kick in the gut.

Affected by the gossip about me, I didn't want anybody to help me. I held Mila on one hip, another bag on the other, plus a third bag with Mila's diapers and food, lugging it all for an hour or so. I carried my burden and a lot of sadness, pain, dark thoughts, and terrible heaviness on the inside. However, as we walked through this majestic forest, in only half an hour's time, the heaviness suddenly cleared away. That's when I understood the immense greatness of trees.

I hope to inspire the reader to try going into a forest during times when they are feeling low or burdened by heavy emotions. Find a big old tree and simply sit by it. Lean on the tree, and stay there in its energetic field. You will see what great helpers the trees are. The healing power of mother nature is present in the trees. My time in the forest amid Mohanji's character assassination was the time when I witnessed the true power of the trees. I did not say a word, none of those thoughts were verbalized, and the whole cloud of negativity was dispersed. After that healing in the forest, I was able to stand by Mohanji with all my heart and soul, through all of the attacks.

In another wave of most-ridiculous accusations, a woman called our host in the US and said, "I never talk bad about people, but I will just tell you this – make sure you never leave your daughter alone in a room with Mohanji."

This character assassination went on for a while and it was quite serious. After the programs in the US, Mohanji found it most convenient that Mila and I go to Serbia, while he opted to go to India alone to face whatever awaited him. There was some risk that these people may have even planned some story that could land Mohanji in jail. There were all sorts of rumors flying around and endless possibilities for further damage; it was a complete fall from his former status. That's exactly what character assassination entails – one being completely disgraced and put down, found guilty without evidence, no matter what anyone says or does. People don't even bother to ask. They hear the rumor and run with it.

But with the grace of Baba and the Tradition, Mohanji slowly lifted himself back up after some time. He continued to focus on social service, loving, and giving. Such determination in the face of rumors, gossip, and humiliation is not humanly possible unless you have the grace of the Divine and you are destined to give something of value to humanity. Human beings alone cannot recover from such negativity.

The Biggest Tests

While Mohanji took the biggest blow, there was quite a lot of darkness directed at me as well. At some point, I faced the biggest test on the path in a period that stretched from the end of 2013 to 2017. It all started when Mila fell and injured her head, and picked up momentum when I traveled to India and decided to change my name to Devi Mohan.

When one changes their name to a higher frequency name such as Devi, it's like changing to a faster lane on the highway – one has to pick up speed. Additionally, further tests in life are inevitable. It is not enough just to want the name Devi Mohan, one has to earn it. In my case, there were a series of challenging experiences, one after the other. Just when I thought something was over, the next blow would come. It was a very tough time for me.

Spiritual ego is the most refined and stealthily camouflaged aspect of our ego, to the point that we could argue that it doesn't even exist. It is only when the spiritual ego is pricked by the Guru that we are made aware of its hidden existence. If one has the wisdom to just hang on to the Guru and do exactly what the Guru says, then the trouble won't be so great.

The way it works is that sometimes the illusion of "something better out there" appears, or someone arrives with a glittering offer of "something better." In any case, true vision is clouded, and inner confirmation is not felt. That's the lure of it, that's the test.

Mila's Fall

Before sharing about the challenges I faced at the time when I changed my name to Devi, I would like to describe the most painful experience of my life. The height of darkness during the phase of attacks on Mohanji manifested during a horrific fall during which we almost lost our precious daughter. On November 5th, 2013, I witnessed Mila fall from a height of 15 feet onto a marble floor. Despite all I had seen as a refugee, I must say, that moment was the scariest experience of my life.

We had gone to a 5-star hotel for a meeting with the purpose of fundraising for our charity, and Mila ran outside while we were waiting for the meeting to commence. She happily ran up a slope covered with green grass, with a green bush fence at the top – it looked safe, and I allowed her to play for some time. She kept climbing up toward the top of the slope and playfully refused to return. I started running after her. When she reached the top, she looked back at me with a smile, and then, as if something behind her pulled her, she disappeared. Unbeknownst to us, there was an opening between the green bushes and the wall behind it, invisible to those at the bottom of the slope.

A couple of seconds later, I witnessed a scene I will never forget – my beloved baby spread out on a marble floor 15 feet from where I stood. For a moment, I felt that I was no longer in my body but hovering above her. For a couple of seconds, I was in a detached witnessing state (one I recognized from my NDE in 2000), ready to cross over with her… It felt as if maybe 20% of me was still connected with the body, and that part of me pushed back, to call for help urgently, to see whether Mila could still be saved… That part of me willed the floating part back into the physical body. In my second attempt, I finally managed to produce a yell: "HELP!" Oblivious to the fact that there is a stone arch above my head, I suddenly straightened my legs in order to run for help, hitting my head. Due to high adrenaline, I did not feel much pain but suddenly felt warm blood gushing down my head. I bent forward, continuing to call for help. (Later on, I came to know that I had an inch-long cut on my head.)

Hotel guards responded immediately. One went to get Mila, and one brought a small towel for me to press against my head. Within a couple of seconds, I was able to hold my beloved Mila in my arms. She was alive! She was conscious and moaning. Our friends who were at the hotel with us were silent and stunned. They just said that the car was ready to take us to a nearby hospital right away.

The minutes it took to reach the hospital seemed so long. I employed passionate prayers and chants to fight the mind's pull toward negative thoughts like, "Will she ever walk again? Will she remain sane?" I didn't know how to hold Mila. I worried about her spine and the possible life-long consequences of not keeping her body straight at this critical time. After reaching the hospital, further traumas ensued – as I placed her on the bed in the Emergency Room, a section of her hair remained in my palm. It scared me, and I did not know what to make of it. Then the doctor asked to hold her to see if she could walk, but oh, she wouldn't… That crushed my heart. However, soon enough, out of protest, she suddenly kicked with both her legs, and that brought a deep sigh of relief…

The doctor said her body seemed to be alright, but that there was a hematoma. Since the back of her head endured such a powerful blow, internal bleeding was surely happening, and that was very dangerous; the accumulated blood was pressing on the brain... He said that considering the height from which she fell, brain surgery might be a possibility, but that could be determined only after a brain scan.

Mohanji rushed to the hospital with my parents-in-law. We were all silent and focused within, our hearts united in continuous prayer, knowing that the outcome of the brain scan was in the hands of the Divine... I later learned that word of Mila's fall had spread very fast among all our friends and family (blood relatives and global spiritual family), and within minutes so many were sending loving rays of light and healing to Mila through deep prayer.

At last, we received the result of the brain scan. There were two hematomas, but the internal bleeding was subsiding, and it was established that brain surgery would not be required. Mila and I (as her companion) were kept under strict observation in the ICU for three days. Happily, we were able to leave the hospital a day before the ACT Fusion charity concert, which actually was the main reason for our trip to Delhi.

I took the bandage off of my head, washed my hair, put on a sari, and got Mila into a colorful dress. It was especially strange when we stood on the stage at this beautiful ACT Fusion concert as if nothing happened. With my head bandage removed and Mila's internal bleeding not visible, we must have appeared normal and as if nothing had happened, to those who did not know about the accident. Life is such a miracle!

Observed from a grand perspective, I am aware that all our experiences have a higher meaning, and if this experience was meant to strengthen my faith and gratitude and give further clarity about the challenges and beauty of our spiritual path, so be it. I am forever grateful to everyone who contributed to Mila's speedy recovery with their prayers, blessings, and loving wishes – they touched my heart deeply, and those energies certainly did reach her. In the lap of our Grand Tradition, in the lap of the Divine, Mila's healing took place miraculously. Mohanji said that when he placed his hands on her in the hospital bed, the energy flowing through the hand that was on her head was so strong that for some time it felt glued to her head. We are forever grateful for the blessing of Mohanji's physical presence in our lives.

During our discussions after the accident, Mohanji shared some profound insights about our path and the following lessons, which I now treasure: "No entity can affect me directly. But beware, they could affect me through you or Mila or others who are close to me or my mission. If you are within my energy field and consciousness, you are safe. Otherwise, you are vulnerable. Their aim is to slow me down. This has happened to almost all masters of the past. Many roadblocks were systematically created in their path, systematically so that they slowed down. Even negative thoughts are given to their followers so that they are distracted and leave the path. The other path option is the path of binding. It is a path of comfort zones, fears, and bindings.

"There are numerous teachers and very few masters on earth today. The masters are connected to the Source. They are the target. The teachers are not affected. Jesus was connected to the Source. He was killed. Socrates and Osho were connected to the Source. Those who are connected to the Source are taking people from earthly binding to the path of liberation. Most of them are avadhootas. Shirdi Sai was even taken to court when He was in His body. Hence, being my wife, you have high responsibility. You should be connected to my consciousness always and operate in that. This is very important to know because if they want to slow me down, they may use you for that.

"Being Mohanji's daughter is not easy for Mila. Lord Krishna, Jesus, and all the higher souls had a tough childhood. How many beings attacked Krishna when he was a baby? The parents of Jesus had to leave Jerusalem in order to save the life of their child. The more powerful the soul is, the more vulnerable he or she is. It depends on the power of the soul. Ammu was powerful as well. We know that now, as she is working through many people to wipe the tears of thousands through Ammucare/ACT. Powerful souls will certainly leave their impressions here, irrespective of their time on earth. But, it is the extraordinary responsibility of parents to take care of their babies. You cannot take chances.

"The Nath tradition or Datta tradition is powerful. Once someone is connected to it, they will always be protected. But this path is the path of liberation, and hence, everyone's free will is well respected. The door of the tradition always stays swinging open for people to come, to stay, or if they choose, to leave. Once inside the house, they are well taken care of."

All this was pondered upon during another week that we were asked to spend in Delhi before Mila could be allowed to fly back to Oman. A day before our return, we visited a beautiful Shirdi Baba temple in Gurgaon. Still recovering from the head injury, Mila had been quite cranky that afternoon, but the moment we entered this temple's energy field, she suddenly became joyous and peaceful.

While offering our prostrations at the murti of Shirdi Baba, we happened to meet a beautiful man with glossy eyes who I presumed was the temple priest. He spoke to me, saying something in Hindi, and I could only make out that he was talking about Baba and the blessings through direct experiences he gives to all those who pray/connect to him. I told him that I had indeed experienced many profound blessings from Baba and that, in fact, the first word that Mila uttered when she was a couple of months old was Baba. He looked into her eyes intently for a couple of seconds and smiled.

We soon parted from the priest with glowing eyes and went on a peaceful walk within the temple grounds, simply soaking in its energy. At one point I noticed that the priest was calling us to come back, mentioning *baccha* (the child).

He held a beautiful mild green scarf in his hand and said, "This is for baccha – from Sai Baba. I watched in wonder how softly he wrapped it around her head, tying it under her chin. She did not complain at all even though she usually doesn't like to be touched by strangers and would normally shout straight away, "Don't touch!" Mila said so sweetly, "Thank you, Sai Baba," and silently wore this scarf on her head for more than 30 minutes.

I was in awe and went into silence – I knew from the basics of energy healing that mild green is the color of healing – and it was surely no coincidence that the priest was asked to place this scarf exactly on Mila's head. From all my past experiences with the Great Sai, I know that whenever he performs a miracle, he also makes sure to leave concrete evidence or a sign to confirm the same to our doubting minds. "No more proofs are required in this body-mind-soul system, dearest Baba," I thought. "I am yours, and you live in my heart forever."

Mohanji also shared with me the loving words of Vittal Babaji, whom he happened to meet soon after we left Delhi, which moved me deeply. He said: "Mila is the child of our tradition, the powerful Datta Tradition. She is the child of all the masters of this tradition. Nobody can harm her permanently. Out of jealousy, they will try. But she is well within our protection ring. Being Mohanji's child, she too will be visible to the world. She will always be protected by the masters."

After this experience, we moved on in life, and in 2015 Mila and I found ourselves settling in Novi Sad, Serbia. Even though Mila was already enrolled in kindergarten in Novi Sad, the two of us had traveled to India and stayed for two months, the entire winter holiday. During December and January, we had been with Mohanji continuously. Ever since we moved to Europe, our stays in India were typically shorter, but not this time. Only later did I realize why it was so important that we were there by his side exactly at that time.

Shadow Attacks

The problems began with the Indian man who initially connected with Mohanji and me way back when we were still in the Middle East. He seemed very sincere and humble and deeply immersed in spiritual practice. In reality however, he was not deeply immersed in any pure practice but a manipulative, dark one. We were all initially quite impressed with his dedication and sincerity and how much he was chanting and meditating. He really seemed like a person who was sincerely moving forward on the spiritual path.

Mohanji supported this man wholeheartedly. His purity often comes with a certain naiveté, the typical Bholenath (Lord of Innocence) quality of Shiva. He allowed this man (whom I shall refer to as the Shadow Man) to stay with us and sometimes even travel with him as part of our closest team.

The Shadow Man was already there when Mila and I reached India in December 2015. He started to go into the dark, manipulative practices (such as black magic) more deeply, and secretly put some black magic powders (or whatever they use) onto our food. The black magic items he was using started to affect us physically, emotionally, mentally, and in every other way. We did not feel normal anymore.

His plan was to affect us in minuscule increments so that the changes would go unnoticed. I simply became very heavy and uninspired to do anything, while Mohanji kept getting angry, so much so that I could not even talk to him. Negativity was piling up. Shadow Man was approximately my age, reasonably good-looking, tall, and slim. He had a knack for hooking women through dark energies and sex and then turning them against the Masters. Later on, I found out that he had already done that with two women connected with Mohanji, but was clearly aiming for many more. I was his next target.

My First-Ever Jealousy

Aside from the Shadow Man, I had an issue with a new devotee from Germany. She had joined us only recently but was already very deeply connected. She was so hands-on with everything, systemizing many things within the Mohanji Foundation, and was of great help at the time when Mohanji was getting more famous and more exposed. Everybody on the Mohanji team was in awe of her performance because she was engaged full-on, doing the work of at least five people. She would wake up at 3:30 a.m. in the morning, do her Kriya, then come to Mohanji to be briefed and assume her tasks for the day. Not only was she very organized, methodical, intelligent, and proactive, but also very beautiful (a former model). She was perfect with coordination, reliable, great with photography and presentation – the list went on and on. She seemed like a Superwoman!!

This German lady also had her own charity, and was much more successful in leading it than I had managed to be with ACT Foundation. I was so busy with Mila and other aspects of our mission work and already bogged down with heaviness and irritability from Shadow Man's diligent dark energy work, that for the first time ever in my life, jealousy was beginning to grow within me as well. Somehow in my life, I had always seemed to be the one to inspire jealousy in others. For me, jealousy felt completely foreign – I just didn't have it in my bones. But one should never underestimate the heaviness of jealousy. We have to be vigilant to notice when it hits.

It was not only this German lady's youth, enthusiasm, and capabilities that were pushing my buttons. It was also the discipline, dedication, innovation, and devotion that she displayed, and just how far she went with it. Whatever was being asked of her, she would do it in record time and add a little something extra on top of it in a proactive way. Simply put, she was just impressive. Deep inside, I felt I should be able to do more, but, especially after becoming a mother, I simply could not. "Are these just my excuses?" I wondered.

Everyone noticed that the German woman could do alone what would take five other people to accomplish. The team members were starting to trust her more and more, and she was assuming increasingly more responsibilities and roles. And as is natural, the higher the responsibility, the greater the power and influence of any individual. Therefore, because she was so responsible and so dedicated, she was growing more and more influential and more powerful in a very short span of time.

Initially, I could say that I was fine with it. We needed really dedicated volunteers, and she was a blessing to the mission. But as a woman, I was sensing something else – and I was probably the only one who sensed this. It was from a woman's perspective that I felt that she was aiming to take over and be "Number One," in terms of being closest to Mohanji, and becoming the Shakti (divine feminine power) of the mission. And at that time, I was still not fully there myself, not fully in my shoes, so to speak. I was not yet fully efficient in my own contribution to the mission.

Mila and I had just moved from the Middle East to Serbia. I was living in my parents' house, was financially unstable, aiming to get my yoga sessions and workshops off the ground, and had my limitations being busy with Mila. It was only natural that I had to be tested. In hindsight, from a higher perspective, all of this was for my highest good, to give me clarity about myself and force me to step up. The status quo could not be maintained. I feel grateful to this woman, for it was through her behavior and her beautiful devotion and dedication that my own shortcomings were revealed to me. But when it was happening, it was not a very pleasant experience at all.

I also noticed that she seemed rather secretive, and that was a red flag for my intuition. For example, while in Tamil Nadu that month, Mohanji, myself, Rajesh Kamath, and the German lady all went for Nadi Reading (reading of the ancient scrolls in which people's destinies were written hundreds of years ago. Truly mind-blowing!). All of us had our scrolls read, but she did not want hers to be read. She was clearly hiding something. Mohanji's started with the following words: "An incarnation of a deity. Global fame." Mine was quite fascinating. It started with syllables of my name, "Bi -lja - na. Father Mi -lan. Mother Mi -le -na." And then it went on about all the main phases of my life. Everything was one hundred percent correct, including my life-long dedication to the mission. For whatever reason, our German friend declined to hear her scroll.

She was indeed very secretive, and I didn't feel that I could fully trust her. I could not feel complete openness and purity like with some other long-term volunteers around Mohanji. She always seemed to be "all up in my face," pointing out my own shortcomings. As a woman, it was not easy to go through that feeling that someone "younger and better" was pretty much taking over. At the same time, the Shadow Man was doing his manipulative stuff and increasing the rift between Mohanji and me. I was reaching for the name "Devi" with two heavy anchors pulling me down.

Changing my Name to Devi

While in Kerala in December 2015, there came a point when it was possible to arrange a Vedic name-changing ceremony with a high priest responsible for such ceremonies. Mohanji's devotee Devadas checked some astrological books and offered a couple of options for my name. I immediately noticed the "Devi" and my intuition was spot on – yes, that sounds like me, Devi Mohan. The moment this thought occurred, there were at least five synchronicities that confirmed this choice of name.

First of all, I remembered what Shirdi Baba said when I received my first shaktipat from him through Mohanji – "the highest version of you is Mother Mary." The Indian equivalent of Mother Mary was indeed Devi, a powerful word that included all aspects of Divine Mother (gentle and motherly such as Mother Mary, but also fierce, courageous, protective, artistic, knowledgeable, etc.). I suddenly got the idea that I would change my name to Devi, in order to strengthen that highest aspect with my personality. The synchronicities that followed came as divine confirmations of my decision.

An old man, who was a clairvoyant and astrologer, once told me that I would become known throughout the world, not as Biljana or Biba, but by some other name. A lady who chanted Devi mantras every day and communed with Divine Mother called to tell me that Devi loved me. Another woman had a vivid dream of Devi with multidimensional arms embracing me, etc.

In the end, I gathered all my strength and made a firm decision, "I will do this." I was aware that changing my name to Devi would test my ability to stand behind my inner truth and ignore the opinions of others, especially their malicious comments. In India, there are many Krishnas (and many other names of Krishna), Ramas, Devis, etc. – it's considered auspicious and smart to attach a higher vibration and divine energy to a child through their name, which they may hear or say or think many times each day. In such a way, that vibration is strengthened in their life. When people call us by a high-vibration name every day, at a subtle level that vibration is strengthened in us at a subtle level.

However, this kind of name would surely raise some eyebrows in the West. For instance, in the Balkans in the Serbo-Croatian language, Devi is pretty much the same as "Devica" or "Djeva," which refers to the purest, virgin aspect of Mother Mary. I knew that this idea wouldn't be easy to introduce, and within the Mohanji Foundation, taking a spiritual name was quite rare. As my natal chart's Uranus willed it, the "Rebel With a Cause" had to be the vanguard, treading unknown territory time and again. There was nobody else who had done this in Serbia, so I would be the first one.

The Shadow Man was carefully observing what was happening, and this was when he ratcheted his manipulative game to the next level. He approached me with the intention of hooking me by playing the card of my spiritual ego. He told me he could teach me a mantra that would raise my spiritual awareness at a record speed and truly make me a Devi. This was a very powerful and very special, super-secret mantra, and he said had inner guidance that I was ready to receive it. This was, of course, very flattering.

At this time, under Shadow Man's influence, Mohanji appeared angry and unapproachable to me. I felt much better if I did not speak to him at all. The moment we spoke about anything, there was just so much negativity that I would regret telling him anything. When the Shadow Man approached me with this mantra proposal, it sounded like something positive that could only help me. I didn't even think or feel that I needed to go to Mohanji to ask him for his approval. At a deeper level, I do agree this was something that appealed to my spiritual ego (the part of me that wanted special recognition and took pleasure in being special, above others), and he knew it. He made me believe that I was the only one privileged enough to be offered this great secret mantra that could really put me into the vibration of Devi. That was the button he was pressing, and he was trying to hook me through that.

He asked to meet me at the most auspicious time (3:30 a.m.) in the puja room to teach me the mantra. He also gave me shaktipat of his own in that puja room and when all was over, he hugged me and I felt he came very close to me in the area of my second chakra, intentionally energizing sexual attraction. Mohanji and Mila were sleeping in the next room, and I felt very uncomfortable at that moment. My intuition was ringing alarm bells, and I started to observe him in a different light.

Fortunately for me, at that point, I had started getting up early in the morning and strengthening my aura through sun-gazing at sunrise. This helped to nullify the Shadow Man's hooking and lessen the effects of his energetic power over me. I could connect with my intuitive guidance better. This was when I decided to speak to Mohanji about this new secret mantra.

I was amazed when Mohanji told me that he was aware of the mantra, but what Shadow man had given me was not a hundred percent correct. I understood that some words in this mantra had been twisted around just a bit, enough to create an effect that did not correspond to our pure White Path. It had an energetic hook in it. This is when Mohanji shared with me one key piece of information that confirmed what my intuition had been telling me. Since the Shadow Man claimed that he was in frequent communion with Devi, at one point Mohanji asked him: "So, when Devi appears to you, how do you see her? How do you recognize it is her?" The Shadow Man replied, "I can always recognize her by a distinct scent of raw flesh."

Mohanji kept quiet at the time but revealed to me later: "That's not Devi. That's not how Devi appears! Her scent is that of the most beautiful celestial fragrance, far from any raw flesh or raw meat."

Mohanji began to understand that something was not right. The Shadow Man was using manipulative methods of hooking people, angling especially for ladies in our group, and the supposed Devi he was connecting to was not the real Devi. A couple of women had already fallen into his trap and were sexually involved with him. Sometimes when we had different gatherings like Mohanji's Satsangs, the Shadow Man would sit in some corner and start giving knowledge. When he spoke, there was a different energy, which he had obtained through all those mantras he chanted. They gave him a special, meditative aura and the appearance of deep calmness and radiance.

The Shadow Man's aim was to position himself as the true guru, and to show or prove that he was smarter and better than Mohanji in every sense, especially in terms of his knowledge and endurance. His aim was to outshine Mohanji, just as the German lady's aim was to outshine me through her outstanding performance.

Thank God that I started talking to Mohanji about this entire situation. That's when I understood that one of the greatest tests on the spiritual path happens when the shadow energies infiltrate the white, and one gets tempted to attain power and fame – in one word, greed. And it is when you have the greed to quickly become something great, rather than going through the process organically as guided by your Guru, that the darkness creeps in very easily.

Dark Light energies always work through fear or greed. They don't work through unconditional love and selflessness, like true Gurus. The shadow energies look for ways to hook a person, and just as with any addiction, a person can no longer feel ok without the substance the darkness is peddling. This is how the manipulative religious sects operate as well. The true guru always gives space, honors free will, empowers, and liberates. As mentioned before, there is no punishment for apostasy with a true Guru. A person can always change their mind and leave. Freedom and free will is always honored. Gurus are after a person's mature choice, deep inner recognition, and conviction based on free will. This is the key difference. The moment I confided in Mohanji, I broke the bubble imposed by the black magic, and the Shadow Man could no longer grip me.

A Woman's Perspective

At this time, I reached my turning point, the actual crescendo of my own experience in this drama. Initially, I did not understand that the manipulative Shadow Man was behind all the negative emotions I harbored, especially the "not good enough" feeling. I connected with all married women who at some point go through this same feeling. As the married woman's life is surrendered to feminine selflessness, supporting her husband with all her heart comes naturally. Their husband becomes someone great and they are in the back, supporting him in the silent ways of the woman.

While masculine energy is more tangible and specific, feminine energy is more ephemeral, but greatly empowering. It is the wind beneath the wings of everyone she supports, but they won't really be aware this subtle feminine energy is what is carrying them through. They are more likely to take that selfless, maternal, purely altruistic energy for granted and not even recognize the help they are receiving. However, with time, one understands that the crucial support they have received came from their nurturing mothers. It came from the Divine Feminine as that unheard, unseen, overlooked and mainly unappreciated wonder of humankind, the jewel of utmost beauty.

This is why I feel we need stories of the Divine Feminine and Divine Masculine to come to life in the minds and hearts of all people, especially our children. We need to appreciate our own mothers and their silent work that we take for granted – all the daily chores that require so much energy but in the end, appear as if nothing was done – work that would be noticed only if she was gone. This is why I can say in full confidence that no woman goes through her life without being taken for granted.

My dear ladies, dear sisters, let us awaken to the truth of our greatest strength: the sacred temple of our deepest intuition and inner guidance, clarity, creativity, and power. Let us look with utmost reverence into that generator of our creative expression, sensuality, and manifestation, the sacred space that gives us energy for deep transformation of ourselves and all others with whom we are in touch. Listen to the primordial sound of its name as you pronounce it – "YONI." The womb. The source. Nature's gateway of all births. The seat of the highest and most unique feminine power. Due to the multidimensionality of the Sanskrit language, *yoni* also connotes the female sexual organs – the vagina, vulva, and uterus.

Lingam and yoni together symbolize the merging of microcosmos and macrocosmos, the divine eternal process of creation and regeneration, and the union of the feminine and the masculine that recreates all of existence through all the cycles of time. Yoni mudra, one of the most famous hand gestures/locks/poses, actually depicts the shape of the yoni, while its variant, Shanmukhi mudra (formed by fingertips being placed on specific points on the face) helps us get detached from the world, just like a baby in mother's womb.

Most women do not even know what their yoni looks like, not to mention its dynamics and secrets. Ladies, at this point, I have a small request for you. It may sound odd, but please do not shy away from it. If you have never done this before, I invite you to hold a small mirror in your hand and take a moment to gaze at the most intimate part of your body, your yoni. As you observe it, recognize the sanctity of this entry point into birth and manifestation of new life on Earth. It is so powerful and special. For centuries, so much shame, guilt, and violence have tainted this sacred entry point into embodiment and union in intimacy. It is time to honor our body as the temple of the soul, and to thank our body for its loving service during this magical earthly experience. It is time to unite in our strength to remain positive no matter what, to remain loving no matter how heavy our surroundings may be, and to create a new reality for all of us.

The sacred feminine and sacred masculine come together. I see them as two archetypes at the foundation of our entire collective, just like the Yin and Yang symbol of the Tao, the Shiva-Shakti symbol of lingam and yoni, etc. I have written blogs about recognizing this principle even at the holiest of locations on Earth, like on mighty Kailash in Tibet and at Machu Picchu in Peru. As discussed in the earlier chapters, the archetypes are the patterns in the collective subconscious and our actual inherited potential, which we actualize only when we bring them into the light of consciousness. Masculine and feminine are not necessarily gendered (masculine does not equal man and feminine does not equal women). Masculine and feminine are archetypes, which means potentials or energies within us.

We need to understand their dynamic within us, and within our organizations and institutions - how they connect and intertwine, and how they balance each other. We need to understand the beauty of these archetypes and aim to always achieve the right balance between them in our own inner and outer worlds. One should never dominate another, neither in nature nor in the human psyche.

MASCULINE	–	*FEMININE*
Logic	–	Intuition
Action	–	Rest
Penetration	–	Receptivity
Cognition	–	Emotion
Structure	–	Fluidity
Singular Focus	–	Big Picture (Wide Frame)

In Vedic terms, "the evolving universe is propelled by the interaction between these two forces of nature - Agni and Soma. Agni represents the 'metabolism' of the universe. It is the agent for causing change. Soma, which stands for all that nourishes, is the fuel that sustains Agni. The pair, Agni and Soma, each need the other; and the two in tandem create, sustain and recycle the substances in the universe, ensuring continuity and evolution of life. [...] It is not possible to say whether food is more important than the eater; fuel more important than the fire; substance more important than action. Both fire and offering are important to one another. Both arise from the same root and both are the essential aspects of all life. Agni and Soma, each compliment the other wonderfully well; and that is the essence of all existence."[49]

The Inner Throne of Devi

As a woman and Mohanji's wife, I knew I had an important role to play within the mission through my feminine qualities of creativity, fluidity, softness, and joy. Still, I was yet to find my place and my true expression within the global platform of Mohanji Foundation. Because I did not appreciate myself fully, I had to undergo all this drama in order to bring certain unintegrated parts of myself

49 Source: https://sreenivasaraos.com/2012/09/30/agni-and-soma-interplay-life-thrives-on-life/

into awareness. I needed to learn how to feel free to create within the platform, not to compete with other women. I realized at one point that I need not invest energy into PROVING something that I ALREADY was! I just needed to step into my shoes fully, expressing myself freely and authentically. That was all.

This is how Baba brought me to this powerful realization at the moment when he raised me from the lowest possible self-confidence, onto the inner throne of Devi. As Mohanji's wife and someone who has been supporting him wholeheartedly from the onset of the mission, I did my best to contribute to so many teams (ACT Foundation, Mai-Tri Method, Himalayan School of Traditional Yoga, Sadhana team, various Balkan teams; to conduct programs, to speak at international event as the Global Ambassador, etc.). There was continuous communication and coordination, most of which was not visible. I was involved with the background support which took a lot of time (and this is something that all Mohanji Foundation volunteers experience), plus there was my own child that needed me as a mother. With all these responsibilities, I often felt dissipated and exhausted. I really was doing my best but now, all of a sudden, I felt there was somebody else better than me, younger than me, possibly more beautiful than me, and maybe more capable and successful than me. What I had to offer was NOT GOOD ENOUGH anymore. As a married woman, I simply had to encounter this issue on the feminine path, to walk over these hurdles at some point in time.

At a deeper level, I also felt that this was karmic. I remembered how, when I was 19 years old, my Croatian Hero had seen those highest qualities in me. I now remembered his wife's elegant message (the little note she inserted into the gift wrapping) and her pain of no longer being good enough, which was felt in the underlying energy of her message. It is possible that at this point, I had to experience the karmic effects of those actions. It was my turn to now experience the feeling of being a married woman outshone by a younger, more talented, and "more everything" one who had appeared on the horizon to dazzle everybody.

The feeling of not being good enough hit me especially hard one day when Mohanji, the German lady, and I were in the car discussing the topic of effective charitable work. In front of her, he told me, "And what have you done for ACT Foundation? Precious nothing." Needless to say, that was an excruciating punch in the gut. The German lady had been far more successful in creating powerful reports and raising funds for her charitable work than I was. I do understand that Mohanji was scolding me because I could have done more. But this particular scolding did not brush off as the earlier blessings of scoldings had. It actually hurt. It brought me to a turning point of self-pity when I started nurturing the following inner narrative, "Maybe I should withdraw gracefully and allow the German lady to take this mission forward with Mohanji and all the other volunteers. Maybe I am really not good enough for this role. Maybe she could do it all so much better. I will not create any fuss and will withdraw peacefully."

These thoughts were boiling in me exactly at the time we reached Shirdi. At that point, I suddenly had this idea: "You know what, Baba, YOU are the one who brought me to Mohanji. So, if I am not good enough for this role, you, dear Baba, should tell me." I really meant it. And if he confirmed it, I would have gracefully withdrawn and looked for another path and another way to serve. That was my final decision. I would not create any drama. I would gracefully withdraw because that would mean I was not the right person for this role of Mohanji's wife after all and that this German lady was better.

The way Baba works is always so special. His leelas are beyond anything one can imagine. Baba gave me a hint through these words from Mohanji: "You know, there is a friend, Hema, a very pure soul from Delhi, who is deeply devoted to Shirdi baba. She is in communion with him every day and prays for people who send her their photos. She lives for Baba, and she got a blessing from him that, if she places somebody's photo on her altar, in her puja room, vibhuti will appear on that photo overnight, along with some message from Baba." Mohanji happened to send her a photo of him and Mila and got a beautiful message back.

At that very moment, I requested he send my photo to this lady as well. Then I prayed to Baba as follows: "Dear Baba, you decide. You tell me what to do. I've just reached my limit. I cannot go on like this, and I leave this to you because it is you brought me on this path. Please give me a sign." I prayed to him and awaited the answer through this woman. Finally, two days later, the message came back. The message was very brief, but so profound, so intimate and so intense, that nothing but tears could come in response. This is the most intimate sharing of mine, more intimate than anything I have expressed in this entire book. Baba's words were: "In terms of her purity, she is Mother Mary. In terms of her devotion, she is Parvati."

I couldn't believe my ears and kept crying. I was at the bottom, in the mud, with no self-respect and self-love left, and Baba had suddenly placed me on a pedestal. Only he can express love in such powerful ways… This took some time to absorb.

That day we were scheduled to perform food seva. We were on the streets of Shirdi early in the morning before 6:00 a.m. and were distributing food to all underprivileged people who wanted to come forward (plus some "Foreignchi Patlin" fans, of course). The German lady was taking photos and on one of them, a huge orb appeared exactly on me, covering my entire head and neck. I was covered in Baba's sacred presence, covered by Baba's grace. I can't express just what kind of a boost that was for me. I was at the very bottom, crushed completely and far away from any Devi, far from even resemblance of anything special. I was the lowliest of the low. And then beloved Baba interfered. These were the signs that he was handling this.

I will never forget this experience and how everything turned around. Baba always knew when I needed a scolding and when I needed a boost. The same was with Mohanji, but at this point both of us were under attack. Baba saved me and helped me stay on the path. At this point, when I was at the very bottom, He helped me by expressing the most loving words and then just brought me up. Like a baby, he lifted me and showered me with his love.

I will never forget this amazing expression of Baba's love. After this, everything was easier. I regained my confidence and was amazed to see how this entire drama resolved and untangled. Even Hollywood movie directors could not have come up with such an ending.

The name change brought us to a turning point. The German lady was in the same car as me when we traveled to the location where the name change would happen. The previous day the two of us had a falling-out so she did not want to speak to me. She wanted to change her name to Mohini

Mohan (interestingly enough, Mohini was the divine seductress – very appropriate). I explained to her that "Mohan" is my married last name. I told her, "Even though we are talking about a spiritual name here, please understand that no one but me can have the last name Mohan. Unless you intend to get married to Mohanji." She was not happy at all, but I could tell that she persisted with this intention.

I spoke to Mohanji that day and put my foot down, for the first time ever. With a very serious tone, I told him, "You know I never interfered with your decisions as a Spiritual Master. I spoke with the German lady and she insists that she wants the name Mohini Mohan, even though I explained to her that Mohan is my last name, my legal married name. I have to tell you, this is really too much for me. If you allow her to change her name to Mohini Mohan, you may as well marry her." And I turned and walked out.

That morning, I woke up early but remained in bed. I didn't mean to eavesdrop, but since I woke up and did not want to interrupt their conversation, it happened that way by default. She came to him in the room next to our bedroom, as always, and the topic of her spiritual name was discussed. Mohanji told her that he gave it serious thought and would recommend a different name for her (it was something like Sri Mohini Bhakta Swaroopa Mohanji). She was not happy with this longer name, but she knew it was pointless to discuss further. This was the moment when she understood that my words still had some relevance, and that she had lost this game.

Similarly, when my self-confidence was boosted by Baba and a change in vibration happened in me, the Shadow Man realized he could not get through to me anymore, and then turned on the German lady full out. Since her plan of becoming the Shakti of Mohanji was shaken, the Shadow Man saw an opening he could use. He used the same strategy on her (probably even the same mantra) and soon they became intimate. The moment he could hook her through sex, she was in his full grip.

They started spending more time together, being intimate, and after a couple of days, they simply eloped and secretly ran away together. What's even worse, later on, he used her in his black magic rituals and dark agendas of maligning Mohanji through unspeakable lies and deceptions. She followed his instructions and maligned Mohanji online, and live at many locations. Her words were very effective and believable because she had been so close to Mohanji and knew how to communicate in a humble but convincing way. Many people, including those who had known us for years, believed her and left Mohanji. However, since the Shadow Man had done this with several other ladies, turning them against Masters and even extorting money from those Masters under threats of defamation, Mohanji would not go for it. He faced it all head-on and did not allow himself to be threatened.

We knew that the German lady would see through the Shadow Man sooner or later, being an essentially good, kind-hearted, and very intelligent young woman. A couple of years later, she indeed left the Shadow Man and found a genuine guru from south India. One day she sent me a loving email and apologized for everything that she had done. I replied lovingly and actually thanked her because I really grew a lot through that entire drama, no matter how painful it was.

I did not say this to her, but I often thought that she even saved me, because the Shadow Man could have been more persistent in getting through to me had it not been for her presence.

After the whole thing was resolved, Devi Amma said, "If Devi [meaning me] was not present there, this could have gone in the wrong direction. The entire mission of Mohanji Foundation was in grave danger." She said that the shadow energies would have penetrated so deeply that it would have been very, very tough for Mohanji to continue. So, this was the time when I was chosen by the Tradition to play that role of Shakti and to protect Mohanji by being present within the eye of the storm, by getting run over, and by then lifting myself back up like a Phoenix bird. Baba sure was the one who gave me the wings in his loving ways.

I must say that the way in which the Shadow Man used this German lady was extremely dangerous. Actions such as defamation of Masters, as shared earlier, is something that attracts really heavy karma on people. It unfortunately takes many lifetimes to come out of it, regardless of the level of spiritual awareness one attains. Imagine having about $100,000 dollars in your spiritual bank account, for which you did many charitable acts and helped many people. But through dark actions, you suddenly accumulate a debt of one billion. That would be the right proportion. In that case, $100,000 is really nothing, as light and insubstantial as a feather. Their loss was immense and the karmic burden unimaginable. Mohanji actually lost nothing. When somebody betrays Mohanji, he loses nothing. But what they lose is irretrievable. And such people cannot come back because the ego will not permit it. I am sharing all this for the purpose of understanding and clarity.

It is very important not to flip while on the path. It is very easy to fall into that trap. Doubt is the main doorway for shadow energies. They create some doubt or they create some fancy where a person on the spiritual path initially gets much more power and benefits. However, it would not be possible to sustain them. Spiritual power and higher states of awareness come hand-in-hand with responsibility and have to be attained gradually, with depth and maturity. It is like exercising in the gym. You don't lift fifty-pound dumbbells on the very first day. The weight has to be loaded gradually as our capacity increases.

However, out of spiritual greed, some people want to take on the heavy weights on their very first day. In the end, they collapse completely. These are the lures and temptations that people like the Shadow Man use. He was tempting people with higher powers and then claiming that Mohanji was denying it to them. But Mohanji was not denying anything. He actually opened up the full gym and allowed those who were ready to lift the big weights to do it. Individual capacities are not the same. The whole manipulation is done in such a way that a powerful path like this is made to look like nothing. But I have to say that this path, for me and those who have recognized it, is everything. It is very powerful and guarantees balanced progress – after all, we are here for the full marathon, not for a sprint.

Chapter 12

In The Flow

The Key Test – Are You In or Out?

People who have volunteered within Mohanji Foundation for a longer time know how beautiful and intensely challenging this path truly is. Mohanji is a fountain of many new initiatives, projects, and programs. It is often challenging to keep up with the speed of his outpouring and the ever-increasing load of responsibility. If one's spiritual practice is poor and inconsistent, it is difficult, if not impossible, to stay in the flow. Many people could not keep up, succumbing to the pressure and falling back into their comfort zones. Those who have been able to diligently maintain their consistency and swim in Mohanji's current – I see them now in a completely different energy, transformed and empowered. However, when it comes to staying on the path or not, everyone has to choose for themselves.

Mohanji once explained that the Masters operate at a very high speed. He gave the example of a fan, its blades spinning so fast that their movement becomes nearly invisible. In the same way, it only appears on the surface that Masters are calm and mainly silent. In reality, they are like fire. They deal with multiple issues simultaneously and are far more active than one can imagine, not just on Earth, but in more than one dimension. Being around Mohanji, especially during travel, and keeping up with his speed is always very challenging. There are no comfort zones to cling to.

There have been volunteers who joined the mission and stayed in Mohanij's vicinity for some time until their comfort zones were challenged. When their core issues and blockages would surface to be worked on, they would find an excuse to leave. And yet, there is that other category of people who want to go deeper and take more responsibility. The Tradition then works on them more – the churning is more turbulent, and karma is more quickly completed. Naturally, the higher the responsibilities, the more the expected maturity, and once the ups and downs increase, one's journey to liberation is fully underway. This process has been my direct experience.

In my case, being not only a volunteer but Mohanji's wife as well, the bar has always been set even higher. Being around him, I could never take it easy, sleeping till late and just taking my time and relaxing. Even after long travels with no sleep, I had to be on my toes. When Mila was little, this was extremely difficult because she always had a lot of energy at night and liked to go to sleep late (while living in Serbia from 2014-2017, she would go to kindergarten around 10:00 a.m.), while Mohanji would wake up by 5:00 a.m. at the very latest. In that scenario, I would need to sleep less than four hours per night in order to attend to both. In the end, especially during travel, I would adjust to Mila's schedule and get up later. By the time I rose, Mohanji would have already had his breakfast.

At some point, it began to look like we were not compatible. One day he told me: "You know... I feel that this whole wife role may be too much for you. Too much pressure. So maybe it's easier for you to be comfortable. Make it easy for yourself. You can continue with all your roles within the mission, but we really don't have to be husband and wife. I feel this is too much for you."

Just when I thought I had handled all possible challenges and attacks, this new bomb landed in my lap. I never expected something like this and was caught completely off guard. That this bomb had come from my beloved Mohanji was very painful, I must say. I didn't know what to say or do. At first, the "not good enough" program was reactivated. The *samskaras* (painful impressions) from the refugee days were ready to take over in a wink. I fought hard and decided to stand my ground.

At first, I thought that he had already made up his mind about divorcing me. I didn't know what to do because I had invested all of myself into our mission and life together, never considering any "Plan B." I had built myself on the platform of the grace of Mohanji and our joint mission. I did not have an alternative – nor did I want one. Yet, if the ground one stands on is cut from beneath their feet, what can be done? This was certainly a huge blow.

At the time when this divorce drama erupted, we were visiting our friends in Switzerland, the wonderful Joshi family whose loving support and selflessness surpassed anything I had ever seen. We were also discussing where Mila and I should live and where we should acquire the land for the main European Mohanji Center, with Slovenia seeming like the best choice.

Just as he was about to leave for the airport, Mohanji said: "I'm going to India now and will be back in two months, in November. So, you have two months to think about all we have discussed, make your decision, and act accordingly." Basically, if I was going to step up, it should be apparent in the depth of my connection, my early morning sadhana, discipline, speed, and the overall energy that I radiated.

With regard to getting up early in the morning, I knew better than to give excuses about Mila sleeping late, my parents, or the central heating that came on only after 7:00 a.m., etc. The truth is that when we are in *tamas* (lethargic energy), we seldom realize it right away. Making excuses and blaming others is typical for the tamasic state. I had other thoughts like, "I'm doing the mission-related work all the time, sometimes till late at night – it's not like I'm watching movies or going out. Why is he saying that?" Yet, when I sincerely contemplated the situation, I realized those thoughts were only excuses as well.

The truth was that I was not managing my time properly. I could do it better. I could build a team of people around me and delegate more. I did not have to do all the work I was doing all by myself. I realized that if I could just focus, get up early in the morning, connect with the consciousness and invoke the Grace, come out of the doership, and surrender, I would then accomplish more and make much better use of my time. I had to admit to myself that this was true.

This goes to say that spiritual awakening is not comfortable and involves a lot of work. Regardless of one's path, one thing is for sure – there will be a lot of churning, and it will never be comfortable. One has to apply a lot of willpower. So, after Mohanji threatened me with divorce, I started waking up early. I started planning my time better. I reached out to other people and asked for help: "Could you please review these applications instead of me?" "Can you please compile the ACT report, and I will just add the final touches and trim it down?" I learned the secret of delegation is not being shy about asking for help, relying on others more, and surrendering perceived control and doership. In this way, I could create the much-needed window of opportunity for the quality time necessary for preplanning, creative work of actual substance, and my higher expression.

This was exactly how I reached the point of creating meditative processes of my own, by connecting with Mohanji's consciousness, relaxing, and following my intuition. The first one to emerge was Awakening Yoga Nidra. This process utilizes the highly receptive alpha state of mind for deep cleansing with the Grace of Guru Tattva; it is an intimate connection with the Divine. The experience is almost like watching one's own inner movie and is very intense and transformative. The aim is to strengthen the inner resolve toward the highest of goals – spiritual liberation in this lifetime.

The time early in the morning, from 3:00 a.m. till 6:00 a.m. is the only golden, *sattvic* (balanced) time of the day when Masters from higher vibratory planes are most active and when our system enters the optimal balance in every way, which then affects the rest of the day. It is already an achievement if one gets up even 15 minutes before 6:00 a.m. Therefore, one can only imagine the blessing and grace of waking up around 4:30 a.m. and completing deep meditative practice or some profound creative work. After that, yoga, brisk walking, or some other form of physical activity is perfect. This has an amazing effect on the entire system including digestion, improves clarity of thinking, and elevates spiritually. After adjusting the rhythm of my sleeping and waking, I started feeling the inner calling to create more transformative processes.

The Birth of Mai-Tri Method & More Challenges

In 2016, after two months spent in India and the entire nightmare with the Shadow Man and German Lady, I returned to Serbia with Mila with some emotional wounds and scars that needed healing. Even though all was resolved outwardly, the heaviness of this experience did leave its mark internally. I was especially longing to speak to a woman who could understand me at a deeper level, to comfort and advise me.

Of course my best friend Marija would have been the perfect confidante, but she was in New York at the time and unfortunately, had been diagnosed with ovarian cancer. I was devastated by this news and was eager to support, not further burden her with my own problems. I decided to turn to Vanja, whose previous session (when my parents from Sirius came) meant so much to me. She was greatly respected by everyone within Mohanji Foundation and during a retreat with Mohanji that year, he advised many people who had more complex challenges to request a session with her.

Just as Consciousness Kriya, or any other profound breakthrough on our path, Mai-Tri Method too had just simply come to life one day, out of the blue. Its moment of birth couldn't have been more casual. There was a sweet lady from Belgrade who had started connecting to Mohanji's consciousness during some other methodology of energy work she used called Shambhala Healing

Sessions. Whenever she was invoking the Masters of Shambhala, inevitably it was Mohanji who would come to perform the necessary energy work, and I was there to translate for her if needed.

She then commented casually, "I may as well call it Mohanji Healing because it is you, Mohanji, whom I see doing the work in every Shambhala Session."

At that moment, Mohanji said, "Ok, go ahead, do it. Devi, you can help systemize it and create the protocol for this method. Just be aware: *prarabdha* karma (the destiny aspect of one's karmic journey) should not be interfered with. I will explain how to deal with that. Also, 50% of any money you receive for the session should be set aside for feeding the hungry. If you follow these two rules, you will have no problems. It will be highly effective because, through my consciousness, you will be able to remove blockages caused by painful impressions even from the deepest and subtlest layer of the aura – the *kaarana shareera* (causal body). This is usually accessible only to Masters, but you will be empowered by me."

My heart expanded immensely! I had been waiting for something like this for years, ever since Devi Amma's comment about the healing energy in my palms. I had been eager to help people through healing energy in this lifetime as well but was determined to wait until I felt the inner confirmation. I just knew it had to be something simple but highly effective. Mai-Tri Method was exactly that. In the end, there were three of us who were tasked with creating the initial standard operating procedure for the Mai-Tri Method to get the ball rolling. Mohanji thought it wiser if his name was not mentioned at all. He also said he would never touch any money from Mai-Tri. It was all to go toward humanitarian work and to the practitioner performing the session.

The moment I started performing Mai-Tri, I was amazed by its depth and the joy I felt being the instrument of that loving heat gushing through my spine and palms. The more sessions I did, the more intense and profound the energy. I never tired from it, once even doing Mai-Tri from 8:00 a.m. till 10:00 p.m. with hardly any breaks. I did not feel tired or hungry, and the love and bliss I would inevitably feel while doing it were deeply fulfilling.

We now have hundreds of Mai-Tri practitioners around the globe and I do not doubt that this number will reach thousands very soon. While performing Mai-Tri, I could see how much my intuition sharpened, along with my ability to sense/see whatever it was that the Higher Self of the client wished to reveal. It would always be something of the greatest importance for that person at that point in time. I don't think any book could have ever taught me more about the subtle laws of karma than what I got to see through this profound method. I am forever grateful to Mohanji for this superb gift to humanity.

I was unaware that our friend Vanja was unhappy about the latest developments with Mai-Tri. It is possible that she enjoyed being the "number one" person when it came to healing sessions recommended by Mohanji and that, to her, Mai-Tri practitioners seemed inexperienced and shallow. On top of that, she worked a lot with people who had issues with curses, spirits, and dark entities. She was really brave and would deal with dark entities head-on. At some point, I believed that she would be the first person I knew whose enlightenment I would get to witness. I admired, loved, and respected her a lot.

It turned out that Vanja was the last person I should have approached for a sincere ladies' talk. She had no male partner and was a total introvert. She did nothing else but her healing sessions within her humble little apartment. She also saw Mohanji only as a Guru, and did not want to know anything about him as my husband. There was something I said the day that we spoke that she really did not like, and she held it against me. I did not realize it at the time because she politely excused herself, but later on, it all came out.

When Mohanji next visited Serbia, Vanja requested a private meeting with him. She proposed that he come to her apartment, but since Mohanji had a rule of not meeting any woman alone in private (to avoid the risk of any potential rumor, which plagued him nonetheless), he asked me to accompany him. I had no idea what awaited me. After all that I had been through, I thought that I had developed a higher tolerance for nonsense, but the opinions about me that Vanja shared in that meeting were the ugliest words that anyone had addressed me with, ever. Nobody had spoken to me that way in my whole life.

The moment we sat down, she gave me a piercing look. I did not know that I had sat on the sofa on which she slept, exactly on the spot where she usually laid her head. That was the initial trigger and yet something I couldn't have known. She spoke directly to Mohanji and ignored me. At some point, I shared a beautiful experience I had during a satsang for 600 people that Mohanji had conducted in Novi Sad that year. When I mentioned something about Mai-Tri, she suddenly turned on me and started shouting, using the most derogatory language about my immaturity, my need to be seen and attract attention, etc. She then said that she knew that I had invented Mai-Tri to show off.

Shocked by what I was hearing, I naturally started defending myself, trying to explain how Mai-Tri came to life. That only caused her tone to rise a couple of notches higher as she shot razor-sharp arrows of even more horrendous words at me. I could clearly feel the energetic hit of each word in my lower belly. When she reached the point of saying the most despicable things that had nothing to do even remotely with reality (including that of me looking forward to Mohanji's death), I realized that such lies did not deserve my response. I simply sat with my spine straight and invoked Baba, thinking: "Baba, I surrender all this at your feet." I visualized myself bowing down at His feet and allowed her to continue her spiteful ranting. The moment I did that, I felt immense blissful, soothing energy like a protective ring of energy around me. Engulfed by Baba's energy, I sat there while the arrows of her preposterous accusations flew around me. My eyes were closed as she continued with the litany of the ugliest possible words. I do feel she was influenced by dark entities because such negativity couldn't have come from her alone.

At some point, her anger amplified, and all the negative energy she had released went back to her. Mohanji had explained this energy rule to me earlier, saying that if one does not accept a package sent by mail, by default, it gets returned to its sender – the same applies to attacks and negative words. Shirdi Baba too has said that people who defame us are licking away our negative karma with their tongues. I witnessed that truth through this intense experience.

At some point, Vanja started to breathe heavily. She did not know what to do with herself, shifting angrily from one side of her chair to the other. An awkward silence followed her tirade. Finally, Mohanji said: "Shall we go?"

“Yes,” I replied calmly. Mohanji and Vanja exchanged some pleasantries, and he and I promptly left. We have not met Vanja ever since.

Later on, reflecting on that occasion, I felt that some karmic leverage was behind the entire drama and that Mohanji’s presence reduced its intensity. There was something I owed her from another life. It could have been that I had put her down in front of other people in another lifetime and the karma between us had to be resolved.

I know that Vanja has continued with her energy work, and I must say in all sincerity, that when I think of her, my first spontaneous reaction is still love and respect. She is incredibly dedicated and very deep. I do feel that she has taken a very tough burden on herself though, especially concerning the often thankless work of battling with dark energy spirits. I do hope she is able to handle it. I found this experience truly amazing and am grateful to Vanja for the same. Without it, I would not have known that I could respond in this way amid such an attack. This was yet another opportunity for spiritual growth through a direct experience.

Blessed by Mother Kali

I traveled to South Africa in July 2017 to conduct my first-ever solo program with the support of dear Milica Bulatović, Swami Bhaktananda from Durban, and our SA team. I was received with lots of love by our Mohanji SA family, and everything went beautifully. With the hectic travel schedule and Mila next to me, I slept less than 3 hours and still managed to get up early the next morning and conduct the full-day program with high energy. That was mind-blowing!

The following day, I woke up spontaneously around 5:00 a.m., hearing the sounds of Swami Bhaktananda’s mantra chanting. It was Navaratri, the celebration of Divine Mother and all of her aspects over nine nights. I was staying at Swami’s home (which was where he created a Datta Tapovan temple within his former garage – simply amazing). There were not many people visiting the temple that early in the morning and I just sat there, enjoying the energy. A little earlier, I received a WhatsApp message from one of our friends in the UK who messaged that he was in the hospital and would greatly appreciate a long-distance Mai-Tri session. While in the beautiful energy of Swami’s chanting, I passed on the energy to this friend. All of a sudden, I felt an immense presence around and above me. It was intense and gigantic. I connected to Mohanji’s consciousness and looked through my third eye – I realized this was none other than Mother Kali. This was my first experience with this fierce, super-powerful aspect of Divine Mother.

Gigantic Mother Kali was lowering her big golden sword right onto me. My mind went blank as I was simply witnessing her pierce me with that mighty sword, which passed right through my crown, all the way down to my perineum. She then wrenched it a bit as if to create more space within my central axis. After some time, she pulled the sword out.

This was yet another experience of something I never knew was possible. My mind was completely silent for a while. I just sat there in awe. I noticed that my meditations improved thereafter, along with the flow of energy through my central axis. And I was filled with sudden love for her! I have loved Mother Kali so much ever since. For somebody from Europe, used to relating to the compassionate and loving Mother Mary as Divine Mother, this was a highly uncommon and very illogical experience. Yet, in the realm of awareness and love, no boundaries imposed by the mind exist. After this experience, I loved Mother Kali's fierceness, especially her ability to conquer and destroy any demonic, manipulative shadow energy. Nothing is impossible for the great Mother Kali.

Little did I know that this was only the beginning of Mother Kali's blessing and presence in my life. My birthday in November 2017 was another powerful turning point marked by Mother Kali's blessings. I will never forget this birthday. Mohanji was to arrive in a week, which meant that the final decision about our marriage would be made. I did my best to elevate my frequency but, in all honesty, I was not sure what else I could do to pass this unique exam.

There was one event with Jan Esmann, a very modest Spiritual Master from Denmark who does "nothing" but deliver individual shaktipat to people for hours, while others sit in silence and await their turn. I came to know about him from our friend Milan from Belgrade, who shared with me a text about Jan's profound inner experience with the Divine. I was in a coffee bar reading this text when I suddenly felt the familiar waves and sensations in the spine (Kundalini experience) – in the midst of a noisy coffee bar! I shared this with Mohanji, and he said that since my Kundalini had responded, there must be something in there for me. Since I was busy with so many of our spiritual activities, the proposition of sitting somewhere in silence for six hours in a row actually sounded really attractive. That event coincided with my 40th birthday, and I decided to treat myself by sitting in silence for six hours and focusing on the Divine.

Towards the very end of this event, while the group energy was immense after so many hours of deep meditation, I was the last one to receive Shaktipat from Jan. He wanted to end the event with 15 min of pure silence, but the moment I returned to my seat, I suddenly felt a strange energetic push from the back of my neck. This happened several times. Whenever I felt that push, I would lean forward a bit and open my mouth. This was really odd, to say the least. I connected to Mohanji's consciousness and asked to see why I was feeling this. At this moment, I clearly saw/sensed Mother Kali, and got a brief telepathic message that I should chant Maha Bhadrakali Mantra (a beautiful mantra that I learned some time back when I first visited Skanda Vale Ashram in the UK). That is why my mouth kept opening – I was supposed to chant.

I have no words to convey how weird it felt to get up, approach Jan, and whisper into his ear, "I apologize to interrupt, but I felt a strong pull to chant something in honor of Divine Mother." Behind me was a hall full of people, mainly people I didn't know. Everyone was seated in pin-drop silence. I got up only because I trusted my intuition that was telling me to do as Mother Kali said. In his casual style, Jan just said "Ok."

My voice broke the perfect silence as I started chanting this mantra. It soon became unusually strong, deep, and clear, and the power behind it was immense. A huge energy descended upon all present – it felt as if a big tent of powerful energy simply fell on our heads. After all the silence, we suddenly had all sorts of sounds in the room – crying, breathing loudly, sniffing, blowing their noses, etc. It was really intense – a huge collective cleansing and release. Some were blissed out, enveloped in Grace, while others went through a huge cleansing. Needless to say, I was amazed. Jan said briefly, "Mother always responds."

After this experience, I engaged in a casual chat with Jan that soon revealed another reason why I was meant to meet him. He mentioned something about a young sadhu appearing to him in his vision several times. He gave Jan a powerful technique "Hong – Sau" with clear instructions on how to focus on the central axis while chanting Hong-Sau. This sadhu told Jan that the Hong-Sau mantra is the essence of Kashmir Shaivism and Shiva-Shakti sutras and would help many people. This is why he had been asked to share it with all the serious, dedicated spiritual seekers he knew. However, since Jan is pretty introverted, he felt a bit shy talking to people about this mantra and kind of sat on it. He said that sadhu had appeared to him again and scolded him. The moment I heard this, I thought, "This sounds like Shirdi Sai Baba." However, since he said "young sadhu," I was unsure and held my tongue.

To my great amazement, a man from Belgrade had a similar thought and showed Jan a photo of Shirdi Sai Baba as a young sadhu (included in the photo section), asking, "Was this the one you saw?"

Jan looked at the photo and said, "Yes, that's him." All of us marveled at this, amazed by Baba's leela. With Jan's permission and Baba's blessing, I am doing my part in spreading this mantra/technique among the people I know. I have also included it in the preparatory techniques before Awakening Yoga Nidra and Group Mai-Tri sessions. I am happy to share it unconditionally with anyone keen to learn it. It is very simple yet amazingly powerful. I have found that it perfectly complements my Consciousness Kriya practice (Hong-Sau can be done at any time of the day, for any amount of time). It helps energize and cleanse the central axis, our inner Stairway to Heaven.

Marriage Exam & the Birth of Conscious Dancing

After this amazing birthday, two weeks passed, and Mohanji arrived just in time for the retreat at Bor Lake in southern Serbia. I knew this would be the location at which the final exam that my marriage depended on would take place. Mohanji was mainly very quiet. He said nothing about when he was going to make the final decision, and I did not want to ask. At the Bor Lake retreat, there were 160 people present and the group energy was amazing. I was on the stage most of the time, next to Mohanji, translating his satsangs or conducting morning yoga and meditations.

During one new process that Mohanji introduced, he divided people into several groups and asked them to articulate certain sounds. There was a bit of confusion, so I suddenly felt an inner prompting to stand up and move my arms to kind of help coordinate the waves of these sounds through the entire audience. As I started waving with my hands, strangely enough, I felt as if I had more than two of them. There was this strangely powerful energy present throughout the hall, and so many people from the audience felt it. I intuitively recognized the mighty vibe of Mother Kali. "Oh wow, again!" I thought. I was zapped by the experience.

The next day, I conducted Awakening Yoga Nidra for the first time, and Mother Kali's mantra was introduced into the part with the most intense cleansing. I could feel Mother Kali cutting off dark chords connecting some people to heavy energy (the result of jealousy, bad wishes, or curses of other people) and then enveloping them in golden light like small babies. There was a lot of crying, and people received it really well. Many shared their experience of unprecedented intimacy with the Divine and a depth of gratitude that literally transformed them. I was deeply grateful to Mother Kali. (I have to point out that invoking and releasing Mother Kali is always done through the Master; I never do it on my own, and always through Mohanji. Just like the protocol with some heads of state or other VIPs – we can't summon the mighty Mother Kali with the snap of our fingers – there is a protocol to be followed, and Masters would know how to do that most respectfully.)

Toward the end of the Bor Lake Retreat, while casually seated near Mohanji in the living room of the hotel, I suddenly had the idea to add some fun and movement to the retreat. What started as a casual thought, ended up in the actual download of a profound technique of vertical alignment through unstructured dance. I named it Conscious Dancing. During this process, eyes would be semi-closed and while dancing, attention would first go to the seven main chakras, and then to the entire central axis covered with golden light. I intuitively found the right song for each part of Conscious Dancing, and we did it for the first time at the Bor Lake retreat. People were simply blown away! One man said that he had tried ayahuasca, marijuana, and whatnot, but nothing took him into such high energy and bliss as this dancing. "And with no side effects or possible addiction," I added. It was truly amazing. Bliss, bliss, bliss!!! "What a special, super eventful retreat," I thought.

At the very end of the retreat, something really interesting happened. As usual, Mohanji started a spontaneous experience-sharing session by asking people about their impressions of the retreat. After that, he called out the names of key organizers of the retreat to acknowledge and thank them, but he did not mention me. I did not mind that because, as his wife, I did not feel he needed to thank me in the same way as he thanked the volunteers. After all, I had been part of the mission from the beginning; we were on this journey together and I did not care much about these formalities or any recognition. Suddenly, one Serbian woman raised her hand. She was visibly excited and her shaky voice conveyed how emotional she was. I translated for her when she said that she had come for our program for the first time and continued: "I am sorry, but I simply have to say something. Mohanji, the program was amazing, and you have thanked everybody, but I strongly feel that this retreat would not be what it was if it weren't for Devi! [At this point, she became very emotional, choked up by her tears for a moment, and the hand holding the microphone was clearly trembling.] I feel Devi is the one who literally CARRIED this retreat! Without HER, this program would not have been what it was. Such a special contribution has to be acknowledged."

I was touched by the statement of this woman, whom I had never met. My heart expanded, and I cried silently not only because I was touched by her loving words, but because I understood right away what that was – a display of approval of Devi Mohan by the Masters. I just knew that they had arranged for this extra bit of drama to convey that I had passed my exam. I could feel it. Mohanji was smiling and there was no need to say anything about my exam. I also realized that he had been playing this game from the beginning, and that this all had been part of his strategy of drilling and uplifting me.

Indeed, from this retreat onward, I felt that some self-imposed limitations which had previously held me back were removed. I felt free to humbly offer my own contribution to the retreats and the entire Mohanji Foundation platform through my authentic expression. I started my website (devimohan.com) and, aside from conducting processes during retreats with Mohanji, I also began conducting smaller programs of my own, preparing the ground for new people to connect with the vast ocean of Mohanji's consciousness and this beautiful path. Mohanji also conducted several Mohanji Acharya trainings, through which other amazing souls who walk this path with conviction were trained and empowered to conduct his programs. During Mohanji Acharya training, they also got a taste of the drilling and ego bashing that I had gone through over the years, and we shared some unforgettable moments of tears, fun, and great depth of connection.

Illusions

During my stay in Bangalore in late 2017, there was a funny incident involving a supposedly clairvoyant woman who visited Mohanji's house with a Sai devotee we knew somewhat. As usual, a group of Mohanji's devotees from different parts of the globe were also present, and without anyone asking for it, the "psychic" woman started offering her predictions. Since Mohanji does not look favorably upon predictions of the future (preferring surrender, hard work, and assuming responsibility in the present), the receptivity within our group was not very high. Moreover, we could see right away that her psychic abilities required significant refinement.

She was telling one man who had been married for years that she saw him finally getting married, etc. She could not even figure out that I was Mohanji's wife and on top of everything told me that I would need two more lifetimes to attain liberation. After she left, Mohanji looked at me and said with a very serious tone: "You mark my words! [I was already trembling.] At the time when I leave my body, all those who are deeply connected to me, with consistency and surrender, all of them will be greatly elevated. And they will have the chance for complete dissolution. I guarantee you that!"

We were all speechless. Though Mohanji doesn't talk about the future much, he made a promise at that moment, highlighting that this is the path of dissolution. Indeed, this is not an entertaining, feel-good path. It is hardcore and it is surely not for everyone. As Mohanji would say, "I am not here to help you become richer, look younger, or be more comfortable in your life. No. This is a path of dissolution, which is even beyond enlightenment." To reach that point, one needs to start walking the path with conviction and have a consistent connection with the Master, based on free will, conscious choice, and mature commitment.

Global Ambassador

When I look back, I can say in all honesty that slowly but surely, Mohanji kept fulfilling all my dreams and aspirations. I have to admit that I was sometimes a bit sad that, after my extremely rigorous studies at Notre Dame, I never really used my Master's degree for anything. Yoga teaching can be done even by someone with only a high school degree. I felt I was not utilizing my full potential. However, all of that changed in a wink when I got to speak at the Parliament of World's Religions

(PoWR) in Toronto in November 2018. This was a truly historic moment. I did not realize that I would be the first Serbian national and the first woman from Former Yugoslavia to speak at this event: the world's oldest, largest, and most inclusive interreligious and interfaith event, which was slowly growing into a full-fledged international interfaith movement.

Since 1893, when the first Parliament was held in Chicago, till date, this incredible event celebrates the beauty and richness of our diversity. My joy knew no bounds as this was fully aligned with my soul's mission and my education. As the representative of Mohanji Foundation and the experiential spirituality that we stand for, I was truly honored to be part of the event which gave voice to some of the greatest spiritual leaders in the history of humankind: Swami Vivekananda, Nelson Mandela, Dalai Lama, Sri Mata Amritanandamayi, Jane Goodall, etc.

I first learned about the Parliament of World's Religions in June 2018, during the peace event called Peace Pledge, in Assisi, Italy. It was a gathering of about twenty representatives of various spiritual paths and religions. Before the event in Assisi, I was a part of the first leg of the Peace Pledge pilgrimage to Greenland organized by a lovely woman called Brigitte von Baren. I joined an amazing group that included an Inuit leader (whom we lovingly called Uncle) and His Holiness Tai Situ Rinpoche, among others, where we witnessed the magnificent glaciers melting at an incredible rate.

During the peace prayer in Assisi, we had a sacred water ceremony during which the water brought from Greenland, the Ganges, and several other locations was merged. The energy during that event was superb. Mohanji was one of the keynote speakers during the event in Assisi, and was allotted just two or three minutes to convey all that he wanted to say. However, when it was his turn to speak, he asked me to join him and then making only a small intro, handed the microphone over to me. I was deeply touched by his forfeiting his moment of fame so that I could speak instead. Such is the selflessness of Mohanji. During my speech, I referred to my NDE and how deeply touched I was to be in a position of actually serving the Unity by participating in this gathering. All of us had teary eyes and my speech was well-received.

It was at this event that I met Audrey Kitagawa, a Chair-elect of the 2018 Parliament of World's Religions, who was the instrument of my participation at this magnificent event in Toronto, representing Mohanji Foundation. Even though I didn't know much about it, I felt intuitively that this event was very important and that, in some way, it would change my life.

In November 2018, when I arrived in Toronto, I felt an incredibly powerful energy at the gigantic convention center that hosted the Parliament, starting with the Opening Ceremony when one of the representatives of the First Nation (the natives of Canada) spoke. Throughout history, the Native tribes in Canada did not fare any better than the Native Americans, but it was wonderful to see that they had finally started to enjoy the attention, recognition, and respect that they have always deserved. I was proud to be there and witness such steps forward in our shared humanity.

All in all, this event was no lip service to tolerance, nor was it an attempt to place all the eggs into one basket. On the contrary, PoWR was about true respect, recognition, and celebration of our unity in diversity. When we see a field full of beautiful flowers of all colors and shapes, we feel happy and remain in awe of the wondrous beauty of nature. Who would want to see the same flower everywhere? How boring would that be? Nature gives us the message of beauty in diversity all the time.

Remembering Swami Vivekananda and his speech, I gave myself the challenge to let all that I had to say simply flow through me. I challenged myself to show up at the panel at which I was scheduled to speak without preparing any notes. My goal was to effectively express my own truth, based on my personal life experiences and insights.

Towards the end of my speech I said, "I realized that, if we want peace as a supreme energy to descend to earth, it must happen through our spine, through experience-based spirituality. The spine is the path to paradise." And that was the moment when I turned to India and the ancient teachings because they had known that truth all along – the vertical dimension of human existence is the solution for peace. My speech was very well received, which was reflected in the fact that I was the only panelist who was asked additional questions. I dared to speak without notes and confirmed to myself the truth of what I felt deep inside – the heart is always more powerful than the mind.

Meeting Other Saints

On this path, I was blessed to witness some really powerful, historic encounters of Mohanji with other great Masters and Siddhas from India (and other countries). Regardless of how he appeared or whether they had heard of him or not, they would inevitably recognize his spiritual stature (which is far more important than status). I already mentioned how big of a role Devi Amma played in my life and would now like to add how the same applied to Mohanji after I introduced him to her. They became deeply connected through the blessing of the great sage Agastya. This connection became so deep that Mohanji now considers Devi Amma his spiritual mother and all of us feel she is indeed our family.

It is important to share some other key details about Devi Amma. She is considered to be Sage Agastya's daughter in consciousness. Sage Agastya, her spiritual Guru, is the leader and foremost among the Masters of the Siddha tradition (*siddha* means "perfected one"). Sage Agastya was the Guru of Mahavatar Babaji, who is one of the eighteen most prominent Masters of the Siddha Tradition. Devi Amma communes with the Siddhas regularly and is also deeply connected to Sathya Sai Baba.

During one of her meetings with Mohanij, Devi Amma showered him with love through the following words, "The Masters are happy with you and your work. They are happy with the way you are doing things and appreciate your honesty and purity. There is nothing for you to learn. When required, the instructions will come. You have to operate in the world in an unorthodox way (compared to traditional Masters) because you have to reach different kinds of people. Yours won't be the role of a typical Guru. It's more like a friend. Sage Agastya gave you the title Jagat-Mitra, the friend of the world. It was he who first brought you to Earth."

These revelations happened back in 2014, right at the time of the attacks which followed the Kailash yatra. At that time, Devi Amma had a telepathic communion with Sage Agastya, which she shared with Mohanji the next day. "Agastya said 'I'm really proud of Mohanji. He is my son. The reason why this is happening is that I have to remove certain things from him. People are not letting him grow. They're not letting him do his job or progress. And he has a big job to do on Earth. Some of these people are very small-minded, and they're not allowing him to take steps forward.'" We were grateful to Devi Amma for the explanation of why Agastya had to remove such people from Mohanji's path.

After that, Devi Amma asked whether Mohanji had any other lessons to learn. Agastya said, "No lessons for him. He came accomplished in this life, and he has nothing to learn. He only has to reveal, and he will reveal – at his time. They have to learn – the people with him – because he is sent by us to bring people back to the Satya Yuga, to raise their awareness sufficiently to enter into the Satya Yuga frequency. So, it is they who have to learn, not him. And if they can't handle him, it's not his problem. It's their problem."

Somewhere around this time, Mohanji met another saint who confirmed the previous message, and said something more. This saint had communion with Sage Boganathar conveying thus: "Mohanji was one of my students, during the time [Mahavatar] Babaji was studying with me. I had given him everything. He has nothing to learn. He only has to reveal. I will help him to reveal his full stature."

Even though Mohanji is a householder in this lifetime, as his wife I was able to recognize over the years that he indeed is an Avadhoota who lives in a completely detached state. You will never see Mohanji being carried away with emotions or harboring any attachments or resentment.

In December 2015, at the time when the drama with the Shadow Man and German Lady was gaining momentum, we met Ganeshananda Giri – a great Master who was more than 100 years old and lived at the time of Shirdi Sai Baba. Though we had visited Shirdi several times, we never knew he was amongst us. What Grace it was to discover such a jewel in Shirdi.

He lived with Shirdi Baba as a little boy and dedicated his life completely to the service of Sai. While walking toward the location where we would meet this Master, Mohanji told us that the reason why Ganeshananda Giri agreed to meet us, was a telepathic instruction by Shirdi Sai several years earlier that he should meet Mohanji. Ganeshananda Giri had never heard of Mohanji but was searching for him because of this message, eagerly awaiting to meet him. And this was the moment in space and time when this magical encounter would happen.

I felt a strange excitement while walking behind Mohanji. As we came to the street of his hotel, the profile of this saint was visible through the glass entrance to the room in which he sat. I will never forget that first moment when we met him. As we were approaching him from his right side, he did not even turn toward us but said firmly, looking ahead: "Welcome Mohanji!" It was obvious that he didn't need his physical eyes to know that it was indeed Mohanji who was entering his room. It was a truly magical moment. After Mohanji, all of us prostrated at his feet and crammed into the small room to enjoy his presence. The warmth and love we experienced from him were beyond words. He spoke profoundly with a thundering voice. He spoke mainly in Hindi, and I could not wait to get the translation of his words.

I learned that he was supposed to be in the hospital but had refused to go. At the age of 106, Ganeshananda Giri looked much younger. His skin was so soft and he exuded very sweet energy. While talking with a strained voice, he had occasional cough attacks. We tried to tell him that it was OK not to talk, but he could not miss this opportunity for which he had waited so long. At one moment, I felt a deep urge from within to place my hand on the back of his heart chakra and pass on healing energy.

I was shy to ask him and, in the end, decided to ask Mohanji instead. Mohanji explained to me that Ganeshananda Giri did not allow anyone to touch him. After many years, we were probably the first to even touch his feet. But because Shirdi Baba's approval was there, the usual rules did not apply. When Mohanji conveyed my question to Ganeshananda Giri, he agreed that I sit next to him and do the healing. My joy knew no bounds! I had no idea where this desire came from, but I just felt so happy to do the healing and see his cough reduce. I was no longer straining to understand what they spoke in Hindi but completely surrendered to the warm energy that was flowing through my spine and palms. The sacred presence and intense energy coursing through the body were all that mattered.

At one point I felt a powerful heat in my *Ananda Gandha* (a sacred point in the body ideal for healing, in which all the chakras converge) just below the rib cage. It was interesting to note that this powerful, loving heat sensation stayed with me for many hours after we left Ganeshananda Giri (whom we also called Babaji). I smiled and thought, "I wonder who did healing for whom in this scenario." All I knew was that this was a great blessing and a true milestone in my life. I also knew that this great Master did something profound that changed my software. I am forever grateful for this blessing.

Another interesting moment during our second visit to Babaji stayed with me. Mohanji was eager to meet Babaji again and again. He was aware of how precious it was to meet someone like him, and suddenly nothing else mattered as much. We thus went to meet him several times more while in Shirdi. Our visits usually took place early in the morning while Mila was sleeping. One time, when we left Mila with our friend Preethi and her two daughters, after some time they all suddenly joined us and Mila happily jumped into the room still wearing her pajamas. It was so sweet to observe just how much she felt at home in Shirdi and especially how comfortable she was with Babaji. He kept showering her with love and attention.

Mila loved to play games on my cell phone, one of which was an app with Santa who would open various gifts and play pranks. Babaji, who had probably never seen an Android phone before, asked her to show him her favorite game. We suddenly heard the sweetest thundering laugh ever! When Mila showed him how Santa removed his pants and showed "Merry Christmas" on his behind, written on his underwear, Babaji laughed loudly and all of us started laughing to no end. It all felt like the most loving family gathering filled with love and sweetness. How could we ever forget this moment of transcendental love?

That day, when I bowed at his feet, he suddenly asked me: "Do you want bhakti or siddhis?" For a moment I was taken aback by this profound question, and my mind went blank. I have experienced questions of such brevity and intensity before, and knew that it was coming from Shirdi Sai himself. And more so, the question came through a man who is such an amazing example of complete and unshakeable devotion. I also understood that Baba wanted me to reflect deeper on that healing experience. It was as if he had asked: "What is the base on which one should build the healing practice – bhakti or the spiritual power of healing? Be aware that it could also inflate the ego and thus block your progress." All this happened in my inner space within a couple of seconds. With full conviction, my reply was: "Babaji, please bless me with bhakti, for only what we gain through true bhakti is right for us."

After leaving Shirdi and reaching Pune, we came to know that Ganeshananda Giri had been admitted to the hospital. Mohanji arranged that Rajesh Kamath, his personal assistant and one of his closest devotees, stay with Babaji and attend to his needs. I was deeply touched by the beauty of Mohanji's devotion, and felt overwhelming love. We also rearranged our schedule to ensure that we visit him in the hospital. The joy of our family reunion was felt again in Babaji's hospital room. He was lying in the hospital bed but his eyes were beaming so beautifully – he did not look like a sick person at all. Our hearts were melting.

We learned that Shirdi Baba had instructed Ganeshananda Giri that he was to construct one more temple, this time in Chennai, and this would be his last task before earning the blessing of samadhi. Mohanji immediately offered his full help in this endeavor and entrusted Madhu, the CEO of Mohanji Foundation and one of his closest devotees from Chennai, to assist Babaji on his behalf in whichever way possible.

Over time, I have witnessed Mohanji's behavior, attitude, and spontaneous demeanor being nothing short of royal. Even though our income was not at all substantial and hardly even covered our personal requirements, he would act as if there were many people and huge funds at his disposal.

Soon after that, I had a profound experience where it became clear to me that Mohanji had been a king or prince in many of his past lives. Some of the recent living Masters, like Baba Vittalananda Saraswati, recognized Mohanji straight away. As soon as Vittal Babaji saw Mohanji, he said: "A precious diamond, a Raja Yogi," and asked Mohanji to sit next to him in a chair that he otherwise never permitted others to use. He treated Mohanji as an equal, and gave him a silver ring which Mohanji still wears. All those present then were simply in awe of the experience because we had been warned that he was a very stern Master.

The same scenario repeated with another Master from Maharashtra – Gorkhe Guruji. He was known for his strictness, and would sometimes even beat people with a stick (especially politicians). Expecting some wild experiences, we were amazed when Gorkhe Guruji gave Mohanji his seat and said, "You sit here." He then publicly declared, "This is Datta (referring to Lord Dattatreya)." I was also worried that I would mess something up when a puja started, but then Gorke Guruji's wife came and recognized me from the "Foreignchi Patlin" movie, which brought great excitement. So I got the VIP treatment as well, and the entire visit was filled with love and joy.

Interestingly enough, at one point Shirdi Sai Baba telepathically conveyed to Ganeshananda Giri to arrange five-star accommodation for Mohanji. He said it had to be royal. Nobody understood why this was so, and Mohanji himself was surprised to hear this because Babaji always believed in a simple, humble lifestyle. But Masters always have their reasons, which are revealed to us at the right point in time.

In a way, I could see the continuity. Mohanji's demeanor exudes a sense of royalty – his benevolence, which often exceeds his capacity, is one example. His ability to lead people, his straightforwardness, innocence, no-nonsense attitude, etc. are all traits of his character which often hide his spiritual stature, but the saints recognize it right away.

Even though at that point in time, Mohanji did not even have an ashram of his own, I could feel and knew beyond any doubt that everything necessary for this spiritual mission would be coming, and would come at the right point in time. (At present, Mohanji Centers of Benevolence are mushrooming around the globe – Canada, Australia, Serbia, Slovenia, and India. The blockage with ashrams was removed after Shirdi Baba passed on a blessing through the Chief Priest of Shirdi, and asked him to donate land of his own to Mohanji at a prime location, not far from Shirdi airport.) Just as everything is revealed at the right time, everything that is needed for the mission of leading people into liberation will surely be given.

In April 2016, when we came to know that our beloved Ganeshananda Giri had entered samadhi. All that remained was deep gratitude for the chance to meet him and be touched by the Grace that flowed through him. May my bhakti and purity increase ever more to enable me to contain the highest energies and merge with that consciousness when all my duties, responsibilities, desires/karmas, and expressions are hopefully exhausted.

Gurupurnima Blessing

In July 2021, just before our very first Festival of Consciousness was organized in Belgrade, we had a powerful experience with Shirdi Sai Baba during a pada puja to Mohanji. This was exactly 11 years after my first pada puja and the samadhi experience that resulted from touching Mohanji's toe.

Even before the Pada Puja began, I could feel an intense presence and a strong pull to go inward. The pull was so strong that I had to make a very strong effort to remain vigilant and resurface from that depth, opening my eyes while waiting for my turn to participate in the puja. I simply could not miss this golden opportunity!

In that unprecedented inner struggle, I somehow did miss the puja. I was deep in inner bliss when I suddenly heard Mohanji's voice say, "OK, done." When I fully opened my eyes, I saw that the pada puja was indeed finished. Subhashree had begun removing the platter with flowers, turmeric, and other puja items. I felt desperate, on the edge of bursting into tears. I pleaded to Mohanji: "Please, can I do it as well? I thought more people wanted to do it. How come it is already over?" He tested my faith a bit, mumbled something about me dragging my feet, and then finally agreed.

My heart was beating fast and my head was heavy from the immense energy. I washed Mohanji's feet with utmost care and placed the yellow and red powders and flower petals on them with utmost care. Then I simply surrendered, once again placing my forehead on his big toe. At that moment, I felt a HUGE PORTAL open above my head – a portal to higher consciousness and purest Grace. I surrendered at its doorstep without a trace of doubt. The Guru's feet truly are the entry point to the highest realms of consciousness. They are tangible, they are real, and they are precious, making the impossible possible, making the unreachable actually reachable to us.

With a heart filled with love, I sat on my pillow on the ground and could finally let go and surrender to the force sucking me inward, letting the mighty inner river carry me wherever it wanted. At that moment, Shirdi Baba spoke through Mohanji with an intensity, love, clarity, and depth far beyond the words I am about to share:

> "What is a Guru? What are you celebrating? Without knowing clearly, it is not a celebration, it's a mechanical action. What do mechanical actions give you? No result. You just had an activity, but no transformation. Many people connect to a Guru without having a clue why they are connecting.
>
> "Some of you just did aarti. You burned camphor. All of you have camphor inside you. Guru is a lit camphor. What happens when unlit camphor comes close to lit camphor? It catches fire. Like that, everyone is Guru material – nobody is lesser and nobody is higher.
>
> "But what is preventing the lighting of your camphor? Either you are not close enough to light the fire, or there is something in between that prevents that fire from catching. Many times, it is the latter. What comes in between? Patterns. Our habitual patterns. Doubts. Usual anxieties, fears, and insecurities connected to patterns. Then you fail to see the lit camphor. You just see the person, the man, the human being, which completely eclipses the state he is in.
>
> "Now a different question – what is a Guru? The material of your aspiration. Which aspiration? To be lit camphor. To be enlightened. To be complete. To be fulfilled. To be expansion, not limitation. That's the Guru. But if you don't achieve that by connecting to a Guru, what are you doing? You are doing nothing. Do you think practices will get you there? No way. Practices are a discipline. Practices are for alignment. A disciplined action for the sake of alignment. That's good of course because without discipline you cannot progress. That's for sure. But, a mechanical activity never takes you there.
>
> "It takes time to become 'dry wood' that catches fire. It requires a lot of sunshine. It is painful. All the emotions and all the things which brought you to Earth, repeatedly, lifetime after lifetime, should become completely dry.
>
> "It's not a boring thing. You experience extraordinary freedom, where you need nothing from Earth. Otherwise, all positions are binding, all possessions are binding, and all relations are binding. Everything is binding. So how do you come out of this? That's when you look at a person who has already come out of it. As an aspiration.

"But please understand. You are unlit camphor – the same material which is lit in a Guru is already sitting inside of you. All it takes is one spark. It doesn't take much effort – when you bring camphor to the fire, it just catches fire. But this camphor should reach the fire in order to catch the fire.

"Usually we don't allow it. By the time it comes closer – oh, old habits, old patterns, they pull you back. What pulls you back? Habits. Patterns. Fears. Confusions. Phobias. Doubts. They take you back. They keep bringing you back. And then, what do you get? Another lifetime of the same patterns, the same thing repeated, over and over again.

"So Guru Purnima is the day when aspirations can have actualization. What is the aspiration? To be free. Simple. Free from what? This binding cycle of birth and death is connected to patterns that bring you back.

"Every Guru's aspiration is to make others reach the same stature. I can only share what I am with you. I cannot share something else. So, when you go to many doors and knock, but don't enter, nothing happens. Knocking is happening, activity is happening, but nowhere you are entering! Until you have entered, you don't get food. Only if you go inside and sit down at the table will you get food.

"If you have clarity, you can get lit. Lit camphor sometimes does not seem like anything. You have to come closer to see they are lit. And to understand, to recognize that, you have to spend time. That's why in Prashna Upanishad, when disciples approached the Master with the question, 'Can you show me God?' the Master said: 'You stay with me for a year. And if you like me and I like you, we will work to find God together.'

"Consistency. Consistency is very, very, important! If there is no consistency, there is no transformation. And sometimes transformation comes much later, like a bamboo shoot. Bamboo, when it's planted, it takes about 5 years to grow a couple of inches. And then it grows rapidly, all of a sudden! It's not like it grows a bit more every year. Sometimes you don't see growth. But something is happening inside. So what you need is consistency."

At this point during this satsang, already sucked into my inner space for a while, enjoying the indescribable bliss of the samadhi state I was blessed to experience once again, all of a sudden the radiant face of Shirdi Sai Baba appeared right in front of me – it was so clear, so intense. I had already felt his presence during the satsang, but now I could also see his face clearly. (Again, he did not wear his usual head cover and looked exactly like in his original photo included in the photo section.)

He was looking straight into my eyes! His piercing eyes were like two transcendental rays, so incredibly intense. There was no "I" to hold back – my awareness was expanded in all directions, so blissful, so empty, so light...

Baba's eyes became even more expressive as he started speaking to me telepathically. At the same moment, those words were given voice somewhere above (or around) my head – through Mohanji's words. This was such a special and unique experience! In the depth of my samadhi, Baba was looking at me, speaking to me. At the same time in a space that felt very far away, somewhere up above, on the surface, Mohanji was uttering the exact same words through his mouth:

> "God is presence! Sun is presence. Soul is presence. Understand – Guru is PRESENCE!
>
> "Guru does nothing. Don't think that Guru does something for you. He does nothing. But Guru's presence lights you up. This is what happens.
>
> "The sun is not doing anything for you, is it? But the sun's presence makes the Earth function. Electricity does nothing for you. But when the electricity comes, lights come. You understand? God is the same. God is not doing anything in particular for the Universe. God's presence makes the Universe alive. You see? Soul's presence makes this body alive. GURU'S PRESENCE makes your PURPOSE ALIVE.
>
> "So don't think that Guru is doing something for you. He doesn't do your karmic laundry. He has his own laundry to clean. Your karmic laundry is your problem. But Guru brings sufficient light so that you know that you have karmic laundry.
>
> "My job is to shake you up. Your job is to stabilize. So my job is not to stabilize you – my job is to shake you up. And in this shake-up, you should stabilize. Then nobody can shake you. Eventually, you become unshakable.
>
> "The moment you realize God is Presence, you will feel God. The moment you realize the soul is the Presence, you will start experiencing and enjoying life. Because when the soul goes, life doesn't exist."

This was such a powerful message from Baba, through beloved Mohanji – I could not complete this book without including the immense blessing these words bring.

Closing the Circle

Finally, I would like to close the circle of my experience-sharing with the Master with whom I started the journey – Mahavatar Babaji. In 2021, Mohanji conducted a retreat at the Bosnian Pyramids in Visoko, near Sarajevo. This is where a complex of huge pyramids was discovered by Dr. Semir (Sam) Osmanagić, which includes the tallest pyramid currently known to the public, the Pyramid of the Sun. Dr. Osmanagić explained that pyramids were never tombs but powerful energy generators. Many revelations await those who visit the mighty Bosnian Pyramids. It has become our tradition since 2016 to conduct a program at the pyramids at least once a year. In the Ravne tunnels, the deeper one goes, the fresher and more pleasant the energy becomes. At some point, the energy becomes so fresh that one feels that breathing happens through the skin instead of the nose.

During one of the previous years, Mohanji pointed out to Dr. Osmanagić one particular stone where he felt the strongest energy. They brought some equipment down and did the necessary measurements – sure enough, the stone was shown to have some unusual energy, and they named it the "Mohanji Stone." They placed a board with Mohanji's silhouette next to it, explaining how this special Mohanji Stone was discovered.

As per what had become our tradition, Mohanji would deliver shaktipat on the last day of the retreat at the Bosnian Pyramids, within the tunnel Ravne, not far from the Mohanji Stone. There was a long line of people awaiting the shaktipat, and I noticed that nobody was sitting on Mohanji Stone. "That is such a pity," I thought. I loved sitting on that stone and meditating. Every time I did that, I would inevitably start feeling my Kundalini. Since the line was long, I put on my headphones, started the vertical Consciousness Kriya breathing, and listened to the Mahatapa mantra that Mohanji received from Mahavatar Babaji, which was recorded by our friend Judith from Switzerland during the COVID lockdown. This was when we got direct confirmation that Mahatapa is one of the names of Mahavatar Babaji, the name he uses in Shambhala or Gyanganj. (I have recorded several episodes on this topic of great Babaji and the Masters of Shambhala, which are available on my Devi Mohan Podcast. I highly recommend them to all who are interested in this topic.)

As I did the Kriya and listened to the Mahatapa mantra, I entered into one of the most powerful samadhi states thus far. My awareness expanded throughout the tunnel Ravne and beyond. The mighty presence of Babaji was felt, but I could not see him. At some point, I connected to Mohanji through my third eye, and for the first time, I entered Mohanji and became one with him. The power of that presence, that mighty energy, cannot be explained in words. Before me, flowing through me, I saw two golden streams. Later on, I came to know that Mohanji was delivering Shaktipat with both hands, which explained that vision.

My mind was completely still, but at one point, Babaji conveyed to me telepathically that he was not revealing his face to me because Mohanji is my Guru, and one's Guru is all the Gurus. This was such a powerful message. On the physical plane and horizontal time, two hours had passed, Shaktipat was over and most of the people had already exited the tunnels in preparation for the satsang with Mohanji in the nearby hall. Someone touched my shoulder and informed me it was time to go. It was not easy to come out of such a deep state, but I did try several times. Two of our volunteers stayed with me to accompany me to the hall. I suddenly got an urge to release some emotional blockage and knew I could not do that silently. Crying turned into loud sobbing, but this blockage simply had to be released. After that, I felt greatly relieved and truly blissed out. My spine was super hot all the time, and this altered state continued for another couple of hours. I could sense many things in people, and all around me.

When I reached the hall, I sat next to one young gentleman from Montenegro whose Kundalini was activated, and I could feel it. Mohanji called Dr. Osmanagić on stage and aside from the speech, that day he took us on an inner journey through guided meditation – to my great amazement, we journeyed to the Great Central Sun, which is my home, Sirius. I knew this was Babaji's leela and simply enjoyed this experience to the maximum.

When we reached our hotel room, I felt a need to lie down for just a bit. I was completely knocked out, just as I had been years before in Rome, after the conscious astral encounter with Babaji. I slept for 12 hours straight! Mohanji's personal assistant Christopher saw me in the same position (all dressed, with my mala around the neck and make-up intact) that evening and the following morning, which surely made him wonder what was going on with me. The only thought I had after getting up was, "Wow!"

George, one of Mohanji's core volunteers from the US, had snapped some photos in the tunnels and showed me one of me with my eyes rolled up in shambhavi mudra. It is not a very pretty photo, but it is very close to my heart because it is a reminder of this powerful experience through which Babaji extended his powerful blessing once again.

I was also reminded of the powerful blessing of Jupiter visible in my natal chart. A lovely lady, Lea Imširagić from Belgrade, once analyzed my natal chart. After the initial glance, she called me to offer an extra hour of reading free of cost. She said that this would be her contribution to our spiritual mission.

I was amazed to hear her words, "In my entire career as an astrologer, I never saw Exalted Jupiter in the natal chart of husband, wife, and child – all three. This is truly remarkable! Only through many lifetimes of purity and selfless service does one earn the blessing of exalted Jupiter in the natal chart. No matter what your other karmas may be, the protective umbrella of Jupiter will always be there. I can see that you as a family have a huge, global mission of serving humanity." This touched my heart. She also said that Mohanji and I are "two engines of the same vehicle." While his task is to vertically download the highest of knowledge – profound knowledge otherwise inaccessible to the human mind, my task is to spread it horizontally (through the work of our foundation, many teams, and volunteers) and make it accessible to people. While I feel there are many other volunteers within Mohanji Foundation who invest more hours and energy in spreading the teachings of Mohanji, I do hope this book is a mighty step in that direction.

Regarding Mila, she once told me, "My mission starts at the age of sixteen." I allow our beloved Mila to enjoy her childhood and discover her talents and soul's mission on her own. Mohanji and I love her unconditionally and convey the same key message to her that we convey to everyone else – just BE YOU.

I will never forget when Mila attracted the attention of the then-President of India, Ram Nath Kovind, during his visit to Slovenia in September 2019. Out of the blue, Mohanji informed me that the President of India was scheduled to arrive in Slovenia the following day. He suggested that Mila and I go to greet him with a copy of our book Kailash with Mohanji — the Inner Kora as a welcoming gift.

My mind immediately construed the scene of hundreds of people gathering to see the Indian President and the two of us trying to elbow our way through with that book. My initial response was "Yeah, right." I would have definitely laughed that idea off if it wasn't Mohanji who had proposed it. After having seen so many miracles and impossible events made possible by Mohanji, I decided to do as he had suggested. As Mohanji would always say, "Just make yourself available and surrender the rest to the Divine." At the last minute, I managed to pick Mila up from school, drive to Ljubljana, the capital of Slovenia, luckily get the last copy of the book from our friend Amina, and then rush to the location where the Indian President was scheduled to be.

To my great surprise, no crowd had gathered; there were only security guards and the Indian Ambassador with his wife. Since I had a bit of experience with official government protocols from my UN days, I decided to locate the person in charge and explain my intention. "Do not even think about it during the main event — the inauguration of the bench of friendship," she said. "After that main event, when the President is walking back to his car, you could possibly give it a try. If willing, he will stop. Otherwise, forget it."

The surprises continued when the entire "main event" lasted only a couple of minutes — the cars arrived, the Indian President and his wife walked toward the bench, snapped a photo, shook hands, and two minutes later, they were already walking back to the car. I glanced at the lady who gave me a nod of approval. Mila and I sprang into action, walking briskly toward the President. It felt funny to break the silence by saying, "Excuse me, Mr. President…"

I introduced myself briefly, saying that I was married to an Indian national, and that (gesturing to Mila) this lovely young girl was our daughter. He glanced at us from the corner of his eye and stopped the moment he noticed Mila, a 100% Indian-presenting child in Slovenia. The moment he smiled and patted Mila's head, more than a dozen video and photo cameras suddenly popped out of nowhere in front of us, clicking and flashing like crazy. I explained that Mila was the only child of Indian ancestry and the only vegetarian in her school, and that oftentimes it was not easy being so different. He said, "Well done, dear child, you are building bridges between nations."

This was an incredibly sweet and exciting moment. I handed over the Kailash Yatra book to the President, and wished him a pleasant stay and a safe journey back to India. Later on, I came to know that our photo with President Ram Nath Kovind was on display at the Indian Embassy in Ljubljana. When I shared this exhilarating experience with Mohanji, he told me, "Well done! You have no idea that in India, even billionaires cannot get an audience with the President. And see how easily you got through. Such are the blessings of our Tradition."

I had no doubt that it was the sweetness and light that Mila carried in her smile that caught the eye of the President of India. We live at a time when children of higher frequency are to become the key change-makers in our world. May we be blessed with many spiritually elevated couples who are blessed to bring such mighty souls to Earth – souls that will help us transform our world as we shift into the new age. I always feel great joy when I see loving, spiritual couples who enter their relationship with the flame of dedication to a higher purpose alive in their hearts.

Speaking of closing the circle, there is one more experience that beckons to be shared. During the Empowered Five program with Mohanji that took place in October 2022 in beautiful Zlatibor (meaning "golden pine tree") in Serbia, I received the rarest of blessings which, as always, was unexpected and arrived in a unique way.

Mohanji guided us through a powerful process of uninterrupted deep meditation for five days in a row. This was the first time we meditated all day long, witnessing our thoughts and doing specific breathing, with the exhalation being two times longer than the inhalation. The energy within the hall was like a woman's womb – we loved being in that hall and sitting in silence. Every day we increased the count, and on the last day, I had an experience I will never forget.

On the inhale, I traveled up the spine and while fixating my inner gaze upward I noticed Mohanji's third eye above my head. I understood that his third eye was a portal into higher dimensions. With every next inhalation, I would come a bit closer to that portal. I kept doing that super-focused breathing until I finally reached and passed through the portal. At that very moment, everything became white, spacious, and ephemeral. I looked further up through my inner vision, and at that moment I sensed/saw the huge presence of Divine Mother. Her head was covered with a white scarf and leaning just a bit to the left, and her most blissful face was indeed "wider than the Heavens."

My next vision was of a silver third hand that miraculously appeared on the icon of Divine Mother in the Serbian Orthodox Church. It is called "Bogorodica Trojeručica." I suddenly felt that both of my hands became silver and super heavy, each weighing hundreds of pounds. These heavy palms were pressing against my thighs, and at the same time, my central axis had an intense flow, while some other sensations were occurring on my face (as if it was getting slightly reshaped). All of this was very intense and required great surrender.

At some point, Mother showed me the shape of my wedding ring and gave clear instructions on how to pass on her blessing to couples who choose to serve a higher purpose. This was unexpected, and I was initially really shy to share it, but over time slowly started to extend this blessing of Divine Mother through her palms which I invoke into mine. The energy during this "Blessing of the Couples" process is very unique and truly special. I look forward to extending my contribution to all such couples on Mother Earth with whom my path will cross and to whom I will be blessed to pass on the energy. When the inner compass is directed toward a higher purpose, the events of life rearrange for everyone's greatest good.

However, if a husband and wife do not allow each other the freedom to be (and over the years become) their highest expression, that marriage is bondage, devoid of a higher, spiritual dimension rooted in the higher purpose of that soul's journey.

In the case of Mila and myself, I must say that Mohanji does not give us any special privileges. We never get pampered. On the contrary, he always raises the bar higher in the terms of our responsibilities and the values that we are meant to live. It is not easy to be Mohanji's wife or Mohanji's child. Responsibilities are many and vigilance is always needed. It is a tall order, but we are doing our best. On this path, we don't get special privileges in terms of monetary benefits either. On the contrary, I have signed a legal document in which I have agreed that all that Mohanji earns during his life, in terms of property, money, etc. will be equally shared by all people who decide to dedicate their lives to our global platform. This is a royal path after all, but royalty comes with the realization that all we need is within, that everything that we desire is indeed already within. True royalty and true richness can only be found in selfless service. This is our truth.

Conclusion

Just a Drop

There is so much to see and experience in this world through our senses. All of it is great fun – for a while. Yet, sooner or later, we remember and recognize at a deeper level that the true ocean of experience lies within, rooted in truth, consciousness, and bliss. Without the light of consciousness, we are slaves to the pendulum of emotional ups and downs and ruled by expectations and disappointments, and repeating patterns in the mind's chase after fame and possessions. All these distractions come with a heavy gravitational pull, leading to bondage.

Can freedom from such bondage be as simple as the act of switching on the light? I do hope that all I have shared in this book has brought the realization behind this question closer to the light of your awareness. Being in the company of saints and Masters brings us so much closer to that inner switch, provided we are ready to recognize them, ready to surrender and let go of the reins held by ego.

Painful experiences of life serve one grand purpose – they create a crack in the hard shell of ego and help us direct our gaze toward what truly matters in life. One of the greatest compliments I have ever received was on the streets of Shirdi in 2019, when a saint I happened to meet told me, "I was just sitting here, witnessing the river of busy minds passing me by. But you were able to notice me in this crowd because you are cracked." I loved it! Being "cracked" is an achievement that may not look good on our résumé, but is crucial in terms of true success in life – our awakening in consciousness.

Only when we are freed from the slavery of ego's endless pretensions and formalities can we expand into the reality of the inner ocean of Unity Consciousness. When we step into our power by choosing to act from the sacred temple of the heart, with the purest of intentions and unconditionality of love, is when we allow the ocean to act through us. Such is our majestic and divine nature. One of the greatest pearls of wisdom I have ever heard comes from the 13th-century Persian poet Rumi, who said it all in only a couple of words: "You are not a drop in the ocean; you are the ocean in a drop." Only one who has experienced that ultimate expansion can say something so profound.

However, under the guise of false humility, our society and the institutions that shape our perception of I-ness, force us into the perception that we are just one tiny speck on the vast canvas of the Divine. The powerful words of Rumi, a man whose every word was a worship of the Sacred Feminine seated on the throne of his heart, flip that restricted view onto its head. We are the entire canvas, the paintbrush, and the hand that holds it. We embody all of it the moment we stop identifying with the ego and open up to manifesting the Divine.

I dare to say that the suppression of the Sacred Feminine is the festering collective wound of separation. All of us are harmed by the masculine dominance in the patriarchy. It beckons to be transformed for the benefit of all men and women, our children, and our Mother Earth. The time has come to undergo that change, individually and collectively. My humble contribution as an authentic contemporary woman is to simply be me. This is the essence of what Mohanji taught me through his simple and profound message: “Be You.” I am aware that, by being me, I become that drop that reveals the power of the ocean in all of us – through acknowledging and surrendering to the inclusive, nurturing, and creative power of the Sacred Feminine, which in turn brings out and honors the Sacred Masculine.

As the entire ocean is contained within the drop, the real possibility of multidimensional worlds resides inside of each one of us – and yes, we are capable of creating from that space. Not only is the Universe abundant, but each one of us individually is abundant. This abundance is one of the pearls on the majestic necklace bestowed upon those who honor the eternal Sacred Feminine presence and principle. This powerful truth reveals that we are capable of what we desire and much beyond that. We are capable of what we are destined for – completion and self-actualization, as individuals and as a collective. The experience and qualities of the Golden Age are ours to claim.

God and Guru – One of Us

After deep retrospection of my life’s dream and my relationship with Mohanji, I concluded that it was unconditionality that made our love much deeper, stronger, and more profound. When we give unconditionally, our true nature is revealed to us in its full glory – as a tangible Presence, a living flame that can only go upward, as the Light beyond the dichotomy of light and shadow. May this unconditionality, symbolized by the wedding ring that manifested in my life, inspire many more couples to join in a sacred union for a higher purpose and serve together, as one.

The fact that Mohanji belongs to the world and I cannot own him never made me the slightest bit insecure; it only reinforced the truth behind our relationship – a truly divine purpose and a cosmic necessity. Mohanji is a powerhouse of purest energy, love, and endless inspiration. What I love the most about him is that he never wanted me to be in the shadow of his greatness and global fame that developed naturally over the years. He always kept bringing out and supporting my authentic expression – the true Devi. Unlike the quiet, introverted, but super powerful Mohanji, I have always been an easily approachable people’s person – joyful, in the flow, recognizable through my laughter, dance, and spontaneous expressions of love. No matter how tough the blows of my life have been, I somehow just danced through them all. The flow showed me the way – the feminine way.

This energy reflects in my life’s work – the processes for deep transformation combined with social service. The bridging of the East and West and offering a union of different approaches to realizing one’s highest expression and purpose is evident in all aspects of my life. I am always reminded of the thundering words of the great Shirdi Sai Baba during one special moment in Muscat, in 2010, soon after we got married. He spoke to me through Mohanji, beaming his unique intensity through

Mohanji's eyes which were fixated on me when he said: "You have now married Mohanji. But have you married his consciousness?" Through that powerful question, Baba conveyed the highest of messages.

One of my favorite songs ever is "One of Us" by Joan Osborne, in which she says: "What if God was one of us? ...Just a stranger on the bus, tryin' to make his way home?" The very idea that God is not aloof, seated in some faraway Heaven, but could be walking among us as a most-humble being, simply making the journey home, was intriguing, to say the least. Walking through life with Mohanji, whom I see as a true embodiment of the Divine, right here by my side, makes me relate to this song ever more deeply.

It was initially such a challenge for me to recognize Mohanji as my Guru when we shared the same bed and toilet, and spoke about common things, among all other topics. It is a natural human tendency to place the Divine on a pedestal or to frame a picture and worship it, projecting our notions onto it. But recognizing a living Master next to me and coping with the speed at which he moves was the greatest challenge that brought the highest of rewards.

I consider myself extremely blessed, in this lifetime and others, to be casual and joke around with the greatest of divine incarnations such as Jesus Christ and Shirdi Sai Baba, and to now enjoy the same privilege with Mohanji. Please note that I am not equating Jesus, Baba, and Mohanji in terms of stature, status, or in any other way. For Christians, Jesus remains the one and only Son of God and the pathway to God. For sincere Shirdi Sai devotees, Baba is the only one (although with a notably less dogmatic point of view). For me, in this lifetime, the Divine has come in such a unique way - as my husband and my Guru, Mohanji.

In India, any true devotee or dedicated disciple will say that the Guru and God are one. This does not make a Godman out of a human but stems from a deep realization that one's stable, tangible, and life-transforming connection with the Source (God, Allah, Parabrahma, etc.) is through the Guru. The power of this connection transcends all boundaries, even that of life and death. A true devotee has nothing to do but maintain the strength and purity of their connection to the Guru – the rest is in the hands of the Divine.

Mohanji once shared an example from the Datta Tradition to which we belong – the example of a baby monkey hanging upside down and holding tight to his mother as she jumps from one branch to another. My dear friend Berislava, a lovely spiritual artist whom I met in Dubai, once shared her own example of the same concept: "Mohanji is like a rocket. Just hold on to him, and he will take you as high as you ever needed to go." To date, this remains the most beautiful example of the Guru-Disciple relationship in my inner vision.

A disciple's connection to their Guru is like a simple rope. When the rocket takes off, this single rope means everything. Maintaining and nurturing the purity and sanctity of one's connection to the Guru, making that rope so strong that nothing can break it, has to be the main focus of a disciple's life. Regardless of where the rocket goes, to which galaxy and dimension, regardless of how tough or blissful the journey may be, or whether others support or ridicule it, one must only focus on the strength of that rope.

Unity and Love

One of the main reasons behind my decision to share the account of my past life regression in this book was to show that Jesus lived among and as one of the common people, the only difference was that he was awakened in consciousness, aware of the truth that he is the embodiment of purest of love and one with Father in that love. All he had to do, and all he could do, was to radiate the frequency of that truth and hold the mirror to others. As Jesus said and showed throughout his life, the greatest commandment is TO LOVE. Love is always the answer. Everything I am today is rooted in love and the service of Unity.

When it comes to unity, what I have realized over the years is that this precious word belongs to the realm of consciousness, not the realm of the mind. This is why true unity inevitably welcomes and honors diversity. Unity does not mean that we should all believe in one religion, converting people from their respective religions that run in their blood and that of their ancestors. No such conversions should ever be done for the sake of someone's idea of unity. Absolutely not.

Unity comes with the maturity of understanding that there is a golden thread, a common denominator that connects all the religions of the world. And that common denominator is unconditional love, selfless service, non-violence (at the level of intention, thought, word, and action) as well as dharma, the innermost feeling of righteousness that we all have, which includes our sacred duty towards our family, society, Mother Earth, and all the souls of any species that come in contact with us. One should never miss the opportunity to express those highest values which are nothing but children of love. This is the way for all of us to unite in the same celebration of the Divine.

Those who find greatest joy in sharing pure love, without any conditions or expectations, walk in the steps of the saints and Masters. This is especially true when we love those who do not love us. At that moment, we who drink from the Source of all remembrance remember their truth for them and invite the same light into their hearts. This is the truth I witnessed when I invoked the golden ball into the heart of the angry Albanian man who was about to attack me.

The same light of love that we project onto others can also illuminate our own inner world. To come out of depression, lethargy, and low self-esteem, one just needs to engage in selfless, loving action, and that energy will immediately trickle down to the level of words, thoughts, and feelings. This is how the transformation happens, and this is why charitable deeds and selfless service have always been the main golden thread that connects all religions and spiritual paths.

May this autobiography be yet another act of service from my side, aimed at those who want to seek the highest in this life but need just a bit of nudge, just a bit of inspiration and encouragement to make that first crucial step, daring to ask that special something from the Universe, whatever it may be. The very fact that you have had the patience to read this long sharing means that you are thirsty and that you are ready to take the plunge. Just go for it!

Only the Beginning

It has been a tremendous honor and pleasure to have you join me on this journey of sharing my most intimate truths, harrowing heartbreaks, and all the immense experiences on my path home. Indeed, the pure consciousness that Mohanji and the Masters embody is the HOME that the refugee in me had always been seeking. In a way, all of us are refugees – having forgotten our original home, the womb of the Divine, and identifying with the earthly plane, making us all walk the same challenging journey Home.

This book has been writing me as well, not just the other way around. It has helped me to realize that the real journey has just begun. I can now freely say that through daring to rise above the circumstances of my life, pulling myself from my comfort zones, and choosing the Truth above all else during every test of life, I have finally stepped fully into the shoes of Devi.

Having shared only the most integral experiences of my life, the pages of this book have reached a number that I had never anticipated. Still, I have realized that on a more subtle level of existence, "Part Two" of my life story is already being written. If the Divine gives that familiar nudge, I shall bring it forth as an earthly expression, humbly offering another book to cover in detail the beautiful experiences and astonishing blessings that could not fit within these pages. Till then, I hold you in the light as family – for all of us, indeed, share the same Home.

May the final words of this book express my highest truth - only Love is real.

—Devi Mohan

Acknowledgements

Writing this book amid my hectic life (that involves frequent travel and many roles within our global platform) took forever. I simply couldn't dedicate enough time to invest my heart and soul as deeply and intimately as this book deserved. "Writing this book is like delivering a child," I recently joked with a friend. Well, I must say that two main *doulas* (spiritual midwives) and many dear friends supported this delivery and deserve mentioning.

The two main doulas from the US who supported this book's unique delivery were dear Aariyah Kaur and Geeta Iyer. Because of their subtlety and utmost dedication, they walked with me through every step and made completing it all possible. Aariyah held my hand through all the phases of this book-writing journey, including the initial steps taken years ago. During the toughest of contractions of the second half of the book writing, when the progress I made seemed too slow to complete the book within the given deadline, Aariyah calmed me down, offering precious words of encouragement at the height of pressure. I must say that Aariyah's talent in tweaking the words just a bit to bring out the true beauty of the English language, while preserving the flavor of my original expression, is truly remarkable. I couldn't have found a better editor than my Divine-sent Aariyah.

Dear Geeta joined us just a bit later, with a humble offer to check the minutest grammar details. Geeta's dedication and patience in going through the long pages of my book with her microscopic precision, that too in the midst of her own storms of life, was beyond remarkable. Thank you, dear Geeta. This book would not be what it is without you.

Finally, I must credit my dear friend and spiritual sister, Jelena Fassbender. She spent years with Mila and me in St. Ana, Slovenia, supporting us in every possible way, until she answered her higher calling of singing. Masters sent me Jelena to help me discern what was too intimate to include in this book and where I needed to be more vulnerable in terms of truthful expression of my own weaknesses. Nobody could do that better than my dear Jelena.

Aside from the above-mentioned, there were a few other supporters whose role was priceless. Wherever I went – Slovenia, Switzerland, Serbia, Croatia, India; at home, in the car, on the airplane – the book writing continued. Therefore, I must thank dear Paula Vouk, the pillar of our Mohanji Slovenia team, who took on the burden of driving me around (including a long drive to Switzerland and back), helping Mila with the homework, grocery shopping and many other everyday duties that would have distracted my focused writing. Our wonderful Lori Werner was also with us from the US for more than a month, volunteering to cook and do all other domestic chores. Her dedication was truly amazing. Finally, my dear mom provided the same essential support and her nourishing food during my days spent in Novi Sad, Serbia.

In terms of graphic design, I must thank the super-talented Ana Berner for this beautiful book cover and all her other graphics through which her subtle feminine creativity complements my higher expressions. My friend Marko Milović gave a wonderful contribution through the software he uses to enhance the resolution of old photos, while dear Mario Brainović stunned me with his talent for capturing the subtle expressions, which is why his photos grace the cover of this book.

I know who is most eager to see me finish this book – my sweetest child Mila, who has been patiently waiting to get her Mom's loving attention back. I thank her for her patience and the many kisses she gave me in support of my persistence to keep writing, no matter what.

I am deeply grateful to everyone else who supported me during this creative process, including dear Subhashree, Rajesh and the entire Gurulight team, who waited for me patiently, way beyond the final deadline, without complaining a single time.

Finally, I would like to thank my beloved Mohanji, who gave me required input whenever I asked for it, be it day or night. As always, he has been my pillar and the golden thread that kept the tapestry of this project together until the very last moment.

Now, after the "final push," I must say I feel truly blissful that this book is finally out – my very first book and a child of the genuine expression of my heart and soul.

About the Author

Devi Mohan wears many hats within the vast global platform called Mohanji Foundation, currently present in more than 90 countries and officially registered in 17. She serves as Global Ambassador of Mohanji Foundation and Global President of the internationally active charity ACT Foundation (with active teams and consistent charitable initiatives and projects in 25 countries). Devi conducts programs and processes aligned with Mohanji's highest teachings, empowering people to connect with the Divine within and overcome all heaviness that dulls their spirit and destroys their willpower.

As a Senior Practitioner of Mai-Tri Method and Mohanji Transformation Method, Devi works with people one-on-one as well as through powerful group processes, some designed by her, in alignment with the Source through Mohanji's consciousness that forever inspires, protects, elevates, and maintains the equilibrium needed to serve tirelessly.

Through Himalayan School of Traditional Yoga, Devi serves the unity consciousness expressed through this ancient practice. It is Devi's direct experience that traditional Yoga uplifts and heals and is needed more than ever in the immense hustle and bustle of the contemporary world.

Through Himalayan School of Traditional Martial Arts, Devi intends to spread the knowledge of the most ancient martial art form, called Kalaripayattu. She intends to focus specifically on effective self-defense methods for the everyday life of women. Devi wishes to see women empowered, and feeling strong, connected, and confident in their skills of self-protection.

As a woman married to an internationally renowned humanitarian, Devi's uniqueness stems from her own authentic space of expression and action, through which she inspires modern women to rise to their highest potential.

More than 40,000 people have experienced her processes since 2014; more than 20 million have benefited from social service through ACT Foundation founded by Mohanji in 2003 and led by Devi as its Global President since 2012. At the heart of ACT are its 550 super-dedicated volunteers leading various initiatives across 25 countries. Women make up 70% of ACT leaders. As their servant leader, she interacts with them regularly, inspiring them to give of themselves evermore.

Devi's authentic contribution is in practicing what she preaches, making her the ambassador of her own work. Devi raised herself from victimhood during her refugee days with the strength, determination, and grace still evident in her life's work. Her presentations and methods for rising above trauma, pain, and shame, are all profoundly transformational. Most importantly, she inspires women to seal the healing process by uplifting others through social service in the true spirit of motherhood. That is how the transformation becomes solid and lasting.

Devi's YouTube video series "My Journey With Mohanji," regular online workshops and retreats around the globe, as well as initiatives like "Festival of Womanhood" (co-founded by Devi), have inspired countless people, especially women. Devi delivers her example of what the world needs most today: a strong, loving, authentic, skilled, and educated woman who acts as the spine of the family and anchors of the energy of peace in the world.

Everything about Devi's present and planned activities can be found on her website: www.devimohan.com.

Said about Devi

Devi Mohan brings positivity, love, enthusiasm, empowerment, and a spirit of collaboration to her work and life's mission wherever she goes. She is the most dedicated human. I have watched her wake up every day to travel to a new place to spread awareness and lift spirits. She is an incredible Light leader in our world and is 100% dedicated to that path. I've had the great honor of traveling with Devi on a couple of beautiful journeys, one through the Holy Land and another in India, in collaboration with the organization "Unity Earth." And at this point, I can say that Devi has become a deep inspirational energy in my life, a mentor, and a dear friend.

—Kristin Hoffman, New York, USA

Listening to Devi Mohan speak at The Parliament of World's Religions in 2018 was a truly amazing experience. I couldn't believe how she could speak without any notes, from the heart. She was so eloquent. Her concept of uplifting humanity truly touched our hearts. We all felt that we wanted to do something more to help the world.

—Andra Baylus, USA

I think of Devi Mohan as a role model for us women. She is a great teacher, a wisdom holder, and a healer in her own right. She can easily inspire people with powerful ideas, which is an awesome gift in this world.

—Jeanetta M. Haley, India

Mother of the world. This is how I would describe Devi. She never says no to someone who needs her. All the time giving her best and never expecting any gratification or applause. Always smiling and serving. Her attitude is my true inspiration.

—Paula Vouk, Slovenia

Devi is a rare kind of woman. Cheerful and bright, deep and wise, open and loving, supportive and genuine. I am forever thankful to my guru Mohanji, who gave me the opportunity to live together with Devi and their daughter Mila. Devi is my friend, my sister, my mother, and my child. She is my soulmate. Brave and authentic, she dares to live her highest Truth, which inspires people all around the world, especially women, to become their best version by sharing her wisdom and love – because she is Love.

—Jelena Fassbender, Germany

It was through the Power of Purity meditation led by the beautiful voice of Devi Mohan in Serbian language that I first connected with Mohanji and Devi. In one word, it felt like a "homecoming."

Her video series "My journey with Mohanji" published on YouTube was priceless to me – enabling me to establish trust and faith in this spiritual path, to surrender myself without (hyper)activity of the mind and constant analysis.

People's hearts easily open to Devi because she is very warm and filled with motherly love, and endlessly charming in her spontaneity and authenticity. She is accessible and does not hide that she, like the rest of us, faces challenges in everyday life, that the spiritual path is challenging, and yet we always have a choice of the path, speed, and level of dedication.

The Yoga classes and Conscious Dancing she leads carry huge transformative energy and enable the practitioners to experience their true nature – unconditional love.

—Nataša Stojkić, Serbia

I used to have a really bad phobia of heights, like being on a plane or even in a tall building. When Devi Mohan came to Doha, Qatar, and conducted her processes, something truly amazing happened as a result of these processes. I was able to overcome my fear of heights and for the first time ever I could come to the 42nd floor of a building and look down through the window, without experiencing panic or anxiety. I'm truly grateful for being free from this fear.

—Diana Lalamova, Qatar

From all the experiences that I shared with Devi over the years, it was Kailash yatra that stood out for me, especially the Inner Kora which was really, really challenging. Even there, in the midst of the harshness and toughest of moments that we experienced, Devi managed to bring in her contagious and healing smile and lightness, her positive attitude, and her readiness for action. I am forever grateful to Devi for existing among us as a living example of joy, purity, and unconditional love.

—Spomenka Dragojević, Serbia

I remember the moment when I was greatly tested and almost left this spiritual path and my beloved Guru Mohanji and just how much Devi helped me at that time. I remember that moment as if it was yesterday, fresh and vivid. It stayed in my mind as a constant reminder that when fears and doubts cloud our vision, the only thing we can do is just hold on and wait for the storm of thoughts and emotions to pass. Devi helped me at that moment by objectively holding a space that is free of doubts and fears, and full of love and acceptance. She was just holding that space, long enough so that I could catch up and match that vibration. Once I was out of the trance of doubts, I could clearly see the play of the mind.

Going through that whole process of falling into disconnection and coming out of it, helped me so many times. The lesson is to just hold on and the storm will pass. Don't make any decisions at that moment. In a few days it will most probably all look so silly. If we miss this chance of merging with the Master's Consciousness in this lifetime, who knows when this chance will come back full circle again? Lifetimes most probably.

I still remember Mohanji saying to me: "Always be like a bird sitting on a dry branch. The branch could break at any time. So, one should be super vigilant and live always in this way." Thank you, dearest Devi.

—Mohana Hanumatananda, Macedonia

When I was young I suffered triple trauma from different forms of physical or sexual abuse. Until my thirties, I never realized that all my thinking and my reactions were based on and came from that trauma material. I realized that I could work with it and start to heal myself. Luckily, the work of Devi Mohan came my way. I've done various processes with her: Awakening Yoga Nidra, The Light Beyond, Group Mai - Tri, as well as one-on-one work with her.

The main thing that really stands out when doing the work with techniques that are developed by Devi and sourced from Mohanji's consciousness is how deep they are. I can say, hand on my heart, that nowhere have I worked with techniques that take me so deep and so to the rawness of the real trauma as those three techniques that I just mentioned. I feel that there is an inner change in me. My heart has opened up. From that space, I really want to serve the world.

Since then I've been involved in various platforms, one of them being ACT Foundation. Recently we've been to Ukraine through ACT4Ukraine initiative once again. I actually took my entire family to Ukraine to help displaced people over there. The feeling of satisfaction that I get from that is actually a healing journey in itself because I've realized that I never experienced that feeling of fullness in my life.

I'm so grateful for these techniques. They make a massive difference and for me, what I've come across so far, they are absolutely unique in what they offer, particularly because they go very, very deep. I highly recommend them, from the heart.

—Selma van Houwelingen, The Netherlands

I had heard so much about Devi long before I had met her; and from her many posts and blogs on Facebook, I found her to be very beautiful, not only in appearance, but I found that she wrote with incredible depth and feeling. I was struck by how humble she came across. And her love and devotion as a wife and first disciple of our Beloved Spiritual Master Mohanji were plain to see, not to mention her love for their precious beautiful daughter Mila. When I saw Devi's pictures on Facebook my heart skipped a beat, and stood still for a moment, for at its core was an instant ancient recognition and knowingness that defies everyday mind logic.

I also noticed how the magnetic Essence and Brightness of her Presence blazed through her pictures. They epitomized that certain radiance and that quality of "aliveness," inherent in people very few and far between.

At the time I thought to myself, yes here's a magnificent daughter of the brilliant stars on her Earth Walk. These were the secret thoughts of my Soul which I shyly share with you now.

Then I met her. My initial thoughts and feelings from her photographs were amplified. The awareness in me arose that the magnificently awakened Devi carries the sun in her. I still remember with vivid clarity the time she made a solo visit to my country South Africa, without Mohanji. There was a retreat just outside Durban in the province of KwaZulu-Natial. Devi was the main guest and facilitator too at this retreat. It was the first day. There was a lovely gathering of Souls, beautiful happy people, all eager and excited to meet Devi. She entered the main hall. From my personal experience, it felt like the room had visibly brightened. Her Soul blazed, and her Heart spoke. I also remember feeling acutely in tune and at home with her energy. It felt faintly familiar, like echoes from a far, far distant past, full memory of which was annoyingly veiled to my present-day senses.

I quietly continue to witness Devi's unfoldment, primarily tutored and nurtured by her Beloved husband, and spiritual mentor and guide, Mohanji. I have observed how she's rapidly healed into her Wholeness, having transcended her painful past, the untold atrocities of the war in her country the former Yugoslavia, despair from displacement, and misery from the endless discrimination as a refugee in her teens. I'm in awe at how she's risen from the ashes of horrors, being pummeled and pounded emotionally and mentally, and honed now into a Being of Diamond Brightness, a Beacon of Hope in the midst of the seemingly never-ending chaos in an ever-changing world. I see how in these turbulent times of uncertainty and instability, people are irresistibly drawn to her, including myself, magnetized by her peaceful presence and positive nature. She has the gift of bringing people together. She is such an incredible empath. Her beautiful heart has blossomed and opened and she's become a magnet for good, and an emissary of unconditional love. Devi is driven by compassion. She inspires trust. Her elegance is further defined by her kindness and humility. She is a fearless advocate for fairness and justice. She is simply guileless. These are my feelings for Devi.

I find that her life is a testament to her inclusive nature. She is spiritually awake, and is guided by higher Awareness and unifying insights. Thus she is innately in tune with the sacred threads of uniqueness inherent in life's varied species including our human race, that co-exist on Earth for the sake of sacred experiences.

Devi's journey of courage and endurance is remarkable. In my view she is perfectly placed to serve as a Peace Ambassador on several international platforms, as well as the many founded by Mohanji to Serve Life and Add Value to the World. Her messages are insightful and underscore the higher values of harmony in diversity, and of positivity and peace. My life has been enriched in many ways and on many levels by Devi's transformational, elevating and healing initiatives and programs. She has the gift of bringing people together. Her actions are imbued with the language and energy of Love. Devi has a Heart that beats to the rhythm of a unified world in the elevating attributes of kindness, compassion, and caring.

—Ami Imzaia, South Africa

Made in United States
Orlando, FL
08 March 2023

30832325R00217